Existentialist Philosophy
An Introduction

EDITED WITH TEXT BY

L. Nathan Oaklander
The University of Michigan—Flint

 PRENTICE HALL, Englewood Cliffs, New Jersey 07632

Library of Congress Cataloging-in-Publication Data

Oaklander, L. Nathan
    Existentialist philosophy : an introduction / edited with text by
  L. Nathan Oaklander.
      p.   cm.
    Includes bibliographical references and index.
    ISBN 0-13-297219-0
    I. Title.
  B819.025   1992
  142'.78—dc20   91-21015
                                                                    CIP

Acquisitions editor: Ted Bolen
Editorial/production supervision
  and interior design: Mary McKinley
Copy editor: Ann Lesser
Cover design: Lundgren Graphics, Ltd.
Prepress buyer: Herb Klein
Manufacturing buyer: Patrice Fraccio

 © 1992 by Prentice-Hall, Inc.
A Simon & Schuster Company
Englewood Cliffs, New Jersey 07632

Printed in the United States of America
10 9 8 7 6 5 4 3 2

ISBN 0-13-297219-0

Prentice-Hall International (UK) Limited, *London*
Prentice-Hall of Australia Pty. Limited, *Sydney*
Prentice-Hall Canada Inc., *Toronto*
Prentice-Hall Hispanoamericana, S.A., *Mexico*
Prentice-Hall of India Private Limited, *New Delhi*
Prentice-Hall of Japan, Inc., *Tokyo*
Simon & Schuster Asia Pte. Ltd., *Singapore*
Editora Prentice-Hall do Brasil, Ltda., *Rio de Janeiro*

For my wife Linda, and my children Lee, Stan, and Rose

Contents

Nietzche selections are taken from these works: *The Gay
Science, Daybreak, The Will to Power, Beyond Good and Evil,
Thus Spoke Zarathustra, The Antichrist, Ecce Homo, On the
Genealogy of Morals, Twilight of the Idols, Human, All Too
Human,* and *The Wanderer and His Shadow*

Chapter Five   Jean-Paul Sartre   240

Preface

It is usual in a text of this sort to begin by offering a definition of "existentialism," but I will break tradition. After all, the subject matter of existentialism is the individual qua individual and thus to offer a definition of it would take us away from its subject matter. Definitions are necessarily general, in that they apply to all individuals picked out by the term being defined. For example, the definition of "bachelor" picks out all those individuals having a certain set of characteristics in common, but it does not tell us anything about an individual as such. Thus, if we attempt to define what it is to be an individual, we create a principle of classification that is necessarily general in its application. The subject matter of existentialism, on the other hand, is so unique and so particular that any attempt to define it would inevitably lose sight of it.

What, then, is this book about? The philosophers whose writings we examine each attempt to direct our attention to ourselves as individuals. They force us to think about our relation to such topics as the existence and nature of God, what it is to be a Christian, the nature of values, and the fact of one's own death. Existentialists encourage us to consider, in a personal way, the meaning of living authentically and inauthentically, our relation to the world and others, and the notions of freedom and responsibility. Thus, we could say that this book is about human life and human existence.

The existentialists included in this anthology intend to have a special effect upon their readers. It is more likely, however, that without some guidance in explicating what they are getting at, their ideas would probably go over the heads of most persons without a background in the field. Thus, I have written long introductions to the selections included in this volume. I hope you will gain an understanding of certain key points from which to build as you carefully read through the text. My interpretations are relatively standard, although I am certain there are teachers and scholars who would disagree with them. In coming to grips with what is rather difficult reading material, getting into a critical discussion of the different interpretations of a concept can be confusing. Consequently, I have not engaged in a critical commentary of alternative interpretations (one exception is my discussion of Sartre on sex). I have, however, supplied a bibliography listing books and articles that discuss, from several different perspectives, most of the topics considered here.

The selections themselves differ from those included in other anthologies on existentialism. My plan has been to include longer selections from fewer philosophers as against the usual procedure of shorter selections from a greater number of philosophers. In this way a more complete (although by no means exhaustive) picture of those represented is given. The choice of Kierkegaard, Nietzsche, Heidegger, and Sartre is based on my opinion that they are the four classic existentialist philosophers. Indeed, it is hard to imagine an undergraduate course in existentialism that would not consider them, and it is likely that, with the possible exception of Heidegger, they all would be included in a section devoted to existentialism in an introductory philosophy course. In addition I have included somewhat shorter selections from Simone de Beauvoir and Albert Camus because de Beauvoir's existentialist ethics nicely compliments and extends Sartre's philosophy and because Camus is generally popular among teachers and students of existentialism.

In editing an anthology it is always difficult to determine what should be included. I have been guided by the following three criteria: (1) selections from the most highly acclaimed works, (2) selections containing ideas for which the author is most famous, and (3) selections that readers would prefer. Fortunately, these criteria have, for the most part, pointed to the same works. Be that as it may, I would hope that in its entirety, this text-anthology will provide you with a concise introduction to existentialist philosophy.

I wish to thank Phyliss Sutton Morris for her comments on a draft of the introductions, my colleague Richard Gull for many conversations on existential topics, and my wife Linda for her encouragement, patience, and support. I have also benefited from various reviewers' suggestions, especially those of Hazel E. Barnes and Winston A. Wilkenson. Others who were helpful in reading and commenting on the manuscript are Richard F. Van Iten, Iowa State University; Eugene Thomas Long, University of South Carolina; Donald Evans, Victoria University, University of Toronto; F. Claude Evans, Washington University; and Hugh Wilder, College of Charleston.

The research for this project was supported (in part) by a grant from the faculty development fund of the University of Michigan–Flint.

1

Introduction

THE SUBJECT MATTER OF EXISTENTIALISM: THE EXISTING INDIVIDUAL

The aim of this book is to introduce you to existentialist philosophy. A natural place to begin is by telling you what existentialism is about, that is, by explaining or discussing its subject matter. In the Preface I suggest that the subject matter of existentialism is human existence or, as I shall also refer to it, the particular, living, existing individual. But to leave it at that is not quite enough, since it would remain unclear how existentialism as a philosophy differs (assuming that it does differ) from philosophy as it has traditionally been conceived, or how it differs from science. After all, throughout the history of philosophy and to the present day, questions concerning human life and existence have been the object of philosophical study. Questions concerning human life such as "What am I?" and "What is the nature of personal identity?" have interested philosophers for centuries. And it seems beyond dispute that science has human life as part of its subject matter. What, then, is it that makes existentialist philosophy distinctive? How are we to distinguish existentialism from traditional philosophical concerns about the nature of human existence on the one hand, and from scientific concerns about human existence on the other?

Before we turn to that question there is a more fundamental distinction needing clarification, namely, the distinction between traditional philosophy and science. Some have thought that all philosophical questions are really scientific questions and that, therefore, philosophy does not have its own distinctive subject matter. Although I believe that to be a mistake, it is not too difficult to see why someone may believe we cannot learn anything from philosophy that we cannot learn from science. The word "philosophy" comes from the Greek words *philo* which means "to love" and *sophia* which means "wisdom." Thus, philosophy is the love of wisdom, and the philosopher is someone who seeks wisdom, truth, and knowledge of reality. All well and good, but doesn't the scientist do the same thing? Isn't the scientist concerned with acquiring truth and knowledge of reality? We are left to wonder how the wisdom that philosophy seeks differs (if it differs) from the wisdom the sciences search after.

We can begin to grasp the distinction between science and philosophy by noting that in our ordinary daily life, thought, and language we make use of a number of concepts in terms of which we interpret our experience. Let me give you an example. Last week I ran into a friend of mine who I had not seen in over ten years. Seeing him, the very same person with whom I had shared so many enjoyable experiences in the past, was a source of great pleasure. We talked about what we had been doing for the past ten years. He told me, among other things, that he hardly recognized me, since I had changed so much, and he also told me how he had been treated unfairly at work, which had caused him a lot of grief. After chatting together for a while, we decided to make plans to meet again before too much time passed. The situation I have described is unproblematic. I had no difficulty understanding the experiences my friend described, nor did he have any difficulty understanding mine. In order to understand them, and in order to have the experiences we did have when we met, we must have been in possession of certain concepts, for example, the concepts of fairness, same person, change, cause, pastness, and the passage of time, to name a few. These concepts and others are employed in our ordinary thought, language, and experience of the world, and they are assumed in science and scientific investigation. That is, the scientist searches for an explanation of why something changes, but does not, qua scientist, consider the questions "What is change?" or "How is change possible?" The scientist looks for the causes of cancer, heart disease, and so on, but does not, qua scientist, ask the question "What is a cause?" Scientists assume that we can have knowledge of substances, and one part of their intellectual endeavor is to impart such knowledge to us, but they do not bother to examine the concept of knowledge or the concept of substance. Thus, we could say the subject matter of philosophy is those fundamental concepts that we uncritically employ and assume in ordinary life and science, and that the wisdom philosophy seeks is that of ascertaining the true nature, or essence, of those fundamental categories or concepts.

To help clarify the distinction between science and traditional philosophy, suppose we consider the philosophical (metaphysical) problem of sameness and difference. If we take two ball bearings with the same size, weight, shape, and so on, then we have two things or objects with all their non-relational qualities in common. Very roughly, the questions of sameness and difference can be stated as follows: "In virtue of what are these two ball bearings the same, and in virtue of what are they different?" Does their sameness and difference have to be grounded in two different kinds of entities—universals and particulars—or will a single sort do? Of course, scientists as well as ordinary people of good common sense may wonder what the fuss is all about. They may simply answer by claiming that the bearings are the same because they have the *same qualities,* and are different because they are *different objects.* However, in so doing, they are saying something that either presupposes there are two kinds (qualities and objects), or they are merely restating the problems without answering them. For to appeal to qualities and objects to solve the problems of sameness and difference leaves unanswered the crucial questions, namely, "What is a quality?" and "What is an object?" These are questions that for scientific (and ordinary) purposes need not, and for philosophical purposes cannot, be answered by the scientist.

Yet even if we admit that there is a distinction between traditional philosophy on the one hand and science on the other, there still remains the question as to where existentialism stands in relation to both these disciplines. Although existentialists have claimed to have discovered a new subject matter, it is perhaps difficult to see how this can be. In what sense can there be a philosophy of human existence that is not a part of traditional philosophy? After all, traditional philosophy deals with fundamental concepts, and certainly the self and human life and existence are among them. So doesn't the subject matter of existentialism fall within the purview of traditional philosophy? Shouldn't we say that existentialism is merely a more specialized aspect of traditional philosophy? Not really, because the subject matter of traditional philosophy is abstract concepts, and although existentialists have offered descriptions of the basic structures of human existence and the world, the fundamental or ultimate subject matter of existentialism is the *existing, concrete, living individual.* Existentialists are not primarily concerned with human life in general, but with the life of particular existing individuals. They are concerned with human life viewed as a series of decisions and choices, and their first goal is to make us aware of ourselves as living individuals who, in our freedom, make decisions and are responsible for them.

Perhaps it is still not clear in what sense human beings can be the subject matter of philosophy, even existentialist philosophy. There are no philosophical questions about cats and dogs, there are just scientific questions about these animals. What, then, can existentialist philosophers say about human existence that cannot be said by scientists? What is the difference between the philosophy of human existence and the various sciences whose subject matter involves human beings? Is there something so special about human life that it cannot be studied by science? Indeed there is, since the scientific facts about human life are *existentially irrelevant.*

To see what is involved in the notions of "existentially irrelevant" and "existentially relevant," let us briefly consider the topic of death. The biologist, physiologist, and physician can tell us all sorts of objective facts about ourselves. They can inform us that a blood pressure reading of 180/110 is considered elevated and may result in heart trouble, kidney failure, or a stroke. They can and do tell us that smoking is hazardous to our health. Indeed, they may inform us of all the objective facts available about the process and inevitability of death. But after they have told us what high blood pressure is and what effects it has on our health, and after they have told us everything they know about the physiological state of death, there will remain one thing that they have not told us, and there will remain one question that they have not answered, namely, *"What do these facts mean to me?"* and *"What do they mean to my life?"* In other words, the scientist never deals with that aspect of death which makes it an existentially relevant issue, namely, "How am I going to personally relate to these facts?"

Insofar as I view the fact of death objectively, as something that happens to everyone, death is an existentially irrelevant phenomenon. It has to do with me only, to use Heidegger's phrase, as a "one like many." Everyone dies, and so will I, but no more significance attaches to my death than to anyone else's death. By looking at death scientifically, objectively, and dispassionately I do not become aware of myself as an existing individual, as an individual who makes decisions and choices which cease at death. For the existentialist, however, the crucial question concerning death does not concern its causes, its effects, or its clinical definition. Rather, the existentially relevant question concerns what the fact of death means to me. It is only by considering death as it relates to my life and to my decisions and choices, that we begin to confront the existentially relevant aspect of death.

There are, naturally, different ways of responding to the question of what the fact of death means to my life. One may claim that since I am going to die, why think of anything as important or why place value on anything that happens? I am going to die anyway, so nothing matters; it makes no difference what I do or how I lead my life. Certainly, this is a possible attitude to take. On the other hand, I may adopt the opposite attitude and claim that since I have only one life and it is going to end,

I better not waste it. The very idea of wasting one's life, or any moment of it, becomes horrifying. What attitude am I to take? Or is there a third or a fourth attitude to adopt toward the fact of my death? Regardless of how one deals with or confronts the question of the relevance of death to the content of one's life we are here dealing with a question that does not arise and cannot be answered by the scientist. Yet in the very process of raising the question of how my death is related to my life, and acting in a certain way in response to it, the topic of death becomes existentially relevant by directing my attention to myself, the subject matter of existentialism.

By briefly considering the philosophical topic of fatalism, we can see how traditional philosophical concerns and certain philosophical "facts" about humans are existentially irrelevant. Fatalism is the view that the laws of logic alone suffice to prove that no person has free will, that no person has it within his or her power to either bring about or prevent an action or event. The argument has its source in Aristotle (384–322 B.C.), but it has also found favor with some contemporary philosophers.[1] Very roughly, it goes like this. According to the logical law of excluded middle, every proposition is either true or false. Thus, for example, the proposition "I will finish writing this chapter tonight" is either now true or now false. If, however, it is now true that I will finish it tonight, then there is now no possibility that I might not. If, on the other hand, it is now false that I will finish it tonight, then there is now no possibility that I might. In either case, "nothing is or takes place fortuitously, either in the present or in the future, and there are no real alternatives, everything takes place of necessity and is fixed."[2]

Of course, not all philosophers, or even most, accept this argument. It is not my intention, however, to discuss the various subtleties surrounding the topic of fatalism, but merely to point out that for most of us the entire issue is existentially irrelevant. That is, for most of us, the fact of the matter—whether or not the logical law of excluded middle entails that no person has free will (i.e., whether or not fatalism is true)—makes no difference to the content of our lives.

Consider an example. Suppose I am convinced that fatalism is true, so I believe that I have no free will to perform or not to perform a given action. Suppose further that circumstances are such that I have to decide whether or not to dive into icy cold water and risk my life to save a drowning child. The decision I have to make at that moment is not made any easier by my belief in fatalism. Moreover, if I had any doubt about whether or not fatalism was true, my attempt to deal with the conflict forced upon me by the circumstances would not be made any easier by madly starting to read books on fatalism. It is glaringly obvious that when we are faced with a life or death situation the issue of whether or not fatalism is true is existentially irrelevant. What is existentially relevant are the phenomena of the situation, the emotional upheaval that we must go through when faced with a conflict of interest and must actually decide what to do.

The example just cited is intended to illustrate that whether or not fatalism is true is not in itself existentially relevant to my life considered as a series of decisions and choices. Of course, an existentialist may admit that though the topic of fatalism is existentially irrelevant, our convictions and attitudes toward the issue may be existentially relevant. Thus, for example, if I think that fatalism is false and my will is free, I might be less likely to think that my decisions and choices are beyond my control and consequently I may become acutely aware of my own responsibility for everything I do. As in the case of death, however, we must distinguish between the objective facts and our attitude toward those facts. It is only by attending to our attitude toward objective facts—what they mean to me as an individual who makes decisions and choices—that we shall approach the existentially relevant.

The philosophers whose works we explore here each have their own particular vehicle for directing our attention to the existentialist subject matter. In addition to challenging us to think personally about topics such as God, death, and values, they use certain terms to direct our attention to ourselves. However, though terms such as "human life," "the existing individual," "the existentially relevant," "the subjective," "the ethical," and "inwardness" may direct our attention to the subject matter of existentialism, they can neither describe it nor *directly* communicate it. There is an important sense in which the existentialist subject matter, unlike the subject matter of science, cannot be directly communicated or described. Here we have another difference between science and existential philosophy.

A science textbook can tell us, by way of description, something about cats, dogs, humans, and the like, but the descriptions that textbooks give us are never about individuals as such. Science can inform us about the genus (animal) to which various species (dog, cat, human) belong, and it can describe the kind (dog) to which an individual of that kind (Rover) belongs. What science cannot do, however, is tell us something about the *individual as such,* for anything that a textbook says about an individual cat, dog, mollusk, or human being could also be said about any other member of the same kind. Thus, in all thought—be it scientific, traditionally philosophical, or ordinary—except existentialist "thought," we cannot have knowledge of an individual entity as such. Only in our own case can we know what it is to be an individual qua individual.

To have knowledge of an individual entity you must be it, yet being the subject matter of existentialism is not sufficient for knowing it. What is required, in addition, is that one undergo a certain sort of experience. The means of arriving at this experience—the vehicle of self-awareness—

is different for each of the philosophers we consider. What we need to emphasize presently, however, is that since in order to describe or communicate something it must be capable of being thought, and since the individual as such cannot be thought, it follows that what it is to be an individual cannot be described or directly communicated.

To see what is involved in the preceding argument, consider the thought expressed by the sentence "Tabby is a cat." Notice that if you take away from that thought the idea of being a cat then there is nothing left to think about. To think of Tabby is to think of a kind of individual, namely, a cat. Thus, although I can think of individual things, it is only by classifying them as belonging to a group or kind. Consequently, since all objective thought is necessarily abstract thought, that is thought about a *kind* of thing, and since the existing individual is not a generality or kind of thing, it appears to follow that the existing individual cannot be known by objective thought.

Another example might help. Consider the sentence, "This is a pencil." Does that sentence express a thought that contains what "this" refers to? No, for if you take away the thought of a pencil from the thought expressed by "this is a pencil" then there is nothing left to think about. I cannot think of what the word "this" refers to without thinking of some kind of thing. Yet if anything refers to an individual qua individual it is the word "this," but what "this" refers to cannot be thought, since it has no content. Thus, once again we see that the individual as such cannot be thought; in any event it cannot be thought of objectively.

It is an easy step from the claim that an individual as such cannot be thought to the conclusion that the (direct) communication of the subject matter of existentialism is impossible. All communication involves the expression and transmission of thought. Although thought may be subtler than language, since there may be thoughts that cannot be expressed in words, all meaningful language is an expression of thought. Thus, if we cannot understand the subject matter of existentialism through objective thought, then we cannot know it through language either. Since, however, (direct) communication involves the transmission of thoughts from one person to another by way of a medium such as written, verbal, body, or sign language, and since we cannot think about the particular as such, it follows that we cannot communicate to another what it is to be a particular existing individual.

For Soren Kierkegaard (1813–1855), it is a contradiction to suppose that one could directly communicate inwardness or subjective existence. In one passage he claims that

> all essential communication is here unthinkable, since everyone must be assumed essentially to possess all, nevertheless wishes to impart himself; and hence desires at one and the same time to have his thinking in the

> inwardness of his subjective existence, and yet also to put himself into communication with others. This contradiction cannot possibly find expression in a direct form.[3]

Since the existing individual is a particular and since all communication involves the universal, if we were to communicate ourselves to another we would have to transform our own particular existence into a universal, and that is impossible. Of course, there is a sense in which what we are is universal and describable in terms that are applicable to others. Virtually all the qualities I possess are possessed by others. Thus, there is a sense in which I can communicate what I am to another. Yet the existentially relevant aspect of my being has to do with what is absolutely unique about me. There is an irreducible particularity about my existence that cannot be transformed into a universal or collection of universals. Thus, in attempting to communicate one's subjective, particular existence the existing individual must turn oneself into a kind of individual and inevitably loses sight of what was intended to be communicated.

Another reason why a direct form of communication of individuality is impossible is that individuality or subjectivity is not a state to be achieved, but rather a constant process of coming to be. To be an individual is to be in a persistent state of striving, but communication presupposes finality and a result, that is, a complete thought to be communicated. Thus, an inwardness or individuality that is never finished and has no result cannot be communicated. For,

> Suppose a man wished to communicate the conviction that it is not the truth but the way which is the truth, i.e. that the truth exists only in the process of becoming, in the process of appropriation, and hence that there is no result . . . suppose he hit upon the excellent shortcut of communicating it in a direct form through the newspapers, thus winning masses of adherents . . . what then? Why then his principle would have turned out to be precisely a result.[4]

Thus, there is no way to communicate what it is to be an individual, but rather "the inwardness of the understanding would consist precisely in each individual coming to understand it by himself."[5]

At this point you may wonder what exactly this book is about and why you should read it. After all, if the existentialist subject matter is incommunicable, then presumably what I have written cannot communicate it. On the other hand, if I do succeed in making the philosophy of existentialism accessible to you then its subject matter *is* communicable! Admittedly, there is an air of paradox about the existence of a book on a topic whose subject matter cannot be directly communicated. Yet I believe the paradox is more apparent than real.

Books on existentialism often stress certain themes that are shared by a variety of philosophers who are called "existentialists." One common theme is the emphasis on human freedom and the related Sartrean slogan that "existence precedes essence," meaning that we have no prepackaged essence or nature, but that what we are is what we choose to be. Another theme stressed by existentialists is the contingency of the world, the fact that the universe has no meaning and is absurd. A third is that there are no objective values. Throughout the book, we explain in detail these and many other existentialist themes. If the interpretations given are intelligible, then in one sense the subject matter of existentialism will be communicated to you. You will have intellectually grasped or comprehended existentialist philosophy as a system of beliefs about the nature of human existence. In another sense, however, to know intellectually what existentialists have said about the nature of human existence is not sufficient (or perhaps even necessary) to know the subject matter of existentialism. Existential understanding involves something else, something more. What existentialists say about the structure of human existence is existentially relevant only if we choose to see it in relation to our own life, incorporate it into our life, and become involved in an intensely personal act of self-transformation as a consequence of it. Only then can we "know" the subject matter of existentialism. Such "knowledge" or self-awareness cannot be directly communicated, but must be lived.

For reasons we discuss, existentialists have noted that we have lost sight of reality, that is, of ourselves as individuals. The philosophers we study attempt to aid us in the discovery of the true reality, the subjective, the existing individual (and they have many fascinating things to tell us about this subject matter). Of course the question remains, "*How* are we to come to an awareness of ourselves as existing individuals?" For Kierkegaard the answer to that question lies in becoming a Christian. To see why he believes that to be the case is the main task of the next chapter.

Before turning to Kierkegaard, I would like to recount an experience in my life that I consider to be one in which I approached the existentialist subject matter. I was nineteen and a sophomore at the University of Iowa. I was living about a mile and a half away from campus and was walking home from the library and stopped at a bridge. It was about 2 A.M. and it was clear and cold. I looked out over the Iowa River and I felt completely alone. I had the realization that what I made of my life depended upon me and me alone; there was nothing in my past, nothing in my background, and nothing in anyone's thoughts about me, that could determine what would become of me. I realized subjectively, and not merely intellectually, that it was up to me to make my future and consequently, that all praise or blame for my life rested entirely on my shoulders. I resolved to make something of myself. Maybe you have had a similar experience and maybe not. If you have, then you have touched the existentialist subject matter, but if you have not, then there is no way I can directly communicate it to you, although I hope that this book will serve to direct your attention to it.

2

Soren Kierkegaard

ON THE IMPOSSIBILITY OF AN EXISTENTIAL SYSTEM

One main aim of Soren Kierkegaard's writings is to enable the individual to come to grips with his or her own "subjectivity" or synonymously, with that "reality." Since, for Kierkegaard, the task of becoming subjective is the task of becoming a Christian, he approaches the subject matter of existentialism through a consideration of religion and the question of the existence of God. Before we can see how the topic of religion can be existentially relevant, that is, how it can be a vehicle to make us aware of our own subjectivity, it is useful to consider Kierkegaard's objections to systematic or speculative philosophy and more generally to place him within the Western philosophical traditions of rationalism and empiricism. For it is often useful to understand a philosopher by considering the views he or she is reacting against as well as the views with which he or she is sympathetic.

Throughout the *Concluding Unscientific Postscript,* Kierkegaard attacks what he calls "speculative" and "systematic" philosophy as well as the objective tendency of the present age. At the heart of his objections is his belief that the way of objective reflection and systematic thought leads us away from the subject and thus away from ourselves. To understand why this is so we first summarize the main elements of the rationalist philosophies of Plato (428–348 B.C.) and Georg Wilhelm Friedrich Hegel (1770–1831), and then we consider Kierkegaard's objections to them. This procedure is appropriate because these two philosophies represent the core of the speculative and systematic philosophy that Kierkegaard so vigorously rejects.

There are two main tenets of rationalism: The first concerns the nature of reality, and the second concerns our knowledge of reality. According to the first tenet, *reality consists of a realm of absolutes, universals, forms, or true essences.* What, then, are universals or absolutes? Suppose we approach this question by drawing a distinction between reality and appearance. Plato, who was one of the first philosophers to make that distinction, claimed that ordinary objects of sense, *particular* things, such as this table, this chair, this tree, this person, and indeed all things existing in space and time, belonged to the realm of appearance. He thought this because all objects in our everyday world of experience are subject to *change.* Such changing particulars are therefore of little interest to the speculative philosopher who searches after knowledge of an unchanging reality.

Accordingly, reality contains non-temporal and non-spatial objects that are not subject to the vicissitudes of earthly existence such as generation, corruption, and change. Universals or absolutes are *unchanging* because they are timeless; *objective* because they do not depend for their existence on anyone thinking of them; and *independent* because their existence does not depend on the existence of spatio-temporal particulars. Thus, for example, Leonardo da Vinci's masterpiece Mona Lisa, like all other beautiful works of art, depends for its beauty on there being a form, ideal, or standard of absolute Beauty, but the form of Beauty itself does not depend on there being any particular instances of it. Absolutes comprise a realm of their own, separate and independent of particulars. Indeed, it is precisely because universals are unchanging, objective, and independent that rationalists claim the totality of absolutes comprise the true Reality.

The second major tenet of rationalism centers on its view concerning the nature of knowledge and the proper way of acquiring it. According to this tradition, we arrive at philosophical truth or knowledge when we understand the nature and relationship between and among universals. Since universals are timeless and unchanging, philosophical truth is also timeless and unchanging. Philosophical truth is absolutely general and necessary truth: truth that holds for all persons and for all times. The proper way of arriving at this truth is through contemplation, abstract thought, and reason. Thus, the passions and the emotions are to be kept in check so as to allow our intellect to have an unbridled opportunity to "see" or more accurately, "intellectually apprehend" the Truth. The speculative philosopher holds that the task of philosophy is to use *reason* and *abstract thought* to build a system based on objective necessary truths that express relations among universals.

Kierkegaard's critique of speculative or systematic philosophy is a critique of all forms of rationalism with their emphasis on the universal as reality and reason as the path to reality. Yet when Kierkegaard argues against the possibility of an existential system, he clearly has Hegel in mind. According to Hegel, the task of philosophy consists in attaining Absolute Truth and Absolute Knowledge. This task is difficult because the concepts (universals) by which we interpret experience are fraught with differences, oppositions, and apparent contradictions. The mind seeks to resolve these inconsistencies through a dialectical process of thesis, antithesis, and synthesis, resulting in a more and more unified understanding of reality. Not only does philosophy seek to resolve the contradictions in our concepts by an appeal to a higher synthesis, but it also attempts to understand world history as the systematic development (the successive generation and overcoming of conflicts) of Reality. It is only the whole of Reality, in all its complexity, that is completely rational and therefore completely real. Hegel calls this totality "The Absolute" and the task of philosophy is to exhibit the rational dynamic structure, the movement of Reason, which culminates in the Absolute's knowledge of itself. For Hegel, the totality—the Absolute Reality—is spiritual; it is identical with the universal thinker that comprehends it.

We can summarize Hegel's philosophy by his statement, "The real is the rational and the rational is the real." This means, on the one hand, that all truths are absolutely necessary truths and in principle these truths can be grasped by reason alone. In other words, in principle we can figure out (deduce) the way the world is (what things exist) solely by reflection on the nature of essences. On the other hand, Hegel's statement means that the knower of the Absolute is pure thought (Reason) knowing itself. Put differently, the history of the universe is the history of Spirit becoming conscious of itself through time. Where, then, does the individual fit into this system? For Hegel the individual human existent is swallowed up in the Absolute, being just a part of the "world-historical" process of the self-realization of Reason or Spirit.

Kierkegaard assails the very idea of rationalism and systematic philosophy at its roots by attacking its central tenets. For Kierkegaard the rationalist is mistaken in thinking that the ultimate reality is the universal or the Absolute and the goal of philosophy is knowledge of the universal or the Absolute. Indeed, the speculative philosopher misses the very point of philosophy, which is to make us aware of that particular element in reality that each one of us is, the existing individual. Clearly, this failure is not due to an oversight on the part of the speculative philosopher, but is the result of the very enterprise itself. For although the goal of systematic or speculative philosophy is to acquire absolute knowledge through abstract thought, the universal is not the real, and abstract thought can never acquaint us with the real. Abstract thought is always about possibilities, kinds, or essences, but the subject matter of existentialism—the true reality—is the particular existing individual. As Kierkegaard says,

> The way of objective reflection makes the subject accidental and thereby transforms existence into something indifferent, something vanishing. . . . The way of objective reflection leads to abstract thought, to mathematics, to historical knowledge of different kinds; and always it leads away from the subject, whose existence or non-existence, and from the objective point of view quite rightly, becomes infinitely indifferent.[1]

Speculative philosophy, with its emphasis on dispassionate objectivity as the basis for arriving at ultimate truth, requires us to move more and more away from ourselves. According to it, if we let our subjectivity enter into our search for objective truth then that which we seek will be clouded by our emotions and passions. For Kierkegaard, however, the striving for objectivity is precisely what is wrong with speculative philosophy because such striving takes us away from our passions and our own subjective reality.

In other passages Kierkegaard criticizes the tendency to think in terms of abstractions and to build philosophical systems that are existentially irrelevant. A consideration of some of them will clarify his attack on systematic philosophy. The following is representative of many:

> Two ways, in general, are open for an existing individual: *Either* he can do his utmost to forget that he is an existing individual, by which he becomes a comic figure, since existence has a remarkable trait of compelling an existing individual to exist whether he will it or not. . . . *Or* he can concentrate his entire energy upon the fact that he is an existing individual. It is from this side, in the first instance, that objection must be made to modern philosophy; not that it has a mistaken presupposition, but that it has a comical presupposition, occasioned by its having forgotten, in a sort of world-historical absent-mindedness, what it means to be a human being. Not indeed, what it means to be a human being in general; for this is the sort of thing that one might even induce a speculative philosopher to agree to; but what it means that you and I and he are human beings, each one for himself. (p. 35)

Kierkegaard's point here is that the greater the emphasis on the objective way, the greater the loss of self-awareness, and yet, even at the height of objectivity and abstraction, it is a contradiction to suppose that the existing subject has vanished completely. After all, who is to write or think the System? Who is to engage in objective reflection? Speculative thought is not a being in its own right who can engage in such reflection. It is only a human being, a living existing human being, who is able to think abstractly. But then we are once again brought back to the existing individual.

People who do their utmost to forget that they are existing individuals are comic figures because reality has a way of forcing us to deal with ourselves as existents. For example, if I try to think of myself as a professor whose job it is to write this book, then I am thinking of myself as a *kind,* and yet at some point I must go through the anguish of making the decision to continue or not to continue to write this book. It is true that in science, philosophy, and our daily life we often think absent-mindedly because we forget what it means to be an individual. We have a natural tendency to think of ourselves as human beings in general, or as a specimen of certain kinds (for example, of our public or private roles), but the philosopher who speculates on what it is to be an individual in general, or on what personal identity in general consists of, does not know what really matters. We are existing individuals, each one for himself or herself. Each of us is not a human being in general, but I am myself and you are yourself.

To be conscious of oneself as a particular existing individual involves not only having beliefs, but also *living in accordance with them.* The objective tendency in modern philosophy does away with subjectivity in the sense of an *active commitment* to what one stands for. In this connection Kierkegaard claims that

> In relation to their systems most systematizers are like a man who builds an enormous castle and lives in a shack close by; *they do not live in their own enormous building.* But spiritually that is the decisive objection. Spiritually speaking a man's thought must be the building in which he lives—otherwise everything is topsy-turvy.[2]

In this passage Kierkegaard is probably thinking of Hegel, but what he says is also applicable to the great French philosopher René Descartes (1596–1650). Descartes, in his effort to combat scepticism and arrive at a firm foundation for the pursuit and development of knowledge, established a method whereby he cast doubt on all his previous beliefs. After arriving at complete scepticism or doubt concerning all his former beliefs, Descartes says,

> In the meantime, I know that no danger or error will result from my plan, and that I cannot possibly go too far in my distrustful attitude. This is because *the task now in hand does not involve action but merely the acquisition of knowledge.*[3]

The emphasized words point to Kierkegaard's fundamental objection to Descartes (or Hegel) in particular and speculative philosophy in general. What Kierkegaard really lacks is a clear understanding of what he is *to do* and not what he is *to know.* Insofar as what one knows does not affect the decisions and choices that constitute the essence of human life, one's knowledge is existentially irrelevant. Subjectivity is rooted in decisiveness and commitment, and they are rooted in passion and action, not in thought.

The question of immortality is another topic that speculative philosophers have, from Kierkegaard's perspective, handled miserably. For

> Systematically, immortality cannot be proved at all. The fault does not lie in the proofs, but in the fact that people will not understand that viewed systematically the whole question is nonsense, so that instead of seeking outward proofs, one had better seek to become a little subjective. Immortality is the most passionate interest of subjectivity; precisely in the interest lies the proof. . . .[4]

Immortality cannot be proved systematically because such a proof would not be of the existence of my immortality, but of immortality in general. For Kierkegaard, however, "such a phantom has no existence."[5] Furthermore, when speculative philosophers consider the question of immortality there is no personal investment. They investigate the problem objectively and in so doing remove the problem from the subjectivity of the individual. It is one thing to think abstractly about life after death, and it is something else entirely to live one's life in accordance with one's belief about such things. Those who offer "proofs do not at all pattern their lives in conformity with the idea. If there is an immortality, it must feel disgust over their lackadaisical manner of life. Can any better refutation be given of the three proofs?" (p. 47). Here Kierkegaard is alluding to his distinction between objective and subjective truth, which we have much to say about later. Presently, however, it is sufficient to note that for Kierkegaard, Socrates was closer to the truth concerning immortality than those speculative philosophers who offer proofs, because only Socrates was willing to risk his life for his beliefs.

There are two major points that emerge from Kierkegaard's critique of systematic, rationalistic, or speculative philosophy. First, the speculative philosopher who emphasizes knowledge of reality is concerned with abstractions, universals, and possibilities and thereby loses sight of the particular, concrete, existing individual. As Kierkegaard puts it,

> Being an individual man is a thing that has been abolished, and every speculative philosopher confuses himself with humanity at large; whereby he becomes something infinitely great, and at the same time nothing at all. (p. 38)

For Kierkegaard, on the other hand, "[T]he real subject is not the cognitive subject, since in knowing he moves in the sphere of the possible; the real subject is the ethically existing subject."[6] The second major criticism is that the objective tendency requires the individual to view issues as a spectator and not as a participant and thereby turns the issues considered into ones that have no significance for the life of an existing individual. In other words, the problems that concern the speculative philosopher do not, as a rule, have any subjective significance; they are existentially irrelevant.

There are other objections that Kierkegaard raises to the System. The System emphasizes finality, whereas the ideal of a *persistent striving* expresses the existing subject's view of life. Moreover, the System deals with the *concept* of existence, but individual existence cannot be reduced to a concept, and the paradoxes which exist for an individual (the concrete problems of what to do when faced with a conflict among choices) cannot be rationally resolved. Furthermore, the System attempts to understand or express reality in writing, but one can no more *directly* communicate the subject matter of existentialism by the use of language than one can by the use of abstract thought.[7] For in order to convey its meaning, language must use general terms such as "human life," or "human existence," but general terms are incapable of expressing the existential subject matter; at best they can only draw our attention to it. Since we cannot know the particular qua particular by means of language or abstract thought (pure reason) and since, for Kierkegaard, the only reality is the ethical, subjective, or particular reality, he concludes that systematic philosophy can never give us knowledge of reality.

Nevertheless, Kierkegaard maintains that we can have knowledge of ourselves. This is possible through a special and unique kind of "experience." Of course, this claim has to be carefully qualified, since for Kierkegaard true self-awareness requires a very special kind of experience, with a very special content, arrived at in a very special way. To begin to understand the nature of this experience and to put Kierkegaard more clearly on the philosophical map, we should say something about another philosophical tradition that resembles, yet is significantly different from Kierkegaard's, namely, the *empiricist* tradition.

For our purposes two key elements of empiricism need emphasis: First, in contrast to the rationalists, the empiricists claim that the world is composed of only one kind of entity, namely, particulars. Universals, construed as abstract objects distinct from particulars, do not exist. Such is the meaning of the empiricist slogan, "All that exists is particular."[8] Second, again in contrast to the rationalists, the empiricists reject pure thought or intellectual apprehension as the primary source of knowledge of reality. For them, experience is the source of knowledge of reality (particulars). By "experience," empiricists mean the awareness of objects through the senses and the awareness, by introspection, of the contents of one's own mind.

In some important respects Kierkegaard can be thought of as an empiricist, since he stresses the particular as the only reality and he emphasizes experience, meaning inwardness or a certain kind of introspection, as the source of knowledge of reality. Yet there are important differences. Whereas empiricists have often shown a tendency to confuse philosophical truth with scientific truth, Kierkegaard, although not against science as such, is against the scientific spirit in philosophy. As he says,

> [A]ll honor to the pursuits of science, and all honor to everyone who assists in driving the cattle away from the sacred precincts of scholarship. But the ethical is and remains the highest task for every human being. One may ask even of the devotee of science that he should acquire an ethical understanding of himself before he devotes himself to scholarship, and that he should continue to understand himself ethically while immersed in his labors; because the ethical is the very breath of the eternal, and constitutes even in solitude the reconciling fellowship with all men.[9]

From Kierkegaard's point of view the trouble with the scientific spirit is that it yields truth that is not about the particular as such, but rather about the kinds to which particulars belong. As we mentioned previously, science informs us about the kinds to which an individual belongs, and thereby necessarily provides us with general truth, that is, truths about all members of the kind it is telling us about. For Kierkegaard, however, philosophical truth *is* applicable to the individual as such, something that is inevitably lost sight of in the pursuit of science. In existentialist thought, unlike scientific thought, we can know something about an individual entity, namely, oneself.

A second important difference is that although both Kierkegaard and empiricists claim that knowledge of reality involves the experience of particulars, their notions of experience are rather different. In the empiricist tradition, to experience an object is to perceive or introspect an outer or inner object. In the empiricist view, as we interpret it for our purposes, the structure of experience is reflected in the structure of language, that is, the structure of experience is relational: expressing a connection between an experiencing subject and an object experienced. For example, when I see an object there is a relation of sensing or perceiving between me and the object perceived. Thus, if I perceive a tree then the structure of the experience could be pictured as shown on page 19.

For Kierkegaard, on the other hand, we cannot perceive our own particular "ethical" reality through the senses, nor can we know the particular by means of an ordinary instance of introspection. Rather, the experience that most fully allows us to have knowledge of our own ethical reality is a unique kind of experience, a unique kind of introspection whose structure and content differ from the relational analysis of experience given by the empiricist. In accordance with Kierkegaard's terminology we

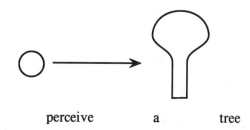

I   perceive   a   tree

may call this experience "inwardness" or "faith." For Kierkegaard, it is only by becoming inward or by having faith that the existing individual can become subjectively in the truth. In other words, subjectivity and existential self-awareness are a consequence of faith, and it is only by having faith that one most clearly becomes aware of oneself as an individual and not merely a specimen of a kind.

What, then, is faith and inwardness, and how does one acquire it? In asking these questions we are considering, in effect, the question of what differentiates "experience," or "introspection" as Kierkegaard conceives of it, from the empiricist analysis. We can begin to get a grip on these questions by noting that faith, for Kierkegaard, is essentially a religious phenomenon, since it concerns the topic of God's existence. However, as in the case of the topic of death, the question of God's existence may be existentially relevant or existentially irrelevant. We may grasp the truth of God's existence subjectively, or we may be related to God in an objective manner. The distinction between objective truth and subjective truth is fundamental to Kierkegaard's thought and to our problem, and we discuss it in the next section.

KIERKEGAARD'S PATH TO THE EXISTING INDIVIDUAL: SUBJECTIVE TRUTH AND FAITH

For Kierkegaard the problem of becoming subjective is the problem of establishing the proper relationship to Christianity. What, then, is the proper relationship, and how is it to be acquired? It should be no surprise to discover that Kierkegaard rejects a purely intellectual or objective relationship to God in favor of a purely subjective or passionate relationship. For that reason the proper place to begin a discussion of Kierkegaard's path to true Christianity and existential self-awareness is by examining his intriguing doctrine that truth is subjectivity.

There is no better place to begin a consideration of the thesis that truth is subjectivity than with the following famous passage:

> *When the question of truth is put forward in an objective manner, reflection is directed objectively to the truth as an object to which the knower is related. The reflection is not on the relationship but on whether he is related to the truth. If that which he is related to is the truth, the subject is in the truth. When the question of truth is put forward in a subjective manner, reflection is directed subjectively to the individual's relationship. If the relation's HOW is in truth, the individual is in truth, even if the WHAT to which he is related is not true.*

We may illustrate this by examining the knowledge of God. Objectively the reflection is on whether the object is the true God; subjectively reflection is on whether the individual is related to a *what* in such a way that his relationship in truth is a God-relationship. (pp. 45–46)

To grasp the truth of the doctrines of Christianity and the existence of God objectively is to come to believe that God's existence is an objective fact that we can come to know on the basis of argument. To have an objective relationship to God is to be a person who assents to all the propositions about God, goes to church, and performs the rituals, but there is no inwardness, no *decisiveness*. Accepting the existence of God is an intellectual accomplishment that does not touch a person's life; it does not make an individual aware of him- or herself as a being that has made, alone and with complete responsibility, the *decision* or *choice* to become a Christian. When truth is considered objectively, it is a matter of correspondence to fact rather than a way of life.

According to Kierkegaard, the degree to which one is objectively secure in one's belief or relationship with God and Christianity is the degree to which one moves away from subjective truth or inwardness. For if God is an objective truth, then one's belief does not require any special relationship or commitment. If there are reasons to uphold or justify being a Christian, then there is no need for the existence of passion or infinite interest to sustain it. In other words, if I believe that the existence of God is supported by reasons, then I stand in a purely cognitive or intellectual relationship to God. Passion and commitment are unnecessary, and therefore subjectivity, inwardness, and self-awareness are at a minimum. Thus, when viewed objectively the question of whether or not God exists is existentially irrelevant, since the question of God's existence has nothing to do with the decisions and choices that make up the content of one's life.

On the other hand, the existence of God can be existentially relevant when one is subjectively in the truth or subjectively related to God. The person who is related to God subjectively comes to see that no arguments for the existence of God are in the slightest degree convincing (or even probable). In fact, it is the very lack of a rational basis for the belief in God that requires the believer to make *a personal, passionate decision and commitment to believe.* It is passion and commitment combined with intellectual doubt that is necessary for subjective truth. The following passage nicely illustrates the distinction between objectivity and subjectivity and where, according to Kierkegaard, the Truth exists.

> If one who lives in a Christian culture goes up to God's house, the house of the true God, with a true conception of God, with knowledge of God and prays—but prays in a false spirit; and one who lives in an idolatrous land prays with the total passion of the infinite, although his eyes rest on the image of an idol; where is there most truth? The one prays in truth to God, although he worships an idol. The other prays in untruth to the true God and therefore really worships an idol. (p. 46)

In other words, passionate inwardness is the mark of truth even if, or rather when, the truth is objectively uncertain.

When one views God subjectively one enters into a God-relationship and thereby achieves inwardness and faith. The true believer recognizes that the existence of God is a paradox—something that is objectively absurd—and yet is willing to allow one's entire life to be determined by the belief in God's existence. What, then, is the absurd? Kierkegaard says,

> The absurd is that the eternal truth has entered time, that God has entered existence, has been born, has grown, and so on, has become precisely like any other human being, quite indistinguishable from other humans. The absurd is precisely by its objective repulsion the measure of the inwardness of faith. (pp. 50–51)

Thus, a person who believes in God believes in the absurd (that the eternal and the temporal are one) and thereby achieves inwardness, since such an individual is doing something on his or her own: committing to a certain way of life even though there is ultimately no rational basis to do so.

When one views God subjectively, one enters into a "God-man" relationship and thereby achieves inwardness and faith. For Kierkegaard, subjectivity, inwardness, and faith are synonymous expressions whose definition is an equivalent expression for truth. Here is such a definition of truth: *"the objective uncertainty, held fast in an appropriation process of the most passionate inwardness is the truth,* the highest truth available for an *existing* person" (p. 48). Thus, faith is not the belief that someday someone will be able to "prove" the objective existence of God. It is, rather, a commitment of oneself, with infinite passion, to something that is not based on any objective fact.

By its very nature, faith involves risk, the risk that what you are believing is not objectively true. In fact, it is only after one recognizes the death of God, the intellectual recognition that God does not exist, that one is free to become genuinely ethical and existentially self-aware. As Kierkegaard puts it,

> Without risk there is no faith. Faith is precisely the contradiction between the infinite passion of inwardness and objective uncertainty. If I can grasp God objectively, I do not believe, but because I cannot know God objectively, I must have faith, and if I will preserve myself in faith, I must constantly be determined to hold fast to the objective uncertainty, so as to remain out upon the ocean's deep, over seventy thousand fathoms of water, and still believe. (p. 48)

Thus, to have faith is to make a decision entirely on one's own without the security of objective reasons to back it up. This is why it is such a difficult decision and one that must be constantly renewed in order to be maintained. Is it any wonder then that Kierkegaard says the danger of subjectivity in its extreme is madness?

The person who has faith arrives at self-awareness because in faith the relationship to God involves one of conscious *self-activity* and *self-creation.* When I subjectively believe that God exists I understand that what I believe cannot be rationally understood or justified, since it is objectively a paradox. Yet if, in spite of the lack of external support, I still believe, then it must be because I consciously decide, with all the passion of the infinite, to choose to bring this commitment into existence. In faith I confront myself as an existing individual, since I am entirely responsible for my faith and I know that I am alone with my faith. Thus, I cannot avoid inwardness and subjectivity in faith, since having faith is solely an act of my own free will. As Kierkegaard puts it,

> Faith has two tasks: to take care in every moment to discover the improbable, the paradox; and then to hold it fast with the passion of inwardness. . . . [F]aith is *self-active* in its relation to the improbable and the paradoxical, *self-active* in its discovery, and *self-active* in every moment holding it fast in order to believe. Merely to lay hold of the improbable requires all the passion of the infinite and its concentration in itself. . . .[10]

If my belief in Christianity rests entirely on me, I must be aware of my decision to become a (true) Christian through faith. Faith, therefore, leads to self-awareness, but why is *Christianity* necessary for a true faith? And, to return to an earlier question, "What precisely is the difference between objective and subjective reflection, between the empiricist account of experience and Kierkegaard's?"

Kierkegaard frequently distinguishes between knowledge and faith or belief. He claims, "the absurd is precisely faith's object and the only positive attitude possible in relation to it is faith, and not knowledge" (p. 51), and thus to attempt to establish that Christianity is something probable or something that can almost be known is to render it impossible to believe through faith. For knowledge involves a cognitive relation between a subject and an object, an object whose existence owes nothing to the passionate interest or commitment of the subject. The structure and content of inwardness, subjective thought, or faith is quite different, for in (existential) belief the object owes its existence to an infinite passion and a continual will (and commitment) to believe in light of objective uncertainty. Moreover, and crucially, in subjective thought or belief we become aware of the paradox of Christianity by becoming aware of ourselves. In other words, as existing individuals we are a mirror image of the contradiction contained in the conception of God. The contradiction within us consists

> in the contradiction that an existing human being is a synthesis of the infinite and the finite situated in time, so that the joy of the eternal in him becomes inexpressible because he is an existing individual. . . . [11]

Like God, we are contradictory beings in that we are, at one and the same time, both universal and particular or abstract and concrete. We are universal by virtue of being human beings and belonging to many other categories (e.g., husband, wife, teacher, mother, etc.), and we are particular in virtue of being the unique and incomparable individuals that we are. Thus, we cannot intellectually apprehend God directly, but we can become involved in a true God-relationship when we look within ourselves and recognize the contradictory beings that we are. As Kierkegaard says,

> For no anonymous author can more cunningly conceal himself, no practitioner of the maieutic art can more carefully withdraw himself from the direct relationship, than God. He is in the creation, and present everywhere in it, but directly he is not there; and *only when the individual turns to his inner self, and hence only in the inwardness of self-activity does he have his attention aroused, and is enabled to see God.*[12]

The faith of the true or subjective Christian gives rise to the greatest degree of inwardness because it is based upon the greatest degree of uncertainty. Nevertheless, a certain degree of inwardness and subjective truth is possible within paganism as Kierkegaard's persistent praise of Socrates makes clear. "The infinite merit of the Socratic position was precisely to accentuate the fact that the knower is an existing individual, and that the task of existing is his essential task."[13] To exist as an individual is to make subjective decisions, decisions ultimately based on passion and not reason. In a certain sense, Socrates was a subjective thinker.

Socrates was judged to have a kind of wisdom called "human" or "Socratic wisdom," the sort of wisdom that accrues to those individuals, if any besides Socrates, who are aware of their own ignorance. Socrates interpreted this judgment as a divine commandment to lead a philosophical life which consisted in searching after truth (by separating the soul from the body), and by questioning others and making them aware of their own ignorance. Socrates' entire life was determined by one eternal and essential truth; namely, that to live a philosophical life is right even if to do so will lead to death. Nevertheless, Socrates was objectively insecure concerning this decisive commitment. Did the gods really mean that he should lead a philosophical life? And what of immortality? Socrates is willing to risk his entire life on the belief that his soul is immortal. But *is* the soul immortal? Socrates believes that it is; he offers several arguments for that thesis, but he concludes his examination of them by claiming that there are still many questions to be asked and that others will no doubt find difficulties with these proofs. In short, Socrates is objectively insecure about the question of immortality and indeed, even the objective validity of the life he has chosen. Nevertheless, he committed himself to living his life in accordance with his beliefs and for that became, in Kierkegaard's eyes, an existing individual and not a mere cognitive subject.

In spite of his praise of Socrates, Kierkegaard does not think that Socrates achieved the level of inwardness achieved by the true Christian, if such a person exists. Christianity gives rise to the greatest degree of inwardness, passion, and commitment because if we are true Christians then *the eternal truth that we commit ourselves to is in itself paradoxical.* Consider the following passage:

> When the eternal truth is related to an existing individual, truth becomes a paradox. The paradox repels the individual because of the objective uncertainty and ignorance towards inwardness. But since this paradox in itself is not paradoxical, it does not push the spirit far enough. For without risk there is no faith, and the greater the risk the greater the faith, and the more objective reliability, the less inwardness (for inwardness is precisely subjectivity). Indeed, the less objective reliability, the deeper becomes the possible inwardness. When the paradox is in itself paradoxical, it repels the individual by the power of the absurd, and the corresponding passion, which is produced in the process, is faith. (p. 50)

This important passage sums up several crucial themes in Kierkegaard's thought. First, faith requires not only that the individual's relationship to the eternal truth be a paradox (that what is true for the individual may be objectively false), but more importantly, that the eternal truth itself be paradoxical. Socrates' belief in the absolutes, the immortality of the soul, and the doctrine of recollection may all be false, but they are not internally inconsistent. The paradox of Christianity, on the other hand, is internally inconsistent and therefore to believe it will be even more difficult. Second, the degree of inwardness is directly proportionate to the degree of objective insecurity one has regarding the object of belief. When the risk is greatest, passion is the greatest, and when passion is greatest, "this absurdity, held fast in the passion of inwardness, is faith". Kierkegaard describes the movements to faith in *Fear and Trembling*. In order to better grasp his concept of faith as well as other central aspects of his philosophy, we turn to a brief discussion of that work.

FEAR AND TREMBLING: THE THREE MOVEMENTS TO FAITH

Fear and Trembling is about the philosophical significance of the story of Abraham and Isaac, and it is also about Kierkegaard's personal experience. The movements to faith that he describes in the "Preliminary Expectoration" are movements that Kierkegaard himself engaged in: pain that he felt when he broke off his engagement to his fiancée Regina. Yet this work is primarily about Abraham, the true father or knight of faith. It is meant to engage us and to lead us toward the path of authenticity by explaining what faith is and by explaining the problems and conflicts that exist for one who tries to arrive at faith.

Let us begin by considering Kierkegaard's discussion of the movements by which one attains faith. He initially illustrates these movements by a case that is basically autobiographical, but we shall see that the case has its parallels in the story of Abraham. The movements of faith involve three steps or stages: (1) commitment or appropriation, (2) infinite resignation, and (3) faith. Kierkegaard illustrates these stages by telling a story of a young lad who falls in love with a princess and yet understands that the situation is such that it is impossible for their love to be realized. The level of commitment involves two substages. First, there is the concentration of the whole content and significance of one's life on a single wish: in this case, the wish for a finite, temporal, loving relationship with the princess. One wishes to see, to touch, to talk to, and to always be with the princess. As a transition to the stage of resignation or renunciation, one recognizes that the finite reality one envisions is impossible. The lad remains alone and isolated and then, in full consciousness, he makes the movement of infinite resignation.

The movement of resignation involves the pain of renouncing the finite temporal realization of the wish, since it is now recognized as objectively impossible. And yet, the wish itself is seen to be possible spiritually. Infinite resignation involves giving up the possibility of the love existing in a human finite sense, but at the same time the renunciation involves a continuation of the love in a spiritual, eternal sense. Love becomes something eternal and remains young. As Kierkegaard puts it,

> From the instant he made the movement the princess is lost to him. He has no need of those erotic tinglings in the nerves at the sight of the beloved, etc., nor does he need to be constantly taking leave of her in a finite sense, because he recollects her in an eternal sense, . . . The knight does not annul his resignation, he preserves his love just as young as it was in its first moment, he never lets it go from him, precisely because he makes the movements infinitely. . . . The two will preserve their love young and sound, she also will have triumphed over her pains, even though she does not, as it is said in the ballad, 'lie every night beside her lord.' These two will to all eternity remain in agreement with one another, with a well-timed *harmonia praestabilita*, ... (pp. 69–70)

Of course, this stage involves pain, the sort of pain that Kierkegaard knew all too well, since it involves the realization that one's love will never be realized in this world. Yet there is, together with this pain, a certain sort of repose and peace, since now the one who gave up the finite becomes self-sufficient in his or her love. The finite element of love no longer matters, since love remains young and possible in a spiritual (ideal) and eternal sense.

The next and final stage involves faith. This stage, if it occurs at all, is practically simultaneous with that of infinite resignation. Here we believe that what we have given up will take place. Thus, in the present case, at the time one renounces all finite possibility in the existence of love, one again believes, by virtue of all the passion of one's soul, and by virtue of the absurd, that one will receive what one has renounced. In faith I believe with all my passion, in virtue of the absurd and not because of any reasons, that the finite love I have given up will be returned to me.

> At the moment when the knight made the act of resignation, he was convinced, humanly speaking, of the impossibility. This was the result reached by the understanding, and he had sufficient energy to think it. On the other hand, in an infinite sense it was possible, namely by renouncing it; but this sort of possessing is at the same time a relinquishing, and yet there is no absurdity in this for the understanding, for the understanding continued to be in the right in affirming that in the world of the finite where it holds sway this was and remains an impossibility. This is quite as clear to the knight of faith, so the only thing that can save him is the absurd, and this he grasps by faith. So he recognizes the impossibility, and at that very instant he believes the absurd; ('I believe nevertheless that I shall get her, in virtue, that is, of the absurd, in virtue of the fact that with God all things are possible.') for, if without recognizing the impossibility with all the passion of his soul and with all his heart, he should wish to imagine that he has faith, he deceives himself, and his testimony has no bearing, since he has not even reached the infinite resignation. (p. 71)

The story of Abraham reflects the three movements of faith in rather clear-cut ways. First, there was one wish dominating the content of Abraham's thought, namely, that he would have a son who would become king. As a test of his faith God asked Abraham to sacrifice his son. Thus, the second movement of infinite resignation occurs when Abraham willingly agrees to sacrifice his son's life and renounce his ethical or moral duty not to murder. Since God wills that his son is to die, Abraham recognizes the finite impossibility of realizing his wish for his son to be king. The final movement or leap of faith occurs when he believes, in virtue of the absurd, that his son will be spared. Indeed,

> a paradoxical and humble courage is required to grasp the whole of the temporal by virtue of the absurd, and this is the courage of faith. By faith Abraham did not renounce his claim upon Isaac, but by faith he got Isaac. (p. 73)

The significance of Abraham's act may be clarified by attending to several questions. First, What is the absurdity involved in Abraham's belief that Isaac would be saved? Why is Abraham's leap to faith done in fear and trembling? What is the "tremendous paradox" that constitutes the significance of Abraham's life? And, finally, how are we to judge Abraham; why is he considered to be such a great person according to Kierkegaard?

A useful way to approach these questions is by considering Kierkegaard's three stages of existence: the aesthetic, the ethical, and the religious, since these three stages closely parallel the movements to faith. In the aesthetic stage, or way of life, the aim of life is pleasure. The main representative of this style of life is Don Juan. Such people admit of no restraint and are constantly satisfying themselves in new and different ways. Of course, aesthetes need not be mere sensualists; their pleasures may be intellectual as well, but the crucial feature is that enjoyment of life is their final aim. What the sensualist and the detached intellectual have in common is selfishness. Both of them live around the question "What interests me?" At the aesthetic stage, the moment is everything; one lives for the *now.* Such a life is in discord and is chaotic, since what one wants is constantly vanishing, and so one is constantly changing one's immediate goals. According to Kierkegaard, the result of pursuing pleasure of the moment is despair. One's life reduces to the pleasure of the moment, but the moment is so short one's life and indeed the individual him- or herself becomes almost nothing.

The ethical stage is arrived at by a leap or decision on the part of the individual to avoid the despair of the aesthetic level. The ethical is a somewhat paradoxical category for Kierkegaard, a paradox that reflects the paradox of human existence. In *Fear and Trembling,* the ethical is the universal, the realm of objective moral truths that everyone ought to accept and live by. The ethical individual is thus the person who has morality as the chief principle of his or her conduct. The ultimate aim of ethical individuals is to perform their duty. In *Fear and Trembling* ethical individuals are those who give up their individuality in order to become the universal, to act as others do. As Kierkegaard says,

> The ethical as such is the universal, and as the universal it applies to everyone, which may be expressed from another point of view by saying that it applies every instant. I . . . conceived immediately as physical and psychical, the particular individual is the individual who has his *telos* in the universal. As soon as the individual would assert himself in his particularity over against the universal he sins, and only by recognizing this can he again reconcile himself with the universal. (pp. 76–77)

In the *Concluding Unscientific Postscript,* however, the ethical is not the universal, but the particular, the concrete, the existing individual. To be "ethical" requires us to concentrate on our own self, and determine for ourselves what we must do. The ethical individual is one who asserts him- or herself as an individual, as being more important than the universal. Consider the following revealing passages:

> *The only reality that exists for an existing individual is his own ethical reality.* . . . The real subject is not the cognitive subject, since in knowing he moves in the sphere of the possible; *the real subject is the ethically existing subject. Ethically the ideality is the real within the individual himself.* The real is an inwardness that is infinitely interested in existing; this is exemplified in the ethical individual. . . . The ethical is concerned with particular human beings, and with each and every one of them by himself.[14]

Ultimately, Kierkegaard is critical of the (universal) ethical sphere of existence insofar as it is understood as a general prescription for how we ought to behave. To exist at the level of the (moral) ethical leads us to think in general terms and to forget that we are existing individuals. In addition to taking us away from the subject matter of existentialism, a second reason why Kierkegaard is critical of the ethical qua universal is that there are problems and paradoxes with the (moral) ethical that cannot be resolved at that level. For example, how, at the ethical level, are we to deal with Abraham's willingness to kill his son Isaac? At the ethical level there is no justification for Abraham's action, and yet Abraham has an "absolute duty" to follow God's command to sacrifice Isaac even if it violates the universal moral law *Thou shalt not kill.* There is a paradox here: It is our duty to follow the moral law and not murder our children, and yet it is also Abraham's duty to obey God's command to sacrifice Isaac. How can these incompatible obligations *both* be our duty? Furthermore, if the ethical is the universal and the ethical is the highest level of existence, then we must view Abraham as a murderer, and we must claim that he was evil in being willing to kill Isaac and violate the moral law. Thus, in order to understand the paradox that constitutes the significance of Abraham's life and to understand his greatness we must turn to the final stage: the movement to faith.

According to Kierkegaard, Abraham was great because he recognized the paradox in doing his duty toward God, and yet he had the faith to act on God's command. That is, Abraham gave up the wish that constituted the content of his life, and he renounced the moral law. Yet, at the same time, he believed in virtue of the absurd, that God would save Isaac. What, then, is the absurd? It is that one must disobey God's command in order to obey God's command. It is that the particular is higher than the universal. In grasping and believing in the absurd with the passion of the infinite within him, Abraham adopted the religious life. The religious stage thus involves a commitment to God's command. One views God's command as an absolute duty even if it involves a violation of the laws of morality which are themselves God's commands!

Naturally, the movement to faith and the movement to the religious stage are made in fear and trembling for, from an ethical point of view, Abraham's act stands without justification. There is no universal value that can justify his act, since there is no objective foundation for renouncing the ethical. Furthermore, his act involves a paradox, namely, that he is breaking the moral law which is God's will, in order to follow God's will. But that is absurd: Since the moral laws are God's will, how can breaking them also be God's will? The justification cannot come from the fact that God commands it, since Abraham has no way of knowing it is God rather than Satan who is commanding him to kill Isaac.

Thus, the movement to the religious stage provides a positive answer to the question "Is there such a thing as a teleological suspension of the ethical?" In overriding the ethical is there some higher end in virtue of which Abraham is "justified" in his willingness to kill Isaac? The answer is yes; one is justified and there is some end greater than the universal. The particular is higher than the universal, for to stand in a relation to a particular qua particular, that is, to stand in a God-relationship is more valuable than any other relationship, since it is one in which passion is at its highest and the individual is greatest. Kierkegaard asks,

> But now when the ethical is teleologically suspended, how does the individual exist in whom it is suspended? He exists as the particular in opposition to the universal. . . . How then did Abraham exist? He believed. This is the paradox which keeps him upon the sheer edge and which he cannot make clear to any other man, for the paradox is that he as the individual puts himself in an absolute relation to the absolute. Is he justified in doing this? His justification is once more the paradox; for if he is justified, it is not by virtue of anything universal, but by virtue of being the particular individual. (p. 82)

The point Kierkegaard is making is that the justification for Abraham's action cannot be objective, since objectively his action constitutes a paradox. Objectively, the universal is higher than the particular, but in faith the individual is higher than the universal. Thus, the "justification" of Abraham's act of faith is that it gives rise to self-awareness: a sense of what it means to exist as an individual and not as a universal. Abraham recognizes that he is obliged to exist alone and that he must give up the comfort of the ethical qua universal in order to do his absolute duty toward God, in order to become an existing individual.

The distinction between the ethical and the religious stage and between infinite resignation and faith can be drawn more clearly by considering the distinction Kierkegaard draws between the *tragic hero* and the *knight of faith*. The tragic hero is one who has to face the difficulty of choosing between what he or she wishes to do and what it is his or her duty to do. The tragic hero renounces a wish and a duty at one level in order to perform a duty at another, higher level. As Kierkegaard puts it,

> When a son is forgetful of his duty, when the state entrusts the father with the sword of justice, when the laws require punishment at the hand of the father, then will the father heroically forget that the guilty one is his son, he will magnanimously conceal his pain, but there will not be a single one among the people, not even the son, who will not admire the father, ... (pp. 79–80)

Or again,

> The difference between the tragic hero and Abraham is clearly evident. The tragic hero still remains with the ethical. He lets one expression of the ethical find its *telos* in a higher expression of the ethical; . . . . (p. 80)

The act of the tragic hero requires courage and renunciation, but it is, nevertheless, an act that has within it the security of the universal. The tragic hero renounces self in order to express the universal, to follow a higher level moral order.

The knight of faith, on the other hand, renounces the universal for the particular. The knight of faith is insecure and completely alone in choosing, since there is no higher level universal that can justify or explain the knight's act. For Abraham

> overstepped the ethical entirely and possessed a higher *telos* outside of it, in relation to which he suspended the former. For I should very much like to know how one would bring Abraham's act into relation with the universal, and whether it is possible to discover any connection whatever between what Abraham did and the universal . . . except the fact that he transgressed it. . . . Therefore, whereas the tragic hero is great by reason of his moral

virtue, Abraham is great by reason of a purely personal virtue. (pp. 80–81)

Thus, for the tragic hero the ethical is the highest level, and obedience to the ethical is the source of his greatness. For Abraham, however, the particular is higher than the moral law and in order to show his faith in God, his absolute duty toward God, and to act on the basis of himself alone, he chose to kill Isaac.

Finally, the difference between the ethical and the religious can be understood in terms of the different relationship we have to God at these levels. At the ethical level, the relationship is one of separation. God is a universal and his commands are our duty, but we are never in a direct relation to God. For,

> The ethical is the universal, and as such it is again the divine. One has therefore a right to say that fundamentally every duty is a duty toward God; but if one cannot say more, then one affirms at the same time that properly I have no duty toward God. Duty becomes duty by being referred to God, but in duty itself I do not come into relation with God. Thus it is a duty to love one's neighbor, but in performing this duty I do not come into relation with God but with the neighbor whom I love. (p. 83)

Thus, at the ethical level we have no special relation to God. Yet there is such a thing as an absolute duty toward God in which we stand in a very special relationship to Him. Our absolute duty toward God may force us to go against the dictates of God at the level of the universal, but an absolute duty forces us to look within and in so doing find God. For "God is Subject and therefore exists only for the subjective individual in inwardness." (p. 46).

Kierkegaard Lexicon

Aesthetic stage. Way of life whose aim is pleasure.

Appropriating process. Continual will to believe, and making one's own what is believed (through decisiveness).

Cognitive subject. Person understood as a knower or objective thinker.

Commitment. Involves decision to live in accordance with one's beliefs and not just to have them.

Dialectics. In Hegel, a process of identifying and resolving contradictions through thesis, antithesis, and synthesis.

Empiricism. All knowledge of reality (the particular) is acquired through experience.

Essence. What a thing is; its true nature. Essences are universals: They are common to many different particular things.

Ethically existing subject. In the *Concluding Unscientific Postscript,* it refers to the existing individual.

Ethical stage. In *Fear and Trembling,* the ethical is the universal, the realm of objective moral truths that everyone ought to accept and live by. The ethical individual is thus the person who has morality as the chief principle of his or her conduct.

Existential system. An impossibility since a system is an abstract construction, but the existential is the concrete particular.

Existentially irrelevant. Has nothing to do with one's life as an existing individual, that is, as an individual who makes decisions and choices.

Existentially relevant. Leads to an awareness of oneself as an existing individual.

Faith. When one believes, with the passion of the infinite, that what is impossible (or absurd), exists or will occur. It involves risk. See also *subjective truth.*

Infinite resignation. Involves the pain of renouncing the finite temporal realization of a wish that is recognized as objectively impossible. And yet, the wish itself is seen to be possible spiritually.

Knight of faith. Renounces both wish and duty, since there is no higher moral law that can be appealed to, to justify the act. In going against one's duty to God one places the particular above the universal (moral order) and shows faith in God.

Necessary truth. Truths that hold for all people for all times; *unchanging* truths.

Objective Christian. Follows customs and rituals, believes the Christian dogmas, and relates to the *what* of Christianity rather than the *how.*

Objective truth. Truth that is based upon and upheld by facts. The individual believer is irrelevant to the truth of the proposition believed. Emphasis is on *what* is believed rather than *how* it is believed.

Particulars. Individual things that exist in space and time.

Rationalism. Reality consists in necessary truths (universals and Absolute Truth), and our knowledge of reality is acquired by reason.

Religious stage. Involves a commitment to God's command. One views God's command as an absolute duty even if it entails a violation of the laws of morality which are themselves God's commands.

Socratic wisdom. Knowledge one possesses when one knows that there is much that one does not know. An awareness of one's own ignorance.

Speculative philosophy. See *rationalism.*

Subjective Christian. Person with a commitment and belief in the absurd. See *faith.*

Subjective thought. Involves passion, an appropriating process, and inwardness (self-reflection).

Subjective truth. *"The objective uncertainty, held fast in an appropriation process of the most passionate inwardness is the truth."* In subjective truth the individual is active in upholding the object believed, and thus the emphasis is on the *how* not the *what.*

Systematic philosophy. See *rationalism.*

Teleological suspension of the ethical. In faith there is an end higher than the universal. The particular is higher than the universal, for to stand in a relation to a particular qua particular, that is, to stand in a God-relationship is more valuable than any other relationship, since it is one in which passion is at its highest and the individual is greatest.

The absurd. For Kierkegaard, that God is eternal and that God was born and died like other humans.

Tragic hero. Individual who renounces a wish and a duty at one level of morality in order to perform a duty at another, higher level. Thus, the tragic hero remains within the realm of the ethical or universal.

KIERKEGAARD SELECTIONS

From *Concluding Unscientific Postscript*

An Existential System Is Impossible

An existential system cannot be formulated. Does this mean that no such system exists? By no means; nor is this implied in our assertion. Reality itself is a system—for God; but it cannot be a system for any existing spirit. System and finality correspond to one another, but existence is precisely the opposite of finality. It may be seen, from a purely abstract point of view, that system and existence are incapable of being thought together; because in order to think existence at all, systematic thought must think it as abrogated, and hence as not existing. Existence separates, and holds the various moments of existence discretely apart; the systematic thought consists of the finality which brings them together. . . .

Respecting the impossibility of an existential system, let us then ask quite simply, as a Greek youth might have asked his teacher (and if the superlative wisdom can explain everything, but cannot answer a simple question, it is clear that the world is out of joint): "Who is to write or complete such a system?" Surely a human being; unless we propose again to begin using the strange mode of speech which assumes that a human being becomes speculative philosophy in the abstract, or becomes the identity of subject and object. So then, a human being—and surely a living human being, i.e. an existing individual. Or if the speculative thought which brings the systems to light is the joint effort of different thinkers: in what last concluding thought does this fellowship finally realize itself, how does it reach the light of day? Surely through some human being? And how are the individual participants related to the joint effort, what are the categories which mediate between the individual and world-process, and who is it again who strings them all together on the systematic thread? Is he a human being, or is he speculative philosophy in the abstract? But if he is a human being, then he is also an existing individual.

Two ways, in general, are open for an existing individual: *Either* he can do his utmost to forget that he is an existing individual, by which he becomes a comic figure, since existence has the remarkable trait of compelling an existing individual to exist whether he wills it or not. (The comical contradiction in willing to be what one is not, as when a man wills to be a bird, is not more comical than the contradiction of not willing to be what one is, as *in casu* an existing individual; just as the language finds it comical that a man forgets his name, which does not so much mean forgetting a designation, as it means forgetting the distinctive essence of one's being.) *Or* he can concentrate his entire energy upon the fact that he is an existing individual. It is from this side, in the first instance, that objection must be made to modern philosophy; not that it has a mistaken presupposition, but that it has a comical presupposition, occasioned by its having forgotten, in a sort of world-historical absent-mindedness, what it means to be a human being. Not indeed, what it means to be a human being in general; for this is the sort of thing that one might even induce a speculative philosopher to agree to; but what it means that you and I and he are human beings, each one for himself.

The existing individual who concentrates all his attention upon the circumstance that he is an existing individual, will welcome these words of Lessing about a persistent striving, as a beautiful saying. To be sure, it did not indeed win for its author an immortal fame, because it is very simple; but every thoughtful individual must needs confirm its truth. The existing individual who forgets that he is an existing individual, will become more and more absent-minded; and as people sometimes embody the fruits of their leisure moments in books, so we may venture to expect as the fruit of his absent-mindedness the expected existential system— well, perhaps not all of us, but only those who are almost as absent-minded as he is. While the Hegelian philosophy goes on and becomes an existential system in sheer distraction of mind, and what is more, is finished—without having an Ethics (where existence properly belongs), the more simple philosophy which is propounded by an existing individual for existing individuals, will more especially emphasize the ethical.

As soon as it is remembered that philosophizing does not consist in addressing fantastic beings in fantastic language, but that those to whom the philosopher addresses himself are human beings; so that we have not to determine fantastically *in abstracto* whether a persistent striving is something lower than the systematic finality, or *vice versa,* but that the question is what existing human beings, in so far as they are existing beings, must needs be content with: then it will be evident that the ideal of a persistent striving is the only view of life that does not carry with it an inevitable disillusionment. Even if a man has attained to the highest, the repetition by which life receives content (if one is to escape retrogression or avoid becoming fantastic) will again constitute a persistent striving; because here again finality is moved further on, and postponed. It is with this view of life as it is with the Platonic interpretation of love as a want; and the principle that not only he is in want who desires something he does not have, but also he who desires the continued possession of what he has. In a speculative-fantastic sense we have a positive finality in the System, and in an aesthetic-fantastic sense we have one in the fifth act of the drama. But this sort of finality is valid only for fantastic beings.

The ideal of a persistent striving expresses the existing subject's ethical view of life. It must therefore not be understood in a metaphysical sense, nor indeed is there any individual who exists metaphysically. One might thus by way of misunderstanding set up an antithesis between finality and the persistent striving for truth. But this is merely a misunderstanding in this sphere. In the ethical sense, on the contrary, the persistent striving represents the consciousness of being an existing individual; the constant learning is the expression for the incessant realization, in no moment complete as long as the subject is in existence; the subject is aware of this fact, and hence is not deceived. But Greek philosophy always had a relation to Ethics. Hence it was not imagined that the principle of always being a learner was a great discovery, or the enthusiastic enterprise of a particular distinguished individual; for it was neither more nor less than the realization that a human being is an existing individual, which it constitutes no great merit to be aware of, but which it is thoughtless to forget.

So-called pantheistic systems have often been characterized and challenged in the assertion that they abrogate the distinction between good and evil, and destroy freedom. Perhaps one would express oneself quite as definitely, if one said that every such system fantastically dissipates the concept *existence.* But we ought to say this not merely of pantheistic systems; it would be more to the point to show that every system must be pantheistic precisely on account of its finality. Existence must be revoked in the eternal before the system can round itself out; there must be no existing remainder, not even such a little minikin as the existing Herr Professor who writes the system. But this is not the way in which the problem is usually dealt with. No, pantheistic systems are attacked, partly in tumultuous aphorisms which again and again promise a new system; and partly by way of scraping together something supposed to be a system, and inserting in it a special paragraph in which it is laid down that the concept *existence,* or actuality, is intended to be especially emphasized. That such a paragraph is a mockery of the entire system, that instead of being a paragraph in a system it is an absolute protest against the system, makes no difference to busy systematists. If the concept of existence is really to be stressed, this cannot be given a direct expression as a paragraph in a system; all direct swearing and oath-supported assurances serve only to make the topsy-turvy profession of the paragraph more and more ridiculous. An actual emphasis on existence must be expressed in an essential form; in view of the elusiveness of existence, such a form will have to be an indirect form, namely, the absence of a system. But this again must not degenerate into an asseverating formula, for the indirect character of the expression will constantly demand renewal and rejuvenation in the form. In the case of committee reports, it may be quite in order to incorporate in the report a dissenting opinion; but an existential system which includes the dissenting opinion as a paragraph in its own logical structure, is a curious monstrosity. What wonder that the System continues to sustain its life as a going concern. In general, objections are haughtily ignored; if a particular objection seems to attract a little attention, the systematic entrepreneurs engage a copyist to copy off the objection, which thereupon is incorporated in the System; and when the book is bound the System is complete.

The systematic Idea is the identity of subject and object, the unity of thought and being. Existence, on the other hand, is their separation. It does not by any means follow that existence is thoughtless; but it has brought about, and brings about, a separation between subject and object, thought and being. In the objective sense, thought is understood as being pure thought; this corresponds in an equally abstract-objective sense to its object, which object is therefore the thought itself, and the truth becomes the correspondence of thought with itself. This objective thought has no relation to the existing subject; and while we are always confronted with the difficult question of how the existing subject slips into this objectivity, where subjectivity is merely pure abstract subjectivity (which again is an objective determination, not signifying any existing human being), it is certain that the existing subjectivity tends more and more to evaporate. And finally, if it is possible for a human being to become anything of the sort, and it is merely something of which at most he becomes aware through the imagination, he becomes the pure abstract conscious participation in and knowledge of this pure relationship between thought and being, this pure identity; aye, this tautology, because this being which is ascribed to the thinker does not signify that he is, but only that he is engaged in thinking.

The existing subject, on the other hand, is engaged in existing, which is indeed the case with every human being. Let us therefore not deal unjustly with the objective tendency, by calling it an ungodly and pantheistic self-deification; but let us rather view it as an essay in the comical. For the notion that from now on until the end of the world nothing could be said except what proposed a further improvement in an almost completed system, is merely a systematic consequence for systematists.

By beginning at once to use ethical categories in criticism of the objective tendency, one does it an injustice, and fails to make contact with it, because one has nothing in common with what is under attack. But by remaining in the metaphysical sphere, one is enabled to use the comical, which also lies in the metaphysical, so as to bring such a transfigured professor to book. If a dancer could leap very high, we would admire him. But if he tried to give the impression that he could fly, let laughter single him out for suitable punishment; even though it might be true that he could leap as high as any dancer ever had done. Leaping is the accomplishment of a being essentially earthly, one who respects the earth's gravitational force, since the leaping is only momentary. But flying carries a suggestion of being emancipated from telluric conditions, a privilege reserved for winged creatures, and perhaps also shared by the inhabitants of the moon—and there perhaps the System will first find its true readers.

Being an individual man is a thing that has been abolished, and every speculative philosopher confuses himself with humanity at large; whereby he becomes something infinitely great, and at the same time nothing at all. He confounds himself with humanity in sheer distraction of mind, just as the opposition press uses the royal "we," and sailors say: "devil take me!" But when a man has indulged in oaths for a long time, he returns at last to the simple utterance, because all swearing is self-nugatory; and when one discovers that every street urchin can say "we," one perceives that it means a little more, after all, to be a particular individual. And when one finds that every cellar-dweller can play the game of being humanity, one learns at last, that being purely and simply a human being is a more significant thing than playing the society game in this fashion. And one thing more. When a cellar-dweller plays this game everyone thinks it ridiculous; and yet it is equally ridiculous for the greatest man in the world to do it. And one may very well permit oneself to laugh at him for this, while still entertaining a just and proper respect for his talents and his learning, and so forth.

From *Concluding Unscientific Postscript*

Subjectivity Is Truth

The problem we are considering is not the truth of Christianity but the individual's relation to Christianity. Our discussion is not about the

Concluding Unscientific Postscript to the Philosophical Fragments (1984) by Soren Kierkegaard, trans. Louis Pojman. Copyright © 1987 by Louis Pojman. Reprinted by permission of Louis Pojman.

scholar's systematic zeal to arrange the truths of Christianity in nice tidy categories but about the individual's personal relationship to this doctrine, a relationship which is properly one of infinite interest to him. Simply stated, "I Johannes Climacus, born in this city, now 30 years old, a decent fellow like most folk, suppose that there awaits me, as it awaits a maid and a professor, a highest good, which is called an eternal happiness. I have heard that Christianity is the way to that good, and so I ask, how may I establish a proper relationship to Christianity?"

I hear an intellectual's response to this, "What outrageous presumption! What egregious egoistic vanity in this theocentric and philosophically enlightened age, which is concerned with global history, to lay such inordinate weight on one's petty self."

I tremble at such a reproof and had I not already inured myself to these kinds of responses, I would slink away like a dog with his tail between his legs. But I have no guilt whatsoever about what I am doing, for it is not I who is presumptuous, but, rather, it is Christianity itself which compels me to ask the question in this way. *For Christianity places enormous significance on my little self, and upon every other self however insignificant it may seem in that it offers each self eternal happiness on the condition that a proper relationship between itself and the individual is established.*

Although I am still an outsider to faith, I can see that the only unpardonable sin against the majesty of Christianity is for an individual to take his relationship to it for granted. However modest it may seem to relate oneself in this way, Christianity considers such a casual attitude to be imprudent. So I must *respectfully decline* all theocentric helpers and the helpers' helpers who would seek to help me *through a detached relationship to this doctrine. I would rather remain where I am with my infinite concern about my spiritual existence, with the problem of how I may become a Christian.* For while it is not impossible for one with an infinite concern for his eternal happiness to achieve salvation, it is entirely impossible for one who has lost all sensitivity to the relationship to achieve such a state.

The objective problem is: Is Christianity true? The subjective problem is: What is the individual's relationship to Christianity? Quite simply, how may I Johannes Climacus participate in the happiness promised by Christianity? The problem concerns myself alone; partly because, if it is properly set forth, it will concern everyone in exactly the same way; and partly because all the other points of view take faith for granted, as trivial.

In order to make my problem clear, I shall first describe the objective problem and show how it should be treated. In this way the historical aspect will be given its due. After this I shall describe the subjective problem.

THE OBJECTIVE PROBLEM OF THE TRUTH OF CHRISTIANITY. From an objective point of view Christianity is an historical fact whose truth must be considered in a purely objective manner, for the modest scholar is far too objective not to leave himself outside—though as a matter of fact, he may count himself as a believer. 'Truth' in this objective sense may mean either (1) historical truth or (2) the philosophical truth. As historical truth, the truth claims must be decided by a critical examination of the various sources in the same way we determine other historical claims. Considered philosophically, the doctrine which has been historically verified must be related to the eternal truth.

The inquiring, philosophical and learned researcher raises the question of the truth, but not the subjective truth, i.e., the truth as appropriated. The inquiring researcher is interested, but he is not infinitely, personally and passionately interested in a way that relates his own eternal happiness to this truth. Far be it for the objective person to be so immodest, so presumptuous as that!

Such an inquirer must be in one of two states. Either he is already in faith convinced of the truth of Christianity—and in such a relationship he cannot be infinitely interested in the objective inquiry, since faith itself consists in being infinitely concerned with Christianity and regards every competing interest as a temptation; or he is not in faith but objectively considering the subject matter, and as such not in a condition of being infinitely interested in the question.

I mention this in order to draw your attention to what will be developed in the second part of this work, viz. that the problem of the truth of Christianity is never appropriately set forth in this objective manner, i.e., it does not arise at all, since Christianity lies in decision. Let the scholarly researcher work with indefatigable zeal even to the point of shortening his life in devoted service to scholarship. Let the speculative philosopher spare neither time nor effort. They are nevertheless not personally and passionately concerned. On the contrary, they wouldn't want to be but will want to develop an objective and disinterested stance. They are only concerned about objective truth, so that the question of personal appropriation is relatively unimportant, something that will follow their findings as a matter of course. In the last analysis what matters to the individual is of minor significance. Herein precisely lies the scholar's exalted equanimity as well as the comedy of his parrot-like pedantry.

THE HISTORICAL POINT OF VIEW. When Christianity is considered through its historical documents, it becomes vital to get a trustworthy account of what Christian doctrine really is. If the researcher is infinitely concerned with his relationship to this truth, he will immediately despair, because it is patently clear that in historical matters the greatest certainty is still only an approximation, and an approximation is too weak for one to build his eternal happiness upon, since its incommensurability with eternal happiness prevents it from obtaining. So the scholar, having only an historical interest in the truth of Christianity, begins his work with tremendous zeal and contributes important research until his 70th year. Then just fourteen days before his death he comes upon a new document which casts fresh light over one whole side of his inquiry. Such an objective personality is the antithesis of the restless concern of the subject who is infinitely interested in eternal happiness and who surely deserves to have a decisive answer to the question concerning that happiness.

When one raises the historical question of the truth of Christianity or of what is and what is not Christian truth, we come directly to the Holy Scriptures as the central document. The historical investigation focuses first on the Bible.

THE HOLY SCRIPTURES. It is very important that the scholar secures the highest possible reliability in his work. In this regard it is important for me not to pretend that I have learning or show that I have none, for my purpose here is more important. And that is to have it understood and remembered that even with the most impressive scholarly credentials and persistence, even if all the intelligence of all the critics met in one single head, still one would get no further than an approximation. We could never show more than that there is an incommensurability between the infinite personal concern for one's eternal happiness and the reliability of the documents.

When the Scriptures are considered as the ultimate arbiter, which determines what is and what is not Christian, it becomes imperative to secure their reliability through a critically historical investigation. So we must deal here with several issues: the canonicity of each book of the Bible, their authenticity, their integrity, the trustworthiness of the authors, and finally, we must assume a dogmatic guarantee: inspiration. When one thinks of the prodigious labors which the English are devoting to digging the tunnel under the Thames, the incredible expenditure of time and effort, and how a little accident can upset the whole project for a long time, one may be able to get some idea of what is involved in the undertaking which we are describing. How much time, what diligence, what glorious acumen, what remarkable scholarship from generation to generation have been requisitioned to accomplish this work of supreme wonder! And yet a single little dialectical doubt can suddenly touch the foundations and for a long time disturb the whole project, closing the underground way to Christianity, which one has tried to establish objectively and scientifically, instead of approaching the problem as it should be approached, above ground—subjectively.

But let us assume first that the critics have established everything that scholarly theologians in their happiest moments ever dreamed to prove about the Bible. These books and no others belong to the canon. They are authentic, complete, their authors are trustworthy,—it is as though every letter was divinely inspired. (One cannot say more than this, for inspiration is an object of faith and is qualitatively dialectical. It cannot be reached by a quantitative increment.) Furthermore, there is not the slightest contradiction in these holy writings. For let us be careful in formulating our hypothesis. If there is even a word that is problematic, the parenthesis of uncertainty begins again, and the critical philological enterprise will lead one astray. In general, all that is needed to cause us to question our findings is a little circumspection, the renunciation of every learned middle-term, which could in a twinkle of the eye degenerate into a hundred year parenthesis.

And so it comes to pass that everything we hoped for with respect to the Scriptures has been firmly established. What follows from this? Has anyone who didn't previously have faith come a single step closer to faith? Of course not, not a single step closer. For faith isn't produced through academic investigations. It doesn't come directly at all, but, on the contrary, it is precisely in objective analysis that one loses the infinite personal and passionate concern which is the requisite condition for faith, its ubiquitous ingredient, wherein faith comes into existence.

Has anyone who had faith gained anything in terms of faith's strength and power? No, not the least. Rather, his prodigious learning which lies like a dragon at faith's door, threatening to devour it, will become a handicap, forcing him to put forth an even greater prodigious effort in fear and trembling in order not to fall into temptation and confuse knowledge with faith. Whereas faith had uncertainty as a useful teacher, it now finds that certainty is its most dangerous enemy. Take passion away and faith disappears, for certainty and passion are incompatible. Let an analogy throw light on this point. He who believes that God exists and providentially rules the world finds it easier to preserve his faith (and not a fantasy) in an imperfect world where passion is kept awake, than in an absolutely perfect world; for in such an ideal world faith is unthinkable. This is the reason that we are taught that in eternity faith will be annulled.

Now let us assume the opposite, that the opponents have succeeded in proving what they desired to establish regarding the Bible and did so with a certainty that transcended their wildest hopes. What then? Has the enemy abolished Christianity? Not a whit. Has he harmed the believer? Not at all. Has he won the right of being free from the responsibility of becoming a believer? By no means. Simply because these books are not by these authors, are not authentic, lack integrity, do not seem to be inspired (though this cannot be demonstrated since it is a matter of faith), it in no way follows that these authors have not existed, and above all it does not follow that Christ never existed. In so far as faith perdures, the believer is at liberty to assume it, just as free (mark well!); for if he accepted the content of faith on the basis of evidence, he would now be on the verge of giving up faith. If things ever came this far, the believer is somewhat to blame, for he invited the procedure and began to play into the hands of unbelief by attempting to prove the content of faith.

Here is the heart of the matter, and I come back to learned theology. For whose sake is the proof sought? Faith does not need it. Yes, it must regard it as an enemy. But when faith begins to feel ashamed, when like a young woman for whom love ceases to suffice, who secretly feels ashamed of her lover and must therefore have it confirmed by others that he really is quite remarkable, so likewise when faith falters and begins to lose its passion, when it begins to cease to be faith, then proof becomes necessary in order to command respect from the side of unbelief.

So when the subject of faith is treated objectively, it becomes impossible for a person to relate himself to the decision of faith with passion, let alone with infinitely concerned passion. It is a self-contradiction and as such comical to be infinitely concerned about what at best can only be an approximation. If in spite of this, we still preserve passion, we obtain fanaticism. For the person with infinite passionate concern every relevant detail becomes something of infinite value. The error lies not in the infinite passion but in the fact that its object has become an approximation.

As soon as one takes subjectivity away—and with it subjectivity's passion—and with passion the infinite concern—it becomes impossible to make a decision—either with regard to this problem or any other; for every decision, every genuine decision, is a subjective action. A contemplator (i.e., an objective subject) experiences no infinite urge to make a decision and sees no need for a commitment anywhere. This is the falsity of objectivity and this is the problem with the Hegelian notion of mediation as the mode of transition in the continuous process, where nothing endures and where nothing is infinitely decided because the movement turns back on itself and again turns back; but the movement itself is a chimera and philosophy becomes wise afterwards. Objectively speaking, this method produces results in great supply, but it does not produce a single decisive result. This is as is expected, since decisiveness inheres in subjectivity, essentially in passion and maximally in the personal passion which is infinitely concerned about one's eternal happiness.

Christianity is spirit, spirit is inwardness, inwardness is subjectivity, subjectivity is essentially passion and at its maximum infinite personal and passionate concern about one's eternal happiness.

BECOMING SUBJECTIVE. Objectively we only consider the subject matter; subjectively we consider the subject and his subjectivity, and, behold, subjectivity is precisely our subject matter. It must constantly be kept in mind that the subjective problem is not about some other subject matter but simply about subjectivity itself. Since the problem is about a decision, and all decisions lie in subjectivity, it follows that not a trace of objectivity remains, for at the moment that subjectivity slinks away from the pain and crisis of decision, the problem becomes to a degree objective. If the Introduction still awaits another work before a judgment can be made on the subject matter, if the philosophical system still lacks a paragraph; if the speaker still has a final argument, the decision is postponed. We do not raise the question of the truth of Christianity in the sense that when it has been decided, subjectivity is ready and willing to accept it. No, the question is about the subject's acceptance of it, and it must be regarded as an infernal illusion or a deceitful evasion which seeks to avoid the decision by taking an objective treatment of the subject matter and assumes that a subjective commitment will follow from the objective deliberation as a matter of course. On the contrary, the decision lies in subjectivity and an objective acceptance is either a pagan concept or one devoid of all meaning.

Christianity will give the single individual eternal happiness, a good, which cannot be divided into parts, but can only be given to one person at a time. Although we presuppose that subjectivity is available to be appropriated, a possibility which involves accepting this good, it is not a subjectivity without qualification, without a genuine understanding of the meaning of this good. Subjectivity's development or transformation, its infinite concentration in itself with regard to an eternal happiness—this highest good of Infinity, an eternal happiness—this is subjectivity's developed possibility. As such, Christianity protests against all objectivity and will infinitely concern itself only with subjectivity. If there is any Christian truth, it first arises in subjectivity. Objectively it does not arise at all. If its truth is only in a single person, then Christianity exists in him alone, and there is greater joy in heaven over this one than over all world history and philosophical systems which, as objective forces, are incommensurable with the Christian idea.

Philosophy teaches that the way to truth is to become objective, but Christianity teaches that the way is to become subjective, i.e., to become a subject in truth. Lest we seem to be trading on ambiguities, let it be said clearly that Christianity aims at intensifying passion to its highest pitch; but passion is subjectivity and does not exist objectively at all.

SUBJECTIVE TRUTH, INWARDNESS; TRUTH IS SUBJECTIVITY. For an objective reflection the truth becomes an object, something objective, and thought points away from the subject. For subjective reflection the truth becomes a matter of appropriation, of inwardness, of subjectivity, and thought must penetrate deeper and still deeper into the subject and his subjectivity. Just as in objective reflection, when objectivity had come into being, subjectivity disappeared, so here the subjectivity of the subject becomes the final stage, and objectivity disappears. It is not for an instant forgotten that the subject is an existing individual, and that existence is a process of becoming, and that therefore the idea of truth being an identity of thought and being is a chimera of abstraction; this is not because the truth is not such an identity but because the believer is an existing individual for whom the truth cannot be such an identity as long as he exists as a temporal being.

If an existing subject really could transcend himself, the truth would be something complete for him, but where is this point outside of himself? The I = I is a mathematical point which does not exist, and in so far as one would take this standpoint, he will not stand in another's way. It is only momentarily that the existential subject experiences the unity of the infinite and the finite, which transcends existence, and that moment is the moment of passion. While scribbling modern philosophy is contemptuous of passion, passion remains the highest point of existence for the individual who exists in time. In passion the existential subject is made infinite in imagination's eternity, and at the same time he is himself.

All essential knowledge concerns existence, or only that knowledge which relates to existence is essential, is essential knowledge. All knowledge, which is not existential, which does not involve inward reflection, is really accidental knowledge, its degree and compass are essentially a matter of no importance. This essential knowledge which relates itself essentially to the existing individual is not to be equated with the above mentioned abstract identity between thought and being. But it means that knowledge must relate itself to the knower, who is essentially an existing individual, and therefore all essential knowledge essentially relates itself to existence, to that which exists. But all ethical and all ethical-religious knowledge has this essential relationship to the existence of the knower.

In order to elucidate the difference between the objective way of reflection and the subjective way, I shall now show how subjective reflection makes its way back into inwardness. The highest point of inwardness in an existing person is passion, for passion corresponds to truth as a paradox, and the fact that the truth becomes a paradox is grounded in its relation to an existing individual. The one corresponds to the other. By forgetting that we are existing subjects, we lose passion and truth ceases to be a paradox, but the knowing subject begins to lose his humanity and becomes fantastic and the truth likewise becomes a fantastic object for this kind of knowledge.

When the question of truth is put forward in an objective manner, reflection is directed objectively to the truth as an object to which the knower is related. The reflection is not on the relationship but on whether he is related to the truth. If that which he is related to is the truth, the subject is in the truth. When the question of truth is put forward in a subjective manner, reflection is directed subjectively to the individual's relationship. If the relation's HOW is in truth, the individual is in truth, even if the WHAT to which he is related is not true.

We may illustrate this by examining the knowledge of God. Objectively the reflection is on whether the object is the true God; subjectively reflection is on whether the individual is related to a *what* in such a way that his relationship in truth is a God-relationship. On which side does the truth lie? Ah, let us not lean towards mediation, and say, it is on neither side but in the mediation of both of them.

The existing individual who chooses the objective way enters upon the entire approximation process which is supposed to bring God into the picture. But this in all eternity cannot be done because God is Subject and therefore exists only for the subjective individual in inwardness. The existing individual who chooses the subjective way comprehends instantly the entire dialectical difficulty involved in having to use some time, perhaps a long time in order to find God objectively. He comprehends this dialectical difficulty in all its pain because every moment without God is a moment lost—so important is the matter of being related to God. In this way God certainly becomes a postulate but not in the useless sense in which it is often taken. It becomes the only way in which an existing individual comes into a relation with God—when the dialectical contradiction brings passion to the point of despair and helps him embrace God with the category of despair (faith). Now the postulate is far from being arbitrary or optional. It becomes a life-saving necessity, so that it is no longer simply a postulate but rather the individual's postulation of the existence of God is a necessity.

Now the problem is to calculate on which side there is the most truth: *either* the side of one who seeks the true God objectively and pursues the approximate truth of the God-idea *or* the side of one who, driven by infinite concern for his relationship to God. No one who has not been corrupted by science can have any doubt in the matter.

If one who lives in a Christian culture goes up to God's house, the house of the true God, with a true conception of God, with knowledge of God and prays—but prays in a false spirit; and one who lives in an idolatrous land prays with the total passion of the infinite, although his eyes rest on the image of an idol; where is there most truth? The one prays in truth to God, although he worships an idol. The other prays in untruth to the true God and therefore really worships an idol.

When a person objectively inquires about the problem of immortality and another person embraces it as an uncertainty with infinite passion, where is there most truth, and who really has the greater certainty? The one has entered into an inexhaustible approximation, for certainty of immortality lies precisely in the subjectivity of the individual. The other is immortal and fights against his uncertainty.

Let us consider Socrates. Today everyone is playing with some proof or other. Some have many, some fewer. But Socrates! He put the question objectively in a hypothetical manner: "*if* there is immortality." Compared to the modern philosopher with three proofs for immortality, should we consider Socrates a doubter? Not at all. On this little *if* he risks his entire life, he dares to face death, and he has directed his life with infinite passion so that the *if* is confirmed—*if* there is immortality. Is there any better proof for life after death? But those who have the three proofs do not at all pattern their lives in conformity with the idea. If there is an immortality, it must feel disgust over their lackadaisical manner of life. Can any better refutation be given of the three proofs? These crumbs of uncertainty helped Socrates because they hastened the process along, inciting the passions. The three proofs that the others have are of no help at all because they are dead to the spirit, and the fact that they need three proofs proves that they are spiritually dead. The Socratic ignorance which Socrates held fast with the entire passion of his inwardness was an expression for the idea that eternal truth is related to an existing individual, and that this will be in the form of a paradox as long as he exists; and yet it is just possible that there is more truth in Socratic ignorance than is contained in the "objective truth" of the philosophical systems, which flirts with the spirit of the times and cuddles up to associate professors.

The objective accent falls on *what* is said; the subjective accent falls on *how* it is said. This distinction is valid even for aesthetics and shows itself in the notion that what may be objectively true may in the mouth of certain people become false. This distinction is illustrated by the saying that the difference between the older days and our day is that in the old days only a few knew the truth while in ours all know it, except that the inwardness towards it is in inverse proportion to the scope of its possession. Aesthetically the contradiction that the truth becomes error in certain mouths is best understood comically. In the ethical-religious domain the accent is again on the *how*. But this is not to be understood as referring to decorum, modulation, delivery etc., but to the individual's relationship to the proposition, the way he relates himself to it. Objectively it is a question simply about the content of the proposition, but subjectively it is a question of inwardness. At its maximum this inward *how* is the passion of infinity and the passion of the infinite is itself the truth. But since the passion of the infinite is exactly subjectivity, subjectivity is the truth. Objectively there is no infinite decision or commitment, and so it is objectively correct to annul the difference between good and evil as well as the law of non-contradiction and the difference between truth and untruth. Only in subjectivity is there decision and commitment, so that to seek this in objectivity is to be in error. It is the passion of infinity that brings forth decisiveness, not its content, for its content is precisely itself. In this manner the subjective *how* and subjectivity are the truth.

But the *how* which is subjectively emphasized because the subject is an existing individual, is also subject to a temporal dialectic. In passion's decisive moment, where the road swings off from the way to objective knowledge, it appears that the infinite decision is ready to be made. But in that moment the existing individual finds himself in time, and the subjective *how* becomes transformed into a striving, a striving which is motivated by and is repeatedly experienced in the decisive passion of the infinite. But this is still a striving.

When subjectivity is truth, subjectivity's definition must include an expression for an opposition to objectivity, a reminder of the fork in the road, and this expression must also convey the tension of inwardness. Here is such a definition of truth: *the objective uncertainty, held fast in an appropriation process of the most passionate inwardness is the truth,* the highest truth available for an *existing* person. There where the way swings off (and where that is cannot be discovered objectively but only subjectively), at that place objective knowledge is annulled. Objectively speaking he has only uncertainty, but precisely there the infinite passion of inwardness is intensified, and truth is precisely the adventure to choose objective uncertainty with the passion of inwardness.

When I consider nature in order to discover God, I do indeed see his omnipotence and wisdom, but I see much more which disturbs me. The result of all this is objective uncertainty, but precisely here is the place for inwardness because inwardness apprehends the objective uncertainty with the entire passion of infinity. In the case of mathematical statements objectivity is already given, but because of the nature of mathematics, this truth is existentially indifferent.

Now the above definition of truth is an equivalent description of faith. Without risk there is no faith. Faith is precisely the contradiction between the infinite passion of inwardness and objective uncertainty. If I can grasp God objectively, I do not believe, but because I cannot know God objectively, I must have faith, and if I will preserve myself in faith, I must constantly be determined to hold fast to the objective uncertainty, so as to remain out upon the ocean's deep, over seventy thousand fathoms of water, and still believe.

In the sentence 'subjectivity, inwardness is truth', we see the essence of Socratic wisdom, whose immortal service is exactly to have recognized the essential meaning of existence, that the knower is an *existing* subject, and for this reason in his ignorance Socrates enjoyed the highest relationship to truth within paganism. This is a truth which speculative philosophy, unhappily, again and again forgets: that the knower is an existing subject. It is difficult enough to recognize this fact in our objective age, long after the genius of Socrates.

When subjectivity, inwardness, is the truth, the truth becomes objectively determined as a paradox, and that it is paradoxical is made clear by the fact that subjectivity is truth, for it repels objectivity, and the expression for the objective repulsion is the intensity and measure of inwardness. The paradox is the objective uncertainty, which is the expression for the passion of inwardness, which is precisely the truth. This is the Socratic principle. The eternal, essential truth, i.e., that which relates itself essentially to the individual because it concerns his existence (all other knowledge is, Socratically speaking, accidental, its degree and scope being indifferent) is a paradox. Nevertheless, the eternal truth is not essentially in itself paradoxical, but it becomes so by relating itself to an existing individual. Socratic ignorance is the expression of this objective uncertainty, the inwardness of the existential subject is the truth. To anticipate what I will develop later, Socratic ignorance is an analogy to the category of the absurd, only that there is still less objective certainty in the absurd, and therefore infinitely greater tension in its inwardness. The Socratic inwardness which involves existence is an analogy to faith, except that this inwardness is repulsed not by ignorance but by the absurd, which is infinitely deeper. Socratically the eternal, essential truth is by no means paradoxical in itself, but only by virtue of its relation to an existing individual.

Subjectivity, inwardness, is the truth. Is there a still more inward expression for this? Yes, there is. If subjectivity is seen as the truth, we may posit the opposite principle: that subjectivity is untruth, error. Socratically speaking, subjectivity is untruth if it fails to understand that subjectivity is truth and desires to understand itself objectively. But now we are presupposing that subjectivity in becoming the truth has a difficulty to overcome in as much as it is in untruth. So we must work backwards, back to inwardness. Socratically, the way back to the truth takes place through recollection, supposing that we have memories of that truth deep within us.

Let us call this untruth of the individual 'sin'. Seen from eternity the individual cannot be in sin, nor can he be eternally presupposed as having been in sin. So it must be that he becomes a sinner by coming into existence (for the beginning point is that subjectivity is untruth). He is not born as a sinner in the sense that he is sinful before he is born, but he is born in sin and as a sinner. We shall call this state *original sin*. But if existence has acquired such power over him, he is impotent to make his way back to eternity through the use of his memory (supposing that there is truth in the Platonic idea that we may discover truth through recollection). If it was already paradoxical that the eternal truth related itself to an existing individual, now it is absolutely paradoxical that it relates itself to such an individual. But the more difficult it is for him through memory to transcend existence, the more inwardness must increase in intense passion, and when it is made impossible for him, when he is held so fast in existence that the back door of recollection is forever closed to him through sin, then his inwardness will be the deepest possible.

Subjectivity is truth. Through this relationship between the eternal truth and the existing individual the paradox comes into existence. Let us now go further and suppose that the eternal truth is essentially a paradox. How does this paradox come into existence? By juxtaposing the eternal, essential truth with temporal existence. When we set them together within the truth itself, the truth becomes paradoxical. The eternal truth has come into time. This is the paradox. If the subject is hindered by sin from making his way back to eternity by looking inward through recollection, he need not trouble himself about this, for now the eternal essential truth is no longer behind him, but it is in front of him, through its being in existence or having existed, so that if the individual does not *existentially* get hold of the truth, he will never get hold of it.

It is impossible to accentuate existence more than this. When the eternal truth is related to an existing individual, truth becomes a paradox. The paradox repels the individual because of the objective uncertainty and ignorance towards inwardness. But since this paradox in itself is not paradoxical, it does not push the spirit far enough. For without risk there is no faith, and the greater the risk the greater the faith, and the more objective reliability, the less inwardness (for inwardness is precisely subjectivity). Indeed, the less objective reliability, the deeper becomes the possible inwardness. When the paradox is in itself paradoxical, it repels the individual by the power of the absurd, and the corresponding passion, which is produced in the process, is faith. But subjectivity, inwardness, is truth, for otherwise we have forgotten the Socratic contribution; but there is no more striking expression for inwardness than when the retreat from existence through recollection back to eternity is made impossible; and when with the truth as paradox encounters the individual who is caught in the vice-grip of sin's anxiety and suffering, but who is also aware of the tremendous risk involved in faith,—when he nevertheless makes the leap of faith—this is subjectivity at its height.

When Socrates believed in the existence of God, he held fast to an objective uncertainty in passionate inwardness, and in that contradiction, in that risk faith came into being. Now it is different. Instead of the objective uncertainty, there is objective certainty about the object—certainty that it is absurd, and it is, again, faith that holds fast to that object in passionate inwardness. Compared with the gravity of the absurd, Socratic ignorance is a joke, and compared with the strenuosity of faith in believing the paradox, Socratic existential inwardness is a Greek life of leisure.

What is the absurd? The absurd is that the eternal truth has entered time, that God has entered existence, has been born, has grown, etc., has become precisely like any other human being, quite indistinguishable from other humans. The absurd is precisely by its objective repulsion the measure of the inwardness of faith. Suppose there is a man who desires to have faith. Let the comedy begin. He desires to obtain faith with the help of objective investigation and what the approximation process of evidential inquiry yields. What happens? With the help of the increment of evidence the absurd is transformed to something else; it becomes probable, it becomes more probable still, it becomes perhaps highly and overwhelmingly probable. Now that there is respectable evidence for the content of his faith, he is ready to believe it, and he prides himself that his faith is not like that of the shoemaker, the tailor, and the simple folk, but comes after a long investigation. Now he prepares himself to believe it. Any proposition that is almost probable, reasonably probable, highly and overwhelmingly probable, is something that is almost known and as good as known, highly and overwhelmingly known—but it is not believed, not through faith; for the absurd is precisely faith's object and the only positive attitude possible in relation to it is faith and not knowledge.

Christianity has declared itself to be the eternal which has entered time, which has proclaimed itself as the *paradox,* and demands faith's inwardness in relation to that which is a scandal to the Jews and folly to the Greeks—and as absurd to the understanding. It is impossible to say this more strongly than by saying: subjectivity is truth, and objectivity is repelled by it—by virtue of the absurd.

Subjectivity culminates in passion. Christianity is the paradox: paradox and passion belong together as a perfect match, and the paradox is perfectly suited to one whose situation is to be in the extremity of existence. Indeed, there never has been found in all the world two lovers more suited to each other than passion and paradox, and the strife between them is a lover's quarrel, when they argue about which one first aroused the other's passion. And so it is here. The existing individual by means of the paradox has come to the extremity of existence. And what is more wonderful for lovers than to be granted a long time together with each other without anything disturbing their relation except that which makes it more inwardly passionate? And this is what is granted to the unspeculative understanding between the passion and paradox, for they will dwell harmoniously together in time and be changed first in eternity.

But the speculative philosopher views things altogether differently. He believes but only to a certain degree. He puts his hand to the plow but quickly looks about for something to know. From a Christian perspective it is hard to see how he could reach the highest good in this manner.

Christianity, Objectively and Subjectively Defined

The Objective Christian

1. A Christian is one who accepts the doctrine of Christianity. But if it is the doctrine which is to decide in the last resort whether one is a Christian, then instantly attention is directed outward, in order to learn to know in the minutest detail what the doctrine of Christianity is, because this indeed is to decide, not what Christianity is, but whether I am a Christian. That same instant begins the erudite, the anxious, the timorous effort at approximation. Approximation can be protracted as long as you please, and in the end the decision whereby one becomes a Christian is relegated to oblivion.

This incongruity has been remedied by the assumption that everyone in Christendom is a Christian, we are all of us what one in a way calls Christians. With this assumption things go better with the objective theories. We are all Christians. The Bible-theory has now to investigate quite objectively what Christianity is (and yet we are in fact Christians, and the objective information is assumed to make us Christians, the objective information which we who are Christians shall now for the first time learn to know—for if we are not Christians, the road here taken will never lead us to become such). The Church theory assumes that we are Christians, but now we have to be assured in a purely objective way what Christianity is, in order that we may defend ourselves against the Turk and the Russian and the Roman yoke, and gallantly fight out the battle of Christianity so that we may make our age, as it were, a bridge to the peerless future which already is glimpsed. This is sheer aesthetics. Christianity is an existence-communication, the task is to become a Christian and continue to be such, and the most dangerous of all illusions is to be so sure of being such that one has to defend the whole of Christendom against the Turk—instead of being alert to defend our own faith against the illusion about the Turk.

2. One says, No, not every acceptance of the Christian doctrine makes one a Christian; what it principally depends upon is appropriation, that one appropriates and holds fast this doctrine quite differently from anything else, that one is ready to live in it and to die in it, to venture one's life for it, etc.

This seems as if it were something. However, the category "quite differently" is a mediocre category, and the whole formula, which makes

Concluding Unscientific Postscript by Soren Kierkegaard, trans. David F. Swenson and Walter Lowrie, pp. 537–541. Copyright 1941 © by Princeton University Press. Reprinted with permission of Princeton University Press.

an attempt to define more subjectively what it is to be a Christian, is neither one thing nor the other, in a way it avoids the difficulty involved in the distraction and deceit of approximation, but it lacks categorical definition. The pathos of approximation which is talked of here is that of immanence; one can just as well say that an enthusiastic lover is so related to his love: he holds fast to it and appropriates it quite differently from anything else, he is ready to live in it and die in it, he will venture everything for it. To this extent there is no difference between a lover and a Christian with respect to inwardness, and one must again recur to the *what,* which is the doctrine—and with that we again come under No. 1.

The pathos of appropriation needs to be so defined that it cannot be confused with any other pathos. The more subjective interpretation is right in insisting that it is appropriation which decides the matter, but it is wrong in its definition of appropriation, which does not distinguish it from every other immediate pathos.

Neither is this distinction made when one defines appropriation as faith, but at once imparts to faith headway and direction towards reaching an understanding, so that faith becomes a provisional function whereby one holds what essentially is to be an object for understanding, a provisional function wherewith poor people and stupid men have to be content, whereas *Privatdocents* and clever heads go further. The mark of being a Christian (i.e. faith) is appropriated, but in such a way that it is not specifically different from other intellectual appropriation where a preliminary assumption serves as a provisional function looking forward to understanding. Faith is not in this case the specific mark of the relationship to Christianity, and again it will be the *what* of faith which decides whether one is a Christian or not. But therewith the thing is again brought back under No. 1.

That is to say, the appropriation by which a Christian is a Christian must be so specific that it cannot be confused with anything else.

3. One defines the thing of becoming and being a Christian, not objectively by the *what* of the doctrine, nor subjectively by appropriation, not by what has gone on in the individual, but by what the individual has undergone: that he was baptized. Though one adjoins to baptism the assumption of a confession of faith, nothing decisive will be gained, but the definition will waver between accentuating the *what* (the path of approximation) and talking indefinitely about acceptance and acceptance and appropriation, etc., without any specific determination.

If being baptized is to be the definition, attention will instantly turn outward towards the reflection, whether I have really been baptized. Then begins the approximation with respect to a historical fact.

If, on the other hand, one were to say that he did indeed receive the Spirit in baptism and by the witness it bears together with his spirit, he knows that he was baptized—then the inference is inverted, he argues from the witness of the Spirit within him to the fact that he was baptized, not from the fact of being baptized to the possession of the Spirit. But if the inference is to be drawn in this way, baptism is quite rightly not regarded as the mark of the Christian, but inwardness is, and so here in turn there is needed a specific definition of inwardness and appropriation whereby the witness of the Spirit in the individual is distinguished from all other (universally defined) activity of spirit in man.

It is noteworthy moreover that the orthodoxy which especially has made baptism the decisive mark is continually complaining that among the baptized there are so few Christians, that almost all, except for an immortal little band, are spiritless baptized pagans—which seems to indicate that baptism cannot be the decisive factor with respect to becoming a Christian, not even according to the latter view of those who in the first form insist upon it as decisive with respect to becoming a Christian.

The Subjective Christian

The decision lies in the subject. The appropriation is the paradoxical inwardness which is specifically different from all other inwardness. The thing of being a Christian is not determined by the *what* of Christianity but by the *how* of the Christian. This *how* can only correspond with one thing, the absolute paradox. There is therefore no vague talk to the effect that being a Christian is to accept, and to accept, and to accept quite differently, to appropriate, to believe, to appropriate by faith quite differently (all of them purely rhetorical and fictitious definitions); but *to believe* is specifically different from all other appropriation and inwardness. Faith is the objective uncertainty due to the repulsion of the absurd held fast by the passion of inwardness, which in this instance is intensified to the utmost degree. This formula fits only the believer, no one else, not a lover, not an enthusiast, not a thinker, but simply and solely the believer who is related to the absolute paradox.

Faith therefore cannot be any sort of provisional function. He who from the vantage point of a higher knowledge would know his faith as a factor resolved in a higher idea has *eo ipso* ceased to believe. Faith *must* not *rest content* with unintelligibility; for precisely the relation to or the repulsion from the unintelligible, the absurd, is the expression for the passion of faith.

This definition of what it is to be a Christian prevents the erudite or anxious deliberation of approximation from enticing the individual into byways so that he becomes erudite instead of becoming a Christian, and in most cases a smatterer instead of becoming a Christian; for the decision lies in the subject. But inwardness has again found its specific mark whereby it is differentiated from all other inwardness and is not disposed of by the chatty category "quite differently" which fits the case of every passion at the moment of passion.

The psychologist generally regards it as a sure sign that a man is beginning to give up a passion when he wishes to treat the object of it objectively. Passion and reflection are generally exclusive of one another. Becoming objective in this way is always retrogression, for passion is man's perdition, but it is his exaltation as well. In case dialectic and reflection are not used to intensify passion, it is a retrogression to become objective; and even he who is lost through passion has not lost so much as he who lost passion, for the former had the possibility.

Thus it is that people in our age have wanted to become objective with relation to Christianity; the passion by which every man is a Christian has become too small a thing for them, and by becoming objective we all of us have the prospect of becoming . . . a *Privatdocent.*

From *Fear and Trembling*

Prelude

Once upon a time there was a man who as a child had heard the beautiful story about how God tempted Abraham, and how he endured temptation, kept the faith, and a second time received again a son contrary to expectation. When the child became older he read the same story with even greater admiration, for life had separated what was united in the pious simplicity of the child. The older he became, the more frequently his mind reverted to that story, his enthusiasm became greater and greater, and yet he was less and less able to understand the story. At last in his interest for that he forgot everything else; his soul had only one wish, to see Abraham, one longing, to have been witness to that event. His desire was not to behold the beautiful countries of the Orient, or the earthly glory of the Promised Land, or that godfearing couple whose old age God

Fear and Trembling/The Sickness Unto Death by Soren Kierkegaard, trans. with introductions and notes by Walter Lowrie, pp. 26, 38–72, 77–82, 86–91. Copyright 1941, 1954, © 1982 renewed by Princeton University Press. Reprinted by permission of Princeton University Press.

had blessed, or the venerable figure of the aged patriarch, or the vigorous young manhood of Isaac whom God had bestowed upon Abraham—he saw no reason why the same thing might not have taken place on a barren heath in Denmark. His yearning was to accompany them on the three days' journey when Abraham rode with sorrow before him and with Isaac by his side. His only wish was to be present at the time when Abraham lifted up his eyes and saw Mount Moriah afar off, at the time when he left the asses behind and went alone with Isaac up unto the mountain; for what his mind was intent upon was not the ingenious web of imagination but the shudder of thought.

That man was not a thinker, he felt no need of getting beyond faith; he deemed it the most glorious thing to be remembered as the father of it, an enviable lot to possess it, even though no one else were to know it.

That man was not a learned exegete, he didn't know Hebrew, if he had known Hebrew, he perhaps would easily have understood the story and Abraham.

Problemata: Preliminary Expectoration

The Story of Abraham and Isaac

An old proverb fetched from the outward and visible world says: "Only the man that works gets the bread." Strangely enough this proverb does not aptly apply in that world to which it expressly belongs. For the outward world is subjected to the law of imperfection, and again and again the experience is repeated that he too who does not work gets the bread, and that he who sleeps gets it more abundantly than the man who works. In the outward world everything is made payable to the bearer, this world is in bondage to the law of indifference, and to him who has the ring, the spirit of the ring is obedient, whether he be Noureddin or Aladdin, and he who has the world's treasure, has it, however he got it. It is different in the world of spirit. Here an eternal divine order prevails, here it does not rain both upon the just and upon the unjust, here the sun does not shine both upon the good and upon the evil, here it holds good that only he who works gets the bread, only he who was in anguish finds repose, only he who descends into the underworld rescues the beloved, only he who draws the knife gets Isaac. He who will not work does not get the bread but remains deluded, as the gods deluded Orpheus with an airy figure in place of the loved one, deluded him because he was effeminate, not courageous, because he was a cithara-player, not a man. Here it is of no use to have Abraham for one's father, nor to have seventeen ancestors—he who will not work must take note of what is written about the maidens of Israel, for he gives birth to wind, but he who is willing to work gives birth to his own father.

There is a knowledge which would presumptuously introduce into the world of spirit the same law of indifference under which the external world sighs. It counts it enough to think the great—other work is not necessary. But therefore it doesn't get the bread, it perishes of hunger, while everything is transformed into gold. And what does it really know? There were many thousands of Greek contemporaries, and countless numbers in subsequent generations, who knew all the triumphs of Miltiades, but only one was made sleepless by them. There were countless generations which knew by rote, word for word, the story of Abraham—how many were made sleepless by it?

Now the story of Abraham has the remarkable property that it is always glorious, however poorly one may understand it; yet here again the proverb applies, that all depends upon whether one is willing to labor and be heavy laden. But they will not labor, and yet they would understand the story. They exalt Abraham—but how? They express the whole thing in perfectly general terms: "The great thing was that he loved God so much that he was willing to sacrifice to Him the best." That is very true, but "the best" is an indefinite expression. In the course of thought, as the tongue wags on, Isaac and "the best" are confidently identified, and he who meditates can very well smoke his pipe during the meditation, and the auditor can very well stretch out his legs in comfort. In case that rich young man whom Christ encountered on the road had sold all his goods and given to the poor, we should extol him, as we do all that is great, though without labor we would not understand him—and yet he would not have become an Abraham, in spite of the fact that he offered his best. What they leave out of Abraham's history is dread; for to money I have no ethical obligation, but to the son the father has the highest and most sacred obligation. Dread, however, is a perilous thing for effeminate natures, hence they forget it, and in spite of that they want to talk about Abraham. So they talk—in the course of the oration they use indifferently the two terms, Isaac and "the best." All goes famously. However, if it chanced that among the auditors there was one who suffered from insomnia—then the most dreadful, the profoundest tragic and comic misunderstanding lies very close. He went home, he would do as Abraham did, for the son is indeed "the best."

If the orator got to know of it, he perhaps went to him, he summoned all his clerical dignity, he shouted, "O abominable man, offscouring of society, what devil possessed thee to want to murder thy son?" And the parson, who had not been conscious of warmth or perspiration in preaching about Abraham, is astonished at himself, at the earnest wrath which he thundered down upon that poor man. He was delighted with himself, for he had never spoken with such verve and unction. He said to himself and to his wife, "I am an orator. What I lacked was the occasion. When I talked about Abraham on Sunday I did not feel moved in the least." In case the same orator had a little superabundance of reason which might be lost, I think he would have lost it if the sinner were to say calmly and with dignity, "That in fact is what you yourself preached on Sunday." How could the parson be able to get into his head such a consequence? And yet it was so, and the mistake was merely that he didn't know what he was saying. Would there were a poet who might resolve to prefer such situations, rather than the stuff and nonsense with which comedies and novels are filled! The comic and the tragic here touch one another at the absolute point of infinity. The parson's speech was perhaps in itself ludicrous enough, but it became infinitely ludicrous by its effect, and yet this consequence was quite natural. Or if the sinner, without raising any objection, were to be converted by the parson's severe lecture, if the zealous clergyman were to go joyfully home, rejoicing in the consciousness that he not only was effective in the pulpit, but above all by his irresistible power as a pastor of souls, who on Sunday roused the congregation to enthusiasm, and on Monday like a cherub with a flaming sword placed himself before the man who by his action wanted to put to shame the old proverb, that "things don't go on in the world as the parson preaches."*

If on the other hand the sinner was not convinced, his situation is pretty tragic. Presumably he would be executed or sent to the lunatic asylum, in short, he would have become unhappy in relation to so-called reality—in another sense I can well think that Abraham made him happy, for he that labors does not perish.

How is one to explain the contradiction illustrated by that orator? Is it because Abraham had a prescriptive right to be a great man, so that what he did is great, and when another does the same it is sin, a heinous sin? In that case I do not wish to participate in such thoughtless eulogy. If faith does not make it a holy act to be willing to murder one's son, then let the same condemnation be pronounced upon Abraham as upon every other man. If a man perhaps lacks courage to carry his thought through, and to say that Abraham was a murderer, then it is surely better to acquire this courage, rather than waste time upon undeserved eulogies. The ethical expression for what Abraham did is, that he would murder Isaac; the religious expression is, that he would sacrifice Isaac; but precisely in this contradiction consists the dread which can well make a man sleepless, and yet Abraham is not what he is without this dread. Or

---

* In the old days they said, "What a pity things don't go on in the world as the parson preaches"—perhaps the time is coming, especially with the help of philosophy, when they will say, "Fortunately things don't go on as the parson preaches; for after all there is some sense in life, but none at all in his preaching."

perhaps he did not do at all what is related, but something altogether different, which is accounted for by the circumstances of his times—then let us forget him, for it is not worth while to remember *that* past which cannot become a present. Or had perhaps that orator forgotten something which corresponds to the ethical forgetfulness of the fact that Isaac was the son? For when faith is eliminated by becoming null or nothing, then there only remains the crude fact that Abraham wanted to murder Isaac—which is easy enough for anyone to imitate who has not faith, the faith, that is to say, which makes it hard for him.

For my part I do not lack the courage to think a thought whole. Hitherto there has been no thought I have been afraid of; if I should run across such a thought, I hope that I have at least the sincerity to say, "I am afraid of this thought, it stirs up something else in me, and therefore I will not think it. If in this I do wrong, the punishment will not fail to follow." If I had recognized that it was the verdict of truth that Abraham was a murderer, I do not know whether I would have been able to silence my pious veneration for him. However, if I had thought that, I presumably would have kept silent about it, for one should not initiate others into such thoughts. But Abraham is no dazzling illusion, he did not sleep into renown, it was not a whim of fate.

Can one then speak plainly about Abraham without incurring the danger that an individual might in bewilderment go ahead and do likewise? If I do not dare to speak freely, I will be completely silent about Abraham, above all I will not disparage him in such a way that precisely thereby he becomes a pitfall for the weak. For if one makes faith everything, that is, makes it what it is, then, according to my way of thinking, one may speak of it without danger in our age, which hardly extravagates in the matter of faith, and it is only by faith one attains likeness to Abraham, not by murder. If one makes love a transitory mood, a voluptuous emotion in a man, then one only lays pitfalls for the weak when one would talk about the exploits of love. Transient emotions every man surely has, but if as a consequence of such emotions one would do the terrible thing which love has sanctified as an immortal exploit, then all is lost, including the exploit and the bewildered doer of it.

So one surely can talk about Abraham, for the great can never do harm when it is apprehended in its greatness; it is like a two-edged sword which slays and saves. If it should fall to my lot to talk on the subject, I would begin by showing what a pious and God-fearing man Abraham was, worthy to be called God's elect. Only upon such a man is imposed such a test. But where is there such a man? Next I would describe how Abraham loved Isaac. To this end I would pray all good spirits to come to my aid, that my speech might be as glowing as paternal love is. I hope that I should be able to describe it in such a way that there would not be many a father in the realms and territories of the King who would dare to affirm that he loved his son in such a way. But if he does not love like Abraham, then every thought of offering Isaac would be not a trial but a base temptation [*Anfechtung*]. On this theme one could talk for several Sundays, one need be in no haste. The consequence would be that, if one spoke rightly, some few of the fathers would not require to hear more, but for the time being they would be joyful if they really succeeded in loving their sons as Abraham loved. If there was one who, after having heard about the greatness, but also about the dreadfulness of Abraham's deed, ventured to go forth upon that road, I would saddle my horse and ride with him. At every stopping place till we came to Mount Moriah I would explain to him that he still could turn back, could repent the misunderstanding that he was called to be tried in such a conflict, that he could confess his lack of courage, so that God Himself must take Isaac, if He would have him. It is my conviction that such a man is not repudiated but may become blessed like all the others. But in time he does not become blessed. Would they not, even in the great ages of faith, have passed this judgment upon such a man? I knew a person who on one occasion could have saved my life if he had been magnanimous. He said, "I see well enough what I could do, but I do not dare to. I am afraid that later I might lack strength and that I should regret it." He was not magnanimous, but who for this cause would not continue to love him?

Having spoken thus and moved the audience so that at least they had sensed the dialectical conflict of faith and its gigantic passion, I would not give rise to the error on the part of the audience that "he then has faith in such a high degree that it is enough for us to hold on to his skirts." For I would add, "I have no faith at all, I am by nature a shrewd pate, and every such person always has great difficulty in making the movements of faith—not that I attach, however, in and for itself, *any value to this difficulty which through the overcoming of it brought the clever head further than the point which the simplest and most ordinary man reaches more easily.*"

After all, in the poets love has its priests, and sometimes one hears a voice which knows how to defend it; but of faith one hears never a word. Who speaks in honor of this passion? Philosophy goes further. Theology sits roughed at the window and courts its favor, offering to sell her charms to philosophy. It is supposed to be difficult to understand Hegel, but to understand Abraham is a trifle. To go beyond Hegel is a miracle, but to get beyond Abraham is the easiest thing of all. I for my part have devoted a good deal of time to the understanding of the Hegelian philosophy, I believe also that I understand it tolerably well, but when in spite of the trouble I have taken there are certain passages I cannot understand, I am foolhardy enough to think that he himself has not been quite clear. All this I do easily and naturally, my head does not suffer from it. But on the other hand when I have to think of Abraham, I am as though annihilated. I catch sight every moment of that enormous paradox which is the substance of Abraham's life, every moment I am repelled, and my thought in spite of all its passion cannot get a hairs-breadth further. I strain every muscle to get a view of it—that very instant I am paralyzed.

I am not unacquainted with what has been admired as great and noble in the world, my soul feels affinity with it, being convinced in all humility that it was in my cause the hero contended, and the instant I contemplate his deed I cry out to myself, *jam tua res agitur.* * I *think* myself *into* the hero, but into Abraham I cannot think myself; when I reach the height I fall down, for what I encounter there is the paradox. I do not however mean in any sense to say that faith is something lowly, but on the contrary that it is the highest thing, and that it is dishonest of philosophy to give something else instead of it and to make light of faith. Philosophy cannot and should not give faith, but it should under-stand itself and know what it has to offer and take nothing away, and least of all should fool people out of something as if it were nothing. I am not unacquainted with the perplexities and dangers of life, I do not fear them, and I encounter them buoyantly. I am not unacquainted with the dreadful, my memory is a faithful wife, and my imagination is (as I myself am not) a diligent little maiden who all day sits quietly at her work, and in the evening knows how to chat to me about it so prettily that I must look at it, though not always, I must say, is it landscapes, or flowers, or pastoral idyls she paints. I have seen the dreadful before my own eyes, I do not flee from it timorously, but I know very well that, although I advance to meet it, my courage is not the courage of faith, nor anything comparable to it. I am unable to make the movements of faith, I cannot shut my eyes and plunge confidently into the absurd, for me that is an impossibility . . . but I do not boast of it. I am convinced that God is love, this thought has for me a primitive lyrical validity. When it is present to me, I am unspeakably blissful, when it is absent, I long for it more vehemently than does the lover for his object; but I do not believe, this courage I lack. For me the love of God is, both in a direct and in an inverse sense, incommensurable with the whole of reality. I am not cowardly enough to whimper and complain, but neither am I deceitful enough to deny that faith is something much higher. I can well endure living in my way, I am joyful and content, but my joy is not that of faith, and in comparison with that it is unhappy. I do not trouble God with my petty sorrows, the particular does not trouble me, I gaze only at my love, and I keep its virginal flame pure and clear. Faith

* Quoted from Horace's *Letters*, I, 18, 84: "It's your affair when the neighbor's house is afire."

is convinced that God is concerned about the least things. I am content in this life with being married to the left hand, faith is humble enough to demand the right hand—for that this is humility I do not deny and shall never deny.

But really is everyone in my generation capable of making the movements of faith, I wonder? Unless I am very much mistaken, this generation is rather inclined to be proud of making what they do not even believe I am capable of making, viz. incomplete movements. It is repugnant to me to do as so often is done, namely, to speak inhumanly about a great deed, as though some thousands of years were an immense distance; I would rather speak humanly about it, as though it had occurred yesterday, letting only the greatness be the distance, which either exalts or condemns. So if (*in the quality of a tragic hero,* for I can get no higher) I had been summoned to undertake such a royal progress to Mount Moriah, I know well what I would have done. I would not have been cowardly enough to stay at home, neither would I have laid down or sauntered along the way, nor have forgotten the knife, so that there might be a little delay—I am pretty well convinced that I would have been there on the stroke of the clock and would have had everything in order, perhaps I would have arrived too early in order to get through with it sooner. But I also know what else I would have done. The very instant I mounted the horse I would have said to myself, "Now all is lost. God requires Isaac, I sacrifice him, and with him my joy—*yet God is love* and continues to be that for me; for in the temporal world God and I cannot talk together, we have no language in common." Perhaps one or another in our age will be foolish enough, or envious enough of the great, to want to make himself and me believe that if I really had done this, I would have done even a greater deed than Abraham; for my prodigious resignation was far more ideal and poetic than Abraham's narrow-mindedness. And yet this is the greatest falsehood, for my prodigious resignation was the surrogate for faith, nor could I do more than make the infinite movement, in order to find myself and again repose in myself. In that case I would not have loved Isaac as Abraham loved. That I was resolute in making the movement might prove my courage, humanly speaking; that I loved him with all my soul is the presumption apart from which the whole thing becomes a crime, but yet I did not love like Abraham, for in that case I would have held back even at the last minute, though not for this would I have arrived too late at Mount Moriah. Besides, by my behavior I would have spoiled the whole story; for if I had got Isaac back again, I would have been in embarrassment. What Abraham found easiest, I would have found hard, namely to be joyful again with Isaac; for he who with all the infinity of his soul, *propio motu et propiis auspiciis* [by his own power and on his own responsibility], has performed the infinite movement [of resignation] and cannot do more, only retains Isaac with pain.

But what did Abraham do? He arrived neither too soon nor too late. He mounted the ass, he rode slowly along the way. All that time he believed—he believed that God would not require Isaac of him, whereas he was willing nevertheless to sacrifice him if it was required. He believed by virtue of the absurd; for there could be no question of human calculation, and it was indeed the absurd that God who required it of him should the next instant recall the requirement. He climbed the mountain, even at the instant when the knife glittered he believed . . . that God would not require Isaac. He was indeed astonished at the outcome, but by a double-movement he had reached his first position, and therefore he received Isaac more gladly than the first time. Let us go further. We let Isaac be really sacrificed. Abraham believed. He did not believe that some day he would be blessed in the beyond, but that he would be happy here in the world. God could give him a new Isaac, could recall to life him who had been sacrificed. He believed by virtue of the absurd; for all human reckoning had long since ceased to function. That sorrow can derange a man's mind, that we see, and it is sad enough. That there is such a thing as strength of will which is able to haul up so exceedingly close to the wind that it saves a man's reason, even though he remains a little queer, that too one sees. I have no intention of disparaging this; but to be able to lose one's reason, and therefore the whole of finiteness of which reason is the broker, and then by virtue of the absurd to gain precisely the same finiteness—that appalls my soul, but I do not for this cause say that it is something lowly, since on the contrary it is the only prodigy. Generally people are of the opinion that what faith produces is not a work of art, that it is coarse and common work, only for the more clumsy natures; but in fact this is far from the truth. The dialectic of faith is the finest and most remarkable of all; it possesses an elevation, of which indeed I can form a conception, but nothing more. I am able to make from the springboard the great leap whereby I pass into infinity, my back is like that of a tight-rope dancer, having been twisted in my childhood, hence I find this easy; with a one-two-three! I can walk about existence on my head; but the next thing I cannot do, for I cannot perform the miraculous, but can only be astonished by it. Yes, if Abraham the instant he swung his leg over the ass's back had said to himself, "Now, since Isaac is lost, I might just as well sacrifice him here at home, rather than ride the long way to Moriah"—then I should have no need of Abraham, whereas now I bow seven times before his name and seventy times before his deed. For this indeed he did not do, as I can prove by the fact that he was glad at receiving Isaac, heartily glad, that he needed no preparation, no time to concentrate upon the finite and its joy. If this had not been the case with Abraham, then perhaps he might have loved

God but not believed; for he who loves God without faith reflects upon himself, he who loves God believingly reflects upon God.

Upon this pinnacle stands Abraham. The last stage he loses sight of is the infinite resignation. He really goes further, and reaches faith; for all these caricatures of faith, the miserable lukewarm indolence which thinks, "There surely is no instant need, it is not worth while sorrowing before the time," the pitiful hope which says, "One cannot know what is going to happen . . . it might possibly be after all"—these caricatures of faith are part and parcel of life's wretchedness, and the infinite resignation has already consigned them to infinite contempt.

Abraham I cannot understand, in a certain sense there is nothing I can learn from him but astonishment. If people fancy that by considering the outcome of this story they might let themselves be moved to believe, they deceive themselves and want to swindle God out of the first movement of faith, the infinite resignation. They would suck worldly wisdom out of the paradox. Perhaps one or another may succeed in that, for our age is not willing to stop with faith, with its miracle of turning water into wine, it goes further, it turns wine into water.

Would it not be better to stop with faith, and is it not revolting that everybody wants to go further? When in our age (as indeed is proclaimed in various ways) they will not stop with love, where then are they going? To earthy wisdom, to petty calculation, to paltriness and wretchedness, to everything which can make man's divine origin doubtful. Would it not be better that they should stand still at faith, and that he who stands should take heed lest he fall? For the movements of faith must constantly be made by virtue of the absurd, yet in such a way, be it observed, that one does not lose the finite but gains it every inch. For my part I can well describe the movements of faith, but I cannot make them. When one would learn to make the motions of swimming one can let oneself be hung by a swimming-belt from the ceiling and go through the motions (describe them, so to speak, as we speak of describing a circle), but one is not swimming. In that way I can describe the movements of faith, but when I am thrown into the water, I swim, it is true (for I don't belong to the beach-waders), but I make other movements, I make the movements of infinity, whereas faith does the opposite: after having made the movements of infinity, it makes those of finiteness. Hail to him who can make those movements, he performs the marvellous, and I shall never grow tired of admiring him, whether he be Abraham or a slave in Abraham's house; whether he be a professor of philosophy or a servant-girl, I look only at the movements. But at them I do look, and do not let myself be fooled, either by myself or by any other man. The knights of the infinite resignation are easily recognized: their gait is gliding and assured. Those on the other hand who carry the jewel of faith are likely to be delusive, because their outward appearance bears a striking resemblance to that which both the infinite resignation and faith profoundly despise . . . to Philistinism.

The Three Movements to Faith

I candidly admit that in my practice I have not found any reliable example of the knight of faith, though I would not therefore deny that every second man may be such an example. I have been trying, however, for several years to get on the track of this, and all in vain. People commonly travel around the world to see rivers and mountains, new stars, birds of rare plumage, queerly deformed fishes, ridiculous breeds of men—they abandon themselves to the bestial stupor which gapes at existence, and they think they have seen something. This does not interest me. But if I knew where there was such a knight of faith, I would make a pilgrimage to him on foot, for this prodigy interests me absolutely. I would not let go of him for an instant, every moment I would watch to see how he managed to make the movements, I would regard myself as secured for life, and would divide my time between looking at him and practising the exercises myself, and thus would spend all my time admiring him. As was said, I have not found any such person, but I can well think him. Here he is. Acquaintance made, I am introduced to him. The moment I set eyes on him I instantly push him from me, I myself leap backwards, I clasp my hands and say half aloud, "Good Lord, is this the man? Is it really he? Why, he looks like a tax-collector!" However, it is the man after all. I draw closer to him, watching his least movements to see whether there might not be visible a little heterogeneous fractional telegraphic message from the infinite, a glance, a look, a gesture, a note of sadness, a smile, which betrayed the infinite in its heterogeneity with the finite. No! I examine his figure from tip to toe to see if there might not be a cranny through which the infinite was peeping. No! He is solid through and through. His tread? It is vigorous, belonging entirely to finiteness; no smartly dressed townsman who walks out to Fresberg on a Sunday afternoon treads the ground more firmly, he belongs entirely to the world, no Philistine more so. One can discover nothing of that aloof and superior nature whereby one recognizes the knight of the infinite. He takes delight in everything, and whenever one sees him taking part in a particular pleasure, he does it with the persistence which is the mark of the earthly man whose soul is absorbed in such things. He tends to his work. So when one looks at him one might suppose that he was a clerk who had lost his soul in an intricate system of book-keeping, so precise is he. He takes a holiday on Sunday. He goes to church. No heavenly glance or any other token of the incommensurable betrays him; if one did not know him, it would be impossible to distinguish him from the rest of the congregation, for his healthy and vigorous hymn-singing proves at the most that he has a good chest. In the afternoon he walks to the forest. He takes delight in everything he sees, in the human swarm, in the new omnibuses, in the water of the Sound; when one meets him on the Beach Road one might suppose he was a shopkeeper taking his fling, that's just the way he disports himself, for his is not a poet, and I have sought in vain to detect in him the poetic incommensurability. Toward evening he walks home, his gait is as indefatigable as that of the postman. On his way he reflects that his wife has surely a special little warm dish prepared for him, e.g. a calf's head roasted, garnished with vegetables. If he were to meet a man like-minded, he could continue as far as East Gate to discourse with him about that dish, with a passion befitting a hotel chef. As it happens, he hasn't four pence to his name, and yet he fully and firmly believes that his wife has that dainty dish for him. If she had it, it would then be an invidious sight for superior people and an inspiring one for the plain man, to see him eat; for his appetite is greater than Esau's. His wife hasn't it—strangely enough, it is quite the same to him. On the way he comes past a building site and runs across another man. They talk together for a moment. In the twinkling of an eye he erects a new building, he has at his disposition all the powers necessary for it. The stranger leaves him with the thought that he certainly was a capitalist, while my admired knight thinks, "Yes, if the money were needed, I dare say I could get it." He lounges at an open window and looks out on the square on which he lives; he is interested in everything that goes on, in a rat which slips under the curb, in the children's play, and this with the nonchalance of a girl of sixteen. And yet he is no genius, for in vain I have sought in him the incommensurability of genius. In the evening he smokes his pipe; to look at him one would swear that it was the grocer over the way vegetating in the twilight. He lives as carefree as a ne'er-do-well, and yet he buys up the acceptable time at the dearest price, for he does not do the least thing except by virtue of the absurd. And yet, and yet—actually I could become furious over it, for envy if for no other reason—this man has made and every instant is making the movements of infinity. With infinite resignation he has drained the cup of life's profound sadness, he knows the bliss of the infinite, he senses the pain of renouncing everything, the dearest things he possesses in the world, and yet finiteness tastes to him just as good as to one who never knew anything higher, for his continuance in the finite did not bear a trace of the cowed and fearful spirit produced by the process of training; and yet he has this sense of security in enjoying it, as though the finite life were the surest thing of all. And yet, and yet the whole earthly form he exhibits is a new creation by virtue of the absurd. He resigned everything infinitely, and then he grasped everything again by virtue of the absurd. He constantly makes the movements of infinity, but he does this with such correctness and assurance that he constantly gets the finite out of it, and there is not a second when one has a notion of anything else. It is supposed to be the most difficult task for a dancer to leap into a definite posture in such a way that there is not a second when he is grasping after the posture, but by the leap itself he stands fixed in that posture. Perhaps no dancer can do it—that is what this knight does. Most people live dejectedly in worldly sorrow and joy; they are the ones who sit along the wall and do not join in the dance. The knights of infinity are dancers and possess elevation. They make the movements upward, and fall down again; and this too is no mean pastime, nor ungraceful to behold. But whenever they fall down they are not able at once to assume the posture, they vacillate an instant, and this vacillation shows that after all they are strangers in the world. This is more or less strikingly evident in proportion to the art they possess, but even the most artistic knights cannot altogether conceal this vacillation. One need not look at them when they are up in the air, but only the instant they touch or have touched the ground— then one recognizes them. But to be able to fall down in such a way that the same second it looks as if one were standing and walking, to transform the leap of life into a walk, absolutely to express the sublime in the pedestrian—that only the knight of faith can do—and this is the one and only prodigy.

But since the prodigy is so likely to be delusive, I will describe the movements in a definite instance which will serve to illustrate their relation to reality, for upon this everything turns. A young swain falls in love with a princess, and the whole content of his life consists in this love, and yet the situation is such that it is impossible for it to be realized, impossible for it to be translated from ideality into reality.* The slaves of paltriness, the frogs in life's swamp, will naturally cry out, "Such a love is foolishness. The rich brewer's widow is a match fully as good and respectable." Let them croak in the swamp undisturbed. It is not so with the knight of infinite resignation, he does not give up his love, not for all the glory of the world. He is no fool. First he makes sure that this really is the content of his life, and his soul is too healthy and too proud to squander the least thing upon an inebriation. He is not cowardly, he is not afraid of letting love creep into his most secret, his most hidden thoughts, to let it twine in innumerable coils about every ligament of his consciousness—if the love becomes an unhappy love, he will never be able to tear himself loose from it. He feels a blissful rapture in letting

---

* Of course any other instance whatsoever in which the individual finds that for him the whole reality of actual existence is concentrated, may, when it is seen to be unrealizable, be an occasion for the movement of resignation. However, I have chosen a love experience to make the movement visible, because this interest is doubtless easier to understand, and so relieves me from the necessity of making preliminary observations which in a deeper sense could be of interest only to a few.

love tingle through every nerve, and yet his soul is as solemn as that of the man who has drained the poisoned goblet and feels how the juice permeates every drop of blood—for this instant is life and death. So when he has thus sucked into himself the whole of love and absorbed himself in it, he does not lack courage to make trial of everything and to venture everything. He surveys the situation of his life, he convokes the swift thoughts, which like tame doves obey his every bidding, he waves his wand over them, and they dart off in all directions. But when they all return, all as messengers of sorrow, and declare to him that it is an impossibility, then he becomes quiet, he dismisses them, he remains alone, and then he performs the movements. If what I am saying is to have any significance, it is requisite that the movement come about normally.*
So for the first thing, the knight will have power to concentrate the whole content of life and the whole significance of reality in one single wish. If a man lacks this concentration, this intensity, if his soul from the beginning is dispersed in the multifarious, he never comes to the point of making the movement, he will deal shrewdly in life like the capitalists who invest their money in all sorts of securities, so as to gain on the one what they lose on the other—in short, he is not a knight. In the next place the knight will have the power to concentrate the whole result of the operations of thought in one act of consciousness. If he lacks this intensity, if his soul from the beginning is dispersed in the multifarious, he will never get time to make the movements, he will be constantly running errands in life, never enter into eternity, for even at the instant when he is closest to it he will suddenly discover that he has forgotten something for which he must go back. He will think that to enter eternity is possible the next instant, and that also is perfectly true, but by such considerations one never reaches the point of making the movements, but by their aid one sinks deeper and deeper into the mire.

So the knight makes the movement—but what movement? Will he forget the whole thing? (For in this too there is indeed a kind of concentration.) No! For the knight does not contradict himself, and it is a contradiction to forget the whole content of one's life and yet remain the

---

* *To this end passion is necessary. Every movement of infinity comes about by passion, and no reflection can bring a movement about. This is the continual leap in existence which explains the movement, whereas mediation is a chimera which according to Hegel is supposed to explain everything, and at the same time this is the only thing he has never tried to explain.* Even to make the well-known Socratic distinction between what one understands and what one does not understand, passion is required, and of course even more to make the characteristic Socratic movement, the movement, namely, of ignorance. What our age lacks, however, is not reflection but passion. Hence in a sense our age is too tenacious of life to die, for dying is one of the most remarkable leaps, and a little verse of a poet has always attracted me much, because, after having expressed prettily and simply in five or six preceding lines his wish for good things in life, he concludes thus:
Ein seliger Sprung in die Ewigkeit. A blissful leap into eternity.

same man. To become another man he feels no inclination, nor does he by any means regard this as greatness. Only the lower natures forget themselves and become something new. Thus the butterfly has entirely forgotten that it was a caterpillar, perhaps it may in turn so entirely forget it was a butterfly that it becomes a fish. The deeper natures never forget themselves and never become anything else than what they were. So the knight remembers everything, but precisely this remembrance is pain, and yet by the infinite resignation he is reconciled with existence. Love for that princess became for him the expression for an eternal love, assumed a religious character, was transfigured into a love for the Eternal Being, which did to be sure deny him the fulfilment of his love, yet reconciled him again by the eternal consciousness of its validity in the form of eternity, which no reality can take from him. Fools and young men prate about everything being possible for a man. That, however, is a great error. Spiritually speaking, everything is possible, but in the world of the finite there is much which is not possible. This impossible, however, the knight makes possible by expressing it spiritually, but he expresses it spiritually by waiving his claim to it. The wish which would carry him out into reality, but was wrecked upon the impossibility, is now bent inward, but it is not therefore lost, neither is it forgotten. At one moment it is the obscure emotion of the wish within him which awakens recollections, at another moment he awakens them himself; for he is too proud to be willing that what was the whole content of his life should be the thing of a fleeting moment. He keeps this love young, and along with him it increases in years and in beauty. On the other hand, he has no need of the intervention of the finite for the further growth of his love. From the instant he made the movement the princess is lost to him. He has no need of those erotic tinglings in the nerves at the sight of the beloved etc., nor does he need to be constantly taking leave of her in a finite sense, because he recollects her in an eternal sense, and he knows very well that the lovers who are so bent upon seeing "her" yet once again, to say farewell for the last time, are right in being bent upon it, are right in thinking that it is the last time, for they forget one another the soonest. He has comprehended the deep secret that also in loving another person one must be sufficient unto oneself. He no longer takes a finite interest in what the princess is doing, and precisely this is proof that he has made the movement infinitely. Here one may have an opportunity to see whether the movement on the part of a particular person is true or fictitious. There was one who also believed that he had made the movement; but lo, time passed, the princess did something else, she married—a prince, let us say—then his soul lost the elasticity of resignation. Thereby he knew that he had not made the movement rightly; for he who has made the act of resignation infinitely is sufficient unto himself. The knight does not annul his resignation, he preserves his love just as young as it was in its first moment, he never lets it go from him, precisely because he makes the movements infinitely. What the princess does, cannot disturb him, it is only the lower natures which find in other people the law for their actions, which find the premises for their actions outside themselves. If on the other hand the princess is like-minded, the beautiful consequence will be apparent. She will introduce herself into that order of knighthood into which one is not received by balloting, but of which everyone is a member who has courage to introduce himself, that order of knighthood which proves its immortality by the fact that it makes no distinction between man and woman. The two will preserve their love young and sound, she also will have triumphed over her pains, even though she does not, as it is said in the ballad, "lie every night beside her lord." These two will to all eternity remain in agreement with one another, with a well-timed *harmonia praestabilita,* so that if ever the moment were to come, the moment which does not, however, concern them finitely (for then they would be growing older), if ever the moment were to come which offered to give love its expression in time, then they will be capable of beginning precisely at the point where they would have begun if originally they had been united. He who understands this, be he man or woman, can never be deceived, for it is only the lower natures which imagine they were deceived. No girl who is not so proud really knows how to love; but if she is so proud, then the cunning and shrewdness of all the world cannot deceive her.

In the infinite resignation there is peace and rest; every man who wills it, who has not abased himself by scorning himself (which is still more dreadful than being proud), can train himself to make this movement which in its pain reconciles one with existence. Infinite resignation is that shirt we read about in the old fable. The thread is spun under tears, the cloth bleached with tears, the shirt sewn with tears; but then too it is a better protection than iron and steel. The imperfection in the fable is that a third party can manufacture this shirt. The secret in life is that everyone must sew it for himself, and the astonishing thing is that a man can sew it fully as well as a woman. In the infinite resignation there is peace and rest and comfort in sorrow—that is, if the movement is made normally. It would not be difficult for me, however, to write a whole book, were I to examine the various misunderstandings, the preposterous attitudes, the deceptive movements, which I have encountered in my brief practice. People believe very little in spirit, and yet making this movement depends upon spirit, it depends upon whether this is or is not a one-sided result of a *dira necessitas,* and if this is present, the more dubious it always is whether the movement is normal. If one means by this that the cold, unfruitful necessity must necessarily be present, one thereby affirms that no one can experience death before he actually dies, and that appears to me a crass materialism. However, in our time people concern themselves rather little about making pure movements. In case one who was about to learn to dance were to say, "For centuries now one generation after another has been learning positions, it is high time I drew some advantage out of this and began straightway with the French dances"—then people would laugh at him; but in the world of spirit they find this exceedingly plausible. What is education? I should suppose that education was the curriculum one had to run through in order to catch up with oneself, and he who will not pass through this curriculum is helped very little by the fact that he was born in the most enlightened age.

The infinite resignation is the last stage prior to faith, so that one who has not made this movement has not faith; for only in the infinite resignation do I become clear to myself with respect to my eternal validity, and only then can there be any question of grasping existence by virtue of faith.

Now we will let the knight of faith appear in the rôle just described. He makes exactly the same movements as the other knight, infinitely renounces claim to the love which is the content of his life, he is reconciled in pain; but then occurs the prodigy, he makes still another movement more wonderful than all, for he says, "I believe nevertheless that I shall get her, in virtue, that is, of the absurd, in virtue of the fact that with God all things are possible." The absurd is not one of the factors which can be discriminated within the proper compass of the understanding: it is not identical with the improbable, the unexpected, the unforeseen. At the moment when the knight made the act of resignation, he was convinced, humanly speaking, of the impossibility. This was the result reached by the understanding, and he had sufficient energy to think it. On the other hand, in an infinite sense it was possible, namely, by renouncing it; but this sort of possessing is at the same time a relinquishing, and yet there is no absurdity in this for the understanding, for the understanding continued to be in the right in affirming that in the world of the finite where it holds sway this was and remained an impossibility. This is quite as clear to the knight of faith, so the only thing that can save him is the absurd, and this he grasps by faith. So he recognizes the impossibility, and that very instant he believes the absurd; for, if without recognizing the impossibility with all the passion of his soul and with all his heart, he should wish to imagine that he has faith, he deceives himself, and his testimony has no bearing, since he has not even reached the infinite resignation.

Faith therefore is not an aesthetic emotion but something far higher, precisely because it has resignation as its presupposition; it is not an immediate instinct of the heart, but is the paradox of life and existence. So when in spite of all difficulties a young girl still remains convinced that her wish will surely be fulfilled, this conviction is not the assurance of faith, even if she was brought up by Christian parents, and for a whole year perhaps has been catechized by the parson. She is convinced in all her childish naïveté and innocence; this conviction also ennobles her nature and imparts to her a preternatural greatness, so that like a thaumaturge she is able to conjure the finite powers of existence and make the very stones weep, while on the other hand in her flurry she may just as well run to Herod as to Pilate and move the whole world by her tears. Her conviction is very lovable, and one can learn much from her, but one thing is not to be learned from her, one does not learn the movements, for her conviction does not dare in the pain of resignation to face the impossibility.

So I can perceive that it requires strength and energy and freedom of spirit to make the infinite movement of resignation, I can also perceive that it is feasible. But the next thing astonishes me, it makes my head swim, for after having made the movement of resignation, then by virtue of the absurd to get everything, to get the wish whole and uncurtailed— that is beyond human power, it is a prodigy. But this I can perceive, that the young girl's conviction is mere levity in comparison with the firmness faith displays notwithstanding it has perceived the impossibility. Whenever I essay to make this movement, I turn giddy, the very instant I am admiring it absolutely a prodigious dread grips my soul—for what is it to tempt God? And yet this movement is the movement of faith and remains such, even though philosophy, in order to confuse the concepts, would make us believe that it has faith, and even though theology would sell out faith at a bargain price.

For the act of resignation faith is not required, for what I gain by resignation is my eternal consciousness, and this is a purely philosophical movement which I dare say I am able to make if it is required, and which I can train myself to make, for whenever any finiteness would get the mastery over me, I starve myself until I can make the movement, for my eternal consciousness is my love to God, and for me this is higher than everything. For the act of resignation faith is not required, but it is needed when it is the case of acquiring the very least thing more than my eternal consciousness, for this is the paradoxical. The movements are frequently confounded, for it is said that one needs faith to renounce the claim to everything, yea, a stranger thing than this may be heard, when a man laments the loss of his faith, and when one looks at the scale to see where he is, one sees, strangely enough, that he has only reached the point where he should make the infinite movement of resignation. In resignation I make renunciation of everything, this movement I make by myself, and if I do not make it, it is because I am cowardly and effeminate and without enthusiasm and do not feel the significance of the lofty dignity which is assigned to every man, that of being his own censor, which is a far prouder title than that of Censor General to the whole Roman Republic. This movement I make by myself, and what I gain is myself in my eternal consciousness, in blissful agreement with my love for the Eternal Being. By faith I make renunciation of nothing, on the contrary, by faith I acquire everything, precisely in the sense in which it is said that he who has faith like a grain of mustard can remove mountains. A purely human courage is required to renounce the whole of the temporal to gain the eternal; but this I gain, and to all eternity I cannot renounce it—that is a self-contradiction. But a paradoxical and humble courage is required to grasp the whole of the temporal by virtue of the absurd, and this is the courage of faith. By faith Abraham did not renounce his claim upon Isaac, but by faith he got Isaac. By virtue of resignation that rich young man should have given away everything, but then when he had done that, the knight of faith should have said to him, "By virtue of the absurd thou shalt get every penny back again. Canst thou believe that?" And this speech ought by no means to have been indifferent to the aforesaid rich young man, for in case he gave away his goods because he was tired of them, his resignation was not much to boast of.

It is about the temporal, the finite, everything turns in this case. I am able by my own strength to renounce everything, and then to find peace and repose in pain. I can stand everything—even though that horrible demon, more dreadful than death, the king of terrors, even though madness were to hold up before my eyes the motley of the fool, and I understood by its look that it was I who must put it on, I still am able to save my soul, if only it is more to me than my earthly happiness that my love to God should triumph in me. A man may still be able at the last instant to concentrate his whole soul in a single glance toward that heaven from which cometh every good gift, and his glance will be intelligible to himself and also to Him whom it seeks as a sign that he nevertheless remained true to his love. Then he will calmly put on the motley garb. He whose soul has not this romantic enthusiasm has sold his soul, whether he got a kingdom for it or a paltry piece of silver. But by my own strength I am not able to get the least of the things which belong to finiteness, for I am constantly using my strength to renounce everything. By my own strength I am able to give up the princess, and I shall not become a grumbler, but shall find joy and repose in my pain; but by my own strength I am not able to get her again, for I am employing all my strength to be resigned. But by faith, says that marvellous knight, by faith I shall get her in virtue of the absurd.

So this movement I am unable to make. As soon as I would begin to make it everything turns around dizzily, and I flee back to the pain of resignation. I can swim in existence, but for this mystical soaring I am too heavy. To exist in such a way that my opposition to existence is expressed as the most beautiful and assured harmony with it, is something I cannot do. And yet it must be glorious to get the princess, that is what I say every instant, and the knight of resignation who does not say it is a deceiver, he has not had one only wish, and he has not kept the wish young by his pain. Perhaps there was one who thought it fitting enough that the wish was no longer vivid, that the barb of pain was dulled, but such a man is no knight. A free-born soul who caught himself entertaining such thoughts would despise himself and begin over again, above all he would not permit his soul to be deceived by itself. And yet it must be glorious to get the princess, and yet the knight of faith is the only happy one, the heir apparent to the finite, whereas the knight of resignation is a stranger and a foreigner. Thus to get the princess, to live with her joyfully and happily day in and day out (for it is also conceivable that the knight of resignation might get the princess, but that his soul had discerned the impossibility of their future happiness), thus to live joyfully and happily every instant by virtue of the absurd, every instant to see the sword hanging over the head of the beloved, and yet not to find repose in the pain of resignation, but joy by virtue of the absurd—this is marvellous. He who does it is great, the only great man. The thought of it stirs my soul, which never was niggardly in the admiration of greatness.

In case then everyone in my generation who will not stop at faith is really a man who has comprehended life's horror, who has understood what Daub means when he says that a soldier who stands alone at his post with a loaded gun in a stormy night beside a powder-magazine . . . will get strange thoughts into his head—in case then everyone who will not stop at faith is a man who had strength of soul to comprehend that the wish was an impossibility, and thereupon gave himself time to remain alone with this thought, in case everyone who will not stop at faith is a man who is reconciled in pain and is reconciled to pain, in case everyone who will not stop at faith is a man who in the next place (and if he has not done all the foregoing, there is no need of his troubling himself about faith)—in the next place did the marvellous thing, grasped the whole of existence by virtue of the absurd . . . then what I write is the highest eulogy of my contemporaries by one of the lowliest among them, who was able only to make the movement of resignation. But why will they not stop at faith, why does one sometimes hear that people are ashamed to acknowledge that they have faith? This I cannot comprehend. If ever I contrive to be able to make this movement, I shall in the future ride in a coach and four.

If it is really true that all the Philistinism I behold in life (which I do not permit my word but my actions to condemn) is not what it seems to be—is it the miracle? That is conceivable, for the hero of faith had in fact a striking resemblance to it—for that hero of faith was not so much an ironist or a humorist, but something far higher. Much is said in our age about irony and humor, especially by people who have never been capable of engaging in the practice of these arts, but who nevertheless know how to explain everything. I am not entirely unacquainted with these two passions, I know a little more about them than what is to be found in German and German-Danish compendiums. I know therefore that these two passions are essentially different from the passion of faith. Irony and humor reflect also upon themselves, and therefore belong within the sphere of the infinite resignation, their elasticity is due to the fact that the individual is incommensurable with reality.

The last movement, the paradoxical movement of faith, I cannot make (be that a duty or whatever it may be), in spite of the fact that I would do it more than gladly. Whether a man has a right to make this affirmation, must be left to him, it is a question between him and the Eternal Being who is the object of faith whether in this respect he can hit upon an amicable compromise. What every man can do is to make the movement of infinite resignation, and I for my part would not hesitate to pronounce everyone cowardly who wishes to make himself believe he can not do it. With faith it is a different matter. But what every man has not a right to do, is to make others believe that faith is something lowly, or that it is an easy thing, whereas it is the greatest and the hardest.

People construe the story of Abraham in another way. They extol God's grace in bestowing Isaac upon him again—the whole thing was only a trial. A trial—that word may say much or little, and yet the whole thing is over as quickly as it is said. One mounts a winged horse, the same instant one is at Mount Moriah, the same instant one sees the ram; one forgets that Abraham rode only upon an ass, which walks slowly along the road, that he had a journey of three days, that he needed some time to cleave the wood, to bind Isaac, and to sharpen the knife.

And yet they extol Abraham. He who is to deliver the discourse can very well sleep till a quarter of an hour before he has to preach, the auditor can well take a nap during the discourse, for all goes smoothly, without the least trouble from any quarter. If there was a man present who suffered from insomnia, perhaps he then went home and sat in a corner and thought: "It's an affair of a moment, this whole thing; if only you wait a minute, you see the ram, and the trial is over." If the orator were to encounter him in this condition, he would, I think, confront him with all his dignity and say, "Wretched man, that thou couldst let thy soul sink into such foolishness! No miracle occurs. The whole of life is a trial." In proportion as the orator proceeds with his outpouring, he would get more and more excited, would become more and more delighted with himself, and whereas he had noticed no congestion of the blood while he talked about Abraham, he now felt how the vein swelled in his forehead. Perhaps he would have lost his breath as well as his tongue if the sinner had answered calmly and with dignity, "But it was about this you preached last Sunday."

Let us then either consign Abraham to oblivion, or let us learn to be dismayed by the tremendous paradox which constitutes the significance of Abraham's life, that we may understand that our age, like every age, can be joyful if it has faith. In case Abraham is not a nullity, a phantom, a show one employs for a pastime, then the fault can never consist in the fact that the sinner wants to do likewise, but the point is to see how great a thing it was that Abraham did, in order that man may judge for himself whether he has the call and the courage to be subjected to such a test. The comic contradiction in the behavior of the orator is that he reduced Abraham to an insignificance, and yet would admonish the other to behave in the same way.

Should not one dare then to talk about Abraham? I think one should. If I were to talk about him, I would first depict the pain of his trial. To that end I would like a leech suck all the dread and distress and torture out of a father's sufferings, so that I might describe what Abraham suffered, whereas all the while he nevertheless believed. I would remind the audience that the journey lasted three days and a good part of the fourth, yea, that these three and a half days were infinitely longer than the few thousand years which separate me from Abraham. Then I would remind them that, in my opinion, every man dare still turn around ere he begins such an undertaking, and every instant he can repentantly turn back. If one does this, I fear no danger, nor am I afraid of awakening in people an inclination to be tried like Abraham. But if one would dispose of a cheap edition of Abraham, and yet admonish everyone to do likewise, then it is ludicrous.

It is now my intention to draw out from the story of Abraham the dialectical consequences inherent in it, expressing them in the form of *problemata,* in order to see what a tremendous paradox faith is, a paradox which is capable of transforming a murder into a holy act well-pleasing to God, a paradox which gives Isaac back to Abraham, which no thought can master, because faith begins precisely there where thinking leaves off.

Problem I: Is There Such a Thing as a Teleological Suspension of the Ethical?

The ethical as such is the universal, and as the universal it applies to everyone, which may be expressed from another point of view by saying that it applies every instant. It reposes immanently in itself, it has nothing without itself which is its *telos,* but is itself *telos* for everything outside it, and when this has been incorporated by the ethical it can go no further. Conceived immediately as physical and psychical, the particular individual is the individual who has his *telos* in the universal, and his ethical task is to express himself constantly in it, to abolish his particularity in order to become the universal. As soon as the individual would assert himself in his particularity over against the universal he sins, and only by recognizing this can he again reconcile himself with the universal. Whenever the individual after he has entered the universal feels an impulse to assert himself as the particular, he is in temptation (*Anfechtung*), and he can labor himself out of this only by penitently abandoning himself as the particular in the universal. If this be the highest thing that can be said of man and of his existence, then the ethical has the same character as man's eternal blessedness, which to all eternity and at every instant is his *telos,* since it would be a contradiction to say that this might be abandoned (i.e. teleologically suspended), inasmuch as this is no sooner suspended than it is forfeited, whereas in other cases what is suspended is not forfeited but is preserved precisely in that higher thing which is its *telos.*

If such be the case, then Hegel is right when in his chapter on "The Good and the Conscience," he characterizes man merely as the particular and regards this character as "a moral form of evil" which is to be annulled in the teleology of the moral, so that the individual who remains in this stage is either sinning or subjected to temptation (*Anfechtung*). On the other hand, Hegel is wrong in talking of faith, wrong in not protesting loudly and clearly against the fact that Abraham enjoys honor and glory as the father of faith, whereas he ought to be prosecuted and convicted of murder.

For faith is this paradox, that the particular is higher than the universal—yet in such a way, be it observed, that the movement repeats itself, and that consequently the individual, after having been in the universal, now as the particular isolates himself as higher than the universal. If this be not faith, then Abraham is lost, then faith has never existed in the world . . . because it has always existed. For if the ethical (i.e. the moral) is the highest thing, and if nothing incommensurable remains in man in any other way but as the evil (i.e. the particular which has to be expressed in the universal), then one needs no other categories besides those which the Greeks possessed or which by consistent thinking can be derived from them. This fact Hegel ought not to have concealed, for after all he was acquainted with Greek thought.

One not infrequently hears it said by men who for lack of losing themselves in studies are absorbed in phrases that a light shines upon the Christian world whereas a darkness broods over paganism. This utterance has always seemed strange to me, inasmuch as every profound thinker and every serious artist is even in our day rejuvenated by the eternal youth of the Greek race. Such an utterance may be explained by the consideration that people do not know what they ought to say but only that they must say something. It is quite right for one to say that paganism did not possess faith, but if with this one is to have said something, one must be a little clearer about what one understands by faith, since otherwise one falls back into such phrases. To explain the whole of existence and faith along with it, without having a conception of what faith is, is easy, and that man does not make the poorest calculation in life who reckons upon admiration when he possesses such an explanation; for, as Boileau says, "*un sot trouve toujours un plus sot qui l'admire.*"

Faith is precisely this paradox, that the individual as the particular is higher than the universal, is justified over against it, is not subordinate but superior—yet in such a way, be it observed, that it is the particular individual who, after he has been subordinated as the particular to the universal, now through the universal becomes the individual who as the particular is superior to the universal, for the fact that the individual as the particular stands in an absolute relation to the absolute. This position cannot be mediated, for all mediation comes about precisely by virtue of the universal; it is and remains to all eternity a paradox, inaccessible to thought. And yet faith is this paradox—or else (these are the logical deductions which I would beg the reader to have *in mente* at every point, though it would be too prolix for me to reiterate them on every occasion)—or else there never has been faith . . . precisely because it always has been. In other words, Abraham is lost.

That for the particular individual this paradox may easily be mistaken for a temptation (*Anfechtung*) is indeed true, but one ought not for this reason to conceal it. That the whole constitution of many persons may be such that this paradox repels them is indeed true, but one ought not for this reason to make faith something different in order to be able to possess it, but ought rather to admit that one does not possess it, whereas those who possess faith should take care to set up certain criteria so that one might distinguish the paradox from a temptation (*Anfechtung*).

Now the story of Abraham contains such a teleological suspension of the ethical. There have not been lacking clever pates and profound investigators who have found analogies to it. Their wisdom is derived from the pretty proposition that at bottom everything is the same. If one will look a little more closely, I have not much doubt that in the whole world one will not find a single analogy (except a later instance which proves nothing), if it stands fast that Abraham is the representative of faith, and that faith is normally expressed in him whose life is not merely the most paradoxical that can be thought but so paradoxical that it cannot be thought at all. He acts by virtue of the absurd, for it is precisely absurd that he as the particular is higher than the universal. This paradox cannot be mediated; for as soon as he begins to do this he has to admit that he was in temptation (*Anfechtung*), and if such was the case, he never gets to the point of sacrificing Isaac, or, if he has sacrificed Isaac, he must turn back repentantly to the universal. By virtue of the absurd he gets Isaac again. Abraham is therefore at no instant a tragic hero but something quite different, either a murderer or a believer. The middle term which saves the tragic hero, Abraham has not. Hence it is that I can understand the tragic hero but cannot understand Abraham, though in a certain crazy sense I admire him more than all other men.

Abraham's relation to Isaac, ethically speaking, is quite simply expressed by saying that a father shall love his son more dearly than himself. Yet within its own compass the ethical has various gradations. Let us see whether in this story there is to be found any higher expression for the ethical such as would ethically explain his conduct, ethically justify him in suspending the ethical obligation toward his son, without in this search going beyond the teleology of the ethical.

When an undertaking in which a whole nation is concerned is hindered, when such an enterprise is brought to a standstill by the disfavor of heaven, when the angry deity sends a calm which mocks all efforts, when the seer performs his heavy task and proclaims that the deity demands a young maiden as a sacrifice—then will the father heroically make the sacrifice. He will magnanimously conceal his pain, even though he might wish that he were "the lowly man who dares to weep," not the king who must act royally. And though solitary pain forces its way into his breast, he has only three confidants among the people, yet soon the whole nation will be cognizant of his pain, but also cognizant of his exploit, that for the welfare of the whole he was willing to sacrifice her, his daughter, the lovely young maiden. O charming bosom! O beautiful cheeks! O bright golden hair! And the daughter will affect him by her tears, and the father will turn his face away, but the hero will raise the knife.—When the report of this reaches the ancestral home, then will the beautiful maidens of Greece blush with enthusiasm, and if the daughter was betrothed, her true love will not be angry but be proud of sharing in the father's deed, because the maiden belonged to him more feelingly than to the father.

When the intrepid judge who saved Israel in the hour of need in one breath binds himself and God by the same vow, then heroically the young maiden's jubilation, the beloved daughter's joy, he will turn to sorrow, and with her all Israel will lament her maiden youth; but every free-born man will understand, and every stout-hearted woman will admire Jephtha, and every maiden in Israel will wish to act as did his daughter. For what good would it do if Jephtha were victorious by reason of his vow if he did not keep it? Would not the victory again be taken from the nation?

When a son is forgetful of his duty, when the state entrusts the father with the sword of justice, when the laws require punishment at the hand of the father, then will the father heroically forget that the guilty one is his son, he will magnanimously conceal his pain, but there will not be a single one among the people, not even the son, who will not admire the father, and whenever the law of Rome is interpreted, it will be remembered that many interpreted it more learnedly, but none so gloriously as Brutus.

If, on the other hand, while a favorable wind bore the fleet on with swelling sails to its goal, Agamemnon had sent that messenger who fetched Iphigenia in order to be sacrificed; if Jephtha, without being bound by any vow which decided the fate of the nation, had said to his daughter, "Bewail now thy virginity for the space of two months, for I will sacrifice thee"; if Brutus had had a righteous son and yet would have ordered the lictors to execute him—who would have understood them? If these three men had replied to the query why they did it by saying, "It is a trial in which we are tested," would people have understood them better?

When Agamemnon, Jephtha, Brutus at the decisive moment heroically overcome their pain, have heroically lost the beloved and have merely to accomplish the outward sacrifice, then there never will be a noble soul in the world who will not shed tears of compassion for their pain and of admiration for their exploit. If, on the other hand, these three men at the decisive moment were to adjoin to their heroic conduct this little word, "But for all that it will not come to pass," who then would understand them? If as an explanation they added, "This we believe by virtue of the absurd," who would understand them better? For who would not easily understand that it was absurd, but who would understand that one could then believe it?

The difference between the tragic hero and Abraham is clearly evident. The tragic hero still remains within the ethical. He lets one expression of the ethical find its *telos* in a higher expression of the ethical; the ethical relation between father and son, or daughter and father, he reduces to a sentiment which has its dialectic in its relation to the idea of morality. Here there can be no question of a teleological suspension of the ethical itself.

With Abraham the situation was different. By his act he overstepped the ethical entirely and possessed a higher *telos* outside of it, in relation to which he suspended the former. For I should very much like to know how one would bring Abraham's act into relation with the universal, and whether it is possible to discover any connection whatever between what Abraham did and the universal . . . except the fact that he transgressed it. It was not for the sake of saving a people, not to maintain the idea of the state, that Abraham did this, and not in order to reconcile angry deities. If there could be a question of the deity being angry, he was angry only with Abraham, and Abraham's whole action stands in no relation to the universal, is a purely private undertaking. Therefore, whereas the tragic hero is great by reason of his moral virtue, Abraham is great by reason of a purely personal virtue. In Abraham's life there is no higher expression for the ethical than this, that the father shall love his son. Of the ethical in the sense of morality there can be no question in this instance. In so far as the universal was present, it was indeed cryptically present in Isaac, hidden as it were in Isaac's loins, and must therefore cry out with Isaac's mouth, "Do it not! Thou art bringing everything to naught."

Why then did Abraham do it? For God's sake, and (in complete identity with this) for his own sake. He did it for God's sake because God required this proof of his faith; for his own sake he did it in order that he might furnish the proof. The unity of these two points of view is perfectly expressed by the word which has always been used to characterize this situation: it is a trial, a temptation (*Fristelse*). A temptation—but what does that mean? What ordinarily tempts a man is that which would keep him from doing his duty, but in this case the temptation is itself the ethical . . . which would keep him from doing God's will. But what then is duty? Duty is precisely the expression for God's will.

Here is evident the necessity of a new category if one would understand Abraham. Such a relationship to the deity paganism did not know. The tragic hero does not enter into any private relationship with the deity, but for him the ethical is the divine, hence the paradox implied in his situation can be mediated in the universal.

Abraham cannot be mediated, and the same thing can be expressed also by saying that he cannot talk. So soon as I talk I express the universal, and if I do not do so, no one can understand me. Therefore if Abraham would express himself in terms of the universal, he must say that his situation is a temptation (*Anfechtung*), for he has no higher expression for that universal which stands above the universal which he transgresses.

Therefore, though Abraham arouses my admiration, he at the same time appalls me. He who denies himself and sacrifices himself for duty gives up the finite in order to grasp the infinite, and that man is secure enough. The tragic hero gives up the certain for the still more certain, and the eye of the beholder rests upon him confidently. But he who gives up the universal in order to grasp something still higher which is not the universal—what is he doing? Is it possible that this can be anything else but a temptation (*Anfechtung*)? And if it be possible . . . but the individual was mistaken—what can save him? He suffers all the pain of the tragic hero, he brings to naught his joy in the world, he renounces everything . . . and perhaps at the same instant debars himself from the sublime joy which to him was so precious that he would purchase it at any price. Him the beholder cannot understand nor let his eye rest confidently upon him. Perhaps it is not possible to do what the believer proposes, since it is indeed unthinkable. Or if it could be done, but if the individual had misunderstood the deity—what can save him? The tragic hero has need of tears and claims them, and where is the envious eye which would be so barren that it could not weep with Agamemnon; but where is the man with a soul so bewildered that he would have the presumption to weep for Abraham? The tragic hero accomplishes his act at a definite instant in time, but in the course of time he does something not less significant, he visits the man whose soul is beset with sorrow, whose breast for stifled sobs cannot draw breath, whose thoughts pregnant with tears weigh heavily upon him, to him he makes his appearance, dissolves the sorcery of sorrow, loosens his corslet, coaxes forth his tears by the fact that in his sufferings the sufferer forgets his own. One cannot weep over Abraham. One approaches him with a *horror religiosus,* as Israel approached Mount Sinai.—If then the solitary man who ascends Mount Moriah, which with its peak rises heaven-high above the plain of Aulis, if he be not a somnambulist who walks securely above the abyss while he who is stationed at the foot of the mountain and is looking on trembles with fear and out of reverence and dread dare not even call to him—if this man is disordered in his mind, if he had made a mistake! Thanks and thanks again to him who proffers to the man whom the sorrows of life have assaulted and left naked—proffers to him the figleaf of the word with which he can cover his wretchedness. Thanks be to thee, great Shakespeare, who art able to express everything, absolutely everything, precisely as it is—and yet why didst thou never pronounce this pang? Didst thou perhaps reserve it to thyself—like the loved one whose name one cannot endure that the world should mention? For the poet purchases the power of words, the power of uttering all the dread secrets of others, at the price of a little secret he is unable to utter . . . and a poet is not an apostle, he casts out devils only by the power of the devil.

But now when the ethical is thus teleologically suspended, how does the individual exist in whom it is suspended? He exists as the particular in opposition to the universal. Does he then sin? For this is the form of sin, as seen in the idea. Just as the infant, though it does not sin, because it is not as such yet conscious of its existence, yet its existence is sin, as seen in the idea, and the ethical makes its demands upon it every instant. If one denies that this form can be repeated [in the adult] in such a way that it is not sin, then the sentence of condemnation is pronounced upon Abraham. How then did Abraham exist? He believed. This is the paradox which keeps him upon the sheer edge and which he cannot make clear to any other man, for the paradox is that he as the individual puts himself in an absolute relation to the absolute. Is he justified in doing this? His justification is once more the paradox; for if he is justified, it is not by virtue of anything universal, but by virtue of being the particular individual. . . .

I return, however, to Abraham. Before the result, either Abraham was every minute a murderer, or we are confronted by a paradox which is higher than all mediation.

The story of Abraham contains therefore a teleological suspension of the ethical. As the individual he became higher than the universal. This is the paradox which does not permit of mediation. It is just as inexplicable how he got into it as it is inexplicable how he remained in it. If such is not the position of Abraham, then he is not even a tragic hero but a murderer. To want to continue to call him the father of faith, to talk of this to people who do not concern themselves with anything but words, is thoughtless. A man can become a tragic hero by his own powers—but not a knight of faith. When a man enters upon the way, in a certain sense the hard way of the tragic hero, many will be able to give him counsel; to him who follows the narrow way of faith no one can give counsel, him no one can understand. Faith is a miracle, and yet no man is excluded from it; for that in which all human life is unified is passion,* and faith is a passion.

Problem II: Is There Such a Thing as an Absolute Duty Toward God?

The ethical is the universal, and as such it is again the divine. One has therefore a right to say that fundamentally every duty is a duty toward God; but if one cannot say more, then one affirms at the same time that properly I have no duty toward God. Duty becomes duty by being referred to God, but in duty itself I do not come into relation with God. Thus it is a duty to love one's neighbor, but in performing this duty I do not come into relation with God but with the neighbor whom I love. If I say then in this connection that it is my duty to love God, I am really uttering only a tautology, inasmuch as "God" is in this instance used in

---

* Lessing has somewhere given expression to a similar thought from a purely aesthetic point of view. What he would show expressly in this passage is that sorrow too can find a witty expression. To this end he quotes a rejoinder of the unhappy English king, Edward II. In contrast to this he quotes from Diderot a story of a peasant woman and a rejoinder of hers. Then he continues: "That too was wit, and the wit of a peasant at that; but the situation made it inevitable. Consequently one must not seek to find the excuse for the witty expressions of pain and of sorrow in the fact that the person who uttered them was a superior person, well educated, intelligent, and witty withal, *for the passions make all men again equal*—but the explanation is to be found in the fact that in all probability everyone would have said the same thing in the same situation. The thought of a peasant woman a queen could have had and must have had, just as what the king said in that instance a peasant too would have been able to say and doubtless would have said." Cf. *Sämtliche Werke,* XXX. p. 223.

an entirely abstract sense as the divine, i.e. the universal, i.e. duty. So the whole existence of the human race is rounded off completely like a sphere, and the ethical is at once its limit and its content. God becomes an invisible vanishing point, a powerless thought, His power being only in the ethical which is the content of existence. If in any way it might occur to any man to want to love God in any other sense than that here indicated, he is romantic, he loves a phantom which, if it had merely the power of being able to speak, would say to him, "I do not require your love. Stay where you belong." If in any way it might occur to a man to want to love God otherwise, this love would be open to suspicion, like that of which Rousseau speaks, referring to people who love the Kaffirs instead of their neighbors.

So in case what has been expounded here is correct, in case there is no incommensurability in a human life, and what there is of the incommensurable is only such by an accident from which no consequences can be drawn, in so far as existence is regarded in terms of the idea, Hegel is right; but he is not right in talking about faith or in allowing Abraham to be regarded as the father of it; for by the latter he has pronounced judgment both upon Abraham and upon faith. In the Hegelian philosophy *das Äussere* (*die Entäusserung*) is higher than *das Innere.* This is frequently illustrated by an example. The child is *das Innere,* the man *das Äussere.* Hence it is that the child is defined by the outward, and conversely, the man, as *das Äussere,* is defined precisely by *das Innere.* Faith, on the contrary, is the paradox that inwardness is higher than outwardness—or, to recall an expression used above, the uneven number is higher than the even.

In the ethical way of regarding life it is therefore the task of the individual to divest himself of the inward determinants and express them in an outward way. Whenever he shrinks from this, whenever he is inclined to persist in or to slip back again into the inward determinants of feeling, mood, etc., he sins, he is in a temptation (*Anfechtung*). The paradox of faith is this, that there is an inwardness which is incommensurable for the outward, an inwardness, be it observed, which is not identical with the first but is a new inwardness. This must not be overlooked. Modern philosophy has permitted itself without further ado to substitute in place of "faith" the immediate. When one does that it is ridiculous to deny that faith has existed in all ages. In that way faith comes into rather simple company along with feeling, mood, idiosyncrasy, vapors, etc. To this extent philosophy may be right in saying that one ought not to stop there. But there is nothing to justify philosophy in using this phrase with regard to faith. Before faith there goes a movement of infinity, and only then, *necopinate,* by virtue of the absurd, faith enters upon the scene. This I can well understand without maintaining on that account that I have faith. If faith is nothing but what philosophy makes it out to be, then Socrates already went further, much further, whereas the contrary is true, that he never reached it. In an intellectual respect he made the movement of infinity. His ignorance is infinite resignation. This task in itself is a match for human powers, even though people in our time disdain it; but only after it is done, only when the individual has evacuated himself in the infinite, only then is the point attained where faith can break forth.

The paradox of faith is this, that the individual is higher than the universal, that the individual (to recall a dogmatic distinction now rather seldom heard) determines his relation to the universal by his relation to the absolute, not his relation to the absolute by his relation to the universal. The paradox can also be expressed by saying that there is an absolute duty toward God; for in this relationship of duty the individual as an individual stands related absolutely to the absolute. So when in this connection it is said that it is a duty to love God, something different is said from that in the foregoing; for if this duty is absolute, the ethical is reduced to a position of relativity. From this, however, it does not follow that the ethical is to be abolished, but it acquires an entirely different expression, the paradoxical expression—that, for example, love to God may cause the knight of faith to give his love to his neighbor the opposite expression to that which, ethically speaking, is required by duty.

If such is not the case, then faith has no proper place in existence, then faith is a temptation (*Anfechtung*), and Abraham is lost, since he gave in to it.

This paradox does not permit of mediation, for it is founded precisely upon the fact that the individual is only the individual. As soon as this individual [who is aware of a direct command from God] wishes to express his absolute duty in [terms of] the universal [i.e. the ethical, and] is sure of his duty in that [i.e. the universal or ethical precept], he recognizes that he is in temptation [i.e. a trial of faith], and, if in fact he resists [the direct indication of God's will], he ends by not fulfilling the absolute duty so called [i.e. what here has been called the absolute duty]; and, if he doesn't do this, [i.e. doesn't put up a resistance to the direct intimation of God's will], he sins, even though *realiter* his deed were that which it was his absolute duty to do. So what should Abraham do? If he would say to another person, "Isaac I love more dearly than everything in the world, and hence it is so hard for me to sacrifice him"; then surely the other would have shaken his head and said, "Why will you sacrifice him then?"—or if the other had been a sly fellow, he surely would have seen through Abraham and perceived that he was making a show of feelings which were in strident contradiction to his act.

In the story of Abraham we find such a paradox. His relation to Isaac, ethically expressed, is this, that the father should love the son. This ethical relation is reduced to a relative position in contrast with the absolute relation to God. To the question, "Why?" Abraham has no answer except that it is a trial, a temptation (*Fristelse*)—terms which, as was remarked above, express the unity of the two points of view: that it is for God's sake and for his own sake. In common usage these two ways of regarding the matter are mutually exclusive. Thus when we see a man do something which does not comport with the universal, we say that he scarcely can be doing it for God's sake, and by that we imply that he does it for his own sake. The paradox of faith has lost the intermediate term, i.e. the universal. On the one side it has the expression for the extremest egoism (doing the dreadful thing it does for one's own sake); on the other side the expression for the most absolute self-sacrifice (doing it for God's sake). Faith itself cannot be mediated into the universal, for it would thereby be destroyed. Faith is this paradox, and the individual absolutely cannot make himself intelligible to anybody. People imagine maybe that the individual can make himself intelligible to another individual in the same case. Such a notion would be unthinkable if in our time people did not in so many ways seek to creep slyly into greatness. The one knight of faith can render no aid to the other. Either the individual becomes a knight of faith by assuming the burden of the paradox, or he never becomes one. In these regions partnership is unthinkable. Every more precise explication of what is to be understood by Isaac the individual can give only to himself. And even if one were able, generally speaking, to define ever so precisely what should be intended by Isaac (which moreover would be the most ludicrous self-contradiction, i.e. that the particular individual who definitely stands outside the universal is subsumed under universal categories precisely when he has to act as the individual who stands outside the universal), the individual nevertheless will never be able to assure himself by the aid of others that this application is appropriate, but he can do so only by himself as the individual. Hence even if a man were cowardly and paltry enough to wish to become a knight of faith on the responsibility of an outsider, he will never become one; for only the individual becomes a knight of faith as the particular individual, and this is the greatness of this knighthood, as I can well understand without entering the order, since I lack courage; but this is also its terror, as I can comprehend even better. . . .

Let us consider a little more closely the distress and dread in the paradox of faith. The tragic hero renounces himself in order to express the universal, the knight of faith renounces the universal in order to become the individual. As has been said, everything depends upon how one is placed. He who believes that it is easy enough to be the individual can always be sure that he is not a knight of faith, for vagabonds and roving geniuses are not men of faith. The knight of faith knows, on the other hand, that it is glorious to belong to the universal. He knows that it is beautiful and salutary to be the individual who translates himself into the universal, who edits as it were a pure and elegant edition of himself, as free from errors as possible and which everyone can read. He knows that it is refreshing to become intelligible to oneself in the universal so that he understands it and so that every individual who understands him understands through him in turn the universal, and both rejoice in the security of the universal. He knows that it is beautiful to be born as the individual who has the universal as his home, his friendly abiding-place, which at once welcomes him with open arms when he would tarry in it. But he knows also that higher than this there winds a solitary path, narrow and steep; he knows that it is terrible to be born outside the universal, to walk without meeting a single traveller. He knows very well where he is and how he is related to men. Humanly speaking, he is crazy and cannot make himself intelligible to anyone. And yet it is the mildest expression, to say that he is crazy. If he is not supposed to be that, then he is a hypocrite, and the higher he climbs on this path, the more dreadful a hypocrite he is.

The knight of faith knows that to give up oneself for the universal inspires enthusiasm, and that it requires courage, but he also knows that security is to be found in this, precisely because it is for the universal. He knows that it is glorious to be understood by every noble mind, so glorious that the beholder is ennobled by it, and he feels as if he were bound; he could wish it were this task that had been allotted to him. Thus Abraham could surely have wished now and then that the task were to love Isaac as becomes a father, in a way intelligible to all, memorable throughout all ages; he could wish that the task were to sacrifice Isaac for the universal, that he might incite the fathers to illustrious deeds— and he is almost terrified by the thought that for him such wishes are only temptations and must be dealt with as such, for he knows that it is a solitary path he treads and that he accomplishes nothing for the universal but only himself is tried and examined. Or what did Abraham accomplish for the universal? Let me speak humanly about it, quite humanly. He spent seventy years in getting a son of his old age. What other men get quickly enough and enjoy for a long time he spent seventy years in accomplishing. And why? Because he was tried and put to the test. Is not that crazy? But Abraham believed, and Sarah wavered and got him to take Hagar as a concubine—but therefore he also had to drive her away. He gets Isaac, then he has to be tried again. He knew that it is glorious to express the universal, glorious to live with Isaac. But this is not the task. He knew that it is a kingly thing to sacrifice such a son for the universal, he himself would have found repose in that, and all would have reposed in the commendation of his deed, as a vowel reposes in its consonant, but that is not the task—he is tried. That Roman general who is celebrated by his name of Cunctator checked the foe by procrastination—but what a procrastinator Abraham is in comparison with him! . . . yet he did not save the state. This is the content of one hundred and thirty years. Who can bear it? Would not his contemporary age, if we can speak of such a thing, have said of him, "Abraham is eternally procrastinating. Finally he gets a son. That took long enough. Now he wants to sacrifice him. So is he not mad? And if at least he could explain why he wants to do it—but he always says that it is a trial." Nor could Abraham explain more, for his life is like a book placed under a divine attachment and which never becomes *publici juris.*

This is the terrible thing. He who does not see it can always be sure that he is no knight of faith, but he who sees it will not deny that even the most tried of tragic heroes walks with a dancing step compared with the knight of faith, who comes slowly creeping forward. And if he has perceived this and assured himself that he has not courage to understand it, he will at least have a presentiment of the marvellous glory this knight attains in the fact that he becomes God's intimate acquaintance, the Lord's friend, and (to speak quite humanly) that he says "Thou" to God in heaven, whereas even the tragic hero only addresses Him in the third person.

The tragic hero is soon ready and has soon finished the fight, he makes the infinite movement and then is secure in the universal. The knight of faith, on the other hand, is kept sleepless, for he is constantly tried, and every instant there is the possibility of being able to return repentantly to the universal, and this possibility can just as well be a temptation as the truth. He can derive evidence from no man which it is, for with that query he is outside the paradox.

So the knight of faith has first and foremost the requisite passion to concentrate upon a single factor the whole of the ethical which he transgresses, so that he can give himself the assurance that he really loves Isaac with his whole soul.* If he cannot do that, he is in temptation (*Anfechtung*). In the next place, he has enough passion to make this

---

* I would elucidate yet once more the difference between the collisions which are encountered by the tragic hero and by the knight of faith. The tragic hero assures himself that the ethical obligation [i.e., the lower ethical obligation, which he puts aside for the higher; in the present case, accordingly, it is the obligation to spare his daughter's life] is totally present in him by the fact that he transforms it into a wish. Thus Agamemnon can say, "The proof that I do not offend against my parental duty is that my duty is my only wish." So here we have wish and duty face to face with one another. The fortunate chance in life is that the two correspond, that my wish is my duty and vice versa, and the task of most men in life is precisely to remain within their duty and by their enthusiasm to transform it into their wish. The tragic hero gives up his wish in order to accomplish his duty. For the knight of faith wish and duty are also identical, but he is required to give up both. Therefore when he would resign himself to giving up his wish he does not find repose, for that is after all his duty. If he would remain within his duty and his wish, he is not a knight of faith, for the absolute duty requires precisely that he should give them up. The tragic hero apprehended a higher expression of duty but not an absolute duty.

assurance available in the twinkling of an eye and in such a way that it is as completely valid as it was in the first instance. If he is unable to do this, he can never budge from the spot, for he constantly has to begin all over again. The tragic hero also concentrated in one factor the ethical which he teleologically surpassed, but in this respect he had support in the universal. The knight of faith has only himself alone, and this constitutes the dreadfulness of the situation. Most men live in such a way under an ethical obligation that they can let the sorrow be sufficient for the day, but they never reach this passionate concentration, this energetic consciousness. The universal may in a certain sense help the tragic hero to attain this, but the knight of faith is left all to himself. The hero does the deed and finds repose in the universal, the knight of faith is kept in constant tension. Agamemnon gives up Iphigenia and thereby has found repose in the universal, then he takes the step of sacrificing her. If Agamemnon does not make the infinite movement, if his soul at the decisive instant, instead of having passionate concentration, is absorbed by the common twaddle that he had several daughters and *vielleicht* [perhaps] the *Ausserordentliche* [extraordinary] might occur—then he is of course not a hero but a hospital-case. The hero's concentration Abraham also has, even though in his case it is far more difficult, since he has no support in the universal; but he makes one more movement by which he concentrates his soul upon the miracle. If Abraham did not do that, he is only an Agamemnon—if in any way it is possible to explain how he can be justified in sacrificing Isaac when thereby no profit accrues to the universal.

Whether the individual is in temptation (*Anfechtung*) or is a knight of faith only the individual can decide. Nevertheless it is possible to construct from the paradox several criteria which he too can understand who is not within the paradox. The true knight of faith is always absolute isolation, the false knight is sectarian. This sectarianism is an attempt to leap away from the narrow path of the paradox and become a tragic hero at a cheap price. The tragic hero expresses the universal and sacrifices himself for it. The sectarian punchinello, instead of that, has a private theatre, i.e. several good friends and comrades who represent the universal just about as well as the beadles in *The Golden Snuffbox* represent justice. The knight of faith, on the contrary, is the paradox, is the individual, absolutely nothing but the individual, without connections or pretensions. This is the terrible thing which the sectarian manikin cannot endure. For instead of learning from this terror that he is not capable of performing the great deed and then plainly admitting it (an act which I cannot but approve, because it is what I do) the manikin thinks that by uniting with several other manikins he will be able to do it. But that is quite out of the question. In the world of spirit no swindling is tolerated. A dozen sectaries join arms with one another, they know nothing whatever of the lonely temptations which await the knight of faith and which he dares not shun precisely because it would be still more dreadful if he were to press forward presumptuously. The sectaries deafen one another by their noise and racket, hold the dread off by their shrieks, and such a hallooing company of sportsmen think they are storming heaven and think they are on the same path as the knight of faith who in the solitude of the universe never hears any human voice but walks alone with his dreadful responsibility.

The knight of faith is obliged to rely upon himself alone, he feels the pain of not being able to make himself intelligible to others, but he feels no vain desire to guide others. The pain is his assurance that he is in the right way, this vain desire he does not know, he is too serious for that. The false knight of faith readily betrays himself by this proficiency in guiding which he has acquired in an instant. He does not comprehend what it is all about, that if another individual is to take the same path, he must become entirely in the same way the individual and have no need of any man's guidance, least of all the guidance of a man who would obtrude himself. At this point men leap aside, they cannot bear the martyrdom of being uncomprehended, and instead of this they choose conveniently enough the worldly admiration of their proficiency. The true knight of faith is a witness, never a teacher, and therein lies his deep humanity, which is worth a good deal more than this silly participation in others' weal and woe which is honored by the name of sympathy, whereas in fact it is nothing but vanity. He who would only be a witness thereby avows that no man, not even the lowliest, needs another man's sympathy or should be abased that another may be exalted. But since he did not win what he won at a cheap price, neither does he sell it out at a cheap price, he is not petty enough to take men's admiration and give them in return his silent contempt, he knows that what is truly great is equally accessible to all.

Either there is an absolute duty toward God, and if so it is the paradox here described, that the individual as the individual is higher than the universal and as the individual stands in an absolute relationto the absolute/or else faith never existed, because it has always existed. . . .

3

Friedrich Nietzsche

THE DEATH OF GOD

Kierkegaard and Friedrich Nietzsche (1844–1900) are both concerned with our coming to grips with the existentialist subject matter. Yet, if there is such a thing, it is not a kind or an abstraction, and so it is not something that can be understood in general terms. Consequently, since all thought and language involves general notions, we cannot come to understand the subject matter of existentialism by means of language or thought. We cannot convey the meaning of "the subjective" or "the existent"; we can only *be* it. Consciousness of being the existentialist subject matter is not, however, sufficient to know what that subject matter is. To know the subject matter one must make a certain kind of discovery. One discovers the existent by discovering oneself, by doing something entirely on the basis of one's own decision and not because of arguments.

For Kierkegaard, one discovers oneself through religion because religion is essentially concerned with faith, and faith involves inwardness. Faith involves a commitment to something, an act of the will, that is entirely one's own free act. It is an act of will that is not based on any objective fact. In order to have faith I must engage in an act by myself without the aid of family, friends, or society. What, then, is the vehicle that Nietzsche utilizes on the road to self-awareness?

Nietzsche came to the discovery of the subject matter of existentialism by way of an inquiry into the nature and significance of ethical matters, and it is easy to see why. The existing individual is a being that makes decisions and choices, but to make a genuine choice or to prefer one thing over another, is to assign a greater value to one than the other. Thus, in talking about values we strike at the heart of what it is to be an existing individual. Of course, the significance of values does not consist merely in the fact that we have them. Their existential significance and relevance concerns what we do with them, how we relate to values. A consideration of values has the capacity to make us existentially self-aware, but values may also be existentially irrelevant.

Recall that in the *Concluding Unscientific Postscript* Kierkegaard claims that the "ethical" individual and not the cognitive individual is the existing individual. For Nietzsche, however, there is another sense in which the "ethical" individual is not the existing individual because the (moral) ethical individual is not aware of the all-important fact of the death of God. That is, the ethical individual still believes that decisions and choices are based on *objective values,* be they the values of God, society, parent, or minister. Although such individuals are ethical because their actions are based on values, they seldom if ever confront themselves in making decisions and choices. The ethical individual is completely unaware and unwilling to face the fact *that values are our own respon-sibility.* Thus, to be ethical, to do what is "objectively right" or to view values as being binding on us, is one way to avoid facing oneself.

If we view values as being objectively valid, as being given to us by some external source, then we may think that we can avoid ultimate responsibility for the values we adopt. We may claim that we are just doing what we are told or what society judges to be right. Of course, even if values are objective it is still up to us to decide whether or not we are to follow them. We cannot avoid taking responsibility for the values we adopt, but we seldom, if at all, are aware of the existentially relevant fact that we have to decide on our own what values to adopt. In the following passage Nietzsche explains why this is so:

> *Our valuations.*—All actions may be referred back to valuations, and all valuations are either one's own or adopted, the latter being by far the more numerous. Why do we adopt them? Through fear, i.e., we think it more advisable to pretend that they are our own, and so well do we accustom ourselves to do so that it at last becomes second nature to us. . . . A valuation of our own . . . is something very rare indeed! But must not our valuation of our neighbor—which is prompted by the motive that we adopt his valuation in most cases—*proceed from ourselves and by our own decision?* Of course, but then we come to these decisions during our childhood, and seldom change them. We often remain during our whole lifetime the dupes of our childish and accustomed judgments in our manner of judging our fellowmen [their minds, rank, morality, character, and reprehensibility], and we find it necessary to subscribe to their valuation.[1]

Although values are our own responsibility, we seldom recognize this because we take for granted that the values instilled in us as children are correct. And then when we are older we fear asserting our own values against the values of others, and consequently we automatically make valuations that coincide with those of others.

Nietzsche believed, however, that some powerful individuals are capable of distinguishing between their own valuations and those of others. Princes or philosophers, for example, are likely to be conscious of their individuality, their difference from others. Thus, for some special individuals, values are existentially relevant; they become vehicles for existential self-awareness. But how is that possible? What is the process whereby a consideration of values may lead to self-awareness? To answer this question let us consider the meaning and significance of the death of God.

Nietzsche's famous slogan that "God is dead" means, first and foremost, that there are no objective values. To view values as objective or absolute is to conceive of an independently existing World or Reality that provides a basis or a ground for all our moral judgments. This Reality may contain certain fixed and indefinable properties, such as *goodness, rightness,* and *justness,* that are possessed by all and only those actions that are good, right, or just. Or, the truth or falsity of our value judgments may be grounded in fixed universal moral rules, or in certain natural facts about humans, for example, that we have an innate desire to seek pleasure. Common to all objectivist or absolutist conceptions of morality is that actions have an intrinsic or inherent positive or negative value and that, consequently, everyone ought to act in accordance with a single code of morality.

In asserting that "God is dead," Nietzsche is not merely claiming that we cannot know which value judgments are true. He is making the more radical claim that we must reject the very idea of a World in itself that could serve as the ultimate standard or foundation for the truth of *any* value judgment. There simply are no universal moral principles, no single moral code, and no non-natural (or natural) properties guaranteeing that a given action is right or wrong. Indeed, for Nietzsche, all judgments of value are objectively false. Since there is no real world and no facts that could provide an objective ground for the truth of any value judgment, we cannot with absolute certainty say that, in all contexts, one course of action rather than another is morally preferable.

The death of God as a Being that is the ground of objective values is of enormous significance. If we think of values as objective, then they have a kind of power over us. Throughout our childhood we have values instilled in us by parents, friends, and mentors. By definition these values do not come from within, but they undoubtedly control us throughout our lives. If we go against these ingrained values we feel guilty, and for that reason there is tremendous psychological pressure to conform. We thereby become slaves to God, and God, as representing objective values, is our master. If, however, God is dead, the effect is *exhilarating*. For if God is dead and there are no objective values, then we are free to create our own values.

Thus, the death of God liberates and frees us to make our own decisions and choices. Before we were slaves to God: We obeyed God, we were ruled by God, and we acted in accordance with His commands. But now we can become legislators of our own values, we can become little gods, we can become masters of ourselves. We no longer need to be ruled by objective values, but can now be ruled by ourselves. As Nietzsche puts it:

> You shall become master over yourself, master also over your virtues. Formerly *they* were your masters; but they must be only your instruments besides other instruments. You shall get control over your For and Against and learn how to display first one and then the other in accordance with your higher goal. (p. 126)

The uncontrollable exhilaration that accompanies our newfound freedom is expressed in the following passage:

> Indeed, we philosophers and "free spirits" feel, when we hear the news that "the old god is dead," as if a new dawn shone on us; our heart overflows with gratitude, amazement, premonitions, expectation. At long last the horizon appears free to us again, even if it should not be bright; at long last our ships may venture out again, venture out to face any danger; all the daring of the lover of knowledge is permitted again; the sea, *our* sea, lies open again, perhaps there has never yet been such an "open sea." (pp. 123–124)

And yet, perhaps this sea is too open. Perhaps our newfound freedom is at once a liberation and at the same time a kind of *terrifying nightmare and an unfreedom.*

Suppose that everything you once believed is thrown into doubt or, worse, that it is shown to be false and completely without foundation. I am not talking here about Descartes who, in an attempt to arrive at certain and indubitable knowledge, argued that since all his former beliefs could be doubted he would treat them as false. For Descartes, doubt was methodological: He doubted not as a matter of practice or action, but as a matter of knowledge. Rather, I am talking about severing the bonds with those cherished moral principles that you once held so dear. I am talking about questioning, doubting, and treating with scepticism those values that provide the underlying framework you either implicitly or explicitly appeal to in making life's important decisions. How is one to bear this newfound freedom now that there are no God-given or objective values; now that we are free to create our own values? What must life be like for the truly "free spirit" who must create values?

According to Nietzsche,

> The great liberation comes for those who are thus fettered suddenly, like the shock of an earthquake: the youthful soul is all at once convulsed, torn loose, torn away—it itself does not know what is happening. . . . A sudden terror and suspicion of what it loved, a lightning-bolt of contempt for what it called 'duty', . . . perhaps a desecrating blow and glance *backwards* to where it formerly loved and worshipped, perhaps a hot blush of shame at what it has just done and at the same time an exultation *that* it has done it, . . . such bad and painful things are part of the history of the great liberation. (pp. 124–125)

Everything that one once loved one now despises. Although one feels powerful and in control of one's life, this awareness

> is at the same time a sickness that can destroy the man who has it, this first outbreak of strength and will to self-determination, to evaluating on one's own account, this will to *free* will. . . . (p. 125)

The scepticism concerning hitherto recognized values leads us to doubt even our own values, *if* we ever had our *own* values. Nietzsche wonders,

> Can *all* values not be turned round? and is good perhaps evil . . . Is everything perhaps in the last resort false? And if we are deceived, are we not for that very reason also deceivers? *must* we not be deceivers?—such thoughts as these tempt him and lead him on, even further away, even further down. Solitude encircles and embraces him, ever more threatening, suffocating, heart-tightening, . . . but who today knows what *solitude* is? . . . (p. 125)

Thus, we are alone with our entire belief and value system shattered. We must suffer the pain and isolation of having rejected what is closest to us without any confidence that what we will put in its place will be "true." Indeed, since there is no such thing as an objectively true value judgment, our freedom becomes terrifying. *How* are we to choose? *What* are we to choose? Our entire life depends on the decisions and choices that we are to make, but the notion of a "right" choice makes no sense in a world without objective value.

Nietzsche expresses the aimlessness of our new "freedom" in the following passage:

> What were we doing when we unchained this earth from its sun? Whither is it moving now? Whither are we moving? Away from all suns? Are we not plunging continually? Backward, sideward, forward, in all directions? Is there still any up or down? Are we not straying as through an infinite nothing? (p. 118)

In this passage, the sun is God or objective values, and we are the earth. When we give up objective values we are left with an infinity of choices none of which are marked out as "right." Our infinite freedom thus becomes a cagelike freedom or an unfreedom in which it is impossible to choose. For the possibility of freedom depends on the possibility of making decisions and choices, that is, if we cannot choose then we are not free. However, in a world in which all value judgments are false, that is, in a world in which there are no values, it can be argued that it is impossible to choose and thus, that it is impossible to be free.

To see what is involved in this last point consider that at present I am faced with the decision to continue writing this book or to get up and walk out of my study. Clearly, if I choose to continue writing this book it is because I place greater value on that act than I do on the alternative. In situations where a choice between two opposing actions is necessary, it is ultimately based upon our *believing* that what we are doing is in some sense more valuable than the alternative. Without that belief choice would be impossible. But for Nietzsche, "great spirits are skeptics."[2]

> The man of faith, the believer, is necessarily a small type of man. Hence, "freedom of spirit" i.e., *unbelief* as an instinct is a precondition of greatness.[3]

Thus, free spirits will *doubt, not believe* that the choices they make are more valuable than the alternatives, and consequently, a "free" spirit would find it impossible to choose, that is, would be unfree.

One might object that it is possible to make a choice even if we do not believe that what we are choosing has value, since we can make an arbitrary choice. Admittedly, we can act arbitrarily, but Nietzsche would certainly not regard such decisions as *free or genuine (authentic) choices.* For arbitrary or capricious choices would not represent a personal commitment to a goal, but would merely be a sign of our upbringing and the influence of the valuations of others.

What, then, is a free choice? And how is a free choice possible in a world without value? The idea that a free choice is a *subjective* choice, that is, a choice based upon one's own self-created values is on the right track, but insufficient as it stands. For the free spirit understands that if all judgments of value are false, then even one's own subjective value judgments are false, and so at one level cannot serve the purpose for which they were introduced, namely, to guide us in our actions and be the foundation for our choices. This point needs some elaboration.

What is a subjective value? Shouldn't we say that a subjective value is an illusory value, a value that does not really exist? Suppose I take a drug that I know will make me hallucinate and as a result I see pink rats coming toward me. Objectively, I know that these pink rats do not really exist and thus I would not let such perceptions influence my decisions and choices. I would not scream for help or reach for a broom to smash them or set traps to kill them. If, on the basis of such perceptions I make the judgment "There are pink rats in my room," I would be making a subjective judgment. Such a judgment would be false, but it would also be existentially irrelevant, since knowing it to be false would render it incapable of directly influencing my life. (Indirectly, however, I may be led to stop taking that drug because of its effects.) Analogously, if subjective value judgments are treated as illusory then they cannot form the basis for our choices. For if subjective values are recognized for what they are, namely, *non-existent values,* then they can no more form the basis for our choices then hallucinations that are understood to be such. Of course, we might *think* that our "subjective" values are objective, that they really do have some independent ground. In that case, they could form a basis of choice. But then, such "subjective" values would not be based upon a realization of the death of God, that is, the non-existence of objective values. Thus, if values are not objective and we do not even think that they are, then subjective values, when correctly understood, cannot perform the task for which they were introduced. Thus, we are again led to the question, "How then is choice possible?" In what sense does the "great liberation" give rise to the birth of a "free spirit"?

Nietzsche recognizes that the freedom left for powerful individuals who set out on their own course without anything to base their decisions on except themselves is a cagelike freedom. He says,

> *In the horizon of the infinite.*—We have left the land and have embarked. We have burned our bridges behind us—indeed, we have gone farther and destroyed the land behind us. Now, little ship, look out! Beside you is the ocean: to be sure, it does not always roar, and at times it lies spread out like silk and gold and reveries of graciousness. But hours will come when you will realize that it is infinite and that there is nothing more awesome than infinity. Oh, the poor bird that felt free and now strikes the ways of this cage! Woe, when you fell homesick for land as if it had offered more *freedom*—and there is no longer any "land." (pp. 120–121)

The ship represents human beings and the land burned behind us represents objective values. We are thus faced with having to make a choice in an infinite sea that contains no path or road marked out as the right one. Has not the infinity of the sea, our monstrous and infinite freedom, become too much to bear? Has not our infinite freedom become an unfreedom? Indeed it has. There is a paradox in Nietzsche's conception of freedom and value, a paradox that requires an enormous strength to overcome, if it is to be overcome. The central concept in Nietzsche's overcoming of the paradox of choice is his doctrine of the *will to power,* which we turn to next.

THE WILL TO POWER AND THE OVERMAN

According to Nietzsche, there is an internal or center of outward force or energy which encounters and opposes the outward expansion of other centers. This will or instinct for power manifests itself in humans as the ultimate psychological explanation or motivating force behind all of our actions, including, as we shall see later, the development of all forms of morality and Christianity. Consider the following relevant passages:

> Life, . . . is specifically a will to the accumulation of force . . . nothing wants to preserve itself, everything is to be added and accumulated.
>   Life as a special case . . . strives after a *maximal feeling of power;* essentially a striving for more power; striving is nothing other than striving for power. . . . (p. 128)
>   And do you know what "the world" is to me? . . . This world: a monster of energy, without beginning, without end; a firm, iron magnitude of force that does not grow bigger or smaller, that does not expend itself but only transforms itself; . . . not something blurry or wasted, not something endlessly extended, but set in a definite space as a definite force, and not a space that might be "empty" here or there, but rather as a force throughout, as a play of forces and waves of forces, at the same time one and many, increasing here and at the same time decreasing there; a sea of forces flowing and rushing together, eternally changing, eternally flooding back, with tremendous years of recurrence, . . . *The world is the will to power—and nothing besides.* And you yourselves are also this will to power—and nothing besides! (pp. 127–128)

Even when we submit ourselves to the will of another we are manifesting our own will to power. Thus, Nietzsche says that "[W]here I found a living creature, there I found will to power: and even in the will of the servant I found the will to be master" (p. 132). Naturally, we appear to have other drives or desires besides the desire for power. The desire to be married, have children, receive a good education, and the like, are wishes that motivate us to act. Yet, Nietzsche maintains that we seek these goals to be "happy," but what is happiness? For Nietzsche it is the "feeling that power is *growing,* that resistance is overcome" (p. 134). Thus, the ultimate goal of all our actions is to achieve power or the feeling of power; even the values we adopt are manifestations of our drive for power. But what does Nietzsche mean by "power" and how is power best realized in an individual, and how does his philosophy of power contribute to a resolution of the paradox of choice?

At the outset we should note that the will to power is not merely a will to exist. In the first place, "the really fundamental instinct of life aims at *the expansion of power,* and, wishing for that, frequently risks and even sacrifices self-preservation."[4] Furthermore, Nietzsche argues that whatever already exists does not need to struggle to exist, and if something does not yet exist then it cannot have a basic drive or will to exist. As Nietzsche puts it,

> Indeed, the truth was not hit by him who shot at it with the word of the 'will to existence': that will does not exist. For, what does not exist cannot will; but what is in existence, how could that still want existence? Only where there is life is there also will: not will to life but—thus I teach you— will to power. (p. 133)

Thus, the will to power is not a will to life, but a will to exist in a certain way. It is a will to perfection, a striving for distinction.

The perfection, distinction, or power we strive for is not necessarily a drive to inflict pain upon others or to do what one wishes without regard for the feeling of others. On the contrary, Nietzsche explicitly claims that such behavior is a sign of the lack of power:

> Certainly the state in which we hurt others is rarely as agreeable, in an unadulterated way, as that in which we benefit others; it is a sign that we are still lacking power. . . . (p. 129)

Admittedly, striving for distinction may manifest itself in tyranny over others, but dominating others is the means, not the end. The end is to increase power and ultimately to attain power over ourselves. Nietzsche says that

> The striving for distinction brings with it *for the next man*—to name only a few steps on the ladder: torment, then blows, then terror, then fearful astonishment, then wonderment, then envy, then admiration, then elevation, then joy, then cheerfulness, then laughter, then derision, then mockery, then ridicule, then giving blows, then imposing torment: here at the end of the ladder stands the *ascetic* and martyr, who feels the highest enjoyment by himself enduring, as a consequence of his drive for distinction, precisely that which, on the first step of the ladder, his counterpart the *barbarian* imposes on others on whom and before whom he wants to distinguish himself. (p. 130)

The point is that the goal of power is self-overcoming or self-mastery, and that overcoming or mastery of others, although not the aim of the drive for power, may aid in the cultivation and strengthening of it.

Thus, the distinction or power that one strives for is not necessarily political or economic power, but the power to create oneself by overcoming those obstacles that would stand in the way of self-realization. Our instinct to power, or as Nietzsche also calls it, our *instinct to freedom,* has as its goal the creation of something that is truly one's own, a monument to one's uniqueness. It also aims at self-mastery: the mastery that comes through being able to set goals for oneself and then overcome the obstacles that might interfere with their realization. In the end, the obstacles that stand in the way of realizing our instinct or will to power are found within. In this connection, Nietzsche distinguishes between the Apollonian, or rational side, of humans and the Dionysian, or passionate, side. According to Nietzsche, the life of rational detachment is not to be desired, but neither is a life of pure passion. The passions are good things in that they spring us into action, but they sometimes get in the way of achieving our goals. So the task is to rechannel our passions, to control their direction with reason. It should be emphasized, however, that the overcoming of passions is not the same thing as eliminating or emasculating them.

In addition to being ruled by the passions, there are other internal impediments to our realizing our will to power, and there are external impediments as well. Some of the external obstacles that prevent us from setting and fulfilling our goals are the values of others, the values of society, and the values of Christianity. Thus, we must overcome or go beyond the traditional values in our attempt to fully realize our will to power. Individuals who can gain control over their own lives, "who are new, unique, incomparable, who give themselves their own laws, who create themselves" (p. 120), are those who most fully realize the fundamental drive to power that, according to Nietzsche, manifests itself in everything we do.

The fundamental will of the spirit is to continually create a new self by surpassing the old. The process of overcoming the old self by continually setting new goals upon the attainment of the old is a process of growth, and in that process power (and freedom) are found. As Nietzsche says,

> That commanding something which people call "the spirit" wants to be master in and around its own house and wants to feel that it is master; . . . Its intent in all this is to incorporate new "experiences," to file new things in old files—growth, in a word—or, more precisely, the *feeling* of growth, the feeling of increased power.[5]

What sort of change, then, is growth? And under what conditions does growth take place?

Nietzsche says that the free, very free spirits grow under special conditions where "the dangerousness of his situation must first grow to the point of enormity, . . ."[6] For Nietzsche, growth "involves the dangerous privilege of living *experimentally*" (p. 125), continually taking risks and at every step of the way accepting responsibility for our actions through a realization that we are those actions. To live dangerously or experimentally involves a continual process of overcoming. Thus spoke Zarathustra,

I teach you the overman. Man is something that should be overcome. What have you done to overcome him? (p. 134)

And in the same vein he says,

And life itself confided this secret to me: "Behold," it said, "I am *that which must always overcome itself.* . . . Whatever I create and however much I love it—soon I must oppose it and my love, thus my will wills it." (pp. 132–133)

The free-spirit is a creating, shaping, changing power whose tireless process of recreation resists the temptation to rest on one's laurels or to be an imitator or parasite of others.

Unfortunately, as Nietzsche sees it, the realization of the will to power in humans is a painful process. For those individuals who want to stand out from the crowd and distinguish their evaluations from the evaluations of others are punished and made to feel guilty. With each level of guilt the fetters and bonds of obligation become all but unbreakable. Thus, the exhilaration that results from breaking away from theology and traditional morality is accompanied by pain and sickness. However, in spite of the pain, the development of a mature freedom of spirit is worth it for those who have the strength to engage in it. For only by overcoming obstacles again and again can we most fully realize our will to power and come to have an awareness of ourselves as those "who are new, unique, incomparable, who give themselves their own laws, who create themselves" (p. 120). Thus, the will to power is the will to create a certain type of person—a *superman* or *overman*—and in this ideal type a resolution of the paradox of choice is to be found.[7]

The truly free individual can overcome the paradox of (free) choice or freedom by having the strength of will to assume responsibility for self-created values by living in accordance with them. The powerful individual on the road to self-mastery and in the midst of the process of growth has the strength to both acknowledge and go beyond the contradiction inherent in decision making and make a choice. Earlier we quoted a passage wherein Nietzsche writes of the terror and pain that results from breaking the bond to custom and duty, and in the same passage he goes on to say that

From this morbid isolation, from the desert of these years of temptation and experiment, it is still a long road to that tremendous overflowing certainty and health which may not dispense even with sickness, as a means and fish-hook of knowledge, so that mature freedom of spirit which is equally self-mastery and discipline of the heart and permits access to many contradictory modes of thought. . . . (p. 125)

The mature freedom of spirit, the individual who achieves a measure of freedom, is what Nietzsche calls a "manly sceptic." Such people are aware that the path they decide to follow is not objectively true or right, but depends entirely on their own perspective and so is a path for which they alone are entirely responsible.

We see, then, that the process leading to a genuine or authentic choice consists in facing the fact about values, realizing that there are no objective values, and yet overcoming that fact by positing goals which form the basis for the growth and development of a life of personal value and personal significance. For Nietzsche,

> The scepticism of audacious manliness which is most closely related to the genius for war and conquest, . . . despises and nevertheless seizes; it undermines and takes possession; it does not believe but does not lose itself in the process; it gives the spirit dangerous freedom, but it is severe on the heart; . . . .[8]

Such dangerous and sceptical choices are possible and are truly free, since they require the individuals who make them to be aware of themselves as existents, as individuals *qua* individuals, and not merely as specimens of the abstract kind of humanity.

A fully developed freedom does not stop, but continues to create new values over and over again, opening itself up to new and different challenges. As he says,

> the strength to create for ourselves our own new eyes—and ever again new eyes that are even more our own: hence man alone among all the animals has no eternal horizons and perspectives. (p. 169)

If we realize our power to create new and even more personal goals and we recognize and act in accordance with the belief that growth is a *processus in infinitum,* then and only then can each of us make genuine choices and become free.

MASTER MORALITY, SLAVE MORALITY, AND TRADITIONAL MORALITY

We have seen that according to Nietzsche the will to power is the basic drive motivating all human behavior. Although he claims that we all have the drive to self-overcoming and self-perfection, we do not all have the strength of will to obtain power over ourselves and create our own values. There are, in other words, degrees of strength of will. The *strong willed* are those who have the strength to chart their own course, create their own values, and live in accordance with them. The *weak willed,* on the other hand, do not have the strength to stand alone and so must satisfy their drive for power in other ways, for example, by following the commands of others. These two types of individuals, roughly characterized as "master" and "slave," are the source or foundation of Nietzsche's famous distinction between *Master* and *Slave Morality.* An examination of these two kinds of morality is a useful place to begin our discussion of Nietzsche's critique of traditional morality.

I

Nietzsche's distinction between Master Morality and Slave Morality is not meant to be exclusive; no society is purely one or the other and no individual is purely one or the other. Societies and individuals are combinations of both, although in modern societies, where Christianity and traditional morality are common, weak-willed slave moralities predominate. What, then, does the distinction between master and slave morality amount to? Let us begin with the morality of the master.

Master morality, as the name suggests, is the morality of the powerful and strong willed. For the masters, the good is the noble, the strong, the powerful, and the bad is the opposite of power: the weak, the cowardly, the timid, the petty. Master morality begins with an *affirmation,* with what is good and what is worthwhile. Those actions which flow from a feeling of power are good; those that proceed from weakness are bad. For the master morality, the good felt themselves to be powerful and those actions were taken to be good, which were the spontaneous outflowing of their abundance of power. As Nietzsche puts it,

> The noble type of man experiences *itself* as determining values; it does not need approval; it judges, "what is harmful to me is harmful in itself"; it knows itself to be that which first accords honor to things; it is *value-creating.* (p. 138)

The good inspire fear, whereas the "bad" are viewed in contrast to the good. In other words, in a master morality, "good" is the fundamental category, and what is not good is bad.

Slave morality, on the other hand, is a morality common to those people who are weak willed, uncertain of themselves, oppressed, and abused. The essence of slave morality is *utility.* The good is what is most useful for the community as a whole. Since the powerful are few in number compared to the masses of the weak, the weak gain power vis-à-vis the strong by treating those qualities that are valued by the powerful as "evil," and those qualities that enable sufferers to endure their lot as "good." Thus, patience, humility, pity, submissiveness to authority, and the like, are considered good.

Slave morality begins in *negation:* a resentment of excellence, achievement, individuality, and power. All these power "virtues" are regarded as evil, and the opposite "virtues" are regarded as good. The slave morality is thus a reactionary morality, since the categories of good and evil are not created from within the individual, but are created as a reaction to the values of the powerful. Whereas the noble person conceives of goodness and later determines what is bad, the slave first conceives of evil—the fearful one—and then fashions a conception of morality. Nietzsche says that

> The slave revolt in morality begins when *ressentiment* itself becomes creative and gives birth to values: . . . While every noble morality develops from a triumphant affirmation of itself, slave morality from the outset says No to what is "outside," what is "different," what is "not itself"; and *this* No is its creative deed. This inversion of the value-positing eye—this *need* to direct one's view outward instead of back to oneself—is of the essence of *ressentiment:* in order to exist, slave morality always first needs a hostile external world; it needs, physiologically speaking, external stimuli in order to act at all—its action is fundamentally reaction. (p. 140)

Slave morality is suspicious of all that is powerful. It is fearful of the strong and it resents the power that the strong possess. Thus, in an attempt to bring down the powerful and attain a modicum of power for themselves, slave moralities render evil precisely those values that the powerful claim are good. Not only does this help bring down the powerful individual, it also provides goals that the weak can attain. In so doing, it provides the weak with a source of power. However, such goals are incompatible with the power that they are aiming at, since it is obviously self-defeating to seek power by giving up power!

Be that as it may, the fact is that the overwhelming majority of people are weak willed and thus societies tend to adopt the values of the weak. Slave moralities, with their emphasis on custom, usefulness, and submission to tradition, are the origin of the powerful individual's *bad conscience.* In a slave morality the instinctual drive to power and freedom, the desire to make individual and original choices, and the desire to think of one's own personal advantage and happiness are killed. The free spirit overflows with power and has an instinct to self-perfection and self-gratification. However, in a slave morality, what the powerful individual thinks of as good is viewed by the *herd* or the masses as evil. Consequently, the will to power in its outward expression is pushed back and made to retreat. Instead of being allowed to discharge itself in outward action, the will to power is turned inward upon itself with the result that the powerful individual becomes guilty and sick with a bad conscience. As Nietzsche puts it,

> This *instinct for freedom* forcibly made latent—this instinct for freedom pushed back and repressed, incarcerated within and finally able to discharge and vent itself only on itself: that, and that alone, is what the *bad conscience* is in its beginnings. (p. 145)

The powerful wants to conquer, be unique, but in being forced to conform, the strong willed is thereby tortured.

Thus, Nietzsche's most fundamental criticism of slave morality is that it views as "evil" and aims to destroy the type of person that society ought to be creating. It calls for a weakening of humans in order to "improve" them, but to weaken is not to improve, but to corrupt: to make us ill by beating down and turning ourselves against our own inner creative energy.

> To call the taming of an animal its "improvement" sounds almost like a joke to our ears. Whoever knows what is going on in menageries doubts that the beasts are "improved" there. They are weakened, they are made less harmful, and through the depressive effect of fear, through pain, through wounds, and through hunger they become sickly beasts. . . . Physiologically speaking: in the struggle with beasts, to make them sick *may* be the only means for making them weak. This the Church understood: it *ruined* man, it weakened him—but it claimed to have "improved" him. (p. 146)

Nietzsche's point here is that the problem with Christianity (a slave morality) is that it creates a milieu in which it is virtually impossible for an individual to be an individual, for one to affirm oneself as a truly autonomous individual. It ruins precisely that type of person who should be improved, revered, and created and it does so as a means of attaining power for the weak. As we shall see, this objection rearises in Nietzsche's critique of traditional morality.

II

Nietzsche's attack on traditional morality and custom is two-pronged. At one level, his criticism consists in tracing the history of present-day morality. His point seems to be that if we see how it is we have come to believe that following tradition and custom is moral, we will also see what is wrong with the morality of custom and how the will to power operates in a perverted form in the development of the morality of custom. From a different direction, Nietzsche criticizes the morality of custom directly by identifying certain intellectual errors and inconsistencies in it. In what follows we discuss these two levels of attack.

Originally, moral actions were those actions that were the natural outgrowth of individuals belonging to the ruling tribes and castes ("the noble, powerful, high-stationed and high-minded"):

> He who has the power to requite, good with good, evil with evil, and also
> actually practices requital—is, that is to say, grateful and revengeful—is
> called good; he who is powerless and cannot requite counts as bad. (p. 148)

Originally, actions were *not* called good because they were considered
"unegoistic" or "useful" for the community; rather actions were good
because they were the creation of those with power. In the soul of the
subjected and powerless a different concept of good and evil emerges.

As Nietzsche sees it, the powerless, like the powerful, have an instinct
to freedom, a drive to be value creating and masters of their own lives,
but their oppression makes it impossible for them to assert their power
in a direct manner. Thus, a different conception of morality develops.
This conception enables the weak to battle the powerful by treating the
values of the strong as "evil" and the welfare of the community as good.
Thus, the chief proposition of common morality is that to be moral is
to act in accordance with custom where "custom" is the *traditional* way
of behaving and evaluating. The tradition is some higher authority that
we must obey because it commands us to do so. Thus, one is commanded
to observe prescriptions *without thinking of oneself as an individual.*
Traditional morality forces the individual to give up the power or the
freedom to depend upon oneself to determine one's own actions.

> The free human being is immoral because in all things he is *determined* to
> depend upon himself and not upon tradition: in all the original conditions
> of mankind, 'evil' signifies the same as 'individual', 'free', 'capricious',
> 'unusual', 'unforeseen', 'incalculable'. . . . Let us not deceive ourselves as
> to the motivation of that morality which demands difficulty of obedience
> to custom as the mark of morality! Self-overcoming is demanded, *not* on
> account of the useful consequences it may have for the individual, but so
> that the hegemony of custom, tradition, shall be made evident in despite
> of the private desires and advantages to the individual: the individual is to
> sacrifice himself—that is the commandment of morality and custom.
> (pp. 150–151)

By losing themselves in the "herd" and by demanding that everyone act
in the same way (in accordance with what is useful for the community),
the weak protect themselves from the strong and attain power for themselves.

According to Nietzsche, however, such a conception of morality is
patently immoral. It not only forgets the original meaning and soil out
of which "the good" grew, but it involves an internal inconsistency. As
a means to gaining power over the strong and realizing their own will to
power, the weak label as "evil" precisely the power that they seek. The
subjected and powerless reduce themselves to a "one like many," a member
of the herd, in order to achieve a measure of self-mastery and power.

But one emasculates power, and does not sublimate it, when one's own source of power is forced to kneel before the dictates of custom.

The internal inconsistency of traditional morality is further evidenced by the fact that the underlying motives for this morality contradict its principles. The argument is as follows. Traditionally selfless acts are praised: those acts which involve the *sacrifice of the individual* for the community, those acts that reflect a lack of concern for one's own elevation, advantage, and amplification of power are praised as being the mark of moral actions. According to Nietzsche, however, "The 'neighbor' praises selflessness *because it brings him advantages*" (p. 155). In other words, the individuals who praise selfless actions do so because of their own *selfish motives,* and thus they are really using morality to attain that which the same people claim is immoral.

Thus, Nietzsche calls for us to go "beyond good and evil." Since "good" and "evil" are distinctions found in traditional morality, one interpretation of this remark is that we should go beyond or reject traditional values. But we should be careful not to misconstrue this interpretation. Nietzsche does not mean that we should no longer do things for other people, or think about anyone else except ourselves. He does not advocate a morality that involves suffering and injury to others. Indeed he says that

> the noble human being, too, helps the unfortunate, but not, or almost not, from pity, but prompted more by an urge begotten by excess of power. (p. 139)

What Nietzsche wants us to get beyond is a blind observance to tradition. As traditional morality would have it, there is a moral code that can cover every situation. But for Nietzsche, the truth is that there is no list of finite rules which will tell us what to do in every situation.

Furthermore, we should go beyond the view that unegoistic and selfless acts are good. Egoism and selfishness are not only unavoidable human characteristics, but their existence is necessary for the attainment of our best. The moral doctrine that treats "good" and "evil" as corresponding to that which is useful and egoistic fails to see that "the strongest and most evil spirits have so far done the most to advance humanity" (p. 154). Those who question the old ideas are really benefiting and preserving the species and themselves. If such individuals are evil, then we ought to promote evil! As Nietzsche says,

> "Man is evil"—thus said all the wisest to comfort me. Alas, if only it were still true today! For evil is man's best strength.
> "Man must become better and more evil"—thus *I* teach. The greatest evil is necessary for the overman's best. (p. 156)

NIETZSCHE'S CRITIQUE OF CHRISTIANITY

In many ways Nietzsche's attack on Christianity parallels his criticisms of traditional morality, and it is easy to see why. Both are examples of slave morality and both, according to Nietzsche, are the result of certain "errors of reason." A useful place to begin our discussion of Nietzsche's critique is with the following passage where he summarizes what he takes to be the intellectual errors of Christianity.

> In Christianity neither morality nor religion has even a single point of contact with reality. Nothing but imaginary *causes* ("God," "soul," "ego," "spirit," "free will"—for that matter, "unfree will"), nothing but imaginary *effects* ("sin," "redemption," "grace," "punishment," "forgiveness of sins,"). Intercourse between imaginary *beings* ("God," "spirits," "souls,"); an imaginary *natural science* (anthropocentric; no trace of any concept of natural causes); an imaginary *psychology* (nothing but self-misunderstandings, interpretations of agreeable or disagreeable general feelings—. . . . "repentance," "pangs of conscience," "temptation by the devil," "the presence of God,"); an *imaginary teleology* ("the kingdom of God," *"the last judgment," "eternal life"*). (p. 159)

For Nietzsche, Christianity is a systematic distortion of reality, since its basic precepts are all "imaginary" and false. These are rather strong statements; let us examine the reasoning that underlies them.

Christianity is not a single belief, but a system of interconnected beliefs that form a systematic way of viewing the world and the actions of people in it. Clearly, the point from which the doctrines of Christianity flow is the existence of God. God is construed as an all-perfect being who created the world and human beings for a purpose. When God created us he instilled in us the faculty of free will, the ability to choose or to avoid a given course of action. It is through the misuse of our free will and not through any fault of God that we err and sin. If we live a Christian, God-fearing life, then we will be rewarded in the next life by entering into the Kingdom of God. On the other hand, if we sin, that is, if we violate God's commands and do not repent, then at death we will begin to serve our sentence of eternal damnation.

Let us begin a consideration of what Nietzsche says about these doctrines by turning to the notions of sin and redemption. One may say that compared to God we are all sinners. God is a being who is wholly love. His actions are always completely unegoistic and unselfish: He acts and desires "everything for others and nothing for himself. . . ." (p. 157). In comparison to God we are selfish and egoistic, constantly struggling and often failing to adhere to divine precepts. We feel guilty for being so evil in the face of God and so look for and feel the need for redemption.

For Nietzsche, this way of viewing the matter is fraught with difficulties. We view ourselves with suspicion and contempt without realizing that we do so by comparing ourselves to a being that cannot possess the properties we attribute to Him. For example, God is alleged to be a completely "unegoistic" being, but for Nietzsche the concept of an "unegoistic action" makes no sense. He says,

> No man has ever done anything that was done wholly for others and with no personal motivation whatever; how, indeed, should a man be *able* to do something that had no reference to himself, that is to say lacked all inner compulsion (which would have its basis in a personal need)? How could the ego act without the ego? (p. 157)

Even those actions that are most obviously altruistic, for example, the sacrifice of one's life for a cause, or in order to save the life of another, are done in the service of a personal ideal. Everything we do satisfies some wish that we have and in that way is egoistic.

Furthermore, no one can act simply on the basis of love for others, since if we cannot love ourselves then we cannot love others. "But if the idea of God [as *wholly* love] falls away, so does the feeling of 'sin' as a transgression against divine precepts, as a blemish on a creature consecrated to God" (p. 157). Thus, we no longer have to fear the eternal damnation of the soul. There is no longer a table of values hanging over our head restricting our freedom by making us feel guilty for wanting to chart our own course.

Not only are the concepts of "sinful" and "redeeming" actions indefensible, but the inner feelings and sensations that accompany actions called "sinful" or "redeeming" are misinterpreted as coming from God. For example, sometimes after having achieved a particularly gratifying result, whether in work, sports, or family life, we have a feeling of strength and pleasure in ourselves. According to Nietzsche, these feelings of power and the glorification of oneself are given a *false psychology*. They are misconstrued as "the wholly underserved flowing down of a radiance of mercy from on high. . . . The love with which fundamentally he loves himself appears as divine love. . . ." (p. 158). Analogously, disagreeable feelings, for example, being depressed, are misconstrued as punishments by God occasioned by sinful action. Thus, Nietzsche says,

> Morality and religion belong altogether to the *psychology of error;* in every single case, cause and effect are confused; or truth is confused with the effects of believing something to be true; or a state of consciousness is confused with its causes. (p. 167)

Typically, we are so afraid of viewing ourselves, we look for a cause for our feelings outside of ourselves, and thus create a false psychology to help us explain them. Yet once we see why we adopt such views we will be able to give them up, or so Nietzsche believes.

Nietzsche speaks of Christianity as involving the *imaginary causes* of God, soul, and free will. By calling these causes "imaginary," Nietzsche means that they do not exist. Recall that according to Christianity a person is essentially a soul or ego. This subject, ego, or substance is construed as an agent or doer that lies behind the deed that it causes. Nietzsche expresses this position in the following passage:

> The subject: interpreted from within ourselves so that the ego counts as a substance, as the cause of all deeds, as a doer.[9]

In this view, the agent or substance is endowed with a simple faculty of free will that enables it to choose or not to choose to perform an action without itself being acted upon by any causes outside or behind it. Free will is thus a God-given faculty implanted in us at creation. A free act or deed is one performed by a substance qua agent that lies outside of the realm of causality and the net of scientific predictability.

In denying free will and the ego as a cause, Nietzsche is denying that the will or self is an entity existing separately and outside the habit, desire, reflection, and act that together go to constitute the action. For Nietzsche,

> there is no such substratum; there is no "being" behind doing, effecting, becoming: "the doer" is merely a fiction added to the deed—the deed is everything. (p. 142)

To be sure, the self exists but not as a mere block of identity distinct from its concrete activities, not as a substance whose freedom is antecedently possessed. Rather, in Nietzsche's view, the doer or subject is nothing more than the totality of its experiences and actions (deeds), and freedom is something that must come to be, mature, and grow. As he says,

> No "substance," rather something that in itself strives after greater strength, and that wants to "preserve" itself only indirectly (it wants to surpass itself—).
> My hypothesis: The subject as multiplicity.[10]

Thus, Nietzsche rejects the Christian doctrine of the soul, and he also rejects the doctrine of free will that is inseparable from it. Although his own view of freedom—as involving growth—is diametrically opposed to the static conception of the substantialist, he does not simply reject the Christian view, he argues against it. His argument is intriguing and worthy of consideration.

Nietzsche attacks the doctrine of freedom of will because he believes that the doctrine, as traditionally conceived, leads to the conclusion that we are neither punishable nor accountable for our actions. The overall structure of his argument can be stated briefly as follows:

1. An agent can be held responsible for an action only if the agent acted intentionally or for some reason, and not unconsciously or under compulsion.
2. No substantialist act of free will is intentional.
3. Therefore, no agent can be held responsible or punishable for a substantialist act of free will.

The argument is valid, but let us turn to his evidence for the two premises in it.

Premise 1 is plausible. For defenders of free will, a necessary condition of responsibility or accountability is that the perpetrator of an act could have deliberated and provided reasons for or against the deed before performing it. In other words, the ability to make a purposeful or rational decision in which motives do play a part is a necessary condition of responsibility. Thus, an agent who is unable to distinguish between good and bad motives for his or her action would not be held responsible, nor would an agent that was forced to perform a "wrongful" act against his or her will. Furthermore, if we can distinguish good and bad motives or reasons, and if we prefer bad reasons or bad motives over good ones, then our deed is one for which we are not only responsible but punishable as well.

An example may help. Suppose a woman has to decide whether or not to have an affair with her best friend's husband. She knows that it is not right because it goes against her religious beliefs, and yet she is motivated to have the affair by what she considers, from her religious perspective, to be an evil motive, namely, self-interest. The final choice she makes is one for which she is responsible because she deliberated and based her decision on reasons. Punishment would be justified in this case only if she intentionally chooses the bad motive to guide her action. At this point the question that troubles Nietzsche is "Whence comes the decision when the scales are weighted with good and bad motives?" (p. 165). Alternatively, "How can anyone intentionally be less intelligent than he has to be?" (p. 165). The response to these questions leads to a justification of Nietzsche's second claim that no act of free will is intentional, which is, of course, the heart of his argument.

The defenders of free will maintain that our choice of bad motives over good ones comes,

> Not from error, not from blindness, not from an external nor from an internal compulsion? . . . Whence? one asks again and again. And here one

> calls 'free-will' to one's aid: it is a *pure* willfulness which is supposed to decide, an impulse is supposed to enter within which motive plays no part, in which the deed, arising out of nothing, occurs as a miracle. (p. 165)

Let us be clear about the view of "free will" that Nietzsche is attempting to reduce to absurdity. There are two main aspects of this conception: First, there exists a self, an agent, that retains its strict identity through time, without temporal parts, and is distinct from the events or happenings that constitute its history. Second, this substance or agent has the capacity to assert its will *uncaused* or *uninfluenced* by its knowledge, environment, history, or heredity. Can the existence of "free will" in the sense just defined ever justify the right to punish? According to Nietzsche, the answer is emphatically *no*.

Recall that the first condition of all punishment is that the perpetrator of the deed acted *intentionally,* that is, on the basis of reason. However, a substantialist act of free will is ultimately *unintentional* because it is not influenced or caused by reason, motive, environment, or anything else. An act of free will is a purely arbitrary, whimsical act *arising out of nothing:* "a deed without a 'for that reason', without motive, without origin, something purposeless and non-rational" (p. 165). Therefore, Nietzsche concludes, "You adherents of 'free-will' *have no right* to punish, or to hold a person responsible, your own principles deny you that right!" (p. 165).

In Nietzsche's own view of freedom a person *is* responsible. Indeed, he maintains that freedom is: "That one has the will to assume respon- sibility for oneself."[11] For Nietzsche a person is responsible and punishable for his or her deeds because these deeds *are* the self and proceed from a person's concrete makeup of habits, desires, and purposes. If our actions are caused by some arbitrary force, agent, or substratum, outside the individual person as he or she actually is, then there is no reason to hold the concrete individual responsible. Freedom and responsibility require an identification of self and deed, an awareness of ourselves as being our deeds. The traditional Christian conception of freedom is false because it separates the self from its acts and thereby makes responsibility im- possible.

For Nietzsche, there is no distinction between the doer of a deed and the totality of its deeds. Concerning the alleged distinction he says,

> The "thing-in-itself" is nonsensical. If I remove all relationships, all the "properties," all the "activities" of a thing, the thing does not remain over; because thingness has only been invented by us owing to the requirements of logic. . . .[12]

Once the "I" as underlying substratum is abandoned, the traditional doctrines of the soul and free will must be abandoned too, and that is precisely what Nietzsche does.

Thus, Nietzsche rejects the very conception of freedom that the Christian conception of sin and guilt are based upon. A freedom that requires an ego or spiritual substance (soul) does not exist because (1) it creates a false dichotomy between doer and deed; (2) it becomes impossible to hold persons responsible, accountable, or punishable for their actions; and (3) it views freedom as something that we possess at creation rather than something that is a process and consequence of activity, development, and growth.

In addition to involving several intellectual errors, Nietzsche claims that Christianity is *nihilistic.* He means several things by this. In one sense, Christianity is nihilistic in that it *is against life.* Christianity distinguishes between this world and the next. The next is a more perfect world where the good will be rewarded and the evil punished. The next world is thought, therefore, to have greater reality than this world, where this world is thought to be corrupt. For Nietzsche, it is the weak, who suffer from this world, who need to create another world.

> The Christian conception of God—God as god of the sick, God as a spider, God as spirit—is one of the most corrupt conceptions of the divine ever attained on earth. . . . God degenerated into the *contradiction* of life, instead of being its transfiguration and eternal Yes! God as the declaration of war against life, against nature, against the will to live! God—the formula for every slander against "this world," for every lie about the "beyond"! God— the deification of nothingness, the will to nothingness pronounced holy. (p. 161)

In adopting an otherworldly and thereby mistaken view of reality, Christians are also adopting a mistaken view of value. What is harmful to life and the development of power is evil, "what elevates it, enhances, affirms, justifies it, and makes it triumphant, is called 'false' " (p. 158). Thus, a second sense in which Christianity is "nihilistic" is that it involves saying "no" to the values of the strong.

Finally, Nietzsche criticizes Christians for having a "nihilistic will." This is the will of the weak who want power, but can only achieve it by distorting reality so as to do away with the autonomy of the powerful individual. That is, one uses Christian values as a way of making the powerful feel guilty and thereby weakening the powerful. Thus Christianity, like traditional morality, is inherently contradictory and perverted. It is contradictory insofar as it attempts to achieve power by denying that power is a virtue. It is perverted because Christians attempt to gain power by practicing obedience to a more powerful figure, that is, by giving up power.

Interestingly, Nietzsche's comments on religion in general and Christianity in particular reveal that his attitude is not entirely negative. Polytheism, the belief in many gods, allows for the possibility of more than one set of moral norms. There need not be a single set of God-given values. The freedom that is recognized by different people to believe in many gods could then be carried over to the freedom for the individual to "posit his own ideal and to derive from it his own law, joys, and rights" (p. 168). Furthermore, religion can serve as a training ground for the strong to practice the art of overcoming. Initially one is ruled, but one can thereby prepare oneself to be a ruler. In addition, religion can serve as a vehicle for the weak to endure their lot. Though the great majority of humans must suffer through a brutish life, "religion and religious significance spread the splendor of the sun over such ever-toiling human beings and make their own sight tolerable to them" (p. 170).

On balance, however, Christianity has done more harm than good. The majority of humans are weak, infirm, sick, and failures and a further weakness of Christianity, with its conception of pity, is that it seeks to preserve these excesses of failures. For Nietzsche, Christianity has "pre-served too much of *what ought to perish*" (p. 171). Christianity encourages the lowly to stay in their place. It places value on the weak willed and teaches them how to deal with their oppression all the while doing so only for the sake of keeping them oppressed.

In keeping humans down and being unwilling to recognize the difference between us (all humans are "equal before God"), Christianity turns values on their head. Christianity has not improved the human race, but worsened it. In the end, we have the European of today—a herd animal. For the strong and higher in rank, only misfortune could result:

> Stand all *valuations on their head—that* is what they had to do. And break the strong, sickly o'er great hopes, cast suspicion on the joy in beauty, bend everything haughty, manly, conquering, domineering, all the instincts characteristic of the highest and best-turned-out type of "man," into unsureness, agony of conscience, self-destruction—indeed, invert all love of the earthly and of dominion over the earth into hatred on the earth and the earthly—that is the task the church posed for itself and had to pose, until in its estimation "becoming unworldly," "unsensual," and "higher men" were fused into a single feeling. (p. 171)

Thus, Christians are *nay-sayers* to this world and destroyers of the powerful person. They knock down and disvalue that which is best, and that, among other things, is what is wrong with Christianity.

We conclude our discussion of Nietzsche's critique of Christianity with a brief consideration of his doctrine of *eternal recurrence*.[13] In *The Will to Power*, Nietzsche expresses a theory of nature, according to which "the world is a circular movement that has already repeated itself infinitely often and plays its game *ad infinitum*."[14] As an empirical theory recurrence has little to recommend it, but as a representation of a psychological attitude toward life it is revealing of several aspects of Nietzsche's views.

The attitude toward life that Nietzsche wishes to express by recurrence is that of nihilism overcome, in particular, the overcoming of the Christian dogma of a more perfect world in the afterlife. Thus, the doctrine of eternal recurrence can be understood as emphasizing that this is the only life, and that the proper attitude toward this life is one of affirmation. To affirm life means to have the courage (and desire) to relive your life again and again. Indeed, this would take great courage. For given Nietzsche's view of the self, every experience and action of a person is essential to that person. Thus, if a person were to recur, then every event in the history of that person would also have to recur. To feel joy at the prospect of recurrence, therefore, involves affirming *everything* in one's life, not wishing for anything to be different. But who could be so well disposed toward their life so as to desire nothing more than the infinite repetition of every aspect of it? Nietzsche's doctrine of eternal recurrence clearly points to the life of an overman as an ideal case, and it teaches us that the task is to live in such a way that you must wish to live it again.

Nietzsche Lexicon

Apollonian. Represents the rational side of humans.

Authentic (free) choice. Choice made on the basis of self-created values for which one accepts responsibility.

Bad conscience. Result of the instinctual drive to power and freedom made to retreat (and turn against itself) in face of the values of the masses.

Dionysian. Represents the passionate side of humans.

Eternal recurrence. As a cosmological theory it holds that "the world is a circular movement that has already repeated itself infinitely often and plays its game *ad infinitum.*" However, in Nietzsche it can more plausibly be understood as emphasizing that this is the only life, and that the proper attitude toward this life is one of affirmation.

Freedom. Involves growth and is an ongoing process, a realization of our will to power. One never truly achieves freedom, as freedom is not a property or faculty that could be possessed by a substance. Freedom is "that one has the will to assume responsibility for oneself."

Free will. Nietzsche rejects free will as a faculty possessed by substantival ego at creation.

Master morality. Morality of the powerful and strong willed. Master morality begins with an *affirmation,* with what is good and what is worthwhile. In a master morality, "good" is the fundamental category and what is not good is bad.

Nihilism. Negative nay-saying attitude toward this life and the values of the strong.

Nihilistic will. Will of the weak who want power, but can only achieve it by distorting reality so as to do away with the autonomy of the powerful individual.

Overman. Ideal type who is able to overcome the obstacles that get in the way of making authentic choices and fully realizing the will to power.

Paradox of choice. Since God is dead, there are no objective values and therefore we are free to choose our own values. Since, however, choice implies value, the death of God makes it impossible to choose.

Resentment. Starting point of slave moralities. Resentment expresses the negative attitude toward those virtues regarded as good by the powerful.

Self-mastery. Mastery that comes through being able to set goals for oneself and then overcome the internal and external obstacles that might interfere with their realization.

Self-overcoming. See *self-mastery.*

Slave morality. Morality common to those people who are weak willed, uncertain of themselves, oppressed, and abused. The essence of slave morality is *utility.* The good is what is most useful for the community as a whole. It is a reactionary morality in which the categories of good and evil are not created from within the individual, but are created as a reaction to the values of the powerful.

Subjective values. Self-created values that one has the strength to live by.

Substantival ego. View of the self that separates the self from its experiences and actions and treats freedom as a property that inheres in the self.

Traditional morality. Slave morality that values custom and traditional ways of behaving.

Will to power. Internal or center of outward force or energy which encounters and opposes the outward expansion of other centers. The will or instinct for power manifests itself in humans as the ultimate psychological explanation or motivating force behind all of our actions.

Note to reader: Asterisks are used at the end of a selection when another selection from a previously cited source begins.

NIETZSCHE SELECTIONS

From *The Gay Science*

The Meaning and Significance of the Death of God

LET US BEWARE.—Let us beware of thinking that the world is a living being. Where should it expand? On what should it feed? How could it grow and multiply? We have some notion of the nature of the organic; and we should not reinterpret the exceedingly derivative, late, rare, accidental, that we perceive only on the crust of the earth and make of it something essential, universal, and eternal, which is what those people do who call the universe an organism. This nauseates me. Let us even beware of believing that the universe is a machine: it is certainly not constructed for one purpose, and calling it a "machine" does it far too much honor.

Let us beware of positing generally and everywhere anything as elegant as the cyclical movements of our neighboring stars; even a glance into the Milky Way raises doubts whether there are not far coarser and more contradictory movements there, as well as stars with eternally linear paths, etc. The astral order in which we live is an exception; this order and the relative duration that depends on it have again made possible an exception of exceptions: the formation of the organic. The total character of the world, however, is in all eternity chaos—in the sense not of a lack of necessity but of a lack of order, arrangement, form, beauty, wisdom, and whatever other names there are for our aesthetic anthropomorphisms. Judged from the point of view of our reason, unsuccessful attempts are by all odds the rule, the exceptions are not the secret aim, and the whole musical box repeats eternally its tune which may never be called a melody—and ultimately even the phrase "unsuccessful attempt" is too anthropomorphic and reproachful. But how could we reproach or praise the universe? Let us beware of attributing to it heartlessness and unreason

The Gay Science by Friedrich Nietzsche, trans. by Walter Kaufmann. Copyright © 1974 Random House. Reprinted with the permission of Random House, Inc.

Hereafter, this work will be cited as *GS*, and in all selections the numbers after the initials at the foot of the extract refer to the section of the work from which it is taken.

or their opposites: it is neither perfect nor beautiful, nor noble, nor does it wish to become any of these things; it does not by any means strive to imitate man. None of our aesthetic and moral judgments apply to it. Nor does it have any instinct for self-preservation or any other instinct; and it does not observe any laws either. Let us beware of saying that there are laws in nature. There are only necessities: there is nobody who commands, nobody who obeys, nobody who trespasses. Once you know that there are no purposes, you also know that there is no accident; for it is only beside a world of purposes that the word "accident" has meaning. Let us beware of saying that death is opposed to life. The living is merely a type of what is dead, and a very rare type.

Let us beware of thinking that the world eternally creates new things. There are no eternally enduring substances; matter is as much of an error as the God of the Eleatics. But when shall we ever be done with our caution and care? When will all these shadows of God cease to darken our minds? When will we complete our de-deification of nature? When may we begin to *"naturalize"* humanity in terms of a pure, newly discovered, newly redeemed nature? [*GS,* 109]

THE MADMAN.—Have you not heard of that madman who lit a lantern in the bright morning hours, ran to the market place, and cried incessantly: "I seek God! I seek God!"—As many of those who did not believe in God were standing around just then, he provoked much laughter. Has he got lost? asked one. Did he lose his way like a child? asked another. Or is he hiding? Is he afraid of us? Has he gone on a voyage? emigrated?—Thus they yelled and laughed.

The madman jumped into their midst and pierced them with his eyes. "Whither is God?" he cried; "I will tell you. *We have killed him—* you and I. All of us are his murderers. But how did we do this? How could we drink up the sea? Who gave us the sponge to wipe away the entire horizon? What were we doing when we unchained this earth from its sun? Whither is it moving now? Whither are we moving? Away from all suns? Are we not plunging continually? Backward, sideward, forward, in all directions? Is there still any up or down? Are we not straying as through an infinite nothing? Do we not feel the breath of empty space? Has it not become colder? Is not night continually closing in on us? Do we not need to light lanterns in the morning? Do we hear nothing as yet of the noise of the gravediggers who are burying God? Do we smell nothing as yet of the divine decomposition? Gods, too, decompose. God is dead. God remains dead. And we have killed him.

"How shall we comfort ourselves, the murderers of all murderers? What was holiest and mightiest of all that the world has yet owned has bled to death under our knives: who will wipe this blood off us? What water is there for us to clean ourselves? What festivals of atonement, what sacred games shall we have to invent? Is not the greatness of this deed too great for us? Must we ourselves not become gods simply to appear worthy of it? There has never been a greater deed; and whoever is born after us—for the sake of this deed he will belong to a higher history than all history hitherto."

Here the madman fell silent and looked again at his listeners; and they, too, were silent and stared at him in astonishment. At last he threw his lantern on the ground, and it broke into pieces and went out. "I have come too early," he said then; "my time is not yet. This tremendous event is still on its way, still wandering; it has not yet reached the ears of men. Lightning and thunder require time; the light of the stars requires time; deeds, though done, still require time to be seen and heard. This deed is still more distant from them than the most distant stars—*and yet they have done it themselves.*"

It has been related further that on the same day the madman forced his way into several churches and there struck up his *requiem aeternam deo.* Led out and called to account, he is said always to have replied nothing but: "What after all are these churches now if they are not the tombs and sepulchers of God?" [*GS,* 125]

LONG LIVE PHYSICS!—How many people know how to observe something? Of the few who do, how many observe themselves? "Everybody is farthest away—from himself"; all who try the reins know this to their chagrin, and the maxim "know thyself!" addressed to human beings by a god, is almost malicious. That the case of self-observation is indeed as desperate as that is attested best of all by the manner in which *almost everybody* talks about the essence of moral actions—this quick, eager, convinced, and garrulous manner with its expression, its smile, and its obliging ardor! One seems to have the wish to say to you: "But my dear friend, precisely this is my specialty. You have directed your question to the one person who is entitled to answer you. As it happens, there is nothing about which I am as wise as about this. To come to the point: when a human being judges *'this is right'* and then infers *'therefore it must be done,'* and then proceeds to *do* what he has thus recognized as right and designated as necessary—then the essence of his action is *moral.*"

But my friend, you are speaking of three actions instead of one. When you judge "this is right," that is an action, too. Might it not be possible that one could judge in a moral and in an immoral manner? *Why* do you consider this, precisely this, right?

"Because this is what my conscience tells me; and the voice of conscience is never immoral, for it alone determines what is to be moral."

But why do you *listen* to the voice of your conscience? And what gives you the right to consider such a judgment true and infallible? For this *faith*—is there no conscience for that? Have you never heard of an intellectual conscience? A conscience behind your "conscience"? Your judgment "this is right" has a pre-history in your instincts, likes, dislikes, experiences, and lack of experiences. "*How* did it originate there?" you must ask, and then also: "What is it that impels me to listen to it?" You can listen to its commands like a good soldier who hears his officer's command. Or like a woman who loves the man who commands. Or like a flatterer and coward who is afraid of the commander. Or like a dunderhead who obeys because no objection occurs to him. In short, there are a hundred ways in which you can listen to your conscience. But that you take this or that judgment for the voice of conscience—in other words, that you feel something to be right—may be due to the fact that you have never thought much about yourself and simply have accepted blindly that what you had been *told* ever since your childhood was right; or it may be due to the fact that what you call your duty has up to this point brought you sustenance and honors—and you consider it "right" because it appears to you as your own "condition of existence" (and that you have a *right* to existence seems irrefutable to you).

For all that, the *firmness* of your moral judgment could be evidence of your personal abjectness, of impersonality; your "moral strength" might have its source in your stubbornness—or in your inability to envisage new ideals. And, briefly, if you had thought more subtly, observed better, and learned more, you certainly would not go on calling this "duty" of yours and this "conscience" of yours duty and conscience. Your understanding *of the manner in which moral judgments have originated* would spoil these grand words for you, just as other grand words, like "sin" and "salvation of the soul" and "redemption" have been spoiled for you.—And now don't cite the categorical imperative, my friend! This term tickles my ear and makes me laugh despite your serious presence. It makes me think of the old Kant who had obtained the "thing in itself" *by stealth*—another very ridiculous thing!—and was punished for this when the "categorical imperative" crept stealthily into his heart and led him *astray—back* to "God," "soul," "freedom," and "immortality," like a fox who loses his way and goes astray back into his cage. Yet it had been *his* strength and cleverness that had *broken open* the cage! . . .

Let us therefore *limit* ourselves to the purification of our opinions and valuations and to the *creation of our own new tables of what is good,* and let us stop brooding about the "moral value of our actions"! We, however, *want to become those we are*—human beings who are new, unique, incomparable, who give themselves laws, who create themselves. [*GS,* 335]

IN THE HORIZON OF THE INFINITE.—We have left the land and have embarked. We have burned our bridges behind us—indeed, we have gone farther and destroyed the land behind us. Now, little ship, look out!

Beside you is the ocean: to be sure, it does not always roar, and at times it lies spread out like silk and gold and reveries of graciousness. But hours will come when you will realize that it is infinite and that there is nothing more awesome than infinity. Oh, the poor bird that felt free and now strikes the walls of this cage! Woe, when you feel homesick for the land as if it had offered more *freedom*—and there is no longer any "land." [*GS,* 124]

From *Daybreak*

WE AERONAUTS OF THE SPIRIT!—All those brave birds which fly out into the distance, into the farthest distance—it is certain! somewhere or other they will be unable to go on and will perch on a mast or a bare cliff-face—and they will even be thankful for this miserable accommodation! But who could venture to infer from that, that there was *not* an immense open space before them, that they had flown as far as one *could* fly! All our great teachers and predecessors have at last come to a stop and it is not with the noblest or most graceful of gestures that weariness comes to a stop: it will be the same with you and me! But what does that matter to you and me! *Other birds will fly farther!* This insight and faith of ours vies with them in flying up and away; it rises above our heads and above our impotence into the heights and from there surveys the distance and sees before it the flocks of birds which, far stronger than we, still strive whither we have striven, and where everything is sea, sea, sea!—And whither then would we go? Would we *cross* the sea? Whither does this mighty longing draw us, this longing that is worth more to us than any pleasure? Why just in this direction, thither where all the suns of humanity have hitherto *gone down?* Will it perhaps be said of us one day that we too, *steering westward, hoped to reach an India*—but that it was our fate to wrecked against infinity? Or, my brothers. Or?—[*D,* 575]

* * *

PREPARATORY HUMAN BEINGS.—I welcome all signs that a more virile, warlike age is about to begin, which will restore honor to courage

Daybreak by Friedrich Nietzsche, trans. by R. J. Hollingdale. Copyright © 1982 by Cambridge University Press. Reprinted with the permission of Cambridge University Press. Hereafter, this work will be cited as *D.*

above all. For this age shall prepare the way for one yet higher, and it shall gather the strength that this higher age will require some day—the age that will carry heroism into the search for knowledge and that will *wage wars* for the sake of ideas and their consequences. To this end we now need many preparatory courageous human beings who cannot very well leap out of nothing, any more than out of the sand and slime of present-day civilization and metropolitanism—human beings who know how to be silent, lonely, resolute, and content and constant in invisible activities; human beings who are bent on seeking in all things for what in them must be *overcome;* human beings distinguished as much by cheerfulness, patience, unpretentiousness, and contempt for all great vanities as by magnanimity in victory and forbearance regarding the small vanities of the vanquished; human beings whose judgment concerning all victors and the share of chance in every victory and fame is sharp and free; human beings with their own festivals, their own working days, and their own periods of mourning, accustomed to command with assurance but instantly ready to obey when that is called for—equally proud, equally serving their own cause in both cases; more endangered human beings, more fruitful human beings, happier beings! For believe me: the secret for harvesting from existence the greatest fruitfulness and the greatest enjoyment is—to *live dangerously!* Build your cities on the slopes of Vesuvius! Send your ships into uncharted seas! Live at war with your peers and yourselves! Be robbers and conquerors as long as you cannot be rulers and possessors, you seekers of knowledge! Soon the age will be past when you could be content to live hidden in forests like shy deer. [*GS,* 285]

EXCELSIOR.—"You will never pray again, never adore again, never again rest in endless trust; you do not permit yourself to stop before any ultimate wisdom, ultimate goodness, ultimate power, while unharnessing your thoughts; you have no perpetual guardian and friend for your seven solitudes; . . . there is no avenger for you any more nor any final improver; there is no longer any reason in what happens, no love in what will happen to you; no resting place is open any longer to your heart, where it only needs to find and no longer to seek; you resist any ultimate peace; you will the eternal recurrence of war and peace: man of renunciation, all this you wish to renounce? Who will give you the strength for that? Nobody yet has had this strength!"

There is a lake that one day ceased to permit itself to flow off; it formed a dam where it had hitherto flown off; and ever since this lake is rising higher and higher. Perhaps this very renunciation will also lend us the strength needed to bear this renunciation; perhaps man will rise ever higher as soon as he ceases to *flow out* into a god. [*GS,* 285]

EMBARK!—Consider how every individual is affected by an overall philosophical justification of his way of living and thinking: he experiences it as a sun that shines especially for him and bestows warmth, blessings, and fertility on him; it makes him independent of praise and blame, self-sufficient, rich, liberal with happiness and good will; incessantly it re-fashions evil into good, leads all energies to bloom and ripen, and does not permit the petty weeds of grief and chagrin to come up at all. In the end one exclaims: How I wish that many such new suns were yet to be created! Those who are evil or unhappy and the exceptional human being—all these should also have their philosophy, their good right, their sunshine! What is needful is not pity for them. We must learn to abandon this arrogant fancy, however long humanity has hitherto spent learning and practicing it. What these people need is not confession, conjuring of souls, and forgiveness of sins; what is needful is a new *justice!* And a new watchword. And new philosophers. The moral earth, too, is round. The moral earth, too, has its antipodes. The antipodes, too, have the right to exist. There is yet another world to be discovered—and more than one. Embark, philosophers! [*GS,* 289]

THE MEANING OF OUR CHEERFULNESS.—The greatest recent event—that "God is dead," that the belief in the Christian god has become unbelievable—is already beginning to cast its first shadows over Europe. For the few at least, whose eyes—the *suspicion* in whose eyes is strong and subtle enough for this spectacle, some sun seems to have set and some ancient and profound trust has been turned into doubt; to them our old world must appear daily more like evening, more mistrustful, stranger, "older." But in the main one may say: The event itself is far too great, too distant, too remote from the multitude's capacity for comprehension even for the tidings of it to be thought of as having *arrived* as yet. Much less may one suppose that many people know as yet *what* this event really means—and how much must collapse now that this faith has been undermined because it was built upon this faith, propped up by it, grown into it; for example, the whole of our European morality. This long plenitude and sequence of breakdown, destruction, ruin, and cataclysm that is now impending—who could guess enough of it today to be compelled to play the teacher and advance pro-claimer of this monstrous logic of terror, the prophet of a gloom and an eclipse of the sun whose like has probably never yet occurred on earth? . . .

Indeed, we philosophers and "free spirits" feel, when we hear the news that "the old god is dead," as if a new dawn shone on us; our heart overflows with gratitude, amazement, premonitions, expectation. At long last the horizon appears free to us again, even if it should not be bright;

at long last our ships may venture out again, venture out to face any danger; all the daring of the lover of the knowledge is permitted again; the sea, *our* sea, lies open again, perhaps there has never yet been such an "open sea."—[*GS,* 343]

From *Human, All Too Human*

One may conjecture that a spirit in whom the type 'free spirit' will one day become ripe and sweet to the point of perfection has had its decisive experience in a *great liberation* and that previously it was all the more a fettered spirit and seemed to be chained for ever to its pillar and corner. What fetters the fastest? What bonds are all but unbreakable? In the case of men of a high and select kind they will be their duties: that reverence proper to youth, that reserve and delicacy before all that is honoured and revered from of old, that gratitude for the soil out of which they have grown, for the hand which led them, for the holy place where they learned to worship—their supreme moments themselves will fetter them the fastest, lay upon them the most enduring obligation. The great liberation comes for those who are thus fettered suddenly, like the shock of an earthquake: the youthful soul is all at once convulsed, torn loose, torn away—it itself does not know what is happening. A drive and impulse rules and masters it like a command; a will and desire awakens to go off, anywhere, at any cost; a vehement dangerous curiosity for an undiscovered world flames and flickers in all its senses. 'Better to die than to go on living *here*'—thus responds the imperious voice and temptation: and this 'here', this 'at home' is everything it had hitherto loved! A sudden terror and suspicion of what it loved, a lightning-bolt of contempt for what it called 'duty', a rebellious, arbitrary, volcanically erupting desire for travel, strange places, estrangements, coldness, soberness, frost, a hatred of love, perhaps a desecrating blow and glance *backwards* to where it formerly loved and worshipped, perhaps a hot blush of shame at what it has just done and at the same time an exultation *that* it has done it, a drunken, inwardly exultant shudder which betrays that a victory has been won—a victory? over what? over whom? an enigmatic, question-packed, questionable victory, but the *first* victory nonetheless: such bad and painful things are part of the history of the great liberation. It is at the same time a sickness that can destroy the man who has it, this first outbreak of strength and will to self-determination, to evaluating on one's own account, this will to *free* will: and how much sickness is expressed in the wild experiments and singularities through which the liberated prisoner now seeks to demonstrate his mastery over things! He prowls cruelly around with an unslaked lasciviousness; what he captures has to expiate the perilous tension of his pride; what excites him he tears apart. With a wicked laugh he turns round whatever he finds veiled and through some sense of shame or other spared and pampered: he puts to the test what these things look like *when* they are reversed. It is an act of willfulness, and pleasure in willfulness, if now he perhaps bestows his favour on that which has hitherto had a bad reputation—if, full of inquisitiveness and the desire to tempt and experiment, he creeps around the things most forbidden. Behind all his toiling and weaving—for he is restlessly and aimlessly on his way as if in a desert—stands the question-mark of a more and more perilous curiosity. 'Can *all* values not be turned round? and is good perhaps evil? and God only an invention and finesse of the Devil? Is everything perhaps in the last resort false? And if we are deceived, are we not for that very reason also deceivers? *must* we not be deceivers?'— such thoughts as these tempt him and lead him on, even further away, even further down. Solitude encircles and embraces him, ever more threatening, suffocating, heart-tightening, that terrible goddess and *mater saeva cupidinum**—but who today knows what *solitude* is? . . .

From this morbid isolation, from the desert of these years of temptation and experiment, it is still a long road to that tremendous overflowing certainty and health which may not dispense even with wickedness, as a means and fish-hook of knowledge, to that *mature* freedom of spirit which is equally self-mastery and discipline of the heart and permits access to many and contradictory modes of thought—to that inner spaciousness and indulgence of superabundance which excludes the danger that the spirit may even on its own road perhaps lose itself and become infatuated and remain seated intoxicated in some corner or other, to that superfluity of formative, curative, moulding and restorative forces which is precisely the sign of *great* health, that superfluity which grants to the free spirit the dangerous privilege of living *experimentally* and of being allowed to offer itself to adventure: the master's privilege of the free spirit! In between there may lie long years of convalescence, years full of variegated, painfully magical transformations ruled and led along by a tenacious *will to health* which often ventures to clothe and disguise itself as health already achieved.

---

* Fierce mother of the cupids

There is a midway condition which a man of such a destiny will not be able to recall without emotion: it is characterized by a pale, subtle happiness of light and sunshine, a feeling of bird-like freedom, bird-like altitude, bird-like exuberance, and a third thing in which curiosity is united with a tender contempt. A 'free-spirit'—this cool expression does one good in every condition, it is almost warming. One lives no longer in the fetters of love and hatred, without yes, without no, near or far as one wishes, preferably slipping away, evading, fluttering off, gone again, again flying aloft; one is spoiled, as everyone is who has at some time seen a tremendous number of things *beneath* him—and one becomes the opposite of those who concern themselves with things which have nothing to do with them. Indeed, the free spirit henceforth has to do only with things—and how many things!—with which he is no longer *concerned* . . .

At that time it may finally happen that, under the sudden illumination of a still stressful, still changeable health, the free, ever freer spirit begins to unveil the riddle of that great liberation which had until then waited dark, questionable, almost untouchable in his memory. If he has for long hardly dared to ask himself: 'why so apart? so alone? renouncing everything I once reverenced? renouncing reverence itself? why this hardness, this suspiciousness, this hatred for your own virtues?'—now he dares to ask it aloud and hears in reply something like an answer. 'You shall become master over yourself, master also over your virtues. Formerly *they* were your masters; but they must be only your instruments beside other instruments. You shall get control over your For and Against and learn how to display first one and then the other in accordance with your higher goal. You shall learn to grasp the sense of perspective in every value judgement—the displacement, distortion and merely apparent teleology of horizons and whatever else pertains to perspectivism; also the quantum of stupidity that resides in antitheses of values and the whole intellectual loss which every For, every Against costs us. You shall learn to grasp the *necessary* injustice in every For and Against, injustice as inseparable from life, life itself as *conditioned* by the sense of perspective and its injustice. You shall above all see with your own eyes where injustice is always at its greatest: where life has developed at its smallest, narrowest, neediest, most incipient and yet cannot avoid taking *itself* as the goal and measure of things and for the sake of its own preservation secretly and meanly and ceaselessly crumbling away and calling into question the higher, greater, richer—you shall see with your own eyes the problem of *order of rank,* and how power and right and spaciousness of perspective grow into the heights together. You shall'—enough: from now on the free spirit *knows* what 'you shall' he has obeyed, and he also knows what he now *can,* what only now he—*may* do . . . [*HAH*, Preface, 3, 4, 6]

From *The Will to Power*

The Will to Power and the Overman

Life, as the form of being most familiar to us, is specifically a will to the accumulation of force; all the processes of life depend on this: nothing wants to preserve itself, everything is to be added and accumulated.

Life as a special case (hypothesis based upon it applied to the total character of being—) strives after a *maximal feeling of power;* essentially a striving for more power; striving is nothing other than striving for power; the basic and innermost thing is still this will. (Mechanics is merely the semeiotics of the results.) [*WP,* 689]

And do you know what "the world" is to me? Shall I show it to you in my mirror? This world: a monster of energy, without beginning, without end; a firm, iron magnitude of force that does not grow bigger or smaller, that does not expend itself but only transforms itself; as a whole, of unalterable size, a household without expenses or losses, but likewise without increase or income; enclosed by "nothingness" as by a boundary; not something blurry or wasted, not something endlessly extended, but set in a definite space as a definite force, and not a space that might be "empty" here or there, but rather as force throughout, as a play of forces and waves of forces, at the same time one and many, increasing here and at the same time decreasing there; a sea of forces flowing and rushing together, eternally changing, eternally flooding back, with tremendous years of recurrence, with an ebb and a flood of its forms; out of the simplest forms striving toward the most complex, out of the stillest, most rigid, coldest forms toward the hottest, most turbulent, most self-contradictory, and then again returning home to the simple out of this abundance, out of the play of contradictions back to the joy of concord, still affirming itself in this uniformity of its courses and its years, blessing itself as that which must return eternally, as a becoming that knows no satiety, no disgust, no weariness: this, my Dionysian world of the eternally self-creating, the eternally self-destroying, this mystery world of the twofold voluptuous delight, my "beyond good and evil," without goal, unless the joy of the circle is itself a goal; without will, unless a ring feels good will toward itself—do you want a *name* for this world? A *solution* for all its riddles? A *light* for you, too, you best-concealed, strongest, most intrepid, most midnightly men?—*This world is the will to power—and nothing besides!* And you yourselves are also this will to power—and nothing besides! [*WP,* 1067]

From *Beyond Good and Evil*

Suppose nothing else were "given" as real except our world of desires and passions, and we could not get down, or up, to any other "reality" besides the reality of our drives—for thinking is merely a relation of these drives to each other: is it not permitted to make the experiment and to ask the question whether this "given" would not be *sufficient* for also understanding on the basis of this kind of thing the so-called mechanistic (or "material") world? I mean, not as a deception, as "mere appearance," an "idea" (in the sense of Berkeley and Schopenhauer) but as holding the same rank of reality as our affect—as a more primitive form of the world of affects in which everything still lies contained in a powerful unity before it undergoes ramifications and developments in the organic process (and, as is only fair, also becomes tenderer and weaker)—as a kind of instinctive life in which all organic functions are still synthetically intertwined along with self-regulation, assimilation, nourishment, excretion, and metabolism—as a *pre-form* of life. . . .

Suppose, finally, we succeeded in explaining our entire instinctive life as the development and ramification of *one* basic form of the will—namely, of the will to power, as *my* proposition has it; suppose all organic functions could be traced back to this will to power and one could also find in it the solution of the problem of procreation and nourishment—it is *one* problem—then one would have gained the right to determine *all* efficient force univocally as—*will to power.* The world viewed from inside, the world defined and determined according to its "intelligible character"—it would be "will to power" and nothing else.—[*BGE,* 36]

* * *

Beyond Good and Evil in *The Basic Writings of Nietzsche* by Friedrich Nietzsche, trans. by Walter Kaufmann. Copyright © 1967, Random House. Reprinted with the permission of Random House, Inc.

Hereafter, this work will be cited as *BGE.*

ON THE DOCTRINE OF THE FEELING OF POWER.—Benefiting and hurting others are ways of exercising one's power upon others; that is all one desires in such cases. One hurts those whom one wants to feel one's power, for pain is a much more efficient means to that end than pleasure; pain always raises the question about its origin while pleasure is inclined to stop with itself without looking back. We benefit and show benevolence to those who are already dependent on us in some way (which means that they are used to thinking of us as causes); we want to increase their power because in that way we increase ours, or we want to show them how advantageous it is to be in our power; that way they will become more satisfied with their condition and more hostile to and willing to fight against the enemies of *our* power.

Whether benefiting or hurting others involves sacrifices for us does not affect the ultimate value of our actions. Even if we offer our lives, as martyrs do for their church, this is a sacrifice that is offered for *our* desire for power or for the purpose of preserving our feeling of power. Those who feel "I possess Truth"—how many possessions would they not abandon in order to save this feeling! What would they not throw overboard to stay "on top"—which means, *above* the others who lack "the Truth"!

Certainly the state in which we hurt others is rarely as agreeable, in an unadulterated way, as that in which we benefit others; it is a sign that we are still lacking power, or it shows a sense of frustration in the face of this poverty; it is accompanied by new dangers and uncertainties for what power we do possess, and clouds our horizon with the prospect of revenge, scorn, punishment, and failure. It is only for the most irritable and covetous devotees of the feeling of power that it is perhaps more pleasurable to imprint the seal of power on a recalcitrant brow—those for whom the sight of those who are already subjected (the objects of benevolence) is a burden and boredom. [*GS,* 13]

* * *

THE STRIVING FOR DISTINCTION.—The striving for distinction keeps a constant eye on the next man and wants to know what his feelings are: but the empathy which this drive requires for its gratification is far from being harmless or sympathetic or kind. We want, rather, to perceive or divine how the next man outwardly or inwardly *suffers* from us, how he loses control over himself and surrenders to the impressions our hand or even merely the sight of us makes upon him; and even when he who strives after distinction makes and wants to make a joyful, elevating or cheering impression, he nonetheless enjoys this success not inasmuch as he has given joy to the next man or elevated or cheered him, but inasmuch as he has *impressed* himself on the soul of the other, changed its shape and ruled over it at his own sweet will. The striving for distinction is the striving for domination over the next man, though it be a very indirect domination and only felt or even dreamed. There is a long scale of degrees of this secretly desired domination, and a complete catalogue of them would be almost the same thing as a history of culture, from the earliest, still grotesque barbarism up to the grotesqueries of over-refinement and morbid idealism. The striving for distinction brings with it *for the next man*—to name only a few steps on the ladder: torment, then blows, then terror, then fearful astonishment, then wonderment, then envy, then admiration, then elevation, then joy, then cheerfulness, then laughter, then derision, then mockery, then ridicule, then giving blows, then imposing torment:—here at the end of the ladder stands the *ascetic* and martyr, who feels the highest enjoyment by himself enduring, as a consequence of his drive for distinction, precisely that which, on the first step of the ladder, his counterpart the *barbarian* imposes on others on whom and before whom he wants to distinguish himself. The triumph of the ascetic over himself, . . . this final tragedy of the drive for distinction in which there is only one character burning and consuming himself—this is a worthy conclusion and one appropriate to the commencement: in both cases an unspeakable happiness at the *sight of torment!* Indeed, happiness, conceived of as the liveliest feeling of power, has perhaps been nowhere greater on earth than in the souls of superstitious ascetics. . . . [*D*, 113]

ON GRAND POLITICS.—However much utility and vanity, those of individuals as of peoples, may play a part in *grand politics:* the strongest tide which carries them forward is the *need for the feeling of power*, which from time to time streams up out of inexhaustible wells not only in the souls of princes and the powerful but not least in the lower orders of the people. There comes again and again the hour when the masses are *ready* to stake their life, their goods, their conscience, their virtue so as to acquire that higher enjoyment and as a victorious, capriciously tyrannical nation to rule over other nations (or to think it rules). Then the impulses to squander, sacrifice, hope, trust, to be over-daring and to fantasise spring up in such abundance that the ambitious or prudently calculating prince can let loose a war and cloak his crimes in the good conscience of his people. The great conquerors have always mouthed the pathetic language of virtue: they have had around them masses in a condition of elevation who wanted to hear only the most elevated language. Strange madness of moral judgments! When man possesses the feeling of power he feels and calls himself *good:* and it is precisely then that the others upon whom he has to *discharge* his power feel and call him *evil!*—[*D*, 189]

DANÄE AND GOD IN GOLD.—Whence comes this immoderate impatience which nowadays turns a man into a criminal under circumstances which would be more compatible with an opposite tendency? For if one man employs false weights, another burns his house down after he has insured it for a large sum, a third counterfeits coins, if three-quarters of the upper classes indulge in permitted fraud and have the stock exchange and speculations on their conscience: what drives them? Not actual need, for they are not so badly off, perhaps they even eat and drink without a care—but they are afflicted day and night by a fearful impatience at the slow way with which their money is accumulating and by an equally fearful pleasure in and love of accumulated money.

In this impatience and this love, however, there turns up again that fanaticism of the *lust for power* which was in former times inflamed by the belief one was in possession of the truth and which bore such beautiful names that one could thenceforth venture to be inhuman *with a good conscience* (to burn Jews, heretics and good books and exterminate entire higher cultures such as those of Peru and Mexico). The means employed by the lust for power have changed, but the same volcano continues to glow, the impatience and the immoderate love demand their sacrifice: and what one formerly did 'for the sake of God' one now does for the sake of money, that is to say, for the sake of that which *now* gives the highest feeling of power and good conscience. [*D,* 204]

From *Thus Spoke Zarathustra*

"Will to truth," you who are wisest call that which impels you and fills you with lust?

A will to the thinkability of all beings: this *I* call your will. You want to *make* all being thinkable, for you doubt with well-founded suspicion that it is already thinkable. But it shall yield and bend for you. Thus your will wants it. It shall become smooth and serve the spirit as its mirror and reflection. That is your whole will, you who are wisest: a will to power—when you speak of good and evil too, and of valuations. You still want to create the world before which you can kneel: that is your ultimate hope and intoxication.

From *Thus Spoke Zarathustra* in *The Portable Nietzsche,* ed. and trans. by Walter Kaufmann. Copyright 1963 by The Viking Press, Inc. Copyright renewed © 1982 by Viking Penguin Inc. All rights reserved. Reprinted by permission of Viking Penguin Inc.

Hereafter, this work will be cited as *Z.*

The unwise, of course, the people—they are like a river on which a bark drifts; and in the bark sit the valuations, solemn and muffled up. Your will and your valuations you have placed on the river of becoming; and what the people believe to be good and evil, that betrays to me an ancient will to power.

It was you who are wisest who placed such guests in this bark and gave them pomp and proud names—you and your dominant will. . . .

But to make you understand my word concerning good and evil, I shall now say to you my word concerning life and the nature of all the living.

I pursued the living; I walked the widest and the narrowest paths that I might know its nature. . . .

But wherever I found the living, there I heard also the speech on obedience. Whatever lives, obeys.

And this is the second point: he who cannot obey himself is commanded. That is the nature of the living.

This, however, is the third point that I heard: that commanding is harder than obeying; and not only because he who commands must carry the burden of all who obey, and because this burden may easily crush him. An experiment and hazard appeared to me to be in all commanding; and whenever the living commands, it hazards itself. Indeed, even when it commands *itself,* it must still pay for its commanding. It must become the judge, the avenger, and the victim of its own law. How does this happen? I asked myself. What persuades the living to obey and command, and to practice obedience even when it commands?

Hear, then, my word, you who are wisest. Test in all seriousness whether I have crawled into the very heart of life and into the very roots of its heart.

Where I found the living, there I found will to power; and even in the will of those who serve I found the will to be master.

That the weaker should serve the stronger, to that it is persuaded by its own will, which would be master over what is weaker still: this is the one pleasure it does not want to renounce. And as the smaller yields to the greater that it may have pleasure and power over the smallest, thus even the greatest still yields, and for the sake of power risks life. That is the yielding of the greatest: it is hazard and danger and casting dice for death.

And where men make sacrifices and serve and cast amorous glances, there too is the will to be master. Along stealthy paths the weaker steals into the castle and into the very heart of the more powerful—and there steals power.

And life itself confided this secret to me: "Behold," it said, "I am *that which must always overcome itself.* Indeed, you call it a will to procreate or a drive to an end, to something higher, farther, more manifold: but all this is one, and one secret.

"Rather would I perish than forswear this; and verily, where there is perishing and a falling of leaves, behold, there life sacrifices itself—for power. That I must be struggle and a becoming and an end and an opposition to ends—alas, whoever guesses what is my will should also guess on what *crooked* paths it must proceed.

"Whatever I create and however much I love it—soon I must oppose it and my love; thus my will wills it. And you too, lover of knowledge, are only a path and footprint of my will; verily, my will to power walks also on the heels of your will to truth.

"Indeed, the truth was not hit by him who shot at it with the word of the 'will to existence': that will does not exist. For, what does not exist cannot will; but what is in existence, how could that still want existence? Only where there is life is there also will: not will to life but—thus I teach you—will to power.

"There is much that life esteems more highly than life itself; but out of the esteeming itself speaks the will to power." [*Z*, Pt. II, "On Self Overcoming"]

Do you want to go the way of your affliction, which is the way to yourself? Then show me your right and your strength to do so. Are you a new strength and a new right? A first movement? A self-propelled wheel? Can you compel the very stars to revolve around you? . . .

Can you give yourself your own evil and your own good and hang your own will over yourself as a law? Can you be your own judge and avenger of your law? Terrible it is to be alone with the judge and avenger of one's own law. Thus is a star thrown out into the void and into the icy breath of solitude. [*Z*, Pt. I, "On the Way of the Creator"]

From *The Antichrist*

What is good? Everything that heightens the feeling of power in man, the will to power, power itself.

What is bad? Everything that is born of weakness.

Hereafter, this work will be cited as *A*.

What is happiness? The feeling that power is *growing*, that resistance is overcome.

Not contentedness but more power; not peace but war; not virtue but fitness (Renaissance virtue, *virtù*, virtue that is moraline-free).

The weak and the failures shall perish: first principle of *our* love of man. And they shall even be given every possible assistance.

What is more harmful than any vice? Active pity for all the failures and all the weak: Christianity.

The problem I thus pose is not what shall succeed mankind in the sequence of living beings (man is an *end*), but what type of man shall be *bred*, shall be *willed*, for being higher in value, worthier of life, more certain of a future.

Even in the past this higher type has appeared often—but as a fortunate accident, as an exception, never as something *willed*. In fact, this has been the type most dreaded—almost *the* dreadful—and from dread the opposite type was willed, bred, and *attained*: the domestic animal, the herd animal, the sick human animal—the Christian.

Mankind does *not* represent a development toward something better or stronger or higher in the sense accepted today. "Progress" is merely a modern idea, that is, a false idea. The European of today is vastly inferior in value to the European of the Renaissance: further development is altogether *not* according to any necessity in the direction of elevation, enhancement, or strength.

In another sense, success in individual cases is constantly encountered in the most widely different places and cultures: here we really do find a *higher type,* which is, in relation to mankind as a whole, a kind of overman. Such fortunate accidents of great success have always been possible and *will* perhaps always be possible. And even whole families, tribes, or peoples may occasionally represent such a *bull's-eye.* [*A,* 2, 3, 4]

* * *

When Zarathustra came into the next town, which lies on the edge of the forest, he found many people gathered together in the market place; for it had been promised that there would be a tightrope walker. And Zarathustra spoke thus to the people:

"I teach you the overman. Man is something that shall be overcome. What have you done to overcome him?

"All beings so far have created something beyond themselves; and do you want to be the ebb of this great flood and even go back to the beasts rather than overcome man? What is the ape to man? A laughingstock or a painful embarrassment. And man shall be just that for the overman: a laughingstock or a painful embarrassment. You have made your way from worm to man, and much in you is still worm. Once you were apes, and even now, too, man is more ape than any ape.

"Whoever is the wisest among you is also a mere conflict and cross between plant and ghost. But do I bid you become ghosts or plants?

"Behold, I teach you the overman. The overman is the meaning of the earth. Let your will say: the overman *shall be* the meaning of the earth! I beseech you, my brothers, *remain faithful to the earth,* and do not believe those who speak to you of otherworldly hopes! Poison-mixers are they, whether they know it or not. Despisers of life are they, decaying and poisoned themselves, of whom the earth is weary: so let them go.

"Once the sin against God was the greatest sin; but God died, and these sinners died with him. To sin against the earth is now the most dreadful thing, and to esteem the entrails of the unknowable higher than the meaning of the earth.

"Once the soul looked contemptuously upon the body, and then this contempt was the highest: she wanted the body meager, ghastly, and starved. Thus she hoped to escape it and the earth. Oh, this soul herself was still meager, ghastly, and starved: and cruelty was the lust of this soul. But you, too, my brothers, tell me: what does your body proclaim of your soul? Is not your soul poverty and filth and wretched contentment?

"Verily, a polluted stream is man. One must be a sea to be able to receive a polluted stream without becoming unclean. Behold, I teach you the overman: he is this sea; in him your great contempt can go under.

"What is the greatest experience you can have? It is the hour of the great contempt. The hour in which your happiness, too, arouses your disgust, and even your reason and your virtue.

"The hour when you say, 'What matters my happiness? It is poverty and filth and wretched contentment. But my happiness ought to justify existence itself.'

"The hour when you say, 'What matters my reason? Does it crave knowledge as the lion his food? It is poverty and filth and wretched contentment.'

"The hour when you say, 'What matters my virtue? As yet it has not made me rage. How weary I am of my good and my evil! All that is poverty and filth and wretched contentment.'

"The hour when you say, 'What matters my justice? I do not see that I am flames and fuel. But the just are flames and fuel.'

"The hour when you say, 'What matters my pity? Is not pity the cross on which he is nailed who loves man? But my pity is no crucifixion.'

"Have you yet spoken thus? Have you yet cried thus? Oh, that I might have heard you cry thus!

"Not your sin but your thrift cries to heaven; your meanness even in your sin cries to heaven.

"Where is the lightning to lick you with its tongue? Where is the frenzy with which you should be inoculated?

"Behold, I teach you the overman: he is this lightning, he is this frenzy." [*Z,* Prologue 3]

* * *

In an age of disintegration that mixes races indiscriminately, human beings have in their bodies the heritage of multiple origins, that is, opposite, and often not merely opposite, drives and value standards that fight each other and rarely permit each other any rest. Such human beings of late cultures and refracted lights will on the average be weaker human beings: their most profound desire is that the war they *are* should come to an end. Happiness appears to them, in agreement with a tranquilizing (for example, Epicurean or Christian) medicine and way of thought, preeminently as the happiness of resting, of not being disturbed, of satiety, of finally attained unity, as a "sabbath of sabbaths," to speak with the holy rhetorician Augustine who was himself such a human being.

But when the opposition and war in such a nature have the effect of one more charm and incentive of life—and if, moreover, in addition to his powerful and irreconcilable drives, a real mastery and subtlety in waging war against oneself, in other words, self-control, self-outwitting, has been inherited or cultivated, too—then those magical, incomprehensible, and unfathomable ones arise, those enigmatic men predestined for victory and seduction, whose most beautiful expression is found in Alcibiades and Caesar (to whose company I should like to add that *first* European after my taste, the Hohenstaufen Frederick II), and among artists perhaps Leonardo da Vinci. They appear in precisely the same ages when that weaker type with its desire for rest comes to the fore: both types belong together and owe their origin to the same causes. [*BGE,* 200]

. . . You want, if possible—and there is no more insane "if possible"—*to abolish suffering.* And we? It really seems that *we* would rather have it higher and worse than ever. Well-being as you understand it— that is no goal, that seems to us an *end,* a state that soon makes man ridiculous and contemptible—that makes his destruction *desirable.* . . .

The discipline of suffering, of *great* suffering—do you not know that only *this* discipline has created all enhancements of man so far? That tension of the soul in unhappiness which cultivates its strength, its shudders face to face with great ruin, its inventiveness and courage in enduring, persevering, interpreting, and exploiting suffering, and whatever has been granted to it of profundity, secret, mask, spirit, cunning, greatness—was it not granted to it through suffering, through the discipline of great suffering? In man *creature* and *creator* are united: in man there is material, fragment, excess, clay, dirt, nonsense, chaos; but in man there is also creator, form-giver, hammer hardness, spectator divinity, and seventh day: do you understand this contrast? And that *your* pity is for the "creature in man," for what must be formed, broken, forged, torn, burnt, made incandescent, and purified—that which *necessarily* must and *should* suffer? [*BGE*, 225]

Refraining mutually from injury, violence, and exploitation and placing one's will on a par with that of someone else—this may become, in a certain rough sense, good manners among individuals if the appropriate conditions are present (namely, if these men are actually similar in strength and value standards and belong together in *one* body). But as soon as this principle is extended, and possibly even accepted as the *fundamental principle of society,* it immediately proves to be what it really is—a will to the *denial* of life, a principle of disintegration and decay.

. . . Life itself is *essentially* appropriation, injury, overpowering of what is alien and weaker; suppression, hardness, imposition of one's own forms, incorporation and at least, at its mildest, exploitation—

Even the body within which individuals treat each other as equals, as suggested before—and this happens in every healthy aristocracy—if it is a living and not a dying body, has to do to other bodies what the individuals within it refrain from doing to each other: it will have to be an incarnate will to power, it will strive to grow, spread, seize, become predominant—not from any morality or immorality but because it is *living* and because life simply *is* will to power. . . . [*BGE*, 259]

From *Ecce Homo*

The word "overman," as the designation of a type of supreme achievement, as opposed to "modern" men, to "good" men, to Christians and other nihilists—a word that in the mouth of a Zarathustra, the annihilator of morality, becomes a very pensive word—has been understood almost everywhere with the utmost innocence in the sense of those very values whose opposite Zarathustra was meant to represent—that is, as an "idealistic" type of a higher kind of man, half "saint," half "genius."

Other scholarly oxen have suspected me of Darwinism on that account. Even the "hero worship" of that unconscious and involuntary counterfeiter, Carlyle, which I have repudiated so maliciously, has been read into it. Those to whom I said in confidence that they should sooner look even for a Cesare Borgia than for a Parsifal, did not believe their own ears. [*EH,* "Why I Write Such Good Books"]

From *Beyond Good and Evil*

Master Morality, Slave Morality, and Traditional Morality

Wandering through the many subtler and coarser moralities which have so far been prevalent on earth, or still are prevalent, I found that certain features recurred regularly together and were closely associated— until I finally discovered two basic types and one basic difference.

There are *master morality* and *slave morality*—I add immediately that in all the higher and more mixed cultures there also appear attempts at mediation between these two moralities, and yet more often the interpenetration and mutual misunderstanding of both, and at times they occur directly alongside each other—even in the same human being, within a *single* soul. The moral discrimination of values has originated either among a ruling group whose consciousness of its difference from the ruled group was accompanied by delight—or among the ruled, the slaves and dependents of every degree.

In the first case, when the ruling group determines what is "good," the exalted, proud states of the soul are experienced as conferring distinction and determining the order of rank. The noble human being separates from himself those in whom the opposite of such exalted, proud states finds expression: he despises them. It should be noted immediately that in this first type of morality the opposition of "good" and *"bad"* means approximately the same as "noble" and "contemptible." (The opposition of "good" and *"evil"* has a different origin.) One feels contempt for the cowardly, the anxious, the petty, those intent on narrow utility; also for the suspicious with their unfree glances, those who humble themselves, the doglike people who allow themselves to be maltreated, the begging flatterers, above all the liars: it is part of the fundamental faith of all aristocrats that the common people lie. "We truthful ones"— thus the nobility of ancient Greece referred to itself.

It is obvious that moral designations were everywhere first applied to *human beings* and only later, derivatively, to actions. Therefore it is a gross mistake when historians of morality start from such questions as: why was the compassionate act praised? The noble type of man experiences *itself* as determining values; it does not need approval; it judges, "what is harmful to me is harmful in itself"; it knows itself to be that which first accords honor to things; it is *value-creating*. Everything it knows as part of itself it honors: such a morality is self-glorification. In the foreground there is the feeling of fullness, of power that seeks to overflow, the happiness of high tension, the consciousness of wealth that would give and bestow: the noble human being, too, helps the unfortunate, but not, or almost not, from pity, but prompted more by an urge begotten by excess of power. The noble human being honors himself as one who is powerful, also as one who has power over himself, who knows how to speak and be silent, who delights in being severe and hard with himself and respects all severity and hardness. . . .

It is the powerful who *understand* how to honor; this is their art, their realm of invention. The profound reverence for age and tradition—all law rests on this double reverence—the faith and prejudice in favor of ancestors and disfavor of those yet to come are typical of the morality of the powerful; and when the men of "modern ideas," conversely, believe almost instinctively in "progress" and "the future" and more and more lack respect for age, this in itself would sufficiently betray the ignoble origin of these "ideas."

A morality of the ruling group, however, is most alien and embarrassing to the present taste in the severity of its principle that one has duties only to one's peers; that against beings of a lower rank, against everything alien, one may behave as one pleases or "as the heart desires," and in any case "beyond good and evil"—here pity and like feelings may find their place. The capacity for, and the duty of, long gratitude and long revenge—both only among one's peers—refinement in repaying, the sophisticated concept of friendship, a certain necessity for having enemies (as it were, as drainage ditches for the affects of envy, quarrelsomeness, exuberance—at bottom, in order to be capable of being good *friends*): all these are typical characteristics of noble morality. . . .

It is different with the second type of morality, *slave morality*. Suppose the violated, oppressed, suffering, unfree, who are uncertain of themselves and weary, moralize: what will their moral valuations have in common? Probably, a pessimistic suspicion about the whole condition of man will find expression, perhaps a condemnation of man along with his condition. The slave's eye is not favorable to the virtues of the powerful: he is skeptical and suspicious, *subtly* suspicious, of all the "good" that is honored there—he would like to persuade himself that even their happiness is not genuine. Conversely, those qualities are brought out and flooded with light which serve to ease existence for those who suffer: here pity, the complaisant and obliging hand, the warm heart, patience, industry, humility, and friendliness are honored—for here these are the most useful qualities and almost the only means for enduring the pressure of existence. Slave morality is essentially a morality of utility.

Here is the place for the origin of that famous opposition of "good" and "evil": into evil one's feelings project power and dangerousness, a certain terribleness, subtlety, and strength that does not permit contempt to develop. According to slave morality, those who are "evil" thus inspire fear; according to master morality it is precisely those who are "good" that inspire, and wish to inspire, fear, while the "bad" are felt to be contemptible.

The opposition reaches its climax when, as a logical consequence of slave morality, a touch of disdain is associated also with the "good" of this morality—this may be slight and benevolent—because the good human being has to be *undangerous* in the slaves' way of thinking: he is good-natured, easy to deceive, a little stupid perhaps, *un bonhomme.* Wherever slave morality becomes preponderant, language tends to bring the words "good" and "stupid" closer together.

One last fundamental difference: the longing for *freedom,* the instinct for happiness and the subtleties of the feeling of freedom belong just as necessarily to slave morality and morals as artful and enthusiastic reverence and devotion are the regular symptom of an aristocratic way of thinking and evaluating. [*BGE,* 260]

From *On the Genealogy of Morals*

The slave revolt in morality begins when *ressentiment* itself becomes creative and gives birth to values: the *ressentiment* of natures that are denied the true reaction, that of deeds, and compensate themselves with an imaginary revenge. While every noble morality develops from a triumphant affirmation of itself, slave morality from the outset says No to what is "outside," what is "different," what is "not itself"; and *this* No is its creative deed. This inversion of the value-positing eye—this *need* to direct one's view outward instead of back to oneself—is of the essence of *ressentiment:* in order to exist, slave morality always first needs a hostile external world; it needs, physiologically speaking, external stimuli in order to act at all—its action is fundamentally reaction.

The reverse is the case with the noble mode of valuation: it acts and grows spontaneously, it seeks its opposite only so as to affirm itself more gratefully and triumphantly—its negative concept "low," "common," "bad" is only a subsequently-invented pale, contrasting image in relation

On the Genealogy of Morals in *The Basic Writings of Nietzsche* by Friedrich Nietzsche, trans. by Walter Kaufmann. Copyright © 1967 Random House. Reprinted with the permission of Random House, Inc.
Hereafter, this work will be cited as *GM.*

to its positive basic concept—filled with life and passion through and through—"we noble ones, we good, beautiful, happy ones!". . . .

To be incapable of taking one's enemies, one's accidents, even one's misdeeds seriously for very long—that is the sign of strong, full natures in whom there is an excess of the power to form, to mold, to recuperate and to forget (a good example of this in modern times is Mirabeau, who had no memory for insults and vile actions done him and was unable to forgive simply because he—forgot). Such a man shakes off with a *single* shrug many vermin that eat deep into others; here alone genuine "love of one's enemies" is possible—supposing it to be possible at all on earth. How much reverence has a noble man for his enemies!—and such reverence is a bridge to love.—For he desires his enemy for himself, as his mark of distinction; he can endure no other enemy than one in whom there is nothing to despise and *very much* to honor! In contrast to this, picture "the enemy" as the man of *ressentiment* conceives him—and here precisely is his deed, his creation: he has conceived "the evil enemy," *"the Evil One,"* and this in fact is his basic concept, from which he then evolves, as an afterthought and pendant, a "good one"—himself!

This, then, is quite the contrary of what the noble man does, who conceives the basic concept "good" in advance and spontaneously out of himself and only then creates for himself an idea of "bad"! This "bad" of noble origin and that "evil" out of the cauldron of unsatisfied hatred—the former an after-production, a side issue, a contrasting shade, the latter on the contrary the original thing, the beginning, the distinctive *deed* in the conception of a slave morality—how different these words "bad" and "evil" are, although they are both apparently the opposite of the same concept "good." But it is *not* the same concept "good": one should ask rather precisely *who* is "evil" in the sense of the morality of *ressentiment.* The answer, in all strictness, is: *precisely* the "good man" of the other morality, precisely the noble, powerful man, the ruler, but dyed in another color, interpreted in another fashion, seen in another way by the venomous eye of *ressentiment.* . . .

But let us return: the problem of the *other* origin of the "good," of the good as conceived by the man of *ressentiment,* demands its solution.

That lambs dislike great birds of prey does not seem strange: only it gives no ground for reproaching these birds of prey for bearing off little lambs. And if the lambs say among themselves: "these birds of prey are evil; and whoever is least like a bird of prey, but rather its opposite, a lamb—would he not be good?" there is no reason to find fault with this institution of an ideal, except perhaps that the birds of prey might view it a little ironically and say: "*we* don't dislike them at all, these good little lambs; we even love them: nothing is more tasty than a tender lamb."

To demand of strength that it should *not* express itself as strength, that it should *not* be a desire to overcome, a desire to throw down, a desire to become master, a thirst for enemies and resistances and triumphs, is just as absurd as to demand of weakness that it should express itself as strength. A quantum of force is equivalent to a quantum of drive, will, effect—more, it is nothing other than precisely this very driving, willing, effecting, and only owing to the seduction of language (and of the fundamental errors of reason that are petrified in it) which conceives and misconceives all effects as conditioned by something that causes effects, by a "subject," can it appear otherwise. For just as the popular mind separates the lightning from its flash and takes the latter for an *action,* for the operation of a subject called lightning, so popular morality also separates strength from expressions of strength, as if there were a neutral substratum behind the strong man, which was *free* to express strength or not to do so. But there is no such substratum; there is no "being" behind doing, effecting, becoming; "the doer" is merely a fiction added to the deed—the deed is everything. The popular mind in fact doubles the deed; when it sees the lightning flash, it is the deed of a deed; it posits the same event first as cause and then a second time as its effect. Scientists do no better when they say "force moves," "force causes," and the like—all its coolness, its freedom from emotion notwithstanding, our entire science still lies under the misleading influence of language and has not disposed of that little changeling, the "subject" (the atom, for example, is such a changeling, as is the Kantian "thing-in-itself"); no wonder if the submerged, darkly glowering emotions of vengefulness and hatred exploit this belief for their own ends and in fact maintain no belief more ardently than the belief that *the strong man is free* to be weak and the bird of prey to be a lamb—for thus they gain the right to make the bird of prey *accountable* for being a bird of prey.

When the oppressed, downtrodden, outraged exhort one another with the vengeful cunning of impotence: "let us be different from the evil, namely good! And he is good who does not outrage, who harms nobody, who does not attack, who does not requite, who leaves revenge to God, who keeps himself hidden as we do, who avoids evil and desires little from life, like us, the patient, humble, and just"—this, listened to calmly and without previous bias, really amounts to no more than: "we weak ones are, after all, weak; it would be good if we did nothing *for which we are not strong enough*"; but this dry matter of fact, this prudence of the lowest order which even insects possess (posing as dead, when in great danger, so as not to do "too much"), has, thanks to the counterfeit and self-deception of impotence, clad itself in the ostentatious garb of the virtue of quiet, calm resignation, just as if the weakness of the weak— that is to say, their *essence,* their effects, their role ineluctable, irremovable reality—were a voluntary achievement, willed, chosen, a *deed,* a *meritorious* act. This type of man *needs* to believe in a neutral independent "subject," prompted by an instinct for self-preservation and self-affirmation in which every lie is sanctified. The subject (or, to use a more popular expression, the *soul*) has perhaps been believed in hitherto more firmly than anything else on earth because it makes possible to the majority of mortals, the weak and oppressed of every kind, the sublime self-deception that interprets weakness as freedom, and their being thus-and-thus as a *merit*. . . . [*GM,* I,10–11, 13]

I regard the bad conscience as the serious illness that man was bound to contract under the stress of the most fundamental change he ever experienced—that change which occurred when he found himself finally enclosed within the walls of society and of peace. The situation that faced sea animals when they were compelled to become land animals or perish was the same as that which faced these semi-animals, well adapted to the wilderness, to war, to prowling, to adventure: suddenly all their instincts were disvalued and "suspended." From now on they had to walk on their feet and "bear themselves" whereas hitherto they had been borne by the water: a dreadful heaviness lay upon them. They felt unable to cope with the simplest undertakings; in this new world they no longer possessed their former guides, their regulating, unconscious and infallible drives: they were reduced to thinking, inferring, reckoning, co-ordinating cause and effect, these unfortunate creatures; they were reduced to their "consciousness," their weakest and most fallible organ! I believe there has never been such a feeling of misery on earth, such a leaden discomfort—and at the same time the old instincts had not suddenly ceased to make their usual demands! Only it was hardly or rarely possible to humor them: as a rule they had to seek new and, as it were, subterranean gratifications.

All instincts that do not discharge themselves outwardly *turn inward*—this is what I call the *internalization* of man: thus it was that man first developed what was later called his "soul." The entire inner world, originally as thin as if it were stretched between two membranes, expanded and extended itself, acquired depth, breadth, and height, in the same measure as outward discharge is *inhibited.* Those fearful bulwarks with which the political organization protected itself against the old instincts of freedom—punishments belong among these bulwarks—brought about that all those instincts of wild, free, prowling man turned backward *against man himself.* Hostility, cruelty, joy in persecuting, in attacking, in change, in destruction—all this turned against the possessors of such instincts: *that* is the origin of the "bad conscience."

The man who, from lack of external enemies and resistances and forcibly confined to the oppressive narrowness and punctiliousness of custom, impatiently lacerated, persecuted, gnawed at, assaulted, and mal-treated himself; this animal that rubbed itself raw against the bars of its cage as one tried to "tame" it; this deprived creature, racked with homesickness for the wild, who had to turn himself into an adventure, a torture chamber, an uncertain and dangerous wilderness—this fool, this yearning and desperate prisoner became the inventor of the "bad conscience." But thus began the gravest and uncanniest illness, from which humanity has not yet recovered, man's suffering *of man, of himself*—the result of a forcible sundering from his animal past, as it were a leap and plunge into new surroundings and conditions of existence, a declaration of war against the old instincts upon which his strength, joy, and terribleness had rested hitherto. . . . From now on, man is *included* among the most unexpected and exciting lucky throws in the dice game of Heraclitus' "great child," be he called Zeus or chance; he gives rise to an interest, a tension, a hope, almost a certainty, as if with him something were announcing and preparing itself, as if man were not a goal but only a way, an episode, a bridge, a great promise.—

Among the presuppositions of this hypothesis concerning the origin of the bad conscience is, first, that the change referred to was not a gradual or voluntary one and did not represent an organic adaptation to new conditions but a break, a leap, a compulsion, an ineluctable disaster which precluded all struggle and even all *ressentiment*. Secondly, however, that the welding of a hitherto unchecked and shapeless populace into a firm form was not only instituted by an act of violence but also carried to its conclusion by nothing but acts of violence—that the oldest "state" thus appeared as a fearful tyranny, as an oppressive and remorseless machine, and went on working until this raw material of people and semi-animals was at last not only thoroughly kneaded and pliant but also *formed.*

I employed the word "state": it is obvious what is meant—some pack of blond beasts of prey, a conqueror and master race which, organized for war and with the ability to organize, unhesitatingly lays its terrible claws upon a populace perhaps tremendously superior in numbers but still formless and nomad. That is after all how the "state" began on earth: I think that sentimentalism which would have it begin with a "contract" has been disposed of. He who can command, he who is by nature "master," he who is violent in act and bearing—what has he to do with contracts! One does not reckon with such natures; they come like fate, without reason, consideration, or pretext; they appear as lightning appears, too terrible, too sudden, too convincing, too "different" even to be hated. Their work is an instinctive creation and imposition of forms; they are the most involuntary, unconscious artists there are—wherever they appear something new soon arises, a ruling structure that *lives,* in which parts and functions are delimited and coordinated, in which nothing whatever finds a place that has not first been assigned a "meaning" in relation to the whole. They do not know what guilt, responsibility, or consideration are, these born organizers; they exemplify that terrible artists' egoism that has the look of bronze and knows itself justified to all eternity in its "work," like a mother in her child. It is not in *them* that the "bad conscience" developed, that goes without saying—but it would not have developed *without them,* this ugly growth, it would be lacking if a tremendous quantity of freedom had not been expelled from the world, or at least from the visible world, and made as it were *latent* under their hammer blows and artists' violence. This *instinct for freedom* forcibly made latent—we have seen it already—this instinct for freedom pushed back and repressed, incarcerated within and finally able to discharge and vent itself only on itself: that, and that alone, is what the *bad conscience* is in its beginnings.

One should guard against thinking lightly of this phenomenon merely on account of its initial painfulness and ugliness. For fundamentally it is the same active force that is at work on a grander scale in those artists of violence and organizers who build states, and that here, internally, on a smaller and pettier scale, directed backward, in the "labyrinth of the breast," to use Goethe's expression, creates for itself a bad conscience and builds negative ideals—namely, the *instinct for freedom* (in my language: the will to power); only here the material upon which the form-giving and ravishing nature of this force vents itself is man himself, his whole ancient animal self—and *not,* as in that greater and more obvious phenomenon, some *other* man, *other* men. This secret self-ravishment, this artists' cruelty, this delight in imposing a form upon oneself as a hard, recalcitrant, suffering material and in burning a will, a critique, a contradiction, a contempt, a No into it, this uncanny, dreadfully joyous labor of a soul voluntarily at odds with itself that makes itself suffer out of joy in making suffer—eventually this entire *active* "bad conscience"—you will have guessed it—as the womb of all ideal and imaginative phenomena, also brought to light an abundance of strange new beauty and affirmation, and perhaps beauty itself.—After all, what would be "beautiful" if the contradiction had not first become conscious of itself, if the ugly had not first said to itself: "I am ugly"? [*GM,* II,16–18]

From *The Twilight of the Idols*

My demand upon the philosopher is known, that he take his stand *beyond* good and evil and leave the illusion of moral judgment *beneath* himself. This demand follows from an insight which I was the first to

Twilight of the Idols by Friedrich Nietzsche, *The Portable Nietzsche,* ed. and trans. by Walter Kaufmann. Copyright © 1963 by The Viking Press, Inc. Copyright renewed (cf. 1982 by Viking Penguin Inc. All rights reserved. Reprinted by permission of Viking Penguin Inc.

Hereafter, this work will be cited as *T.*

formulate: that *there are altogether no moral facts.* Moral judgments agree
with religious ones in believing in realities which are no realities. Morality
is merely an interpretation of certain phenomena—more precisely, a
misinterpretation. Moral judgments, like religious ones, belong to a stage
of ignorance at which the very concept of the real and the distinction
between what is real and imaginary, are still lacking; thus "truth," at this
stage, designates all sorts of things which we today call "imaginings."
Moral judgments are therefore never to be taken literally: so understood,
they always contain mere absurdity. Semeiotically, however, they remain
invaluable: they reveal, at least for those who know, the most valuable
realities of cultures and inwardnesses which did not know enough to
"understand" themselves. Morality is mere sign language, mere symptom-
atology: one must know what it is all about to be able to profit from it.

A first example, quite provisional. At all times they have wanted to
"improve" men: this above all was called morality. Under the same word,
however, the most divergent tendencies are concealed. Both the *taming*
of the beast, man, and the *breeding* of a particular kind of man have
been called "improvement." Such zoological terms are required to express
the realities—realities, to be sure, of which the typical "improver," the
priest, neither knows anything, nor wants to know anything.

To call the taming of an animal its "improvement" sounds almost
like a joke to our ears. Whoever knows what goes on in menageries
doubts that the beasts are "improved" there. They are weakened, they
are made less harmful, and through the depressive effect of fear, through
pain, through wounds, and through hunger they become sickly beasts. It
is no different with the tamed man whom the priest has "improved." In
the early Middle Ages, when the church was indeed, above all, a menagerie,
the most beautiful specimens of the "blond beast" were hunted down
everywhere; and the noble Teutons, for example, were "improved." But
how did such an "improved" Teuton who had been seduced into a
monastery look afterward? Like a caricature of man, like a miscarriage:
he had become a "sinner," he was stuck in a cage, imprisoned among
all sorts of terrible concepts. And there he lay, sick, miserable, malevolent
against himself: full of hatred against the springs of life, full of suspicion
against all that was still strong and happy. In short, a "Christian."

Physiologically speaking: in the struggle with beasts, to make them
sick *may* be the only means for making them weak. This the church
understood: it *ruined* man, it weakened him—but it claimed to have
"improved" him. [*T,* "The 'Improvers' of Mankind,"* 1, 2]

* * *

HERD INSTINCT —Wherever we encounter a morality, we also encounter valuations and an order of rank of human impulses and actions.
These valuations and orders of rank are always expressions of the needs

of a community and herd: whatever benefits it most—and second most, and third most—that is also considered the first standard for the value of all individuals. Morality trains the individual to be a function of the herd and to ascribe value to himself only as a function. The conditions for the preservation of different communities were very different; hence there were very different moralities. Considering essential changes in the forms of future herds and communities, states and societies, we can prophesy that there will yet be very divergent moralities. Morality is herd instinct in the individual. [*GS,* 116]

* * *

. . . the judgment "good" did *not* originate with those to whom "goodness" was shown! Rather it was "the good" themselves, that is to say, the noble, powerful, high-stationed and high-minded, who felt and established themselves and their actions as good, that is, of the first rank, in contradistinction to all the low, low-minded, common and plebeian. It was out of this *pathos of distance* that they first seized the right to create values and to coin names for values: what had they to do with utility! The viewpoint of utility is as remote and inappropriate as it possibly could be in face of such a burning eruption of the highest rank-ordering, rank-defining value judgments: for here feeling has attained the antithesis of that low degree of warmth which any calculating prudence, any calculus of utility, presupposes—and not for once only, not for an exceptional hour, but for good. The pathos of nobility and distance, as aforesaid, the protracted and domineering fundamental total feeling on the part of a higher ruling order in relation to a lower order, to a "below"— *that* is the origin of the antithesis "good" and "bad." . . .

It follows from this origin that the word "good" was definitely *not* linked from the first and by necessity to "unegoistic" actions. . . . Rather it was only when aristocratic value judgments *declined* that the whole antithesis "egoistic" "unegoistic" obtruded itself more and more on the human conscience—it is, to speak in my own language, the *herd instinct* that through this antithesis at last gets its word (and its *words*) in. And even then it was a long time before that instinct attained such dominion that moral evaluation was actually stuck and halted at this antithesis (as, for example, is the case in contemporary Europe: the prejudice that takes "moral," "unegoistic," *"désintéressé"* as concepts of equivalent value already rules today with the force of a "fixed idea" and brain-sickness). [*GM,* I,2]

* * *

The falseness of a judgment is for us not necessarily an objection to a judgment; in this respect our new language may sound strangest. The question is to what extent it is life-promoting, life-preserving, species-preserving, perhaps even species-cultivating. And we are fundamentally inclined to claim that the falsest judgments (which include the synthetic judgments *a priori*) are the most indispensable for us; that without accepting the fictions of logic, without measuring reality against the purely invented world of the unconditional and self-identical, without a constant falsification of the world by means of numbers, man could not live— that renouncing false judgments would mean renouncing life and a denial of life. To recognize untruth as a condition of life—that certainly means resisting accustomed value feelings in a dangerous way; and a philosophy that risks this would by that token alone place itself beyond good and evil. [*BGE,* 4]

There are no moral phenomena at all, but only a moral interpretation of phenomena—[*BGE,* 108]

* * *

TWOFOLD PREHISTORY OF GOOD AND EVIL.—The concept good and evil has a twofold prehistory: *firstly* in the soul of the ruling tribes and castes. He who has the power to requite, good with good, evil with evil, and also actually practices requital—is, that is to say, grateful and revengeful—is called good; he who is powerless and cannot requite counts as bad. As a good man one belongs to the 'good', a community which has a sense of belonging together because all the individuals in it are combined with one another through the capacity for requital. As a bad man one belongs to the 'bad', to a swarm of subject, powerless people who have no sense of belonging together. The good are a caste, the bad a mass like grains of sand. Good and bad is for a long time the same thing as noble and base, master and slave. On the other hand, one does not regard the enemy as evil: he can requite. In Homer the Trojan and the Greek are both good. It is not he who does us harm but he who is contemptible who counts as bad. . . . *Then* in the soul of the subjected, the powerless. Here every *other* man, whether he be noble or base, counts as inimical, ruthless, cruel, cunning, ready to take advantage. Evil is the characterizing expression for man, indeed for every living being one supposes to exist, for a god, for example; human, divine mean the same thing as diabolical, evil. Signs of goodness, benevolence, sympathy are received fearfully as a trick, a prelude with a dreadful termination, a means of confusing and outwitting, in short as refined wickedness. When this disposition exists in the individual a community can hardly arise, at best the most rudimentary form of community: so that wherever this conception of good and evil reigns the downfall of such individuals, of their tribes and races, is near.—Our present morality has grown up in the soil of the *ruling* tribes and castes. [*HAH, 45]*

ORIGIN OF JUSTICE.—Justice (fairness) originates between parties of approximately *equal power,* as Thucydides correctly grasped (in the terrible colloquy between the Athenian and Melian ambassadors): where there is no clearly recognizable superiority of force and a contest would result in mutual injury producing no decisive outcome the idea arises of coming to an understanding and negotiating over one another's demands: the characteristic of *exchange* is the original characteristic of justice. Each satisfies the other, inasmuch as each acquires what he values more than the other does. One gives to the other what he wants to have, to be henceforth his own, and in return receives what one oneself desires. Justice is thus requital and exchange under the presupposition of an approximately equal power position: revenge therefore belongs originally within the domain of justice, it is an exchange. Gratitude likewise.—Justice goes back naturally to the viewpoint of an enlightened self-preservation, thus to the egoism of the reflection: 'to what end should I injure myself uselessly and perhaps even then not achieve my goal?'—so much for the *origin* of justice. Since, in accordance with their intellectual habit, men have *forgotten* the original purpose of so-called just and fair actions, and especially because children have for millennia been trained to admire and imitate such actions, it has gradually come to appear that a just action is an unegoistic one: but it is on this appearance that the high value accorded it depends; and this high value is, moreover, continually increasing, as all valuations do: for something highly valued is striven for, imitated, multiplied through sacrifice, and grows as the worth of the toil and zeal expended by each individual is added to the worth of the valued thing.—How little moral would the world appear without forgetfulness! A poet could say that God has placed forgetfulness as a doorkeeper on the threshold of the temple of human dignity. [*HAH, 92*]

CUSTOM AND WHAT IS IN ACCORDANCE WITH IT.—To be moral, to act in accordance with custom, to be ethical means to practise obedience towards a law or tradition established from of old. Whether one subjects oneself with effort or gladly and willingly makes no difference, it is enough that one does it. He is called 'good' who does what is customary as if by nature, as a result of a long inheritance, that is to say easily and gladly, and this is so whatever what is customary may be (exacts revenge, for example, when exacting revenge is part of good custom, as it was with the ancient Greeks). He is called good because he is good 'for something'; since, however, benevolence, sympathy and the like have throughout all the changes in customs always been seen as 'good for something', as useful, it is now above all the benevolent, the helpful who are called 'good.' To be evil is 'not to act in accordance with custom,' to practise things not sanctioned by custom, to resist tradition, however rational or stupid that tradition may be; in all the laws of custom of all times, however, doing injury to one's neighbour has been seen as injurious above all else, so that now at the word 'evil' we think especially of voluntarily doing injury to one's neighbour. 'Egoistic' and 'unegoistic' is not the fundamental antithesis which has led men to make the distinction between 'in accordance with custom' and 'in defiance of custom', between good and evil, but adherence to a tradition, a law, and severance from it. How the tradition has *arisen* is here a matter of indifference, and has in any event nothing to do with good and evil or with any kind of immanent categorical imperative,* it is above all directed at the preservation of a *community,* a people; every superstitious usage which has arisen on the basis of some chance event mistakenly interpreted enforces a tradition which it is in accordance with custom to follow; for to sever oneself from it is dangerous, and even more injurious to the *community* than to the individual (because the gods punish the community for misdeeds and for every violation of their privileges and only to that extent punish the individual). Every tradition now continually grows more venerable the farther away its origin lies and the more this origin is forgotten; the respect paid to it increases from generation to generation, the tradition at last becomes holy and evokes awe and reverence; and thus the morality of piety is in any event a much older morality than that which demands unegoistic actions. [*HAH,* 96]

* * *

CONCEPT OF MORALITY OF CUSTOM.—In comparison with the mode of life of whole millennia of mankind we present-day men live in a very immoral age: the power of custom is astonishingly enfeebled and the moral sense so rarefied and lofty it may be described as having more or less evaporated. That is why the fundamental insights into the origin of morality are so difficult for us latecomers, and even when we have acquired them we find it impossible to enunciate them, because they sound so uncouth or because they seem to slander morality! This is, for example, already the case with the *chief proposition:* morality is nothing other (therefore *no more!*) than obedience to customs, of whatever kind they may be; customs, however, are the *traditional* way of behaving and evaluating. In things in which no tradition commands there is no morality; and the less life is determined by tradition, the smaller the circle of morality. The free human being is immoral because in all things he is *determined* to depend upon himself and not upon a tradition: in all the original conditions of mankind, 'evil' signifies the same as 'individual,' 'free', 'capricious', 'unusual', 'unforeseen', 'incalculable'. Judged by the standard of these conditions, if an action is performed *not* because tradition

---

* Kant considered the categorical imperative—defined in the *Groundwork for a Metaphysic of Morals* as 'Act as if the maxim of your action were to become through your will a universal natural law'—to derive from the nature of rationality.

commands it but for other motives (because of its usefulness to the individual, for example), even indeed for precisely the motives which once founded the tradition, it is called immoral and is felt to be so by him who performed it: for it was not performed in obedience to tradition. What is tradition? A higher authority which one obeys, not because it commands what is *useful* to us, but because it *commands.*—What distinguishes this feeling in the presence of tradition from the feeling of fear in general? It is fear in the presence of a higher intellect which here commands, of an incomprehensible, indefinite power, of something more than personal—there is *superstition* in this fear.—Originally all education and care of health, marriage, cure of sickness, agriculture, war, speech and silence, traffic with one another and with the gods belonged within the domain of morality: they demanded one observe prescriptions *without thinking of oneself* as an individual. Originally, therefore, everything was custom, and whoever wanted to elevate himself above it had to become lawgiver and medicine man and a kind of demi-god: that is to say, he had to *make customs*—a dreadful, mortally dangerous thing! . . . Let us not deceive ourselves as to the motivation of that morality which demands difficulty of obedience to custom as the mark of morality! Self-overcoming is demanded, *not* on account of the useful consequences it may have for the individual, but so that the hegemony of custom, tradition, shall be made evident in despite of the private desires and advantages of the individual: the individual is to sacrifice himself—that is the commandment of morality of custom.—Those moralists, on the other hand, who, following in the footsteps of Socrates, offer the *individual* a morality of self-control and temperance as a means to his own *advantage,* as his personal key to happiness, *are the exceptions*—and if it seems otherwise to us that is because we have been brought up in their after-effect: they all take a new path under the highest disapprobation of all advocates of morality of custom—they cut themselves off from the community, as immoral men, and are in the profoundest sense evil. Thus to a virtuous Roman of the old stamp every *Christian* who 'considered first of all his *own* salvation', appeared—evil. [*D, 9*]

DISTANT PROSPECT.—If only those actions are moral which are performed for the sake of another and only for his sake, as one definition has it, then there are no moral actions! If only those actions are moral which are performed out of freedom of will, as another definition says, then there are likewise no moral actions!—What is it then which is so *named* and which in any event exists and wants explaining? It is the effects of certain intellectual mistakes.—And supposing one freed oneself from these errors, what would become of 'moral actions'?—By virtue of these errors we have hitherto accorded certain actions a higher value than they possess: we have segregated them from the 'egoistic' and 'unfree' actions. If we now realign them with the latter, as we shall have to do, we shall certainly *reduce* their value (the value we feel they possess), and indeed shall do so to an unfair degree, because the 'egoistic' and 'unfree' actions were hitherto evaluated too low on account of their supposed profound and intrinsic difference.—Will they from then on be performed less often because they are now valued less highly?—Inevitably! At least for a good length of time, as long as the balance of value-feelings continues to be affected by the reaction of former errors! But our counter-reckoning is that we shall restore to men their goodwill towards the actions decried as egoistic and restore to these actions their *value—we shall deprive them of their bad conscience!* And since they have hitherto been by far the most frequent actions, and will continue to be so for all future time, we thus remove from the entire aspect of action and life its *evil appearance!* This is a very significant result! When man no longer regards himself as evil he ceases to be so! [*D,* 148]

* * *

THE INNOCENT ELEMENT IN SO-CALLED EVIL ACTS.—All 'evil' acts are motivated by the drive to preservation or, more exactly, by the individual's intention of procuring pleasure and avoiding displeasure; so motivated, however, they are not evil. 'Procuring pain as such' *does not exist,* except in the brains of philosophers, neither does 'procuring pleasure as such' (pity in the Schopenhauerian sense).—The evil acts at which we are now most indignant rest on the error that he who perpetrates them against us possesses free will, that is to say, that he could have *chosen* not to cause us this harm. It is this belief in choice that engenders hatred, revenge-fulness, deceitfulness, all the degrading our imagination undergoes, while we are far less censorious towards an animal because we regard it as unaccountable. To do injury not from the drive to preservation but as requital—is the consequence of a mistaken judgment and therefore likewise innocent. [*HAH,* 99]

'MAN'S ACTIONS ARE ALWAYS GOOD.'—We do not accuse nature of immorality when it sends us a thunderstorm and makes us wet: why do we call the harmful man immoral? Because in the latter case we assume a voluntarily commanding free will, in the former necessity. But this distinction is an error. And then: we do not call even intentional harming immoral under all circumstances; one unhesitatingly kills a fly intention-ally, for example, merely because one does not like its buzzing, one punishes the criminal intentionally and does him harm so as to protect ourselves and society. In the first instance it is the individual who, to preserve himself or even merely to avoid displeasure, intentionally does harm; in the second it is the state. All morality allows the intentional causing of harm in the case of self-defence: that is, when it is a matter of *self-preservation.* But these two points of view *suffice* to explain all evil acts perpetrated by men against men: one desires pleasure or to ward off displeasure; it is always in some sense a matter of self-preservation. Socrates and Plato are right: whatever man does he always does the good, that is to say: that which seems to him good (useful) according to the relative degree of his intellect, the measure of his rationality. [*HAH,* 102]

UNACCOUNTABILITY AND INNOCENCE.—The complete unaccountability of man for his actions and his nature is the bitterest draught the man of knowledge has to swallow if he has been accustomed to seeing in accountability and duty the patent of his humanity. All his evaluations, all his feelings of respect and antipathy have thereby become disvalued and false: his profoundest sentiment, which he accorded to the sufferer, the hero, rested upon an error; he may no longer praise, no longer censure, for it is absurd to praise and censure nature and necessity. As he loves a fine work of art but does not praise it since it can do nothing for itself, as he stands before the plants, so must he stand before the actions of men and before his own. He can admire their strength, beauty, fullness, but he may not find any merit in them: the chemical process and the strife of the elements, the torment of the sick man who yearns for an end to his sickness, are as little merits as are those states of distress and psychic convulsions which arise when we are torn back and forth by conflicting motives until we finally choose the most powerful of them— as we put it (in truth, however, until the most powerful motive chooses us). But all these motives, whatever exalted names we may give them, have grown up out of the same roots as those we believe evilly poisoned; between good and evil actions there is no difference in kind, but at the most one of degree. Good actions are sublimated evil ones; evil actions are coarsened, brutalized good ones. It is the individual's sole desire for self-enjoyment (together with the fear of losing it) which gratifies itself in every instance, let a man act as he can, that is to say as he must: whether his deeds be those of vanity, revenge, pleasure, utility, malice, cunning, or those of sacrifice, sympathy, knowledge. Degrees of intelligent judgement decide whither each person will let his desire draw him; every society, every individual always has present an order of rank of things considered good, according to which he determines his own actions and judges those of others. But this standard is continually changing, many actions are called evil but are only stupid, because the degree of intelligence which decided for them was very low. Indeed, in a certain sense *all* present actions are stupid, for the highest degree of human intelligence which can now be attained will certainly be exceeded in the future: and then all our actions and judgements will seem in retrospect as circumscribed and precipitate as the actions and judgements of still existing primitive peoples now appear to us. To perceive all this can be very painful, but then comes a consolation: such pains are birth-pangs. The butterfly wants to get out of its cocoon, it tears at it, it breaks it open: then it is blinded and confused by the unfamiliar light, the realm of freedom. It is in such men as are *capable* of that suffering—how few they will be!—that the first attempt will be made to see whether mankind could *transform itself from a moral to a knowing mankind.* The sun of a new gospel is casting its first beam on the topmost summits in the soul of every individual: there the mists are gathering more thickly than ever, and the brightest glitter and the gloomiest twilight lie side by side. Everything is necessity— thus says the new knowledge; and this knowledge itself is necessity. Everything is innocence: and knowledge is the path to insight into this innocence. If pleasure, egoism, vanity are *necessary* for the production of the moral phenomena and their finest flower, the sense for truth and justice in knowledge; if error and aberration of the imagination was the only means by which mankind was able gradually to raise itself to this degree of self-enlightenment and self-redemption—who could venture to denigrate those means? Who could be despondent when he becomes aware of the goal to which those paths lead? It is true that everything in the domain of morality has become and is changeable, unsteady, everything is in flux: but *everything is also flooding forward,* and towards *one* goal. Even if the inherited habit of erroneous evaluation, loving, hating does continue to rule in us, under the influence of increasing knowledge it will grow weaker: a new habit, that of comprehending, not-loving, not-hating, surveying is gradually implanting itself in us on the same soil and will in thousands of years' time perhaps be strong enough to bestow on mankind the power of bringing forth the wise, innocent (conscious of innocence) man as regularly as it now brings forth—*not his antithesis but necessary preliminary*—the unwise, unjust, guilt-conscious man. [*HAH,* 107]

* * *

WHAT PRESERVES THE SPECIES.—The strongest and most evil spirits have so far done the most to advance humanity: again and again they relumed the passions that were going to sleep—all ordered society puts the passions to sleep—and they reawakened again and again the sense of comparison, of contradiction, of the pleasure in what is new, daring, untried; they compelled men to pit opinion against opinion, model against model. Usually by force of arms, by toppling boundary markers, by violating pieties—but also by means of new religions and moralities. In every teacher and preacher of what is *new* we encounter the same "wickedness" that makes conquerors notorious, even if its expression is subtler and it does not immediately set the muscles in motion, and therefore also does not make one that notorious. What is new, however, is always *evil*, being that which wants to conquer and overthrow the old boundary markers and the old pieties; and only what is old is good. The good men are in all ages those who dig the old thoughts, digging deep and getting them to bear fruit—the farmers of the spirit. But eventually all land is exploited, and the ploughshare of evil must come again and again.

Nowadays there is a profoundly erroneous moral doctrine that is celebrated especially in England: this holds that judgments of "good" and "evil" sum up experiences of what is "expedient" and "inexpedient." One holds that what is called good preserves the species, while what is called evil harms the species. In truth, however, the evil instincts are expedient, species-preserving, and indispensable to as high a degree as the good ones; their function is merely different. [*GS*, 4]

TO THE TEACHERS OF SELFISHNESS.—A man's virtues are called *good* depending on their probable consequences not for him but for us and society: the praise of virtues has always been far from "selfless," far from "unegoistic." Otherwise one would have had to notice that virtues (like industriousness, obedience, chastity, filial piety, and justice) are usually harmful for those who possess them, being instincts that dominate them too violently and covetously and resist the efforts of reason to keep them in balance with their other instincts. When you have a virtue, a real, whole virtue (and not merely a mini-instinct for some virtue), you are its *victim*. But your neighbor praises your virtue precisely on that account. . . . The praise of the selfless, the self-sacrificial, the virtuous— that is, of those who do not apply their whole strength and reason to their own preservation, development, elevation, promotion, and the expansion of their power, but rather live, in relation to themselves, modestly and thoughtlessly, perhaps even with indifference or irony—this praise certainly was not born from the spirit of selflessness. The "neighbor" praises selflessness *because it brings him advantages.* If the neighbor himself were "selfless" in his thinking, he would repudiate this diminution of strength, this mutilation for *his* benefit; he would work against the development of such inclinations, and above all he would manifest his selflessness by *not* calling it *good!*

This indicates the fundamental contradiction in the morality that is very prestigious nowadays: the *motives* of this morality stand opposed to its *principle*. What this morality considers its proof is refuted by its criterion of what is moral. [*GS*, 21]

* * *

The most concerned ask today: "How is man to be preserved?" But Zarathustra is the first and only one to ask: "How is man to be overcome?"

I have the overman at heart, *that* is my first and only concern—

and *not* man: not the neighbor, not the poorest, not the most ailing, not the best.

O my brothers, what I can love in man is that he is an overture and a going under. And in you too there is much that lets me love and hope. That you despise, you higher men, that lets me hope. For the great despisers are the great reverers. That you have despaired, in that there is much to revere. For you did not learn how to surrender, you did not learn petty prudences. For today the little people lord it; they all preach surrender and resignation and prudence and industry and consideration and the long etcetera of the small virtues. . . .

Overcome these masters of today, O my brothers—these small people, *they* are the overman's greatest danger.

You higher men, overcome the small virtues, the small prudences, the grain-of-sand consideration, the ants' riffraff, the wretched contentment, the "happiness of the greatest number"!

"Man is evil"—thus said all the wisest to comfort me. Alas, if only it were still true today! For evil is man's best strength.

"Man must become better and more evil"—thus *I* teach. The greatest evil is necessary for the overman's best. It may have been good for that preacher of the little people that he suffered and tried to bear man's sin. But I rejoice over great sin as my great consolation. [*Z*, Pt. IV, "On the Higher Man," 3, 5]

From *Human, All Too Human*

Nietzsche's Critique of Christianity

Before we go on to exhibit this condition the Christian need of redemption in its further consequences let us confess to ourselves that the man in this condition has got into it, not through his 'guilt' and 'sin,' but through a succession of errors of reason, that it was the fault of the mirror if his nature appeared to him dark and hateful to such a degree, and that this mirror was *his* work, the very imperfect work of human imagination and judgement. Firstly, a being capable of nothing but unegoistic actions is more fabulous than the phoenix; it cannot even be imagined clearly, if only because under strict examination the whole concept 'unegoistic action' vanishes into thin air. No man has ever done anything that was done wholly for others and with no personal motivation whatever; how, indeed, should a man be *able* to do something that had no reference to himself, that is to say lacked all inner compulsion (which would have its basis in a personal need)? How could the ego act without the ego?—On the other hand, a God who was *wholly* love, as is occasionally supposed, would be incapable of a single unegoistic action: in connection with which one should recall a thought of Lichtenberg's, though it was, to be sure, taken from a somewhat lower sphere: 'It is impossible, as is commonly said, for us to *feel* for others; we feel only for ourselves. The proposition sounds hard, but is not if it is correctly understood. One loves neither father, nor mother, nor wife, nor child, one loves the pleasant sensations they produce in us', or as La Rochefoucauld says: *si on croit aimer sa maîtresse pour l'amour d'elle, on est bien trompé'*. . . . If, however, a man should wish to be, like that God, wholly love, and to do and desire everything for others and nothing for himself, then the latter is impossible simply because he has to do a *great deal* for himself if he is to be able to do anything whatever for the sake of others. . . .— Further: the idea of a God is disturbing and humiliating as long as it is believed, but how it *originated* can at the present stage of comparative ethnology no longer admit of doubt; and with the insight into this origination that belief falls away. But if the idea of God falls away, so does the feeling of 'sin' as a transgression against divine precepts, as a blemish on a creature consecrated to God. Then there probably still remains over that feeling of depression which is very much entwined with and related to fear of punishment by secular justice or the disapprobation of other men; the depression caused by the pang of conscience, the sharpest sting in the feeling of guilt, is nonetheless abolished when one sees that, although one may by one's actions have offended against human tradition, human laws and ordinances, one has not therewith endangered the 'eternal salvation of the soul' and its relationship to the divinity. If a man is, finally, able to attain to the philosophical conviction of the unconditional necessity of all actions and their complete unaccountability and to make it part of his flesh and blood, then that remainder of the pang of conscience also disappears.

Now if, as has been said, the Christian has got into the feeling of self-contempt through certain errors, that is to say through a false, un-scientific interpretation of his actions and sensations, he also notices with the highest astonishment that this condition of contempt, the pang of conscience, displeasure in general, does not persist, but that occasionally there are hours when all this is wafted away from his soul and he again feels free and valiant. What has happened is that his pleasure in himself, his contentment at his own strength, has, in concert with the weakening which every profound excitation must necessarily undergo, carried off the victory: he loves himself again, he feels it—but precisely this love, this new self-valuation seems to him incredible, he can see in it only the wholly undeserved flowing down of a radiance of mercy from on high. If he earlier believed he saw in every event warnings, menaces, punishments and every sort of sign of divine wrath, he now *interprets* divine goodness *into* his experiences: this event appears to him to exhibit kindness, that is like a helpful signpost, a third and especially the whole joyful mood he is in seems to him proof that God is merciful. If he earlier in a condition of depression interpreted his actions falsely, now he does the same with his experiences; he conceives his mood of consolation as the effect upon him of an external power, the love with which fundamentally he loves himself appears as divine love; that which he calls mercy and the prelude to redemption is in truth self-pardon, self-redemption.

Thus: a certain false psychology, a certain kind of fantasy in the interpretation of motives and experiences is the necessary presupposition for becoming a Christian and for feeling the need of redemption. With the insight into this aberration of reason and imagination one ceases to be a Christian. [*HAH,* 133–135]

* * *

Against this theologians' instinct I wage war: I have found its traces everywhere. Whoever has theologians' blood in his veins, sees all things in a distorted and dishonest perspective to begin with. The pathos which develops out of this condition calls itself *faith:* closing one's eyes to oneself once and for all, lest one suffer the sight of incurable falsehood. This faulty perspective on all things is elevated into a morality, a virtue, a holiness; the good conscience is tied to faulty vision; and no *other* perspective is conceded any further value once one's own has been made sacrosanct with the names of "God," "redemption," and "eternity." I have dug up the theologians' instinct everywhere: it is the most widespread, really *subterranean,* form of falsehood found on earth.

Whatever a theologian feels to be true *must* be false: this is almost a criterion of truth. His most basic instinct of self-preservation forbids him to respect reality at any point or even to let it get a word in. Wherever the theologians' instinct extends, *value judgments* have been stood on their heads and the concepts of "true" and "false" are of necessity reversed: whatever is most harmful to life is called "true"; whatever elevates it, enhances, affirms, justifies it, and makes it triumphant, is called "false." When theologians reach out for *power* through the "conscience" of princes (*or* of peoples), we need never doubt what really happens at bottom: the will to the end, the *nihilistic* will, wants power.

In Christianity neither morality nor religion has even a single point of contact with reality. Nothing but imaginary *causes* ("God," "soul," "ego," "spirit," "free will"—for that matter, "unfree will"), nothing but imaginary *effects* ("sin," "redemption," "grace," "punishment," "forgiveness of sins"). Intercourse between imaginary *beings* ("God," "spirits," "souls"); an imaginary *natural* science (anthropocentric; no trace of any concept of natural causes); an imaginary *psychology* (nothing but self-misunderstandings, interpretations of agreeable or disagreeable general feelings—for example, of the states of the *nervus sympathicus*—with the aid of the sign language of the religio-moral idiosyncrasy: "repentance," "pangs of conscience," "temptation by the devil," "the presence of God"); an imaginary *teleology* ("the kingdom of God," "the Last Judgment," "eternal life").

This *world of pure fiction* is vastly inferior to the world of dreams insofar as the latter *mirrors* reality, whereas the former falsifies, devalues, and negates reality. Once the concept of "nature" had been invented as the opposite of "God," "natural" had to become a synonym of "reprehensible": this whole world of fiction is rooted in *hatred* of the natural (of reality!); it is the expression of a profound vexation at the sight of reality.

But this explains everything. Who alone has good reason to lie his way out of reality? He who suffers from it. But to suffer from reality is to be a piece of reality that has come to grief. The preponderance of feelings of displeasure over feelings of pleasure is the cause of this fictitious morality and religion; but such a preponderance provides the very formula for decadence.

A critique of the *Christian conception of God* forces us to the same conclusion. A people that still believes in itself retains its own god. In him it reveres the conditions which let it prevail, its virtues: it projects its pleasure in itself, its feeling of power, into a being to whom one may offer thanks. Whoever is rich wants to give of his riches; a proud people needs a god: it wants to *sacrifice.* Under such conditions, religion is a form of thankfulness. Being thankful for himself, man needs a god. Such a god must be able to help and to harm to be friend and enemy—he is admired whether good or destructive. The *anti-natural* castration of a god to make him a god of the good alone, would here be contrary to everything desirable. The evil god is needed no less than the good god: after all, we do not owe our own existence to tolerance and humanitarianism.

What would be the point of a god who knew nothing of wrath, revenge, envy, scorn, cunning, and violence? who had perhaps never experienced the delightful *ardeurs* of victory and annihilation? No one would understand such a god: why have him then?

To be sure, when a people is perishing, when it feels how its faith in the future and its hope of freedom are waning irrevocably, when submission begins to appear to it as the prime necessity and it becomes aware of the virtues of the subjugated as the conditions of self-preservation, then its god *has to* change too. Now he becomes a sneak, timid and modest; he counsels "peace of soul," hate-no-more, forbearance, even "love" of friend and enemy. He moralizes constantly, he crawls into the cave of every private virtue, he becomes god for everyman, he becomes a private person, a cosmopolitan.

Formerly he represented a people, the strength of a people, everything aggressive and power-thirsty in the soul of a people; now he is merely the good god.

Indeed, there is no other alternative for gods: *either* they are the will to power, and they remain a people's gods, *or* the incapacity for power, and then they necessarily become *good.*

Wherever the will to power declines in any form, there is invariably also a physiological retrogression, decadence. The deity of decadence, gelded in his most virile virtues and instincts, becomes of necessity the god of the physiologically retrograde, of the weak. Of course, they do not *call* themselves the weak; they call themselves "the good."

No further hint is required to indicate the moments in history at which the dualistic fiction of a good and an evil god first became possible. The same instinct which prompts the subjugated to reduce their god to the "good-in-itself" also prompts them to eliminate all the good qualities from the god of their conquerors; they take revenge on their masters by turning their god into the *devil.* The *good* god and the devil—both abortions of decadence.

How can anyone today still submit to the simplicity of Christian theologians to the point of insisting with them that the development of the conception of God from the "God of Israel," the god of a people, to the Christian God, the quintessence of everything good, represents *progress?* Yet even Renan does this. As if Renan had the right to be simple-minded! After all, the opposite stares you in the face. When the presuppositions of *ascending* life, when everything strong, brave, masterful, and proud is eliminated from the conception of God; when he degenerates step by step into a mere symbol, a staff for the weary, a sheet-anchor for the drowning; when he becomes the god of the poor, the sinners, and the sick par excellence, and the attribute "Savior" or "Redeemer" remains in the end as the one essential attribute of divinity—just *what* does such a transformation signify? what, such as *reduction* of the divine?

To be sure, "the kingdom of God" has thus been enlarged. Formerly he had only his people, his "chosen" people. Then he, like his people, became a wanderer and went into foreign lands; and ever since, he has not settled down anywhere—until he finally came to feel at home anywhere, this great cosmopolitan—until "the great numbers" and half the earth were on his side. Nevertheless, the god of "the great numbers," the democrat among the gods, did not become a proud pagan god: he remained a Jew, he remained a god of nooks, the god of all the dark corners and places, of all the unhealthy quarters the world over!

His world-wide kingdom is, as ever, an underworld kingdom, a hospital, a *souterrain* kingdom, a ghetto kingdom. And he himself: so pale, so weak, so decadent. Even the palest of the pale were able to master him: our honorable metaphysicians, those concept-albinos. They spun their webs around him until, hypnotized by their motions, he himself became a spider, another metaphysician. Now he, in turn, spun the world out of himself—*sub specie Spinozae.* Now he transfigured himself into something ever thinner and paler; he became an "ideal," he became "pure spirit," the "Absolute," the "thing-in-itself." The deterioration of a god: God became the "thing-in-itself."

The Christian conception of God—God as god of the sick, God as a spider, God as spirit—is one of the most corrupt conceptions of the divine ever attained on earth. It may even represent the low-water mark in the descending development of divine types. God degenerated into the *contradiction* of life, instead of being its transfiguration and eternal Yes! God as the declaration of war against life, against nature, against the will to live! God—the formula for every slander against "this world," for every lie about the "beyond"! God—the deification of nothingness, the will to nothingness pronounced holy! [*A,* 9, 15–18]

*   *   *

Philosophers are accustomed to speak of the will as if it were the best-known thing in the world; indeed, Schopenhauer has given us to understand that the will alone is really known to us, absolutely and completely known, without subtraction or addition. But again and again it seems to me that in this case, too, Schopenhauer only did what philosophers are in the habit of doing—he adopted a *popular prejudice* and exaggerated it. Willing seems to me to be above all something *complicated,* something that is a unit only as a word—and it is precisely in this one word that the popular prejudice lurks, which has defeated the always inadequate caution of philosophers. So let us for once be more cautious, let us be "unphilosophical": let us say that in all willing there is, first, a plurality of sensations, namely, the sensation of the state *"away from which,"* the sensation of the state *"towards which,"* the sensations of this *"from"* and *"towards"* themselves, and then also an accompanying muscular sensation, which, even without our putting into motion "arms and legs," begins its action by force of habit as soon as we "will" anything.

Therefore, just as sensations (and indeed many kinds of sensations) are to be recognized as ingredients of the will, so, secondly, should thinking also: in every act of the will there is a ruling thought—let us not imagine it possible to sever this thought from the "willing," as if any will would then remain over!

Third, the will is not only a complex of sensation and thinking, but it is above all an *affect,* and specifically the affect of the command. That which is termed "freedom of the will" is essentially the affect of superiority in relation to him who must obey: "I am free, 'he' must obey"—this consciousness is inherent in every will; and equally so the straining of the attention, the straight look that fixes itself exclusively on one aim, the unconditional evaluation that "this and nothing else is necessary now," the inward certainty that obedience will be rendered—and whatever else belongs to the position of the commander. A man who *wills* commands something within himself that renders obedience, or that he believes renders obedience.

But now let us notice what is strangest about the will—this manifold thing for which the people have only one word: inasmuch as in the given circumstances we are at the same time the commanding *and* the obeying parties, and as the obeying party we know the sensations of constraint, impulsion, pressure, resistance, and motion, which usually begin immediately after the act of will; inasmuch as, on the other hand, we are accustomed to disregard this duality, and to deceive ourselves about it by means of the synthetic concept "I," a whole series of erroneous conclusions, and consequently of false evaluations of the will itself, has become attached to the act of willing—to such a degree that he who wills believes sincerely that willing *suffices* for action. Since in the great majority of cases there has been exercise of will only when the effect of the command—that is, obedience; that is, the action—was to be *expected,* the *appearance* has translated itself into the feeling, as if there were *a necessity of effect.* In short, he who wills believes with a fair amount of certainty that will and action are somehow one; he ascribes the success, the carrying out of the willing, to the will itself, and thereby enjoys an increase of the sensation of power which accompanies all success.

"Freedom of the will"—that is the expression for the complex state of delight of the person exercising volition, who commands and at the same time identifies himself with the executor of the order—who, as such, enjoys also the triumph over obstacles, but thinks within himself that it was really his will itself that overcame them. In this way the person exercising volition adds the feelings of delight of his successful executive instruments, the useful "underwills" or under-souls—indeed, our body is but a social structure composed of many souls—to his feelings of delight as commander. . . . In all willing it is absolutely a question of commanding and obeying, on the basis, as already said, of a social structure composed of many "souls." Hence a philosopher should claim the right to include willing as such within the sphere of morals—morals being understood as the doctrine of the relations of supremacy under which the phenomenon of "life" comes to be. [*BGE,* 19]

* * *

THE FABLE OF INTELLIGIBLE FREEDOM.—The principal stages in the history of the sensations by virtue of which we make anyone accountable for his actions, that is to say, of the moral sensations, are as follows. First of all, one calls individual actions good or bad quite irrespective of their motives but solely on account of their useful or harmful consequences. Soon, however, one forgets the origin of these designations and believes that the quality 'good' and 'evil' is inherent in the actions themselves, irrespective of their consequences: thus committing the same error as that by which language designates the stone itself as hard, the tree itself as green—that is to say, by taking for cause that which is effect. Then one consigns the being good or being evil to the motives and regards the deeds in themselves as morally ambiguous. One goes further and accords the predicate good or evil no longer to the individual motive but to the whole nature of a man out of whom the motive grows as the plant does from the soil. Thus one successively makes men accountable for the effects they produce, then for their actions, then for their motives, and finally for their nature. Now one finally discovers that this nature, too, cannot be accountable, inasmuch as it is altogether a necessary consequence and assembled from the elements and influence of things past and present: that is to say, that man can be made accountable for nothing, not for his nature, nor for his motives, nor for his actions, nor for the effects he produces. One has thereby attained to the knowledge that the history of the moral sensations is the history of an error, the error of accountability, which rests on the error of freedom of will. . . . No one is accountable for his deeds, no one for his nature; to judge is the same thing as to be unjust. This also applies when the individual judges himself. The proposition is as clear as daylight, and yet here everyone prefers to retreat back into the shadows and untruth: from fear of the consequences. [*HAH*, 39]

From *The Wanderer and His Shadow*

WHERE THE THEORY OF FREEDOM OF WILL ORIGINATED.—Over one man *necessity* stands in the shape of his passions, over another as the habit of hearing and obeying, over a third as a logical conscience, over

The Wanderer and His Shadow, Part Two of Vol. 2, *Human, All Too Human* by Friedrich Nietzsche, trans. by R. J. Hollingdale. Copyright © 1986 by Cambridge University Press. Reprinted with the permission of Cambridge University Press.
    Hereafter, this work will be cited as *WS*.

a fourth as caprice and a mischievous pleasure in escapades. These four will, however, seek the *freedom* of their will precisely where each of them is most firmly fettered: it is as if the silkworm sought the freedom of its will in spinning. How does this happen? Evidently because each considers himself most free where his *feeling of living* is greatest; thus, as we have said, in passion, in duty, in knowledge, in mischievousness respectively. That through which the individual human being is strong, wherein he feels himself animated, he involuntarily thinks must also always be the element of his freedom: he accounts dependence and dullness, independence and the feeling of living as necessarily coupled.—Here an experience in the social-political domain has been falsely transferred to the farthest metaphysical domain: in the former the strong man is also the free man; the lively feeling of joy and sorrow, high hope, boldness in desire, powerfulness in hatred is the property of the rulers and the independent, while the subjected man, the slave, lives dull and oppressed.—The theory of freedom of will is an invention of *ruling* classes.

FEELING NO NEW CHAINS.—So long as we do not *feel* that we are dependent on anything we regard ourselves as independent: a false conclusion that demonstrates how proud and lusting for power man is. For he here assumes that as soon as he experiences dependence he must under all circumstances notice and recognize it, under the presupposition that he is *accustomed* to living in independence and if, exceptionally, he lost it, he would at once perceive a sensation antithetical to the one he is accustomed to.—But what if the opposite were true: that he is *always* living in manifold dependence but regards himself *as free* when, out of long habituation, he *no longer perceives* the weight of the chains? It is only from *new* chains that he now suffers:—'freedom of will' really means nothing more than feeling no new chains. [*WS*, 9, 10]

HAVE THE ADHERENTS OF THE THEORY OF FREE-WILL THE RIGHT TO PUNISH?—People who judge and punish as a profession try to establish in each case whether an ill-doer is at all accountable for his deed, whether he was *able* to employ his intelligence, whether he acted for *reasons* and not unconsciously or under compulsion. If he is punished, he is punished for having preferred the worse reasons to the better: which he must therefore have *known*. Where this knowledge is lacking a man is, according to the prevailing view, unfree and not responsible: except if his lack of knowledge, his *ignorantia legis** for example, is a result of an intentional neglect to learn; in which case, when he failed to learn what he should have learned he had already preferred the worse reasons to the better and must now suffer the consequences of his bad choice. If, on the other

---

* *ignorantia legis:* ignorance of the law

hand, he did not see the better reasons, perhaps from dull-wittedness or weakness of mind, it is not usual to punish him: he lacked, one says, the capacity to choose, he acted as an animal would. For an offence to be punishable presupposes that its perpetrator intentionally acted contrary to the better dictates of his intelligence. But how can anyone intentionally be less intelligent than he has to be? Whence comes the decision when the scales are weighted with good and bad motives? Not from error, from blindness, not from an external nor from an internal compulsion? (Consider, moreover, that every so-called 'external compulsion' is nothing more than the internal compulsion of fear and pain.) Whence? one asks again and again. The *intelligence* is not the cause, because it could not decide against the better reasons? And here one calls 'free-will' to one's aid: it is *pure wilfulness* which is supposed to decide, an impulse is supposed to enter within which motive plays no part, in which the deed, arising out of nothing, occurs as a miracle. It is this supposed *wilfulness,* in a case in which wilfulness ought not to reign, which is punished: the rational intelligence, which knows law, prohibition and command, ought to have permitted no choice, and to have had the effect of compulsion and a higher power. Thus the offender is punished because he employs 'free-will', that is to say, because he acted without a reason where he ought to have acted in accordance with reasons. Why did he do this? But it is precisely this question that can no longer even be *asked:* it was a deed without a 'for that reason', without motive, without origin, something purposeless and non-rational.—*But such a deed too ought,* in accordance with the first condition of all punishability laid down above, *not to be punished*! It is not as if something had *not* been done here, something omitted, the intelligence had *not* been employed: for the omission is under all circumstances *unintentional*! and only the intentional omission to perform what the law commands counts as punishable. The offender certainly preferred the worse reasons to the better, but *without* reason or intention: he certainly failed to employ his intelligence, but not *for the purpose* of not employing it. The presupposition that for an offence to be punishable its perpetrator must have intentionally acted contrary to his intelligence—it is precisely this presupposition which is annulled by the assumption of 'free-will'. You adherents of the theory of 'free-will' *have no right* to punish, your own principles deny you that right!—But these are at bottom nothing but a very peculiar conceptual mythology; and the hen that hatched it sat on her eggs in a place far removed from reality. [*WS,* 23]

THE ERROR OF A FALSE CAUSALITY.—People have believed at all times that they knew what a cause is; but whence did we take our knowledge— or more precisely, our faith that we had such knowledge? From the realm of the famous "inner facts," of which not a single one has so far proved to be factual. We believed ourselves to be causal in the act of willing: we thought that here at least we caught causality in the act. Nor did one doubt that all the antecedents of an act, its causes, were to be sought in consciousness and would be found there once sought—as "motives": else one would not have been free and responsible for it. Finally, who would have denied that a thought is caused? that the ego causes the thought?

Of these three "inward facts" which seem to guarantee causality, the first and most persuasive is that of the will as cause. The conception of a consciousness ("spirit") as a cause, and later also that of the ego as cause (the "subject"), are only afterbirths: first the causality of the will was firmly accepted as given, as *empirical.*

Meanwhile we have thought better of it. Today we no longer believe a word of all this. The "inner world" is full of phantoms and will-o'-the-wisps: the will is one of them. The will no longer moves anything, hence does not explain anything either—it merely accompanies events; it can also be absent. The so-called *motive:* another error. Merely a surface phenomenon of consciousness, something alongside the deed that is more likely to cover up the antecedents of the deeds than to represent them. And as for the *ego!* That has become a fable, a fiction, a play on words: it has altogether ceased to think, feel, or will!

What follows from this? There are no mental causes at all. The whole of the allegedly empirical evidence for that has gone to the devil. That is what follows! And what a fine abuse we had perpetrated with this "empirical evidence"; we *created* the world on this basis as a world of causes, a world of will, a world of spirits. The most ancient and enduring psychology was at work here and did not do anything else: all that happened was considered a doing, all doing the effect of a will; the world became to it a multiplicity of doers; a doer (a "subject") was slipped under all that happened. It was out of himself that man projected his three "inner facts"—that in which he believed most firmly, the will, the spirit, the ego. He even took the concept of being from the concept of the ego; he posited "things" as "being," in his image, in accordance with his concept of the ego as a cause. Small wonder that later he always found in things only that *which he had put into them.* The thing itself, to say it once more, the concept of thing is a mere reflex of the faith in the ego as cause. And even your atom, my dear mechanists and physicists—how much error, how much rudimentary psychology is still residual in your atom! Not to mention the "thing-in-itself," the *horrendum pudendum* of the metaphysicians! The error of the spirit as cause mistaken for reality! And made the very measure of reality! And called God!

THE WHOLE REALM OF MORALITY AND RELIGION BELONGS UNDER THIS CONCEPT OF IMAGINARY CAUSES.—The "explanation" of *disagreeable* general feelings. They are produced by beings that are hostile to us (evil spirits: the most famous case—the misunderstanding of the hysterical as witches). They are produced by acts which cannot be approved (the feeling of "sin," of "sinfulness," is slipped under a physiological discomfort; one always finds reasons for being dissatisfied with oneself). They are produced as punishments, as payment for something we should not have done, for what we should not have *been* (impudently generalized by Schopenhauer into a principle in which morality appears as what it really is—as the very poisoner and slanderer of life: "Every great pain, whether physical or spiritual, declares what we deserve; for it could not come to us if we did not deserve it." *World as Will and Representation* II, 666). They are produced as effects of ill-considered actions that turn out badly. (Here the affects, the senses, are posited as causes, as "guilty"; and physiological calamities are interpreted with the help of other calamities as "deserved.")

The "explanation" of *agreeable* general feelings. They are produced by trust in God. They are produced by the consciousness of good deeds (the so-called "good conscience"—a physiological state which at times looks so much like good digestion that it is hard to tell them apart). They are produced by the successful termination of some enterprise (a naive fallacy: the successful termination of some enterprise does not by any means give a hypochondriac or a Pascal agreeable general feelings). They are produced by faith, charity, and hope—the Christian virtues.

In truth, all these supposed explanations are resultant states and, as it were, translations of pleasurable or unpleasurable feelings into a false dialect: one is in a state of hope *because* the basic physiological feeling is once again strong and rich; one trusts in God *because* the feeling of fullness and strength gives a sense of rest. Morality and religion belong altogether to the *psychology of error:* in every single case, cause and effect are confused; or truth is confused with the effects of *believing* something to be true; or a state of consciousness is confused with its causes.

THE ERROR OF FREE WILL.—Today we no longer have any pity for the concept of "free will": we know only too well what it really is—the foulest of all theologians' artifices, aimed at making mankind "responsible" in their sense, that is, *dependent upon them.* Here I simply supply the psychology of all "making responsible."

Wherever responsibilities are sought, it is usually the instinct of wanting to judge and punish which is at work. Becoming has been deprived of its innocence when any being-such-and-such is traced back to will, to purposes, to acts of responsibility: the doctrine of the will has been invented essentially for the purpose of punishment, that is, because one wanted to impute guilt. The entire old psychology, the psychology of will, was conditioned by the fact that its originators, the priests at the head of ancient communities, wanted to create for themselves the right to punish—or wanted to create this right for God. Men were considered "free" so that they might be judged and punished—so that they might become *guilty:* consequently, every act had to be considered as willed, and the origin of every act had to be considered as lying within the consciousness (and thus the most fundamental counterfeit *in psychologicis* was made the principle of psychology itself).

Today, as we have entered into the reverse movement and we immoralists are trying with all our strength to take the concept of guilt and the concept of punishment out of the world again, and to cleanse psychology, history, nature, and social institutions and sanctions of them, there is in our eyes no more radical opposition than that of the theologians, who continue with the concept of a "moral world-order" to infect the innocence of becoming by means of "punishment" and "guilt." Christianity is a metaphysics of the hangman.

What alone can be *our* doctrine? That no one *gives* man his qualities—neither God, nor society, nor his parents and ancestors, nor he himself. (The nonsense of the last idea was taught as "intelligible freedom" by Kant—perhaps by Plato already.) No one is responsible for man's being there at all, for his being such-and-such, or for his being in these circumstances or in this environment. The fatality of his essence is not to be disentangled from the fatality of all that has been and will be. Man is not the effect of some special purpose, of a will, and end; nor is he the object of an attempt to attain an "ideal of humanity" or an "ideal of happiness" or an "ideal of morality." It is absurd to wish to devolve one's essence on some end or other. We have invented the concept of "end": in reality there is no end.

One is necessary, one is a piece of fatefulness, one belongs to the whole, one is in the whole; there is nothing which could judge, measure, compare, or sentence our being, for that would mean judging, measuring, comparing, or sentencing the whole. But there is nothing besides the whole. That nobody is held responsible any longer, that the mode of being may not be traced back to a *causa prima,* that the world does not form a unity either as a sensorium or as "spirit"—that alone is the great liberation; with this alone is the innocence of becoming restored. The concept of "God" was until now the greatest objection to existence. We deny God, we deny the responsibility in God: only thereby do we redeem the world. [*T,* The Four Great Errors, 3, 6–8]

* * *

THE GREATEST ADVANTAGE OF POLYTHEISM.—For an individual to posit his own ideal and to derive from it his own law, joys, and rights—that may well have been considered hitherto as the most outrageous human aberration and as idolatry itself. The few who dared as much always felt the need to apologize to themselves, usually by saying: "It wasn't I! Not I! But *a god* through me." The wonderful art and gift of creating gods—polytheism—was the medium through which this impulse could discharge, purify, perfect, and ennoble itself; for originally it was a very undistinguished impulse, related to stubbornness, disobedience, and envy. Hostility against this impulse to have an ideal of one's own was formerly the central law of all morality. There was only one norm, *man;* and every people thought that it possessed this one ultimate norm. But above and outside, in some distant overworld, one was permitted to behold a *plurality of norms;* one god was not considered a denial of another god, nor blasphemy against him. It was here that the luxury of individuals was first permitted; it was here that one first honored the rights of individuals. The invention of gods, heroes, and overmen of all kinds, as well as near-men and undermen, dwarfs, fairies, centaurs, satyrs, demons, and devils was the inestimable preliminary exercise for the justification of the egoism and sovereignty of the individual: the freedom that one conceded to a god in his relation to other gods—one eventually also granted to oneself in relation to laws, customs, and neighbors.

Monotheism, on the other hand, this rigid consequence of the doctrine of one normal human type—the faith in one normal god beside whom there are only pseudo-gods—was perhaps the greatest danger that has yet confronted humanity. It threatened us with the premature stagnation that, as far as we can see, most other species have long reached; for all of them believe in one normal type and ideal for their species, and they have translated the morality of mores definitively into their own flesh and blood. In polytheism the free-spiriting and many-spiriting of man attained its first preliminary form—the strength to create for ourselves our own new eyes—and ever again new eyes that are even more our own: hence man alone among all the animals has no eternal horizons and perspectives. [*GS,* 143]

* * *

The philosopher as *we* understand him, we free spirits—as the man of the most comprehensive responsibility who has the conscience for the over-all development of man—this philosopher will make use of religions for his project of cultivation and education, just as he will make use of whatever political and economic states are at hand. The selective and cultivating influence, always destructive as well as creative and form-giving, which can be exerted with the help of religions, is always multiple and different according to the sort of human beings who are placed under its spell and protection. For the strong and independent who are prepared and predestined to command and in whom the reason and art of a governing race become incarnate, religion is one more means for overcoming resistances, for the ability to rule—as a bond that unites rulers and subjects and betrays and delivers the consciences of the latter, that which is most concealed and intimate and would like to elude obedience, to the former. And if a few individuals of such noble descent are inclined through lofty spirituality to prefer a more withdrawn and contemplative life and reserve for themselves only the most subtle type of rule (over selected disciples or brothers in some order), then religion can even be used as a means for obtaining peace from the noise and exertion of *cruder* forms of government, and purity from the *necessary* dirt of all politics. . . .

Meanwhile religion also gives to some of the ruled the instruction and opportunity to prepare themselves for future ruling and obeying: those slowly ascending classes—in which, thanks to fortunate marital customs, the strength and joy of the will, the will to self-control is ever growing—receive enough nudges and temptations from religion to walk the paths to higher spirituality, to test the feelings of great self-overcoming, of silence and solitude. . . .

To ordinary human beings, finally—the vast majority who exist for service and the general advantage, and who *may* exist only for that— religion gives an inestimable contentment with their situation and type, manifold peace of the heart, an ennobling of obedience, one further happiness and sorrow with their peers and something transfiguring and beautifying, something of a justification for the whole everyday character, the whole lowliness, the whole half-brutish poverty of their souls. Religion and religious significance spread the splendor of the sun over such ever-toiling human beings and make their own sight tolerable to them.

In the end, to be sure—to present the other side of the account of these religions, too, and to expose their uncanny dangerousness—one always pays dearly and terribly when religions do *not* want to be a means of education and cultivation in the philosopher's hand but insist on having their own *sovereign* way, when they themselves want to be ultimate ends and not means among other means. There is among men as in every other animal species an excess of failures, of the sick, degenerating, infirm, who suffer necessarily; the successful cases are, among men too, always the exception—and in view of the fact that man is the *as yet undetermined animal,* the rare exception. But still worse: the higher the type of man that a man represents, the greater the improbability that he will turn out *well.* The accidental, the law of absurdity in the whole economy of mankind, manifests itself most horribly in its destructive effect on the higher men whose complicated conditions of life can only be calculated with great subtlety and difficulty.

What, then, is the attitude of the above-mentioned two greatest religions toward this *excess* of cases that did not turn out right? They seek to preserve, to preserve alive whatever can possibly be preserved; indeed, as a matter of principle, they side with these cases as religions for *sufferers;* they agree with all those who suffer life like a sickness and would like to make sure that every other feeling about life should be considered false and should become impossible. Even if the very highest credit is given to this considerate and preserving care, which, besides being directed toward all the others, was and is also directed toward the highest type of man, the type that so far has almost always suffered most; nevertheless, in a total accounting, the *sovereign* religions we have had so far are among the chief causes that have kept the type "man" on a lower rung—they have preserved too much of *what ought to perish*. What we have to thank them for is inestimable; and who could be rich enough in gratitude not to be impoverished in view of all that the "spiritual men" of Christianity, for example, have so far done for Europe! And yet, when they gave comfort to sufferers, courage to the oppressed and despairing, a staff and support to the dependent, and lured away from society into monasteries and penitentiaries for the soul those who had been destroyed inwardly and who had become savage: how much more did they have to do besides, in order to work with a good conscience and on principle, to preserve all that was sick and that suffered—which means, in fact and in truth, to *worsen the European race?* Stand all valuations *on their head—that* is what they had to do. And break the strong, sickly o'er great hopes, cast suspicion on the joy in beauty, bend everything haughty, manly, conquering, domineering, all the instincts characteristic of the highest and best-turned-out type of "man," into unsureness, agony of conscience, self-destruction—indeed, invert all love of the earthly and of dominion over the earth into hatred of the earth and the earthly— *that* is the task the church posed for itself and had to pose, until in its estimation "becoming unworldly," "unsensual," and "higher men" were fused into a single feeling. . . .

I meant to say: Christianity has been the most calamitous kind of arrogance yet. Men, not high and hard enough to have any right to try to form *man* as artists; men, not strong and farsighted enough to *let* the foreground law of thousandfold failure and ruin prevail, though it cost them sublime self-conquest; men, not noble enough to see the abysmally different order of rank, chasm of rank, between man and man—*such* men have so far held sway over the fate of Europe, with their "equal before God," until finally a smaller, almost ridiculous type, a herd animal, something eager to please, sickly, and mediocre has been bred, the European of today—[*BGE,* 61–62]

* * *

FOR THE NEW YEAR.—I still live, I still think: I still have to live, for I still have to think. . . . Today everybody permits himself the expression of his wish and his dearest thought; hence I, too, shall say what it is that I wish from myself today, and what was the first thought to run across my heart this year—what thought shall be for me the reason, warranty, and sweetness of my life henceforth. I want to learn more and more to see as beautiful what is necessary in things; then I shall be one of those who make things beautiful. *Amor fati:* let that be my love henceforth! I do not want to wage war against what is ugly. I do not want to accuse; I do not even want to accuse those who accuse. *Looking away* shall be my only negation. And all in all and on the whole: some day I wish to be only a Yes-sayer. [*GS,* 276]

THE GREATEST WEIGHT.—What, if some day or night a demon were to steal after you into your loneliest loneliness and say to you: "This life as you now live it and have lived it, you will have to live once more and innumerable times more; and there will be nothing new in it, but every pain and every joy and every thought and sigh and everything unutterably small or great in your life will have to return to you, all in the same succession and sequence—even this spider and this moonlight between the trees, and even this moment and I myself. The eternal hourglass of existence is turned upside down again and again, and you with it, speck of dust!"

Would you not throw yourself down and gnash your teeth and curse the demon who spoke thus? Or have you once experienced a tremendous moment when you would have answered him: "You are a god and never have I heard anything more divine." If this thought gained possession of you, it would change you as you are or perhaps crush you. The question in each and every thing, "Do you desire this once more and innumerable times more?" would lie upon your actions as the greatest weight. Or how well disposed would you have to become to yourself and to life *to crave nothing more fervently* than this ultimate eternal confirmation and seal? [*GS,* 341]

4

Martin Heidegger

HEIDEGGER AND THE PROBLEM OF BEING

Martin Heidegger (1889–1976), like the other philosophers we have previously considered, is concerned with directing our attention to the existentialist subject matter, the existing individual, or in his terminology *Dasein*. Unlike Kierkegaard and Nietzsche, however, he approaches this subject matter by way of a technical philosophical problem in metaphysics, namely, the problem of Being. Although Heidegger gives us a detailed account of the Dasein and has many interesting things to say about the human situation, he is not primarily concerned with the existing individual, or Dasein. Rather the central task of *Being and Time* is to clarify the problem of Being, and his examination of Dasein is of importance primarily because it is an essential preparatory step to accomplish that task. To see why he thought that a consideration of Dasein is the only way we can become clear about Being, we must first try to understand the problem of Being.

Suppose I call the piece of chalk I am holding in my hand "x." Then to the question "What is x?" one may give the following replies:

1. X is, or X is an existent.
2. X is a piece of chalk.
3. The x I am holding in my hand is the x you are looking at.

4. This x is white.
5. This x is chalk.

As these responses make clear, the verb *to be* can be used in several different senses: It corresponds (1) to the "is" of existence; (2) to the "is" of essence; (3) to the "is" of identity; (4) to the "is" of predication; and (5) to the "is" of composition. The problem of Being qua Being, the problem of Being in its most general form, is the problem of understanding what the verb to be signifies in all its various senses. The first two uses; (1) the "is" of existence and (2) the "is" of essence, are the most fundamental, for we would not bother with (3) through (5) unless we first knew that x existed and what x is. The "is" of existence, however, is the most fundamental of all senses of the verb *to be* because unless something exists the question of what kind of being it is does not arise.

Heidegger's fundamental concern is with Being in the sense of "existence." He does not mean "existence" merely as applied to human existence; nor is his concern with Being a concern with the question of whether or not a certain particular entity or kind of entity exists. Rather, Heidegger is concerned with the general metaphysical question of what it means for something to exist: What is the meaning of Being?

To get a sense of the puzzling nature of this question, all we need to do is consider some of the ways in which it has been answered. Some have said that "to exist" means "to be perceived," or more plausibly, "to be perceivable." But that will not do, since for something to be perceived or perceivable, it must already exist. Similarly, the familiar account of existence, according to which "x exists" means that "x is in space and time," is also circular. Since x must exist in order to be in space and time, we are left with the question at the start of our inquiry, namely, "What does it mean *to be* in space and time?"

Another possibility, explicitly rejected by Heidegger, is the view that the meaning of Being is an entity—existence—that some entities possess and some do not. The paradoxical nature of this gambit should be evident. Since x would not exist if existence did not attach onto it, how could x or anything else for that matter come to exist? Before existence attached onto an entity it would be nothing, but then how could existence attach onto it? How could nothing come to possess existence? We would have to claim that an entity must pre-exist in order for existence to attach onto it, but then we would have to explain what it means to say that an entity "pre-exists." Are we not merely presupposing the concept of existence once again?

Furthermore, if existence is an entity, then either it exists or it does not. If it does not, then it cannot attach onto anything. And if existence exists, then existence must attach onto it, and we are off on an infinite regress in which existence attaches onto existence, which attaches onto existence ad infinitum. For reasons such as these Heidegger is quite explicit in maintaining that "The Being of entities 'is' not itself an entity" (p. 194).

What, then, is the meaning of Being? The question is difficult for us to answer because Being is peculiar: It is, in a sense, hidden from us. Whenever we think of or perceive a thing we are at once confronted with its essence or nature. When we perceive that a thing exists we are at once confronted by what it is. Conversely, we have difficulty grasping a thing's nature without at the same time grasping that it exists. Even when we think of an abstract possibility, we must think of that possibility as existing. Thus, as a result of the hidden nature of being, its indistinguishability from essence, the problem of the meaning of Being has tended to be forgotten; we have "fallen from Being." And yet, there is a distinction between existence and essence, and there is a problem of existence. For if it is sometimes true to say that "this chalk might not have existed," then it is also intelligible to assert that "this chalk exists." What, then, are we asserting when we assert that "this (x) exists"?

All entities, including Dasein, have Being and thus in some vague sense we must already know what it is that we are seeking. But which entity shall we take for our example, and why shall we assign it priority? Heidegger has claimed to have discovered a way in which we can grasp the nature of existence, namely by attending to human being, Dasein. For in Dasein the distinction between essence and existence is most clear. As Heidegger puts it,

> Dasein always understands itself in terms of its existence—in terms of a possibility of itself: to be itself or not itself. Dasein has either chosen these possibilities itself, or got itself into them, or grown up in them already. Only the particular Dasein decides its existence, whether it does so by taking hold or by neglecting. The question of existence never gets straightened out except through existing itself. (p. 196)

There is a sense in which what we are—our essence—is a result of what we do—our existence. What I am is the result of what I choose, design, or wish to be. Thus, to the extent that we think of ourselves as persons who make decisions and choices, what we are is determined by the decisions and choices we have made, are making, and will make. Since, however, these choices and this essence are produced by me, there must be a distinction between my existence and my essence: I exist in order to produce my essence, which is completed only at death. For it is only at death that I cease to make those choices that go into determining my essence. Thus, in Dasein there is a chasm separating existence from essence. Since I must first exist in order to be what I am, I must have an understanding of existence. Thus,

> Dasein is an entity which does not just occur among other entities. Rather it is ontically distinguished by the fact that, in its very Being, that Being is an issue for it. . . . And this means . . . that there is some way in which Dasein understands itself in its Being, and that to some degree it does so explicitly. It is peculiar to this entity that which and through its Being, this Being is disclosed to it. *Understanding of Being is itself a definite characteristic of Dasein's Being.* (p. 196)

Look at it this way. Suppose that we include in our essence everything that can be said about us up to the present moment. Considering myself I can truly say that I am a white American male, I weigh (approximately) 150 pounds, I am a teacher, have green eyes, I was born in the Bronx, I went to the University of Iowa, and so on. All these facts about me are part of what I am, they are part of my essence, but they do not constitute my complete essence. My essence continues to grow, expand, and change throughout the period of my existence. Although many of these facts are such before I am aware of them, eventually there comes a time in our lives when we become self-conscious: conscious of what we are and what we have been and that we exist as Beings who must choose a possible future or essence for ourselves. That is, at some point in our lives we become conscious that our existence—that we are—is separate from our essence—what we are—since we must first exist in order to produce our essence.

That I have a body is part of my essence and so is not something that I have any control over, but what I do with my body, for example, the presence or absence of my body from this room, is up to me. In our own case we can and do distinguish between what we are and what we will be, and recognize that what we will be, our future and completed essence, depends upon what we choose to be and not upon what we have been. Thus, since our complete essence is not determined until our last act is complete, it follows that we must first exist in order to determine what we are and moreover, that each of us must, in our own case, understand what existence is. Or, to use a slogan made popular by Jean-Paul Sartre, in the case of human Being, existence precedes essence. In this respect Dasein differs from objects that are "ready-at-hand"—objects that are made by humans in a state of civilization—since with regard to such objects essence precedes existence. What they are and what they will do is fixed before they exist, but in the case of Dasein there is first an understanding, however vague, of one's own existence. Only then does the individual through this or that particular decision create its essence.[1]

Thus, Heidegger offers an analysis of Dasein not for its own sake but because he thinks that we can best grasp the meaning of Being by attending to the peculiar and unique kind of Being that belongs to Dasein. His inquiry into the Being of Dasein takes the form of an existential analysis, which concerns giving an account of the basic constitution of human existence as such, specifying the various structures or levels in terms of which we can understand the essence of human life. Yet, his approach to the "existential" question takes its cue from a consideration of Dasein in its everydayness. That is, by a phenomenological investigation into the "existentiell" issue of how Dasein is to understand and decide its own existence in concrete situations, we will be led to an existential understanding of the theoretical structure of Dasein.

Heidegger believes that an examination of the several structures of human Being will enable us to understand the structure of existence as such. However, our concern with the structures of Dasein will only relate to them as they are applicable to human life apart from their relation to the philosophical question of the meaning of Being.

It is useful to outline the different levels or structures in virtue of which Dasein can be understood, since they form the framework of the discussion to follow.

1. Being-in-the world
   a. State-of-mind *(Befindlichkeit)*
   b. Discourse or talk
   c. Understanding
2. Care
   a. Being-already-in (a world)
   b. Being-alongside (entities encountered within the world).
   c. Being-ahead-of itself.
3. Inauthentic
   a. Facticity
   b. Fallenness
   c. Existentiality
4. Authentic
   a. Guilt
   b. Conscience
   c. Resolve
5. Time
   a. Past
   b. Present
   c. Future

Heidegger refers to these structures and the moments or aspects of them as "ontological" features of human life, by which he means that they state necessary or essential features of Dasein. Yet one might wonder how a being as unique and unlike all other kinds of objects in the world can have an essence. This apparent difficulty can be resolved by distinguishing two senses of "essence." According to the first, something has an "essence" if there are laws that govern the behavior of all members of the kind to which it belongs. Dasein does not, in that sense, have an essence because, according to the existentialists, there are no laws that can predict all human behavior. We are basically agents free from the causal process.

The typical existentialist argument for this anti-deterministic stance is not based on dialectical arguments, but on phenomenological considerations. Thus, in connection with the question of whether all human behavior is governed by laws of nature, the existentialist typically appeals to the phenomenological awareness of freedom—the obviously observable features of choice situations—as the basis for a denial of "essence."

On the other hand, we can make necessarily true claims about the existing individual. That is, although we cannot invariably predict how humans will behave, we can assert absolute truths about the human condition and the various structures of Dasein. The various existentialia within those structures do just that. We should note, however, that these different levels are not separate and distinct, but should be thought of as being superimposed on one another. There is a single Being, Dasein, who is all of these things. Indeed, the different aspects of each level are themselves inseparable from each other because Dasein's Being cannot be understood piecemeal; Dasein is a unitary Being. We can begin to see this by considering the first primordial structure of Dasein, Being-in-the-world. (When Heidegger talks about the "primordial" structures of Dasein, he is referring to those features of Dasein that result from an accurate description of our "primitive" (untheoretical) experience of the world.) Before we turn to Heidegger's description of Dasein as a "Being-in-the-world," we will briefly consider the method by which Heidegger (and Sartre) attempt to accomplish their purposes, namely, the *phenomenological method.*

The phenomenological method was developed by Edmund Husserl (1859–1938), and although Husserl was not himself an existentialist his method of analysis has been taken over by existentialists. In contrast to the rationalist approach to reality where knowledge of reality is obtained through reason alone, the phenomenological approach is radically empiricist. That is, the data that forms the starting point of phenomenological investigations are not how we think about or conceptualize a certain subject matter, but how we directly encounter and experience it, how it is given to us in experience. Thus, for example, when we experience the world, we take it for granted that there is a world, and our theoretical speculations (science and traditional philosophy) seek to understand the nature of the world and not our experience of it. When we adopt a phenomenological attitude, however, we attend to our experience (awareness) of the world. Once this "shift" of attention or focus is accomplished, the phenomenological method (as Heidegger and Sartre practice it) involves a detailed description of how the world, including the self, is given to the awareness of the phenomenological observer. In phenomenological description and analysis we make explicit what "presents itself" in our experience of the world and our place in it. For Heidegger the method is intended to disclose Being as such, but for reasons we have considered he approaches this task through a phenomenological investigation of Dasein.

DASEIN AS BEING-IN-THE-WORLD

How is Dasein related to the world? Indeed, what is the world for Dasein? Essentially, Dasein is a Being-in-the-world. The hyphens are meant to indicate that there is a sense in which Dasein cannot be separated from the world and the world cannot be separated from Dasein, for Dasein is the world and the world is Dasein. We can come to grasp the meaning of these enigmatic remarks by contrasting Heidegger's attitude about the relation between Dasein and the world with two opposing attitudes.

When we speak of ordinary objects of practical life such as tables, chairs, beds, sofas, pencils, and the like, as being in the world, we are viewing the world as something like a huge container with various things in it. Thus, we speak of the sofa as being in the living room. This involves a spatial relationship between one thing and another completely different thing. On this model, Dasein is like any other object: It exists as one among many objects in the world.

Another relationship that Dasein has with the world is a cognitive relationship: Dasein knows the world. Dasein as an I or a knowing subject is somehow apart from the world, separated from the world, and standing in a detached intellectual relationship to it. Viewed in this way Dasein is not an object in the world at all, but rather the world is an object for Dasein, a subject that lies beyond the world.

For Heidegger, neither of these two attitudes captures the meaning of the relationship between Dasein and the world. Dasein is not a Being outside the world, nor is Dasein an object among objects within the world. The connection between Dasein and the world is much too intimate to be understood spatially, and Dasein's primitive relation to the world is not a cognitive one. Rather, there is a sense in which I am inseparable from the world and the world is inseparable from me. That is, Being-in-the-world is a unitary phenomenon.

To see what is involved, recall that Dasein is a Being whose essence is determined by what it makes of itself. What I am is what I have created, what I am creating, and what I will create. There are, of course, objects that Dasein has not created, for example, the air, the oceans, the moon, and so on, but much of the world is what Dasein has created. Insofar as we think of Dasein as human being in a state of civilization, much of the world is an organized set of objects that Dasein has created. Thus, when we think of the world in terms of objects "ready-at-hand" we recognize that to grasp the world we must grasp Dasein, since Dasein makes there to be a world. Conversely, to grasp Dasein we must grasp the world, since human beings cannot be understood apart from what they do, and what they do is create objects in the world. Moreover, Dasein is not simply located in the world, but may be said more accurately to "dwell alongside" the world understood as a vast instrumental system held together by Dasein's concerns and creations. Thus, for Heidegger, the world and Dasein are inseparable, for "Ontologically, 'world' is not a way of characterizing those entities which Dasein essentially is not; it is rather a characteristic of Dasein itself."[2]

With this background we are ready to consider the different aspects of Dasein's Being-in-the-world. To understand Dasein as a Being-in-the-world is to understand Dasein as a being with a place in the world, as a being that understands its place in the world, and as a being that has dealings with the world. We are agents that choose some possible world and some possible essence for ourselves on the basis of our situation and through communication. These are the aspects of Being-in-the-world: State-of-mind, understanding, and discourse, and in what follows we attempt to explain them.

Moods are a familiar and obvious everyday sort of occurrence. For Heidegger they are phenomena that reveal very fundamental aspects of our Being. He says that

> In having a mood, Dasein is always disclosed moodwise as that entity to which it has been delivered over in its Being; and in this way it has been delivered over to the Being which, in existing, it has to be. (p. 208)

In other words, our moods reveal to us the fact that we are "thrown" into the world and thus to a certain extent our life has a definite character regardless of our choices. In my own case there are certain facts that I can do nothing about. For example, I was born in the twentieth century to white Jewish parents in New York City. These and many others are facts that I must deal with. Through our moods we become conscious that our present essence is partially determined by the place in the world in which we find ourselves, and thus that there are certain facts about ourselves and our situation over which we have no control. Our state-of-mind points to the fact that our situation in life already contains a great many givens that we can do nothing about.

An equally primordial or fundamental state of Being-in-the-world is understanding. Our state of mind makes us aware of our being thrown into a situation already created, but together with that awareness is an equally basic awareness of our having a future and of there being possibilities awaiting our future. As Heidegger puts it,

> . . . as thrown, Dasein is thrown into the kind of Being which we call "projecting." Projecting has nothing to do with comporting oneself towards a plan that has been thought out, and in accordance with which Dasein arranges its Being. On the contrary, any Dasein has, as Dasein, already projected itself; and as long as it is, it is projecting. As long as it is, Dasein always has understood itself and always will understand itself in terms of possibilities. (p. 210)

Dasein, in sharp contrast to things that are "present-at-hand" (objects there by nature) and "ready-at-hand" (objects created by humans in a state of civilization), projects itself into the future. Dasein is "thrown potentiality," since the awareness of our place in the world carries with it understanding: *"the existential Being of Dasein's own potentiality-for-Being"* (p. 209). Thrownness carries with it a disclosure of possible ways of structuring the world in the future. Indeed, I cannot be conscious of my situation without at the same time realizing that I have a future situation to create, that I have to go someplace from where I presently find myself. Thus, state-of-mind and understanding are inseparable, and they are equally inseparable from discourse. To emphasize the unity of the aspects of Being-in-the-world Heidegger maintains that *"Discourse is existentially equiprimordial with state-of-mind and understanding"* (p. 211).

This entity which is placed in the world is necessarily dealing with the world, and our dealings with the world essentially involve speech, discourse, or talk. By "discourse" Heidegger means any meaningful behavior between human beings, a spontaneous and natural behavior that we engage in. Discourse is inseparable from our state-of-mind, since our conception of ourselves as having a place in the world is dependent on our interaction with other people, and this is primarily through discourse. Indeed, without discourse we would have no conception of the world at all. Furthermore, discourse is equiprimordial with understanding, in that we express our future and make our future understood through speech. Indeed, Dasein could not intelligibly deal with the world through speech unless it understood itself. How, for example, could I communicate my thoughts to you in this section unless I had some idea of what I will be communicating in the next paragraph and the next section?

Thus, the three aspects of Being-in-the-world are inseparable; none can be made intelligible apart from the other. These three notions signify how we understand ourselves in the world. We have a place in the world, we are agents with a task awaiting us, a future to create, and we are dealing with the world through discourse.

DASEIN'S BEING AS CARE

To understand Dasein's Being as *Care* is to grasp the sense in which the different structures of Dasein and the different existentialia within each structure comprise a *single entity.* For Heidegger, the various aspects of human life

> . . . are not pieces belonging to something composite, one of which might sometimes be missing; but there is woven together in them a primordial context which makes up the totality of the structural whole which we are seeking. . . . How is this unity itself to be characterized? (p. 213)

In response to this question Heidegger claims, *"Temporality reveals itself as the meaning of authentic care"* (p. 234). In what follows we endeavor to explain the sense in which temporality provides a unity to Dasein.

There is one point we need to emphasize at the outset. Like Nietzsche and (as we shall see) Sartre, Heidegger rejects the conception of the self as consisting of a substratum or separately existing entity that is only contingently connected to its experiences and the world it inhabits. For Heidegger, I am not a Being that could be separated from the world or from others. Rather my Being is inseparably connected with my Being-in-the-world and my Being-with-others. Although the self is not a substance distinct from its experiences, the self is a single unity, not capable of being broken up into temporal parts. Thus, he rejects any conception of the self that would treat it as a succession of different experiences somehow related to form a single whole. For Heidegger, the "I" is

> what maintains itself as something identical throughout changes in its Experiences and ways of behavior, and which relates itself to this changing multiplicity in so doing. (p. 205)

Dasein is a *continuant* that retains its strict identity through time: It cannot be divided into a multiplicity of temporal parts. What, then, constitutes the unity of Dasein?

In order to answer the question, "What makes the unity of a single life possible?" we must, according to Heidegger, take into account what I *have been,* what *I am,* and what *I will be,* that is, the past, present, and future of Dasein. We must not, however, think of the past, present, and future of Dasein as three separate entities that are somehow connected. The past, present, and future of Dasein are *one* in a sense in which the past, present, and future of a piece of chalk are not. In the case of a piece of chalk you can divide its history into successive slices and you can understand what the chalk is at each moment without knowing anything about any of its other temporal parts. What the chalk was in the past can be understood without knowing what it is, or if it is, in the present. And we can completely understand the past of a piece of chalk even if we know nothing of its future. In other words, ordinary objects *can* be thought of as a succession of temporal parts, some of which are past, others of which are future, and one of which is present. Moreover, we can understand what a piece of chalk is by viewing any temporal part of it in isolation from any other. In the case of Dasein, however, you cannot separate the past, present, and future and regard them as three distinct features of Dasein. For you cannot understand what Dasein is by examining one temporal part. You cannot understand Dasein's past apart from Dasein's present and future, its present apart from its past and future, or its future apart from its present and past. The past, present, and future of Dasein are one, and each cannot be understood apart from the other. Indeed, it is precisely the inseparability of Dasein's past, present, and future that constitute the unity of Care.

To see why and how this is so, note that to understand Dasein's future, it is necessary to understand the future that Dasein projects for itself. However, the future that Dasein projects for itself can be understood only as the future that has grown out of the past and present of a single Dasein. It is the past and present of Dasein that makes intelligible our future choices. For example, I cannot understand what it would be like to be faced with a certain choice thirty minutes from now apart from my past and present. I have to decide in the future whether or not to keep writing this text, but I can only understand what it would be like to be faced with that decision because in the past I have spent time working on this book and at present I am writing it. What I am going to do, the future essence I shall create for myself, can be made intelligible only in the light of what I have made of myself in the past and what I am making of myself at the present moment. In short, my future is inseparable from my past and present.

Furthermore, my present is inseparably connected with my past and future. I can understand what I am doing only if I connect it with what I have done in the past. For what I am doing now makes sense only if it is seen as a logical outgrowth of what I have done before. For example, my present writing of this text makes sense only insofar as it is understood to be the logical continuation of what I have written before. Similarly, to understand who I am now, you must understand what I intend to be, for my present actions make sense only in the light of what I see them as leading to. To understand me now you must understand how my present actions are related to what I want to be. Thus, each element of the human story is logically dependent on the other in such a way that Dasein cannot be understood piecemeal. We cannot understand Dasein by viewing an isolated temporal aspect. To understand Dasein we must view Dasein as an indivisible whole, a single being that does not have distinct temporal parts.

The unity of Dasein can also be seen by noting that my past cannot be understood apart from my present and future. I can understand my past only insofar as I can understand how and why my past gave rise to what I am now and what I hope to be in the future. Still differently, the interpretation that we give to our past actions must take into account what I am doing and what I will do: my present and my future. Thus, the different aspects of *Care* and *Temporality* are not really different. They are different aspects of Dasein that are really inseparable characteristics of one and the same entity. There is a single Dasein that is past, present, and future.

DASEIN AS AUTHENTIC AND INAUTHENTIC AND AS BEING-TOWARDS-DEATH

To grasp the Being of Dasein is to grasp that Dasein is not simply a composite totality with many different aspects, but a structural whole, all of whose characteristics are inseparably united. Thus, we should not view the different levels, or even the different aspects of each level, as isolated phenomena but rather picture each level as superimposed on the other. Since Dasein is a unity our task is to see how these various ways of structuring Dasein are interrelated. Accordingly, in approaching the levels of inauthentic and authentic we shall ask, "In what ways is Dasein as inauthentic and authentic related to Dasein as a Being-in-the-world, Care, and Temporality?" A useful place to begin our discussion is with what Heidegger has to say about the topic of *death.*

At the levels of authentic and inauthentic, Heidegger is primarily concerned with the uniqueness of Dasein—how Dasein is totally unlike anything else—and that is why Heidegger reaches these two levels of Dasein by a consideration of the phenomenon of death. For by viewing Dasein as something which faces death we get at the inner nature of Dasein, Dasein's uniqueness. This is because *death individualizes each of us from all other objects* (present-at-hand and ready-at-hand), and it *individualizes us from all other human beings.*

Death individualizes us from all other objects because only Dasein reaches its "wholeness" in death. At death Dasein comes to an end; there are no longer any possibilities in its future, since Dasein is no longer a Being-in-the-world capable of projecting and acting on future possibilities.

Yet, in the very ceasing to be of Dasein there is a coming to be of the essence of Dasein. In other words, Dasein is not "whole" until death, for when it ceases to exist it then acquires a kind of Being that it never had when it was alive and making choices.

Look at it this way: Until my last act I am "thrown potentiality," in that I am placed into a world in which I must choose a possible future for myself. I must first exist in order to create my Being, which Being is not whole until I cease to exist. Thus, when I die I achieve a certain kind of being—an essence—that I never really had when I was alive. In the case of a piece of chalk or a tree, on the other hand, the reverse is true. For ordinary objects, their essence precedes their existence. On the basis of this difference we may say that death individualizes Dasein from all objects.

A consideration of death points to our uniqueness in a second way. *Death individualizes or isolates each of us from all other individuals.* What Heidegger has in mind is this. In general, and with regard to virtually everything that we do, we are replaceable. As Heidegger says, "Indisputably, the fact that one Dasein *can be represented* by another belongs to its possibilities of Being in Being-with-one-another in the world" (p. 216). Heidegger's point here is that since one is what one does, and since what we do can always be done by someone else, we are, as it were, specimens of a kind substitutable without qualification by any other member of the species *homo sapiens.* And yet there is a sense in which this is not true, for there is something that is absolutely unique about me, and about which I am irreplaceable, namely, my death. As Heidegger puts it,

> [T]his possibility of representing breaks down completely if the issue is one of representing that possibility-of-Being which makes up Dasein's coming to an end, and which, as such, gives to it its wholeness. *No one can take the Other's dying away from him. . . .* Dying is something that every Dasein itself must take upon itself at the time. By its very essence, death is in every case mine, in so far as it 'is' at all. (p. 216)

Thus, dying has existential significance. It is that about which Dasein is absolutely unique and irreplaceable, and it constitutes the wholeness of Dasein. The phenomenon of death because it is unique to each existing individual can help us to understand the distinction between Dasein as inauthentic and Dasein as authentic, and it can also lead to existential self-awareness. Before we see why and how this is so we briefly consider Heidegger's *Preliminary Sketch of the Existential-Ontological Structure of Death* (p. 217).

We have seen that for Heidegger, death constitutes the totality of Dasein and it is the point at which Dasein reaches wholeness. We have also seen that for Heidegger, death is not just one event among many for Dasein, but that it is a basic and distinctive feature of the Being of

Dasein. In his preliminary sketch of death Heidegger attempts to reinforce these points by defining death in terms of the characteristics of Care and Being-in-the-world.

Heidegger claims that "death reveals itself as that *possibility which is one's ownmost, which is non-relational, and which is not to be outstripped*" (p. 218). These crucial aspects of death can be understood in terms of the distinctive elements of Care and Being-in-the-world. Death as a possibility is not one possibility among many; it is the possibility of there being no more possibilities. In this respect death corresponds to understanding and Being-ahead-of-itself. Dasein is thrown into the world of its concern (Being-already-in-the world), and through its state-of-mind has disclosed to itself its Being-towards-the-end. It is thrown into a possibility which is not to be outstripped, in that death is an inevitable and necessary possible. It is a fact that we are thrown into Being-towards-the-end just as it is a fact that we are thrown into living in a nuclear age. However, our communicating about death (Being-alongside) primarily and for the most part is by way of *falling*. That is, our typical dealings with death involve fleeing in the face of it, attempting to avoid it. Thus, death is essential to Dasein's Being, for we can understand the basic structures of death in terms of the basic structures of Being that we have so far considered. According to Heidegger, this brief existential-ontological account of death asserting as it does the connection between Being-in-the-world, Care, and death needs to be given a phenomenological justification where "we must be able to see this connection above all in that concretion which lies closest to Dasein—its everydayness" (p. 219).

In our everydayness we live in the "they," in that we tend to think of ourselves as "das man" or human being in general. We view ourselves not as individuals, but as members of a kind. In much the same way the common everyday mode of Being-towards-death is inauthentic. Our ordinary attitude toward death treats it as something that happens to everyone in the end, but right now it has nothing to do with me. Someone or other dies or "one dies," and one's own death is thought of as a "one like many." It is a biological fact, an event that happens to all living things, but not one that I must especially concern myself with.

This way of viewing death amounts to a flight from the fact of one's own individual death. We avoid facing our own death by viewing it as a certain objective event that is encountered in the world. But to view death as an event among events is to fail to face the fact of the uniqueness of one's own death and the uniqueness of oneself. It avoids the realization that death constitutes the end of one's own Dasein and that therefore one has to continually create what one will be until the possibility of there being no more possibilities is realized.

The attempt to avoid facing the fact of one's own death takes ingenious forms. We try to convince the dying person that he or she will escape death as a way of consoling the person and keeping his or her ownmost non-relational possibility-of-Being completely concealed.

> In this manner the "they" provides *a constant tranquillization about death.* At bottom, however, this is a tranquillization not only for him who is 'dying' but just as much for those who 'console' him. (p. 220)

Further, the "they" tries to tranquilize our anxiety in the face of death by transforming it into an approaching event which it is cowardly to fear. The result of branding the anxiety over death, fear, and fear, cowardice, is to alienate Dasein from its ownmost possibility, and this is the mark of *falling:*

> As falling, everyday Being-towards-death is a constant *fleeing in the face of death.* Being-*towards*-the-end has the mode of *evasion in the face of it*— giving new explanations for it, understanding it inauthentically, and concealing it. . . . But in thus falling and fleeing *in the face of* death, Dasein's everydayness attests that the very "they" itself already has the definite character of *Being-towards-death,* even when it is not explicitly engaged in 'thinking about death.' (p. 221)

In other words, however much we try to avoid facing the fact of our own death, we are inevitably confronted with it. Indeed, the very act of concealing death assumes that there is something to be concealed and that we know it. This feature of self-deception is given a careful analysis by Sartre. Now we turn to a consideration of the possibility of Dasein's understanding authentically its Being-towards-death.

To view death authentically does not necessarily involve acting in a different way, but it does involve understanding one's own death differently. Dasein is authentic insofar as it understands its uniqueness. Thus, to view one's own death authentically involves facing the fact that one's own death is unique and not a "one like many." It involves facing the fact of one's own death and not trying to escape it by viewing it as an objective fact that happens to everyone. Further, to view death authentically is to realize that death is the end of our possibilities or potentialities and that one is free to determine what possibilities or choices will precede the one that cannot be overcome. As Heidegger puts it,

> Anticipation, . . . unlike inauthentic Being-towards-death, does not evade the fact that death is not to be outstripped; instead, anticipation frees itself *for* accepting this. When, by anticipation, one becomes free *for* one's own death, one is liberated from one's lostness in those possibilities which may accidently thrust themselves upon one; and one is liberated in such a way that for the first time one can authentically understand and choose among the factical possibilities lying ahead of that possibility which is not to be outstripped. (pp. 224–225)

Death is of the utmost significance because it can make us existentially self-aware if it is viewed authentically. For the recognition of death as something unique forces us to view ourselves apart from our general conception of human beings or the conception that others have of us. It forces us to realize that what we are is determined only after we have completed our last act, and, therefore, we are free to choose what we are to be.

By examining these different ways of understanding death, we can generalize to what it is to understand oneself authentically or inauthentically. Inauthentic individuals think of themselves as specimens of certain kinds and what they do is done on the basis of such an understanding. Authentic individuals realize that the kinds to which they belong are accidental.[3] They realize that we are each unique and cannot be understood solely in terms of the kinds to which we belong. Authentic individuals recognize the incompleteness of their being, their freedom to determine what they are by selecting this or that kind of future and in so doing are aware of themselves as existing individuals. Thus, the distinction between authentic and inauthentic is a distinction between kinds of self-understanding. We should remind ourselves, however, that no individual is wholly authentic or inauthentic, although one or the other mode of existence may predominate.

As inauthentic, Dasein can be understood in terms of its *facticity, fallenness,* and *existentiality.* These three moments, or "existentialia," are ways of understanding our "Being-in-the-world" in its various moments, and are employed in the preliminary definition of "Care." Facticity is that mode of Being-in-the-world which corresponds to state-of-mind. It suggests that what Dasein finds itself to be, what it already is, has the character of an established matter of fact. One's facticity is like the sort of place which a square has on a chessboard. It does not make sense for a square on a chessboard to change its place; it is fixed. Analogously, at the level of facticity, I think of myself as necessarily being what I am. I think of myself as being like a chair or a piece of chalk, as being one of the many in the world, as a brute matter of fact. Thus, for example, I think of the roles that I play and the categories to which I belong as being necessarily part of what I am. While I think of myself in this way I must also think of my *fallenness.*

I am dealing with the world, I am an agent in the world, and I have *fallen* into the world to the extent that I think of my dealings with the world as a piece of chalk deals with the world. A chalk does not make choices among future possibilities. What it will do is determined in advance by the essence given to it by its creator. To think of myself as having fallen into the world is to view my decisions and choices as being the natural and inevitable result of the kind of entity that I am. For example, I am an author and a teacher. As an author I signed a contract to complete this book, and that is that. My decision to complete this book, or even to continue writing this sentence, when viewed in terms of fallenness, is seen as the natural and inevitable consequence of what I am, an author. I think of my decisions as being like the flowing of a stream; the stream keeps going and my actions keep flowing from my essence. Thus, when I view my place in the world and my being thrown into this particular situation in the world in terms of my fallenness, I think of myself as necessarily being in that place. What I do is the result of the place that I am in. I am free, but "free" only to act in accordance with my essence or what I am, to act in accordance with the "they" or what others take me to be.

We have considered Dasein's relation to the past and the present, but Dasein is also Being that makes its future, and this can be inauthentically understood if Dasein regards its future as merely a part of its nature. Thus, I may think that my future is fixed because I have an essence, and what I will do is the result of what I project myself to be and what I project myself to be is based upon what I am, my essence. To characterize one's future choices in terms of *existentiality* is to understand them inauthentically.

To regard Dasein as authentic is not to make a different kind of decision, but it is to understand the decisions that we do make in a certain fashion. First, in terms of the relationship of our decisions to the past, the past is not viewed as an established matter of fact which determines our present and future choices, but as a *debt* which we must take into account. You cannot get rid of your *guilt,* that is, you cannot avoid responsibility for your past, but to describe Dasein's relationship to the past by the term "guilt" is to recognize that Dasein has achieved an awareness of freedom from and lack of necessary connection with the past. As Heidegger says,

> Everyday common sense first takes 'Being-guilty' in the sense of 'owing', and 'having something due on account'. . . . "Being-guilty" also has the signification of *'being responsible for'*—that is, being the cause or author of something, or even 'being the occasion' for something. . . . These ordinary significations of "Being-guilty" as 'having debts to someone' and 'having responsibility for something' go together and define a kind of behavior which we call *'making oneself responsible'*. . . . (p. 229)

To be guilty is not to regard what was done as something which ought not to have been done. Rather Dasein acknowledges the past as a kind of debt, something that one has to live with, but something that one can be separated from. My past is there and influences my present and future. However, it is something to take into account, and not something that determines our present and future decisions.

The *call of conscience* occurs when I free myself from my past, and my lostness in the "they." Dasein "Losing itself in the publicness and idle talk of the 'they', it *fails to hear* its own Self in listening to the they-self" (p. 227). In conscience one frees oneself from one's past and one's surroundings by experiencing the ultimate responsibility for what one decides to choose. In conscience, one is in a state, when facing a decision, in which one recognizes that one is completely alone and on one's own; nothing other than Dasein is regarded as relevant, no event or anything in Dasein's past. Dasein faces the fact of its loneliness, its recognition that it alone has complete responsibility for its decisions and choices. You follow your conscience when you do something regardless of what you think yourself to be, or what you are in public life, or what you are reputed to be. Consequently, to be authentic is to recognize one's freedom. We are authentic in regard to our awareness of our Self when we recognize that nothing that you are (teacher, student, author, etc.) determines your actions.

Resolve, or *resoluteness,* is an authentic projection of the future, a way of considering the future. When we are faced with the task of making our future, this task is all important and must be performed completely by oneself. We are thrown into the world, and we are faced with the task of making our future. We must choose from the different possible ways of structuring the world. To project a future for oneself authentically with resolve is to recognize that the future one projects must be decided upon completely by oneself. We can get advice from others, but ultimately our future Being is an issue for us, and we must settle it on our own account.

In resolve we recognize that what we will be is not determined entirely by what we have been, but that we are free to choose a way of Being in the future that differs from what we were in the past. In resolve one accepts one's past and present as providing the context in which one's future decisions will be made, but one does not view one's future as the future of an object in the world whose essence is fixed. Thus, when viewed authentically, the future is seen connected with the past and the present and yet not necessarily determined by the past and present.

Existentiality and resolve are the primary modes of Dasein, for they concern the future. The future is primary, in the sense that we tend to distinguish ourselves in the past from what we are and will be. I can think about what I am now and distinguish it from what I was when I was twelve, and what I will be at fifty. Thus, what we have been is not so essential to ourselves. Because of this, I may think of myself primarily as a future Being and not a past Being. If I am primarily what I will be then what I am, my essence, is not yet. Hence once again we see the sense in which my existence precedes my essence.

DASEIN AND TEMPORALITY

According to Heidegger, temporality is the fundamental basis of the unity of Dasein, since all the other structures are ultimately unified and understood in terms of past, present, and future. To understand Dasein as temporality is to understand Dasein as the Being who is the fundamental ground or basis for our ordinary conception of time. Heidegger argues that since our ordinary conception of time is really an abstraction from the temporality of Dasein, we must first understand the temporality of Dasein in order to understand our ordinary way of conceiving time. What he has in mind can be seen by recalling the problem of accounting for or explaining our possession of the ordinary concept of time.

Heidegger claims that we ordinarily conceive of time as a single thing that is composed of an infinite sequence of moments each of which is *now.* Some of these moments are past, others present, and others future. The past and future have some kind of reality, but not the reality of the present. This concept is, however, problematic. For if we think of our experience of time as a sequence of *nows,* as events flowing by, then we can have the experience of the present, but we cannot have the experience of past and future. How, then, can we account for our notion of time in which one thing is past, present, and future? In other words, How does our ordinary conception of time as a single thing that is past, present, and future arise? How can we think of the *now* as being past, present, and future?

Heidegger's answer is that Dasein originates time because Dasein itself is a single Being, a unity, that is now (and always) past, present, and future. But what does this mean, and how is it possible? Well, I am now past because what I am *now* is in part determined by my past. At this moment my past has some reality, since my past is part of me. Similarly, I am now in the future, in that what I will be is part of what I take myself to be. In other words, my present conception of myself depends in part on what I intend to be in the future. So even my future is now, insofar as what I am now is in part determined by what I take myself to be in the future. In short, Dasein is now (and always) past, present, and future. Thus, in reflecting upon Dasein's temporality, Dasein can come to think that time is a single entity in which past, present, and future are all real. In other words, ordinary time is an abstraction from the temporality of Dasein.

The ordinary conception of time as an endless sequence of *nows,* although founded upon the temporality of Dasein is not an authentic way of viewing time, according to Heidegger. For the ordinary conception of time allows us to conceive of the present solely as a time for us to do something. The present is when we become very busy meeting people and making appointments. One loses one's own time as the present is viewed in isolation from one's own past and future. One loses one's own time because in the view of time as an endless sequence of *nows* one tends to forget the fact into which Dasein has entered, namely the Being-towards-death. Thus, the inauthentic individual by viewing time solely in terms of the *now* does not become aware of the potentiality for the future, one's own freedom. Nor does one become aware of the influences of one's past on the present.

To become aware of one's potentiality of the future is to become aware of one's freedom. By concentrating or thinking of time as being in the *now* and what is going on *now,* one doesn't think in terms of the future. One doesn't think of the fact that I could make this or that future for myself. One is fixated on the *now* and so loses the sense of there being different possible alternative ways of viewing the future.

The correct, or rather the authentic, conception of time is one in which the present is viewed as the point at which we must project a future for ourselves while retaining a knowledge of one's past as having contributed to that present. One is not captured or consumed by the present, but always views his or her entire life. One is continuously projecting and acting on possibilities for the future at the same time one is viewing one's past, not as something over and done with, but as something that must be taken into account in determining the possibilities for the future.

HEIDEGGER LEXICON

Authentic. Basic structure of Dasein that represents a manner of self-understanding.

Being-ahead-of-itself. Aspect of Care that corresponds to the future of Dasein with its realm of possibilities.

Being-alongside (entities encountered within the world). Aspect of Care that corresponds to the present of Dasein and discourse.

Being-already-in (a world). Aspect of Care that corresponds to Dasein's past and indicates that we are thrown into a world that is not our making.

Being-in-the-world. Basic structure of Dasein which reveals that Dasein cannot be separated from the world and the world cannot be separated from Dasein, for Dasein is the world and the world is Dasein.

Care. Basic structure of Dasein that allows us to grasp the sense in which the different structures of Dasein and the different existentialia within each structure comprise a single entity.

Conscience. Aspect of authenticity in which one frees oneself from one's past and one's surroundings by experiencing the ultimate responsibility for what one decides to choose.

Dasein. Human being.

Death. "[T]hat *possibility which is one's ownmost, which is non-relational, and which is not to be outstripped.*"

Discourse or talk. Any meaningful behavior between human beings: a spontaneous and natural behavior that we engage in.

Existential analysis. Concerns giving an account of the basic constitution of human existence as such; specifying the various structures or levels in terms of which we can understand the essence of human life.

Existentiality. Aspect or moment of inauthentic Dasein. One views one's future as fixed and what one projects oneself to be is based upon what one is, one's fixed essence.

Existentiell. Phenomenological investigation into how Dasein understands itself and makes decisions concerning its own existence in concrete everyday situations.

Facticity. Aspect of inauthentic Dasein which suggests that what Dasein finds itself to be, what it already is, has the character of an established matter of fact. At the level of facticity, I think of myself as necessarily being what I am.

Fallenness. When I view my place in the world and my being thrown into this particular situation in the world in terms of my fallenness, I think of myself as necessarily being in that place. What I do is the result of the place that I am in.

Guilt. Aspect of authentic Dasein. To describe Dasein's relationship to the past by the term "guilt" is to recognize that Dasein has achieved an awareness of freedom from and lack of necessary connection with the past.

Inauthentic. Basic structure of Dasein that represents a manner of self-understanding.

Phenomenological method. Radical empiricism which takes as its subject matter how we directly encounter and experience the world. It seeks to give an accurate and unprejudiced description of how the world, including the self, is experienced.

Present-at-hand. Objects there by nature, for example, moon, trees, oceans.

Ready-at-hand. Objects created by humans in a state of civilization.

Resolve. Authentic projection of the future. To project a future for oneself authentically with resolve is to recognize that the future one projects must be decided upon completely by oneself.

State-of-mind *(Befindlichkeit).* Moment or aspect of Being-in-the-world that is disclosed through our moods. It consists in our awareness that there are certain facts about ourselves and our situation over which we have no control.

"They" or "das man." Inauthentic mode of existence in which we forget that we are existing individuals and become lost in the "one like many."

Thrown potentiality. I am placed into a world in which I must choose a possible future for myself.

Time. Fundamental structure which provides basis for the unity of Dasein, since all the other structures are ultimately unified and understood in terms of past, present, and future.

Understanding. Moment or aspect of Being-in-the-world which consists in an awareness of our having a future and of there being possibilities awaiting our future.

HEIDEGGER SELECTIONS

From *Being and Time*

The Problem of Being, Dasein as Being-in-the-World, and Dasein as Care

THE QUESTION OF BEING. The question about the meaning of Being is to be *formulated*. We must therefore discuss it with an eye to these structural items.

Inquiry, as a kind of seeking, must be guided beforehand by what is sought. So the meaning of Being must already be available to us in some way. As we have intimated, we always conduct our activities in an understanding of Being. Out of this understanding arise both the explicit question of the meaning of Being and the tendency that leads us towards its conception. We do not *know* what 'Being' means. But even if we ask, 'What *is* "Being"?', we keep within an understanding of the 'is', though we are unable to fix conceptionally what that 'is' signifies. We do not even know the horizon in terms of which that meaning is to be grasped and fixed. *But this vague average understanding of Being is still a Fact.* . . .

Further, this vague average understanding of Being may be so infiltrated with traditional theories and opinions about Being that these remain hidden as sources of the way in which it is prevalently understood. What we seek when we inquire into Being is not something entirely unfamiliar, even if proximally we cannot grasp it at all.

In the question which we are to work out, *what is asked about* is Being—that which determines entities as entities, that on the basis of which [woraufhin] entities are already understood, however we may discuss them in detail. The Being of entities 'is' not itself an entity. If we are to understand the problem of Being, our first philosophical step consists in not μῦθόν τινα διηγεῖσθαι, in not 'telling a story'—that is to say, in not defining entities as entities by tracing them back in their origin to some other entities, as if Being had the character of some possible entity. Hence

Being, as that which is asked about, must be exhibited in a way of its own, essentially different from the way in which entities are discovered. Accordingly, *what is to be found out by the asking*—the meaning of Being—also demands that it be conceived in a way of its own, essentially contrasting with the concepts in which entities acquire their determinate signification.

In so far as Being constitutes what is asked about, and "Being" means the Being of entities, then entities themselves turn out to be *what is interrogated.* These are, so to speak, questioned as regards their Being. But if the characteristics of their Being can be yielded without falsification, then these entities must, on their part, have become accessible as they are in themselves. When we come to what is to be interrogated, the question of Being requires that the right way of access to entities shall have been obtained and secured in advance. But there are many things which we designate as 'being' ["seiend"], and we do so in various senses. Everything we talk about, everything we have in view, everything towards which we comport ourselves in any way, is being; what we are is being, and so is how we are. Being lies in the fact that something is, and in its Being as it is; in Reality; in presence-at-hand; in subsistence; in validity; in Dasein; in the 'there is'. In *which* entities is the meaning of Being to be discerned? From which entities is the disclosure of Being to take its departure? Is the starting-point optional, or does some particular entity have priority when we come to work out the question of Being? Which entity shall we take for our example, and in what sense does it have priority?

If the question about Being is to be explicitly formulated and carried through in such a manner as to be completely transparent to itself, then any treatment of it in line with the elucidations we have given requires us to explain how Being is to be looked at, how its meaning is to be understood and conceptually grasped; it requires us to prepare the way for choosing the right entity for our example, and to work out the genuine way of access to it. Looking at something, understanding and conceiving it, choosing, access to it—all these ways of behaving are constitutive for our inquiry, and therefore are modes of Being for those particular entities which we, the inquirers, are ourselves. Thus to work out the question of Being adequately, we must make an entity—the inquirer—transparent in his own Being. The very asking of this question is an entity's mode of *Being;* and as such it gets its essential character from what is inquired about—namely, Being. This entity which each of us is himself and which includes inquiring as one of the possibilities of its Being, we shall denote by the term *"Dasein".* If we are to formulate our question explicitly and transparently, we must first give a proper explication of an entity (Dasein), with regard to its Being.

THE ONTICAL PRIORITY OF THE QUESTION OF BEING. Science in general may be defined as the totality established through an interconnection of true propositions. This definition is not complete, nor does it reach the meaning of science. As ways in which man behaves, sciences have the manner of Being which this entity—man himself—possesses. This entity we denote by the term *"Dasein"*. Scientific research is not the only manner of Being which this entity can have, nor is it the one which lies closest. Moreover, Dasein itself has a special distinctiveness as compared with other entities, and it is worth our while to bring this to view in a provisional way. Here our discussion must anticipate later analyses, in which our results will be authentically exhibited for the first time.

Dasein is an entity which does not just occur among other entities. Rather it is ontically distinguished by the fact that, in its very Being, that Being is an *issue* for it. But in that case, this is a constitutive state of Dasein's Being, and this implies that Dasein, in its Being, has a relationship towards that Being—a relationship which itself is one of Being. And this means further that there is some way in which Dasein understands itself in its Being, and that to some degree it does so explicitly. It is peculiar to this entity that with and through its Being, this Being is disclosed to it. *Understanding of Being is itself a definite characteristic of Dasein's Being.* Dasein is ontically distinctive in that it *is* ontological.

Here "Being-ontological" is not yet tantamount to "developing an ontology". So if we should reserve the term "ontology" for that theoretical inquiry which is explicitly devoted to the meaning of entities, then what we have had in mind in speaking of Dasein's "Being-ontological" is to be designated as something "pre-ontological". It does not signify simply "being-ontical", however, but rather "being in such a way that one has an understanding of Being".

That kind of Being towards which Dasein can comport itself in one way or another, and always does comport itself somehow, we call *"existence" [Existenz]*. And because we cannot define Dasein's essence by citing a "what" of the kind that pertains to a subject-matter [eines sachhaltigen Was], and because its essence lies rather in the fact that in each case it has its Being to be, and has it as its own, we have chosen to designate this entity as "Dasein", a term which is purely an expression of its Being.

Dasein always understands itself in terms of its existence—in terms of a possibility of itself: to be itself or not itself. Dasein has either chosen these possibilities itself, or got itself into them, or grown up in them already. Only the particular Dasein decides its existence, whether it does so by taking hold or by neglecting. The question of existence never gets straightened out except through existing itself. The understanding of oneself which leads *along this way* we call *"existentiell"*. The question of existence is one of Dasein's ontical 'affairs'. This does not require that the ontological structure of existence should be theoretically transparent. The question about that structure aims at the analysis [Auseinanderlegung] of what constitutes existence. The context [Zusammenhang] of such structures we call *"existentiality"*. Its analytic has the character of an understanding which is not existentiell, but rather *existential*. The task of an existential analytic of Dasein has been delineated in advance, as regards both its possibility and its necessity, in Dasein's ontical constitution.

So far as existence is the determining character of Dasein, the ontological analytic of this entity always requires that existentiality be considered beforehand. By "existentiality" we understand the state of Being that is constitutive for those entities that exist. But in the idea of such a constitutive state of Being, the idea of Being is already included. And thus even the possibility of carrying through the analytic of Dasein depends on working out beforehand the question about the meaning of Being in general. . . . We must choose such a way of access and such a kind of interpretation that this entity can show itself in itself and from itself. And this means that it is to be shown as it is *proximally and for the most part*—in its average *everydayness*. In this everydayness there are certain structures which we shall exhibit—not just any accidental structures, but essential ones which, in every kind of Being that factical Dasein may possess, persist as determinative for the character of its Being. Thus by having regard for the basic state of Dasein's everydayness, we shall bring out the Being of this entity in a preparatory fashion. . . .

We shall point to *temporality* as the meaning of the Being of that entity which we call "Dasein". If this is to be demonstrated, those structures of Dasein which we shall provisionally exhibit must be Interpreted over again as modes of temporality. In thus interpreting Dasein as temporality, however, we shall not give the answer to our leading question as to the meaning of Being in general. But the ground will have been prepared for obtaining such an answer.

THE ONTOLOGICAL ANALYTIC OF DASEIN. In designating the tasks of 'formulating' the question of Being, we have shown not only that we must establish which entity is to serve as our primary object of interrogation, but also that the right way of access to this entity is one which we must explicitly make our own and hold secure. We have already discussed which entity takes over the principal role within the question of Being. But how are we, as it were, to set our sights towards this entity, Dasein, both as something accessible to us and as something to be understood and interpreted?

In demonstrating that Dasein in ontico-ontologically prior, we may have misled the reader into supposing that this entity must also be what is given as ontico-ontologically primary not only in the sense that it can itself be grasped 'immediately', but also in that the kind of Being which it possesses is presented just as 'immediately'. Ontically, of course, Dasein is not only close to us—even that which is closest: we *are* it, each of us, we ourselves. In spite of this, or rather for just this reason, it is ontologically that which is farthest. To be sure, its ownmost Being is such that it has an understanding of that Being, and already maintains itself in each case as if its Being has been interpreted in some manner. But we are certainly not saying that when Dasein's own Being is thus interpreted pre-ontologically in the way which lies closest, this interpretation can be taken over as an appropriate clue, as if this way of understanding Being is what must emerge when one's ownmost state of Being is considered as an ontological theme. The kind of Being which belongs to Dasein is rather such that, in understanding its own Being, it has a tendency to do so in terms of that entity towards which it comports itself proximally and in a way which is essentially constant—in terms of the 'world'. In Dasein itself, and therefore in its own understanding of Being, the way the world is understood is, as we shall show, reflected back ontologically upon the way in which Dasein itself gets interpreted.

A Preparatory Analysis of Dasein

THE THEME OF THE ANALYTIC OF DASEIN. We are ourselves the entities to be analysed. The Being of any such entity is *in each case mine*. These entities, in their Being, comport themselves towards their Being. As entities with such Being, they are delivered over to their own Being. *Being* is that which is an issue for every such entity. This way of characterizing Dasein has a double consequence:

1. The 'essence' ["Wesen"] of this entity lies in its "to be" [Zusein]. Its Being-what-it-is [Was-sein] *(essentia)* must, so far as we can speak of it at all, be conceived in terms of its Being *(existentia)*. But here our ontological task is to show that when we choose to designate the Being of this entity as "existence" [Existenz], this term does not and cannot have the ontological signification of the traditional term *"existentia"*; ontologically, *existentia* is tantamount to *Being-present-at-hand,* a kind of Being which is essentially inappropriate to entities of Dasein's character. To avoid getting bewildered, we shall always use the Interpretative expression *"presence-at-hand"* for the term *"existentia",* while the term "existence", as a designation of Being, will be allotted solely to Dasein.

The essence of Dasein lies in its existence. Accordingly those characteristics which can be exhibited in this entity are not 'properties' present-at-hand of some entity which 'looks' so and so and is itself present-at-hand; they are in each case possible ways for it to be; and no more than that. All the Being-as-it-is [So-sein] which this entity possesses is primarily

Being. So when we designate this entity with the term 'Dasein', we are expressing not its "what" (as if it were a table, house or tree) but its Being.

2. That Being which is an *issue* for this entity in its very Being, is in each case mine. Thus Dasein is never to be taken ontologically as an instance or special case of some genus of entities as things that are present-at-hand. To entities such as these, their Being is 'a matter of indifference'; or more precisely, they 'are' such that their Being can be neither a matter of indifference to them, nor the opposite. Because Dasein has *in each case mineness [Jemeinigkeit]*, one must always use a *personal* pronoun when one addresses it: 'I am', 'you are'.

Furthermore, in each case Dasein is mine to be in one way or another. Dasein has always made some sort of decision as to the way in which it is in each case mine [je meines]. That entity which in its Being has this very Being as an issue, comports itself towards its Being as its ownmost possibility. In each case Dasein *is* its possibility, and it 'has' this possibility, but not just as a property [eigenschaftlich], as something present-at-hand would. And because Dasein is in each case essentially its own possibility, it *can,* in its very Being, 'choose' itself and win itself; it can also lose itself and never win itself; or only 'seem' to do so. But only in so far as it is essentially something which can be *authentic*—that is, something of its own—can it have lost itself and not yet won itself. As modes of Being, *authenticity* and *inauthenticity* (these expressions have been chosen terminologically in a strict sense) are both grounded in the fact that any Dasein whatsoever is characterized by mineness. But the inauthenticity of Dasein does not signify any 'less' Being or any 'lower' degree of Being. Rather it is the case that even in its fullest concretion Dasein can be characterized by inauthenticity—when busy, when excited, when interested, when ready for enjoyment.

The two characteristics of Dasein which we have sketched—the priority of *'existentia'* over *essentia,* and the fact that Dasein is in each case mine [die Jemeinigkeit]—have already indicated that in the analytic of this entity we are facing a peculiar phenomenal domain. Dasein does not have the kind of Being which belongs to something merely present-at-hand within the world, nor does it ever have it. So neither is it to be presented thematically as something we come across in the same way as we come across what is present-at-hand. The right way of presenting it is so far from self-evident that to determine what form it shall take is itself an essential part of the ontological analytic of this entity. Only by presenting this entity in the right way can we have any understanding of its Being. No matter how provisional our analysis may be, it always requires the assurance that we have started correctly.

In determining itself as an entity, Dasein always does so in the light of a possibility which it *is* itself and which, in its very Being, it somehow understands. This is the formal meaning of Dasein's existential constitution. But this tells us that if we are to Interpret this entity *ontologically,* the problematic of its Being must be developed from the existentiality of its existence. This cannot mean, however, that "Dasein" is to be construed in terms of some concrete possible idea of existence. At the outset of our analysis it is particularly important that Dasein should not be Interpreted with the differentiated character [Differenz] of some definite way of existing, but that it should be uncovered [aufgedeckt] in the undifferentiated character which it has proximally and for the most part. This undifferentiated character of Dasein's everydayness is *not nothing,* but a positive phenomenal characteristic of this entity. Out of this kind of Being—and back into it again—is all existing, such as it is. We call this everyday undifferentiated character of Dasein *"averageness" [Durchschnittlichkeit].*

And because this average everydayness makes up what is ontically proximal for this entity, it has again and again been *passed over* in explicating Dasein. That which is ontically closest and well known, is ontologically the farthest and not known at all; and its ontological signification is constantly overlooked. . . .

Dasein's average everydayness, however, is not to be taken as a mere 'aspect'. Here too, and even in the mode of inauthenticity, the structure of existentiality lies *a priori.* And here too Dasein's Being is an issue for it in a definite way; and Dasein comports itself towards it in the mode of average everydayness, even if this is only the mode of fleeing *in the face of it* and forgetfulness *thereof.*

Being-in-the-world in General as the Basic State of Dasein

A PRELIMINARY SKETCH OF BEING-IN-THE-WORLD, IN TERMS OF AN ORIENTATION TOWARDS BEING-IN AS SUCH. Dasein is an entity which, in its very Being, comports itself understandingly towards that Being. In saying this, we are calling attention to the formal concept of existence. Dasein exists. Furthermore, Dasein is an entity which in each case I myself am. Mineness belongs to any existent Dasein, and belongs to it as the condition which makes authenticity and inauthenticity possible. In each case Dasein exists in one or the other of these two modes, or else it is modally undifferentiated.

But these are both ways in which Dasein's Being takes on a definite character, and they must be seen and understood *a priori* as grounded upon that state of Being which we have called *"Being-in-the-world".* An interpretation of this constitutive state is needed if we are to set up our analytic of Dasein correctly.

The compound expression "Being-in-the-world" indicates in the very way we have coined it, that it stands for a *unitary* phenomenon. This primary datum must be seen as a whole. But while Being-in-the-world cannot be broken up into contents which may be pieced together, this does not prevent it from having several constitutive items in its structure. Indeed the phenomenal datum which our expression indicates is one which may, in fact, be looked at in three ways. If we study it, keeping the whole phenomenon firmly in mind beforehand, the following items may be brought out for emphasis:

First, the *'in-the-world'*. With regard to this there arises the task of inquiring into the ontological structure of the 'world' and defining the idea of *worldhood* as such.

Second, that *entity* which in every case has Being-in-the-world as the way in which it is. Here we are seeking that which one inquires into when one asks the question 'Who?' By a phenomenological demonstration we shall determine who is in the mode of Dasein's average everydayness.

Third, *Being-in [In-sein]* as such. We must set forth the ontological Constitution of inhood [Inheit] itself. Emphasis upon any one of these constitutive items signifies that the others are emphasized along with it; this means that in any such case the whole phenomenon gets seen. Of course Being-in-the-world is a state of Dasein which is necessary *a priori,* but it is far from sufficient for completely determining Dasein's Being. Before making these three phenomena the themes for special analyses, we shall attempt by way of orientation to characterize the third of these factors.

What is meant by *"Being-in"?* Our proximal reaction is to round out this expression to "Being-in 'in the world'", and we are inclined to understand this Being-in as 'Being in something' ["Sein in . . ."]. This latter term designates the kind of Being which an entity has when it is 'in' another one, as the water is 'in' the glass, or the garment is 'in' the cupboard. By this 'in' we mean the relationship of Being which two entities extended 'in' space have to each other with regard to their location in that space. Both water and glass, garment and cupboard, are 'in' space and 'at' a location, and both in the same way. This relationship of Being can be expanded: for instance, the bench is in the lecture-room, the lecture-room is in the university, the university is in the city, and so on, until we can say that the bench is 'in world-space'. All entities whose Being 'in' one another can thus be described have the same kind of Being—that of Being-present-at-hand—as Things occurring 'within' the world. Being-present-at-hand 'in' something which is likewise present-at-hand, and Being-present-at-hand-along-with [Mitvorhandensein] in the sense of a definite location-relationship with something else which has the same kind of Being, are ontological characteristics which we call *"categorical":* they are of such a sort as to belong to entities whose kind of Being is not of the character of Dasein.

Being-in, on the other hand, is a state of Dasein's Being; it is an existentiale. So one cannot think of it as the Being-present-at-hand of some corporeal Thing (such as a human body) 'in' an entity which is present-at-hand. Nor does the term "Being-in" mean a spatial 'in-one-another-ness' of things present-at-hand, any more than the word 'in' primordially signifies a spatial relationship of this kind. 'In' is derived from *"innan"*—"to reside", *"habitare"*, "to dwell" [sich auf halten]. 'An' signifies "I am accustomed", "I am familiar with", "I look after something". It has the signification of *"colo"* in the senses of *"habito"* and *"diligo"*. The entity to which Being-in in this signification belongs is one which we have characterized as that entity which in each case I myself am [bin]. The expression *'bin'* is connected with *'bei'*, and so *'ich bin'* ['I am'] means in its turn "I reside" or "dwell alongside" the world, as that which is familiar to me in such and such a way. "Being" [Sein], as the infinitive of *'ich bin'* (that is to say, when it is understood as an *existentiale*), signifies "to reside alongside. . .", "to be familiar with. . .". *"Being-in" is thus the formal existential expression for the Being of Dasein, which has Being-in-the-world as its essential state.*

A FOUNDED MODE IN WHICH BEING-IN IS EXEMPLIFIED. KNOWING THE WORLD. When Dasein directs itself towards something and grasps it, it does not somehow first get out of an inner sphere in which it has been proximally encapsulated, but its primary kind of Being is such that it is always 'outside' alongside entities which it encounters and which belong to a world already discovered. Nor is any inner sphere abandoned when Dasein dwells alongside the entity to be known, and determines its character; but even in this 'Being-outside' alongside the object, Dasein is still 'inside', if we understand this in the correct sense; that is to say, it is itself 'inside' as a Being-in-the-world which knows. And furthermore, the perceiving of what is known is not a process of returning with one's booty to the 'cabinet' of consciousness after one has gone out and grasped it; even in perceiving, retaining, and preserving, the Dasein which knows *remains outside,* and it does so *as Dasein.* If I 'merely' know [Wissen] about some way in which the Being of entities is interconnected, if I 'only' represent them, if I 'do no more' than 'think' about them, I am no less alongside the entities outside in the world than when I *originally* grasp them. Even the forgetting of something, in which every relationship of Being towards what one formerly knew has seemingly been obliterated, must be conceived *as a modification of the primordial Being-in;* and this holds for every delusion and for every error.

We have now pointed out how those modes of Being-in-the-world which are constitutive for knowing the world are interconnected in their foundations; this makes it plain that in knowing, Dasein achieves a new *status of Being [Seinsstand]* towards a world which has already been discovered in Dasein itself. This new possibility of Being can develop itself autonomously; it can become a task to be accomplished, and as scientific knowledge it can take over the guidance for Being-in-the-world. But a *'commercium'* of the subject with a world does not get *created* for the first time by knowing, nor does it *arise* from some way in which the world acts upon a subject. Knowing is a mode of Dasein founded upon Being-in-the-world. Thus Being-in-the-world, as a basic state, must be Interpreted *beforehand*.

THE BEING OF THE ENTITIES ENCOUNTERED IN THE ENVIRONMENT. The Being of those entities which we encounter as closest to us can be exhibited phenomenologically if we take as our clue our everyday Being-in-the-world, which we also call our *"dealings" in* the world and *with* entities within-the-world. Such dealings have already dispersed themselves into manifold ways of concern. The kind of dealing which is closest to us is as we have shown, not a bare perceptual cognition, but rather that kind of concern which manipulates things and puts them to use; and this has its own kind of 'knowledge'. The phenomenological question applies in the first instance to the Being of those entities which we encounter in such concern. To assure the kind of seeing which is here required, we must first make a remark about method.

In the disclosure and explication of Being, entities are in every case our preliminary and our accompanying theme [das Vor-und Mitthema-tische]; but our real theme is Being. In the domain of the present analysis, the entities we shall take as our preliminary theme are those which show themselves in our concern with the environment. Such entities are not thereby objects for knowing the 'world' theoretically; they are simply what gets used, what gets produced, and so forth. As entities so encountered, they become the preliminary theme for the purview of a 'knowing' which, as phenomenological, looks primarily towards Being, and which, in thus taking Being as its theme, takes these entities as its accompanying theme. This phenomenological interpretation is accordingly not a way of knowing those characteristics of entities which themselves are [seiender Beschaffenheiten des Seienden]; it is rather a determination of the structure of the Being which entities possess. But as an investigation of Being, it brings to completion, autonomously and explicitly, that understanding of Being which belongs already to Dasein and which 'comes alive' in any of its dealings with entities. Those entities which serve phenomenologically as our preliminary theme—in this case, those which are used or which are to be found in the course of production—become accessible when we put ourselves into the position of concerning ourselves with them in some such way. Taken strictly, this talk about "putting ourselves into such a position" [Sichversetzen] is misleading; for the kind of Being which belongs to such concernful dealings is not one into which we need to put ourselves first. This is the way in which everyday Dasein always *is:* when I open the door, for instance, I use the latch. The achieving of phenomenological access to the entities which we encounter, consists rather in thrusting aside our interpretative tendencies, which keep thrusting themselves upon us and running along with us, and which conceal not only the phenomenon of such 'concern', but even more those entities themselves *as* encountered of their own accord *in* our concern with them. These entangling errors become plain if in the course of our investigation we now ask which entities shall be taken as our preliminary theme and established as the pre-phenomenal basis for our study.

Being-in-the-world as Being-with and Being-one's-self. The "They"

Our analysis of the worldhood of the world has constantly been bringing the whole phenomenon of Being-in-the-world into view, although its constitutive items have not all stood out with the same phenomenal distinctness as the phenomenon of the world itself. We have Interpreted the world ontologically by going through what is ready-to-hand within-the-world; and this Interpretation has been put first, because Dasein, in its everydayness (with regard to which Dasein remains a constant theme for study), not only is in a world but comports itself towards that world with one predominant kind of Being. Proximally and for the most part Dasein is fascinated with its world. Dasein is thus absorbed in the world; the kind of Being which it thus possesses, and in general the Being-in which underlies it, are essential in determining the character of a phenomenon which we are now about to study. We shall approach this phenomenon by asking *who* it is that Dasein is in its everydayness. All the structures of Being which belong to Dasein, together with the phenomenon which provides the answer to this question of the "who", are ways of its Being. To characterize these ontologically is to do so existentially. We must therefore pose the question correctly and outline the procedure for bringing into view a broader phenomenal domain of Dasein's everydayness. By directing our researches towards the phenomenon which is to provide us with an answer to the question of the "who", we shall be led to certain structures of Dasein which are equiprimordial with Being-in-the-world: *Being-with* and *Dasein-with [Mitsein* und *Mitdasein].* In this kind of Being is grounded the mode of everyday Being-one's-Self [Selbstsein]; the explication of this mode will enable us to see what we may call the 'subject' of everydayness—the *"they"*. Our chapter on the 'who' of the average Dasein will thus be divided up as follows: 1. an approach to the existential question of the "who" of Dasein; 2. the Dasein-with of Others, and everyday Being-with; 3. everyday Being-one's-Self and the "they".

AN APPROACH TO THE EXISTENTIAL QUESTION OF THE "WHO" OF DAS-

EIN. The answer to the question of who Dasein is, . . . indicated formally [by] the basic characteristics of Dasein. Dasein is an entity which is in each case I myself; its Being is in each case mine. This definition *indicates* an *ontologically* constitutive state, but it does no more than indicate it. At the same time this tells us *ontically* (though in a rough and ready fashion) that in each case an "I"—not Others—is this entity. The question of the "who" answers itself in terms of the "I" itself, the 'subject', the 'Self'. The "who" is what maintains itself as something identical throughout changes in its Experiences and ways of behaviour, and which relates itself to this changing multiplicity in so doing. Ontologically we understand it as something which is in each case already constantly present-at-hand, both in and for a closed realm, and which lies at the basis, in a very special sense, as the *subjectum*. As something selfsame in manifold otherness, it has the character of the *Self*. Even if one rejects the "soul substance" and the Thinghood of consciousness, or denies that a person is an object, ontologically one is still positing something whose Being retains the meaning of present-at-hand, whether it does so explicitly or not. Substantiality is the ontological clue for determining which entity is to provide the answer to the question of the "who". Dasein is tacitly conceived in advance as something present-at-hand. This meaning of Being is always implicated in any case where the Being of Dasein has been left indefinite. Yet presence-at-hand is the kind of Being which belongs to entities whose character is not that of Dasein.

According to the analysis which we have now completed, Being with Others belongs to the Being of Dasein, which is an issue for Dasein in its very Being. Thus as Being-with, Dasein 'is' essentially for the sake of Others. This must be understood as an existential statement as to its essence. Even if the particular factical Dasein does *not* turn to Others, and supposes that it has no need of them or manages to get along without them, it *is* in the way of Being-with. In Being-with, as the existential "for-the-sake-of" of Others, these have already been disclosed in their Dasein. With their Being-with, their disclosedness has been constituted beforehand; accordingly, this disclosedness also goes to make up significance—that is to say, worldhood. And, significance, as worldhood, is tied up with the existential "for-the-sake-of-which". Since the worldhood of that world in which every Dasein essentially is already, is thus constituted, it accordingly lets us encounter what is environmentally ready-to-hand as something with which we are circumspectively concerned, and it does so in such a way that together with it we encounter the Dasein-with of Others. The structure of the world's worldhood is such that Others are not proximally present-at-hand as free-floating subjects along with other Things, but show themselves in the world in their special environmental Being, and do so in terms of what is ready-to-hand in that world.

Being-with is such that the disclosedness of the Dasein-with of Others belongs to it; this means that because Dasein's Being is Being-with, its understanding of Being already implies the understanding of Others. This understanding, like any understanding, is not an acquaintance derived from knowledge about them, but a primordially existential kind of Being, which, more than anything else, makes such knowledge and acquaintance possible. Knowing oneself [Sichkennen] is grounded in Being-with, which understands primordially. It operates proximally in accordance with the kind of Being which is closest to us—Being-in-the-world as Being-with; and it does so by an acquaintance with that which Dasein, along with the Others, comes across in its environmental circumspection and concerns itself with—an acquaintance in which Dasein understands. Solicitous concern is understood in terms of what we are concerned with, and along with our understanding of it. Thus in concernful solicitude the Other is proximally disclosed.

EVERYDAY BEING-ONE'S-SELF AND THE "THEY". The *ontologically* relevant result of our analysis of Being-with is the insight that the 'subject character' of one's own Dasein and that of Others is to be defined existentially—that is, in terms of certain ways in which one may be. In that with which we concern ourselves environmentally the Others are encountered as what they are; they *are* what they do.

In one's concern with what one has taken hold of, whether with, for, or against, the Others, there is constant care as to the way one differs from them, whether that difference is merely one that is to be evened out, whether one's own Dasein has lagged behind the Others and wants to catch up in relationship to them, or whether one's Dasein already has some priority over them and sets out to keep them suppressed. The care about this distance between them is disturbing to Being-with-one-another, though this disturbance is one that is hidden from it. If we may express this existentially, such Being-with-one-another has the character of *distantiality [Abständigkeit]*. The more inconspicuous this kind of Being is to everyday Dasein itself, all the more stubbornly and primordially does it work itself out.

But this distantiality which belongs to Being-with, is such that Dasein, as everyday Being-with-one-another, stands in *subjection [Botmässigkeit]* to Others. It itself *is* not; its Being has been taken away by the Others. Dasein's everyday possibilities of Being are for the Others to dispose of as they please. These Others, moreover, are not *definite* Others. On the contrary, any Other can represent them. What is decisive is just that inconspicuous domination by Others which has already been taken over unawares from Dasein as Being-with. One belongs to the Others oneself and enhances their power. 'The Others' whom one thus designates in order to cover up the fact of one's belonging to them essentially oneself, are those who proximally and for the most part *'are there'* in everyday

Being-with-one-another. The "who" is not this one, not that one, not oneself [man selbst], not some people [einige], and not the sum of them all. The 'who' is the neuter, *the "they" [das Man].*

Being-in as Such

THE TASK OF A THEMATIC ANALYSIS OF BEING-IN. In the preparatory stage of the existential analytic of Dasein, we have for our leading theme this entity's basic state, Being-in-the-World. Our first aim is to bring into relief phenomenally the unitary primordial structure of Dasein's Being, in terms of which its possibilities and the ways for it 'to be' are ontologically determined. Up till now, our phenomenal characterization of Being-in-the-world has been directed towards the world, as a structural item of Being-in-the-world, and has attempted to provide an answer to the question about the "who" of this entity in its everydayness. But even in first marking out the tasks of a preparatory fundamental analysis of Dasein, we have already provided an advance orientation as to *Being-in as such,* and have illustrated it in the concrete mode of knowing the world. . . .

What we have hitherto set forth needs to be rounded out in many ways by working out fully the existential *a priori* of philosophical anthropology and taking a look at it. But this is not the aim of our investigation. *Its aim is one of fundamental ontology.* Consequently, if we inquire about Being-in as our theme, we cannot indeed consent to nullify the primordial character of this phenomenon by deriving it from others—that is to say, by an inappropriate analysis, in the sense of a dissolving or breaking up. But the fact that something primordial is underivable does not rule out the possibility that a multiplicity of characteristics of Being may be constitutive for it. If these show themselves, then existentially they are equiprimordial. The phenomenon of the *equiprimordiality* of constitutive items has often been disregarded in ontology, because of a methodologically unrestrained tendency to derive everything and anything from some simple 'primal ground'.

The Existential Constitution of the "There"

BEING THERE AS STATE-OF-MIND. What we indicate *ontologically* by the term "state-of-mind"* is *ontically* the most familiar and everyday sort of thing; our mood, our Being-attuned. Prior to all psychology of moods,

---

* 'Befindlichkeit'. More literally: 'the state in which one may be found'. (The common German expression 'Wie befinden Sie sich?' means simply 'How are you?' or 'How are you feeling?') Our translation, 'state-of-mind', comes fairly close to what is meant; but it should be made clear that the 'of-mind' belongs to English idiom, has no literal counterpart in the structure of the German word, and fails to bring out the important connotation of finding oneself.

a field which in any case still lies fallow, it is necessary to see this phenomenon as a fundamental *existentiale,* and to outline its structure.

Both the undisturbed equanimity and the inhibited ill-humour of our everyday concern, the way we slip over from one to the other, or slip off into bad moods, are by no means nothing ontologically, even if these phenomena are left unheeded as supposedly the most indifferent and fleeting in Dasein. The fact that moods can deteriorioate [verdorben werden] and change over means simply that in every case Dasein always has some mood [gestimmt ist]. The pallid, evenly balanced lack of mood [Ungestimmtheit], which is often persistent and which is not to be mistaken for a bad mood, is far from nothing at all. Rather, it is in this that Dasein becomes satiated with itself. Being has become manifest as a burden. Why that should be, one does not *know.* And Dasein cannot know anything of the sort because the possibilities of disclosure which belong to cognition reach far too short a way compared with the primordial disclosure belonging to moods, in which Dasein is brought before its Being as "there". Furthermore, a mood of elation can alleviate the manifest burden of Being; that such a mood is possible also discloses the burdensome character of Dasein, even while it alleviates the burden. A mood makes manifest 'how one is, and how one is faring' ["wie einem ist und wird"]. In this 'how one is', having a mood brings Being to its "there".

In having a mood, Dasein is always disclosed moodwise as that entity to which it has been delivered over in its Being; and in this way it has been delivered over to the Being which, in existing, it has to be. "To be disclosed" does not mean "to be known as this sort of thing". And even in the most indifferent and inoffensive everydayness the Being of Dasein can burst forth as a naked 'that it is and has to be' [als nacktes "Dass es est ist und zu sein hat"]. The pure 'that it is' shows itself, but the "whence" and the "whither" remain in darkness. The fact that it is just as everyday a matter for Dasein not to 'give in' ["nachgibt"] to such moods—in other words, not to follow up [nachgeht] their disclosure and allow itself to be brought before that which is disclosed—is no evidence *against* the phenomenal facts of the case, in which the Being of the "there" is disclosed moodwise in its "that-it-is"; it is rather evidence for it. In an *ontico-*existentiell sense, Dasein for the most part evades the Being which is disclosed in the mood. In an *ontologico-*existential sense, this means that even in that to which such a mood pays no attention, Dasein is unveiled in its Being-delivered-over to the "there". In the evasion itself the "there" *is* something disclosed.

This characteristic of Dasein's Being—this 'that it is'—is veiled in its "whence" and "whither", yet disclosed in itself all the more unveiledly; we call it the *"thrownness"* of this entity into its "there"; indeed, it is thrown in such a way that, as Being-in-the-world, it is the "there". The expression "thrownness" is meant to suggest the *facticity of its being delivered over.* The 'that it is and has to be' which is disclosed in Dasein's state-of-mind is not the same 'that-it-is' which expresses ontologico-categorially the factuality belonging to presence-at-hand. This factuality becomes accessible only if we ascertain it by looking at it. The "that-it-is" which is disclosed in Dasein's state-of-mind must rather be conceived as an existential attribute of the entity which has Being-in-the-world as its way of Being. *Facticity is not the factuality of the factum brutum of something present-at-hand, but a characteristic of Dasein's Being—one which has been taken up into existence, even if proximally it has been thrust aside.* The "that-it-is" of facticity never becomes something that we can come across by beholding it.

BEING-THERE AS UNDERSTANDING. State-of-mind is *one* of the existential structures in which the Being of the 'there' maintains itself. Equiprimordial with it in constituting this Being is *understanding.* A state-of-mind always has its understanding, even if it merely keeps it suppressed. Understanding always has its mood. If we Interpret understanding as a fundamental *existentiale,* this indicates that this phenomenon is conceived as a basic mode of Dasein's *Being.* On the other hand, 'understanding' in the sense of *one* possible kind of cognizing among others (as distinguished, for instance, from 'explaining'), must, like explaining, be Interpreted as an existential derivative of that primary understanding which is one of the constituents of the Being of the "there" in general.

Understanding is the existential Being of Dasein's own potentiality-for-Being; and it is so in such a way that this Being discloses in itself what its Being is capable of. We must grasp the structure of this *existentiale* more precisely.

As a disclosure, understanding always pertains to the whole basic state of Being-in-the-world. As a potentiality-for-Being, any Being-in is a potentiality-for-Being-in-the-world. Not only is the world, *qua* world, disclosed as possible significance, but when that which is within-the-world is itself freed, this entity is freed for *its own* possibilities. That which is ready-to-hand is discovered as such in its service*ability,* its us*ability,* and its detriment*ality.* The totality of involvements is revealed as the categorial whole of a *possible* interconnection of the ready-to-hand. But even the 'unity' of the manifold present-at-hand, of Nature, can be discovered only if a *possibility* of it has been disclosed. Is it accidental that the question about the *Being* of Nature aims at the 'conditions of its *possibility*'? On what is such an inquiry based? When confronted with this inquiry, we cannot leave aside the question: *why* are entities which are not of the character of Dasein understood in their Being, if they are disclosed in accordance with the conditions of their possibility? Kant presupposes something of the sort, perhaps rightly. But this presupposition itself is something that cannot be left without demonstrating how it is justified.

Why does the understanding—whatever may be the essential dimensions of that which can be disclosed in it—always press forward into possibilities? It is because the understanding has in itself the existential structure which we call *"projection"*. With equal primordiality the understanding projects Dasein's Being both upon its "for-the-sake-of-which" and upon significance, as the worldhood of its current world. The character of understanding as projection is constitutive for Being-in-the-world with regard to the disclosedness of its existentially constitutive state-of-Being by which the factical potentiality-for-Being gets its leeway [Spielraum]. And as thrown, Dasein is thrown into the kind of Being which we call "projecting". Projecting has nothing to do with comporting oneself towards a plan that has been thought out, and in accordance with which Dasein arranges its Being. On the contrary, any Dasein has, as Dasein, already projected itself; and as long as it is, it is projecting. As long as it is, Dasein always has understood itself and always will understand itself in terms of possibilities. Furthermore, the character of understanding as projection is such that the understanding does not grasp thematically that upon which it projects—that is to say, possibilities. Grasping it in such a manner would take away from what is projected its very character as a possibility, and would reduce it to the given contents which we have in mind; whereas projection, in throwing, throws before itself the possibility as possibility, and lets it *be* as such. As projecting, understanding is the kind of Being of Dasein in which it *is* its possibilities as possibilities.

As *existentialia,* states-of-mind and understanding characterize the primordial disclosedness of Being-in-the-world. By way of having a mood, Dasein 'sees' possibilities, in terms of which it is. In the projective disclosure of such possibilities, it already has a mood in every case. The projection of its ownmost potentiality-for-Being has been delivered over to the Fact of its thrownness into the "there". Has not Dasein's Being become more enigmatical now that we have explicated the existential constitution of the Being of the "there" in the sense of thrown projection? It has indeed. We must first let the full enigmatical character of this Being emerge, even if all we can do is to come to a genuine breakdown over its 'solution', and to formulate anew the question about the Being of thrown projective Being-in-the-world.

But in the first instance, even if we are just to bring into view the everyday kind of Being in which there is understanding with a state-of-mind, and if we are to do so in a way which is phenomenally adequate to the full disclosedness of the "there", we must work out these *existentialia* concretely.

BEING-THERE AND DISCOURSE. LANGUAGE. The fundamental *existentialia* which constitute the Being of the "there", the disclosedness of Being-in-the-world, are states-of-mind and understanding. In understanding, there lurks the possibility of interpretation—that is, of appropriating what is understood. In so far as a state-of-mind is equiprimordial with an act of understanding, it maintains itself in a certain understanding. Thus there corresponds to it a certain capacity for getting interpreted. We have seen that assertion is derived from interpretation, and is an extreme case of it. In clarifying the third signification of assertion as communication (speaking forth), we were led to the concepts of "saying" and "speaking", to which we had purposely given no attention up to that point. The fact that language *now* becomes our theme *for the first time* will indicate that this phenomenon has its roots in the existential constitution of Dasein's disclosedness. *The existential-ontological foundation of language is discourse or talk.* This phenomenon is one of which we have been making constant use already in our foregoing Interpretation of state-of-mind, understanding, interpretation, and assertion; but we have, as it were, kept it suppressed in our thematic analysis.

Discourse is existentially equiprimordial with state-of-mind and understanding. The intelligibility of something has always been articulated, even before there is any appropriative interpretation of it. Discourse is the Articulation of intelligibility. Therefore it underlies both interpretation and assertion. That which can be Articulated in interpretation, and thus even more primordially in discourse, is what we have called "meaning". That which gets articulated as such in discursive Articulation, we call the "totality-of-significations" [Bedeutungsganze]. This can be dissolved or broken up into significations. Significations, as what has been Articulated from that which can be Articulated, always carry meaning [. . . sind . . . sinnhaft]. If discourse, as the Articulation of the intelligibility of the "there", is a primordial *existentiale* of disclosedness, and if disclosedness is primarily constituted by Being-in-the-world, then discourse too must have essentially a kind of Being which is specifically *worldly.* The intelligibility of Being-in-the-world—an intelligibility which goes with a state-of-mind—*expresses itself as discourse.* The totality-of-significations of intelligibility is *put into words.* To significations, words accrue. But word-Things do not get supplied with significations.

The way in which discourse gets expressed is language. Language is a totality of words—a totality in which discourse has a 'worldly' Being of its own; and as an entity within-the-world, this totality thus becomes something which we may come across as ready-to-hand. Language can be broken up into word-Things which are present-at-hand. Discourse is existentially language, because that entity whose disclosedness it Articulates according to significations, has, as its kind of Being, Being-in-the-world—a Being which has been thrown and submitted to the 'world'.

As an existential state in which Dasein is disclosed, discourse is constitutive for Dasein's existence. *Hearing* and *keeping silent [Schweigen]* are possibilities belonging to discursive speech. In these phenomena the constitutive function of discourse for the existentiality of existence becomes entirely plain for the first time. But in the first instance the issue is one of working out the structure of discourse as such.

Discoursing or talking is the way in which we articulate 'significantly' the intelligibility of Being-in-the-world. Being-with belongs to Being-in-the-world, which in every case maintains itself in some definite way of concernful Being-with-one-another. Such Being-with-one-another is discursive as assenting or refusing, as demanding or warning, as pronouncing, consulting, or interceding, as 'making assertions', and as talking in the way of 'giving a talk'. Talking is talk about something. That which the discourse is *about* [das *Worüber* der Rede] does not necessarily or even for the most part serve as the theme for an assertion in which one gives something a definite character. Even a command is given about something; a wish is about something. And so is intercession. What the discourse is about is a structural item that it necessarily possesses; for discourse helps to constitute the disclosedness of Being-in-the-world, and in its own structure it is modelled upon this basic state of Dasein. What is talked about [das Beredete] in talk is always 'talked to' ["angeredet"] in a definite regard and within certain limits. In any talk or discourse, there is *something said-in-the-talk* as such [ein *Geredetes* as solches]—something said as such [das . . . Gesagte als solches] whenever one wishes, asks, or expresses oneself about something. In this "something said", discourse communicates.

FALLING AND THROWNNESS. Idle talk, curiosity and ambiguity characterize the way in which, in an everyday manner, Dasein is its 'there'—the disclosedness of Being-in-the-world. As definite existential characteristics, these are not present-at-hand in Dasein, but help to make up its Being. In these, and in the way they are interconnected in their Being, there is revealed a basic kind of Being which belongs to everydayness; we call this the *"falling"* of Dasein.

This term does not express any negative evaluation, but is used to signify that Dasein is proximally and for the most part *alongside* the 'world' of its concern. This "absorption in. . ." [Aufgehen bei . . .] has mostly the character of Being-lost in the publicness of the "they". Dasein has, in the first instance, fallen away [abgefallen] from itself as an authentic potentiality for Being its Self, and has fallen into the 'world'. "Fallenness" into the 'world' means an absorption in Being-with-one-another, in so far as the latter is guided by idle talk, curiosity, and ambiguity. Through the Interpretation of falling, what we have called the "inauthenticity" of Dasein may now be defined more precisely. On no account, however, do the terms "inauthentic" and "non-authentic" signify 'really not', as if in this mode of Being, Dasein were altogether to lose its Being. "In-authenticity" does not mean anything like Being-no-longer-in-the-world, but amounts rather to a quite distinctive kind of Being-in-the-world—the kind which is completely fascinated by the 'world' and by the Dasein-with of Others in the "they". Not-Being-its-self [Das Nicht-es-selbst-sein] functions as a *positive* possibility of that entity which, in its essential concern, is absorbed in a world. This kind of *not-Being* has to be conceived as that kind of Being which is closest to Dasein and in which Dasein maintains itself for the most part.

DASEIN'S BEING AS CARE. Since our aim is to grasp the totality of this structural whole ontologically, we must first ask whether the phenomenon of anxiety and that which is disclosed in it, can give us the whole of Dasein in a way which is phenomenally equiprimordial, and whether they can do so in such a manner that if we look searchingly at this totality, our view of it will be filled in by what has thus been given us. The entire stock of what lies therein may be counted up formally and recorded: anxiousness as a state-of-mind is a way of Being-in-the-world; that in the face of which we have anxiety is thrown Being-in-the-world; that which we have anxiety about is our potentiality-for-Being-in-the-world. Thus the entire phenomenon of anxiety shows Dasein as factically existing Being-in-the-world. The fundamental ontological characteristics of this entity are existentiality, facticity, and Being-fallen. These existential characteristics are not pieces belonging to something composite, one of which might sometimes be missing; but there is woven together in them a primordial context which makes up that totality of the structural whole which we are seeking. In the unity of those characteristics of Dasein's Being which we have mentioned, this Being becomes something which it is possible for us to grasp as such ontologically. How is this unity itself to be characterized?

Dasein is an entity for which, in its Being, that Being is an issue. The phrase 'is an issue' has been made plain in the state-of-Being of understanding—of understanding as self-projective Being towards its ownmost potentiality-for-Being. This potentiality is that for the sake of which any Dasein is as it is. In each case Dasein has already compared itself, in its Being, with a possibility of itself. Being-free *for* one's ownmost potentiality-for-Being, and therewith for the possibility of authenticity and inauthenticity, is shown, with a primordial, elemental concreteness, in anxiety. But ontologically, Being towards one's ownmost potentiality-for-Being means that in each case Dasein is already *ahead* of itself [ihm selbst . . . *vorweg]* in its Being. Dasein is always 'beyond itself' ["über sich hinaus"], not as a way of behaving towards other entities which it is *not,* but as Being towards the potentiality-for-Being which it is itself. This structure of Being, which belongs to the essential 'is an issue', we shall denote as Dasein's *"Being-ahead-of-itself"*.

But this structure pertains to the whole of Dasein's constitution.

"Being-ahead-of-itself" does not signify anything like an isolated tendency in a worldless 'subject', but characterizes Being-in-the-world. To Being-in-the-world, however, belongs the fact that it has been delivered over to itself—that it has in each case already been thrown *into a world*. The abandonment of Dasein to itself is shown with primordial concreteness in anxiety. "Being-ahead-of-itself" means, if we grasp it more fully, *"ahead-of-itself-in-already-being-in-a-world"*. As soon as this essentially unitary structure is seen as a phenomenon, what we have set forth earlier in our analysis of worldhood also becomes plain. The upshot of that analysis was that the referential totality of significance (which as such is constitutive for worldhood) has been 'tied up' with a "for-the-sake-of-which". The fact that this referential totality of the manifold relations of the 'in-order-to' has been bound up with that which is an issue for Dasein, does not signify that a 'world' of Objects which is present-at-hand has been welded together with a subject. It is rather the phenomenal expression of the fact that the constitution of Dasein, whose totality is now brought out explicitly as ahead-of-itself-in-Being-already-in . . . , is primordially a whole. To put it otherwise, existing is always factical. Existentiality is essentially determined by facticity.

Furthermore, Dasein's factical existing is not only generally and without further differentiation a thrown potentiality-for-Being-in-the-world; it is always also absorbed in the world of its concern. In this falling Being-alongside . . . , fleeing in the face of uncanniness (which for the most part remains concealed with latent anxiety, since the publicness of the "they" suppresses everything unfamiliar), announces itself, whether it does so explicitly or not, and whether it is understood or not. Ahead-of-itself-Being-already-in-a-world essentially includes one's falling and one's *Being alongside* those things ready-to-hand within-the-world with which one concerns oneself.

The formally existential totality of Dasein's ontological structural whole must therefore be grasped in the following structure: the Being of Dasein means ahead-of-itself-Being-already-in-(the-world) as Being-alongside (entities encountered within-the-world). This Being fills in the signification of the term *"care" [Sorge]*, which is used in a purely ontologico-existential manner. From this signification every tendency of Being which one might have in mind ontically, such a worry [Besorgnis] or carefreeness [Sorglosigkeit], is ruled out. . . .

One thing has become unmistakable: *our existential analysis of Dasein up till now cannot lay claim to primordiality*. Its fore-having never included more than the *inauthentic* Being of Dasein, and of Dasein as *less* than a *whole [als unganzes]*. If the Interpretation of Dasein's Being is to become primordial, as a foundation for working out the basic question of ontology, then it must first have brought to light existentially the Being of Dasein in its possibilities of *authenticity* and *totality*.

Thus arises the task of putting Dasein as a whole into our fore-having. This signifies, however, that we must first of all raise the question of this entity's potentiality-for-Being-a-whole. As long as Dasein is, there is in every case something still outstanding, which Dasein can be and will be. But to that which is thus outstanding, the 'end' itself belongs. The 'end' of Being-in-the-world is death. This end, which belongs to the potentiality-for-Being—that is to say, to existence—limits and determines in every case whatever totality is possible for Dasein. If, however, Dasein's Being-at-an-end in death, and therewith its Being-a-whole, are to be included in the discussion of its possibly *Being-a-whole,* and if this is to be done in a way which is appropriate to the phenomena, then we must have obtained an ontologically adequate conception of death—that is to say an *existential* conception of it. But as something of the character of Dasein, death *is* only in an existentiell *Being towards death [Sein zum Tode].*

Dasein as Being-Towards-Death
and as Authentic and Inauthentic

Dasein's Being-Towards-Death

THE POSSIBILITY OF EXPERIENCING THE DEATH OF OTHERS, AND THE POSSIBILITY OF GETTING A WHOLE DASEIN INTO OUR GRASP. When Dasein reaches its wholeness in death, it simultaneously loses the Being of its "there". By its transition to no-longer-Dasein [Nichtmehr-dasein], it gets lifted right out of the possibility of experiencing this transition and of understanding it as something experienced. Surely this sort of thing is denied to any particular Dasein in relation to itself. But this makes the death of Others more impressive. In this way a termination [Beendigung] of Dasein becomes 'Objectively' accessible. Dasein can thus gain an experience of death, all the more so because Dasein is essentially Being with Others. In that case, the fact that death has been thus 'Objectively' given must make possible an ontological delimitation of Dasein's totality.

Thus from the kind of Being which Dasein possesses as Being with one another, we might draw the fairly obvious information that when the Dasein of Others has come to an end, it might be chosen as a substitute theme for our analysis of Dasein's totality. But does this lead us to our appointed goal?

Even the Dasein of Others, when it has reached its wholeness in death, is no-longer-Dasein, in the sense of Being-no-longer-in-the-world.

Does not dying mean going-out-of-the-world, and losing one's Being-in-the-world? Yet when someone has died, his Being-no-longer-in-the-world (if we understand it in an extreme way) is still a Being, but in the sense of the Being-just-present-at-hand-and-no-more of a corporeal Thing which we encounter. In the dying of the Other we can experience that remarkable phenomenon of Being which may be defined as the change-over of an entity from Dasein's kind of Being (or life) to no-longer-Dasein. The *end* of the entity *qua* Dasein is the *beginning* of the same entity *qua* something present-at-hand.

Indisputably, the fact that one Dasein *can be represented* by another belongs to its possibilities of Being in Being-with-one-another in the world. In everyday concern, constant and manifold use is made of such representability. Whenever we go anywhere or have anything to contribute, we can be represented by someone within the range of that 'environment' with which we are most closely concerned. The great multiplicity of ways of Being-in-the-world in which one person can be represented by another, not only extends to the more refined modes of publicly being with one another, but is likewise germane to those possibilities of concern which are restricted within definite ranges, and which are cut to the measure of one's occupation, one's social status, or one's age. But the very meaning of such representation is such that it is always a representation 'in' ["in" und "bei"] something—that is to say, in concerning oneself with something. But proximally and for the most part everyday Dasein understands itself in terms of that with *which* it is customarily concerned. 'One *is*' what one does. In relation to this sort of Being (the everyday manner in which we join with one another in absorption in the 'world' of our concern) representability is not only quite possible but is even constitutive for our being with one another. *Here* one Dasein can and must, within certain limits, *'be'* another Dasein.

However, this possibility of representing breaks down completely if the issue is one of representing that possibility-of-Being which makes up Dasein's coming to an end, and which, as such, gives to it its wholeness. *No one can take the Other's dying away from him.* Of course someone can 'go to his death for another'. But that always means to sacrifice oneself for the Other *'in some definite affair'*. Such "dying for" can never signify that the Other has thus had his death taken away in even the slightest degree. Dying is something that every Dasein itself must take upon itself at the time. By its very essence, death is in every case mine, in so far as it 'is' at all. And indeed death signifies a peculiar possibility-of-Being in which the very Being of one's own Dasein is an issue. In dying, it is shown that mineness and existence are ontologically constitutive for death. Dying is not an event; it is a phenomenon to be understood existentially; and it is to be understood in a distinctive sense which must be still more closely delimited.

PRELIMINARY SKETCH OF THE EXISTENTIAL-ONTOLOGICAL STRUCTURE OF DEATH. From our considerations of totality, end, and that which is still outstanding, there has emerged the necessity of Interpreting the phenomenon of death as Being-towards-the-end, and of doing so in terms of Dasein's basic state. Only so can it be made plain to what extent Being-a-whole, as constituted by Being towards-the-end, is possible in Dasein itself in conformity with the structure of its Being. We have seen that care is the basic state of Dasein. The ontological signification of the expression "care" has been expressed in the 'definition': "ahead-of-itself-Being-already-in (the world) as Being-alongside entities which we encounter (within-the-world)". In this are expressed the fundamental characteristics of Dasein's Being: existence, in the "ahead-of-itself"; facticity, in the "Being-already-in"; falling, in the "Being-alongside". If indeed death belongs in a distinctive sense to the Being of Dasein, then death (or Being-towards-the-end) must be defined in terms of these characteristics.

We must, in the first instance, make plain in a preliminary sketch how Dasein's existence, facticity, and falling reveal themselves in the phenomenon of death.

The Interpretation in which the "not-yet—and with it even the uttermost "not-yet", the end of Dasein—was taken in the sense of something still outstanding, has been rejected as inappropriate in that it included the ontological perversion of making Dasein something present-at-hand. Being-at-an-end implies existentially Being-towards-the-end. The uttermost "not-yet" has the character of something *towards which* Dasein *comports itself.* The end is impending [steht . . . bevor] for Dasein. Death is not something not yet present-at-hand, nor is it that which is ultimately still outstanding but which has been reduced to a minimum. *Death is something that stands before us—something impending.*

However, there is much that can impend for Dasein as Being-in-the-world. The character of impendence is not distinctive of death. On the contrary, this Interpretation could even lead us to suppose that death must be understood in the sense of some impending event encountered environmentally. For instance, a storm, the remodelling of the house, or the arrival of a friend, may be impending; and these are entities which are respectively present-at-hand, ready-to-hand, and there-with-us. The death which impends does not have this kind of Being.

But there may also be impending for Dasein a journey, for instance, or a disputation with Others, or the forgoing of something of a kind which Dasein itself can be—its own possibilities of Being, which are based on its Being with Others.

Death is a possibility-of-Being which Dasein itself has to take over in every case. With death, Dasein stands before itself in its ownmost potentiality-for-Being. This is a possibility in which the issue is nothing less than Dasein's Being-in-the-world. Its death is the possibility of no-longer being-able-to-be-there. If Dasein stands before itself as this possibility, it has been *fully* assigned to its ownmost potentiality-for-Being. When it stands before itself in this way, all its relations to any other Dasein have been undone. This ownmost non-relational possibility is at the same time the uttermost one.

As potentiality-for-Being, Dasein cannot outstrip the possibility of death. Death is the possibility of the absolute impossibility of Dasein. Thus death reveals itself as that *possibility which is one's ownmost, which is non-relational, and which is not to be outstripped [unüberholbare].* As such, death is something *distinctively* impending. Its existential possibility is based on the fact that Dasein is essentially disclosed to itself, and disclosed, indeed, as ahead-of-itself. This item in the structure of care has its most primordial concretion in Being-towards-death. As a phenomenon, Being-towards-the-end becomes plainer as Being towards that distinctive possibility of Dasein which we have characterized.

This ownmost possibility, however, non-relational and not to be outstripped, is not one which Dasein procures for itself subsequently and occasionally in the course of its Being. On the contrary, if Dasein exists, it has already been *thrown* into this possibility. Dasein does not, proximally and for the most part, have any explicit or even any theoretical knowledge of the fact that it has been delivered over to its death, and that death thus belongs to Being-in-the-world. Thrownness into death reveals itself to Dasein in a more primordial and impressive manner in that state-of-mind which we have called "anxiety". Anxiety in the face of death is anxiety 'in the face of' that potentiality-for-Being which is one's ownmost, nonrelational, and not to be outstripped. That in the face of which one has anxiety is Being-in-the-world itself. That about which one has this anxiety is simply Dasein's potentiality-for-Being. Anxiety in the face of death must not be confused with fear in the face of one's demise. This anxiety is not an accidental or random mood of 'weakness' in some individual; but, as a basic state-of-mind of Dasein, it amounts to the disclosedness of the fact that Dasein exists as thrown Being *towards* its end. Thus the existential conception of "dying" is made clear as thrown Being towards its ownmost potentiality-for-Being, which is non-relational and not to be outstripped. Precision is gained by distinguishing this from pure disappearance, and also from merely perishing, and finally from the 'Experiencing' of a demise.

Being-towards-the-end does not first arise through some attitude which occasionally emerges, nor does it arise as such an attitude; it belongs essentially to Dasein's thrownness, which reveals itself in a state-of-mind (mood) in one way or another. The factical 'knowledge' or 'ignorance' which prevails in any Dasein as to its ownmost Being-towards-the-end, is only the expression of the existentiell possibility that there are different ways of maintaining oneself in this Being. Factically, there are many who, proximally and for the most part, do not know about death; but this must not be passed off as a ground for proving that Being-towards-death does not belong to Dasein 'universally'. It only proves that proximally and for the most part Dasein covers its ownmost Being-towards-death, fleeing *in the face* of it. Factically, Dasein is dying as long as it exists, but proximally and for the most part, it does so by way of *falling*. For factical existing is not only generally and without further differentiation a thrown potentiality-for-Being-in-the-world, but it has always likewise been absorbed in the 'world' of its concern. In this falling Being-alongside, fleeing from uncanniness announces itself; and this means now, a fleeing in the face of one's ownmost Being-towards-death. Existence, facticity, and falling characterize Being-towards-the-end, and are therefore constitutive for the existential conception of death. *As regards its ontological possibility, dying is grounded in care.*

But if Being-towards-death belongs primordially and essentially to Dasein's Being, then it must also be exhibitable in everydayness, even if proximally in a way which is inauthentic. And if Being-towards-the-end should afford the existential possibility of an existentiell Being-a-whole for Dasein, then this would give phenomenal confirmation for the thesis that "care" is the ontological term for the totality of Dasein's structural whole. If, however, we are to provide a full phenomenal justification for this principle, a *preliminary sketch* of the connection between Being-towards-death and care is not sufficient. We must be able to see this connection above all in that *concretion* which lies closest to Dasein—its everydayness.

BEING-TOWARDS-DEATH AND THE EVERYDAYNESS OF DASEIN. In setting forth average everyday Being-towards-death, we must take our orientation from those structures of everydayness at which we have earlier arrived. In Being-towards-death, Dasein comports itself *towards itself* as a distinctive potentiality-for-Being. But the Self of everydayness is the "they". The "they" is constituted by the way things have been publicly interpreted, which expresses itself in idle talk. Idle talk must accordingly make manifest the way in which everyday Dasein interprets for itself its Being-towards-death. The foundation of any interpretation is an act of understanding, which is always accompanied by a state-of-mind, or, in other words, which has a mood. So we must ask how Being-towards-death is disclosed by the kind of understanding which, with its state-of-mind, lurks in the idle talk of the "they". How does the "they" comport itself understandingly towards that ownmost possibility of Dasein, which is non-relational and is not to be outstripped? What state-of-mind discloses to the "they" that it has been delivered over to death, and in what way?

In the publicness with which we are with one another in our everyday manner, death is 'known' as a mishap which is constantly occurring—as a 'case of death'. Someone or other 'dies', be he neighbour or stranger [Nächste oder Fernerstehende]. People who are no acquaintances of ours are 'dying' daily and hourly. 'Death' is encountered as a well-known event occurring within-the-world. As such it remains in the inconspicuousness characteristic of what is encountered in an everyday fashion. The "they" has already stowed away [gesichert] an interpretation for this event. It talks of it in a 'fugitive' manner, either expressly or else in a way which is mostly inhibited, as if to say, "One of these days one will die too, in the end; but right now it has nothing to do with us."

The analysis of the phrase 'one dies' reveals unambiguously the kind of Being which belongs to everyday Being-towards-death. In such a way of talking, death is understood as an indefinite something which, above all, must duly arrive from somewhere or other, but which is proximally *not yet present-at-hand* for oneself, and is therefore no threat. The expression 'one dies' spreads abroad the opinion that what gets reached, as it were, by death, is the "they". In Dasein's public way of interpreting, it is said that 'one dies', because everyone else and oneself can talk himself into saying that "in no case is it I myself", for this "one" is *the "nobody"*. 'Dying' is levelled off to an occurrence which reaches Dasein, to be sure, but belongs to nobody in particular. If idle talk is always ambiguous, so is this manner of talking about death. Dying, which is essentially mine in such a way that no one can be my representative, is perverted into an event of public occurrence which the "they" encounters. In the way of talking which we have characterized, death is spoken of as a 'case' which is constantly occurring. Death gets passed off as always something 'actual'; its character as a possibility gets concealed, and so are the other two items that belong to it—the fact that it is non-relational and that it is not to be outstripped. By such ambiguity, Dasein puts itself in the position of losing itself in the "they" as regards a distinctive potentiality-for-Being which belongs to Dasein's ownmost Self. The "they" gives its approval, and aggravates the *temptation* to cover up from oneself one's ownmost Being-towards-death. This evasive concealment in the face of death dominates everydayness so stubbornly that, in Being with one another, the 'neighbours' often still keep talking the 'dying person' into the belief that he will escape death and soon return to the tranquillized everydayness of the world of his concern. Such 'solicitude' is meant to 'console' him. It insists upon bringing him back into Dasein, while in addition it helps him to keep his ownmost non-relational possibility-of-Being completely concealed. In this manner the "they" provides [besorgt] a *constant tranquillization about death*. At bottom, however, this is a tranquillization not only for him who is 'dying' but just as much for those who 'console' him. And even in the case of a demise, the public is still not to have its own tranquillity upset by such an event, or be disturbed in the carefreeness with which it concerns itself. Indeed the dying of Others is seen often enough as a social inconvenience, if not even a downright tactlessness, against which the public is to be guarded.

But along with this tranquillization, which forces Dasein away from its death, the "they" at the same time puts itself in the right and makes itself respectable by tacitly regulating the way in which *one* has to comport oneself towards death. It is already a matter of public acceptance that 'thinking about death' is a cowardly fear, a sign of insecurity on the part of Dasein, and a sombre way of fleeing from the world. *The "they" does not permit us the courage for anxiety in the face of death.* The dominance of the manner in which things have been publicly interpreted by the "they", has already decided what state-of-mind is to determine our attitude towards death. In anxiety in the face of death, Dasein is brought face to face with itself as delivered over to that possibility which is not to be outstripped. The "they" concerns itself with transforming this anxiety into fear in the face of an oncoming event. In addition, the anxiety which has been made ambiguous as fear, is passed off as a weakness with which no self-assured Dasein may have any acquaintance. What is 'fitting' [Was sich . . . "gehört"] according to the unuttered decree of the "they", is indifferent tranquillity as to the 'fact' that one dies. The cultivation of such a 'superior' indifference *alienates* Dasein from its ownmost non-relational potentiality-for-Being.

But temptation, tranquillization, and alienation are distinguishing marks of the kind of Being called *"falling"*. As falling, everyday Being-towards-death is a constant *fleeing in the face of death*. Being-*towards-*the-end has the mode of *evasion in the face of it*—giving new explanations for it, understanding it inauthentically, and concealing it. Factically one's own Dasein is always dying already; that is to say, it is in a Being-towards-its-end. And it hides this Fact from itself by recoining "death" as just a "case of death" in Others—an everyday occurrence which, if need be, gives us the assurance still more plainly that 'oneself' is still 'living'. But in thus falling and fleeing *in the face of* death, Dasein's everydayness attests that the very "they" itself already has the definite character of *Being-towards-death,* even when it is not explicitly engaged in 'thinking about death'. *Even in average everydayness, this ownmost potentiality-for-Being, which is non-relational and not to be outstripped, is constantly an issue for Dasein. This is the case when its concern is merely in the mode of an untroubled indifference* **towards** *the uttermost possibility of existence.*

In setting forth everyday Being-towards-death, however, we are at the same time enjoined to try to secure a full existential conception of Being-towards-the-end, by a more penetrating Interpretation in which falling Being-towards-death is taken as an evasion *in the face of death.* *That in the face of which one flees* has been made visible in a way which is phenomenally adequate. Against this it must be possible to project phenomenologically the way in which evasive Dasein itself understands its death. . . .

Factically, Dasein maintains itself proximally and for the most part in an inauthentic Being-towards-death. How is the ontological possibility of an *authentic* Being-towards-death to be characterized 'Objectively', if, in the end, Dasein never comports itself authentically towards its end, or if, in accordance with its very meaning, this authentic Being must remain hidden from the Others? Is it not a fanciful undertaking, to project the existential possibility of so questionable an existentiell potentiality-for-Being? What is needed, if such a projection is to go beyond a merely fictitious arbitrary construction? Does Dasein itself give us any instructions for carrying it out? And can any grounds for its phenomenal legitimacy be taken from Dasein itself? Can our analysis of Dasein up to this point give us any prescriptions for the ontological task we have now set ourselves, so that what we have before us may be kept on a road of which we can be sure?

The existential conception of death has been established; and therewith we have also established what it is that an authentic Being-towards-the-end should be able to comport itself towards. We have also characterized inauthentic Being-towards-death, and thus we have prescribed in a negative way [prohibitiv] how it is possible for authentic Being-towards-death *not* to be. It is with these positive and prohibitive instructions that the existential edifice of an authentic Being-towards-death must let itself be projected.

Dasein is constituted by disclosedness—that is, by an understanding with a state-of-mind. *Authentic* Being-towards-death can *not evade* its own most non-relational possibility, or *cover up* this possibility by thus fleeing from it, or *give a new explanation* for it to accord with the common sense of the "they". In our existential projection of an authentic Being-towards-death, therefore, we must set forth those items in such a Being which are constitutive for it as an understanding of death—and as such an understanding in the sense of Being towards this possibility without either fleeing it or covering it up.

In the first instance, we must characterize Being-towards-death as a *Being towards a possibility*—indeed, towards a distinctive possibility of Dasein itself. "Being towards" a possibility—that is to say, towards something possible—may signify "Being out for" something possible, as in concerning ourselves with its actualization. Such possibilities are constantly encountered in the field of what is ready-to-hand and present-at-hand—what is attainable, controllable, practicable, and the like. In concernfully Being out for something possible, there is a tendency to *annihilate the possibility* of the possible by making it available to us. But the concernful actualization of equipment which is ready-to-hand (as in producing it, getting it ready, readjusting it, and so on) is always merely relative, since even that which has been actualized is still characterized in terms of some involvements—indeed this is precisely what characterizes its Being. Even though actualized, it remains, as actual, something possible for doing something; it is characterized by an "in-order-to". What our analysis is to make plain is simply how Being out for something concernfully, comports itself towards the possible: it does so not by the theoretico-thematical consideration of the possible as possible, and by having regard for its possibility as such, but rather by looking *circum*spectively *away* from the possible and looking at that for which it is possible. . . .

But Being towards this possibility, as Being-towards-death, is so to comport ourselves towards *death* that in this Being, and for it, death reveals itself *as a possibility.* Our terminology for such Being towards this possibility is *"anticipation" of this possibility.* But in this way of behaving does there not lurk a coming-close to the possible, and when one is close to the possible, does not its actualization emerge? In this kind of coming close, however, one does not tend towards concernfully making available something actual; but as one comes closer understandingly, the possibility of the possible just becomes 'greater'. *The closest closeness which one may have in Being towards death as a possibility, is as far as possible from anything actual.* The more unveiledly this possibility gets understood, the more purely does the understanding penetrate into it *as the possibility of the impossibility of any existence at all.* Death, as possibility, gives Dasein nothing to be 'actualized', nothing which Dasein, as actual, could itself *be.* It is the possibility of the impossibility of every way of comporting oneself towards anything, of every way of existing. In the anticipation of this possibility it becomes 'greater and greater'; that is to say, the possibility reveals itself to be such that it knows no measure at all, no more or less, but signifies the possibility of the measureless impossibility of existence. In accordance with its essence, this possibility offers no support for becoming intent on something, 'picturing' to oneself the actuality which is possible, and so forgetting its possibility. Being-towards-death, as anticipation of possibility, is what first *makes* this possibility *possible,* and sets it free as possibility.

Being-towards-death is the anticipation of a potentiality-for-Being of that entity whose kind of Being is anticipation itself. In the anticipatory revealing of this potentiality-for-Being, Dasein discloses itself to itself as regards its uttermost possibility. But to project itself on its ownmost potentiality-for-Being means to be able to understand itself in the Being of the entity so revealed—namely, to exist. Anticipation turns out to be the possibility of understanding one's *ownmost* and uttermost potentiality-for-Being—that is to say, the possibility of *authentic existence.* The on-tological constitution of such existence must be made visible by setting forth the concrete structure of anticipation of death. How are we to delimit this structure phenomenally? Manifestly, we must do so by determining those characteristics which must belong to an anticipatory disclosure so that it can become the pure understanding of that ownmost possibility which is non-relational and not to be outstripped—which is certain and, as such, indefinite. It must be noted that understanding does not primarily mean just gazing at a meaning, but rather understanding oneself in that potentiality-for-Being which reveals itself in projection.

Death is Dasein's *ownmost* possibility. Being towards this possibility discloses to Dasein its *ownmost* potentiality-for-Being, in which its very Being is the issue. Here it can become manifest to Dasein that in this distinctive possibility of its own self, it has been wrenched away from the "they". This means that in anticipation any Dasein can have wrenched itself away from the "they" already. But when one understands that this is something which Dasein 'can' have done, this only reveals its factical lostness in the everydayness of the they-self.

The ownmost possibility is *non-relational*. Anticipation allows Dasein to understand that that potentiality-for-being in which its ownmost Being is an issue, must be taken over by Dasein alone. Death does not just 'belong' to one's own Dasein in an undifferentiated way; death *lays claim* to it as an *individual* Dasein. The non-relational character of death, as understood in anticipation, individualizes Dasein down to itself. This individualizing is a way in which the 'there' is disclosed for existence. It makes manifest that all Being-alongside the things with which we concern ourselves, and all Being-with Others, will fail us when our ownmost potentiality-for-Being is the issue. Dasein can be *authentically itself* only if it makes this possible for itself of its own accord. But if concern and solicitude fail us, this does not signify at all that these ways of Dasein have been cut off from its authentically Being-its-Self. As structures essential to Dasein's constitution, these have a share in conditioning the possibility of any existence whatsoever. Dasein is authentically itself only to the extent that, *as* concernful Being-alongside and solicitous Being-with, it projects itself upon its ownmost potentiality-for-Being rather than upon the possibility of the they-self. The entity which anticipates its non-relational possibility, is thus forced by that very anticipation into the possibility of taking over from itself its ownmost Being, and doing so of its own accord.

The ownmost, non-relational possibility is *not to be outstripped*. Being towards this possibility enables Dasein to understand that giving itself up impends for it as the uttermost possibility of its existence. Anticipation, however, unlike inauthentic Being-towards-death, does not evade the fact that death is not to be outstripped; instead, anticipation frees itself *for* accepting this. When, by anticipation, one becomes free *for* one's own death, one is liberated from one's lostness in those possibilities which may accidentally thrust themselves upon one; and one is liberated in such a way that for the first time one can authentically understand and choose among the factical possibilities lying ahead of that possibility which is not to be outstripped. Anticipation discloses to existence that its uttermost possibility lies in giving itself up, and thus it shatters all one's tenaciousness to whatever existence one has reached. In anticipation, Dasein guards itself against falling back behind itself, or behind the potentiality-for-Being which it has understood. It guards itself against 'becoming too old for its victories' (Nietzsche). Free for its ownmost possibilities, which are determined by the *end* and so are understood as *finite [endliche]*, Dasein dispels the danger that it may, by its own finite understanding of existence, fail to recognize that it is getting outstripped by the existence-possibilities of Others, or rather that it may explain these possibilities wrongly and force them back upon its own, so that it may divest itself of its ownmost factical existence. As the non-relational possibility, death individualizes—but only in such a manner that, as the possibility which is not to be outstripped, it makes Dasein, as Being-with, have some understanding of the potentiality-for-Being of Others. Since anticipation of the possibility which is not to be outstripped discloses also all the possibilities which lie ahead of that possibility, this anticipation includes the possibility of taking the *whole* of Dasein in advance [Vorwegnehmens] in an existentiell manner; that is to say, it includes the possibility of existing as a *whole potentiality-for-Being.*

The ownmost, non-relational possibility, which is not to be outstripped, is *certain.* The way *to be* certain of it is determined by the kind of truth which corresponds to it (disclosedness). The certain possibility of death, however, discloses Dasein as a possibility, but does so only in such a way that, in anticipating this possibility, Dasein *makes* this possibility *possible* for itself as its ownmost potentiality-for-Being. The possibility is disclosed because it is made possible in anticipation. To maintain oneself in this truth—that is, to be certain of what has been disclosed—demands all the more that one should anticipate. . . .

Holding death for true (death *is* just one's own) shows another kind of certainty, and is more primordial than any certainty which relates to entities encountered within-the-world, or to formal objects; for it is certain of Being-in-the-world. As such, holding death for true does not demand just *one* definite kind of behaviour in Dasein, but demands Dasein itself in the full authenticity of its existence. In anticipation Dasein can first make certain of its ownmost Being in its totality—a totality which is not to be outstripped. Therefore the evidential character which belongs to the immediate givenness of Experiences of the "I", or of consciousness, must necessarily lag behind the certainty which anticipation includes. Yet this is not because the way in which these are grasped would not be a rigorous one, but because in principle such a way of grasping them cannot hold *for true* (disclosed) something which at bottom it insists upon 'having there' as true: namely, Dasein itself, which I myself *am,* and which, as a potentiality-for-Being, I can be authentically only by anticipation.

The ownmost possibility, which is non-relational, not to be outstripped, and certain, is *indefinite* as regards its certainty. How does anticipation disclose this characteristic of Dasein's distinctive possibility? How does the anticipatory understanding project itself upon a potentiality-for-Being which is certain and which is constantly possible in such a way that the "when" in which the utter impossibility of existence becomes possible remains constantly indefinite? In anticipating [zum] the indefinite certainty of death, Dasein opens itself to a constant *threat* arising out of its own "there". In this very threat Being-towards-the-end must maintain itself. So little can it tone this down that it must rather cultivate the indefiniteness of the certainty. How is it existentially possible for this constant threat to be genuinely disclosed? All understanding is accompanied by a state-of-mind. Dasein's mood brings it face to face with the thrownness of its 'that it is there'. *But the state-of-mind which can hold open the utter and constant threat to itself arising from Dasein's ownmost individualized Being, is anxiety.* In this state-of-mind, Dasein finds itself *face to face* with the "nothing" of the possible impossibility of its existence. Anxiety is anxious *about* the potentiality-for-Being of the entity so destined [des so bestimmten Seienden], and in this way it discloses the uttermost possibility. Anticipation utterly individualizes Dasein, and allows it, in this individualization of itself, to become certain of the totality of its potentiality-for-Being. For this reason, anxiety as a basic state-of-mind belongs to such a self-understanding of Dasein on the basis of Dasein itself. Being-towards-death is essentially anxiety. This is attested unmistakably, though 'only' indirectly, by Being-towards-death as we have described it, when it perverts anxiety into cowardly fear and, in surmounting this fear, only makes known its own cowardliness in the face of anxiety.

We may now summarize our characterization of authentic Being-towards-death as we have projected it existentially: *anticipation reveals to Dasein its lostness in the they-self, and brings it face to face with the possibility of being itself, primarily unsupported by concernful solicitude, but of being itself, rather, in an impassioned* **freedom towards death**—*a freedom which has been released from the Illusions of the "they", and which is factical, certain of itself, and anxious.*

Dasein as an Authentic Potentiality-for-Being, and Resoluteness

THE EXISTENTIAL-ONTOLOGICAL FOUNDATIONS OF CONSCIENCE. In the phenomenon of conscience we find, without further differentiation, that in some way it gives us something to understand. Our analysis of it takes its departure from this finding. Conscience discloses, and thus belongs within the range of those existential phenomena which constitute the *Being of the "there"* as disclosedness. We have analysed the most universal structures of state-of-mind, understanding, discourse and falling. If we now bring conscience into this phenomenal context, this is not a matter of applying these structures schematically to a special 'case' of Dasein's disclosure. On the contrary, our Interpretation of conscience not only will carry further our earlier analysis of the disclosedness of the "there", but it will also grasp it more primordially with regard to Dasein's authentic Being.

Through disclosedness, that entity which we call "Dasein" is in the possibility of *being* its "there". With its world, it is there for itself, and indeed—proximally and for the most part—in such a way that it has disclosed to itself its potentiality-for-Being in terms of the 'world' of its concern. Dasein exists as a potentiality-for-Being which has, in each case, already abandoned itself to definite possibilities. And it has abandoned itself to these possibilities because it is an entity which has been thrown, and an entity whose thrownness gets disclosed more or less plainly and impressively by its having a mood. To any state-of-mind or mood, understanding belongs equiprimordially. In this way Dasein 'knows' what it is itself capable of [woran es mit ihm selbst ist], inasmuch as it has either projected itself upon possibilities of its own or has been so absorbed in the "they" that it has let such possibilities be presented to it by the way in which the "they" has publicly interpreted things. The presenting of these possibilities, however, is made possible existentially through the fact that Dasein, as a Being-with which understands, can *listen* to Others. Losing itself in the publicness and the idle talk of the "they", it *fails to hear [überhört]* its own Self in listening to the they-self. If Dasein is to be able to get brought back from this lostness of failing to hear itself, and if this is to be done through itself, then it must first be able to find itself—to find itself as something which has failed to hear itself, and which fails to hear in that it *listens away* to the "they". This listening-away must get broken off; in other words, the possibility of another kind of hearing which will interrupt it, must be given by Dasein itself. The possibility of its thus getting broken off lies in its being appealed to without mediation. Dasein fails to hear itself, and listens away to the "they"; and this listening-away gets broken by the call if that call, in accordance with its character as such, arouses another kind of hearing, which, in relationship to the hearing that is lost, has a character in every way opposite. If in this lost hearing, one has been fascinated with the 'hubbub' of the manifold ambiguity which idle talk possesses in its everyday 'newness', then the call must do its calling without any hubbub and unambiguously, leaving no foothold for curiosity. *That which, by calling in this manner, gives us to understand, is the conscience.*

THE CHARACTER OF CONSCIENCE AS A CALL. To any discourse there belongs that which is talked about in it. Discourse gives information about something, and does so in some definite regard. From what is thus talked about, it draws whatever it is saying as this particular discourse—what is said in the talk as such. In discourse as communication, this becomes accessible to the Dasein-with of Others, for the most part by way of uttering it in language.

In the call of conscience, what is it that is talked about—in other words, to what is the appeal made? Manifestly Dasein itself. This answer is as incontestable as it is indefinite. If the call has so vague a target, then it might at most remain an occasion for Dasein to pay attention to itself. But it is essential to Dasein that along with the disclosedness of its world it has been disclosed to itself, so that it always *understands itself.* The call reaches Dasein in this understanding of itself which it always has, and which is concernful in an everyday, average manner. The call reaches the they-self of concernful Being with Others.

And to what is one called when one is thus appealed to? To one's *own Self.* Not to what Dasein counts for, can do, or concerns itself with in being with one another publicly, nor to what it has taken hold of, set about, or let itself be carried along with. The sort of Dasein which is understood after the manner of the world both for Others and for itself, gets *passed over* in this appeal; this is something of which the call to the Self takes not the slightest cognizance. And because only the *Self* of the they-self gets appealed to and brought to hear, the *"they"* collapses. But the fact that the call *passes over* both the "they" and the manner in which Dasein has been publicly interpreted, does not by any means signify that the "they" is not *reached too.* Precisely *in passing over* the "they" (keen as it is for public repute) the call pushes it into insignificance [Bedeutungslosigkeit]. But the Self, which the appeal has robbed of this lodgement and hiding-place, gets brought to itself by the call.

When the they-self is appealed to, it gets called to the Self. But it does not get called to that Self which can become for itself an 'object' on which to pass judgment, nor to that Self which inertly dissects its 'inner life' with fussy curiosity, nor to that Self which one has in mind when one gazes 'analytically' at psychical conditions and what lies behind them. The appeal to the Self in the they-self does not force it inwards upon itself, so that it can close itself off from the 'external world'. The call passes over everything like this and disperses it, so as to appeal solely to that Self which, notwithstanding, is in no other way than Being-in-the-world.

But how are we to determine *what is said in the talk* that belongs to this kind of discourse? *What* does the conscience call to him to whom it appeals? Taken strictly, nothing. The call asserts nothing, gives no information about world-events, has nothing to tell. Least of all does it try to set going a 'soliloquy' in the Self to which it has appealed. 'Nothing' gets called *to [zu*-gerufen] this Self, but it has been *summoned [aufgerufen]* to itself—that is, to its ownmost potentiality-for-Being. The tendency of the call is not such as to put up for 'trial' the Self to which the appeal is made; but it calls Dasein forth (and 'forward') into its ownmost possibilities, as a summons to its ownmost *potentiality*-for-Being-its-Self.

GUILT. Everyday common sense first takes 'Being-guilty' in the sense of 'owing', of 'having something due on account'. One is to give back to the Other something to which the latter has a claim. This 'Being-guilty' as *'having debts' ["Schulden haben"]* is a way of Being with Others in the field of concern, as in providing something or bringing it along. Other modes of such concern are: depriving, borrowing, withholding, taking, stealing—failing to satisfy, in some way or other, the claims which Others have made as to their possessions. This kind of Being-guilty is related to *that with which one can concern oneself.*

"Being-guilty" also has the signification of *'being responsible for' ["schuld sein an"]*—that is, being the cause or author of something, or even 'being the occasion' for something. In this sense of 'having responsibility' for something, one can 'be guilty' of something without 'owing' anything to someone else or coming to 'owe' him. On the other hand, one can owe something to another without being responsible for it oneself. Another person can 'incur debts' with Others 'for me'.

These ordinary significations of "Being-guilty" as 'having debts to someone' and 'having responsibility for something' can go together and define a kind of behaviour which we call *'making oneself responsible';* that is, by having the responsibility for having a debt, one may break a law and make oneself punishable. Yet the requirement which one fails to satisfy need not necessarily be related to anyone's possessions; it can regulate the very manner in which we are with one other publicly. 'Making oneself responsible' by breaking a law as we have thus defined it, can indeed also have the character of *'coming to owe something to Others'.* This does not happen merely through law-breaking as such, but rather through my having the responsibility for the Other's becoming endangered in his existence, led astray, or even ruined. This way of coming to owe something to Others is possible without breaking the 'public' law. Thus the formal conception of "Being-guilty" in the sense of having come to owe something to an Other, may be defined as follows: *"Being-the-basis* for a lack of something in the Dasein of an Other, and in such a manner that this very Being-the-basis determines itself as 'lacking in some way' in terms of that for which it is the basis." This kind of lacking is a failure to satisfy some requirement which applies to one's existent Being with Others. . . .

Nevertheless, in the idea of 'Guilty!' there lies the character of the *"not"*. If the 'Guilty!' is something that can definitely apply to existence, then this raises the ontological problem of clarifying existentially the *character* of this "not" *as a "not"*. Moreover, to the idea of 'Guilty!' belongs what is expressed without further differentiation in the conception of guilt as 'having responsibility for'—that is, as Being-the basis for . . . Hence we define the formally existential idea of the 'Guilty!' as "Being-the-basis for a Being which has been defined by a 'not' "—that is to say, as *"Being-the-basis of a nullity"*. The idea of the "not" which lies in the concept of guilt as understood existentially, excludes relatedness to anything present-at-hand which is possible or which may have been required; furthermore, Dasein is altogether incommensurable with anything present-at-hand or generally accepted [Geltenden] which is not it itself, or which is not *in the way Dasein is*—namely, *existing;* so any possibility that, with regard to Being-the-basis for a lack, the entity which is itself such a basis might be reckoned up as 'lacking in some manner', is a possibility which drops out. If a lack, such as failure to fulfil some requirement, has been 'caused' in a manner characteristic of Dasein, we cannot simply reckon back to there being something lacking [Mangelhaftigkeit] in the 'cause'. Being-the-basis-for-something need not have the same "not"-character as the *privativum* which is based upon it and which arises from it. The basis need not acquire a nullity of its own from that for which it is the basis [seinem Begründeten]. This implies, however, that *Being-guilty does not first result from an indebtedness [Verschuldung], but that, on the contrary, indebtedness becomes possible only 'on the basis' of a primordial Being-guilty.*

THE EXISTENTIAL STRUCTURE OF THE AUTHENTIC POTENTIALITY-FOR-BEING WHICH IS ATTESTED IN THE CONSCIENCE. The disclosedness of Dasein in wanting to have a conscience, is thus constituted by anxiety as state-of-mind, by understanding as a projection of oneself upon one's ownmost Being-guilty, and by discourse as reticence. This distinctive and authentic disclosedness, which is attested in Dasein itself by its conscience—*this reticent self-projection upon one's ownmost Being-guilty, in which one is ready for anxiety*—we call *"resoluteness"*.

Resoluteness is a distinctive mode of Dasein's disclosedness. In an earlier passage, however, we have Interpreted disclosedness existentially as the *primordial truth*. Such truth is primarily not a quality of 'judgment' nor of any definite way of behaving, but something essentially constitutive for Being-in-the-world as such. Truth must be conceived as a fundamental *existentiale*. In our ontological clarification of the proposition that 'Dasein is in the truth' we have called attention to the primordial disclosedness of this entity as the *truth of existence;* and for the delimitation of its character we have referred to the analysis of Dasein's authenticity.

In resoluteness we have now arrived at that truth of Dasein which is most primordial because it is *authentic.* Whenever a "there" is disclosed, its whole Being-in-the-world—that is to say, the world, Being-in, and the Self which, as an 'I am', this entity is—is disclosed with equal primordiality. Whenever the world is disclosed, entities within-the-world have been discovered already. The discoveredness of the ready-to-hand and the present-at-hand is based on the disclosedness of the world for if the current totality of involvements is to be freed, this requires that significance be understood beforehand. In understanding significance, concernful Dasein submits itself circumspectively to what it encounters as ready-to-hand. Any discovering of a totality of involvements goes back to a "for-the-sake-of-which"; and on the understanding of such a "for-the-sake-of-which" is based in turn the understanding of significance as the disclosedness of the current world. In seeking shelter, sustenance, livelihood, we do so "for the sake of" constant possibilities of Dasein which are very close to it; upon these the entity for which its own Being is an issue, has already projected itself. Thrown into its 'there', every Dasein has been factically submitted to a definite 'world'—its 'world'. At the same time those factical projections which are closest to it, have been guided by its concernful *lostness* in the "they". To this lostness, one's own Dasein can appeal, and this appeal can be understood in the way of resoluteness. But in that case this *authentic* disclosedness modifies with equal primordiality both the way in which the 'world' is discovered (and this is founded upon that disclosedness) and the way in which the Dasein-with of Others is disclosed. The 'world' which is ready-to-hand does not become another one 'in its content', nor does the circle of Others get exchanged for a new one; but both one's Being towards the ready-to-hand understandingly and concernfully, and one's solicitous Being with Others, are now given a definite character in terms of their ownmost potentiality-for-Being-their-Selves.

Resoluteness, as *authentic Being-one's-Self,* does not detach Dasein from its world, nor does it isolate it so that it becomes a free-floating "I". And how should it, when resoluteness as authentic disclosedness, is *authentically* nothing else than *Being-in-the-world?* Resoluteness brings the Self right into its current concernful Being-alongside what is ready-to-hand, and pushes it into solicitous Being with Others.

In the light of the "for-the-sake-of-which" of one's self-chosen potentiality-for-Being, resolute Dasein frees itself for its world. Dasein's resoluteness towards itself is what first makes it possible to let the Others who are with it 'be' in their ownmost potentiality-for-Being, and to co-disclose this potentiality in the solicitude which leaps forth and liberates. When Dasein is resolute, it can become the 'conscience' of Others. Only by authentically Being-their-Selves in resoluteness can people authentically be with one another—not by ambiguous and jealous stipulations and talkative fraternizing in the "they" and in what "they" want to undertake.

Resoluteness, by its ontological essence, is always the resoluteness of some factical Dasein at a particular time. The essence of Dasein as an entity is its existence. Resoluteness 'exists' only as a resolution [Entschluss] which understandingly projects itself. But on what basis does Dasein disclose itself in resoluteness? On what is it to resolve? *Only* the resolution itself can give the answer. One would completely misunderstand the phenomenon of resoluteness if one should want to suppose that this consists simply in taking up possibilities which have been proposed and recommended, and seizing hold of them. *The resolution is precisely the disclosive projection and determination of what is factically possible at the time.* To resoluteness, the *indefiniteness* characteristic of every potentiality-for-Being into which Dasein has been factically thrown, is something that necessarily *belongs.* Only in a resolution is resoluteness sure of itself. The *existentiell indefiniteness* of resoluteness never makes itself definite except in a resolution; yet it has, all the same, its *existential definiteness.*

What one resolves upon in resoluteness has been prescribed onto-logically in the existentiality of Dasein in general as a potentiality-for-Being in the manner of concernful solicitude. As care, however, Dasein has been Determined by facticity and falling. Disclosed in its 'there', it maintains itself both in truth and in untruth with equal primordiality. This 'really' holds in particular for resoluteness as authentic truth. Resoluteness appropriates untruth authentically. Dasein is already in irresoluteness [Unentschlossenheit], and soon, perhaps, will be in it again. The term "irresoluteness' merely expresses that phenomenon which we have Interpreted as a Being-surrendered to the way in which things have been prevalently interpreted by the "they". Dasein, as a they-self, gets 'lived' by the common-sense ambiguity of that publicness in which nobody resolves upon anything but which has always made its decision. "Resoluteness" signifies letting oneself be summoned out of one's lostness in the "they". The irresoluteness of the "they" remains dominant notwithstanding, but it cannot impugn resolute existence. In the counter-concept to irresoluteness, as resoluteness as existentially understood, we do not have in mind any ontico-psychical characteristic in the sense of Being-burdened with inhibitions. Even resolutions remain dependent upon the "they" and its world. The understanding of this is one of the things that a resolution discloses, inasmuch as resoluteness is what first gives authentic transparency to Dasein. In resoluteness the issue for Dasein is its ownmost potentiality-for-Being, which, as something thrown, can project itself only upon definite factical possibilities. Resolution does not withdraw itself from 'actuality', but discovers first what is factically possible; and it does so by seizing upon it in whatever way is possible for it as its ownmost potentiality-for-Being in the "they".

TEMPORALITY AS THE ONTOLOGICAL MEANING OF CARE. In characterizing the 'connection' between care and Selfhood, our aim was not only to clarify the special problem of "I"-hood, but also to help in the final preparation for getting into our grasp phenomenally the totality of Dasein's structural whole. We need the *unwavering discipline* of the existential way of putting the question, if, for our ontological point of view, Dasein's kind of Being is not to be finally perverted into a mode of presence-at-hand, even one which is wholly undifferentiated. Dasein becomes 'essentially' Dasein in that authentic existence which constitutes itself as anticipatory resoluteness. Such resoluteness, as a mode of the authenticity of care, contains Dasein's primordial Self-constancy and to-tality. We must take an undistracted look at these and understand them existentially if we are to lay bare the ontological meaning of Dasein's Being.

What are we seeking ontologically with the meaning of care? What does *"meaning"* signify? In our investigation, we have encountered this phenomenon in connection with the analysis of understanding and inter-pretation. According to that analysis, meaning is that wherein the un-derstandability [Verstehbarkeit] of something maintains itself—even that of something which does not come into view explicitly and thematically. "Meaning" signifies the "upon-which" [das Woraufhin] of a primary projection in terms of which something can be conceived in its possibility as that which it is. Projecting discloses possibilities—that is to say, it discloses the sort of thing that makes possible.

To lay bare the "upon-which" of a projection, amounts to disclosing that which makes possible what has been projected. To lay it bare in this way requires methodologically that we study the projection (usually a tacit one) which underlies an interpretation, and that we do so in such a way that what has been projected in the projecting can be disclosed and grasped with regard to its "upon-which". To set forth the meaning of care means, then, to follow up the projection which guides and underlies the primordial existential Interpretation of Dasein, and to follow it up in such a way that in what is here projected, its "upon-which" may be seen. What has been projected is the Being of Dasein, and it is disclosed in what constitutes that Being as an authentic potentiality-for-Being-a-whole. That upon which the Being which has been disclosed and is thus constituted has been projected, is that which itself makes possible this Constitution of Being as care. When we inquire about the meaning of care, we are asking *what makes possible the totality of the articulated structural whole of care, in the unity of its articulation as we have unfolded it.* . . .

Anticipatory resoluteness discloses the current Situation of the "there" in such a way that existence, in taking action, is circumspectively concerned with what is factically ready-to-hand environmentally. Resolute Being-alongside what is ready-to-hand in the Situation—that is to say, taking action in such a way as to let one encounter what *has presence* environ-mentally—is possible only by *making* such an entity *present*. Only as the *Present [Gegenwart]* in the sense of making present, can resoluteness be what it is: namely, letting itself be encountered undisguisedly by that which it seizes upon in taking action.

Coming back to itself futurally, resoluteness brings itself into the Situation by making present. The character of "having been" arises from the future, and in such a way that the future which "has been" (or better, which "is in the process of having been") releases from itself the Present. This phenomenon has the unity of a future which makes present in the process of having been; we designate it as *"temporality"*. Only in so far as Dasein has the definite character of temporality, is the authentic potentiality-for-Being-a-whole of anticipatory resoluteness, as we have described it, made possible for Dasein itself. *Temporality reveals itself as the meaning of authentic care. . . .*

If resoluteness makes up the mode of authentic care, and if this itself is possible only through temporality, then the phenomenon at which we have arrived by taking a look at resoluteness, must present us with only a modality of temporality, by which, after all, care as such is made possible. Dasein's totality of Being as care means: ahead-of-itself-already-being-in (a world) as Being-alongside (entities encountered within-the-world). When we first fixed upon this articulated structure, we suggested that with regard to this articulation on the ontological question must be pursued still further back until the unity of the totality of this structural manifoldness has been laid bare. *The primordial unity of the structure of care lies in temporality.*

The "ahead-of-itself" is grounded in the future. In the "Being-already-in . . .", the character of "having been" is made known. "Being-alongside . . ." becomes possible in making present. While the "ahead" includes the notion of a "before", neither the 'before' in the 'ahead' nor the 'already' is to be taken in terms of the way time is ordinarily understood; this has been automatically ruled out by what has been said above. With this 'before' we do not have in mind 'in advance of something' [das "Vorher"] in the sense of 'not yet now—but later'; the 'already' is just as far from signifying 'no longer now—but earlier'. If the expressions 'before' and 'already' were to have a time-oriented [zeithafte] signification such as *this* (and they can have this signification too), then to say that care has temporality would be to say that it is something which is 'earlier' and 'later', 'not yet' and 'no longer'. Care would then be conceived as an entity which occurs and runs its course 'in time'. The *Being* of an entity having the character of Dasein would become something *present-at-hand*. If this sort of thing is impossible, then any time-oriented sig-nification which the expressions we have mentioned may have, must be different from this. The 'before' and the 'ahead' indicate the future as of a sort which would make it possible for Dasein to be such that its potentiality-for-Being is an issue. Self-projection upon the 'for-the-sake-of-oneself' is grounded in the future and is an essential characteristic of *existentiality. The primary meaning of existentiality is the future.*

Likewise, with the 'already' we have in view the existential temporal meaning of the Being of that entity which, in so far as it *is,* is already something that has been thrown. Only because care is based on the character of "having been", can Dasein exist as the thrown entity which it is. 'As long as' Dasein factically exists, it is never past [vergangen], but it always is indeed as already having *been,* in the sense of the "I *am*-as-having-been". And only as long as Dasein is, *can* it *be* as having been. On the other hand, we call an entity "past", when it is no longer present-at-hand. Therefore Dasein, in existing, can never establish itself as a fact which is present-at-hand, arising and passing away 'in the course of time', with a bit of it past already. Dasein never 'finds itself' except as a thrown Fact. In the *state-of-mind in which it finds itself,* Dasein is assailed by itself as the entity which it still is and already was—that is to say, which it constantly *is* as having been. The primary existential meaning of facticity lies in the character of "having been". In our formulation of the structure of care, the temporal meaning of existentiality and facticity is indicated by the expressions 'before' and 'already'.

On the other hand, we lack such an indication for the third item which is constitutive for care—the Being-alongside which falls. This should not signify that falling is not also grounded in temporality; it should instead give us a hint that *making-present,* as the *primary* basis for *falling* into the ready-to-hand and present-at-hand with which we concern ourselves, remains *included* in the future and in having been, and is included in these in the mode of primordial temporality. When resolute, Dasein has brought itself back from falling, and has done so precisely in order to be more authentically 'there' in the 'moment of *vision*' as regards the Situation which has been disclosed.

Temporality makes possible the unity of existence, facticity, and falling, and in this way constitutes primordially the totality of the structure of care. The items of care have not been pieced together cumulatively any more than temporality itself has been put together 'in the course of time' ["mit der Zeit"] out of the future, the having been, and the Present. Temporality 'is' not an *entity* at all. It is not, but it *temporalizes* itself. Nevertheless, we cannot avoid saying, 'Temporality "is" . . . the meaning of care', 'Temporality "is" . . . defined in such and such a way'; the reason for this can be made intelligible only when we have clarified the idea of Being and that of the 'is' in general. Temporality temporalizes, and indeed it temporalizes possible ways of itself. These make possible the multiplicity of Dasein's modes of Being, and especially the basic possibility of authentic or inauthentic existence.

The future, the character of having been, and the Present, show the phenomenal characteristics of the 'towards-oneself', the 'back-to', and the 'letting-oneself-be-encountered-*by*'. The phenomena of the "towards . . .", the "to . . .", and the "alongside . . .", make temporality manifest as the εκστατικόν pure and simple. *Temporality is the primordial 'outside-of-itself' in and for itself.* We therefore call the phenomena of the future, the character of having been, and the Present, the *"ecstases"* of temporality. Temporality is not, prior to this, an entity which first emerges from *itself;* its essence is a process of temporalizing in the unity of the ecstases. What is characteristic of the 'time' which is accessible to the ordinary under-standing, consists, among other things, precisely in the fact that it is a pure sequence of "nows", without beginning and without end, in which the ecstatical character of primordial temporality has been levelled off. But this very levelling off, in accordance with its existential meaning, is grounded in the possibility of a definite kind of temporalizing, in con-formity with which temporality temporalizes as inauthentic the kind of 'time' we have just mentioned. If, therefore, we demonstrate that the 'time' which is accessible to Dasein's common sense is *not* primordial, but arises rather from authentic temporality, then, in accordance with the principle, *"a potiori fit denominatio",* we are justified in designating as *"primordial time"* the *temporality* which we have now laid bare.

In enumerating the ecstases, we have always mentioned the future first. We have done this to indicate that the future has a priority in the ecstatical unity of primordial and authentic temporality. This is so, even though temporality does not first arise through a cumulative sequence of the ecstases, but in each case temporalizes itself in their equiprimordiality. But within this equiprimordiality, the modes of temporalizing are different. The difference lies in the fact that the nature of the temporalizing can be determined primarily in terms of the different ecstases. Primordial and authentic temporality temporalizes itself in terms of the authentic future and in such a way that in having been futurally, it first of all awakens the Present. *The primary phenomenon of primordial and authentic tem-porality is the future.* The priority of the future will vary according to the ways in which the temporalizing of inauthentic temporality itself is modified, but it will still come to the fore even in the derivative kind of 'time'.

Dasein and Temporality

Genesis of the Ordinary Conception of Time

The principal thesis of the ordinary way of interpreting time—namely, that time is 'infinite'—makes manifest most impressively the way in which world-time and accordingly temporality in general have been levelled off and covered up by such an interpretation. It is held that time presents itself proximally as an uninterrupted sequence of "nows". Every "now", moreover, is already either a "just-now" or a "forthwith". If in characterizing time we stick primarily and exclusively *to such a sequence,* then in principle neither beginning nor end can be found in it. Every last "now", *as "now",* is always *already* a "forthwith" that is no longer [ein Sofort-nicht-mehr]; thus it is time in the sense of the "no-longer-now"— in the sense of the past. Every first "now" is a "just-now" that is not yet [ein Soeben-noch-nicht]; thus it is time in the sense of the "not-yet-now"—in the sense of the 'future'. Hence time is endless 'on both sides'. This thesis becomes possible only on the basis of an orientation *towards a free-floating "in-itself" of a course of "nows" which is present-at-hand*— an orientation in which the full phenomenon of the "now" has been covered up with regard to its datability, its worldhood, its spannedness, and its character of having a location of the same kind as Dasein's, so that it has dwindled to an unrecognizable fragment. If one directs one's glance towards Being-present-at-hand and not-Being-present-at-hand, and thus 'thinks' the sequence of "nows" through 'to the end', then an end can never be found. In *this* way of *thinking* time through to the end, one *must* always *think* more time; from this one infers that time *is* infinite.

But wherein are grounded this levelling-off of world-time and this covering-up of temporality? In the Being of Dasein itself, which we have, in a preparatory manner, Interpreted as *care.* Thrown and falling, Dasein is proximally and for the most part lost in that with which it concerns itself. In this lostness, however, Dasein's fleeing in the face of that authentic existence which has been characterized as "anticipatory resoluteness", has made itself known; and this is a fleeing which covers up. In this concernful fleeing lies a fleeing *in the face of* death—that is, a looking-away *from* the end of Being-in-the-world. This looking-away from it, is in itself a mode of that Being-*towards*-the-end which is ecstatically *futural.* The inauthentic temporality of everyday Dasein as it falls, must, as such a looking-away from finitude, fail to recognize authentic futurity and therewith temporality in general. And if indeed the way in which Dasein is ordinarily understood is guided by the "they", only so can the self-forgetful 'representation' of the 'infinity' of public time be strengthened. The "they" never dies because it *can*not die; for death is in each case mine, and only in anticipatory resoluteness does it get authentically understood in an existentiell manner. Nevertheless, the "they", which never dies and which misunderstands Being-towards-the-end, gives a characteristic interpretation to fleeing in the face of death. To the very end 'it always has more time'. Here a way of "having time" in the sense that one can lose it makes itself known. 'Right now, this! then that! And that is barely over, when . . .' Here it is not as if the finitude of time were getting understood; quite the contrary, for concern sets out to snatch as much as possible from the time which still keeps coming and 'goes on'. Publicly, time is something which everyone takes and can take. In the everyday way in which we are with one another, the levelled-off sequence of "nows" remains completely unrecognizable as regards its origin in the temporality of the individual Dasein. How is 'time' in its course to be touched even the least bit when a man who has been present-at-hand 'in time' no longer exists? Time goes on, just as indeed it already 'was' when a man 'came into life'. The only time one knows is the public time which has been levelled off and which belongs to everyone—and that means, to nobody.

But just as he who flees in the face of death is pursued by it even as he evades it, and just as in turning away from it he must see it none the less, even the innocuous infinite sequence of "nows" which simply runs its course, imposes itself 'on' Dasein in a remarkably enigmatical way. Why do we say that time *passes away,* when we do not say with *just as much* emphasis that it arises? Yet with regard to the pure sequence of "nows" we have as much right to say one as the other. When Dasein talks of time's *passing away,* it understands, in the end, more of time than it wants to admit; that is to say, the *temporality* in which world-time temporalizes itself has *not been completely closed off,* no matter how much it may get covered up. Our talk about time's passing-away gives expression to this 'experience': time does not let itself be halted. This 'experience' in turn is possible only because the halting of time is something that we want. Herein lies an inauthentic *awaiting* of 'moments'—an awaiting in which these are already *forgotten* as they glide by. The *awaiting* of inauthentic existence—the awaiting which forgets as it makes present— is the condition for the possibility of the ordinary experience of time's passing-away. Because Dasein is futural in the "ahead-of-itself", it must, in awaiting, understand the sequence of "nows" as one which *glides by* as it passes away. *Dasein knows fugitive time in terms of its 'fugitive' knowledge about its death.* In the kind of talk which emphasizes time's passing away, the *finite futurity* of Dasein's temporality is publicly reflected. And because even in talk about time's passing away, death can remain covered up, time shows itself as a passing-away 'in itself'.

But even in this pure sequence of "nows" which passes away in itself, primordial time still manifests itself throughout all this levelling off and covering up. In the ordinary interpretation, the stream of time is defined as an *irreversible* succession. Why cannot time be reversed? Especially if one looks exclusively at the stream of "nows", it is incomprehensible in itself why this sequence should not present itself in the reverse direction. The impossibility of this reversal has its basis in the way public time originates in temporality, the temporalizing of which is primarily futural and 'goes' to its end ecstatically in such a way that it 'is' already towards its end.

The ordinary way of characterizing time as an endless, irreversible sequence of "nows" which passes away, arises from the temporality of falling Dasein. *The ordinary representation of time has its natural justi-fication.* It belongs to Dasein's average kind of Being, and to that un-derstanding of Being which proximally prevails. Thus proximally and for the most part, even *history* gets understood *publicly* as happening *within-time.* This interpretation of time loses its exclusive and pre-eminent justification only if it claims to convey the 'true' conception of time and to be able to prescribe the sole possible horizon within which time is to be Interpreted. On the contrary, it has emerged that *why and how world-time belongs to Dasein's temporality* is intelligible only in terms of that temporality and its temporalizing. From temporality the full structure of world-time has been drawn; and only the Interpretation of this structure gives us the clue for 'seeing' at all that in the ordinary conception of time something has been covered up, and for estimating how much the ecstatico-horizontal constitution of temporality has been levelled off. This orientation by Dasein's temporality indeed makes it possible to exhibit the origin and the factical necessity of this levelling off and covering up, and at the same time to test the arguments for the ordinary theses about time.

On the other hand, within the horizon of the way time is ordinarily understood, *temporality is inaccessible in the reverse direction.* Not only must the now-time be oriented primarily by temporality in the order of possible interpretation, but it temporalizes itself only in the inauthentic temporality of Dasein; so if one has regard for the way the now-time is derived from temporality, one is justified in considering temporality as the *time which is primordial.*

Ecstatico-horizonal temporality temporalizes itself *primarily* in terms of the *future.* In the way time is ordinarily understood, however, the basic phenomenon of time is seen in the *"now",* and indeed in that pure "now" which has been shorn in its full structure—that which they call the 'Present'. One can gather from this that there is in principle no prospect that *in terms of this kind of "now"* one can clarify the ecstatico-horizonal phenomenon of the *moment of vision* which belongs to temporality, or even that one can derive it thus. Correspondingly, the future as ecstatically understood—the datable and significant 'then'—does not coincide with the ordinary conception of the 'future' in the sense of a pure "now" which has not yet come along but is only coming along. And the concept of the past in the sense of the pure "now" which has passed away, is just as far from coinciding with the ecstatical "having-been"—the datable and significant 'on a former occasion'. The "now" is not pregnant with the "not-yet-now", but the Present arises from the future in the primordial ecstatical unity of the temporalizing of temporality.

5

Jean-Paul Sartre

SARTRE ON THE NATURE OF CONSCIOUSNESS: A CRITIQUE OF CARTESIANISM

The philosophers we have been considering have all been concerned with a special subject matter. Jean-Paul Sartre (1905–1980) approaches this subject matter via an examination of the nature of consciousness, which is quite appropriate. For if we really want to identify the subject matter of existentialism, then we should identify it as consciousness because consciousness is most obviously involved in our decisions and choices. That is, insofar as human life is conceived of as a continuous series of decisions and choices, it is essentially the life of a conscious being. Thus, to examine Sartre's account of consciousness is, in effect, to examine his account of human life. What, then, is Sartre's account of consciousness?

Sartre's treatment of consciousness is multifaceted, and in this section we do not attempt a complete analysis. Nevertheless, we can begin to get an idea of his view by considering selections from his early work, *The Transcendence of the Ego,* and also from the introduction to his most famous book, *Being and Nothingness.*[1] In those works Sartre uses the term *consciousness* as the most general term for what we would ordinarily describe by the verbs "see," "feel," "think about," "imagine," "desire," and so on. All these terms imply that an individual is conscious of something. Consciousness in any and all of its forms is directed toward an object. In other words, consciousness is intentional. This is a truism accepted by all; the philosophical question concerns the nature or structure of intentionality. Rather than turn directly to Sartre's analysis of intentionality and the nature of consciousness, we begin by briefly discussing René Descartes, for in order to clarify Sartre's own view of consciousness it is useful to understand the Cartesian analysis he is rejecting and why he is rejecting it.

Descartes was the first modern philosopher to make a sharp distinction between what consciousness is in itself and what physical processes may occur during consciousness. He recognized that consciousness is the most fundamental item in the subject matter of philosophy because we cannot investigate anything—we cannot have knowledge of the world or of mathematics and geometry—without presupposing a conscious act. Descartes' famous *Cogito,* or "I think," is meant to indicate the fundamental role that consciousness plays in his philosophy. Consciousness is the starting point of all knowledge.

What, then, is Descartes' analysis of consciousness? More specifically, how would he analyze the statement "I am thinking of X"? In Descartes' view the "I" refers to an unextended immaterial mental substance or self. This substance serves to account for the unity of the various thoughts belonging to one mind at a moment, as well as the unity of a succession of thoughts through time. The "I" is a separately existing entity, over and above the particular conscious acts, thoughts, experiences, and feelings that belong to a person through time. It also serves to individuate one person from another. Each person has his or her own "ego" or substantial self. Mental or conscious acts like perceiving, imagining, and hoping are construed as properties of the self. Indeed, consciousness, taken quite generally, as either thinking, perceiving, imagining, and the like, is the essential property of the self. It is, according to Descartes, a property without which "I" could not exist. The mind or substantial self has or "owns" thoughts.

Under the sway of his methodological doubt on the one hand, and the rise of the new science on the other, Descartes was committed to representationalism, the view maintaining that when we think, we are not directly in touch with the object or fact we are thinking about. For Descartes, to think about X is to have an idea, mental image, representation, or concept of X which, like the act of thinking itself, exists "in" the mind. How exactly the idea or concept of X represents or is related to X, whether by resemblance, causation, or a basic intentional nexus, is not clear in Descartes and need not detain us. What is important to note is that in Descartes' view, (1) the structure of consciousness requires a substantial self or ego as the subject or owner of consciousness; (2) consciousness of an object involves some relation between the substantial

"I" and an object; and (3) consciousness contains ideas, concepts, or more generally representations, of what it is about.

Sartre rejects each of these three aspects of the Cartesian view. Consciousness is neither a substance nor a property; it is neither "owned" nor inhabited by a mental substance; and it is neither a relation between a mental substance and an object nor a container with something in it. Sartre's own analysis of consciousness makes the Cartesian view otiose. He maintains that the first essential feature of consciousness is its intentionality. There is nothing more to consciousness than its intentionality (its being consciousness of an object) and because it is intentional it exhausts itself in reaching to an object. Furthermore, the intentionality of consciousness implies that consciousness is a direction to a transcendent object, an object that exists outside of consciousness. Thus, neither the object of consciousness nor a representation (an idea) of the object of consciousness is "in" consciousness; that is, consciousness has no contents.

In claiming that consciousness has no contents, Sartre does not mean that consciousness is a container with nothing in it, but rather that it is nothing in itself. What consciousness is, its essence, is determined by its object, but if you take away the object of consciousness then there is nothing left. Thus, on the one hand, the object of consciousness is the essence of consciousness, and on the other hand, consciousness is not its object, but is separated from it. In short, in and of itself consciousness is nothingness; it is not a self-contained thing or substance in the world. It exists, but exists as a *lack* of the being it intends or is about.

Sartre expresses some of these ideas in the following passage:

> All consciousness, as Husserl has shown, is consciousness of something. This means that there is no consciousness which is not a *positing* of a transcendent object, or if you prefer, that consciousness has no "content." . . . All consciousness is positional consciousness in that it transcends itself in order to reach an object, and exhausts itself in this same positing. (pp. 287–288)

Since consciousness exhausts itself in positing or intending an object, the Cartesian conception of consciousness as having a substantial ego as an ingredient of consciousness or as a subject of consciousness must be mistaken. From Sartre's point of view, the Cartesian clutters consciousness with a being which it is not. Furthermore, Sartre argues that introducing a substantival ego into consciousness leads to insurmountable dialectical and phenomenological difficulties. We can begin to see what those difficulties are by turning to a second essential feature of consciousness, namely self-consciousness.

According to Sartre, "The type of existence of consciousness is to be conscious of itself. And consciousness is conscious of itself insofar as it is conscious of a transcendent object" (p. 282). Sartre is making a phenomenological point here about how consciousness is given to us:

Whenever I am conscious of an object or whenever I intend some state of affairs, I am conscious of being conscious of that object or state of affairs. Suppose, for example, that I am seeing a table. In order for me to have this consciousness, in order for me to perceive or see a table, I must be conscious of perceiving or seeing the table and not, say, imagining or remembering it. Or suppose that I am thinking of my mother. Can this thinking be unconscious? Can I be conscious of a transcendent object (an object for consciousness), unconsciously? For Sartre the idea of being conscious of X unconsciously makes no sense. According to Sartre, "the necessary and sufficient condition for a knowing consciousness to be knowledge of its object, is that it be conscious of itself as being that knowledge" (p. 288).

Since consciousness is essentially self-consciousness, an adequate account of consciousness must provide an adequate account of self-consciousness and that, Sartre maintains, the Cartesian analysis cannot do. Recall that according to Descartes, if we think of consciousness, then we must think of it according to the following picture. Suppose that I am conscious of X. For Descartes I am a pure ego or substance that engages in consciousness, and consciousness is a relation between the I (an immaterial substance) and its object. That is, consciousness is a relation possessed by a substance or thing in the world. By calling consciousness a relation we mean that it relates or connects two terms: One term is the self or the "I" and the other is the object of consciousness.

Sartre rejects this model of consciousness as incoherent. The general line of his argument may be stated as follows:

1. All consciousness is self-consciousness.
2. Therefore, any adequate account of consciousness must be an adequate account of self-consciousness.
3. The Cartesian account of self-consciousness is inadequate.
4. Therefore, the Cartesian account of consciousness is inadequate.

Since we have already considered (1) and since (2) follows from (1), the crucial premise to consider is (3). Sartre states his argument for (3) in the following passage:

> What is the consciousness of consciousness? We suffer to such an extent from the illusion of the primacy of knowledge that we are immediately ready to make of the consciousness of consciousness an idea ideae in the manner of Spinoza; that is, a knowledge of knowledge . . . It does not seem possible for us to accept this interpretation of the consciousness of consciousness. If we accept the law of the knower-known dyad, then a third term will be necessary in order for the knower to become known in turn, and we will be faced with this dilemma: either we stop at any one term of the series. . . In this case the totality of the phenomenon falls into the unknown; that is, we always bump up against a non-self-conscious reflection

and a final term. Or else we affirm the necessity of an infinite regress *(idea ideae ideae, etc.),* which is absurd. (p. 288)

The problem with the Cartesian analysis is that it is impaled on the horns of a dilemma. It implies either that there is an infinite regress of conscious acts (if there is one conscious act) or there is an unconscious consciousness (which is absurd). Since it treats consciousness as a relation between two entities, it must treat self-consciousness or consciousness of consciousness as a relation between two entities, as a second consciousness that orients itself toward the first. Thus, self-consciousness would look like this:

$$S \xrightarrow{\text{conscious of}} \quad [S \xrightarrow{\text{conscious of}} X]$$

But this account leads to an infinite regress. Since all consciousness is conscious of itself, there must be a consciousness that takes the second consciousness as its object, and so on. That is,

$$S \xrightarrow{\text{conscious of}} \quad \{S \xrightarrow{\text{conscious of}} \quad [S \xrightarrow{\text{conscious of}} X]\}$$

Since there is no end to the number of acts of consciousness that are necessary in order to be conscious of an object, I would have to perform an infinite number of acts in order to be conscious of an object, and that is absurd.

Of course, one may attempt to nip the regress in the bud by claiming that consciousness of consciousness is not conscious of itself. The structure of self-consciousness would then be

$$S \xrightarrow[\text{conscious of}]{\text{unconscious}} \quad [S \xrightarrow{\text{conscious of}} X]$$

However, if you say that the second or final consciousness is not self-consciousness, but is a non-conscious consciousness, then there cannot be an original consciousness of an object. That is, if the second consciousness of consciousness is not conscious of itself, then it does not exist (given that all consciousness is self-consciousness). However, if the consciousness of consciousness does not exist, then the original consciousness of *X* does not exist because there is nothing that is conscious of it.

There is a third account of consciousness and self-consciousness that gets blurred with the other two and is worth mentioning because it may be thought of as an intermediary between the substantival Cartesian view and the non-substantial Sartrean view of consciousness. On this view, there is no substantial ego, but in self-consciousness there is a consciousness that orients itself toward consciousness. For example, *I am conscious of perceiving a chair* would be analyzed as

$$\underline{\text{conscious of}} > \qquad [\underline{\text{conscious of}} > \text{X}]$$

Of course, we are still stuck with the same dilemma of having either an infinite regress of conscious acts or of a non-self-conscious consciousness. In either case, we cannot, however, account for our consciousness of an object.

The main difficulty with the Cartesian account of self-consciousness is that it treats self-consciousness as a knowing (positional) consciousness. That is, for the Cartesian the *Cogito* ("I think") is taken to be a reflective or cognitive act: a substantial ego directed toward, conscious of, or knowing, its own thinking. However, if the consciousness of consciousness is positional, then the dilemma Sartre raises appears unavoidable. Thus, Sartre claims that we must draw a distinction between the pre-reflective and the reflective *cogito*. At the pre-reflective level "I think" involves my actually thinking of an object together with consciousness (of) that thinking, but it does not posit thinking as an object. We could, however, come to reflect, or know, our thinking. For example, I could reflect on my perception of a streetcar and when I do I am having a positional consciousness whose object is "my" earlier consciousness of the streetcar. This is the reflective *Cogito* (what Descartes thought was the *Cogito*) and occurs when I posit consciousness as an object of consciousness. Sartre emphasizes, however, that one need not reflect on consciousness in order to be conscious of consciousness. As Sartre puts it,

> It is not reflection which reveals the consciousness reflected-on to itself. Quite the contrary, it is the non-reflective consciousness which renders the reflection possible; there is a pre-reflective *cogito* which is the condition of the Cartesian *cogito*. (p. 289)

Sartre's point is that in order for me to *know* that "I think" I must first be non-reflectively conscious (of) thinking. The reflective Cogito presupposes that I am conscious of consciousness in a non-cognitive, non-positional way.

With this background we can see how Sartre explicates the relation between consciousness and self-consciousness so as to avoid the infinite regress associated with the Cartesian view. His gambit involves distinguishing between *positional (thetic) consciousness* and *non-positional (non-thetic) consciousness,* on the one hand, and identifying them on the other. To see what is involved consider the following passage:

> this consciousness of consciousness—except in the case of reflective consciousness to be dealt with later—is not positional, i.e., consciousness is not for itself its own object. Its object is by nature outside it, and this is why consciousness posits and grasps the object in the same act. Consciousness

only knows itself only as absolute inwardness. We shall call such a consciousness consciousness in the first degree or unreflected consciousness. . . . Consciousness of self is not dual. If we wish to avoid an infinite regress, there must be an immediate, non-cognitive relation of the self to itself. (pp. 282, 289)

A positional consciousness is an intentional consciousness that is directed toward an object other than itself. For example, if I am reading a book or running after a streetcar, then I posit the book to be read, or the streetcar to be caught. During an act of positional consciousness we are not, however, reflectively aware of our consciousness of the book or the streetcar. Of course, later we may remember reading the book or running after the streetcar, in which case there exists a reflecting consciousness that takes an earlier consciousness as its object. Sartre's interesting idea is to insist that self-consciousness, that is, consciousness (of) consciousness is non-positional and non-reflective, meaning that it does not posit an object other than or outside itself. When I am conscious (of) "my" consciousness of a streetcar, there is not one consciousness that posits a second, but rather there is a positional consciousness of an object and a non-positional consciousness (of) the positional consciousness not being the same as its object. There is a distinction, but there is no real difference between positional and non-positional consciousness.

According to Sartre, consciousness and self-consciousness are two aspects of a single phenomenon. Consciousness is essentially intentional in that it posits an object, and consciousness is essentially self-consciousness in that it does not posit an object. This unity in difference is possible because non-positional consciousness is one with positional consciousness. As Sartre puts it,

> The idea can be expressed in these terms: every conscious existence exists as consciousness of existing. We understand now why the first consciousness of consciousness is not positional; it is because it is one with the consciousness of which it is consciousness. With one move it determines itself as consciousness of perception and a perception . . . This self-consciousness we ought to consider not as a new consciousness, but as *the only mode of existence which is possible for a consciousness of something.* (p. 290)

Thus, Sartre rejects the Cartesian view and replaces it with an analysis of consciousness as an indivisible unity of consciousness and self-consciousness. Sartre's ontological analysis of consciousness is in turn supported by phenomenological considerations that provide a further argument against a Cartesian mental substance.

Sartre's view of the non-reflective nature of self-consciousness takes its starting point from the phenomenological fact that when I am reading a book, or running after a streetcar, or counting the number of people in a room, I am positionally conscious of words and their meaning, or the streetcar having to be caught, or the number of people in this room, but there is no "I" present in consciousness. For the *I* to be present is for it to be present as an object, and that only for reflective consciousness. In unreflective consciousness, however, I am immersed in the world; there is nothing I can identify myself with. There is self-consciousness, but in consciousness (of) consciousness the self that I am conscious (of) is nothing (not a thing or substance) in itself. Sartre says that

> The Cogito affirms too much. The certain content of the pseudo-"Cogito" is not "I have consciousness of this chair," but "There is consciousness of this chair."[2]

And later,

> It is certain however, that the *I* does appear on the unreflected level. If someone asks me "What are you doing?" and I reply, all preoccupied, "I am trying to hang this picture," or "I am repairing the rear tire," these statements do not transport us to the level of reflection. But this "I" which is here in question nevertheless is no mere syntactical form. It has a meaning; it is quite simply an empty concept which is destined to remain empty. Just as I can think of a chair in the absence of any chair merely by a concept, I can in the same way think of the *I* in the absence of the *I*."[3]

Again, Sartre is making the point that there is no *I* qua substance present to intuition when I am conscious of the world. Even though there is the linguistic locution "I am conscious of the chair," all that really exists is a consciousness (of) the consciousness of the chair, and qua consciousness I am nothing.

A question and possible objection seems to arise at this point. Sartre has argued that I am nothing, since when I am conscious of the world I am immersed in the world and conscious of myself as nothingness, a pure direction to a transcendent object (i.e., an object for consciousness). Since, however, I can be positionally conscious of consciousness, does it not follow that I am something, that I am in the world as an object or an entity? How then can Sartre claim that we are not objects, that we are nothing?

This objection contains a fallacy, for my positional consciousness of the streetcar having to be caught, for example, is myself only so long as I am not (positionally) conscious of it. For if I am conscious of the consciousness of the streetcar then I am not the first order consciousness, but the second order consciousness. Thus, insofar as there is no positional consciousness of consciousness, I am not in the world, and insofar as consciousness is an object of consciousness, the object posited is no longer me. To put the point otherwise, I cannot be an object of consciousness for myself, for when I become an object of consciousness I cease to be myself; what I am is the second order consciousness and not the object of consciousness.

Hence there is a sense in which self-knowledge is impossible. I cannot know myself, since knowledge is always of objects or entities in the world, but I (qua consciousness) can never be an object for myself. For whenever I am aware of something I regard it as separate from myself; I distance myself from it, since what I am is the consciousness of the object and not the object itself. Thus, when I am conscious of myself, that is, my past consciousness, I am not an object of consciousness, but rather I am the consciousness that is aware of "my past." Thus I can never know what "I" am, since insofar as "I" am consciousness, I am nothing. I am a being, but we can grasp the kind of being we are only by grasping that we are beings that are not things.

A further consequence of the nothingness of consciousness is that there are no laws governing consciousness.

> It is futile to try to invoke pretended *laws* of consciousness of which the articulated whole would constitute the essence. A law is a transcendent object of knowledge; there can be consciousness of a law, not a law of consciousness. For the same reason it is impossible to assign to consciousness a motivation other than itself. (p. 291)

According to Sartre, one's decision to do *X* can never be explained causally. Causal explanation makes sense only if we are talking about things, or events in a thing. Since, however, all consciousness is self-consciousness, and since all non-positional consciousness is nothing, consciousness is nothing, and what is nothing cannot be caused or explained causally.

Consciousness is completely free: It has no causes and it has no effects. At each moment it must create itself spontaneously from nothing.

> We may therefore formulate our thesis: transcendental consciousness is an impersonal spontaneity. It determines its existence at each instant, without our being able to conceive anything before it. Thus, each instant of our conscious life reveals to us a creation *ex nihilo*. Not a new arrangement, but a new existence. (p. 284)

Perhaps you would reply that I can cause consciousness by simply deciding to be conscious of something. That is, I can will to decide to do something and thereby do it. But Sartre denies that we can will consciousness or explain consciousness by appealing to an act of will. For, first, such an analysis would be circular. We are attempting to explain consciousness (our conscious decisions) by an appeal to willing, but willing is itself a consciousness and so to speak of it as causing consciousness would be irrelevant because we want an explanation of what causes the willing. Second, insofar as I will something I cannot bring it about. For example, if I will to fall asleep then I cannot sleep; if I will not to think about something then I think about it. Finally, willing cannot cause consciousness because one's will has no power over one's future decisions and choices. The will is essentially concerned with the future, but what I will do in the future is not determined by what I will do now. I can will to do X and then at the next instant do Y. I will to go to the library to study, but then after I walk to the library I turn around at the entrance gate. I will to stop smoking and then I light up a cigarette. I'm in the library and I will to read a book, but a member of the opposite sex walks by and my consciousness is directed to him or her and not my studies.

Thus, for Sartre, consciousness is spontaneous because we have no power over it. Our consciousness has no causes, not even I cause consciousness, and so it is out of control. Thus, there is a sense in which freedom no longer applies to consciousness. Because consciousness has no cause, it is perfectly free, and yet this perfect freedom amounts to a complete lack of freedom. Since what I will be conscious of (what I will choose to do ten seconds from now has no cause), my future decision is beyond my freedom. I have no control over what I will do, and this is a source of anguish when we become conscious of it.

Sartre illustrates this monstrous freedom by describing the anguish a young woman experiences when she worries that when her husband has gone she would sit by the window and solicit passersby. There is nothing in her past, her upbringing, or environment that would suggest she would do such a thing, and yet she is anguished because she is conscious of her nothingness. That is, she realizes she cannot decide now what she will do later, and yet later, when her husband leaves, she will have to make a decision. The future decision is, however, beyond her freedom. There is nothing that she can do now which will help her to make the later decision, she has no power over what she will choose later because she is completely free, and this is the source of her anguish.

One way in which we avoid anguish is by constructing for ourselves an *I* or an ego that serves to give structure and character to our life. That is, we think of the ego as a self whose character determines how we will act. Indeed, it is true, we do have a character. Our past actions reflect a pattern and character that we believe will extend beyond the present. Anguish appears when we realize that we are not what we take ourselves to be. For the self we identify with is always behind us, always a "has been" that depends for its existence on our continually recreating it. Or, if we think of it as extending into the future, then it is an ideal object that is constituted by future states and actions. Such future recreation is purely spontaneous, however, and beyond our control.[4]

A good passage indicating the role the ego plays in our attempt to avoid anguish is the following:

> Perhaps, in reality, the essential function of the ego is not so much theoretical as practical. . . . [P]erhaps the essential role of the ego is to mask from consciousness its very spontaneity. . . . Everything happens, therefore, as if consciousness constituted the ego as a false representation of itself, as if consciousness hypnotized itself before this ego which it has constituted, absorbing itself in the ego as if to make the ego its guardian and its law. (p. 285)

By creating an ego for ourselves, we think both that what we will do is caused by us, we are agents that bring about our own futures, and furthermore, that this ego is endowed with an essence from which our future choices flow. Through such a construction we manage to avoid facing the anguish of having to tirelessly create what we are. Of course, when we try to avoid anguish we are really just deceiving ourselves, since our nothingness prevents us from being an ego with a fixed nature. In later sections we delve further into Sartre's account of freedom, anguish, and our mechanisms of defense. We conclude this section here by briefly discussing another key element of Sartre's analysis of consciousness.

At the end of *The Transcendence of the Ego*, Sartre says that consciousness is "impersonal" and "absolute." To see what he means let us once again contrast Descartes and Sartre. Recall that for Descartes consciousness is always *personal,* that is, consciousness is either mine or yours depending upon whether or not it is owned or exemplified by my mind or by your mind. A natural by-product of this view is the belief in a subject/object dualism, a fundamental distinction between the ego, or me, and the world. Sartre rejects these elements of Cartesianism, since in his view consciousness is not a subject, nor is it a property "owned" by an immaterial substance. Rather, consciousness is *impersonal* not only because there is no me in it, but also because it does not belong to me or you or anyone else: It is purely a direction to a transcendent object. Furthermore, Sartre also rejects the idea that there is a distinction between subject and object, between me and the world. He says that

> It is enough that the *Me* be contemporary with the World and that the subject-object dualism, which is purely logical, finally disappear from philosophical preoccupations. The World has not created the *Me*, the *Me* has not created the World. They are two objects for the absolute, impersonal consciousness, and it is by virtue of this consciousness that they are connected. (p. 287)

Although Sartre emphasizes the *nothingness* of consciousness and spells out the implications of that nothingness concerning self-knowledge and freedom, there is an important sense in which consciousness is *everything* or *absolute.*

When Sartre says that consciousness is a "non-substantial absolute," he means, in part, that consciousness, although dependent on its objects for its existence, is not caused by the objects it intends. In addition, consciousness is absolute in that it constitutes everything including egos. That is, consciousness, although not responsible for the existence of objects in themselves, is responsible for what those objects are taken to be. For example, I am not responsible for the political structure of the United States, and yet my consciousness is responsible for what I take that structure to be. Thus, the meaning or significance of ordinary objects and events is determined by consciousness. But if consciousness constitutes objects, then it also constitutes egos. For apart from consciousness of my past, my future, and what people think of me, I am nothing to myself. Apart from all consciousness I am nothing. I come to be something, I come to think of myself as a person and distinguish myself from others only insofar as I become conscious of my past. What I take myself to be depends on consciousness. Thus, consciousness constitutes my ego and every other ego. Indeed, it constitutes everything, for how the world is understood depends on consciousness. Consequently, consciousness is a being that is both nothing and everything. It is *nothing,* since it is not an object in the world, and it is *everything,* since it constitutes everything. Since human life is consciousness, it, too, is both *everything* and *nothing.*

THE RELATION BETWEEN CONSCIOUSNESS (BEING-FOR-ITSELF) AND THE WORLD (BEING-IN-ITSELF)

Toward the end of the introduction to *Being and Nothingness,* Sartre distinguishes between conscious being or being-for-itself and unconscious being or being-in-itself (p. 294). The argument for these two kinds of being is based on the very nature of consciousness. The nature of consciousness is such that it is always of an object which is eventually not itself consciousness. That is, since all consciousness is intentional, the being of consciousness ultimately depends on the being of something other than consciousness. Thus, some being must exist in-itself or as such, and some being must exist for-itself, that is, as of some object.

The argument for the existence of these two kinds of being also implies two differences between them. First, being-in-itself does not depend on consciousness for its existence, it is self-dependent, but being-for-itself does depend on some thing other than consciousness, namely, the object it intends. Second, since all positional consciousness is self-consciousness, that is, a non-positional consciousness of itself, there cannot be a consciousness of an object unless there is a non-positional consciousness. On the other hand, being-in-itself is not conscious of an object and thus can exist even though it is not conscious of itself.

We thus have two kinds of being: being-for-itself or conscious being, and being-in-itself or unconscious being. The question Sartre raises next is, "What is the connection between these two kinds of being?" Since the distinctive feature of human beings is consciousness, in asking how the two kinds of beings are related Sartre is asking for an explanation of the connection between human reality and the world. Or, as he puts it, "What is the synthetic relation which we call being-in-the-world?" Sartre's answer to that question involves the heart of his account of human life and to it we now turn.

According to Sartre, we can only understand the connection between human life and the world by examining human behavior, the sort of behavior that includes physical behavior, and certain attitudes and activities such as questioning. Humans stand before the world with a questioning attitude, an attitude that is filled with meaning. For Sartre, our questioning attitude reveals that we grasp the world as involving *negation* or *nothingness*. To see what is involved, we should note that our questioning attitude makes sense only if we admit the possibility of either a positive or a negative reply. If, for example, I wonder whether or not there are cigarettes in my top drawer (an unlikely event since I do not smoke), then it makes sense to say that I have discovered cigarettes in the drawer only if it is possible that there are no cigarettes to be found.

Suppose that I am looking for cigarettes in the drawer, and they are not there. In that case I have discovered that the world contains a little pool of nothingness. To use an example of Sartre's,

> at the moment when I ask, "Is there any behavior which can reveal to me the relation of man with the world?" I admit *on principle* the possibility of a negative reply such as, "No, such conduct does not exist." This means that we admit to being faced with the transcendent fact of the non-existence of such conduct. (p. 295)

Thus, the existence of the questioning attitude reveals to us the being of non-being, the existence of negative facts.

To clarify Sartre's point let us consider still another case. Suppose I enter a café looking for Pierre. I was supposed to meet him at four o'clock, but I am fifteen minutes late. Will he wait for me?

> I look at the room, the patrons, and I say, "He is not here." Is there an intuition of Pierre's absence, or does negation indeed enter in only with judgment? At first sight it seems absurd to speak here of intuition since to be exact there could not be an intuition of *nothing* since the absence of Pierre is this nothing. Popular consciousness, however, bears witness to this

intuition. Do we not say, for example, "I suddenly saw that he was not there." Is this just a matter of misplaced negation? Let us look a little closer. (p. 296)

Sartre is wondering if negation is merely a feature of negative judgment or whether, perhaps, negative judgment is fundamentally dependent on the existence of negation. Sartre goes on to claim that a closer look reveals that objective negative facts are the basis of negative judgments and thus that the world contains objective negative facts, beings that are non-beings.

Sartre's argument for the existence of pools of nothingness is based upon the phenomenology of the situation. When I enter the café looking for Pierre the café is the ground, and upon this ground I direct consciousness to the various faces, but I do not see Pierre. I expect to find him, I look for him, but I do not see him or, more accurately, I see that Pierre is not in the café. I am confronted with a particular nothingness in the world. Since I am looking for Pierre and do not find him, I am conscious of Pierre's not being in the world, his not being there as an object of consciousness. Thus, consciousness finds pools of nothingness that are in the world as objectively and clearly as anything else.

It is, however, important to distinguish Pierre's not being in the café from, say, de Gaulle's not being in the café. Pierre's not being in the café is an objective fact that conditions the judgment, since I am looking for Pierre. De Gaulle's not being there is not an objective negative fact, since there is no consciousness that is looking for de Gaulle. Sartre expresses this point in the following passage:

> I myself expected to see Pierre, and my expectation brought about the occurrence of Pierre's absence as a real event concerning this café. It is an objective fact at present that I have discovered this absence, and it presents itself as a synthetic relation between Peter and the setting in which I am looking for him. . . . By contrast, judgments which I can make subsequently to amuse myself, such as, "Wellington is not in this café, Paul Valéry is no longer here, etc."—these have a purely abstract meaning; . . . . Here the relation "is not" is merely *thought*. This example is sufficient to show that non-being does not come to things by a negative judgment, it is the negative judgment, on the contrary, which is conditioned and supported by non-being. (p. 297)

Thus, negative facts or pools of nothingness are in the world as objectively and truly as any positive fact. Still, we may wonder where this nothingness comes from.

According to Sartre, the nothingness in the world comes from human consciousness, for if I was not looking for Pierre the negative fact of Pierre's not being in the café would not exist. Nothingness emerges as a possibility only under my gaze. In other words, the fact of Pierre's absence is not itself a conscious being and yet its existence depends on a conscious being. Thus, since it makes sense to describe nothingness as being in the world only if someone is conscious of it, *there is a sense in which the nothingness that is found in the world is produced by consciousness.*

But how can *I* qua consciousness produce nothingness in the world? What must consciousness be like in order for it to produce non-being? Sartre claims that consciousness cannot be a being-in-itself, since if it were then the only relation it could have to nothingness would be a causal relation. But consciousness cannot produce non-being or nothingness by causing it to exist, for a real cause can only produce a real effect. In other words, in order for consciousness to cause non-being, non-being would have to be some*thing* in-itself because only things or events in things can be part of the causal series. Since, however, nothingness is not a thing or an event, it cannot be caused. How then, can consciousness produce nothingness? Sartre's answer is that this is possible only because consciousness itself is nothing. Only that which is itself nothing can produce nothing. As Sartre argues,

> It is essential therefore that the questioner have the permanent possibility of disassociating himself from the causal series which constitutes being and which can only produce being. . . . A real cause, in fact, produces a real effect and the caused being is wholly engaged by the cause in what is; to the extent that its being depends on the cause, it cannot have within itself the tiniest germ of nothingness. Thus, insofar as the questioner must be able to effect in relation to the questioned a kind of nihilating withdrawal, he is not subject to the causal order of the world; he detaches himself from Being. (p. 298)

Thus, nothingness is produced by consciousness because consciousness is nothing in-itself and so is well suited to introduce nothingness into the world. Sartre says,

> Man presents himself at least in this instance as a being which causes Nothingness to arise in the world, inasmuch as he himself is affected with non-being to this end. . . . (p. 298)

In what sense is consciousness nothingness? We have already considered several senses in which this is so, but in its most fundamental sense consciousness is nothingness and human life is nothingness because we are free. Human freedom is precisely the nothingness of consciousness. Thus, to understand the nothingness of human life is to understand the nature of human freedom. What, then, is the nature of human freedom, according to Sartre?

Before we turn to that question, which is the subject of the next section, let us return to the question that formed the starting point of our discussion, namely, what is the relation between consciousness and the world or being-for-itself and being-in-itself? In brief, the connection may be summarized by saying that consciousness produces nothingness in the world and therefore, in a sense we explain shortly, consciousness creates the world, or makes there to be the "worldliness" of the world.

The significance of the fact that humans produce nothingness in the world is that without consciousness there would be no "world." Apart from consciousness, being-in-itself is an undifferentiated totality of being. This totality exists in itself independent of consciousness, but it is not yet a world. In order to become a world, a being that can be understood to be such and such, there must be differences within being-in-itself. An undifferentiated totality cannot be a world. Furthermore, the existence of differences or diversities imply the existence of negation. More specifically, in order for there to be different kinds of things, for example, land, sea, stars, earth, animals, and the like, we must be able to say "this is not that." We must be able to say, for example, that "this table is not that chair." But to make distinctions between things, to see something as distinct and different from something else, is precisely to be confronted with negation or nothingness. Thus, in order for there to be a world there must be nothingness, but in order for the world to contain nothingness there must be consciousness, since consciousness produces nothingness in the world.

With this point we return once again to the sense in which consciousness is *everything* or *absolute*. For, although consciousness is not responsible for the existence of being-in-itself it is responsible for the worldliness of being-in-itself. It is responsible for the existence of the world as we understand it. For suppose we distinguish the world as it is in-itself, call it "world$_1$," from the world as we understand or interpret it, call that "world$_2$." Then, we may say that for Sartre, in order for there to be a world$_2$ for consciousness there must be diversities. Since, however, the existence of diversity implies the existence of negations, and negation implies consciousness, we may conclude that consciousness introduces nothingness into being-in-itself (world$_1$) and thereby creates the worldliness or the world, and makes there to be a world$_2$.

SARTRE ON FREEDOM

In freedom the human being is his own past (and also his own future) in the form of nihilation. (p. 299)

Our freedom consists in our nothingness, and our nothingness consists in our containing within ourselves a contradiction. The contradiction in our existence—our freedom—consists in our not being what we are and our being what we are not. The meaning of this claim can be stated briefly as follows: It is essential to human life that we regard ourselves as separated or disengaged from what we are. I am disengaged or separated from myself in that what I am is independent of what I was and what I was is *independent* of what I will be. The notion of "independence" is liable to be misunderstood here, since it is not intended primarily in a causal sense. Like Heidegger, Sartre believes that we should not picture a person as a succession of momentary selves or states of consciousness (decisions and experiences), where freedom consists in one's past experiences not determining the present and one's present experiences not determining the future. The independence of our present from our past, our future from our present is not the causal independence of three separate individuals. Rather, the lack of causal connection between my past and my present, and my present and my future is the result of my freedom. It is because I am not myself and because I am separated from what I am by consciousness, that my past cannot cause my present and my present cannot cause my future.

Look at it this way: Insofar as I have an essence it is my past and so I am my past. Indeed, I can identify a past as mine only by assuming that I am identical with that past individual. I am, however, also my future: When I anticipate the future of several individuals the fact that one of them is me has a special importance. I have a great concern for the future welfare of one of those future individuals because that person is me. In other words, it makes sense to say that I have a selfish concern for one person in the future because what happens to one of those future individuals will make a difference to what happens to *me*. Thus, there is a fundamental sense in which I am past and I am future; that one and the same individual is past, present, and future. And yet, our past does not determine our present, and our present does not determine our future. To say these two things amounts to saying that I do not determine myself. This is not a causal claim, but rather it is the claim that I am not myself, since I really am (my past and future) what I really am not (my past and future), I am nothing.

Thus, my freedom consists in being my past (and future) and yet not being my past (and future), my being separated from my past (and future) by the nothingness that I am at present. On the one hand, I am not my past, since what I am now depends on what I do now, and nothing that I have been determines what decision I will now make. On the other hand, I am my past, since what I am now depends on what I have done, since I am constituted by my past. That is, my essence (insofar as I have one) is my past—and I am strictly identical with the individual who did such and such in the past.

The paradox of human life being what it is not and not being what it is, can be clarified by recalling the nature of consciousness. The past is not me, since my past can only be an object for consciousness, and so when I become conscious of my past I separate myself from it. I am not my past, but the consciousness of it. Furthermore, the past is not me, since no past decision is binding on me at present. If my past constituted a fixed essence that determined who or what I am, then my present decisions could be understood as the inevitable outcome of a being with such and such a nature. And yet the past cannot cause the present, since now I am not my past. At present I am separated from my past by the nothingness that I am. But this is only half of the story. The past is me, since I cannot understand myself at present apart from what I remember myself to have been in the past. Insofar as I have an identity it is founded upon what "has been," what I have done. Thus, I am one person then and now, but I am my past in the mode of not being it.

Sartre gives an example of our freedom from the past by discussing a gambler

> who has freely and sincerely decided not to gamble anymore . . . [but] approaches the gaming table, [and] suddenly sees all his resolutions melt away. . . . The earlier resolution of "not playing anymore" is always *there,* and in the majority of cases the gambler, when in the presence of the gaming table turns toward it as if to ask it for help; for he does not wish to play, or rather having taken his resolution the day before, he thinks of himself still as not wishing to play anymore; he believes in the effectiveness of this resolution. But what he apprehends then in anguish is precisely the total inefficacy of the past resolution. It is there doubtless but congealed, ineffectual, transcended by the very fact that I am conscious of it. The resolution is still me to the extent that I realize constantly my identity with myself across the temporal flux, but it is no longer me—due to the fact that it has become an object for my consciousness. I am not subject to it. It fails in the mission which I have given it. The resolution is there still, I *am* it in the mode of not-being. (pp. 301–302)

In the situation Sartre describes, the gambler has decided not to gamble. The gambler is not his past, in that the decision he made last night is ineffective unless it is renewed now. But this is to make a new decision, a decision in which what I decided or thought yesterday no longer has any power. On the other hand, the person who decided not to gamble is the same as the person who must now make the decision whether to gamble or not. Thus, there is a sense in which the person who has to make a decision in the present has already decided. The gambler can only understand his present decision in the light of his past. Thus, his decision lives in the present. Yet at the moment when the gambler *is* the decision not to gamble, he is not what he is, since the past does not determine what he will do now, and so he must remake that decision.

Sartre's point is that on the one hand I am completely alone in the present, since whatever I am now is solely dependent on what I do now. It does not make sense to say that my decision to gamble is the effect of the decision I made last night. I am disengaged from my past, restricted to my present, and yet I am my past, since I cannot understand myself except in terms of my past. There is a sense in which my past lives in my present. My past decisions are what I am. There is no separately existing ego that has these decisions, and there is no substantial self that underlies them. These decisions are what I am: I am now what I was. There are not two selves, a past self and a present self. The past self *is* the present self, and thus the past self lives in the present. Yet, I am not my past, since in virtue of being conscious of my past I separate myself from it. I am separate from what I am (in the past) by the nothingness (consciousness) that I am (in the present). Moreover, I am not my past, in that my past decisions are ineffective; I must remake the resolution which I am. Thus, I am my past in the mode of not being it.

Freedom is also that what I will be is not determined by what I am. We are free from our future as well as from our past. This means on the one hand that what I now choose is not something that will *cause* me to choose something in the future. I have no more control over my future decisions than I do over yours. Yet this is only part of the story, since what the person in the future will be depends entirely on what I do now, since I am now the same person as the person who exists in the future. Sartre makes these points by claiming that I am my future in the mode of not-being it: What I do now will affect what I am, that is, my future, yet I am not that future person, since I am separated from it by time, and I have no control over what that person (I) will be. Sartre puts the matter as follows:

> This means that in establishing a certain conduct as a possibility and precisely because it is *my* possibility, I am aware that *nothing* can compel me to adopt that conduct. Yet I am indeed already there in the future; it is for the sake of that being which I will be there at the turning of the path that I now exert all my strength, and in this sense there is already a relation between my future being and my present being. But a nothingness has slipped into the heart of this relation; I *am* not the self which I will be. First I am not that self because time separates me from it. Secondly, I am not that self because what I am is not the foundation of what I will be. Finally I am not that self because no actual existent can determine strictly what I am going to be. Yet as I am already what I will be (otherwise I would not be interested in any one being more than another), *I am the self which I will be, in the mode of not being it.* (p. 301)

The split of consciousness at every instant even separates me from what I am at present. That is, I am the consciousness that I choose to be at present, but not for-myself:

> Let us imagine that moved by jealousy, curiosity, or vice I have just glued my ear to the door and looked through a keyhole. I am alone and on the

level of a non-thetic self-consciousness. This means first of all that there is no self to inhabit my consciousness, nothing therefore to which I can refer my acts in order to qualify them. They are in no way *known; I am my* acts and hence they carry in themselves their whole justification. . . . No transcending view comes to confer upon my acts the character of a given on which a judgment can be brought to bear. (pp. 336–337)

At present I am jealous, but I am not jealous for-myself. For myself I am immersed in the world and not what I am. Thus, I am my past, present, and future, and I am not my past, present, and future, but separated from it. I am what I am not, and I am not what I am. At its deepest level, the nothingness of human existence, the meaninglessness of human life, is its freedom.

ANGUISH, FEAR, AND FLIGHT

A situation provokes fear if there is a possibility of my life being changed from without; my being provokes *anguish* to the extent that I distrust myself and my own reactions in that situation. (p. 299)

According to Sartre, anguish is the consciousness of our freedom. Anguish in the face of the past is our consciousness that we are always separated from our past essence by nothingness and thus that we are free to be what we are (our past essence) or not to be it. According to Sartre,

Anguish as the manifestation of freedom in the face of self means that man is always separated by nothingness from his essence. Essence is what has been. . . . Man continually carries with him a pre-judicative comprehension of his essence, but due to this very fact he is separated from it by nothingness. . . . The overflow of our consciousness progressively constitutes this nature, but it remains always behind us and it dwells in us as the permanent object of our retrospective comprehension. It is insofar as this nature is a demand without being a recourse that it is apprehended in anguish. (p. 304)

Anguish in the face of the future is the realization that my future decisions are of the utmost importance to me, and yet I am not at present in control of them. Regardless of what good intentions I am or have now, I must in the future recreate myself from nothing.

Sartre distinguishes anguish from fear. Fear is when I am worried about a certain decision someone else will make, or when I am worried about some physical event that will cause me harm. Fear is always fear of some being-in-the-world, some transcendent object of consciousness. Fear is when I am walking on a precipice and I think that the ground might fall under me or that I might slip off the ledge and fall. In fear, I view myself as a destructible object, a being-in-itself that is subject to the effects of other objects.

Anguish, on the other hand, is always of oneself. One does not anguish over what someone or something will do to me, but what I will do to myself. Thus, I am not in anguish when I realize that I could slip off the precipice, but when I realize that I could throw myself off. In anguish I am conscious that the decisions I make in the future are of the utmost importance to me now, since I am that future person, and yet now I am powerless to affect my future. Anguish with respect to the future involves the realization that, because of my radical freedom (that is, the spontaneity of consciousness), I have no more control over my future than I have over your future. In anguish "I apprehend my freedom as being the possible destroyer in the present and in the future of what I am."

Throughout most of our lives we avoid being conscious of our freedom, that is, we avoid anguish. This fact gives rise to a problem, according to Sartre. If all consciousness is self-consciousness so that nothing is hidden from consciousness, and the essence of consciousness is anguish or freedom, then how come we so seldom experience anguish? If at each moment I have to make decisions *ex nihilo,* then why am I so seldom aware of this? How come we do not always think that actions about which we have to make decisions are actions that require a decision to be made?

According to Sartre, one reason we so easily avoid anguish is that we are creatures of habit. We find ourselves in a situation and act by habit. For example, I hear an alarm clock and I apprehend it as a signal to get up and go to work or to school. I don't stop to consider my possibilities, nor do I reflect on the fact that the ringing of the alarm clock does not intrinsically mean "get up and go to work," but that its meaning depends on me. It is true that in the past I have decided that the alarm clock should mean that it's time to go to work, but I am not my past. Thus, I am in anguish when I realize that I must remake that decision now. Yet, in acting by habit and by always being busy, we distract ourselves from realizing that we must remake our decisions and thus we avoid the agony of anguish. That is why, incidentally, a person with leisure is more likely to become conscious of anguish.

The environment and everyday morality also help us to avoid anguish. The environment is replete with signs telling us what to do, for example, "no smoking in this section," "keep off the grass," and so on. Moreover, the sight of the police also serves to make decisions for us. But most of all, everyday morality excludes ethical anguish. We are trained from childhood to make certain decisions because they are objectively the right things to do. One ought to keep one's promises; one ought not to steal; one ought to tell the truth. We interpret morality as having an objective foundation. In this way values would be required because they have a foundation outside ourselves. If values are required then we would not have to constantly make decisions to obey or disobey values. Thus, by viewing values as objective, we avoid the anguish that comes about from a realization that we need not obey them. Of course, this is just an escape, since the truth is that values depend on us. We confer value on something by choosing it, and since we are not our past choices we must continually reaffirm or disavow our commitment to values previously chosen, and that requires making another choice.

A third way in which we attempt to avoid anguish occurs when we begin to become conscious of anguish, when we can no longer be in the situation, but are faced with a moral crisis that necessitates our making a decision. Suppose, for example, that I am a student and doing poorly in a class, but must get at least a B or be withdrawn from school. I have to decide whether to try to give a phony excuse so as to get extra time to study, or work hard to attempt to get a good grade. I am faced with a decision that has to be made now. I can still avoid facing the fact of my freedom by means of various intellectual illusions or rationalizations. One method involves accepting psychological determinism. I can say to myself that whatever I do is determined and I have no power over my present actions, so why worry about having to make a decision. Unfortunately, this mechanism does not enable us to avoid anguish for long. Since even if we believe that our decisions are determined we are still in anguish over the fact that phenomenologically we are the ones that have to decide what to do among various possibilities and we are the ones who are completely responsible for the act.

A more sophisticated rationalization consists in accepting that there are several possibilities for the future. For example, I could say to myself that I realize I could either continue to write this book or stop writing it. I could still avoid experiencing anguish about the future by thinking of these possibilities as purely logical possibilities that I could do, or as possibilities that someone other than myself in the same situation might do, but not ones that I would actually do. They become purely external possibilities, but not possibilities that I need concern myself with. I could, in other words, treat myself as another person.

A final rationalization that one might use to avoid anguish begins by accepting that one is free, that the decisions one makes are one's own and for which one is completely responsible. One then claims to be a person with a fixed essence who freely chooses to act in accordance with that essence. For example, suppose I am faced with the decision to keep talking to my students. I may avoid the anguish concerning that decision by objectifying myself. I think of myself as a teacher, and I continue to talk because teachers are supposed to lecture to students. I regard my decisions as flowing freely from what I am and thus the anguish of having to choose my being *ex nihilo* does not arise.

Sartre characterizes this form of flight in the following passage:

> What I attempt to flee here is my very transcendence in so far as it sustains and surpasses my essence. I assert that I *am* my essence in the mode of being of the in-itself. At the same time I always refuse to consider that essence as being historically constituted as implying my action as a circle implies its properties. I apprehend it, or at least I try to apprehend it as the original beginning of my possible, and I do not admit at all that it has in itself a beginning. I assert then that an act is free when it exactly reflects my essence. However, this freedom which would disturb me if it were freedom before myself, I attempt to bring back to the heart of my essence— i.e., of my self. It is a matter of envisaging the self as a little God which inhabits me and which possesses my freedom as a metaphysical virtue. (p. 310)

To think of oneself as a "little God" is to think of one's essence determining one's spontaneous and free actions. In that way we can finally avoid the anguish of having to continually choose to reaffirm what we want to be. Of course, this is an illusion and an escape. It is an illusion because we do not have a fixed essence that determines our present, and it is an escape from facing the reality of several alternative possibilities about which we have to decide.

We have discussed some of the mechanisms that enable us to avoid ourselves, but we have not discussed how such avoidance is possible. One might argue that it is not possible because (1) all consciousness is self-consciousness, hence nothing is hidden from consciousness, and (2) the essence of consciousness is freedom. Therefore (3) it follows that all consciousness is consciousness (of) freedom. Yet the characteristic state of human life is that we flee from ourselves. How can one flee from oneself? How, at one and the same time, can we be conscious that we have a decision to make and yet believe that we do not have to make one? How is it possible to know the truth—that we are free—and to deny it?

The difficulty of understanding self-deception can be clarified by comparing it with a case of ordinary deception or lying. In ordinary deception there is always a duality involved. The person who is the deceiver is in complete possession of the truth, and he is conscious that he is telling a lie. The other person, the person who is being deceived, is, of course, not in possession of the truth. Thus, ordinary deception could accurately be described as one self or consciousness hiding the truth from another self or consciousness. Yet this cannot be the model according to which we are to understand self-deception, since self-deception does not involve *two* persons. When I lie to myself there is not one self lying to another distinct self, but rather there is only one person, one consciousness, deceiving itself. "Bad faith . . . implies in essence the unity of a *single* consciousness" (p. 314). Furthermore, in ordinary deception the person deceived is not in possession of the truth, but in self-deception I must be both conscious of the truth and believe a lie. I must be conscious of what I am avoiding.

To the extent that we flee anguish we are in bad faith and are deceiving ourselves. Self-deception may take different forms: We may deceive ourselves into thinking that we do not have to make a decision when in fact we do. We can deceive ourselves into thinking that we are not really what we really are, for example, that we are not cowardly when in fact we are. Or we may think that we are what we are not, for example, that we are popular when we are not. Whatever form of bad faith we engage in we run up against the difficult question of trying to understand how it is possible. In the next section we consider Sartre's phenomenological description of the patterns of bad faith and his ontological analysis of their possibility.

SARTRE'S ACCOUNT OF BAD FAITH

> What then are we to say that consciousness must be in the instantaneity of the pre-reflective *cogito*—if the human being is to be capable of bad faith? (p. 312)

As we have seen from our discussion of Sartre's account of freedom, human existence is contradictory. One and the same person has an essence and does not have an essence. In virtue of our past we have an essence. Our past is what we are: There is no denying the truth that since I have been engaged in the teaching profession for the past fifteen years, I am a teacher. Yet in virtue of my future I do not have an essence, but rather I create my essence as I continue to make decisions and choices. So, on the one hand we create our essence, and on the other hand, the person who will create his or her essence already has an essence and is a certain kind of being. These two distinct features of human existence, which Sartre calls "facticity" and "transcendence," are what we are. We are a combination of *Being* (facticity) and *Nothingness* (transcendence).

Although we are both fixed and free, or have nature and at any moment are capable of changing our nature, we frequently avoid facing one or the other of these aspects of ourselves. We frequently deceive ourselves into thinking that we are not what we are, and that we are what we are not. Thus the question arises as to how can I, at one and the same time, both believe, for example, that I am a teacher and also that I am not one? Sartre's answer consists in claiming that in cases of self-deception or bad faith there is a disintegration or falling apart of a single consciousness into two poles (one of which it is and one of which it is not) and an oscillation back and forth into one and then the other of the elements (poles) into which it has disintegrated. Thus, when I become conscious of one aspect of myself (what I am) I deny it by shifting and identifying myself with what I am not. And when I become conscious of what I am not I avoid facing that aspect of my being by shifting and identifying myself with what I am. Thus, if we think of consciousness as being split into two: then self-deception consists in an individual first identifying with A and then with B and then shifting back and forth. There is a sense in which $C=A$ and $C=B$ and yet $A \neq B$.

Sartre mentions three specific ways in which consciousness disintegrates. The first is due to the possibility of regarding myself as I am *for myself* or as I am *for others*. The second way is due to the possibility of regarding myself as either *being in the midst of the world* or as *being in the world*. The third way is due to our ability to distinguish *what we are* from *what we will be*. Each specific form of disintegration involves the distinction between facticity and transcendence. I can think of myself in terms of my relationship to the world (facticity), or I can think of myself in terms of what I originate and what I am responsible for (transcendence). *Bad faith occurs when I shift from one pole to the other and affirm the one pole as being the other.* The shift allows me to see the truth and deny it at a single instant.

The essence of all specific forms of bad faith is summarized by Sartre in the following crucial passage:

> What unity do we find in these various aspects of bad faith? It is a certain art of forming contradictory concepts which unite in themselves both an idea and the negation of that idea. The basic concept which is thus engendered utilizes the double property of the human being, who is at once a *facticity* and a *transcendence*. These two aspects of human reality are and ought to be capable of a valid coordination. But bad faith does not wish either to coordinate them or to surmount them in a synthesis. Bad faith seeks to affirm their identity while preserving their differences. It must affirm facticity as *being* transcendence and transcendence as *being* facticity, in such a way that at the instant when a person apprehends the one he can find himself abruptly faced with the other. (p. 317)

Perhaps we can best explain what Sartre has in mind by these distinctions by considering each of his examples of bad faith.

Sartre distinguishes between being in the world and being in the midst of the world. *To be in the world* is to be in the world as consciousness, to consider oneself as a free agent with no pre-determined essence. To consider oneself as *being in the midst of the world* is to think of oneself as a being-in-itself; as an object among objects, a formed entity. Sartre illustrates these two poles into which consciousness may split by talking about the waiter. Consider a waiter who is playing or acting the role of being a waiter. To the extent to which he regards himself as a formed entity with a certain fixed essence, he must also regard everything he does as proceeding from his essence. On the other hand, it is possible for the waiter to conceive of himself as one who chooses to be a waiter, and thus cannot be identified with being a waiter. Since he can distinguish what *he is* from what he *can be,* that is, although he is a waiter he need not continue to be one, there is a sense in which he is not a waiter. Thus, there is a distinction between what I am in the midst of the world (my essence or facticity) and what I am in the world (my transcendence), but there is no difference, since if you take away what I am in the midst of the world, there is nothing left for me to identify myself with. It is precisely because of this distinction without a difference that the waiter can be in bad faith.

Suppose that the waiter's entire life is devoted to being a waiter: collecting tips, carrying his tray properly, and so on. Surely, such a person is a waiter, that is what he is. He is not a diplomat! He can, however, attempt to avoid this truth about himself by thinking that he is not really concerned with tips, serving meals properly, and so on. He can shift from what he is in the midst of the world to what he is as a free project. He may say or think to himself that tips are unimportant; it is the waiter who is really working for tips. He "sees" that he is a waiter, but at that very instant he shifts to what he is as a free project and claims that in himself tips are unimportant. He shifts to what he is (in the world) as a free agent and claims that he is (in the midst of the world) not a waiter.

Thus, the waiter is in bad faith, since he denies that his essence is to be a waiter and believes, by virtue of his transcendence, that he *is* (essentially) not a waiter. Admittedly, by virtue of his transcendence he is not a waiter "in the world," but bad faith occurs when he believes that he is not a waiter "in the midst of the world." He denies his essence by shifting to himself as a free project, and infecting his essence with what it is not, namely, his freedom. In short, he avoids facing what he is in the midst of the world by viewing his essence as not being what it is.

Bad faith occurs when the waiter views himself as a free agent whose essence is not to be a waiter. However, that awareness leads to anguish, for if he is a free project whose essence *is not* to be a waiter, then he must decide what his essence *is* to be. He must make some choices for which he alone is completely responsible. At that moment anguish arises and he must decide what he is to be, and in bad faith he avoids facing the need to make a decision by shifting to what he is in the midst of the world, that is, by infecting freedom with facticity. The waiter is conscious of being a free agent, alone and responsible for creating his essence, but denies it by identifying himself with what he is as a formed entity. He thereby "sees" his freedom as being fixed by his essence, and he is in bad faith.

Another pair of poles into which consciousness disintegrates so as to make bad faith possible is between what we are *for ourselves* from what we are *for others*. Although this is a distinction that is possible to make, what is crucial to see is that it is a distinction without a difference. What I am is determined by my relationships with other people and what other people know and think about me on the basis of my relations with them. Thus, apart from the other I am nothing, I have no essence. Consequently, there are not really two I's, the I for others and the I for myself, since apart from the other I can have no conception of myself.

Nevertheless, there is a sense in which what I am for myself is distinct from what I am for others. The distinction exists because even though what others know about me, or how I appear to others, is what I am (my essence), I can conceive of myself as not being fixed in my actions by the essence that others give me. I can conceive of myself as being free to act in ways contrary to how others see me, and for that reason there is a distinction between what I am for myself and what I am for others. What is crucial to note, however, is that this distinction does not imply a difference. When I take away from myself how others conceive of me or how I appear to others, then there is nothing left. In virtue of this distinction without a difference, it is possible to shift back and forth and identify myself first with what I am for-myself and then with what I am for-others.

Sartre uses the example of the homosexual to illustrate how this particular disintegration of consciousness makes bad faith possible. Suppose a person wants to deny to himself that he is a homosexual. The person admits to having engaged in homosexual acts, and so is aware of being a homosexual, but nevertheless denies being a homosexual. He claims that being a homosexual is the external me, what I am for others. Others may conceive of me in this way, but this is not the real me, the inner me, or what I am for myself. In myself and for myself I am not a homosexual. He may say that these acts were due to bad luck or accidental circumstances but for myself I am (essentially) not a homosexual. Thus, the homosexual is in bad faith when he is aware of his being a homosexual (for others) and shifts to what he is for himself and claims that "I am not a homosexual," meaning that he has a different essence, the essence of *not being a homosexual*.

In this instance, bad faith involves distinguishing what I am for others (my essence, or facticity), and what I am for myself (my freedom, or transcendence) and, at the same time, affirming that what I am for myself is my essence. Since I am (for myself) not a homosexual, I conclude that the judgment of others is mistaken: I am (essentially) not a homosexual. Of course this is just a deception for insofar as I *am* (for myself) not a homosexual I am nothing—I do not have the essence of "not being a homosexual" or the essence of "being a homosexual"—I am completely natureless, and I am conscious (of) my nothingness.

Thus, when I identify myself with what I am for myself so as to avoid the label of the crowd, a new form of anguish arises. Since what I am for myself is really *nothing,* I have a pre-judicative consciousness (of) having to choose what my essence will be: If my essence is not to be a homosexual, then what is it to be? At this stage, I can avoid facing the anguish of freedom, that for myself I am nothing since I have to continually create my essence, by viewing my freedom as fixed by what others take me to be. I distinguish what others think of me from myself, and at the same moment I identify what I am with their conception. Thus, I assert, in bad faith, that "I am (for myself) a homosexual."

In these cases the homosexual avoids facing himself by turning his transcendence into what it is not (facticity), and his facticity into what it is not (transcendence). This is possible because there is a distinction between our facticity and transcendence, but there is no difference. There are not two entities, but one entity that is both facticity and transcendence. Thus, when viewing one aspect we can deny it by affirming that aspect as being the other. An important passage in which Sartre summarizes this analysis is the following:

> The homosexual recognizes his faults, but he struggles with all his strength against the crushing view that his misdeeds constitute for him a *destiny.* He does not wish to let himself be considered as a thing. He has an obscure but strong feeling that a homosexual is not a homosexual as this table is a table or as this red-haired man is red-haired. It seems to him that he has escaped from each misdeed as soon as he has posited it and recognized it; he even feels that the psychic duration by itself cleanses him from each sin, constitutes for him an undetermined future, enables him to be born anew. Is he wrong? Does he not recognize in himself the peculiar, irreducible character of human reality? His attitude includes then an undeniable comprehension of truth. But at the same time he needs this perpetual rebirth, this constant escape in order to live; he must constantly put himself beyond reach in order to avoid the terrible judgment of the social group. Thus he plays on the word *being.* He would be right actually if he understood the phrase, "I am not a pederast" in the sense of "I am not what I am." That is, if he declared to himself, "To the extent that a pattern of behavior is defined as the behavior of a pederast and to the extent that I have adopted this conduct, I am a pederast. But to the extent that human reality cannot be finally defined by patterns of behavior, I am not one." But instead he slides surreptitiously towards a different connotation of the word "being." He understands "not being" in the sense of "not-being-in-itself." He lays claim to "not being a pederast" in the sense in which this table is *not* an inkwell. He is in bad faith. (pp. 323–324)

The point here is that the homosexual sees a glimmer of truth. On the one hand, he recognizes that he is (for-others) a homosexual insofar as he has engaged in these acts. His past actions constitute his essence insofar as he has one. But he also recognizes that he is not a homosexual in the way in which chalk is brittle. It is not a fixed quality that determines his behavior. Thus, he could in good faith claim that he is (for-himself) not a homosexual. In virtue of freedom he *is not* (in the future) what he *is* (in the past) or at least he does not have to be. His future is open, his past does not determine what he will choose to be, and so on. Yet, he falls into bad faith when he affirms his facticity as being his transcendence. Qua facticity he *is* (in-itself) a homosexual, qua transcendence he *is* (for-itself) nothing. Bad faith arises when he claims that he *is* (in-itself or essentially) *not* a homosexual, or when he claims that he *is* (for-himself) a homosexual. Bad faith involves a shifting from one sense of "being" to the other and at the same time identifying the one being as being the other.

Sartre's discussion of the girl in the café reveals several mechanisms that perpetuate bad faith. On the one hand, she distinguishes what she *will be* from what she *is now* and so avoids facing the truth about either her possible future or actual present. More specifically, when the young woman becomes conscious of her date's remarks as transcending the present to the future, she is forced to become conscious that she will have to make a decision concerning the man's advances sooner or later. She is aware of the desire she instills in him, but it embarrasses her and she does not want to face it, so she shifts to the present and treats his remarks and his behavior as pertaining to the present. If he claims that she is attractive, she treats that as a remark concerning her intellectual qualities. On the other hand, she may then become bothered that he is just concerned with having an intellectual relationship and since "she would find no charm in a respect which would be only respect" (p. 316), she shifts to the future. Then he takes her hand. This calls for a decision, but she deceives herself into thinking that a decision need not be made by turning her hand into an inert being-in-itself, and she just leaves it there. Yet she maintains her being for herself—her transcendence—by drawing "her companion up to the most lofty regions of sentimental speculation; she speaks of life, of her life, and she shows in her essential aspect—a personality, a consciousness." (p. 316). Again, we have the typical pattern of bad faith—a shifting between our facticity and our transcendence.

Sartre has some interesting things to say about the ideal of sincerity and the champion of sincerity. He claims that to be sincere is impossible and so those who believe that they have achieved sincerity are in bad faith. Moreover, the person who demands sincerity of his or her friends is also in bad faith. The idea behind these claims is this: To be sincere involves *being what one is,* but that is impossible because in order to be sincere we must simultaneously be conscious of what we are and be what we are. Yet, in the very act of positing our essence, at the very moment that we assert, or set about to be what we are, we separate ourselves from what we are. We become non-positionally conscious of our not being what we are and thereby cease to be it. Thus, sincerity is bad faith, since it aims at denying our transcendence and treating our transcendence as a being-in-itself. Sincerity aims at being in the present what we were in the past, but in the present we are not our past, rather we are separated from our past by the nothingness that we are at present. In short, I cannot decide to be what I am, since at the moment I do I am not that thing.

The champion of sincerity is in bad faith because he or she treats the freedom of the other as the freedom of a thing. More specifically, the champion of sincerity demands of the other that she admit what she is. The champion holds out for the other the hope that if she recognizes for herself what she is, then she will be separated from her essence and free from it. One achieves freedom, since in confession you will no longer be what you confess to be. However, the champion falls into bad faith when, at the moment the Other admits what she is—her essence—the Other's freedom is treated as the "freedom" of a thing. Thus, the champion of sincerity does not really want to deal with the Other as a consciousness and so demands that the Other admit her essence. In that way the Other can be treated as a thing whose actions follow from her fixed essence. Thus, the champion of sincerity infects the Other's transcendence with facticity and is in bad faith.

Let us sum up the discussion to this point. Sartre claims that bad faith or self-deception consists in the oscillation between the two poles with which a person can identify him- or herself. It is possible to combine these special cases into one: the shift between facticity and transcendence. A human being's facticity is what he is for others, what he has been, and what he is in the midst of the world. In a sense, human beings are like tables and chairs and other ordinary objects. There is, however, another side to us: our transcendence. This block of identity that we are is, in some sense, made by us, since what we are is determined by our choices. Thus, we are in the peculiar state of being like books and chairs and not being like those entities. Bad faith is possible because there is a single being that is not what it is and is what it is not.

There is still something missing from Sartre's account. We may recognize the phenomenon that Sartre is talking about but may still be puzzled. After all, how is it possible for there to be an entity that is both facticity and transcendence? How is it possible to unite facticity and transcendence in one instantaneous act of bad faith? Sartre suggests an answer. He claims that the contradiction in human beings that makes bad faith possible is grounded in the double disintegrated character of every individual consciousness. For each individual act of consciousness is what it is not and is not what it is.

Recall that for Sartre human reality is essentially consciousness and that all consciousness is self-consciousness. Suppose we take an individual consciousness. I believe *X*. As soon as I have the belief I am non-positionally conscious (of) it, but as soon as I am conscious (of) it, I am not that belief. And yet I am that belief, since I am conscious of the object and that consciousness is one with the belief. Thus, the double nature of an atomic consciousness reveals that consciousness is what it is, and is what it is not. Consider the following relevant passage:

> Thus the non-thetic consciousness (of) believing is destructive of belief. But at the same time the very law of the pre-reflective *cogito* implies that the being of believing ought to be the consciousness of believing.
> Thus belief is a being which questions its own being, which can realize itself only in its destruction, which can manifest itself to itself only by denying itself. It is a being for which to be is to appear and to appear is to deny itself. To believe is not-to-believe. We see the reason for it; the being of consciousness is to exist by itself, then to make itself be and thereby to pass beyond itself. In this sense consciousness is perpetually escaping itself, belief becomes non-belief, the immediate becomes mediation, the absolute becomes relative, and the relative becomes absolute. The ideal of good faith (to believe what one believes) is, like that of sincerity (to be what one is), an ideal of being-in-itself. Every belief is a belief that falls short; one never wholly believes what one believes. Consequently the primitive project of bad faith is only the utilization of this self-destruction of the fact of consciousness. (p. 327)

Look at it this way. When I believe that *X* I am the belief, but as soon as I have the belief I become non-positionally conscious of it, and thus I am not the belief. There is a distinction at a moment between what I am and what I am not. Yet, although there is a distinction there is no difference. There is nothing left to the consciousness of *X* when you take away self-consciousness; but non-positional consciousness is nothing apart from the consciousness of *X*. Thus, the very nature of consciousness is to be identical with something it is not (non-positional consciousness) and something which it is (intentional consciousness), and to oscillate between the two poles contained in every instantaneous act of consciousness. Thus, ultimately, it is the structure of consciousness itself that makes possible the phenomenon of bad faith.

SARTRE ON SEX

Sartre's analysis of sexual desire is the culmination of some of the most central themes of *Being and Nothingness*. It has, however, scarcely received the attention it deserves, and when it is considered, some of his interpreters seem to misunderstand him.[5] Perhaps the reason why Sartre's analysis of sexual desire is misunderstood is that once it is clearly spelled out, it seems to lead to the rather paradoxical conclusion that all sexual activity is a kind of perversion. Some are unwilling to accept that Sartre could have maintained such a view, and misinterpretations arise. It seems, however, that in some sense Sartre's analysis of sexual desire does entail that all sexual activity is a "perversion." One aim of this section is to defend that claim. Since Sartre's analysis of sexuality cannot be understood apart from some of his most fundamental ontological views, it is necessary and useful to review some of the main themes that we have developed up to this point in our exposition. Then, after criticizing a recent account of Sartre's views on sex, we offer what we consider to be the correct interpretation of Sartre.

Consciousness and the World

In examining the system of a great philosopher, we inevitably are led to one or more basic gambits that serve as the foundation of what is to follow. In Sartre's philosophy of human reality, one basic gambit is his analysis of consciousness as an "indivisible, indissoluble unity" of both positional and non-positional consciousness. His idea, you will recall, is that all consciousness is a unity that involves both a positional or thetic consciousness of an object and a non-positional or non-thetic consciousness of itself. For example, at the moment when I am perceiving a tree I am conscious of the tree and (non-positionally) conscious of perceiving, as opposed to, say, remembering or thinking of the tree. These are the phenomenological facts; the original Sartrean thesis concerning them is that the non-positional consciousness of the positional perceiving consciousness is one with the perceiving consciousness.

One consequence of Sartre's gambit is that consciousness is nothing. That is, consciousness is not an entity, a thing, or an object in the world. He reasons that all objects or things in the world have a hidden nature. When I look at a table I can only see its front surface; consequently, much of the table is hidden from me. By contrast, since all consciousness is self-consciousness, when I see a table there is nothing about my seeing that is hidden from me. Consciousness is entirely translucent; it is what it appears to be and appears to be what it is. Thus, in virtue of his first gambit which asserts the unity of positional and non-positional consciousness, consciousness is nothing.

In virtue of Sartre's second basic gambit, consciousness may be said to be everything. His second gambit is that consciousness, although not responsible for the existence of its objects, is responsible for producing out of being-in-itself a world in which classifications can be made and distinctions can be drawn. In other words, it is in virtue of consciousness that objects can be divided into kinds, and actions can be given meaning and valuations. Thus, consciousness is everything because it determines what objects and actions are understood to be.

Given Sartre's two basic gambits and some consequences of them, the relations between consciousness and the world may be stated briefly: Consciousness is not an object or thing in the world, but rather consciousness is the creator of the worldliness of the world in virtue of introducing meaning, values, and differences into the undifferentiated totality of being-in-itself.

The Meaning of the Other's Look

A good passage that connects these two Sartrean gambits with his view on the Other is the following:

> . . . My objectivity cannot itself derive *for me* from the objectivity of the world since I am precisely the one by whom *there is* a world; that is the one who on principle cannot be an object for himself. (p. 336)

In other words, for me, apart from my relations with the Other, I cannot have a conception of myself as an object. Sartre's point is that when I reflect upon "my" past consciousness, I am not the consciousness reflected upon (i.e., the object), but rather, I am the reflecting consciousness. For myself, I am, as it were, at the center of the world. I am the creator and master of the world in the sense that qua consciousness I am the source of the world's structure and I am responsible for creating myself in the light of all the possibilities that are open to me. For myself I am *nothing* except consciousness (transcendence).

Yet, there is another aspect to my being—my facticity—my body and my nature or essence as revealed through my actions. The look of the Other makes me non-positionally conscious of this other aspect of me. For, from the point of view of the Other's consciousness, I have become a part of the world. Consequently, I have lost myself as a for-itself (or consciousness), and for the first time I discover myself as a being-in-the-world. As Sartre says,

> To apprehend myself as seen is, in fact, to apprehend myself as seen in the world and from the standpoint of the world. . . . For the Other *I am seated* as this inkwell *is on* the table; for the Other, *I am leaning over* the keyhole as this tree *is bent* by the wind. Thus for the Other I have stripped myself of my transcendence. (pp. 340, 341)

It is consciousness which creates the world, and thus the appearance of the Other's consciousness signals the loss of my world, that is, the loss of my freedom to structure the world and create myself. Sartre makes this point in the following passage:

> . . . Suddenly the alienation of myself, which is the act of being-looked-at, involves the alienation of the world which I organize. The appearance of the Other in the world corresponds therefore to a congealed sliding of the whole universe, to a decentralization of the world which undermines the centralization which I am simultaneously effecting. (p. 334)

The Other steals my world and reduces me to a mere object. Here we have the most fundamental sense of alienation: I am alienated from what I am as a for-itself.

The loss of my transcendence, or myself as for-itself, does have some compensation. Insofar as I am an object for the Other I avoid my being "nothing," and thus I avoid the infinite responsibilities accruing to the consciousness that lies at the center of the world. And yet, "conflict is the original meaning of being-for-others" (p. 345). I want to recover my world and freedom, for although my emergence in the world as an entity with a certain kind of character depends on the Other, I am responsible for what the Other finds. Herein lies the rub: The Other is the foundation of what I am for-myself—the Other determines my essence or nature (that is, the meaning of my acts)—and yet, in virtue of my transcendence, I am responsible for what the Other creates or determines. Thus, I want to reaffirm myself as a for-itself. The question we must now consider is how, according to Sartre, are we to recapture our identity as a for-itself (consciousness)?

Sartre's views on sex are inextricably bound up with his answer to that question, but the connection between sex and the reaffirmation of our freedom is not as simple as some of Sartre's critics would have us believe. One interpretation of Sartre's views on sex is that the sole aim or goal of sex is domination or power over the Other. It is maintained that in the sexual situation we recover our freedom by making the Other into an object. Robert Solomon expresses this understanding of Sartre in the following passage:

> For Sartre, sexual desire is the desire to possess, to gain recognition of one's own freedom at the expense of the Other. By 'incarnating' and degrading him/her in flesh, one reduces him/her to an object. Sadism is but an extension of this domination over the Other. Or one allows himself to be 'incarnated' as a devious route to the same end, making the Other his/her sexual slave. . . . On this model, *degradation is the central activity of sex,* to convince the Other that he/she is a slave, to persuade the Other of one's own power, whether it be through the skills of sexual technique or through the passive demands of being sexually served.[6]

Solomon seems to be claiming that, for Sartre, the central aim of both sexual desire and sexual activity is to reduce the Other to an object and elevate oneself in power. We argue that, for Sartre, the goal of sexual desire is never to reduce the Other to a mere object, and that in sexual activity that goal is sometimes but by no means always sought after. Our argument begins by first considering Sartre's analysis of sexual desire.

Sexual Desire

Sexual desire is a unique state of consciousness in which, as Sartre says, "it seems that one is invaded by facticity" (p. 348). In sexual desire I am not only a clear and translucent for-itself, since my consciousness becomes immersed in and identical with my body. To see what is involved, let us follow Sartre and explain sexual desire by means of a contrast and an analogy. Sartre contrasts sexual desire with the desire for food. Both hunger and sexual desire presuppose a certain state of the body, but in hunger the desiring consciousness flees the body and is completely absorbed in its future possibilities, that is, the future ways of satisfying hunger. On the other hand, in sexual desire one does not flee from one's body but rather one coalesces with it. According to Sartre,

> the desiring consciousness exists this facticity; *it is in terms of this facticity*— we could even say *through it*—that the desired body appears as desirable. (p. 347)

In other words, when I desire another I am conscious of the Other's body and at the same time non-positionally conscious of my own body. To quote Sartre once more,

> Desire is not only the desire of the Other's body; it is—within the unity of a single act—the nonthetically lived project of being swallowed up in the body. (p. 349)

Sartre calls a sexual-desiring consciousness a "troubled" consciousness and compares it with "troubled" or muddy water. "Troubled" water remains water, but it is disturbed and changed by the presence of something that is not clearly distinguishable from the water itself. Similarly, a desiring consciousness is consciousness, that is, it is a direction toward an object, and a non-positional consciousness of itself, but it is not only that. For in sexual desire my consciousness is disturbed by my body which at that time is indistinguishable from it. Thus, using Sartre's terminology we may say that in sexual desire and only in sexual desire there is an "incarnation of consciousness" (p. 350). Or, as Sartre also puts it, "The being which desires is consciousness *making itself body*" (p. 349). We are now ready to understand how, according to Sartre, we are to reaffirm our identity as a consciousness or a for-itself.

Sexual desire is the mechanism by which I recover my world from the Other, but that does not mean that through sexual desire I degrade the Other or turn him or her into an object. Rather, it means that I recover my world by producing in the Other sexual desire toward me. In sexual desire I incarnate my own consciousness (I make myself "flesh") so as to produce a similar incarnation in the Other. That is, sexual desire is intentionally seductive: The goal of sexual desire is to produce an identity of consciousness and body in the Other as exists in myself. Sartre sums up the matter in a quote that the foregoing should make clear:

> Thus, the revelation of the Other's flesh is made through my own flesh; in desire and in the caress which expresses desire, I incarnate myself in order to realize the incarnation of the Other . . . I make her enjoy my flesh through her flesh in order to compel her to feel herself flesh. And so possession truly appears as a *double reciprocal incarnation.* (p. 350)

In sexual desire there is a positional consciousness of the Other's consciousness and body and a non-positional consciousness of one's own consciousness and body. The motive for this reciprocal incarnation is twofold: (1) insofar as the other is conscious of his or her body, I reaffirm my identity as a consciousness, and (2) insofar as the other is conscious of me, I can retain my identity as an object in the midst of the world. Thus, in sexual desire lies the resolution of the conflict in human relationships, for in sexual desire I achieve and the Other achieves an ideal situation in which we preserve our freedom (consciousness, transcendence) while retaining our security as beings in the midst of the world. Therefore, Solomon is mistaken when he says that sexual desire aims at the recognition of one's own freedom at the expense of the Other.[7]

The question remains regarding whether Sartre maintains that the goal of all sexual activity is power or domination over the Other. In the next section we consider that question and explain our belief that, according to Sartre, all sexual activity is a kind of perversion.

Sexual Activity and Sexual Perversion

There is, as we all know, a connection between sexual desire and sexual activity: The former, given the appropriate conditions, leads to the latter. Now, it is precisely because sexual desire leads to sexual activity that Sartre says, "Desire is itself doomed to failure" (p. 353). Sartre's point is that sexual activity entails a breakdown of the double reciprocal incarnation brought about by sexual desire, because sexual activity involves either a concentration on one's own bodily pleasure or "a desire of *taking* and of *appropriating*" (p. 354) the Other's body. If I concentrate on my own pleasure, then I am forgetful of the Other's incarnation and reduce myself to an object, thus remaining a slave to the Other. If, on the other hand, I ignore my own pleasure and concentrate on appropriating the Other's body, that is, I attempt to seize the Other's body, to unite with it, and so on, then the Other ceases to be an incarnated consciousness and becomes a mere object in the midst of the world. Thus, Sartre says that desire "brings about the rupture of that reciprocity of incarnation which was precisely the unique goal of desire" (p. 355). Or, still differently, sexual desire issues in the death of desire, and hence it is "doomed to failure."

Given the foregoing understanding of sexual activity, it follows that domination or power is not the sole aim of sexual activity. For, when I pay attention to my own pleasure the Other-as-object (or incarnated consciousness) disappears, and the Other-as-consciousness (or look) appears. If one is to speak of an aim of this sort of activity, then we can best quote Sartre where he says,

> . . . Consciousness apprehending itself in its facticity demands to be apprehended and transcended as body-for-the-Other by means of the Other's consciousness. (p. 354)

Clearly then, the aim of all sexual activity is not to dominate, or to degrade the Other by reducing him or her into an object.

It remains to be shown that it follows from Sartre's analysis of sex that all sexual activity is a kind of perversion. Fortunately, the argument is really quite simple. We have seen that for Sartre, sexual desire is the ideal state for individuals to be in because it involves a double reciprocal incarnation and thus a solution to the fundamental conflict between ourselves and Others. In sexual desire I desire the Other as the Other desires me; not as a body, and not as a consciousness, but as a human being, that is, as a unity of consciousness and body. To quote Sartre once more,

> I desire a human being, not an insect or a mollusk, and I desire him (or her) as he is and I am in situation in the world and as he is an Other for me and as I am an Other for him. (p. 346)

We have also seen that sexual desire leads to sexual activity, which destroys the reciprocal incarnation. If the destruction is accomplished by attention to pleasure, then the situation is masochistic; if the destruction is accomplished by appropriating the Other, then the situation is sadistic. In either case, sexual activity is a kind of perversion, that is, a movement away from the state of sexual desire. This way of reading Sartre is not only structurally sound, it also has textual support. Consider, for example, a passage that occurs during Sartre's discussion of sadism:

> . . . as soon as I seek to take the Other's body which through my own incarnation I have induced to incarnate itself, I break the reciprocity of incarnation, I transcend my body toward its own possibles, and I orient myself in the direction of sadism. Thus, sadism and masochism are the two reefs on which desire may founder—whether I transcend my troubled disturbance toward an appropriation of the other's flesh or, intoxicated with my own disturbance, pay attention only to my flesh and ask nothing of the Other except that he should be the look which aids me in realizing my flesh. It is because of this inconstancy on the part of desire and its perpetual oscillation between these two perils that 'normal' sexuality is commonly designated as 'sadomasochistic.' (p. 355)

This passage, I submit, supports my thesis that for Sartre, all sexual activity is a kind of perversion. In other words, even normal sexuality, what Thomas Nagel calls "unadorned sexual intercourse," will be a perversion, since it involves a rupture of the double reciprocal incarnation brought about by sexual desire.

The case for interpreting Sartre as we do depends on supposing that according to him, the goal of sexual desire is realizable, for it is only by allowing sexuality to achieve its goal on occasion that we can provide the concept of perversion with a foothold. Fortunately, there are passages which do strongly suggest that the goal of sexual desire is realizable. For example, after a brief discussion of the caress, Sartre says,

> At this moment the communion of desire is realized; each consciousness by incarnating itself has realized the incarnation of the Other; each one's disturbance has caused disturbance to be born in the Other and is thereby so much enriched. By each caress I experience my own flesh, and I am conscious that this flesh which I feel and appropriate through my flesh is flesh-realized-by-the-Other. (p. 353)

In spite of that passage, Nagel has claimed that in Sartre's view the aim of sexual desire cannot be accomplished and thus he cannot admit the concept of perversion. Nagel writes,

> According to Sartre, all attempts to incorporate the other into my world as subject, that is, to apprehend him at once as an object for me and a subject for whom I am an object, are unstable and doomed to collapse into one or the other of the two aspects. This has the consequence that there can be no such thing as a successful sexual relation, since the deep aim of sexual desire cannot in principle be accomplished. It seems likely, therefore, that this view will not permit a basic distinction between successful or complete, and unsuccessful, or incomplete, sex and therefore cannot admit the concept of perversion.[8]

Although Nagel does not give any textual support for his interpretation, there are passages that do indeed suggest that the goal of sexual desire is unattainable. Sartre says that desire is "doomed to failure," "that it bears within itself the cause of its own failure," and that it is an "impossible ideal" (p. 353). In light of these and other passages can it still be maintained that sexual desire is realizable and consequently that sexual activity is a perversion of desire? We think, perhaps, that it can.

When Sartre says that "desire bears within itself the cause of its own failure," we suggest he means that the necessary result of attaining desire is the collapse or destruction of desire. A sexually desiring consciousness is, in a sense, a contradiction. For is it not contradictory to suppose that two radically different kinds of being—my facticity and my transcendence—can be indivisibly united in desire? Indeed, it is a contradiction, but why should that prove it has no being? If my account of Sartre's analysis of consciousness as being an indivisible unity of positional and non-positional consciousness is correct, then he has already admitted a contradictory being into his ontology. (The contradiction is that positional consciousness is intentional, non-positional consciousness is unintentional, and yet together they form a single consciousness.) The fact that sexual desire is a contradictory being does entail that desire contains within itself the cause of its own failure. For, due to its being contradictory, a desiring consciousness is radically unstable, in that the immediate result of its realization is a disintegration into one or another of the aspects that comprise it. More specifically, at the moment at which desire is realized there is a shift of consciousness to my own incarnation or the incarnation of the Other. In other words, the result of attaining the goal of sexual desire is the breakdown of the double reciprocal incarnation into a subject-object or sadomasochistic dichotomy. In either case, as Sartre says, "there is a rupture of contact and desire misses its goal" (p. 354). It is this "rupture of contact" that constitutes a perversion, and since all sexual activity involves such a breakdown, it follows that all sexual activity is a perversion.

We close this section with two remarks. First, a common theme in existentialist literature is that life is meaningless and that the human condition is hopeless. My interpretation of Sartre on sex makes clear at least one meaning of these vague slogans. What makes the human condition so hopeless is that unperverted relationships between human beings require an ideal state of sexual desire that is fleeting and rarely achieved. And further, shortly after it is achieved, it inevitably leads to its own destruction. Second, Sartre's views on sex would also make clear why the basic problems of human relationships cannot be solved in bed. As Solomon facetiously, but perhaps not inaccurately puts it, "Sartre's notion of sexuality, taken seriously, would be enough to keep us out of bed for a month."[9]

THE DESIRE TO BE GOD

We have seen that for Sartre, consciousness is the essence of human reality and that, to put it paradoxically, for consciousness, to be is not to be. That is, to be conscious of an object is not to be an object of consciousness. Thus, consciousness is a *lack of being* and because of that lack, Sartre maintains our most fundamental desire (or project) is the desire to complete our being, to merge our being for-itself with being in-itself. As Sartre puts it,

> Fundamentally man is the *desire to be.* . . . As for the being which is the object of this desire, we know *a priori* what this is. The for-itself is the being which is to itself its own lack of being. The being which the for-itself lacks is the in-itself. . . . Thus the end and goal of the nihilation which I am is the in-itself. Thus human reality is the desire of being-in-itself. (pp. 355–356)

The project to become a being-in-itself-for-itself is the desire to become a cause of one's own being, that is, to have one's essence be the foundation of one's free choice; to be an *ens causa sui,* a "self-cause." "Thus the best way to conceive of the fundamental project of human reality is to say that man is the being whose project is to be God" (p. 357).

According to Sartre, the desire to be God is known a priori, since it is the very nature of consciousness, and not any empirical discovery, that reveals this universal human passion. On the other hand, the manifestation of the fundamental project in particular existing individuals is unique and in principle empirically discoverable by the method of existential psychoanalysis. That is, we each choose to complete our being (to realize the project of being God) in our own particular way and "each example of human conduct . . . even our most insignificant and superficial behavior" (p.   ) reveals something about our *original* or *fundamental choice* of being. The task of existential psychoanalysis is, therefore, to make the individual aware of the self it wants to be, and also aware that this ultimate project is not objective, that is, that the individual is the source of the fundamental choice and as such it is not fixed but can be changed.

In the section on "Existential Ethics" Sartre says,

> But the principal result of existential psychoanalysis must be to make us repudiate the *spirit of seriousness.* The spirit of seriousness has two characteristics: it considers values as transcendent givens independent of human subjectivity, and it transfers the quality of "desirable" from the ontological structure of things to their simple material constitution. (p. 365)

The problem with the spirit of seriousness, that is, the attempt to treat values as objective properties of objects and actions, is that it serves to hide our freedom from us. "Objects are mute demands, and [we are] nothing in [ourselves] but the passive obedience to these demands" (p. 365). In other words, if we treat values as objective (beings-in-them-selves) then we fall into bad faith by treating our freedom as fixed by those values.

Sartre believes, however, that existential psychoanalysis can reveal to us that our real reason for treating values as objective is the ultimate project or desire to fuse the in-itself with the for-itself. When we come to see that that desire is doomed to failure, and that we are the beings by whom values and projects exist, then "freedom will become conscious of itself and will reveal itself in anguish as the unique source of value and the nothingness by which the *world* exists" (p. 366).

What is anguishing is the realization that our ultimate value, namely, the desire to be an *ens causa sui,* is unattainable. Thus we are confronted with the question, "What ultimate project are we to put in its place?" Could freedom choose itself for a value? What would that mean if, as Sartre insists, we can never merge a being *for* consciousness with a consciousness *of* being? We turn to Simone de Beauvoir to find a response to these questions.

Sartre Lexicon

Anguish. Consciousness of our freedom.

Bad faith. Self-deception that occurs when we see what we are and deny it, or see what we are not and affirm it. Bad faith occurs when I shift from one pole (facticity) to the other (transcendence) or vice versa, and affirm the one pole as being the other.

Being in the midst of the world. To think of oneself as a Being-in-itself, as an object among objects, a formed entity.

Being-in-the-world. To be in the world as consciousness, to consider oneself as a free agent with no predetermined essence.

Being-for-itself. Conscious being.

Being-for-others. What we are in terms of how others see us.

Being-for-ourselves. What we are for ourselves apart from our relationships with others.

Being-in-itself. Unconscious being, matter.

Consciousness. Most general term for what we would ordinarily describe by the verbs "see," "feel," "think about," "imagine," "desire," and so on. The "essence" of human reality. See *nothingness, non-positional,* and *positional.*

Ens causa sui. Cause of itself.

Existential psychoanalysis. Task is to make a person aware of his or her original project.

Facticity. We find ourselves existing at a certain time, in a certain place, with certain qualities and capacities. We are a biological conception. We can predict all kinds of things about each other. We are explainable in scientific terms. When viewed in this light we are a mere block of identity, a concrete thing.

Fear. Concern over what some being-in-the-world might do to me. I view myself as a destructible object, a being-in-itself that is subject to the effects of other objects.

Freedom. Consists in our not being what we are and our being what we are not.

Intentionality. Indicates that consciousness is always directed toward an object, is always *of* or *about* something.

Negation. As expressed in a negative judgment such as "Peter is not in the café," it represents a fact in the world that exists because a consciousness was aware of it.

Non-positional consciousness. Consciousness (of) a consciousness of an object that forms an indivisible unity with the positional consciousness.

Non-thetic consciousness. See *non-positional consciousness.*

Nothingness. There are several senses in which consciousness is nothingness. (1) Consciousness is not a thing or a substance in the world. (2) Unlike things, consciousness is completely translucent, there is nothing about consciousness that is hidden from us. (3) In virtue of its intentionality consciousness is a *lack;* its essence is "outside" itself. (4) Consciousness is free.

Original project. Our conception of what we want ourselves to be. It is not a choice among choice, but a choice of a being. It represents the meaning of each particular concrete choice we make.

Positional consciousness. Consciousness that is directed toward (posits) an object other than itself.

Pre-reflective cogito. At the pre-reflective level "I think" involves my actually thinking of an object together with (non-positional, non-cognitive) consciousness (of) that thinking.

Reflective cogito. Occurs when I posit consciousness as an object of consciousness, for example, when I remember that I was thinking.

Self-consciousness. Consciousness (of) consciousness as, for example, when I am counting the number of people in the room I am conscious that I am counting and not, say, running after a bus.

Sexual desire. State of "reciprocal incarnation" in which I am conscious of the Other and non-positionally conscious of myself as the object of the Other's consciousness, and the Other is related in the same way to me. "The being which desires is consciousness making itself body."

Shame. Non-reflective awareness of yourself as being an object.

Sincerity. To be sincere is to be what you are and is, for Sartre, a form of bad faith.

Thetic consciousness. See *positional consciousness.*

Transcendence. This block of identity that we are is, in some sense, made by us, since what we are is determined by our choices. That aspect of us in virtue of which we are capable of changing our past "essence."

Transcendent object. Object for consciousness.

SARTRE SELECTIONS

From *The Transcendence of the Ego*

The Nature of Consciousness

The type of existence of consciousness is to be consciousness of itself. And consciousness is aware of itself *in so far as it is consciousness of a transcendent object.* All is therefore clear and lucid in consciousness: the object with its characteristic opacity is before consciousness, but consciousness is purely and simply consciousness of being consciousness of that object. This is the law of its existence.

We should add that this consciousness of consciousness—except in the case of reflective consciousness which we shall dwell on later—is not *positional,* which is to say that consciousness is not for itself its own object. Its object is by nature outside of it, and that is why consciousness *posits* and *grasps* the object in the same act. Consciousness knows itself only as absolute inwardness. We shall call such a consciousness: consciousness in the first degree, or *unreflected* consciousness.

Now we ask: is there room for an *I* in such a consciousness? The reply is clear: evidently not. . . .

Thus, if one introduces this opacity into consciousness, one thereby destroys the fruitful definition cited earlier. One congeals consciousness, one darkens it. Consciousness is then no longer a spontaneity; it bears within itself the germ of opaqueness. But in addition we would be forced to abandon that original and profound view which makes of consciousness a *non-substantial* absolute. A pure consciousness is an absolute quite simply because it is consciousness of itself. It remains therefore a "phenomenon" in the very special sense in which "to be" and "to appear" are one. It is all lightness, all translucence. This it is which differentiates the *Cogito* of Husserl from the Cartesian *Cogito.* But if the *I* were a necessary structure of consciousness, this opaque *I* would at once be raised

The Transcendence of the Ego by Jean-Paul Sartre, trans. by Forrest Williams and Robert Kirkpatrick, pp. 40–42, 44–49, and 98–106. Translation copyright © 1957 Farrar, Straus and Giroux, Inc. Reprinted by permission of Farrar, Straus and Giroux, Inc. and by Librarie Hatier SA

to the rank of an absolute. We would then be in the presence of a monad. And this, indeed, is unfortunately the orientation of the new thought of Husserl (see *Cartesianische Meditationen*). Consciousness is loaded down; consciousness has lost that character which rendered it the absolute existent *by virtue of non-existence*. It is heavy and *ponderable*. All the results of phenomenology begin to crumble if the *I* is not, by the same title as the world, a relative existent: that is to say, an object *for* consciousness.

But it must be remembered that all the writers who have described the *Cogito* have dealt with it as a reflective operation, that is to say, as an operation of the second degree. Such a *Cogito* is performed by a consciousness *directed upon consciousness,* a consciousness which takes consciousness as an object. Let us agree: the certitude of the *Cogito* is absolute, for, as Husserl said, there is an indissoluble unity of the reflecting consciousness and the reflected consciousness (to the point that the reflecting consciousness could not exist without the reflected consciousness). But the fact remains that we are in the presence of a synthesis of two consciousnesses, one of which is consciousness *of* the other. Thus the essential principle of phenomenology, "all consciousness is consciousness *of* something," is preserved. Now, my reflecting consciousness does not take itself for an object when I effect the *Cogito*. What it affirms concerns the reflected consciousness. Insofar as my reflecting consciousness is consciousness of itself, it is *non-positional* consciousness. It becomes positional only by directing itself upon the reflected consciousness which itself was not a positional consciousness of itself before being reflected. Thus the consciousness which says *I Think* is precisely not the consciousness which thinks. Or rather it is not *its own* thought which it posits by this thetic act. We are then justified in asking ourselves if the *I* which thinks is common to the two superimposed consciousnesses, or if it is not rather the *I* of the reflected consciousness. All reflecting consciousness is, indeed, in itself unreflected, and a new act of the third degree is necessary in order to posit it. Moreover, there is no infinite regress here, since a consciousness has no need at all of a reflecting consciousness in order to be conscious of itself. It simply does not posit itself as an object.

But is it not precisely the reflective act which gives birth to the *me* in the reflected consciousness? Thus would be explained how every thought apprehended by intuition possesses an *I*, without falling into the difficulties noted in the preceding section. Husserl would be the first to acknowledge that an unreflected thought undergoes a radical modification in becoming reflected. But need one confine this modification to a loss of "naïveté"? Would not the appearance of the *I* be what is essential in this change?

One must evidently revert to a concrete experience, which may seem impossible, since by definition such an experience is reflective, that is to say, supplied with an *I*. But every unreflected consciousness, being non-thetic consciousness of itself, leaves a non-thetic memory that one can consult. To do so it suffices to try to reconstitute the complete moment in which this unreflected consciousness appeared (which by definition is always possible). For example, I was absorbed just now in my reading. I am going to try to remember the circumstances of my reading, my attitude, the lines that I was reading. I am thus going to revive not only these external details but a certain depth of unreflected consciousness, since the objects could only have been perceived *by* that consciousness and since they remain relative to it. That consciousness must not be posited as object of a reflection. On the contrary, I must direct my attention to the revived objects, but *without losing sight of the unreflected consciousness,* by joining in a sort of conspiracy with it and by drawing up an inventory of its content in a non-positional manner. There is no doubt about the result: while I was reading, there was consciousness *of* the book, *of* the heroes of the novel, but the *I* was not inhabiting this consciousness. It was only consciousness of the object and non-positional consciousness of itself. I can now make these a-thetically apprehended results the object of a thesis and declare: there was no *I* in the unreflected consciousness. It should not be thought that this operation is artificial or conceived for the needs of the case. . . .

When I run after a streetcar, when I look at the time, when I am absorbed in contemplating a portrait, there is no *I.* There is consciousness *of the streetcar-having-to-be-overtaken,* etc., and non-positional consciousness of consciousness. In fact, I am then plunged into the world of objects; it is they which constitute the unity of my consciousnesses; it is they which present themselves with values, with attractive and repellant qualities—but *me,* I have disappeared; I have annihilated myself. There is no place for *me* on this level. And this is not a matter of chance, due to a momentary lapse of attention, but happens because of the very structure of consciousness. . . .

We may therefore formulate our thesis: transcendental consciousness is an impersonal spontaneity. It determines its existence at each instant, without our being able to conceive anything *before* it. Thus each instant of our conscious life reveals to us a creation *ex nihilo.* Not a new *arrangement,* but a new existence. There is something distressing for each of us, to catch in the act this tireless creation of existence of which *we* are not the creators. At this level man has the impression of ceaselessly escaping from himself, of overflowing himself, of being surprised by riches which are always unexpected. And once more it is an unconscious from which he demands an account of this surpassing of the *me* by consciousness. Indeed, the *me* can do nothing to this spontaneity, for *will is an object which constitutes itself for and by this spontaneity.* The will directs itself upon states, upon emotions, or upon things, but it never turns back upon consciousness. We are well aware of this in the occasional cases in which we try *to will* a consciousness (I *will* fall asleep, I *will* no longer think about that, etc.). In these various cases, it is *by essence* necessary that the will be maintained and preserved *by that consciousness which is radically opposed* to the consciousness it wants to give rise to (if I *will* to fall asleep, I stay awake; if I *will* not to think about this or that, I think about it *precisely on that account*). It seems to us that this monstrous spontaneity is at the origin of numerous psychasthenic ailments. Consciousness is frightened by its own spontaneity because it senses this spontaneity as *beyond* freedom. This is clearly seen in an example from Janet. A young bride was in terror, when her husband left her alone, of sitting at the window and summoning the passers-by like a prostitute. Nothing in her education, in her past, nor in her character could serve as an explanation of such a fear. It seems to us simply that a negligible circumstance (reading, conversation, etc.) had determined in her what one might call "a vertigo of possibility." She found herself monstrously free, and this vertiginous freedom appeared to her *at the opportunity* for this action which she was afraid of doing. But this vertigo is comprehensible only if consciousness suddenly appeared to itself as infinitely overflowing in its possibilities the *I* which ordinarily serves as its unity.

Perhaps, in reality, the essential function of the ego is not so much theoretical as practical. We have noticed, indeed, that it does not bind up the unity of phenomena; that it is limited to reflecting an *ideal* unity, whereas the real and concrete unity has long been effected. But perhaps the essential role of the ego is to mask from consciousness its very spontaneity.

Everything happens, therefore, as if consciousness constituted the ego as a false representation of itself, as if consciousness hypnotized itself before this ego which it has constituted, absorbing itself in the ego as if to make the ego its guardian and its law. It is thanks to the ego, indeed, that a distinction can be made between the possible and the real, between appearance and being, between the willed and the undergone.

But it can happen that consciousness suddenly produces itself on the pure reflective level. Perhaps not without the ego, yet as escaping from the ego on all sides, as dominating the ego and maintaining the ego outside the consciousness by a continued creation. On this level, there is no distinction between the possible and the real, since the appearance is the absolute. There are no more barriers, no more limits, nothing to hide consciousness from itself. Then consciousness, noting what could be called the fatality of its spontaneity, is suddenly anguished: it is this dread, absolute and without remedy, this fear of itself, which seems to us constitutive of pure consciousness, and which holds the key to the psychasthenic ailment we spoke of. If the *I* of the *I Think* is the primary structure of consciousness, this dread is impossible. If, on the contrary, our point of view is adopted, not only do we have a coherent explanation of this ailment, but we have, moreover, a permanent motive for carrying out the phenomenological reduction. As we know, in his article in *Kants-tudien* Fink admits, not without some melancholy, that as long as one remains in the "natural" attitude, there is *no reason,* no "motive" for exercising the ἐπόχη. In fact, this natural attitude is perfectly coherent. There one will find none of those contradictions which, according to Plato, lead the philosopher to effect a philosophical conversion. Thus, the ἐπόχη appears in the phenomenology of Husserl as a miracle. Husserl himself, in *Cartesianische Meditationen,* made an extremely vague allusion to certain psychological motives which would lead to undertaking reduc-tion. But these motives hardly seem sufficient. Moreover, reduction seems capable of being performed only at the end of lengthy study. It appears, then, as a *knowledgeable* operation, which confers on it a sort of gratui-tousness. On the other hand, if "the natural attitude" appears wholly as an effort made by consciousness to escape from itself by projecting itself into the *me* and becoming absorbed there, and if this effort is never completely rewarded, and if a simple act of reflection suffices in order for conscious spontaneity to tear itself abruptly away from the *I* and be given as independent, then the ἐπόχη is no longer a miracle, an intellectual method, an erudite procedure: it is an anxiety which is imposed on us and which we cannot avoid: it is both a pure event of transcendental origin and an ever possible accident of our daily life.

But if the *I* becomes a transcendent, it participates in all the vicis-situdes of the world. It is no absolute; it has not created the universe; it falls like other existences at the stroke of the ἐπόχη; and solipsism becomes unthinkable from the moment that the *I* no longer has a privileged status. Instead of expressing itself in effect as "I alone exist as absolute," it must assert that "absolute consciousness alone exists as absolute," which is obviously a truism. My *I,* in effect, is *no more certain for consciousness than the I of other men.* It is only more intimate.

The theorists of the extreme Left have sometimes reproached phe-nomenology for being an idealism and for drowning reality in the stream of ideas. But if idealism is the philosophy without evil of Brunschvieg, if it is a philosophy in which the effort of spiritual assimilation never meets external resistances, in which suffering, hunger, and war are diluted in a slow process of the unification of ideas, nothing is more unjust than to call phenomenologists "idealists." On the contrary, for centuries we have not felt in philosophy so realistic a current. The phenomenologists have plunged man back into the world; they have given full measure to man's agonies and sufferings, and also to his rebellions. Unfortunately, as long as the *I* remains a structure of absolute consciousness, one will still be able to reproach phenomenology for being an escapist doctrine, for again pulling a part of man out of the world and, in that way, turning our attention from the real problems. It seems to us that this reproach no longer has any justification if one makes the *me* an existent, strictly contemporaneous with the world, whose existence has the same essential characteristics as the world. It has always seemed to me that a working hypothesis as fruitful as historical materialism never needed for a foundation the absurdity which is metaphysical materialism. In fact, it is not necessary that the object precede the subject for spiritual pseudo-values to vanish and for ethics to find its bases in reality. It is enough that the *me* be contemporaneous with the World, and that the subject-object duality, which is purely logical, definitively disappear from philosophical preoccupations. The World has not created the *me;* the *me* has not created the World. These are two objects for absolute, impersonal consciousness, and it is by virtue of this consciousness that they are connected. This absolute consciousness, when it is purified of the *I,* no longer has anything of the *subject.* It is no longer a collection of representations. It is quite simply a first condition and an absolute source of existence. And the relation of interdependence established by this absolute consciousness between the *me* and the World is sufficient for the *me* to appear as "endangered" before the World, for the *me* (indirectly and through the intermediary of states) to draw the whole of its content from the World. No more is needed in the way of a philosophical foundation for an ethics and a politics which are absolutely positive.

From Sartre, *Being and Nothingness*

The Pre-Reflective *Cogito*

All consciousness, as Husserl has shown, is consciousness *of* something. This means that there is no consciousness which is not a *positing* of a transcendent object, or if you prefer, that consciousness has no "content." We must renounce those neutral "givens" which, according to the system of reference chosen, find their place either "in the world" or "in the psyche." A table is not *in* consciousness—not even in the capacity of a representation. A table is *in* space, beside the window, *etc.* The existence of the table in fact is a center of opacity for consciousness; it would require an infinite process to inventory the total contents of a thing. To introduce this opacity into consciousness would be to refer to infinity the inventory which it can make of itself, to make consciousness a thing, and to deny the cogito. The first procedure of a philosophy ought

Being and Nothingness by Jean-Paul Sartre, trans. by Hazel Barnes, excerpts from pp. 11–17, 23–24, 33–44, 58–59, and 64–116. Copyright © 1956 by the Philosophical Library. Reprinted by permission of the Philosophical Library.

to be to expel things from consciousness and to reestablish its true connection with the world, to know that consciousness is a positional consciousness *of* the world. All consciousness is positional in that it transcends itself in order to reach an object, and it exhausts itself in this same positing. All that there is of *intention* in my actual consciousness is directed toward the outside, toward the table; all my judgments or practical activities, all my present inclinations transcend themselves; they aim at the table and are absorbed in it. Not all consciousness is knowledge (there are states of affective consciousness, for example), but all knowing consciousness can be knowledge only of its object.

However, the necessary and sufficient condition for a knowing consciousness to be knowledge *of* its object, is that it be consciousness of itself as being that knowledge. This is a necessary condition, for if my consciousness were not consciousness of being consciousness of the table, it would then be consciousness of that table without consciousness of being so. In other words, it would be a consciousness ignorant of itself, an unconscious—which is absurd. This is a sufficient condition, for my being conscious of being conscious of that table suffices in fact for me to be conscious of it. That is of course not sufficient to permit me to affirm that this table exists *in itself*—but rather that it exists *for me*.

What is this consciousness of consciousness? We suffer to such an extent from the illusion of the primacy of knowledge that we are immediately ready to make of the consciousness of consciousness an *idea ideae* in the manner of Spinoza; that is, a knowledge of knowledge. Alain, wanting to express the obvious "To know is to be conscious of knowing," interprets it in these terms: "To know is to know that one knows." In this way we should have defined *reflection* or positional consciousness of consciousness, or better yet *knowledge of consciousness*. This would be a complete consciousness directed toward something which is not it; that is, toward consciousness as object of reflection. It would then transcend itself and like the positional consciousness *of* the world would be exhausted in aiming at its object. But that object would be itself a consciousness.

It does not seem possible for us to accept this interpretation of the consciousness of consciousness. The reduction of consciousness to knowledge in fact involves our introducing into consciousness the subject-object dualism which is typical of knowledge. But if we accept the law of the knower-known dyad, then a third term will be necessary in order for the knower to become known in turn, and we will be faced with this dilemma: Either we stop at any one term of the series—the known, the knower known, the knower known by the knower, *etc.* In this case the totality of the phenomenon falls into the unknown; that is, we always bump up against a non-self-conscious reflection and a final term. Or else we affirm the necessity of an infinite regress *(idea ideae ideae, etc.),* which is absurd. Thus to the necessity of ontologically establishing consciousness we would add a new necessity: that of establishing it epistemologically. Are we obliged after all to introduce the law of this dyad into consciousness? Consciousness of self is not dual. If we wish to avoid an infinite regress, there must be an immediate, non-cognitive relation of the self to itself.

Furthermore the reflecting consciousness posits the consciousness reflected-on, as its object. In the act of reflecting I pass judgment on the consciousness reflected-on; I am ashamed of it, I am proud of it, I will it, I deny it, *etc.* The immediate consciousness which I have of perceiving does not permit me either to judge or to will or to be ashamed. It does not *know* my perception, does not *posit* it; all that there is of intention in my actual consciousness is directed toward the outside, toward the world. In turn, this spontaneous consciousness of my perception is *constitutive* of my perceptive consciousness. In other words, every positional consciousness of an object is at the same time a non-positional consciousness of itself. If I count the cigarettes which are in that case, I have the impression of disclosing an objective property of this collection of cigarettes: *they are a dozen.* This property appears to my consciousness as a property existing in the world. It is very possible that I have no positional consciousness of counting them. Then I do not know myself as counting. Proof of this is that children who are capable of making an addition spontaneously can not *explain* subsequently how they set about it. Piaget's tests, which show this, constitute an excellent refutation of the formula of Alain—To know is to know that one knows. Yet at the moment when these cigarettes are revealed to me as a dozen, I have a non-thetic consciousness of my adding activity. If anyone questioned me, indeed, if anyone should ask, "What are you doing there?" I should reply at once, "I am counting." This reply aims not only at the instantaneous consciousness which I can achieve by reflection but at those fleeting consciousnesses which have passed without being reflected-on, those which are forever not-reflected-on in my immediate past. Thus reflection has no kind of primacy over the consciousness reflected-on. It is not reflection which reveals the consciousness reflected-on to itself. Quite the contrary, it is the non-reflective consciousness which renders the reflection possible; there is a pre-reflective cogito which is the condition of the Cartesian cogito. At the same time it is the non-thetic consciousness of counting which is the very condition of my act of adding. If it were otherwise, how would the addition be the unifying theme of my consciousness? In order that this theme should preside over a whole series of syntheses of unifications and recognitions, it must be present to itself, not as a thing but as an operative intention which can exist only as the revealing-revealed *(révélante-révélée),* to use an expression of Heidegger's. Thus in order to count, it is necessary to be conscious of counting.

Of course, someone may say, but this makes a circle. For is it not necessary that I count *in fact* in order to *be conscious* of counting? That is true. However there is no circle, or if you like, it is the very nature of consciousness to exist "in a circle." The idea can be expressed in these terms: Every conscious existence exists as consciousness of existing. We understand now why the first consciousness of consciousness is not positional; it is because it is one with the consciousness of which it is consciousness. At one stroke it determines itself as consciousness of perception and as perception. The necessity of syntax has compelled us hitherto to speak of the "non-positional consciousness of self." But we can no longer use this expression in which the *"of self"* still evokes the idea of knowledge. (Henceforth we shall put the "of" inside parentheses to show that it merely satisfies a grammatical requirement.)

This self-consciousness we ought to consider not as a new consciousness, but as *the only mode of existence which is possible for a consciousness of something.* Just as an extended object is compelled to exist according to three dimensions, so an intention, a pleasure, a grief can exist only as immediate self-consciousness. If the intention is not a thing in consciousness, then the being of the intention can be only consciousness. It is not necessary to understand by this that on the one hand, some external cause (an organic trouble, an unconscious impulse, another *Erlebnis*) could determine that a psychic event—a pleasure, for example—produce itself, that on the other hand, this event so determined in its material structure should be compelled to produce itself as self-consciousness. This would be to make the non-thetic consciousness a *quality* of the positional consciousness (in the sense that the perception, positional consciousness of that table, would have as addition the quality of self-consciousness) and would thus fall back into the illusion of the theoretical primacy of knowledge. This would be moreover to make the psychic event a thing and to *qualify* it with "conscious" just as I can qualify this blotter with "red." Pleasure can not be distinguished—even logically—from consciousness of pleasure. Consciousness (of) pleasure is constitutive of the pleasure as the very mode of its own existence, as the material of which it is made, and not as a form which is imposed by a blow upon a hedonistic material. Pleasure can not exist "before" consciousness of pleasure—not even in the form of potentiality or potency. A potential pleasure can exist only as consciousness (of) being potential. Potencies of consciousness exist only as consciousness of potencies.

Conversely, as I showed earlier, we must avoid defining pleasure by the consciousness which I have of it. This would be to fall into an idealism of consciousness which would bring us by indirect means to the primacy of knowledge. Pleasure must not disappear behind its own self-consciousness; it is not a representation, it is a concrete event, full and absolute. It is no more a quality of self-consciousness than self-consciousness is a quality of pleasure. There is no more first a consciousness which receives *subsequently* the affect "pleasure" like water which one stains, than there is first a pleasure (unconscious or psychological) which receives subsequently the quality of "conscious" like a pencil of light rays. There is an indivisible, indissoluble being—definitely not a substance supporting its qualities like particles of being, but a being which is existence through and through. Pleasure is the being of self-consciousness and this self-consciousness is the law of being of pleasure. This is what Heidegger expressed very well when he wrote (though speaking of *Dasein,* not of consciousness): "The 'how' *(essentia)* of this being, so far as it is possible to speak of it generally, must be conceived in terms of its existence *(existentia)*." This means that consciousness is not produced as a particular instance of an abstract possibility but that in rising to the center of being, it creates and supports its essence—that is, the synthetic order of its possibilities.

This means also that the type of being of consciousness is the opposite of that which the ontological proof reveals to us. Since consciousness is not *possible* before being, but since its being is the source and condition of all possibility, its existence implies its essence. Husserl expresses this aptly in speaking of the "necessity of fact." In order for there to be an essence of pleasure, there must be first the *fact* of a consciousness (of) this pleasure. It is futile to try to invoke pretended *laws* of consciousness of which the articulated whole would constitute the essence. A law is a transcendent object of knowledge; there can be consciousness of a law, not a law of consciousness. For the same reasons it is impossible to assign to a consciousness a motivation other than itself. Otherwise it would be necessary to conceive that consciousness to the degree to which it is an effect, is not conscious (of) itself. It would be necessary in some manner that it should be without being conscious (of) being. We should fall into that too common illusion which makes consciousness semi-conscious or a passivity. But consciousness is consciousness through and through. It can be limited only by itself.

This self-determination of consciousness must not be conceived as a genesis, as a becoming, for that would force us to suppose that consciousness is prior to its own existence. Neither is it necessary to conceive of this self-creation as an act, for in that case consciousness would be conscious (of) itself as an act, which it is not. Consciousness is a plenum of existence, and this determination of itself by itself is an essential characteristic. It would even be wise not to misuse the expression "cause of self," which allows us to suppose a progression, a relation of self-cause to self-effect. It would be more exact to say very simply: The existence of consciousness comes from consciousness itself. By that we need not understand that consciousness "derives from nothingness." There can not be "nothingness of consciousness" *before* consciousness. "Before" consciousness one can conceive only of a plenum of being of which no element can refer to an absent consciousness. If there is to be nothingness of consciousness, there must be a consciousness which has been and which is no more and a witnessing consciousness which poses the nothingness of the first consciousness for a synthesis of recognition. Consciousness is prior to nothingness and "is derived" from being.*

One will perhaps have some difficulty in accepting these conclusions. But considered more carefully, they will appear perfectly clear. The paradox is not that there are "self-activated" existences but that there is no other kind. What is truly unthinkable is passive existence; that is, existence which perpetuates itself without having the force either to produce itself or to preserve itself. From this point of view there is nothing more incomprehensible than the principle of inertia. Indeed where would consciousness "come" from if it did "come" from something? From the limbo of the unconscious or of the physiological. But if we ask ourselves how this limbo in its turn can exist and where it derives its existence, we find ourselves faced with the concept of passive existence; that is, we can no more absolutely understand how this non-conscious given (unconscious or physiological) which does not derive its existence from itself, can nevertheless perpetuate this existence and find in addition the ability to produce a consciousness. This demonstrates the great favor which the proof *a contingentia mundi* has enjoyed.

Thus by abandoning the primacy of knowledge, we have discovered the *being* of the *knower* and encountered the absolute, that same absolute which the rationalists of the seventeenth century had defined and logically constituted as an object of knowledge. But precisely because the question concerns an absolute of existence and not of knowledge, it is not subject to that famous objection according to which a known absolute is no longer an absolute because it becomes relative to the knowledge which one has of it. In fact the absolute here is not the result of a logical construction on the ground of knowledge but the subject of the most concrete of experiences. And it is not at all *relative* to this experience because it *is* this experience. Likewise it is a non-substantial absolute. The ontological error of Cartesian rationalism is not to have seen that if the absolute is defined by the primacy of existence over essence, it can not be conceived as a substance. Consciousness has nothing substantial, it is pure "appearance" in the sense that it exists only to the degree to which it appears. But it is precisely because consciousness is pure appearance, because it is total emptiness (since the entire world is outside it)—it is because of this identity of appearance and existence within it that it can be considered as the absolute.

---

* That certainly does not mean that consciousness is the foundation of its being. On the contrary, as we shall see later, there is a full contingency of the being of consciousness. We wish only to show (1) That *nothing* is the cause of consciousness. (2) That consciousness is the cause of its own way of being.

The Ontological Proof

Consciousness is consciousness of something. This means that transcendence is the constitutive structure of consciousness; that is that consciousness emerges *supported by* a being which is not itself. This is what we call the ontological proof. No doubt someone will reply that the existence of a requirement of consciousness does not prove that this requirement must be satisfied. But this objection cannot hold up against an analysis of what Husserl calls intentionality, though, to be sure, he misunderstood its essential character. To say that consciousness is consciousness of something means that for consciousness there is no being outside of that precise obligation to be a revealing intuition of something— *i.e.,* of a transcendent being. Not only does pure subjectivity, if initially given, fail to transcend itself to posit the objective; but it would also lose its purity. What can properly be called subjectivity is consciousness (of) consciousness. But this consciousness (of being) consciousness must be qualified in some way, and it can be qualified only as revealing intuition or it is nothing. Now a revealing intuition implies something revealed. Absolute subjectivity can be established only in the face of something revealed; immanence can be defined only within the apprehension of a transcendent. It might appear that there is an echo here of Kant's refutation of problematical idealism. But we ought rather to think of Descartes. We are here on the ground of being, not of knowledge. It is not a question of showing that the phenomena of inner sense imply the existence of objective spatial phenomena, but that consciousness implies in its being a non-conscious and transphenomenal being. In particular there is no point in replying that in fact subjectivity implies objectivity and that it constitutes itself in constituting the objective; we have seen that subjectivity is powerless to constitute the objective. To say that consciousness is consciousness of something is to say that it must occur as a revealed-revelation of a being which is not it and which gives itself as already existing when consciousness reveals it.

Thus we have left pure appearance and have arrived at full being. Consciousness is a being whose existence posits its essence, and inversely it is consciousness of a being, whose essence implies its existence; that is, in which appearance lays claim to *being*. Being is everywhere. Certainly we could apply to consciousness the definition which Heidegger reserves for *Dasein* and say that it is a being such that in its being, its being is in question. But it would be necessary to complete the definition and formulate it more like this: *consciousness is a being such that in its being, its being is in question insofar as this being implies a being other than itself.*

We must understand that this being is no other than the transphenomenal being of phenomena and not a noumenal being which is hidden behind them. It is the being of this table, of this package of tobacco, of the lamp, more generally the being of the world which is implied by consciousness. It requires simply that the being of that which *appears* does not exist *only* insofar as it appears. The transphenomenal being of what exists *for consciousness* is itself in itself *(lui-même en soi)*. . . .

On the Relation Between Consciousness and the World

The Question

Our inquiry has led us to the heart of being. But we have been brought to an impasse since we have not been able to establish the connection between the two regions of being which *we have* discovered. . . .

The relation of the regions of being is an original emergence and is a part of the very structure of these beings. But we discovered this in our first observations. It is enough now to open our eyes and question ingenuously this totality which is man-in-the-world. It is by the description of this totality that we shall be able to reply to these two questions: (1) What is the synthetic relation which we call being-in-the-world? (2) What must man and the world be in order for a relation between them to be possible? In truth, the two questions are interdependent, and we can not hope to reply to them separately. But each type of human conduct, being the conduct of man in the world, can release for us simultaneously man, the world, and the relation which unites them, only on condition that we envisage these forms of conduct as realities objectively apprehensible and not as subjective affects which disclose themselves only in the face of reflection.

We shall not limit ourselves to the study of a single pattern of conduct. We shall try on the contrary to describe several and, proceeding from one kind of conduct to another, attempt to penetrate into the profound meaning of the relation "man-world." But first of all we should choose a single pattern which can serve us as a guiding thread in our inquiry.

Now this very inquiry furnishes us with the desired conduct; this man that *I am*—if I apprehend him such as he is at this moment in the world, I establish that he stands before being in an attitude of interrogation. At the very moment when I ask, "Is there any conduct which can reveal to me the relation of man with the world?" I pose a question. This question I can consider objectively, for it matters little whether the questioner is myself or the reader who reads my work and who is questioning along with me. But on the other hand, the question is not simply the objective totality of the words printed on this page; it is indifferent to the symbols which express it. In a word, it is a human attitude filled with meaning. What does this attitude reveal to us?

In every question we stand before a being which we are questioning. Every question presupposes a being who questions and a being which is questioned. This is not the original relation of man to being-in-itself, but rather it stands within the limitations of this relation and takes it for granted. On the other hand, this being which we question, we question *about* something. That *about which* I question the being participates in the transcendence of being. I question being about its ways of being or about its being. From this point of view the question is a kind of expectation; I expect a reply from the being questioned. That is, on the basis of a pre-interrogative familiarity with being, I expect from this being a revelation of its being or of its way of being. The reply will be a "yes" or a "no." It is the existence of these two equally objective and contradictory possibilities which on principle distinguishes the question from affirmation or negation. There are questions which on the surface do not permit a negative reply—like, for example, the one which we put earlier, "What does this attitude reveal to us?" But actually we see that it is always possible with questions of this type to reply, "Nothing" or "Nobody" or "Never." Thus at the moment when I ask, "Is there any conduct which can reveal to me the relation of man with the world?" I admit *on principle* the possibility of a negative reply such as, "No, such a conduct does not exist." This means that we admit to being faced with the transcendent fact of the non-existence of such conduct. . . .

The question can be put in these terms: Is negation as the structure of the judicative proposition at the origin of nothingness? Or on the contrary is nothingness as the structure of the real, the origin and foundation of negation? Thus the problem of being had referred us first to that of the question as a human attitude, and the problem of the question now refers us to that of the being of negation.

It is evident that non-being always appears within the limits of a human expectation. It is because I expect to find fifteen hundred francs that I find *only* thirteen hundred. It is because a physicist *expects* a certain verification of his hypothesis that nature can tell him no. It would be in vain to deny that negation appears on the original basis of a relation of man to the world. The world does not disclose its non-beings to one who has not first posited them as possibilities. But is this to say that these non-beings are to be reduced to pure subjectivity? . . . We think not. . . .

The Origin of Negation

We need only to consider an example of a negative judgment and to ask ourselves whether it causes non-being to appear at the heart of being or merely limits itself to determining a prior revelation. I have an appointment with Pierre at four o'clock. I arrive at the café a quarter of an hour late. Pierre is always punctual. Will he have waited for me? I look at the room, the patrons, and I say, "He is not here." Is there an intuition of Pierre's absence, or does negation indeed enter in only with judgment? At first sight it seems absurd to speak here of intuition since to be exact there could not be an intuition of *nothing* and since the absence of Pierre is this nothing. Popular consciousness, however, bears witness to this intuition. Do we not say, for example, "I suddenly saw that he was not there." Is this just a matter of misplacing the negation? Let us look a little closer.

It is certain that the café by itself with its patrons, its tables, its booths, its mirrors, its light, its smoky atmosphere, and the sounds of voices, rattling saucers, and footsteps which fill it—the café is a fullness of being. And all the intuitions of detail which I can have are filled by these odors, these sounds, these colors, all phenomena which have a trans-phenomenal being. Similarly Pierre's actual presence in a place which I do not know is also a plenitude of being. We seem to have found fullness everywhere. But we must observe that in perception there is always the construction of a figure on a ground. No one object, no group of objects is especially designed to be organized as specifically either ground or figure; all depends on the direction of my attention. When I enter this café to search for Pierre, there is formed a synthetic organization of all the objects in the café, on the ground of which Pierre is given as about to appear. This organization of the café as the ground is an original nihilation. Each element of the setting, a person, a table, a chair, attempts to isolate itself, to lift itself upon the ground constituted by the totality of the other objects, only to fall back once more into the undifferentiation of this ground; it melts into the ground. For the ground is that which is seen only in addition, that which is the object of a purely marginal attention. Thus the original nihilation of all the figures which appear and are swallowed up in the total neutrality of a *ground* is the necessary condition for the appearance of the principle figure, which is here the person of Pierre. This nihilation is given to my intuition; I am witness to the successive disappearance of all the objects which I look at—in particular of the faces, which detain me for an instant (Could this be Pierre?) and which as quickly decompose precisely because they "are not" the face of Pierre. Nevertheless if I should finally discover Pierre, my intuition would be filled by a solid element, I should be suddenly arrested by his face and the whole café would organize itself around him as a discrete presence.

But now Pierre is not here. This does not mean that I discover his absence in some precise spot in the establishment. In fact Pierre is absent from the *whole* café; his absence fixes the café in its evanescence; the café remains *ground;* it persists in offering itself as an undifferentiated totality to my only marginal attention; it slips into the background; it pursues its nihilation. Only it makes itself ground for a determined figure; it carries the figure everywhere in front of it, presents the figure everywhere to me. This figure which slips constantly between my look and the solid, real objects of the café is precisely a perpetual disappearance; it is Pierre raising himself as nothingness on the ground of the nihilation of the café. So that what is offered to intuition is a flickering of nothingness; it is the nothingness of the ground, the nihilation of which summons and demands the appearance of the figure, and it is the figure—the nothingness which slips as a *nothing* to the surface of the ground. It serves as foundation for the judgment—"Pierre is not here." It is in fact the intuitive apprehension of a double nihilation. To be sure Pierre's absence supposes an original relation between me and this café; there is an infinity of people who are without any relation with this café for want of a real expectation which establishes their absence. But, to be exact, I myself expected to see Pierre, and my expectation has caused the absence of Pierre *to happen* as a real event concerning this café. It is an objective fact at present that I have *discovered* this absence, and it presents itself as a synthetic relation between Pierre and the setting in which I am looking for him. Pierre absent haunts this café and is the condition of its self-nihilating organization as ground. By contrast, judgments which I can make subsequently to amuse myself, such as, "Wellington is not in this café, Paul Valéry is no longer here, *etc.*"—these have a purely abstract meaning; they are pure applications of the principle of negation without real or efficacious foundation, and they never succeed in establishing a *real* relation between the café and Wellington or Valéry. Here the relation "is not" is merely *thought*. This example is sufficient to show that non-being does not come to things by a negative judgment; it is the negative judgment, on the contrary, which is conditioned and supported by non-being. . . .

But where does nothingness come from? If it is the original condition of the questioning attitude and more generally of all philosophical or scientific inquiry, what is the original relation of the human being to nothingness? What is the original nihilating conduct?

We shall be helped in our inquiry by a more complete examination of the conduct which served us as a point of departure. We must return to the question. We have seen, it may be recalled, that every question in essence posits the possibility of a negative reply. In a question we question a being about its being or its way of being. This way of being or this being is veiled; there always remains the possibility that it may unveil itself as a Nothingness. But from the very fact that we presume that an Existent can always be revealed as *nothing,* every question supposes that we realize a nihilating withdrawal in relation to the given, which becomes a simple *presentation,* fluctuating between being and Nothingness.

It is essential therefore that the questioner have the permanent possibility of dissociating himself from the causal series which constitutes being and which can produce only being. If we admitted that the question is determined in the questioner by universal determinism, the question would thereby become unintelligible and even inconceivable. A real cause, in fact, produces a real effect and the caused being is wholly engaged by the cause in positivity; to the extent that its being depends on the cause, it can not have within itself the tiniest germ of nothingness. Thus in so far as the questioner must be able to effect in relation to the questioned a kind of nihilating withdrawal, he is not subject to the causal order of the world; he detaches himself from Being. This means that by a double movement of nihilation he nihilates the thing questioned in relation to himself by placing it in a *neutral* state, between being and non-being—and that he nihilates himself in relation to the thing questioned by wrenching himself from being in order to be able to bring out of himself the possibility of a non-being. Thus in posing a question, a certain negative element is introduced into the world. We see nothingness as making the world iridescent, casting a shimmer over things. But at the same time the question emanates from a questioner who, in order to motivate himself in his being as one who questions, disengages himself from being. This disengagement is then by definition a human process. Man presents himself at least in this instance as a being who causes Nothingness to arise in the world, inasmuch as he himself is affected with non-being to this end.

Freedom, Anguish, and Flight

Thus the condition on which human reality can deny all or part of the world is that human reality carry nothingness within itself as the *nothing* which separates its present from all its past. But this is still not all, for the *nothing* envisaged would not yet have the sense of nothingness; a suspension of being which would remain unnamed, which would not be consciousness of suspending being would come from outside consciousness and by reintroducing opacity into the heart of this absolute lucidity, would have the effect of cutting it in two. Furthermore this nothing would by no means be negative. Nothingness, as we have seen above, is the ground of the negation because it conceals the negation within itself, because it is the negation as being. It is necessary then that conscious being constitute itself in relation to its past as separated from this past by a nothingness. It must necessarily be conscious of this cleavage in being, but not as a phenomenon which it experiences, rather as a structure of consciousness which it is. Freedom is the human being putting his past out of play by secreting his own nothingness. Let us understand indeed that this original necessity of being its own nothingness does not belong to consciousness intermittently and on the occasion of particular negations. This does not happen just at a particular moment in psychic life when negative or interrogative attitudes appear; consciousness continually experiences itself as the nihilation of its past being.

But someone doubtless will believe that he can use against us here an objection which we have frequently raised ourselves: if the nihilating consciousness exists only as consciousness of nihilation, we ought to be able to define and describe a constant mode of consciousness, present *qua* consciousness, which would be consciousness of nihilation. Does this consciousness exist? Behold, a new question has been raised here: if freedom is the being of consciousness, consciousness ought to exist as consciousness of freedom. What form does this consciousness of freedom assume? In freedom the human being *is* his own past (as also his own future) in the form of nihilation. If our analysis has not led us astray, there ought to exist for the human being, in so far as he is conscious of being, a certain mode of standing opposite his past and his future, as being both this past and this future and as not being them. We shall be able to furnish an immediate reply to this question; it is in anguish that man gets the consciousness of his freedom, or if you prefer, anguish is the mode of being of freedom as consciousness of being; it is in anguish that freedom is, in its being, in question for itself.

Kierkegaard describing anguish in the face of what one lacks characterizes it as anguish in the face of freedom. But Heidegger, whom we know to have been greatly influenced by Kierkegaard, considers anguish instead as the apprehension of nothingness. These two descriptions of anguish do not appear to us contradictory; on the contrary the one implies the other.

First we must acknowledge that Kierkegaard is right; anguish is distinguished from fear in that fear is fear of beings in the world whereas anguish is anguish before myself. Vertigo is anguish to the extent that I am afraid not of falling over the precipice, but of throwing myself over. A situation provokes fear if there is a possibility of my life being changed from without; my being provokes anguish to the extent that I distrust myself and my own reactions in that situation. The artillery preparation which precedes the attack can provoke fear in the soldier who undergoes the bombardment, but anguish is born in him when he tries to foresee the conduct with which he will face the bombardment, when he asks himself if he is going to be able to "hold up." Similarly the recruit who reports for active duty at the beginning of the war can in some instances be afraid of death, but more often he is "afraid of being afraid"; that is, he is filled with anguish before himself. Most of the time dangerous or threatening situations present themselves in facets; they will be apprehended through a feeling of fear or of anguish according to whether we envisage the situation as acting on the man or the man as acting on the situation. The man who has just received a hard blow—for example, losing a great part of his wealth in a crash—can have the fear of threatening poverty. He will experience anguish a moment later when nervously wringing his hands (a symbolic reaction to the action which is imposed but which remains still wholly undetermined), he exclaims to himself: "What am I going to do? But what am I going to do?" In this sense fear and anguish are exclusive of one another since fear is unreflective apprehension of the transcendent and anguish is reflective apprehension of the self; the one is born in the destruction of the other. The normal process in the case which I have just cited is a constant transition from the one to the other. But there exist also situations where anguish appears pure; that is, without ever being preceded or followed by fear. If, for example, I have been raised to a new dignity and charged with a delicate and flattering mission, I can feel anguish at the thought that I will not be capable perhaps of fulfilling it, and yet I will not have the least fear in the world of the consequences of my possible failure.

What is the meaning of anguish in the various examples which I have just given? Let us take up again the example of vertigo. Vertigo announces itself through fear; I am on a narrow path—without a guard rail—which goes along a precipice. The precipice presents itself to me as *to be avoided;* it represents a danger of death. At the same time I conceive of a certain number of causes, originating in universal determinism, which can transform that threat of death into reality: I can slip on a stone and fall into the abyss; the crumbling earth of the path can give way under my steps. Through these various anticipations, I am given to myself as a thing; I am passive in relation to these possibilities; they come to me from without; in so far as I am also an object in the world, subject to gravitation, they are *my* possibilities. At this moment *fear* appears, which in terms of the situation is the apprehension of myself as a destructible transcendent in the midst of transcendents, as an object which does not contain in itself the origin of its future disappearance. My reaction will be of the reflective order; I will pay attention to the stones in the road; I will keep myself as far as possible from the edge of the path. I realize myself as pushing away the threatening situation with all my strength, and I project before myself a certain number of future conducts destined to keep the threats of the world at a distance from me. These conducts are *my* possibilities. I escape fear by the very fact that I am placing myself on a plane where *my own* possibilities are substituted for the transcendent probabilities where human action had no place. . . .

Now as we have seen, consciousness of being is the being of consciousness. There is no question here of a contemplation which I could make after the event, of a horror already constituted; it is the very being of horror to appear to itself as "not being the cause" of the conduct it calls for. In short, to avoid fear, which reveals to me a transcendent future strictly determined, I take refuge in reflection, but the latter has only an undetermined future to offer. This means that in establishing a certain conduct as a possibility and precisely because it is *my* possibility, I am aware that *nothing* can compel me to adopt that conduct. Yet I am indeed already there in the future; it is for the sake of that being which I will be there at the turning of the path that I now exert all my strength, and in this sense there is already a relation between my future being and my present being. But a nothingness has slipped into the heart of this relation; I *am* not the self which I will be. First I am not that self because time separates me from it. Secondly, I am not that self because what I am is not the foundation of what I will be. Finally I am not that self because no actual existent can determine strictly what I am going to be. Yet as I am already what I will be (otherwise I would not be interested in any one being more than another), *I am the self which I will be, in the mode of not being it.* It is through my horror that I am carried toward the future, and the horror nihilates itself in that it constitutes the future as possible. Anguish is precisely my consciousness of being my own future, in the mode of not-being. To be exact, the nihilation of horror as a *motive,* which has the effect of reinforcing horror as a *state,* has as its positive counterpart the appearance of other forms of conduct (in particular that which consists in throwing myself over the precipice) as *my* possible *possibilities.* If *nothing* compels me to save my life, *nothing* prevents me from precipitating myself into the abyss. The decisive conduct will emanate from a self which I am not yet. Thus the self which I am depends on the self which I am not yet to the exact extent that the self which I am not yet does not depend on the self which I am. Vertigo appears as the apprehension of this dependence. I approach the precipice, and my scrutiny is searching for myself in my very depths. In terms of this moment, I play with my possibilities. My eyes, running over the abyss from top to bottom, imitate the possible fall and realize it symbolically; at the same time suicide, from the fact that it becomes a *possibility* possible for *me,* now causes to appear possible motives for adopting it (suicide would cause anguish to cease). Fortunately these motives in their turn, from the sole fact that they are motives of a possibility, present themselves as ineffective, as non-determinant; they can no more *produce* the suicide than my horror of the fall can *determine me* to avoid it. It is this counter-anguish which generally puts an end to anguish by transmuting it into indecision. Indecision in its turn calls for decision. I abruptly put myself at a distance from the edge of the precipice and resume my way.

The example which we have just analyzed has shown us what we could call "anguish in the face of the future." There exists another: anguish in the face of the past. It is that of the gambler who has freely and sincerely decided not to gamble anymore and who, when he approaches the gaming table, suddenly sees all his resolutions melt away. This phenomenon has often been described as if the sight of the gaming table reawakened in us a tendency which entered into conflict with our former resolution and ended by drawing us in spite of this. Aside from the fact that such a description is done in materialistic terms and peoples the mind with opposing forces (there is, for example, the moralists' famous "struggle of reason with the passions"), it does not account for the facts. In reality—the letters of Dostoevsky bear witness to this—there is nothing in us which resembles an inner *debate* as if we had to weigh motives and incentives before deciding. The earlier resolution of "not playing anymore" is always *there,* and in the majority of cases the gambler when in the presence of the gaming table, turns toward it as if to ask it for help; for he does not wish to play, or rather having taken his resolution the day before, he thinks of himself still as not wishing to play anymore; he believes in the effectiveness of this resolution. But what he apprehends then in anguish is precisely the total inefficacy of the past resolution. It is there doubtless but fixed, ineffectual, surpassed by the very fact that I am conscious *of* it. The resolution is still *me* to the extent that I realize constantly my identity with myself across the temporal flux, but it is no longer *me*—due to the fact that it has become an object *for* my consciousness. I am not subject to it, it fails in the mission which I have given it. The resolution is there still, I *am* it in the mode of not-being. What the gambler apprehends at this instant is again the permanent rupture in determinism; it is nothingness which separates him from himself; I should have liked so much not to gamble anymore; yesterday I even had a synthetic apprehension of the situation (threatening ruin, disappointment of my relatives) as *forbidding me* to play. It seemed to me that I had established a *real barrier* between gambling and myself, and now I suddenly perceive that my former understanding of the situation is no more than a memory of an idea, a memory of a feeling. In order for it to come to my aid once more, I must remake it *ex nihilo* and freely. The not-gambling is only one of my possibilities, as the fact of gambling is another of them, neither more nor less. I *must rediscover* the fear of financial ruin or of disappointing my family, *etc.,* I must re-create it as experienced fear. It stands behind me like a boneless phantom. It depends on me alone to lend it flesh. I am alone and naked before temptation as I was the day before. After having patiently built up barriers and walls, after enclosing myself in the magic circle of a resolution, I perceive with anguish that *nothing* prevents me from gambling. The anguish *is me* since by the very fact of taking my position in existence as consciousness of being, I make myself *not to be* the past of good resolutions *which I am.*

It would be in vain to object that the sole condition of this anguish is ignorance of the underlying psychological determinism. According to such a view my anxiety would come from lack of knowing the real and effective incentives which in the darkness of the unconscious determine my action. In reply we shall point out first that anguish has not appeared to us as a *proof* of human freedom; the latter was given to us as the necessary condition for the question. We wished only to show that there exists a specific consciousness of freedom, and we wished to show that this consciousness is anguish. This means that we wished to establish anguish in its essential structure as consciousness of freedom. Now from this point of view the existence of a psychological determinism could not invalidate the results of our description. Indeed anguish either is actually an unrealized ignorance of this determinism—and then anguish apprehends itself in fact as freedom—or else one may claim that anguish is consciousness of being ignorant of the real causes of our acts. In the latter case anguish would come from that of which we have a presentiment, a screen deep within ourselves for monstrous motives which would suddenly release guilty acts. But in this case we should suddenly appear to ourselves as *things in the world;* we should be to ourselves or own transcendent situation. Then anguish would disappear to give way to *fear,* for fear is a synthetic apprehension of the transcendent as dreadful.

This freedom which reveals itself to us in anguish can be characterized by the existence of that *nothing* which insinuates itself between motives and act. It is not *because* I am free that my act is not subject to the determination of motives; on the contrary, the structure of motives as ineffective is the condition of my freedom. If someone asks what this *nothing* is which provides a foundation for freedom, we shall reply that we can not describe it since it *is not,* but we can at least hint at its meaning by saying that this nothing is made-to-be by the human being in his relation with himself. The nothing here corresponds to the necessity for the motive to appear as motive only as a correlate of a consciousness *of* motive. In short, as soon as we abandon the hypothesis of the contents of consciousness, we must recognize that there is never a motive *in* consciousness; motives are only *for* consciousness. And due to the very fact that the motive can arise only as appearance, it constitutes itself as ineffective. Of course it does not have the externality of a temporal-spatial thing; it always belongs to subjectivity and it is apprehended as *mine.* But it is by nature transcendence in immanence, and consciousness is not subject to it because of the very fact that consciousness posits it; for consciousness has now the task of conferring on the motive its meaning and its importance. Thus the *nothing* which separates the motive from consciousness characterizes itself as transcendence in immanence. It is by arising as immanence that consciousness nihilates the nothing which makes consciousness exist for itself as transcendence. But we see that the nothingness which is the condition of all transcendent negation can be elucidated only in terms of two other original nihilations: (1) Consciousness *is not* its own motive inasmuch as it is *empty* of all content. This refers us to a nihilating structure of the pre-reflective *cogito*. (2) Consciousness confronts its past and its future as facing a self which it is in the mode of not-being. This refers us to a nihilating structure of temporality.

There can be for us as yet no question of elucidating these two types of nihilation; we do not at the moment have the necessary techniques at our disposal. It is sufficient to observe here that the definitive explanation of negation can not be given without a description of self-consciousness and of temporality.

What we should note at present is that freedom, which manifests itself through anguish, is characterized by a constantly renewed obligation to remake the *Self* which designates the free being. As a matter of fact when we showed earlier that my possibilities were filled with anguish because it depended on *me* alone to sustain them in their existence, that did not mean that they derived from a *Me* which, to itself at least, would first be given and would then pass in the temporal flux from one consciousness to another consciousness. The gambler who must realize anew the synthetic apperception of a *situation* which would forbid him to play, must rediscover at the same time the *self* which can appreciate that situation, which "is in situation." This *self* with its *a priori* and historical content is the *essence* of man. Anguish as the manifestation of freedom in the face of self means that man is always separated by a nothingness from his essence. We should refer here to Hegel's statement: *"Wesen ist was gewesen ist."* Essence is what has been. Essence is everything in the human being which we can indicate by the words—that *is*. Due to this fact it is the totality of characteristics which *explain* the act. But the act is always beyond that essence; it is a human act only in so far as it surpasses every explanation which we can give of it, precisely because the very application of the formula "that is" to man causes all that is designated, *to have-been.* Man continually carries with him a pre-judicative comprehension of his essence, but due to this very fact he is separated from it by a nothingness. Essence is all that human reality apprehends in itself as *having been.* It is here that anguish appears as an apprehension of self inasmuch as it exists in the perpetual mode of detachment from what is; better yet, in so far as it makes itself exist as such. For we can never apprehend an *Erlebnis* as a living consequence of that *nature* which is ours. The overflow of our consciousness progressively constitutes that nature, but it remains always behind us and it dwells in us as the permanent object of our retrospective comprehension. It is in so far as this nature is a demand without being a recourse that it is apprehended in anguish.

In anguish freedom is anguished before itself inasmuch as it is instigated and bound by nothing. Someone will say, freedom has just been defined as a permanent structure of the human being; if anguish manifests it, then anguish ought to be a permanent state of my affectivity. But, on the contrary, it is completely exceptional. How can we explain the rarity of the phenomenon of anguish?

We must note first of all that the most common situations of our life, those in which we apprehend our possibilities as such by means of actively realizing them, do not manifest themselves to us through anguish because their very structure excludes anguished apprehension. Anguish in fact is the recognition of a possibility as *my* possibility; that is, it is constituted when consciousness sees itself cut from its essence by nothingness or separated from the future by its very freedom. This means that a nihilating nothing removes from me all excuse and that at the same time what I project as my future being is always nihilated and reduced to the rank of simple possibility because the future which I am remains out of my reach. But we ought to remark that in these various instances we have to do with a temporal form where I await myself in the future, where I "make an appointment with myself on the other side of that hour, of that day, or of that month." Anguish is the fear of not finding myself at that appointment, of no longer even wishing to bring myself there. But I can also find myself engaged in acts which reveal my possibilities to me at the very instant when they are realized. In lighting this cigarette I learn my concrete possibility, or if you prefer, my desire of smoking. It is by the very act of drawing toward me this paper and this pen that I give to myself as my most immediate possibility the act of working at this book; there I am engaged, and I discover it at the very moment when I am already throwing myself into it. At that instant, to be sure, it remains my possibility, since I can at each instant turn myself away from my work, push away the notebook, put the cap on my fountain pen. But this possibility of interrupting the action is rejected on a second level by the fact that the action which discovers itself to me through my act tends to crystallize as a transcendent, relatively independent form. The consciousness of man *in action* is non-reflective consciousness. It is consciousness of something, and the transcendent which discloses itself to this consciousness is of a particular nature; it is a *structure of exigency* in the world, and the world correlatively discloses in it complex relations of instrumentality. In the act of tracing the letters which I am writing, the whole sentence, still unachieved, is revealed as a passive exigency to be written. It is the very meaning of the letters which I form, and its appeal is not put into question, precisely because I can not write the words without transcending them toward the sentence and because I discover it as the necessary condition for the meaning of the words which I am writing. At the same time in the very framework of the act an indicative complex of instruments reveals itself and organizes itself (pen-ink-paper-lines-margin, *etc.*), a complex which can not be apprehended for itself but which rises in the heart of the transcendence which discloses to me as a passive exigency the sentence to be written. Thus in the quasi-generality of everyday acts, I am engaged, I have ventured, and I discover my possibilities by realizing them and in the very act of realizing them as exigencies, urgencies, instrumentalities. . . .

Now at each instant we are thrust into the world and engaged there. This means that we act before positing our possibilities and that these possibilities which are disclosed as realized or in process of being realized refer to meanings which necessitate special acts in order to be put into question. The alarm which rings in the morning refers to the possibility of my going to work, which is *my* possibility. But to apprehend the summons of the alarm as a summons is to get up. Therefore the very act of getting up is reassuring, for it eludes the question, "Is work *my* possibility?" Consequently it does not put me in a position to apprehend the possibility of quietism, of refusing to work, and finally the possibility of refusing the world and the possibility of death. In short, to the extent that I apprehend the meaning of the ringing, I am already up at its summons; this apprehension guarantees me against the anguished intuition that it is I who confer on the alarm clock its exigency—I and I alone.

In the same way, what we might call everyday morality is exclusive of ethical anguish. There is ethical anguish when I consider myself in my original relation to values. Values in actuality are demands which lay claim to a foundation. But this foundation can in no way be *being,* for every value which would base its ideal nature on its being would thereby cease even to be a value and would realize the heteronomy of my will. Value derives its being from its exigency and not its exigency from its being. It does not deliver itself to a contemplative intuition which would apprehend it as *being* value and thereby would remove from it its right over my freedom. On the contrary, it can be revealed only to an active freedom which makes it exist as value by the sole fact of recognizing it as such. It follows that my freedom is the unique foundation of values and that *nothing,* absolutely nothing, justifies me in adopting this or that particular value, this or that particular scale of values. As a being by whom values exist, I am unjustifiable. My freedom is anguished at being the foundation of values while itself without foundation. It is anguished in addition because values, due to the fact that they are essentially revealed to a freedom, can not disclose themselves without being at the same time "put into question," for the possibility of overturning the scale of values appears complementarily as *my* possibility. It is anguish before values which is the recognition of the ideality of values.

Ordinarily, however, my attitude with respect to values is eminently reassuring. In fact I am engaged in a world of values. The anguished apperception of values as sustained in being by my freedom is a secondary and mediated phenomenon. The immediate is the world with its urgency; and in this world where I engage myself, my acts cause values to spring up like partridges. My indignation has given to me the negative value "baseness," my admiration has given the positive value "grandeur." Above all my obedience to a multitude of tabus, which is real, reveals these tabus to me as existing in fact. The bourgeois who call themselves "respectable citizens" do not become respectable as the result of contemplating moral values. Rather from the moment of their arising in the world they are thrown into a pattern of behavior the meaning of which is respectability. Thus respectability acquires a being; it is not put into question. Values are sown on my path as thousands of little real demands, like the signs which order us to keep off the grass.

Thus in what we shall call the world of the immediate, which delivers itself to our unreflective consciousness, we do not first appear to ourselves, to be thrown subsequently into enterprises. Our being is immediately "in situation"; that is, it arises in enterprises and knows itself first in so far as it is reflected in those enterprises. We discover ourselves then in a world peopled with demands, in the heart of projects "in the course of realization." I write. I am going to smoke. I have an appointment this evening with Pierre. I must not forget to reply to Simon. I do not have the right to conceal the truth any longer from Claude. All these trivial passive expectations of the real, all these commonplace, everyday values, derive their meaning from an original projection of myself which stands as my choice of myself in the world. But to be exact, this projection of myself toward an original possibility, which causes the existence of values, appeals, expectations, and in general a world, appears to me only beyond the world as the meaning and the abstract, logical signification of my enterprises. For the rest, there exist concretely alarm clocks, signboards, tax forms, policemen, so many guard rails against anguish. But as soon as the enterprise is held at a distance from me, as soon as I am referred to myself because I must await myself in the future, then I discover myself suddenly as the one who gives its meaning to the alarm clock, the one who by a signboard forbids himself to walk on a flower bed or on the lawn, the one from whom the boss's order borrows its urgency, the one who decides the interest of the book which he is writing, the one finally who makes the values exist in order to determine his action by their demands. I emerge alone and in anguish confronting the unique and original project which constitutes my being; all the barriers, all the guard rails collapse, nihilated by the consciousness of my freedom. I do not have nor can I have recourse to any value against the fact that it is I who sustain values in being. Nothing can ensure me against myself, cut off from the world and from my essence by this nothingness which I *am*. I have to realize the meaning of the world and of my essence; I make my decision concerning them—without justification and without excuse.

Anguish then is the reflective apprehension of freedom by itself. In this sense it is mediation, for although it is immediate consciousness of itself, it arises from the negation of the appeals of the world. It appears at the moment that I disengage myself from the world where I had been engaged—in order to apprehend myself as a consciousness which possesses a pre-ontological comprehension of its essence and a pre-judicative sense of its possibilities. Anguish is opposed to the mind of the serious man who apprehends values in terms of the world and who resides in the reassuring, materialistic substantiation of values. In the serious mood I define myself in terms of the object by pushing aside *a priori* as impossible all enterprises in which I am not engaged at the moment; the meaning which my freedom has given to the world, I apprehend as coming from the world and constituting my obligations. In anguish I apprehend myself at once as totally free and as not being able to derive the meaning of the world except as coming from myself.

We should not however conclude that being brought on to the reflective plane and envisaging one's distant or immediate possibilities suffice to apprehend oneself in *pure* anguish. In each instance of reflection anguish is born as a structure of the reflective consciousness in so far as the latter considers consciousness as an object of reflection; but it still remains possible for me to maintain various types of conduct with respect to my own anguish—in particular, patterns of flight. Everything takes place, in fact, as if our essential and immediate behavior with respect to anguish is flight. Psychological determinism, before being a theoretical conception, is first an attitude of excuse, or if you prefer, the basis of all attitudes of excuse. It is reflective conduct with respect to anguish; it asserts that there are within us antagonistic forces whose type of existence is comparable to that of things. It attempts to fill the void which encircles us, to re-establish the links between past and present, between present and future. It provides us with a *nature* productive of our acts, and these very acts it makes transcendent; it assigns to them a foundation in something other than themselves by endowing them with an inertia and externality eminently reassuring because they constitute a permanent game of *excuses*. Psychological determinism denies that transcendence of human reality which makes it emerge in anguish beyond its own essence. At the same time by reducing us to *never being anything but what we are,* it reintroduces in us the absolute positivity of being-in-itself and thereby reinstates us at the heart of being.

But this determinism, a reflective defense against anguish, is not given as a reflective *intuition.* It avails nothing against the *evidence* of freedom; hence it is given as a faith to take refuge in, as the ideal end toward which we can flee to escape anguish. That is made evident on the philosophical plane by the fact that deterministic psychologists do not claim to found their thesis on the pure givens of introspection. They present it as a satisfying hypothesis, the value of which comes from the fact that it accounts for the facts—or as a necessary postulate for establishing all psychology. They admit the existence of an immediate consciousness of freedom, which their opponents hold up against them under the name of "proof by intuition of the inner sense." They merely focus the debate on the *value* of this inner revelation. Thus the intuition which causes us to apprehend ourselves as the original cause of our states and our acts has been discussed by nobody. It is within the reach of each of us to try to mediate anguish by rising above it and by *judging* it as an illusion due to the mistaken belief that we are the real causes of our acts. The problem which presents itself then is that of the degree of faith in this mediation. Is an anguish placed under judgment a disarmed anguish? Evidently not. However here a new phenomenon is born, a process of "distraction" in relation to anguish which, once again, supposes within it a nihilating power.

By itself determinism would not suffice to establish distraction since determinism is only a postulate or an hypothesis. This process of detachment is a more complete activity of flight which operates on the very level of reflection. It is first an attempt at distraction in relation to the possibles opposed to *my* possible. When I constitute myself as the comprehension of a possible as *my* possible, I must recognize its existence at the end of my project and apprehend it as myself, awaiting me down .there in the future and separated from me by a nothingness. In this sense I apprehend myself as the original source of my possibility, and it is this which ordinarily we call the consciousness of freedom. It is this structure of consciousness and this alone that the proponents of free will have in mind when they speak of the intuition of the inner sense. But it happens that I force myself at the same time to *be distracted* from the constitution of other possibilities which contradict *my* possibility. In truth I can not avoid positing their existence by the same movement which generates the chosen possibility as mine. I can not help constituting them as *living* possibilities; that is, *as having the possibility of becoming my possibilities.* But I force myself to see them as endowed with a transcendent, purely logical being, in short, as things. If on the reflective plane I envisage the possibility of writing this book as *my* possibility, then between this possibility and my consciousness I cause a nothingness of being to arise which constitutes the writing of the book as a possibility and which I apprehend precisely in the permanent possibility that the possibility of not writing the book is *my* possibility. But I attempt to place myself on the other side of the possibility of not writing it as I might do with respect to an observable object, and I let myself be penetrated with what I wish to see there; I try to apprehend the possibility of not writing as needing to be mentioned merely as a reminder, as not concerning me. It must be an external possibility in relation to me, like movement in relation to the motionless billiard ball. If I could succeed in this, the possibilities hostile to *my* possibility would be constituted as logical entities and would lose their effectiveness. They would no longer be threatening since they would be "outsiders," since they would surround my possible as purely *conceivable* eventualities; that is, fundamentally, conceivable *by another* or as *possibles of another who might find himself in the same situation.* They would belong to the objective situation as a transcendent structure, or if you prefer (to utilize Heidegger's terminology)—*I* shall write this book but *anybody* could also not write it. Thus I should hide from myself the fact that the possibles are *myself* and that they are immanent conditions of the possibility of my possible. They would preserve just enough being to preserve for my possible its character as gratuitous, as a free possibility for a free being, but they would be disarmed of their threatening character. They would not *interest* me; the chosen possible would appear—due to its selection—as my only concrete possible, and consequently the nothingness which separates me from it and which actually confers on it its possibility would collapse.

But flight before anguish is not only an effort at distraction before the future; it attempts also to disarm the past of its threat. What I attempt to flee here is my very transcendence in so far as it sustains and surpasses my essence. I assert that I *am* my essence in the mode of being of the in-itself. At the same time I always refuse to consider that essence as being historically constituted and as implying my action as a circle implies its properties. I apprehend it, or at least I try to apprehend it as the original beginning of my possible, and I do not admit at all that it has in itself a beginning. I assert then that an act is free when it exactly reflects my essence. However, this freedom which would disturb me if it were freedom before myself, I attempt to bring back to the heart of my essence—*i.e.,* of my self. It is a matter of envisaging the self as a little God which inhabits me and which possesses my freedom as a metaphysical virtue. It would be no longer my being which would be free qua being but my Self which would be free in the heart of my consciousness. It is a fiction eminently reassuring since freedom has been driven down into the heart of an opaque being; to the extent that my essence is not translucency, that it is transcendent in immanence, freedom would become one of its properties. In short, it is a matter of apprehending my freedom in my self as the freedom of another. We see the principal themes of this fiction: My self becomes the origin of its acts as the other of his, by virtue of a personality already constituted. To be sure, he (the self) lives and transforms himself; we will admit even that each of his acts can contribute to transforming him. But these harmonious, continued transformations are conceived on a biological order. They resemble those which I can establish in my friend Pierre when I see him after a separation. Bergson expressly satisfied these demands for reassurance when he conceived his theory of the profound self which endures and organizes itself, which is constantly contemporary with the consciousness which I have of it and which can not be surpassed by consciousness, which is found at the origin of my acts not as a cataclysmic power but as a father begets his children, in such a way that the act without following from the essence as a strict consequence, without even being foreseeable, enters into a reassuring relation with it, a family resemblance. The act goes farther than the self but along the same road; it preserves, to be sure, a certain irreducibility, but we recognize ourselves in it, and we find ourselves in it as a father can recognize himself and find himself in the son who continues his work. Thus by a projection of freedom—which we apprehend in ourselves—into a psychic object which is the self, Bergson has contributed to disguise our anguish, but it is at the expense of consciousness itself. What he has established and described in this manner is not our freedom as it appears to itself; *it is the freedom of the Other.*

Such then is the totality of processes by which we try to hide anguish from ourselves; we apprehend our particular possible by avoiding considering all other possibles, which we make the possibles of an undifferentiated Other. The chosen possible we do not wish to see as sustained in being by a pure nihilating freedom, and so we attempt to apprehend it as engendered by an object already constituted, which is no other than our self, envisaged and described as if it were another person. We should like to preserve from the original intuition what it reveals to us as our independence and our responsibility but we tone down all the original nihilation in it; moreover we are always ready to take refuge in a belief in determinism if this freedom weighs upon us or if we need an excuse. Thus we flee from anguish by attempting to apprehend ourselves from without as an Other or as *a thing.* What we are accustomed to call a revelation of the inner sense or an original intuition of our freedom contains nothing original; it is an already constructed process, expressly designed to hide from ourselves anguish, the veritable "immediate given" of our freedom.

Do these various constructions succeed in stifling or hiding our anguish? It is certain that we can not overcome anguish, for we *are* anguish. As for veiling it, aside from the fact that the very nature of consciousness and its translucency forbid us to take the expression literally, we must note the particular type of behavior which it indicates. We can hide an external object because it exists independently of us. For the same reason we can turn our look or our attention away from it—that is, very simply, fix our eyes on some other object; henceforth each reality— mine and that of the object—resumes its own life, and the accidental relation which united consciousness to the thing disappears without thereby altering either existence. But if I *am* what I wish to veil, the question takes on quite another aspect. I can in fact wish "not to see" a certain aspect of my being only if I am acquainted with the aspect which I do not wish to see. This means that in my being I must indicate this aspect in order to be able to turn myself away from it; better yet, I must think of it constantly in order to take care not to think of it. In this connection it must be understood not only that I must of necessity perpetually carry within me what I wish to flee but also that I must aim at the object of my flight in order to flee it. This means that anguish, the intentional aim of anguish, and a flight from anguish toward reassuring myths must all be given in the unity of the same consciousness. In a word, I flee in order not to know, but I can not avoid knowing that I am fleeing; and the flight from anguish is only a mode of becoming conscious of anguish. Thus anguish, properly speaking, can be neither hidden nor avoided.

Yet to flee anguish and to be anguish can not be exactly the same thing. If I am my anguish in order to flee it, that presupposes that I can decenter myself in relation to what I am, that I can be anguish in the form of "not-being it," that I can dispose of a nihilating power at the heart of anguish itself. This nihilating power nihilates anguish in so far as I flee it and nihilates itself in so far as *I am anguish in order to flee it*. This attitude is what we call *bad faith*. There is then no question of expelling anguish from consciousness nor of constituting it in an unconscious psychic phenomenon; very simply I can make myself guilty of bad faith while apprehending the anguish which I am, and this bad faith, intended to fill up the nothingness which I *am* in my relation to myself, precisely implies the nothingness which it suppresses.

Bad faith is going to be the next object of our investigation. For man to be able to question, he must be capable of being his own nothingness; that is, he can be at the origin of non-being in being only if his being—in himself and by himself—is transfixed with nothingness. Thus the transcendences of past and future appear in the temporal being of human reality. But bad faith is instantaneous. What then are we to say that consciousness must be in the instantaneity of the pre-reflective *cogito*—if the human is to be capable of bad faith?

Bad Faith

I. Bad Faith and Falsehood

The human being is not only the being by whom *négatités* are disclosed in the world; he is also the one who can take negative attitudes with respect to himself. In our Introduction we defined consciousness as "a being such that in its being, its being is in question in so far as this being implies a being other than itself." But now that we have examined the meaning of "the question," we can at present also write the formula thus: "Consciousness is a being, the nature of which is to be conscious of the nothingness of its being." In a prohibition or a veto, for example, the human being denies a future transcendence. But this negation is not explicative. My consciousness is not restricted to *envisioning* a *négatité*. It constitutes itself in its own flesh as the nihilation of a possibility. For that reason it must arise in the world as a *No;* it is as a No that the slave first apprehends the master, or that the prisoner who is trying to escape sees the guard who is watching him. There are even men (*e.g.,* caretakers, overseers, gaolers), whose social reality is uniquely that of the No, who will live and die, having forever been only a No upon the earth. Others, so as to make the No a part of their very subjectivity, establish their human personality as a perpetual negation. This is the meaning and function of what Scheler calls "the man of resentment"—in reality, the No. But there exist more subtle behaviors, the description of which will lead us further into the inwardness of consciousness. Irony is one of these. In irony a man annihilates what he posits within one and the same act; he leads us to believe in order not to be believed; he affirms to deny and denies to affirm; he creates a positive object but it has no being other than its nothingness. Thus attitudes of negation toward the self permit us to raise a new question: What are we to say is the being of man who has the possibility of denying himself? But it is out of the question to discuss the attitude of "self-negation" in its universality. The kinds of behavior which can be ranked under this heading are too diverse; we risk retaining only the abstract form of them. It is best to choose and to examine one determined attitude which is essential to human reality and which is such that consciousness instead of directing its negation outward turns it toward itself. This attitude, it seems to me, is *bad faith (mauvaise foi)*.

Frequently this is identified with falsehood. We say indifferently of a person that he shows signs of bad faith or that he lies to himself. We shall willingly grant that bad faith is a lie to oneself, on condition that we distinguish the lie to oneself from lying in general. Lying is a negative attitude, we will agree to that. But this negation does not bear on consciousness itself; it aims only at the transcendent. The essence of the lie implies in fact that the liar actually is in complete possession of the truth which he is hiding. A man does not lie about what he is ignorant of; he does not lie when he spreads an error of which he himself is the dupe; he does not lie when he is mistaken. The ideal description of the liar would be a cynical consciousness, affirming truth within himself, denying it in his words, and denying that negation as such. Now this double negative attitude rests on the transcendent; the fact expressed is transcendent since it does not exist, and the original negation rests on a *truth;* that is, on a particular type of transcendence. As for the inner negation which I effect correlatively with the affirmation for myself of the truth, this rests on *words;* that is, on an event in the world. Furthermore the inner disposition of the liar is positive; it could be the object of an affirmative judgment. The liar intends to deceive and he does not seek to hide this intention from himself nor to disguise the translucency of consciousness; on the contrary, he has recourse to it when there is a question of deciding secondary behavior. It explicity exercises a regulatory control over all attitudes. As for his flaunted intention of telling the truth ("I'd never want to deceive you! This is true! I swear it!")—all this, of course, is the object of an inner negation, but also it is not recognized by the liar as *his* intention. It is played, imitated, it is the intention of the character which he plays in the eyes of his questioner, but this character, precisely because he *does not exist,* is a transcendent. Thus the lie does not put into the play the inner structure of present consciousness; all the negations which constitute it bear on objects which by this fact are removed from consciousness. The lie then does not require special ontological foundation, and the explanations which the existence of negation in general requires are valid without change in the case of deceit. Of course we have described the ideal lie; doubtless it happens often enough that the liar is more or less the victim of his lie, that he half persuades himself of it. But these common, popular forms of the lie are also degenerate aspects of it; they represent intermediaries between falsehood and bad faith. The lie is a behavior of transcendence.

The lie is also a normal phenomenon of what Heidegger calls the *"mit-sein."** It presupposes my existence, the existence of the *Other,* my existence *for* the Other, and the existence of the Other *for* me. Thus there is no difficulty in holding that the liar must make the project of the lie in entire clarity and that he must possess a complete comprehension of the lie and of the truth which he is altering. It is sufficient that an over-all opacity hide his intentions from the *Other;* it is sufficient that the Other can take the lie for truth. By the lie consciousness affirms that it exists by nature as *hidden from the Other;* it utilizes for its own profit the ontological duality of myself and myself in the eyes of the Other.

The situation can not be the same for bad faith if this, as we have said, is indeed a lie to oneself. To be sure, the one who practices bad faith is hiding a displeasing truth or presenting as truth a pleasing untruth. Bad faith then has in appearance the structure of falsehood. Only what changes everything is the fact that in bad faith it is from myself that I am hiding the truth. Thus the duality of the deceiver and the deceived does not exist here. Bad faith on the contrary implies in essence the unity of a *single* consciousness. This does not mean that it can not be conditioned by the *mit-sein* like all other phenomena of human reality, but the *mit-sein* can call forth bad faith only by presenting itself as *a situation* which

* Tr. A "being-with" others in the world.

bad faith permits surpassing; bad faith does not come from outside to human reality. One does not undergo his bad faith; one is not infected with it; it is not a *state*. But consciousness affects itself with bad faith. There must be an original intention and a project of bad faith; this project implies a comprehension of bad faith as such and a pre-reflective apprehension (of) consciousness as affecting itself with bad faith. It follows first that the one to whom the lie is told and the one who lies are one and the same person, which means that I must know in my capacity as deceiver the truth which is hidden from me in my capacity as the one deceived. Better yet I must know the truth very exactly *in order* to conceal it more carefully—and this not at two different moments, which at a pinch would allow us to re-establish a semblance of duality—but in the unitary structure of a single project. How then can the lie subsist if the duality which conditions it is suppressed?

To this difficulty is added another which is derived from the total translucency of consciousness. That which affects itself with bad faith must be conscious (of) its bad faith since the being of consciousness is consciousness of being. It appears then that I must be in good faith, at least to the extent that I am conscious of my bad faith. But then this whole psychic system is annihilated. We must agree in fact that if I deliberately and cynically attempt to lie to myself, I fail completely in this undertaking; the lie falls back and collapses beneath my look; it is ruined *from behind* by the very consciousness of lying to myself which pitilessly constitutes itself well within my project as its very condition. We have here an *evanescent* phenomenon which exists only in and through its own differentiation. To be sure, these phenomena are frequent and we shall see that there is in fact an "evanesence" of bad faith, which, it is evident, vacillates continually between good faith and cynicism: Even though the existence of bad faith is very precarious, and though it belongs to the kind of psychic structures which we might call *metastable,* it presents nonetheless an autonomous and durable form. It can even be the normal aspect of life for a very great number of people. A person can *live* in bad faith, which does not mean that he does not have abrupt awakenings to cynicism or to good faith, but which implies a constant and particular style of life. Our embarrassment then appears extreme since we can neither reject nor comprehend bad faith.

II. Patterns of Bad Faith

If we wish to get out of this difficulty, we should examine more closely the patterns of bad faith and attempt a description of them. This description will permit us perhaps to fix more exactly the conditions for the possibility of bad faith; that is, to reply to the questions we raised at the outset: "What must be the being of man if he is to be capable of bad faith?"

Take the example of a woman who has consented to go out with a particular man for the first time. She knows very well the intentions which the man who is speaking to her cherishes regarding her. She knows also that it will be necessary sooner or later for her to make a decision. But she does not want to realize the urgency; she concerns herself only with what is respectful and discreet in the attitude of her companion. She does not apprehend this conduct as an attempt to achieve what we call "the first approach"; that is, she does not want to see possibilities of temporal development which his conduct presents. She restricts this behavior to what is in the present; she does not wish to read in the phrases which he addresses to her anything other than their explicit meaning. If he says to her, "I find you so attractive!" she disarms this phrase of its sexual background; she attaches to the conversation and to the behavior of the speaker, the immediate meanings, which she imagines as objective qualities. The man who is speaking to her appears to her sincere and respectful as the table is round or square, as the wall coloring is blue or gray. The qualities thus attached to the person she is listening to are in this way fixed in a permanence like that of things, which is no other than the projection of the strict present of the qualities into the temporal flux. This is because she does not quite know what she wants. She is profoundly aware of the desire which she inspires, but the desire cruel and naked would humiliate and horrify her. Yet she would find no charm in a respect which would be only respect. In order to satisfy her, there must be a feeling which is addressed wholly to her *personality— i.e.,* to her full freedom—and which would be a recognition of her freedom. But at the same time this feeling must be wholly desire; that is, it must address itself to her body as object. This time then she refuses to apprehend the desire for what it is; she does not even give it a name; she recognizes it only to the extent that it transcends itself toward admiration, esteem, respect and that it is wholly absorbed in the more refined forms which it produces, to the extent of no longer figuring anymore as a sort of warmth and density. But then suppose he takes her hand. This act of her companion risks changing the situation by calling for an immediate decision. To leave the hand there is to consent in herself to flirt, to engage herself. To withdraw it is to break the troubled and unstable harmony which gives the hour its charm. The aim is to postpone the moment of decision as long as possible. We know what happens next; the young woman leaves her hand there, but she *does not notice* that she is leaving it. She does not notice because it happens by chance that she is at this moment all intellect. She draws her companion up to the most lofty regions of sentimental speculation; she speaks of Life, of her life, she shows herself in her essential aspect—a personality, a consciousness. And during this time the divorce of the body from the soul is accomplished; the hand rests inert between the warm hands of her companion—neither consenting nor resisting—a thing.

We shall say that this woman is in bad faith. But we see immediately that she uses various procedures in order to maintain herself in this bad faith. She has disarmed the actions of her companion by reducing them to being only what they are; that is, to existing in the mode of the in-itself. But she permits herself to enjoy his desire, to the extent that she will apprehend it as not being what it is, will recognize its transcendence. Finally while sensing profoundly the presence of her own body—to the point of being aroused, perhaps—she realized herself as *not being* her own body, and she contemplates it as though from above as a passive object to which events can *happen* but which can neither provoke them nor avoid them because all its possibilities are outside of it. What unity do we find in these various aspects of bad faith? It is a certain art of forming contradictory concepts which unite in themselves both an idea and the negation of that idea. The basic concept which is thus engendered utilizes the double property of the human being, who is at once a *facticity* and a *transcendence*. These two aspects of human reality are and ought to be capable of a valid coordination. But bad faith does not wish either to coordinate them or to surmount them in a synthesis. Bad faith seeks to affirm their identity while preserving their differences. It must affirm facticity as *being* transcendence and transcendence as *being* facticity, in such a way that at the instant when a person apprehends the one, he can find himself abruptly faced with the other.

We can find the prototype of formulae of bad faith in certain famous expressions which have been rightly conceived to produce their whole effect in a spirit of bad faith. Take for example the title of a work by Jacques Chardonne, *Love Is Much More than Love*. We see here how unity is established between *present* love in its facticity—"the contact of two skins," sensuality, egoism, Proust's mechanism of jealousy, Adler's battle of the *sexes, etc.*—and love as transcendence—Mauriac's "river of fire," the longing for the infinite, Plato's *eros,* Lawrence's deep cosmic intuition, *etc.* Here we leave facticity to find ourselves suddenly beyond the present and the factual condition of man, beyond the psychological, in the heart of metaphysics. On the other hand, the title of a play by Sarment, *I Am Too Great for Myself,* which also presents characters in bad faith, throws us first into full transcendence in order suddenly to imprison us within the narrow limits of our factual essence. We will discover this structure again in the famous sentence: "He has become what he was" or in its no less famous opposite: "Eternity at last changes each man into himself." It is well understood that these various formulae have only the appearance of bad faith; they have been conceived in this paradoxical form explicitly to shock the mind and discountenance it by an enigma. But it is precisely this appearance which is of concern to us. What counts here is that the formulae do not constitute new, solidly structured ideas; on the contrary, they are formed so as to remain in perpetual disintegration and so that we may slide at any time from naturalistic present to transcendence and *vice versa.*

We can see the use which bad faith can make of these judgments which all aim at establishing that I am not what I am. If I were only what I *am,* I could, for example, seriously consider an adverse criticism which someone makes of me, question myself scrupulously, and perhaps be compelled to recognize the truth in it. But thanks to transcendence, I am not subject to all that I am. I do not even have to discuss the justice of the reproach. As Suzanne says to Figaro, "To prove that I am right would be to recognize that I can be wrong." I am on a plane where no reproach can touch me since what I really am is my transcendence. I flee from myself, I escape myself, I leave my tattered garment in the hands of the fault-finder. But the ambiguity necessary for bad faith comes from the fact that I affirm here that I *am* my transcendence in the mode of being of a thing. It is only thus, in fact, that I can feel that I escape all reproaches. It is in the sense that our young woman purifies the desire of anything humiliating by being willing to consider it only as pure transcendence, which she avoids even naming. But inversely "I Am Too Great for Myself," while showing our transcendence changed into facticity, is the source of an infinity of excuses for our failures or our weaknesses. Similarly the young coquette maintains transcendence to the extent that the respect, the esteem manifested by the actions of her admirer are already on the plane of the transcendent. But she arrests this transcendence, she glues it down with all the facticity of the present; respect is nothing other than respect, it is an arrested surpassing which no longer surpasses itself toward anything.

But although this *metastable* concept of "transcendence-facticity" is one of the most basic instruments of bad faith, it is not the only one of its kind. We can equally well use another kind of duplicity derived from human reality which we will express roughly by saying that its being-for-itself implies complementarily a being-for-others. Upon any one of my conducts it is always possible to converge two looks, mine and that of the Other. The conduct will not present exactly the same structure in each case. But as we shall see later, as each look perceives it, there is between these two aspects of my being, no difference between appearance and being—as if I were to my self the truth of myself and as if the Other possessed only a deformed image of me. The equal dignity of being, possessed by my being-for-others and by my being-for-myself, permits a perpetually disintegrating synthesis and a perpetual game of escape from the for-itself to the for-others and from the for-others to the for-itself. We have seen also the use which our young lady made of our being-in-the-midst-of-the-world—*i.e.,* of our inert presence as a passive object among other objects—in order to relieve herself suddenly from the functions of her being-in-the-world—that is, from the being which causes there to be a world by projecting itself beyond the world toward its own possibilities. Let us note finally the confusing syntheses which play on the nihilating ambiguity of these temporal ekstases, affirming at once that I am what I have been (the man who deliberately *arrests himself* at one period in his life and refuses to take into consideration the later changes) and that I am not what I have been (the man who in the face of reproaches or rancor dissociates himself from his past by insisting on his freedom and on his perpetual re-creation). In all these concepts, which have only a transitive role in the reasoning and which are eliminated from the conclusion (like the imaginaries in the computations of physicists), we find again the same structure. We have to deal with human reality as a being which is what it is not and which is not what it is.

But what exactly is necessary in order for these concepts of disintegration to be able to receive even a pretence of existence, in order for them to be able to appear for an instant to consciousness, even in a process of evanescence? A quick examination of the idea of sincerity, the antithesis of bad faith, will be very instructive in this connection. Actually sincerity presents itself as a demand and consequently is not a *state.* Now what is the ideal to be attained in this case? It is necessary that a man be *for himself* only what he *is.* But is this not precisely the definition of the in-itself—or if you prefer—the principle of identity? To posit as an ideal the being of things, is this not to assert by the same stroke that this being does not belong to human reality and that the principle of identity, far from being a universal axiom universally applied, is only a synthetic principle enjoying a merely regional universality? Thus in order that the concepts of bad faith can put us under illusion at least for an instant, in order that the candor of "pure hearts" (*cf.* Gide, Kessel) can have validity for human reality as an ideal, the principle of identity must not represent a constitutive principle of human reality and human reality must not be necessarily what it is but must be able to be what it is not. What does this mean?

If man is what he is, bad faith is forever impossible and candor ceases to be his ideal and becomes instead his being. But is man what he is? And more generally, how can he *be* what he is when he exists as consciousness of being? If candor or sincerity is a universal value, it is evident that the maxim "one must be what one is" does not serve solely as a regulating principle for judgments and concepts by which I express what I am. It posits not merely an ideal of knowing but an ideal of *being;* it proposes for us an absolute equivalence of being with itself as a prototype of being. In this sense it is necessary that we *make ourselves* what we are. But what *are we* then if we have the constant obligations to make ourselves what we are, if our mode of being is having the obligation to be what we are?

Let us consider this waiter in the café. His movement is quick and forward, a little too precise, a little too rapid. He comes toward the patrons with a step a little too quick. He bends forward a little too eagerly; his voice, his eyes express an interest a little too solicitous for the order of the customer. Finally there he returns, trying to imitate in his walk the inflexible stiffness of some kind of automaton while carrying his tray with the recklessness of a tight-rope-walker by putting it in a perpetually unstable, perpetually broken equilibrium which he perpetually re-estab-lishes by a light movement of the arm and hand. All his behavior seems to us a game. He applies himself to chaining his movements as if they were mechanisms, the one regulating the other; his gestures and even his voice seem to be mechanisms; he gives himself the quickness and pitiless rapidity of things. He is playing, he is amusing himself. But what is he playing? We need not watch long before we can explain it: he is playing at *being* a waiter in a café. There is nothing there to surprise us. The game is a kind of marking out and investigation. The child plays with his body in order to explore it, to take inventory of it; the waiter in the café plays with his condition in order to *realize* it. This obligation is not different from that which is imposed on all tradesmen. Their condition is wholly one of ceremony. The public demands of them that they realize it as a ceremony; there is the dance of the grocer, of the tailor, of the auctioneer, by which they endeavor to persuade their clientele that they are nothing but a grocer, an auctioneer, a tailor. A grocer who dreams is offensive to the buyer, because such a grocer is not wholly a grocer. Society demands that he limit himself to his function as a grocer, just as the soldier at attention makes himself into a soldier-thing with a direct regard which does not see at all, which is no longer meant to see, since it is the rule and not the interest of the moment which determines the point he must fix his eyes on (the sight "fixed at ten paces"). There are indeed many precautions to imprison a man in what he is, as if we lived in perpetual fear that he might escape from it, that he might break away and suddenly elude his condition.

In a parallel situation, from within, the waiter in the café can not be immediately a café waiter in the sense that this inkwell *is* an inkwell, or the glass is a glass. It is by no means that he can not form reflective judgments or concepts concerning his condition. He knows well what it "means": the obligation of getting up at five o'clock, of sweeping the floor of the shop before the restaurant opens, of starting the coffee pot going, *etc.* He knows the rights which it allows: the right to the tips, the right to belong to a union, *etc.* But all these concepts, all these judgments refer to the transcendent. It is a matter of abstract possibilities, of rights and duties conferred on a "person possessing rights." And it is precisely this person *who I have to be* (if I am the waiter in question) and who I am not. It is not that I do not wish to be this person or that I want this person to be different. But rather there is no common measure between his being and mine. It is a "representation" for others and for myself, which means that I can be he only in *representation*. But if I represent myself as him, I am not he; I am separated from him as the object from the subject, separated *by nothing,* but this nothing isolates me from him. I can not be he, I can only play *at being* him; that is, imagine to myself that I am he. And thereby I affect him with nothingness. In vain do I fulfill the functions of a café waiter. I can be he only in the neutralized mode, as the actor is Hamlet, by mechanically making the *typical gestures* of my state and by aiming at myself as an imaginary café waiter through those gestures taken as an "analogue." What I attempt to realize is a being-in-itself of the café waiter, as if it were not just in my power to confer their value and their urgency upon my duties and the rights of my position, as if it were not my free choice to get up each morning at five o'clock or to remain in bed, even though it meant getting fired. As if from the very fact that I sustain this role in existence I did not transcend it on every side, as if I did not constitute myself as one *beyond* my condition. Yet there is no doubt that I *am* in a sense a café waiter— otherwise could I not just as well call myself a diplomat or a reporter? But if I am one, this can not be in the mode of being in-itself. I am a waiter in the mode of *being what I am not.*

Furthermore we are dealing with more than mere social positions; I am never any one of my attitudes, any one of my actions. The good speaker is the one who *plays* at speaking, because he can not *be speaking.* The attentive pupil who wishes to *be* attentive, his eyes riveted on the teacher, his ears wide open, so exhausts himself in playing the attentive role that he ends up by no longer hearing anything. Perpetually absent to my body, to my acts, I am despite myself that "divine absence" of which Valéry speaks. I can not say either that I *am* here or that I *am* not here, in the sense that we say "that box of matches *is* on the table"; this would be to confuse my "being-in-the-world" with a "being-in-the-midst-of-the-world." Nor that I *am* standing, nor that I *am* seated; this would be to confuse my body with the idiosyncratic totality of which it is only one of the structures. On all sides I escape being and yet—I am. . . .

The Other's consciousness is what it is not.

Furthermore the being of my own consciousness does not appear to me as the consciousness of the Other. It *is* because it makes itself, since its being is consciousness of being. But this means that making sustains being; consciousness has to be its own being, it is never sustained by being; it sustains being in the heart of subjectivity, which means once again that it is inhabited by being but that it is not being; *consciousness is not what it is.*

Under these conditions what can be the significance of the ideal of sincerity except as a task impossible to achieve, of which the very meaning is in contradiction with the structure of my consciousness. To be sincere, we said, is to be what one is. That supposes that I am not originally what I am. But here naturally Kant's "You ought, therefore you can" is implicly understood. I can *become* sincere; this is what my duty and my effort to achieve sincerity imply. But we definitely establish that the original structure of "not being what one is" renders impossible in advance all movement toward being in itself of "being what one is." And this impossibility is not hidden from consciousness; on the contrary, it is the very stuff of consciousness; it is the embarrassing constraint which we constantly experience; it is our very incapacity to recognize ourselves, to constitute ourselves as being what we are. It is this necessity which means that, as soon as we posit ourselves as a certain being, by a legitimate judgment, based on inner experience or correctly deduced from *a priori* or empirical premises, then by that very positing we surpass this being— and that not toward another being but toward emptiness, toward *nothing.*

How then can we blame another for not being sincere or rejoice in our own sincerity since this sincerity appears to us at the same time to be impossible? How can we in conversation, in confession, in introspection, even attempt sincerity since the effort will by its very nature be doomed to failure and since at the very time when we announce it we have a prejudicative comprehension of its futility? In introspection I try to determine exactly what I am, to make up my mind to be my true self without delay—even though it means consequently to set about searching for ways to change myself. But what does this mean if not that I am constituting myself as a thing? Shall I determine the ensemble of purposes and motivations which have pushed me to do this or that action? But this is already to postulate a causal determinism which constitues the flow of my states of consciousness as a succession of physical states. Shall I uncover in myself "drives," even though it be to affirm them in shame? But is this not deliberately to forget that these drives are realized with my consent, that they are not forces of nature but that I lend them their efficacy by a perpetually renewed decision concerning their value? Shall I pass judgment on my character, on my nature? Is this not to veil from myself at that moment what I know only too well, that I thus judge a past to which by definition my present is not subject? The proof of this is that the same man who in sincerity posits that he is what in actuality he was, is indignant at the reproach of another and tries to disarm it by asserting that he can no longer be what he was. We are readily astonished and upset when the penalites of the court affect a man who in his new freedom *is no longer* the guilty person he was. But at the same time we require of this man that he recognize himself as *being* this guilty one. What then is sincerity except precisely a phenomenon of bad faith? Have we not shown indeed that in bad faith human reality is constitued as a being which is what it is not and which is not what it is?

Let us take an example: A homosexual frequently has an intolerable feeling of guilt, and his whole existence is determined in relation to this feeling. One will readily foresee that he is in bad faith. In fact it frequently happens that this man, while recognizing his homosexual inclination, while avowing each and every particular misdeed which he has committed, refuses with all his strength to consider himself *"a paederast."* His case is always "different," peculiar; there enters into it something of a game, of chance, of bad luck; the mistakes are all in the past; they are explained by a certain conception of the beautiful which women can not satisfy; we should see in them the results of a restless search, rather than the manifestations of a deeply rooted tendency, *etc., etc.* Here is assuredly a man in bad faith who borders on the comic since, acknowledging all the facts which are imputed to him, he refuses to draw from them the conclusion which they impose. His friend, who is his most severe critic, becomes irritated with this duplicity. The critic asks only one thing—and perhaps then he will show himself indulgent: that the guilty one recognize himself as guilty, that the homosexual declare frankly—whether humbly or boastfully matters little—"I am a paederast." We ask here: Who is in bad faith? The homosexual or the champion of sincerity?

The homosexual recognizes his faults, but he struggles with all his strength against the crushing view that his mistakes constitute for him a *destiny.* He does not wish to let himself be considered as a thing. He has an obscure but strong feeling that a homosexual is not a homosexual as this table is a table or as this red-haired man is red-haired. It seems to him that he has escaped from each mistake as soon as he has posited it and recognized it; he even feels that the psychic duration by itself cleanses him from each misdeed, constitutes for him an undetermined future, causes him to be born anew. Is he wrong? Does he not recognize in himself the peculiar, irreducible character of human reality? His attitude includes then an undeniable comprehension of truth. But at the same time he needs this perpetual rebirth, this constant escape in order to live; he must constantly put himself beyond reach in order to avoid the terrible judgment of collectivity. Thus he plays on the word *being.* He would be right actually if he understood the phrase "I am not a paederast" in the sense of "I am not what I am." That is, if he declared to himself, "To the extent that a pattern of conduct is defined as the conduct of a pacdcrast and to the extent that I have adopted this conduct, I am a paederast. But to the extent that human reality can not be finally defined by patterns of conduct, I am not one." But instead he slides surreptitiously toward a different connotation of the word "being." He understands "not being"

in the sense of "not-being-in-itself." He lays claim to "not being a paederast" in the sense in which this table *is not* an inkwell. He is in bad
faith.

But the champion of sincerity is not ignorant of the transcendence
of human reality, and he knows how at need to appeal to it for his own
advantage. He makes use of it even and brings it up in the present
argument. Does he not wish, first in the name of sincerity, then of freedom,
that the homosexual reflect on himself and acknowledge himself as a
homosexual? Does he not let the other understand that such a confession
will win indulgence for him? What does this mean if not that the man
who will acknowledge himself as a homosexual will no longer be *the same*
as the homosexual whom he acknowledges being and that he will escape
into the region of freedom and of good will? The critic asks the man
then to be what he is in order no longer to be what he is. It is the
profound meaning of the saying, "A sin confessed is half pardoned." The
critic demands of the guilty one that he constitute himself as a thing,
precisely in order no longer to treat him as a thing. And this contradiction
is constitutive of the demand of sincerity. Who can not see how offensive
to the Other and how reassuring for me is a statement such as, "He's
just a paederast," which removes a disturbing freedom from a trait and
which aims at henceforth constituting all the acts of the Other as consequences following strictly from his essence. That is actually what the
critic is demanding of his victim—that he constitute himself as a thing,
that he should entrust his freedom to his friend as a fief, in order that
the friend should return it to him subsequently—like a suzerain to his
vassal. The champion of sincerity is in bad faith to the degree that in
order to reassure himself, he pretends to judge, to the extent that he
demands that freedom as freedom constitute itself as a thing. We have
here only one episode in that battle to the death of consciousness which
Hegel calls "the relation of the master and the slave." A person appeals
to another and demands that in the name of his nature as consciousness
he should radically destroy himself as consciousness, but while making
this appeal he leads the other to hope for a rebirth beyond this destruction. . . .

In the final analysis the goal of sincerity and the goal of bad faith
are not so different. To be sure, there is a sincerity which bears on the
past and which does not concern us here; I am sincere if I confess *having
had* this pleasure or that intention. We shall see that if this sincerity is
possible, it is because in his fall into the past, the being of man is
constituted as a being-in-itself. But here our concern is only with the
sincerity which aims at itself in present immanence. What is its goal? To
bring me to confess to myself what I am in order that I may finally
coincide with my being; in a word, to cause myself to be, in the mode

of the in-itself, what I am in the mode of "not being what I am." Its assumption is that fundamentally I am already, in the mode of the in-itself, what I have to be. Thus we find at the base of sincerity a continual game of mirror and reflection, a perpetual passage from the being which is what it is to the being which is not what it is and inversely from the being which is not what it is to the being which is what it is. And what is the goal of bad faith? To cause me to be what I am, in the mode of "not being what one is," or not to be what I am in the mode of "being what one is." We find here the same game of mirrors. In fact in order for me to have an intention of sincerity, I must at the outset simultaneously be and not be what I am. Sincerity does not assign to me a mode of being or a particular quality, but in relation to that quality it aims at making me pass from one mode of being to another mode of being. This second mode of being, the ideal of sincerity, I am prevented by nature from attaining; and at the very moment when I struggle to attain it, I have a vague prejudicative comprehension that I shall not attain it. But all the same, in order for me to be able to conceive an intention in bad faith, I must have such a nature that within my being I escape from my being. If I were sad or cowardly in the way in which this inkwell is an inkwell, the possibility of bad faith could not even be conceived. Not only should I be unable to escape from my being; I could not even imagine that I could escape from it. But if bad faith is possible by virtue of a simple project, it is because so far as my being is concerned, there is no difference between being and non-being if I am cut off from my project.

Bad faith is possible only because sincerity is conscious of missing its goal inevitably, due to its very nature. I can try to apprehend myself as *"not being cowardly,"* when I *am* so, only on condition that the "being cowardly" is itself "in question" at the very moment when it exists, on condition that it is itself *one* question, that at the very moment when I wish to apprehend it, it escapes me on all sides and annihilates itself. The condition under which I can attempt an effort in bad faith is that in one sense, I *am not* this coward which I do not wish to be. But if I *were not* cowardly in the simple mode of not-being-what-one-is-not, I would be "in good faith" by declaring that I am not cowardly. Thus this inapprehensible coward is evanescent; in order for me not to be cowardly, I must in some way also be cowardly. That does not mean that I must be "a little" cowardly, in the sense that "a little" signifies "to a certain degree cowardly—and not cowardly to a certain degree." No. I must at once both be and not be totally and in all respects a coward. Thus in this case bad faith requires that I should not be what I am; that is, that there be an imponderable difference separating being from non-being in the mode of being of human reality.

But bad faith is not restricted to denying the qualities which I possess, to not seeing the being which I am. It attempts also to constitute myself as being what I am not. It apprehends me positively as courageous when I am not so. And that is possible, once again, only if I am what I am not; that is, if non-being in me does not have being even as non-being. Of course necessarily I *am not* courageous; otherwise bad faith would not be *bad* faith. But in addition my effort in bad faith must include the ontological comprehension that even in my usual being what I *am,* I am not it really and that there is no such difference between the being of "being-sad," for example—which I *am* in the mode of not being what I am—and the "non-being" of not-being-courageous which I wish to hide from myself. Moreover it is particularly requisite that the very negation of being should be itself the object of a perpetual nihilation, that the very meaning of "non-being" be perpetually in question in human reality. If I *were not* courageous in the way in which this inkwell is not a table; that is, if I were isolated in my cowardice, propped firmly against it, incapable of putting it in relation to its opposite, if I were not capable of *determining* myself as cowardly—that is, to deny courage to myself and thereby to escape my cowardice in the very moment that I posit it— if it were not on principle *impossible* for me to coincide with my *not-being-courageous* as well as with my being-courageous—then any project of bad faith would be prohibited me. Thus in order for bad faith to be possible, sincerity itself must be in bad faith. The condition of the possibility for bad faith is that human reality, in its most immediate being, in the intra-structure of the pre-reflective *cogito,* must be what it is not and not be what it is.

III. The "Faith " of Bad Faith

We have indicated for the moment only those conditions which render bad faith conceivable, the structures of being which permit us to form concepts of bad faith. We can not limit ourselves to these considerations; we have not yet distinguished bad faith from falsehood. The two-faced concepts which we have described would without a doubt be utilized by a liar to discountenance his questioner, although their two-faced quality being established on the being of man and not on some empirical circumstance, can and ought to be evident to all. The true problem of bad faith stems evidently from the fact that bad faith is *faith.* It can not be either a cynical lie or certainty—if certainty is the intuitive possession of the object. But if we take belief as meaning the adherence of being to its object when the object is not given or is given indistinctly, then bad faith is belief; and the essential problem of bad faith is a problem of belief.

I believe that my friend Pierre feels friendship for me. I believe it *in good faith.* I believe it but I do not have for it any self-evident intuition, for the nature of the object does not lend itself to intuition. I *believe it;* that is, I allow myself to give in to all impulses to trust it; I decide to believe in it, and to maintain myself in this decision; I conduct myself, finally, as if I were certain of it—and all this in the synthetic unity of one and the same attitude. This which I define as good faith is what Hegel would call the *immediate.* It is simple faith. Hegel would demonstrate at once that the immediate calls for mediation and that belief, by becoming *belief for itself,* passes to the state of non-belief. If I *believe* that my friend Pierre likes me, this means that his friendship appears to me as the meaning of all his acts. Belief is a particular consciousness of *the meaning* of Pierre's acts. But if I know that I believe, the belief appears to me as pure subjective determination without exteral correlative. This is what makes the very word "to believe" a term utilized indifferently to indicate the unwavering firmness of belief ("My God, I believe in you") and its character as disarmed and strictly subjective ("Is Pierre my friend? I do not know; I believe so"). But the nature of consciousenss is such that in it the mediate and the immediate are one and the same being. To believe is to know that one believes, and to know that one believes is no longer to believe. Thus to believe is not to believe any longer because that is only to believe—this in the unity of one and the same non-thetic self-consciousness. To be sure, we have here forced the description of the phenomenon by designating it with the word *to know;* non-thetic consciousness is not to *know.* But it is in its very translucency at the origin of all knowing. Thus the non-thetic consciousness (of) believing is destructive of belief. But at the same time the very law of the pre-reflective *cogito* implies that the being of believing ought to be the consciousness of believing.

Thus belief is a being which questions its own being, which can realize itself only in its destruction, which can manifest itself to itself only by denying itself. It is a being for which to be is to appear and to appear is to deny itself. To believe is not-to-believe. We see the reason for it; the being of consciousness is to exist by itself, then to make itself be and thereby to pass beyond itself. In this sense consciousness is perpetually escaping itself, belief becomes non-belief, the immediate becomes mediation, the absolute becomes relative, and the relative becomes absolute. The ideal of good faith (to believe what one believes) is, like that of sincerity (to be what one is), an ideal of being-in-itself. Every belief is a belief that falls short; one never wholly believes what one believes. Consequently the primitive project of bad faith is only the utilization of this self-destruction of the fact of consciousness.

From *The War Diaries, November 1939– March 1940*

On Authenticity

Tuesday, 20 February

I rather think I was authentic before my leave. Probably because I was alone. In Paris, I was not authentic. At present, I'm no longer anything. This leads me to clarify a few points regarding authenticity. First of all, the following: authenticity is achieved en bloc, one either is or is not authentic. But that doesn't at all mean that one acquires authenticity once and for good. I've already pointed out that the present has no purchase on the future, nor the past on the present. According to Gide, one does not 'benefit by acquired momentum' in moral conduct, anymore than in the novel. And the authenticity of your previous momentum doesn't protect you in any way against falling next instant into the inauthentic. The most one can say is that it's less difficult to preserve authenticity than to acquire it. But, in fact, can one even talk about 'preserving'? The instant that arrives is novel, the situation is novel: a new authenticity has to be invented. It's still the case, people will say, that the memory of the authentic must protect us somewhat from inauthenticity. But the memory of the authentic, in inauthenticity, is itself inauthentic.

This leads me to clarify also what I said about the desire for authenticity. It is customary to consider that this desire for authenticity is 'something, after all—better than nothing'. In this way, the continuity at first set aside is reintroduced, unobtrusively and by a roundabout route. A distinction will then be made between inauthentic beings wallowing in their inauthenticity, those whom an already meritorious desire torments in their mire and, lastly, those who enjoy the authentic. But this detour will bring us back to the morality of the virtues. It must be said, there are just two alternatives: either the desire for authenticity torments us in the midst of inauthenticity, and then it's itself inauthentic; or else it's already full authenticity, though it's unaware of itself and hasn't yet taken stock of itself. There's no room for a third estate.

I see, for example, how L.'s desire for authenticity is poisoned by inauthenticity.* She'd like to be authentic, from affection for us, from trust in us, in order to join us—and also from an idea of merit. She suffers at seeing a supreme value posited that is alien to her; she'd like to be authentic, just as she might want to become a good skier or a clever philosopher. It seems to her, too, that if she acquired this authenticity she'd *merit* more from life and from men. And doubtless she has clearly understood that the authentic man rejects a priori any idea of merit; but she cannot rid herself of the idea that he's all the more meritorious in his very manner of refusing merit. I see only a totally poisoned desire there; one which, whatever plane of reflection one views it on, remains poisoned through and through. And I don't even say that, given the right circumstances, this desire might not be the occasion for a total transformation that would precisely confer authenticity. I say only that it cannot of itself lead to the authentic. It must be recovered and transformed within an already authentic consciousness.

On the other hand, I can very well imagine how authenticity acquired through a free mutation may first manifest itself in the guise of a desire for authenticity. So this expresses merely the fact that the cause is won. For though authenticity is all of a piece, it isn't enough to have acquired it once, in respect of a particular, concrete circumstance, in order for it to extend itself spontaneously to all the situations into which we are plunged. For example, I can imagine someone being called up who was a highly inauthentic bourgeois, who used to live inauthentically in all the various social situations into which he was thrown—family, job, etc. I can grant that the shock of war may suddenly have induced him to a conversion towards the authentic, which leads him to be authentically *in situation* vis-à-vis the war. But this authenticity, if it is *true,* needs to conquer new territory. It first presents itself in the form of a desire to revise old situations in the light of this change. It first gives itself as anxiety and critical desire. Here, this way of *extending* authenticity mustn't be confused in any sense with an increase in authenticity. The authenticity *is already there.* Only it must be consolidated and extended.

The question wouldn't present itself in that way if the previously experienced situations were present. But they've receded. The person who has been called up is no longer 'a family man', he's no longer practising his profession, etc. He's led to *think* about those situations, to make resolutions for the future, and to establish guidelines for *keeping* authen-

---

* L. = 'Lise Oblanoff', or Nathalie Sorokine (see de Beauvoir, *The Prime of Life,* pp. 347–8 and *Lettres au Castor,* pp. 484, 503, etc.).

ticity as he moves on to other events. The desire to acquire authenticity, ultimately, is only a desire to see things more clearly and not lose it. And resistance comes, not from residues of inauthenticity which may remain here and there in a badly dusted-off consciousness, but simply from the fact that his previous situations resist the change as *things*. He has lived them until then in a certain way, and by living them he has *constituted* them. They have become *institutions:* they have their own permanence outside him, and they even evolve in spite of him. It is necessary to *call* into question. The desire to call into questions, if it is sincere, can appear only against a background of authenticity. And it's not enough to call into question: it's necessary to change. But the revolutionary changes revealed by a struggle against the solidity of institutions are no different, in nature, from the changes a politician wishes to introduce into social institutions—and they encounter the same resistance.

So it is by no means enough to be authentic: it's necessary to adapt one's life to one's authenticity. Whence that deep desire, that fear and that anguish at the heart of all authenticity—which are apprehensions *before life.* Yet it must be clearly understood that authenticity cannot be divided. This fear is due to the fact that the situations envisaged are on the horizon, out of reach; to the fact that one will encounter them later, without being immersed in them for the time being. Whoever one is, there are always a large number of faraway situations on the horizon, about which one 'worries' in the authentic. But if one of those situations is assumed to re-form unexpectedly around me, and if I'm authentic, I shall show myself to be authentic without stopping to think of this restored situation—without needing to prepare any transition—simply because I *am* so.

If, for example, the wife of this person who has been called up comes to visit him at the front, he'll be *different* with her—without any effort or premeditation or thematic preparation—simply because he *is* different. But, you may say, she'll very soon present him with the image of his former inauthenticity. Yes—and that will be the touchstone, not of his actual authenticity, but of how determined he is to cling to it. Perhaps he'll yield, but he can't revert to his old errors vis-à-vis that woman without, at a stroke, tumbling headlong into inauthenticity—and even his very being-in-war will thereby be affected. For, presumably, a being who expects the inauthentic of us will freeze us to the marrow with inauthenticity, by reviving our old love. It's an imposed inauthenticity, against which it is easy but painful to defend oneself. . . .

If the war doesn't last too long, I'm very afraid, since my leave, of finding myself just as I was last year, at the rendezvous I'd fixed with myself for after the war.

From *Being and Nothingness*

The Existence of Others

The Problem

We have described human reality from the standpoint of negating conduct and from the standpoint of the *cogito*. Following this lead we have discovered that human reality is-for-itself. Is this *all* that it is? Without going outside our attitude of reflective description, we can encounter modes of consciousness which seem, even while themselves remaining strictly in for-itself, to point to a radically different type of ontological structure. This ontological structure is *mine;* it is in relation to myself as subject that I am concerned about myself, and yet this concern (for-myself) reveals to me a being which is *my* being without being-for-me.

Consider for example shame. Here we are dealing with a mode of consciousness which has a structure identical with all those which we have previously described. It is a non-positional self-consciousness, conscious (of) itself as shame; as such, it is an example of what the Germans call *Erlebnis,* and it is accessible to reflection. In addition its structure is intentional; it is a shameful apprehension *of* something and this something is *me.* I am ashamed of what I *am.* Shame therefore realizes an intimate relation of myself to myself. Through shame I have discovered an aspect of *my* being. Yet although certain complex forms derived from shame can appear on the reflective plane, shame is not originally a phenomenon of reflection. In fact no matter what results one can obtain in solitude by the religious *practice* of shame, it is in its primary structure shame *before somebody.* I have just made an awkward or vulgar gesture. This gesture clings to me; I neither judge it nor blame it. I simply live it. I realize it in the mode of for-itself. But now suddenly I raise my head. Somebody was there and has seen me. Suddenly I realize the vulgarity of my gesture, and I am ashamed. It is certain that my shame is not reflective, for the presence of another in my consciousness, even as a

Being and Nothingness, trans. Hazel E. Barnes. Excerpts from pp. 301–303, 341–355, 383–387, 474–475, 497–517, 722–734, and 795–798. Copyright © 1956 by the Philosophical Library.

catalyst, is incompatible with the reflective attitude; in the field of my reflection I can never meet with anything but the consciousness which is mine. But the Other is the indispensable mediator between myself and me. I am ashamed of myself *as I appear* to the Other.

By the mere appearance of the Other, I am put in the position of passing judgment on myself as on an object, for it is as an object that I appear to the Other. Yet this object which has appeared to the Other is not an empty image in the mind of another. Such an image, in fact, would be imputable wholly to the Other and so could not "touch" me. I could feel irritation, or anger before it as before a bad portrait of myself which gives to my expression an ugliness or baseness which I do not have, but I could not be touched to the quick. Shame is by nature *recognition*. I recognize that I *am* as the Other sees me. There is however no question of a comparison between what I am for myself and what I am for the Other as if I found in myself, in the mode of being of the For-itself, an equivalent of what I am for the Other. In the first place this comparison is not encountered in us as the result of a concrete psychic operation. Shame is an immediate shudder which runs through me from head to foot without any discursive preparation. In addition the comparison is impossible; I am unable to bring about any relation between what I am in the intimacy of the For-Itself, without distance, without recoil, without perspective, and this unjustifiable being-in-itself which I am for the Other. There is no standard here, no table of correlation. Moreover the very notion of *vulgarity* implies an inter-monad relation. Nobody can be vulgar all alone!

Thus the Other has not only revealed to me what I was; he has established me in a new type of being which can support new qualifications. This being was not in me potentially before the appearance of the Other, for it could not have found any place in the For-itself. Even if some power had been pleased to endow me with a body wholly constituted before it should be for-others, still my vulgarity and my awkwardness could not lodge there potentially; for they are meanings and as such they surpass the body and at the same time refer to a witness capable of understanding them and to the totality of my human reality. But this new being which appears *for* the other does not reside *in* the Other; I am responsible for it as is shown very well by the education system which consists in making children ashamed of what they are.

Thus shame is shame *of oneself before the Other;* these two structures are inseparable. But at the same time I need the Other in order to realize fully all the structures of my being. The For-itself refers to the For-others. Therefore if we wish to grasp in its totality the relation of man's being to being-in-itself, we can not be satisfied with the descriptions outlined in the earlier chapters of this work. We must answer two far more formidable questions: first that of the existence of the Other, then that of the relation of my *being* to the being of the Other.

The Look

I am in a public park. Not far away there is a lawn and along the edge of that lawn there are benches. A man passes by those benches. I see this man; I apprehend him as an object and at the same time as a man. What does this signify? What do I mean when I assert that this object *is a man?*

If I were to think of him as being only a puppet, I should apply to him the categories which I ordinarily use to group temporal-spatial "things." That is, I should apprehend him as being "beside" the benches, two yards and twenty inches from the lawn, as exercising a certain pressure on the ground, *etc.* His relation with other objects would be of the purely additive type; this means that I could have him disappear without the relations of the other objects around him being perceptibly *changed.* In short, no new relation would appear *through him* between those things in my universe: grouped and synthesized *from my point of view* into instrumental complexes, they would *from his* disintegrate into multiplicities of indifferent relations. Perceiving him as a *man,* on the other hand, is not to apprehend an additive relation between the chair and him; it is to register an organization *without distance* of the things in my universe around that privileged object. To be sure, the lawn remains two yards and twenty inches away from him, but it is also *as a lawn* bound to him in a relation which at once both transcends distance and contains it. Instead of the two terms of the distance being indifferent, interchangeable, and in a reciprocal relation, the distance *is unfolded starting from* the man whom I see and *extending up to* the lawn as the synthetic upsurge of a univocal relation. We are dealing with a relation which is without *parts,* given at one stroke, inside of which there unfolds a spatiality which is not *my* spatiality; for instead of a grouping *toward me* of the objects, there is now an orientation *which flees from me.*

Of course this relation without distance and without parts is in no way that original relation of the Other to me which I am seeking. In the first place, it concerns only the man and the things in the world. In addition it is still an object of knowledge; I shall express it, for example, by saying that this man sees the lawn, or that in spite of the prohibiting sign he is preparing to walk on the grass, *etc.* Finally it still retains a pure character of probability: First, it is *probable* that this object is a man. Second, even granted that he is a man, it remains only probable that he sees the lawn at the moment that I perceive him; it is possible that he is dreaming of some project without exactly being aware of what is around him, or that he is blind, *etc., etc.* Nevertheless this new relation of the object-man to the object-lawn has a particular character; it is simultaneously given to me as a whole, since it is there in the world as an object which I can know (it is, in fact, an objective relation which I express by saying: Pierre has glanced at this watch, Jean has looked out the window, *etc.*), and at the same time it entirely escapes me. To the extent that the man-as-object is the fundamental term of this relation, to the extent that the relation *reaches toward him,* it escapes me. I can not put myself at the center of it. The distance which unfolds between the lawn and the man across the synthetic upsurge of this primary relation is a negation of the distance which I establish—as a pure type of external negation—between these two objects. The distance appears as a pure *disintegration* of the relations which I apprehend between the objects of my universe. It is not I who realize this disintegration; it appears to me as a relation which I aim at emptily across the distances which I originally established between things. It stands as a background of things, a background which on principle escapes me and which is conferred on them from without. Thus the appearance among the objects of *my* universe of an element of disintegration in that universe is what I mean by the appearance of a man in my universe.

The Other is first the permanent flight of things toward a goal which I apprehend as an object at a certain distance from me but which escapes me inasmuch as it unfolds about itself its own distances. Moreover this disintegration grows by degrees; if there exists between the lawn and the Other a relation which is without distance and which creates distance, then there exists necessarily a relation between the Other and the statue which stands on a pedestal *in the middle of* the lawn, and a relation between the Other and the big chestnut trees which border the walk; there is a total space which is grouped around the Other, and this space is made *with my space;* there is a regrouping in which I take part but which escapes me, a regrouping of all the objects which people my universe. This regrouping does not stop there. The grass is something qualified; it is *this* green grass which exists for the Other; in this sense the very quality of the object, its deep, raw green is in direct relation to this man. This green turns toward the Other a face which escapes me. I apprehend the relation of the green to the Other as an objective relation, but I can not apprehend the green *as* it appears to the Other. Thus suddenly an object has appeared which has stolen the world from me. Everything is in place; everything still exists for me; but everything is traversed by an invisible flight and fixed in the direction of a new object. The appearance of the Other in the world corresponds therefore to a fixed sliding of the whole universe, to a decentralization of the world which undermines the centralizaton which I am simultaneously effecting.

But *the Other* is still an object *for me.* He belongs to *my distances;*

the man is there, twenty paces from me, he is turning his back on me. As such he is again two yards, twenty inches from the lawn, six yards from the statue; hence the disintegration of my universe is contained within the limits of this same universe; we are not dealing here with a flight of the world toward nothingness or outside itself. Rather it appears that the world has a kind of drain hole in the middle of its being and that it is perpetually flowing off through this hole. The universe, the flow, and the drain hole are all once again recovered, reapprehended, and fixed as an object. All this is there *for me* as a partial structure of the world, even though the total disintegration of the universe is involved. Moreover these disintegrations may often be contained within more narrow limits. There, for example, is a man who is reading while he walks. The disintegration of the universe which he represents is purely virtual: he has ears which do not hear, eyes which see nothing except his book. Between his book and him I apprehend an undeniable relation without distance of the same type as that which earlier connected the walker with the grass. But this time the form has closed in on itself. There is a full object for me to grasp. In the midst of the world I can say "man-reading" as I could say "cold stone," "fine rain." I apprehend a closed "Gestalt" in which the *reading* forms the essential quality; for the rest, it remains blind and mute, lets itself be known and perceived as a pure and simple temporal-spatial thing, and seems to be related to the rest of the world by a purely indifferent externality. The quality "man-reading" as the relation of the man to the book is simply a little particular crack in my universe. At the heart of this solid, visible form he makes himself a particular emptying. The form is massive only in appearance; its peculiar meaning is to be—in the midst of my universe, at ten paces from me, at the heart of that massity—a closely consolidated and localized flight.

None of this enables us to leave the level on which the Other is an *object.* At most we are dealing with a particular type of objectivity akin to that which Husserl designated by the term *absence* without, however, his noting that the Other is defined not as the absence of a consciousness in relation to the body which I see but by the absence of the world which I perceive, an absence discovered at the very heart of my perception of this world. On this level the Other is an object in the world, an object which can be defined by the world. But this relation of flight and of absence on the part of the world in relation to me is only probable. If it is this which defines the objectivity of the Other, then to what original presence of the Other does it refer? At present we can give this answer: of the Other-as-object is defined in connection with the world as the object which sees what I see, then my fundamental connection with the Other-as-subject must be able to be referred back to my permanent possibility of *being seen* by the Other. It is in and through the revelation of my being-as-object for the Other that I must be able to apprehend the presence of his being-as-subject. For just as the Other is a probable object for me-as-subject, so I can discover myself in the process of becoming a probable object for only a certain subject. This relation can not derive from the fact that *my universe is an object for the Other-as-object, as if* the Other's look after having wandered over the lawn and the surrounding objects came following a definite path to place itself on me. I have observed that I can not be an object for an object. A radical conversion of the Other is necessary if he is to escape objectivity. Therefore I can not consider the look which the Other directs on me as one of the possible manifestations of his objective being; the Other can not look at *me* as he looks at the grass. Furthermore my objectivity can not itself derive *for me* from the objectivity of the world since I am precisely the one by whom *there is* a world; that is, the one who on principle can not be an object for himself.

Thus this relation which I call "being-seen-by-another," far from being merely one of the relations signified by the word *man,* represents an irreducible fact which can not be deduced either from the essence of the Other-as-object, or from my being-as-subject. On the contrary, if the concept of the Other-as-object is to have any meaning, this can be only as the result of the conversion and the degradation of that original relation. In a word, my apprehension of the Other in the world as *probably being* a man refers to my permanent possibility of *being-seen-by-him;* that is, to the permanent possibility that a subject who sees me may be substituted for the object seen by me. "Being-seen-by-the-Other" is the *truth* of "seeing-the-Other." Thus the notion of the Other can not under any circumstances aim at a solitary, extra-mundane consciousness which I can not even think. The man is defined by his relation to the world and by his relation to myself. He is that object in the world which determines an internal flow of the universe, an internal hemorrhage. He is the subject who is revealed to me in that flight of myself toward objectivation. But the original relation of myself to the Other is not only an absent truth aimed at across the concrete presence of an object in my universe; it is also a concrete, daily relation which at each instant I experience. At each instant the Other *is looking at me.* It is easy therefore for us to attempt with concrete examples to describe this fundamental connection which must form the basis of any theory concerning the Other. If the Other is on principle the *one who looks at me,* then we must be able to explain the meaning of the Other's look. . . .

Shame

Let us imagine that moved by jealousy, curiosity, or vice I have just glued my ear to the door and looked through a keyhole. I am alone and on the level of a non-thetic self-consciousness. This means first of all that there is no self to inhabit my consciousness, nothing therefore to which I can refer my acts in order to qualify them. They are in no way *known;* I *am my acts* and hence they carry in themselves their whole justification. I am a pure consciousness *of* things, and things, caught up in the circuit of my selfness, offer to me their potentialities as the proof of my non-thetic consciousness (of) my own possibilities. This means that behind that door a spectacle is presented as "to be seen," a conversation as "to be heard." The door, the keyhole are at once both instruments and obstacles; they are presented as "to be handled with care"; the keyhole is given as "to be looked through close by and a little to one side," *etc.* Hence from this moment "I do what I have to do." No transcending view comes to confer upon my acts the character of a *given* on which a judgment can be brought to bear. My consciousness sticks to my acts, it *is* my acts; and my acts are commanded only by the ends to be attained and by the instruments to be employed. My attitude, for example, has no "outside"; it is a pure process of relating the instrumet (the keyhole) to the end to be attained (the spectacle to be seen), a pure mode of losing myself in the world, of causing myself to be drunk in by things as ink is by a blotter in order that an instrumental-complex oriented :oward an end may be synthetically detached on the ground of the world. The order is the reverse of causal order. It is the end to be attained which organizes all the moments which precede it. The end justifies the means; the means do not exist for themselves and outside the end.

Moreover the ensemble exists only in relation to a free project of my possibilities. Jealousy, as the possibility which I *am,* organizes this instrumental complex by transcending it toward itself. But I *am* this jealousy; I do not *know* it. If I contemplated it instead of making it, then only the worldly complex in instrumentality could teach it to me. This ensemble in the world with its double and inverted determination (there is a spectacle to be seen behind the door only because I am jealous, but my jealousy is nothing except the simple objective fact that *there is* a sight *to be seen* behind the door)—this we shall call *situation*. This situation reflects to me at once both my facticity and my freedom; on the occasion of a certain objective structure of the world which surrounds me, it refers my freedom to me in the form of tasks to be freely done. There is no constraint here since my freedom eats into my possibles and since correlatively the potentialities of the world indicate and offer only themselves. Moreover I can not truly define myself as *being* in a situation: first because I am not a positional consciousness of myself; second because I am my own nothingness. In this sense—and since I am what I am not and since I am not what I am—I can not even define myself as truly *being* in the process of listening at doors. I escape this provisional definition of myself by means of all my transcendence. There as we have seen is the origin of bad faith. Thus not only am I unable to *know* myself, but my very being escapes—although I *am* that very escape from my being—and I am absolutely nothing. There is nothing *there* but a pure nothingness encircling a certain objective ensemble and throwing it onto relief outlined upon the world, but this ensemble is a real system, a disposition of means in a view of an end.

But all of a sudden I hear footsteps in the hall. Someone is looking at me! What does this mean? It means that I am suddenly affected in my being and that essential modifications appear in my structure—modifications which I can apprehend and fix conceptually by means of the reflective *cogito.*

First of all, I now exist as *myself* for my unreflective consciousness. It is this irruption of the self which has been most often described: I see *myself* because *somebody* sees me—as it is usually expressed. This way of putting it is not wholly exact. But let us look more carefully. So long as we considered the for-itself in its isolation, we were able to maintain that the unreflective consciousness can not be inhabited by a self; the self was given in the form of an object and only for the reflective consciousness. But here the self comes to haunt the unreflective consciousness. Now the unreflective consciousness is a consciousness *of* the world. Therefore for the unreflective consciousness the self exists on the level of objects in the world; this role which devolved only on the reflective consciousness— the making-present of the self—belongs now to the unreflective consciousness. Only the reflective consciousness has the self directly for an object. The unreflective consciousness does not apprehend the *person* directly or as *its* object; the person is presented to consciousness *in so far as the person is an object for the Other.* This means that all of a sudden I am conscious of myself as escaping myself, not in that I am the foundation of my own nothingness but in that I have my foundation outside myself. I am for myself only as I am a pure reference to the Other.

Nevertheless we must not conclude here that the object is the Other and that the *Ego* present to my consciousness is a secondary structure or a meaning of the Other-as-object; the Other is not an object here and can not be an object, as we have shown, unless by the same stroke *my* self ceases to be an object-for-the-Other and vanishes. Thus I do not aim at the Other as an object nor at my *Ego* as an object for myself; I do not even direct an empty intention toward that *Ego* as toward an object presently out of my reach. In fact it is separated from me by a nothingness which I can not fill since I apprehend it *as not being for me* and since on principle it exists for the *Other.* Therefore I do not aim at it as if it could someday be given me but on the contrary in so far as it on principle flees from me and will never belong to me. Nevertheless I *am that Ego;* I do not reject it as a strange image, but it is present to me as a self which I *am* without *knowing* it; for I discover it in shame and, in other

SARTRE SELECTIONS   339

instances, in pride. It is shame or pride which reveals to me the Other's
look and myself at the end of that look. It is the shame or pride which
makes me *live,* not *know* the situation of being looked at.

Now, shame, as we noted at the beginning of this chapter, is shame
of *self;* it is the *recognition* of the fact that I *am* indeed that object which
the Other is looking at and judging. I can be ashamed only as my freedom
escapes me in order to become a *given* object. Thus originally the bond
between my unreflective consciousness and my *Ego,* which is being looked
at, is a bond not of knowing but of being. Beyond any knowledge which
I can have, I am this self which another knows. And this self which I
am—this I am in a world which the Other has made alien to me, for
the Other's look embraces my being and correlatively the walls, the door,
the keyhole. All these instrumental-things, in the midst of which I am,
now turn toward the Other a face which on principle escapes me. Thus
I am my *Ego* for the Other in the midst of a world which flows toward
the Other. Earlier we were able to call this internal hemorrhage the flow
of *my* world toward the Other-as-object. This was because the flow of
blood was trapped and localized by the very fact that I fixed as an object
in my world that Other toward which this world was bleeding. Thus not
a drop of blood was lost; all was recovered, surrounded, localized although
in a being which I could not penetrate. Here on the contrary the flight
is without limit; it is lost externally; the world flows out of the world
and I flow outside myself. The Other's look makes me be beyond my
being in this world and puts me in the midst of the world which is at
once *this world* and beyond this world. What sort of relations can I enter
into with this being which I am and which shame reveals to me?

In the first place there is a relation of being. I *am* this being. I do
not for an instant think of denying it; my shame is a confession. I shall
be able later to use bad faith so as to hide it from myself, but bad faith
is also a confession since it is an effort to flee the being which I am. But
I am this being, neither in the mode of "having to be" nor in that of
"was"; I do not found it in its being; I can not produce it directly. But
neither is it the indirect, strict effect of my acts as when my shadow on
the ground or my reflection in the mirror is moved in correlation with
the gestures which I make. This being which I am preserves a certain
indetermination, a certain unpredictability. And these new characteristics
do not come only from the fact that I can not *know* the Other; they stem
also and especially from the fact that the Other is free. Or to be exact
and to reverse the terms, the Other's freedom is revealed to me across
the uneasy indetermination of the being which I am for him. Thus this
being is not my possible; it is not always in question at the heart of my
freedom. On the contrary, it is the limit of my freedom, its "backstage"
in the sense that we speak of "behind the scenes." It is given to me as
a burden which I carry without ever being able to turn back to know it,

without even being able to realize its weight. If it is comparable to my shadow, it is like a shadow which is projected on a moving and unpredictable material such that no table of reference can be provided for calculating the distortions resulting from these movements. Yet we still have to do with *my* being and not with an image of my being. We are dealing with my being as it is written in and by the Other's freedom. Everything takes place as if I had a dimension of being from which I was separated by a radical nothingness; and this nothingness is the Other's freedom. The Other has to make my being-for-him *be* in so far as he has to be his being. Thus each of my free conducts engages me in a new environment where the very stuff of my being is the unpredictable freedom of another. Yet by my very shame I claim as mine that freedom of another. I affirm a profound unity of consciousness, not that harmony of monads which has sometimes been taken as a guarantee of objectivity but a unity of being; for I accept and wish that others should confer upon me a being which I recognize.

Shame reveals to me that I *am* this being, not in the mode of "was" or of "having to be" but *in-itself.* When I am alone, I can not realize my "being-seated"; at most it can be said that I simultaneously both am it and am not it. But in order for me to be what I am, it suffices merely that the Other look at me. It is not for myself, to be sure; I myself shall never succeed at realizing this being-seated which I grasp in the Other's look. I shall remain forever a consciousness. But it is for the Other. Once more the nihilating escape of the for-itself is fixed, once more the in-itself closes in upon the for-itself. But once more this metamorphosis is effected *at a distance.* For the Other *I am seated* as this inkwell *is on* the table; for the Other, *I am leaning over* the keyhole as this tree *is bent* by the wind. Thus for the Other I have stripped myself of transcendence. This is because my transcendence becomes for whoever makes himself a witness of it (*i.e.,* determines himself *as not being* my transcendence) a purely established transcendence, a given-transcendence; that is, it acquires a nature by the sole fact that the *Other* confers on it an outside. This is accomplished, not by any distortion or by a refraction which the Other would impose on my transcendence through his categories, but by his very being. If there is an Other, whatever or whoever he may be, whatever may be his relations with me, and without his acting upon me in any way except by the pure upsurge of his being—then I have an outside, I have a *nature.* My original fall is the existence of the Other. Shame—like pride—is the apprehension of myself as a nature although that very nature escapes me and is unknowable as such. Strictly speaking, it is not that I perceive myself losing my freedom in order to become a *thing,* but my nature is—over there, outside my lived freedom—as a given attribute of this being which I am for the Other.

I grasp the Other's look at the very center of my *act* as the solidification and alienation of my own possibilities. In fear or in anxious or prudent anticipation, I perceive that these possibilities which I *am* and which are the condition of my transcendence are given also to another, given as about to be transcended in turn by his own possibilities. The Other as a look is only that—my transcendence transcended. Of course I still *am* my possibilities in the mode of non-thetic consciousness (of) these possibilities. But at the same time the look alienates them from me. Hitherto I grasped these possibilites thetically on the world and in the world in the form of the potentialities of instruments: the dark corner in the hallway referred to me the possibility of hiding—as a simple potential quality of its shadow, as the invitation of its darkness. This quality or instrumentality of the object belonged to it alone and was given as an objective, ideal property marking its real belonging to that complex which we have called *situation*. But with the Other's look a new organization of complexes comes to superimpose itself on the first. To apprehend myself as seen is, in fact, to apprehend myself as seen *in the world* and from the standpoint of the world. The look does carve me out in the universe; it comes to search for me at the heart of my situation and grasps me only in irresolvable relations with instruments. If I am seen as seated, I must be seen as "seated-on-a-chair," if I am grasped as bent over, it is as "bent-over-the-keyhole," *etc.* But suddenly the alienation of myself, which is the act of being-looked-at, involves the alienation of the world which I organize. I am seen as seated on this chair with the result that I do not see it at all, that it is impossible for me to see it, that it escapes me so as to organize itself into a new and differently oriented complex—with other relations and other distances in the midst of other objects which simlarly have for me a secret face.

Thus I, who in so far as I am my possibles, am what I am not and am not what I am—behold now I *am* somebody! And the one who I am—and who on principle escapes me—I am he *in the midst of the world* in so far as he escapes me. Due to this fact my relation to an object or the potentiality of an object decomposes under the Other's look and appears to me in the world as my possibility of utilizing the object, but only as this possibility on principle escapes me; that is, in so far as it is surpassed by the Other toward his own possibilities. For example, the potentiality of the dark corner becomes a given possibility of hiding in the corner by the sole fact that the Other can pass beyond it toward his possibility of illuminating the corner with his flashlight. This possibility is there, and I apprehend it but as absent, as *in the Other;* I apprehend it through my anguish and through my decision to give up that hiding place which is *"too risky."*

With the Other's look the "situation" escapes me. To use an everyday expression which better expresses our thought, I *am no longer master of the situation.* Or more exactly, I remain master of it, but it has one real dimension by which it escapes me, by which unforeseen reversals cause it *to be* otherwise than it appears for me. To be sure it can happen that in strict solitude I perform an act whose consequences are completely opposed to my anticipations and to my desires; for example I gently draw toward me a small platform holding this fragile vase, but this movement results in tipping over a bronze statuette which breaks the vase into a thousand pieces. Here, however, there is nothing which I could not have foreseen if I had been more careful, if I had observed the arrangement of the objects, *etc.—nothing which on principle escapes me.* The appearance of the Other, on the contrary, causes the appearance in the situation of an aspect which I did not wish, of which I am not the master, and which on principle escapes me since it is *for the Other.*

Fear and Pride

Fear implies that I appear to myself as threatened by virtue of my being a presence in the world, not in my capacity as a for-itself which makes a world exist. It is the object which *I* am which is in danger in the world and which as such, because of its indissoluble unity of being with the being which I have to be, can involve in its own ruin the ruin of the for-itself which I have to be. Fear is therefore the discovery of my being-as-object on the occasion of the appearance of another object in my perceptive field. It reflects the origin of all fear, which is the fearful discovery of my pure and simple object-state insofar as it is transcended by possibles which are not my possibles. It is by thrusting myself toward my possibles that I shall escape fear to the extent that I shall consider my objectivity as non-essential. This can happen only if I apprehend myself as being responsible for the Other's being. The Other becomes then *that which I make myself not-be,* and his possibilities are possibilities which I refuse and which I can simply contemplate—hence dead-possibilities. Therefore I transcend my present possibilities insofar as I consider them as always able to be transcended by the Other's possibilities, but I also transcend the Other's possibilities by considering them from the point of view of the only quality which he has which is not his own possibility— his very character as Other inasmuch as I make there to be an Other. I transcend the Other's possibilities by considering them as possibilities of transcending me which I can always transcend toward new possibilities. Thus at one and the same time I have regained my being-for-itself through my consciousness (of) myself as a perpetual center of infinite possibilities, and I have transformed the Other's possibilities into dead-possibilities by affecting them all with the character of *"not-lived-by-me"*—that is as *simply given.* . . .

Shame motivates the reaction which surpasses and overcomes the shame inasmuch as the reaction encloses within it an implicit and non-thematized comprehension of being-able-to-be-an-object on the part of the subject for whom I am an object. This implicit comprehension is nothing other than the consciousness (of) my "being-myself"; that is, of my selfness reinforced. In fact in the structure which expresses the experience "I am ashamed of myself," shame supposes a me-as-object for the Other but also a selfness which is ashamed and which is imperfectly expressed by the "I" of the formula. Thus shame is a unitary apprehension with three dimensions: "*I* am ashamed of *myself* before the *Other*."

If any one of these dimensions disappears, the shame disappears as well. If, however, I conceive of the "they" as a subject before whom I am ashamed, then it can not become an object without being scattered into a plurality of Others; and if I posit it as the absolute unity of the subject which can in no way become an object, I thereby posit the eternity of my being-as-object and so perpetuate my shame. This is shame before God; that is, the recognition of my being-an-object before a subject which can never become an object. By the same stroke I *realize* my object-state in the absolute and hypostasize it. The position of God is accompanied by a reification of my object-ness. Or better yet, I posit my being-an-object-for-God as more real than my For-itself; I exist alienated and I cause myself to learn from outside what I must be. This is the origin of fear before God. Black masses, desecration of the host, demonic associations, *etc.*, are so many attempts to confer the character of object on the absolute Subject. In desiring Evil for Evil's sake I attempt to contemplate the divine transcendence—for which Good is the peculiar possibility—as a purely given transcendence and one which I transcend toward Evil. Then I "make God suffer," I "irritate him," *etc.* These attempts, which imply the absolute *recognition* of God as a subject who can not be an object, carry their own contradiction within them and are always failures.

Pride does not exclude original shame. In fact it is on the ground of fundamental shame or shame of being an object that pride is built. It is an ambiguous feeling. In pride I recognize the Other as the subject through whom my being gets its object-state, but I recognize as well that I myself am also responsible for my objectivity. I emphasize my responsibility and I assume it. In one sense therefore pride is at first resignation: in order to be proud of *being that,* I must of necessity first resign myself to *being only that.* We are therefore dealing with a primary reaction to shame, and it is already a reaction of flight and of bad faith; for without ceasing to hold the Other as a subject, I try to apprehend myself as *affecting* the Other by my object-state. In short there are two authentic attitudes: that by which I recognize the Other as the subject through whom I get my objectivity—this is shame; and that by which I apprehend myself as the free object by which the Other gets his being-other—this is arrogance or the affirmation of my freedom confronting the Other-as-object. But pride—or vanity—is a feeling without equilibrium, and it is in bad faith. In vanity I attempt in my capacity as object to act upon the Other. I take this beauty or this strength or this intelligence which he confers on me—insofar as he constitutes me as an object—and I attempt to make use of the recoil so as to affect him passively with a feeling of admiration or of love. But at the same time I demand that this feeling as the sanction of my being-as-object should be entertained by the Other in his capacity as subject—*i.e.,* as a freedom. This is, in fact, the only way of conferring an absolute objectivity on my strength or on my beauty. Thus the feeling which I demand from the other carries within itself its own contradiction since I must affect the Other with it insofar as he is free. The feeling is entertained in the mode of bad faith, and its internal development leads it to disintegration. In fact as I play my assumed role of my being-as-object, I attempt to recover it *as an object.* Since the Other is the key to it, I attempt to lay hold of the Other so that he may release to me the secret of my being. Thus vanity impels me to get hold of the Other and to constitute him as an object in order to burrow into the heart of this object to discover there my own object-state. But this is to kill the hen that lays the golden eggs. By constituting the Other as object, I constitute myself as an image at the heart of the Other-as-object; hence the disillusion of vanity. In that image which I wanted to grasp in order to recover it and merge it with my own being, I no longer recognize myself. I must willy-nilly impute the image to the Other as one of his own subjective properties. Freed in spite of myself from my object-state, I remain alone confronting the Other-as-object in my unqualifiable selfness which I have to be forever without reprieve.

Shame, fear, and pride are my original reactions; they are only various ways by which I recognize the Other as a subject beyond reach, and they include within them a comprehension of my selfness which can and must serve as my motivation for constituting the Other as an object. . . .

Concrete Relations with Others: Sexual Desire

Everything which may be said of me in my relations with the Other applies to him as well. While I attempt to free myself from the hold of the Other, the Other is trying to free himself from mine; while I seek to enslave the Other, the Other seeks to enslave me. We are by no means dealing with unilateral relations with an object-in-itself, but with reciprocal and moving relations. The following descriptions of concrete behavior must therefore be envisaged within the perspective of *conflict*. Conflict is the original meaning of being-for-others.

If we start with the first revelation of the Other as a *look,* we must recognize that we experience our inapprehensible being-for-others in the form of a *possession.* I am possessed by the Other; the Other's look fashions my body in its nakedness, causes it to be born, sculptures it, produces it as it *is,* sees it as I shall never see it. The Other holds a secret—the secret of what I am. He makes me be and thereby he possesses me, and this possession is nothing other than the consciousness of possessing me. I in the recognition of my object-state have proof that he has this consciousness. By virtue of consciousness the Other is for me simultaneously the one who has stolen my being from me and the one who causes "there to be" a being which is my being. Thus I have a comprehension of this ontological structure: I am responsible for my being-for-others, but I am not the foundation of it. It appears to me therefore in the form of a contingent given for which I am nevertheless responsible; the Other founds my being in so far as this being is in the form of the "there is." But he is not responsible for my being although he founds it in complete freedom—in and by means of his free transcendence. Thus to the extent that I am revealed to myself as responsible for my being, I *lay claim* to this being which I am; that is, I wish to recover it, or, more exactly, I am the project of the recovery of my being. I want to stretch out my hand and grab hold of this being which is presented to me as *my being* but at a distance—like the dinner of Tantalus; I want to found it by my very freedom. For if in one sense my being-as-object is an unbearable contingency and the pure "possession" of myself by another, still in another sense this being stands as the indication of what I should be obliged to recover and found in order to be the foundation of myself. But this is conceivable only if I assimilate the Other's freedom. Thus my project of recovering myself is fundamentally a project of absorbing the Other.

My original attempt to get hold of the Other's free subjectivity through his objectivity-for-me is *sexual desire.* Perhaps it will come as a surprise to see a phenomenon which is usually classified among "psycho-physiological reactions" now mentioned on the level of primary attitudes which manifest our original mode of realizing Being-for-Others. For the majority of psychologists indeed, desire, as a fact of consciousness, is in strict correlation with the nature of our sexual organs, and it is only in connection with an elaborate study of these that sexual desire can be understood. . . .

But does this mean that the For-itself is sexual "accidentally," by the pure contingency of having this particular body? Can we admit that this tremendous matter of the sexual life comes as a kind of addition to the human condition? Man, it is said, is a sexual being because he possesses a sex. And if the reverse were true? If sex were only the instrument and, so to speak, the *image* of a fundamental sexuality? If man possessed a sex only because he is originally and fundamentally a sexual being as a being who exists in the world in relation with other men? Infantile sexuality precedes the physiological maturation of the sex organs. Men who have become eunuchs do not thereby cease to feel desire. Nor do many old men. The fact of being able to *make use of* a sex organ fit to fertilize and to procure enjoyment represents only one phase and one aspect of our sexual life. There is one mode of sexuality "with the possibility of satisfaction," and the developed sex represents and makes concrete this possibility. But there are other modes of sexuality of the type which can not get satisfaction, and if we take these modes into account we are forced to recognize that sexuality appears with birth and disappears only with death. Moreover neither the tumescence of the penis nor any other physiological phenomenon can ever explain or provoke sexual desire— no more than the vaso-constriction or the dilation of the pupils (or the simple consciousness of these physiological modifications) will be able to explain or to provoke fear. In one case as in the other although the body plays an important role, we must—in order to understand it—refer to being-in-the-world and to being-for-others. I desire a human being, not an insect or a mollusk, and I desire him (or her) as he is and as I am in situation in the world and as he is an Other for me and as I am an Other for him.

The fundamental problem of sexuality can therefore be formulated thus: is sexuality a contingent accident bound to our physiological nature, or is it a necessary structure of being-for-itself-for-others? From the sole fact that the question can be posited in these terms, we see that we must go back to ontology to decide it. Moreover ontology can decide this question only by determining and fixing the meaning of sexual existence for-the-Other. To have sex means—in accordance with the description of the body which we attempted in the preceding chapter—to exist sexually for an Other who exists sexually for me. And it must be well understood that at first this Other is not necessarily *for me*—nor I for him—a *heterosexual* existent but only a being who has sex. Considered from the point of view of the For-itself, this apprehension of the Other's sexuality could not be the pure disinterested contemplation of his primary or secondary sexual characteristics. *My first* apprehension of the Other as having sex does not come when I conclude from the distribution of his hair, from the coarseness of his hands, the sound of his voice, his strength that he is of the masculine sex. We are dealing there with derived conclusions which refer to an original state. The first apprehension of the Other's sexuality in so far as it is lived and suffered can be only *desire;* it is by desiring the Other (or by discovering myself as incapable of desiring him) or by apprehending his desire for me that I discover his being-sexed. Desire reveals to me simultaneously *my* being-sexed and *his* being-sexed, *my* body as sex and *his* body. Here therefore in order to decide the nature and ontological position of sex we are referred to the study of desire. What therefore is desire? . . .

The man who desires *exists* his body in a particular mode and thereby places himself on a particular level of existence. In fact everyone will agree that desire is not only *longing,* a clear and translucent *longing* which directs itself through our body toward a certain object. Desire is defined as *trouble.* The notion of "trouble" can help us better to determine the nature of desire. We contrast troubled water with transparent water, a troubled look with a clear look. Troubled water remains water; it preserves the fluidity and the essential characteristics of water; but its translucency is "troubled" by an inapprehensible presence which makes one with it, which is everywhere and nowhere and which is given as a clogging of the water by itself. To be sure, we can explain the troubled quality by the presence of fine solid particles suspended in the liquid, but this explanation is that of the *scientist.* Our original apprehension of the troubled water is given us as changed by the presence of an invisible *something* which is not itself distinguished and which is manifested as a pure factual resistance. If the desiring consciousness is *troubled,* it is because it is analogous to the troubled water.

To make this analogy precise, we should compare sexual desire with another form of desire—for example, with hunger. Hunger, like sexual desire, supposes a certain state of the body, defined here as the impoverishment of the blood, abundant salivary secretion, contractions of the tunica, *etc.* These various phenomena are described and classified from the point of view of the Other. For the For-itself they are manifested as pure facticity. But this facticity *does not compromise* the nature of the For-itself, for the For-itself immediately flees it toward its possibles; that is, toward a certain state of satisfied-hunger which, as we have pointed out in Part Two, is the In-itself-for-itself of hunger. Thus hunger is a pure surpassing of corporal facticity; and to the extent that the For-itself becomes conscious of this facticity in a non-thetic form, the For-itself becomes conscious of it as a surpassed facticity. The body here is indeed the *past, the passed-beyond.* In sexual desire, to be sure, we can find that structure common to all appetites—a state of the body. The Other can note various physiological modifications (the erection of the penis, the turgescence of the nipples of the breasts, changes in the circulatory system, rise in temperature, *etc.*). The desiring consciousness exists this facticity; it is *in terms of this facticity*—we could even say *through* it—that the desired body appears as desirable. Nevertheless if we limited ourselves to this description, sexual desire would appear as a *distinct and clear desire,* comparable to the desire of eating and drinking. It would be a pure flight from facticity toward other possibles. Now everyone is aware that there is a great abyss between sexual desire and other appetites. We all know the famous saying, "Make love to a pretty woman when you want her just as you would drink a glass of cold water when you are thirsty." We know also how unsatisfactory and even shocking this statement is to the mind. This is because when we do desire a woman, we do not keep ourselves wholly outside the desire; the desire *compromises* me; I am the accomplice of my desire. Or rather the desire has fallen wholly into complicity with the body. Let any man consult his own experience; he knows how consciousness is clogged, so to speak, by sexual desire; it seems that one is invaded by facticity, that one ceases to flee it and that one slides toward a *passive* consent to the desire. At other moments it seems that facticity invades consciousness in its very flight and renders consciousness opaque to itself. It is like a yeasty tumescence of *fact*.

The expressions which we use to designate desire sufficiently show its specificity. We say that it *takes hold of you*, that it *overwhelms you*, that it *paralyzes you*. Can one imagine employing the same words to designate hunger? Can one think of a hunger which "would overwhelm" one? Strictly speaking, this would be meaningful only when applied to impressions of emptiness. But, on the contrary, even the feeblest desire is already overwhelming. One can not hold it at a distance as one can with hunger and "think of something else" while keeping desire as an undifferentiated tonality of non-thetic consciousness which would be desire and which would serve as a sign of the body-as-ground. But *desire is consent to desire*. The heavy, fainting consciousness slides toward a languor comparable to sleep. Everyone has been able to observe the appearance of desire in another. Suddenly the man who desires becomes a heavy tranquility which is frightening, his eyes are fixed and appear half-closed, his movements are stamped with a heavy and sticky sweetness; many seem to be falling asleep. And when one "struggles against desire," it is precisely this languor which one resists. If one succeeds in resisting it, the desire before disappearing will become wholly distinct and clear, like hunger. And then there will be "an awakening." One will feel that one is lucid but with heavy head and beating heart. Naturally all these descriptions are inexact; they show rather the way in which we interpret desire. However they indicate the primary fact of desire: in desire consciousness chooses to exist its facticity on another plane. It no longer flees it; it attempts to subordinate itself to its own contingency—as it apprehends another body—*i.e.*, another contingency—as desirable. In this sense desire is not only the revelation of the Other's body but the revelation of my own body. And this, not in so far as this body *is an instrument* or a *point of view*, but in so far as it is pure facticity; that is, a simple contingent form of the necessity of my contingency. I *feel* my skin and my muscles and my breath, and I feel them not in order to transcend them *toward* something as in emotion or appetite but as a living and inert datum, not simply as the pliable and discrete instrument of my action upon the world but as a *passion* by which I am engaged in the world and in danger in the world. The For-itself *is not* this contingency; it continues to exist but it experiences the vertigo of its own body. Or, if you prefer, this vertigo is precisely its way of existing its body. The non-thetic consciousness allows itself to go over to the body, *wishes to be* the body and to be only body. In desire the body, instead of being only the contingency which the For-itself flees toward possibles which are peculiar to it, becomes at the same time the most immediate possible of the For-itself. Desire is not only the desire of the Other's body; it is— within the unity of a single act—the non-thetically lived project of being swallowed up in the body. Thus the final state of sexual desire can be swooning as the final stage of consent to the body. It is in this sense that desire can be called the desire of one body for another body. It is in fact an appetite directed *toward* the Other's body, and it is lived as the vertigo of the For-itself before its own body. The being which desires is consciousness *making itself body.*

But granted that desire is a consciousness which makes itself body in order to appropriate the Other's body apprehended as an organic totality in situation with consciousness on the horizon—what then is the meaning of desire? That is, why does consciousness make itself body—or vainly attempt to do so—and what does it expect from the object of its desire? The answer is easy if we realize that in desire I make myself flesh *in the presence of the Other in order to appropriate* the Other's flesh. This means that it is not merely a question of my grasping the Other's shoulders or thighs or of my drawing a body over against me; it is necessary as well for me to apprehend them with this particular instrument which is the body as it produces a clogging of consciousness. In this sense when I grasp these shoulders, it can be said not only that my body is a means for touching the shoulders but that the Other's shoulders are a means for my discovering my body as the fascinating revelation of facticity—that is, as flesh. Thus desire is the desire to appropriate a body as this appropriation reveals to me my body as flesh. But this body which I wish to appropriate, I wish to appropriate as *flesh.* Now at first the Other's body is not flesh for me; it appears as a synthetic form in action. As we have seen, we can not perceive the Other's body as pure flesh; that is, in the form of an isolated object maintaining external relations with other *thises.* The Other's body is originally a body in situation; flesh, on the contrary, appears as the *pure contingency of presence.* Ordinarily it is hidden by cosmetics, clothing, *etc.;* in particular it is hidden by *movements.* Nothing is less "in the flesh" than a dancer even though she is nude. Desire is an attempt to strip the body of its movements as of its clothing and to make it exist as pure flesh; it is an attempt to *incarnate* the Other's body. . . .

Desire is expressed by the caress as thought is by language. The caress reveals the Other's flesh as flesh to myself *and to the Other.* But it reveals this flesh in a very special way. To take hold of the Other reveals to her her inertia and her passivity as a transcendence-transcended; but this is not to caress her. In the caress it is not only my body as a synthetic form in action which caresses the Other; it is my body as flesh which causes the Other's flesh to be born. The caress is designed to cause the Other's body to be born, through pleasure, for the Other—and for myself—as a *touched* passivity in such a way that my body is made flesh in order to touch the Other's body with its own passivity; that is, by caressing itself with the Other's body rather than by caressing her. This is why amorous gestures have a language which could almost be said to be studied; it is not a question so much of taking hold of a part of the Other's body as of placing one's own body against the Other's body. Not so much to push or to touch in the active sense but to place against. It seems that I lift my own arm as an inanimate object and that I *place* it against the flank of the desired woman, that my fingers which I run over her arm are inert at the end of my hand. Thus the revelation of the Other's flesh is made through my own flesh; in desire and in the caress which expresses desire, I incarnate myself in order to realize the incarnation of the Other. The caress by *realizing* the Other's incarnation reveals to me my own incarnation; that is, I make myself flesh in order to impel the Other to realize *for-herself* and *for me* her own flesh, and my caresses cause my flesh to be born for me in so far as it is for the Other *flesh causing her to be born as flesh.* I make her enjoy my flesh through her flesh in order to compel her to feel herself flesh. And so possession truly appears as a *double reciprocal incarnation.* Thus in desire there is an attempt at the incarnation of consciousness (this is what we called earlier the clogging of consciousness, a troubled consciousness, *etc.*) in order to realize the incarnation of the Other. . . .

We are now in a position to make explicit the profound meaning of desire. In the primordial reaction to the Other's look I constitute myself as a look. But if I look at his look in order to defend myself against the Other's freedom and to transcend it as freedom, then both the freedom and the look of the Other collapse. I see eyes; I see a being-in-the-midst-of-the-world. Henceforth the Other escapes me. I should like to act upon his freedom, to appropriate it, or at least, to make the Other's freedom recognize my freedom. But this freedom is death; it is no longer absolutely *in the world* in which I encounter the Other-as-object, for his characteristic is to be transcendent to the world. To be sure, I can *grasp* the Other, grab hold of him, knock him down. I can, providing I have the power, compel him to perform this or that act, to say certain words. But everything happens as if I wished to get hold of a man who runs away and leaves only his coat in my hands. It is the coat, it is the outer shell which I possess. I shall never get hold of more than a body, a psychic object in the midst of the world. And although all the acts of this body can be interpreted in terms of freedom, I have completely lost the key to this interpretation; I can act only upon a facticity. If I have preserved my awareness of a transcendent freedom in the Other, this awareness provokes me to no purpose by indicating a reality which is on principle beyond my reach and by revealing to me every instant the fact that I *am missing* it, that everything which I do is done "blindly" and takes on a meaning elsewhere in a sphere of existence from which I am on principle excluded. I can make the Other beg for mercy or ask my pardon, but I shall always be ignorant of what this submission means for and in the Other's freedom.

Moreover at the same time my *awareness* is altered; I lose the exact comprehension of *being-looked-at,* which is, as we know, the only way in which I can make proof of the Other's freedom. Thus I am engaged in an enterprise the meaning of which I have forgotten. I am dismayed confronting this Other as I see him and touch him but am at a loss as to what to do with him. It is exactly as if I had preserved the vague memory of a certain *Beyond* which is beyond what I see and what I touch, a Beyond concerning which I know that this is precisely what I want to appropriate. It is now that I *make myself desire.* Desire is an attitude aiming at enchantment. Since I can grasp the Other only in his objective facticity, the problem is to ensnare his freedom within this facticity. It is necessary that he be "caught" in it as the cream is caught up by a person skimming milk. So the Other's For-itself must come to play on the surface of his body, and be extended all through his body; and by touching this body I should finally touch the Other's free subjectivity. This is the true meaning of the word *possession.* It is certain that I want to *possess* the Other's body, but I want to possess it in so far as it is itself a "possessed"; that is, in so far as the Other's consciousness is identified with his body. Such is the impossible ideal of desire: to possess the Other's transcendence as pure transcendence and at the same time as *body,* to reduce the Other to his simple *facticity* because he is then in the midst of my world but to bring it about that this facticity is a perpetual appresentation of his nihilating transcendence. . . .

I desire a woman *in the world,* standing *near a table,* lying naked *on a bed,* or seated *at my side.* But if the desire flows back from the situation upon the being who is in situation, it is in order to dissolve the situation and to corrode the Other's relations in the world. The movement of desire which goes from the surrounding "environment" to the desired person is an isolating movement which destroys the environment and cuts off the person in question in order to effect the emergence of his pure facticity. But this is possible only if each object which refers me to the person is fixed in its pure contingency at the same time that it indicates him to me; consequently this return movement to the Other's being is a movement of return to myself as pure being-there. I destroy my possibilities in order to destroy those of the world and to constitute the world as a "world of desire"; that is, as a destructured world which has lost its meaning, a world in which things jut out like fragments of pure matter, like brute qualities. Since the For-itself is a choice, this is possible only if I project myself toward a new possibility: that of being "absorbed by my body as ink is by a blotter," that of being reduced to my pure being-there. This project, inasmuch as it is not simply conceived and thematically posited but rather lived—that is, inasmuch as its real-ization is not distinct from its conception—is "disturbance" or "trouble." Indeed we must not understand the preceding descriptions as meaning that I deliberately put myself in a state of disturbance with the purpose of rediscovering the Other's pure "being-there." Desire is a lived project which does not suppose any preliminary deliberation but which includes within itself its meaning and its interpretation. As soon as I throw myself toward the Other's facticity, as soon as I wish to push aside his acts and his functions so as to touch him in his flesh, I incarnate myself, for I can neither wish nor even conceive of the incarnation of the Other except in and by means of my own incarnation. Even the empty outline of a desire (as when one absentmindedly "undresses a woman with one's look") is an empty outline of troubled disturbance, for I desire only with my trouble, and I disrobe the Other only by disrobing myself; I foreshadow and outline the Other's flesh only by outlining my own flesh.

But my *incarnation* is not only the preliminary condition of the appearance of the Other as flesh *to my eyes.* My goal is to cause him to be incarnated as flesh in *his own eyes.* It is necessary that I drag him onto the level of pure facticity; he must be reduced for himself to being only flesh. Thus I shall be reassured as to the permanent possibilities of a transcendence which can at any instant transcend me on all sides. This transcendence *will be no more than this;* it will remain enclosed within the limits of an object; in addition and because of this very fact, I shall be able to touch it, feel it, possess it. Thus the other meaning of my incarnation—that is, of my troubled disturbance—is that it is a magical language. I make myself flesh so as to fascinate the Other by my nakedness and to provoke in her the desire for my flesh—exactly because this desire will be nothing else in the Other but an incarnation similar to mine. Thus desire is an invitation to desire. It is my flesh alone which knows how to find the road to the Other's flesh and I lay my flesh next to her flesh so as to awaken her to the meaning of flesh. In the caress when I slowly lay my inert hand against the Other's flank, I am making that flank feel my flesh, and this can be achieved only if it renders itself inert. The shiver of pleasure which it feels is precisely the awakening of its consciousness as flesh. If I extend my hand, remove it, or clasp it, then it becomes again body in action; but by the same stroke I make my hand disappear as flesh. To let it run indifferently over the length of her body, to reduce my hand to a soft brushing almost stripped of meaning, to a pure existence, to a pure matter slightly silky, slightly satiny, slightly rough—this is to give up for oneself being the one who establishes references and unfolds distances; it is to be made pure mucous membrane. At this moment the communion of desire is realized; each consciousness by incarnating itself has realized the incarnation of the other; each one's disturbance has caused disturbance to be born in the Other and is thereby so much enriched. By each caress I experience my own flesh and the Other's flesh through my flesh, and I am conscious that this flesh which I feel and appropriate through my flesh is flesh-realized-by-the Other. . . .

Nevertheless desire is itself doomed to failure. As we have seen, coitus, which ordinarily terminates desire, is not its essential goal. To be sure, several elements of our sexual structure are the necessary expression of the nature of desire, in particular the erection of the penis and the clitoris. This is nothing else in fact but the affirmation of the flesh by the flesh. Therefore it is absolutely necessary that it should not be accomplished *voluntarily;* that is, that we can not use it as an instrument but that we are dealing with a biological and autonomous phenomenon whose autonomous and involuntary expression accompanies and signifies the submerging of consciousness in the body. It must be clearly understood that no fine, prehensile organ provided with striated muscles can be a sex organ, a *sex.* If sex were to appear as an organ, it could be only one manifestation of the vegetative life. But contingency reappears if we consider that *there are* sexes and *particular* sexes. Consider especially the penetration of the female by the male. This does, to be sure, conform to that radical incarnation which desire wishes to be. (We may in fact observe the organic passivity of sex in coitus. It is the whole body which advances and withdraws, which *carries* sex forward or withdraws it. Hands help to introduce the penis; the penis itself appears as an instrument which one manages, which one makes penetrate, which one withdraws, which one utilizes. And similarly the opening and the lubrication of the vagina can not be obtained voluntarily.) Yet coitus remains a perfectly contingent modality of our sexual life. It is as much a pure contingency as sexual pleasure proper. In truth the ensnarement of consciousness in the body normally has its own peculiar result—that is, a sort of particular ecstasy in which consciousness is no more than consciousness (of) the body and consequently a reflective consciousness *of* corporeality. Pleasure in fact—like too keen a pain—motivates the appearance of reflective consciousness which is *"attention to pleasure."*

But pleasure is the death and the failure of desire. It is the death of desire because it is not only its fulfillment but its limit and its end.

This, moreover, is only an organic contingency: it *happens that* the incarnation is manifested by erection and that the erection ceases with ejaculation. But in addition pleasure closes the sluice to desire because it motivates the appearance of a reflective consciousness *of* pleasure, whose object becomes a reflective enjoyment; that is, it is *attention to the incarnation of the For-itself which is reflected-on* and by the same token it is forgetful of the Other's incarnation. Here we are no longer within the province of contingency. Of course it remains contingent that the passage to the fascinated reflection should be effected on the occasion of that particular mode of incarnation which is pleasure (although there are numerous cases of passage to the reflective without the intervention of pleasure), but there is a permanent danger for desire in so far as it is an attempt at incarnation. This is because consciousness by incarnating itself loses sight of the Other's incarnation, and its own incarnation absorbs it to the point of becoming the ultimate goal. In this case the pleasure of caressing is transformed into the pleasure of being caressed; what the For-itself demands is to feel within it its own body expanding to the point of nausea. Immediately there is a rupture of contact and desire misses its goal. It happens very often that this failure of desire motivates a passage to masochism; that is, consciousness apprehending itself in its facticity demands to be apprehended and transcended as body-for-the-Other by means of the Other's consciousness. In this case the Other-as-object collapses, the Other-as-look appears, and my consciousness is a consciousness swooning in its flesh beneath the Other's look.

Yet conversely desire stands at the origin of its own failure inasmuch as it is a desire of *taking* and of *appropriating*. It is not enough merely that troubled disturbance should effect the Other's incarnation; desire is the desire to appropriate this incarnated consciousness. Therefore desire is naturally continued not by *caresses* but by acts of taking and of penetration. The caress has for its goal only to impregnate the Other's body with consciousness and freedom. Now it is necessary to take this saturated body, to seize it, to enter into it. But by the very fact that I now attempt to seize the Other's body, to pull it toward me, to grab hold of it, to bite it, my own body ceases to be flesh and becomes again the synthetic instrument *which I am.* And by the same token the *Other* ceases to be an incarnation; she becomes once more an instrument in the midst of the world which I apprehend in terms of its situation. Her consciousness, which played on the surface of her flesh and which I tried to *taste* with my flesh, disappears under my sight; she remains no more than an *object* with object-images inside her. At the same time my disturbance disappears. This does not mean that I cease to desire but that desire has lost its matter; it has become *abstract;* it is a desire to handle and to take. I insist on taking the Other's body but my very insistence makes my incarnation disappear. At present I surpass my body anew toward my own possibilities (here the possibility of taking), and similarly the Other's body which is surpassed toward its potentialities falls from the level of *flesh* to the level of pure object. This situation brings about the rupture of that reciprocity of incarnation which was precisely the unique goal of desire. The Other may remain troubled; she may remain flesh *for herself,* and I can understand it. But it is a flesh which I no longer apprehend through my flesh, a flesh which is no longer anything but the *property* of an Other-as-object and not the incarnation of an Other-as-consciousness. Thus I *am body* (a synthetic totality in situation) confronting a *flesh.* I find myself in almost the same situation as that from which I tried to escape by means of desire; that is, I try to use the object-Other so as to make her deliver her transcendence, and precisely because she is *all* object she escapes me with *all* her transcendence. Once again I have even lost the precise comprehension of what I seek and yet I am engaged in the search. I take and discover myself in the process of taking, but what I take in my hands is *something else* than what I wanted to take. I feel this and I suffer from it but without being capable of saying what I wanted to take; for along with my troubled disturbance the very comprehension of my desire escapes me. I am like a sleepwalker who wakens to find himself in the process of gripping the edge of the bed while he can not recall the nightmare which provoked his gesture. It is this situation which is at the origin of *sadism.*

These few remarks do not aim at exhausting the problem of sadism. We wanted only to show that it is as a seed in desire itself, as the failure of desire; in fact as soon as I seek to *take* the Other's body, which through my incarnation I have induced to incarnate itself, I break the reciprocity of incarnation, I surpass my body toward its own possibilities, and I orient myself in the direction of sadism. Thus sadism and masochism are the two reefs on which desire may founder—whether I surpass my troubled disturbance toward an appropriation of the Other's flesh or, intoxicated with my own trouble, pay attention only to my flesh and ask nothing of the Other except that he should be the look which aids me in realizing my flesh. It is because of this inconstancy on the part of desire and its perpetual oscillation between these two perils that "normal" sexuality is commonly designated as "sadistic-masochistic."

Existential Psychoanalysis

Fundamentally man is *the desire to be,* and the existence of this desire is not to be established by an empirical induction; it is the result of an *a priori* description of the being of the for-itself, since desire is a lack and since the for-itself is the being which is to itself its own lack of being. The original project which is expressed in each of our empirically observable tendencies is then the *project of being;* or, if you prefer, each empirical tendency exists with the original project of being, in a relation of expression and symbolic satisfaction just as conscious drives, with Freud, exist in relation to the complex and to the original libido. Moreover the desire to be by no means exists *first* in order to cause itself to be expressed subsequently by desires *a posteriori.* There is nothing outside of the symbolic expression which it finds in concrete desires. There is not first a single desire of being, then a thousand particular feelings, but the desire to be exists and manifests itself only in and through jealousy, greed, love of art, cowardice, courage, and a thousand contingent, empirical expressions which always cause human reality to appear to us only as *manifested* by *a particular man,* by a specific person.

As for the being which is the object of this desire, we know *a priori* what this is. The for-itself is the being which is to itself its own lack of being. The being which the for-itself lacks is the in-itself. The for-itself arises as the nihilation of the in-itself and this nihilation is defined as the project toward the in-itself. Between the nihilated in-itself and the projected in-itself the for-itself is nothingness. Thus the end and the goal of the nihilation which I am is the in-itself. Thus human reality is the desire of being-in-itself. But the in-itself which it desires can not be pure contingent, absurd in-itself, comparable at every point to that which it encounters and which it nihilates. The nihilation, as we have seen, is in fact like a revolt of the in-itself, which nihilates itself against its contingency. To say that the for-itself lives its facticity, as we have seen in the chapter concerning the body, amounts to saying that the nihilation is the vain effort of a being to found its own being and that it is the withdrawal to found being which provokes the minute displacement by which nothingness enters into being. The being which forms the object of the desire of the for-itself is then an in-itself which would be to itself its own foundation; that is, which would be to its facticity in the same relation as the for-itself is to its motivations. In addition the for-itself, being the negation of the in-itself, could not desire the pure and simple return to the in-itself. Here as with Hegel, the negation of the negation can not bring us back to our point of departure. Quite the contrary, what the for-itself demands of the in-itself is precisely the totality detotalized—"In-itself nihilated in for-itself." In other words the for-itself projects *being as for-itself,* a being which is what it is. It is as being which is what it is not, and which is not what it is, that the for-itself projects being what it is. It is as consciousness that it wishes to have the impermeability and infinite density of the in-itself. It is as the nihilation of the in-itself and a perpetual evasion of contingency and of facticity that it wishes to be its own foundation. This is why the possible is projected in general as what the for-itself lacks in order to become in-itself-for-itself. The fundamental value which presides over this project is exactly the in-itself-for-itself; that is, the ideal of a consciousness which would be the foundation of its own being-in-itself by the pure consciousness which it would have of itself. It is this ideal which can be called God. Thus the best way to conceive of the fundamental project of human reality is to say that man is the being whose project is to be God. Whatever may be the myths and rites of the religion considered, God is first "sensible to the heart" of man as the one who identifies and defines him in his ultimate and fundamental project. If man possesses a pre-ontological comprehension of the being of God, it is not the great wonders of nature nor the power of society which have conferred it upon him. God, value and supreme end of transcendence, represents the permanent limit in terms of which man makes known to himself what he is. To be man means to reach toward being God. Or if you prefer, man fundamentally is the desire to be God. . . .

It should be possible to establish the human truth of the person, as we have attempted to do by an ontological phenomenology. The catalogue of empirical desires ought to be made the object of appropriate psychological investigations, observation and induction and, as needed, experience can serve to draw up this list. They will indicate to the philosopher the comprehensible relations which can unite to each other various desires and various patterns of behaviors, and will bring to light certain concrete connections between the subject of experience and "situations" experientially defined (which at bottom originate only from limitations applied in the name of positivity to the fundamental situation of the subject in the world). But in establishing and classifying fundamental desires of *individual persons* neither of these methods is appropriate. Actually there can be no question of determining *a priori* and ontologically what appears in all the unpredictability of a free act. This is why we shall limit ourselves here to indicating very summarily the possibilities of such a quest and its perspectives. The very fact that we can subject any man whatsoever to such an investigation—that is what belongs to human reality in general. Or, if you prefer, this is what can be established by an ontology. But the inquiry itself and its results are on principle wholly outside the possibilities of an ontology.

On the other hand, pure, simple empirical description can only give us catalogues and put us in the presence of pseudo-irreducibles (the desire to write, to swim, a taste for adventure, jealousy, *etc.*). It is not enough in fact to draw up a list of behavior patterns, of drives and inclinations, it is necessary also to *decipher* them; that is, it is necessary to know how to *question* them. This research can be conducted only according to the rules of a specific method. It is this method which we call existential psychoanalysis.

The *principle* of this psychoanalysis is that man is a totality and not a collection. Consequently he expresses himself as a whole in even his most insignificant and his most superficial behavior. In other words there is not a taste, a mannerism, or a human act which is not *revealing*.

The *goal* of psychoanalysis is to *decipher* the empirical behavior patterns of man; that is to bring out in the open the revelations which each one of them contains and to fix them conceptually.

Its *point of departure* is *experience;* its pillar of support is the fundamental, pre-ontological comprehension which man has of the human person. Although the majority of people can well ignore the indications contained in a gesture, a word, a sign and can look with scorn on the revelation which they carry, each human individual nevertheless possesses *a priori* the *meaning* of the revelatory value of these manifestations and is capable of deciphering them, at least if he is aided and guided by a helping hand. Here as elsewhere, truth is not encountered by chance; it does not belong to a domain where one must seek it without ever having any presentiment of its location, as one can go to look for the source of the Nile or of the Niger. It belongs *a priori* to human comprehension and the essential task is an hermeneutic; that is, a deciphering, a determination, and a conceptualization.

Its *method* is comparative. Since each example of human conduct symbolizes in its own manner the fundamental choice which must be brought to light, and since at the same time each one disguises this choice under its occasional character and its historical opportunity, only the comparison of these acts of conduct can effect the emergence of the unique revelation which they all express in a different way. The first outline of this method has been furnished for us by the psychoanalysis of Freud and his disciples. For this reason it will be profitable here to indicate more specifically the points where existential psychoanalysis will be inspired by psychoanalysis proper and those where it will radically differ from it.

Both kinds of psychoanalysis consider all objectively discernible manifestations of "psychic life" as symbols maintaining symbolic relations to the fundamental, total structures which constitute the individual person. Both consider that there are no primary givens such as hereditary dispositions, character, *etc.* Existential psychoanalysis recognizes nothing *before* the original upsurge of human freedom; empirical psychoanalysis holds that the original affectivity of the individual is virgin wax *before* its history. The libido is nothing besides its concrete fixations, save for a permanent possibility of fixing anything whatsoever upon anything whatsoever. Both consider the human being as a perpetual, searching historization. Rather than uncovering static, constant givens they discover the meaning, orientation, and adventures of this history. Due to this fact both consider man in the world and do not imagine that one can question the being of a man without taking into account all his *situation.* Psychological investigations aim at reconstituting the life of the subject from birth to the moment of the cure; they utilize all the objective documentation which they can find: letters, witnesses, intimate diaries, "social" information of every kind. What they aim at restoring is less a pure psychic event than a twofold structure: the crucial event of infancy and the psychic crystallization around this event. Here again we have to do with a *situation.* Each "historical" fact from this point of view will be considered at once as a *factor* of the psychic evolution and as a *symbol* of that evolution. For it is nothing in itself. It operates only according to the way in which it is taken and this very manner of taking it expresses symbolically the internal disposition of the individual.

Empirical psychoanalysis and existential psychoanalysis both search within an existing situation for a fundamental attitude which can not be expressed by simple, logical definitions because it is prior to all logic, and which requires reconstruction according to the laws of specific syntheses. Empirical psychoanalysis seeks to determine the *complex,* the very name of which indicates the polyvalence of all the meanings which are referred back to it. Existential psychoanalysis seeks to determine the *original choice.* This original choice operating in the face of the world and being a choice of position in the world is total like the complex, it is prior to logic like the complex. It is this which decides the attitude of the person when confronted with logic and principles, therefore there can be no possibility of questioning it in conformance to logic. It brings together in a prelogical synthesis the totality of the existent, and as such it is the center of reference for an infinity of polyvalent meanings.

Both our psychoanalyses refuse to admit that the subject is in a privileged position to proceed in these inquiries concerning himself. They equally insist on a strictly objective method, using as documentary evidence the data of reflection as well as the testimony of others. Of course the subject *can* undertake a psychoanalytic investigation of himself. But in this case he must renounce at the outset all benefit stemming from his peculiar position and must question himself exactly as if he were someone else. Empirical psychoanalysis in fact is based on the hypothesis of the existence of an unconscious psyche, which on principle escapes the intuition of the subject. Existential psychoanalysis rejects the hypothesis of the unconscious; it makes the psychic act co-extensive with consciousness. But if the fundamental project is fully experienced by the subject and hence wholly conscious, that certainly does not mean that it must by the same token be *known* by him; quite the contrary. The reader will perhaps recall the care we took in the Introduction to distinguish between consciousness and knowledge. To be sure, as we have seen earlier, reflection can be considered as a quasi-knowledge. But what it grasps at each moment is not the pure project of the for-itself as it is symbolically expressed—

often in several ways at once—by the concrete behavior which it apprehends. It grasps the concrete behavior itself; that is, the specific dated desire in all its characteristic network. It grasps at once symbol and symbolization. This apprehension, to be sure, is entirely constituted by a pre-ontological comprehension of the fundamental project; better yet, in so far as reflection is almost a non-thetic consciousness of itself as reflection, it *is* this same project, as well as the non-reflective consciousness. But it does not follow that it commands the instruments and techniques necessary to isolate the choice symbolized, to fix it by concepts, and to bring it forth into the full light of day. It is penetrated by a great light without being able to express what this light is illuminating. We are not dealing with an unsolved riddle as the Freudians believe; all is there, luminous; reflection is in full possession of it, apprehends all. But this "mystery in broad daylight" is due to the fact that this possession is deprived of the means which would ordinarily permit *analysis* and *conceptualization*. It grasps everything, all at once, without shading, without relief, without connections of grandeur—not that these shades, these values, these reliefs exist somewhere and are hidden from it, but rather because they must be established by another human attitude and because they can exist only *by means of* and *for* knowledge. Reflection, unable to serve as the basis for existential psychoanalysis, will then simply furnish us with the brute materials toward which the psychoanalyst must take an objective attitude. Thus only will he be able to *know* what he *already understands*. The result is that complexes uprooted from the depths of the unconscious, like projects revealed by existential psychoanalysis, will be apprehended *from the point of view of the Other*. Consequently the *object* thus brought into the light will be articulated according to the structures of the transcended-transcendence; that is, its being will be the being-for-others even if the psychoanalyst and the subject of the psychoanalysis are actually the same person. Thus the project which is brought to light by either kind of psychoanalysis can be only the totality of the individual human being, the irreducible element of the transcendence with the structure of *being-for-others*. What always escapes these methods of investigation is the project as it is for itself, the complex in its own being. This project-for-itself can be experienced only as a living possession; there is an incompatibility between existence for-itself and objective existence. But the object of the two psychoanalyses has in it nonetheless the *reality of a being;* the subject's knowledge of it can in addition contribute to *clarify* reflection, and that reflection can then become a possession which will be a quasi-knowing.

At this point the similarity between the two kinds of psychoanalysis ceases. They differ fundamentally in that empirical psychoanalysis has decided upon its own irreducible instead of allowing this to make itself known in a self-evident intuition. The libido or the will to power in actuality constitutes a psycho-biological residue which is not clear in itself and which does not appear to us as *being beforehand* the irreducible limit of the investigation. Finally it is experience which establishes that the foundation of complexes is this libido or this will to power; and these results of empirical inquiry are perfectly contingent, they are not convincing. Nothing prevents our conceiving *a priori* of a "human reality" which would not be expressed by the will to power, for the libido would not constitute the original, undifferentiated project.

On the other hand, the choice to which existential psychoanalysis will lead us, precisely because it is a choice, accounts for its original contingency, for the contingency of the choice is the reverse side of its freedom. Furthermore, inasmuch as it is established on the *lack of being,* conceived as a fundamental characteristic of being, it receives its legitimacy *as a choice,* and we know that we do not have to push further. Each result then will be at once fully contingent and legitimately irreducible. Moreover it will always remain *particular;* that is, we will not achieve as the ultimate goal of our investigation and the foundation of all behavior an abstract, general term, libido for example, which would be differentiated and made concrete first in complexes and then in detailed acts of conduct, due to the action of external facts and the history of the subject. On the contrary, it will be a choice which remains unique and which is from the start absolute concreteness. Details of behavior can express or *particularize* this choice, but they can not make it more concrete than it already is. That is because the choice is nothing other than the being of each human reality; this amounts to saying that a particular partial behavior *is* or expresses the original choice of this human reality since for human reality there is no difference between existing and choosing for itself. From this fact we understand that existential psychoanalysis does not have to proceed from the fundamental "complex," which is exactly the choice of being, to an abstraction like the libido which would explain it. The complex is the ultimate choice, it is the choice of being and *makes itself such.* Bringing it into the light will reveal it each time as evidently irreducible. It follows necessarily that the libido and the will to power will appear to existential psychoanalysis neither as general characteristics common to all mankind nor as irreducibles. At most it will be possible after the investigation to establish that they express by virtue of particular ensembles in certain subjects a fundamental choice which can not be reduced to either one of them. We have seen in fact that desire and sexuality in general express an original effort of the for-itself to recover its being which has become estranged through contact with the Other. The will to power also originally supposes being-for-others, the comprehension of the Other, and the choice of winning its own salvation by means of the Other. The foundation of this attitude must

be an original choice which would make us understand the radical identification of being-in-itself-for-itself with being-for-others.

The fact that the ultimate term of this existential inquiry must be
a *choice* distinguishes even better the psychoanalysis for which we have
outlined the method and principal features. It thereby abandons the
supposition that the environment acts mechanically on the subject under
consideration. The environment can act on the subject only to the exact
extent that he comprehends it; that is, transforms it into a situation.
Hence no objective description of this environment could be of any use
to us. From the start the environment conceived as a situation refers to
the for-itself which is choosing, just as the for-itself refers to the environment by the very fact that the for-itself is in the world. By renouncing
all mechanical causation, we renounce at the same time all *general*
interpretation of the symbolization confronted. Our goal could not be to
establish empirical laws of succession, nor could we constitute a universal
symbolism. Rather the psychoanalyst will have to rediscover at each step
a symbol functioning in the particular case which he is considering. If
each being is a totality, it is not conceivable that there can exist elementary
symbolic relationships (*e.g.,* the faeces = gold, or a pincushion = the
breast) which preserve a constant meaning in all cases; that is, which
remain unaltered when they pass from one meaningful ensemble to another
ensemble. Furthermore the psychoanalyst will never lose sight of the fact
that the choice is living and consequently can be *revoked* by the subject
who is being studied. We have shown in the preceding chapter the
importance of the *instant,* which represents abrupt changes in orientation
and the assuming of a new position in the face of an unalterable past.
From this moment on, we must always be ready to consider that symbols
change meaning and to abandon the symbol used hitherto. Thus existential
psychoanalysis will have to be completely flexible and adapt itself to the
slightest observable changes in the subject. Our concern here is to understand what is *individual* and often even instantaneous. The method
which has served for one subject will not necessarily be suitable to use
for another subject or for the same subject at a later period.

Precisely because the goal of the inquiry must be to discover a *choice*
and not a *state,* the investigator must recall on every occasion that his
object is not a datum buried in the darkness of the unconscious but a
free, conscious determination—which is not even resident in consciousness, but which is one with this consciousness itself. Empirical psychoanalysis, to the extent that its method is better than its principles, is often
in sight of an existential discovery, but it always stops part way. When
it thus approaches the fundamental choice, the resistance of the subject
collapses suddenly and he *recognizes* the image of himself which is
presented to him as if he were seeing himself in a mirror. This involuntary
testimony of the subject is precious for the psychoanalyst; he sees there

the sign that he has reached his goal; he can pass on from the investigation proper to the cure. But nothing in his principles or in his initial postulates permits him to understand or to utilize this testimony. Where could he get any such right? If the complex is really unconscious—that is, if there is a barrier separating the sign from the thing signified—how could the subject *recognize* it? Does the unconscious complex recognize itself? But haven't we been told that it lacks *understanding?* And if of necessity we granted to it the faculty of understanding the signs, would this not be to make of it by the same token a conscious unconscious? What is understanding if not to be conscious of what is understood? Shall we say on the other hand that it is the subject as conscious who recognizes the image presented? But how could he compare it with his true state since that is out of reach and since he has never had any knowledge of it? At most he will be able to judge that the psychoanalytic explanation of his case is a *probable* hypothesis, which derives its probability from the number of behavior patterns which it explains. His relation to this interpretation is that of a third party, that of the psychoanalyst himself; he has no privileged position. And if he *believes* in the probability of the psychoanalytic hypothesis, is this simple belief, which lives in the limits of his consciousness, able to effect the breakdown of the barriers which dam up the unconscious tendencies? The psychoanalyst doubtless had some obscure picture of an abrupt coincidence of conscious and unconscious. But he has removed all methods of conceiving of this coincidence in any positive sense.

Still, the enlightenment of the subject is a fact. There is an intuition here which is accompanied by evidence. The subject guided by the psychoanalyst does more and better than to give his agreement to an hypothesis; he touches it, he sees what it is. This is truly understandable only if the subject has never ceased being conscious of his deep tendencies; better yet, only if these drives are not distinguished from his conscious self. In this case as we have seen, the traditional psychoanalytic interpretation does not cause him to attain *consciousness* of what he is; it causes him to attain *knowledge* of what he is. It is existential psychoanalysis then which claims the final intuition of the subject as decisive.

This comparison allows us to understand better what an existential psychoanalysis must be if it is entitled to exist. It is a method destined to bring to light, in a strictly objective form, the subjective choice by which each living person makes himself a person; that is, makes known to himself what he is. Since what the method seeks is a *choice of being* at the same time as a *being,* it must reduce particular behavior patterns to fundamental relations—not of sexuality or of the will to power, but *of being*—which are expressed in this behavior. It is then guided from the start toward a comprehension of being and must not assign itself any other goal than to discover being and the mode of being of the being confronting this being. It is forbidden to stop before attaining this goal. It will utilize the comprehension of being which characterizes the investigator inasmuch as he is himself a human reality; and as it seeks to detach being from its symbolic expressions, it will have to rediscover each time on the basis of a comparative study of acts and attitudes, a symbol destined to decipher them. Its criterion of success will be the number of facts which its hypothesis permits it to explain and to unify as well as the self-evident intuition of the irreducibility of the end attained. To this criterion will be added in all cases where it is possible, the decisive testimony of the subject. The results thus achieved—that is, the ultimate ends of the individual—can then become the object of a classification, and it is by the comparison of these results that we will be able to establish general considerations about human reality as an empirical choice of its own ends. The behavior studied by this psychoanalysis will include not only dreams, failures, obsessions, and neuroses, but also and especially the thoughts of waking life, successfully adjusted acts, style, *etc.* This psychoanalysis has not yet found its Freud. At most we can find the foreshadowing of it in certain particularly successful biographies. We hope to be able to attempt elsewhere two examples in relation to Flaubert and Dostoevsky. But it matters little to us whether it now exists; the important thing is that it is possible.

Ethical Implications

Ontology itself can not formulate ethical precepts. It is concerned solely with what is, and we can not possibly derive imperatives from ontology's indicatives. It does, however, allow us to catch a glimpse of what sort of ethics will assume its responsibilities when confronted with a *human reality in situation.* Ontology has revealed to us, in fact, the origin and the nature of *value;* we have seen that value is the *lack* in relation to which the for-itself determines its being as *a lack.* By the very fact that the for-itself *exists,* as we have seen, value arises to haunt its being-for-itself. It follows that the various tasks of the for-itself can be made the object of an existential psychoanalysis, for they all aim at producing the missing synthesis of consciousness and being in the form of value or self-cause. Thus existential psychoanalysis is *moral description,* for it releases to us the ethical meaning of various human projects. It indicates to us the necessity of abandoning the psychology of interest along with any utilitarian interpretation of human conduct—by revealing to us the *ideal* meaning of all human attitudes. These meanings are beyond egoism and altruism, beyond also any behavior which is called *disinterested*. Man makes himself man in order to be God, and selfness considered from this point of view can appear to be an egoism; but precisely because there is no common measure between human reality and the self-cause which it wants to be, one could just as well say that man loses himself in order that the self-cause may exist. We will consider then that all human existence is a passion, the famous *self-interest* being only one way freely chosen among others to realize this passion.

But the principal result of existential psychoanalysis must be to make us repudiate the *spirit of seriousness*. The spirit of seriousness has two characteristics: it considers values as transcendent givens independent of human subjectivity, and it transfers the quality of "desirable" from the ontological structure of things to their simple material constitution. For the spirit of seriousness, for example, *bread* is desirable because it is *necessary* to live (a value written in an intelligible heaven) and because bread *is* nourishing. The result of the serious attitude, which as we know rules the world, is to cause the symbolic values of things to be drunk in by their empirical idiosyncrasy as ink by a blotter; it puts forward the opacity of the desired object and posits it in itself as a desirable irreducible. Thus we are already on the moral plane but concurrently on that of bad faith, for it is an ethics which is ashamed of itself and does not dare speak its name. It has obscured all its goals in order to free itself from anguish. Man pursues being blindly by hiding from himself the free project which is this pursuit. He makes himself such that he is *waited for* by all the tasks placed along his way. Objects are mute demands, and he is nothing in himself but the passive obedience to these demands.

Existential psychoanalysis is going to reveal to man the real goal of his pursuit, which is being as a synthetic fusion of the in-itself with the for-itself; existential psychoanalysis is going to acquaint man with his passion. In truth there are many men who have practiced this psychoanalysis on themselves and who have not waited to learn its principles in order to make use of them as a means of deliverance and salvation. Many men, in fact, know that the goal of their pursuit is being; and to the extent that they possess this knowledge, they refrain from appropriating things for their own sake and try to realize the symbolic appropriation of their being-in-itself. But to the extent that this attempt still shares in the spirit of seriousness and that these men can still believe that their mission of effecting the existence of the in-itself-for-itself is written in things, they are condemned to despair; for they discover at the same time that all human activities are equivalent (for they all tend to sacrifice man in order that the self-cause may arise) and that all are on principle doomed to failure. Thus it amounts to the same thing whether one gets drunk alone or is a leader of nations. If one of these activities takes precedence over the other, this will not be because of its real goal but because of the degree of consciousness which it possesses of its ideal goal; and in this case it will be the quietism of the solitary drunkard which will take precedence over the vain agitation of the leader of nations.

But ontology and existential psychoanalysis (or the spontaneous and empirical application which men have always made of these disciplines) must reveal to the moral agent that he is *the being by whom values exist.* It is then that his freedom will become conscious of itself and will reveal itself in anguish as the unique source of value and the nothingness by which the *world* exists. As soon as freedom discovers the quest for being and the appropriation of the in-itself as *its own possibles,* it will apprehend by and in anguish that they are possibles only on the ground of the possibility of other possibles. But hitherto although possibles could be chosen and rejected *ad libitum,* the theme which made the unity of all choices of possibles was the value or the ideal presence of the *ens causa sui.* What will become of freedom if it turns its back upon this value? Will freedom carry this value along with it whatever it does and even in its very turning back upon the in-itself-for-itself? Will freedom be reapprehended from behind by the value which it wishes to contemplate? Or will freedom, by the very fact that it apprehends itself as a freedom in relation to itself, be able to put an end to the reign of this value? In particular is it possible for freedom to take itself for a value as the source of all value, or must it necessarily be defined in relation to a transcendent value which haunts it? And in case it could will itself as its own possible and its determining value, what would this mean? A freedom which wills itself freedom is in fact a being-which-is-not-what-it-is and which-is-what-it-is-not, and which chooses as the ideal of being, being-what-it-is-not and not-being-what-it-is.

This freedom chooses then not to *recover* itself but to flee itself, not to coincide with itself but to be always at a distance *from* itself. What are we to understand by this being which wills to hold itself in awe, to be at a distance from itself? Is it a question of bad faith or of another fundamental attitude? And can one *live* this new aspect of being? In particular will freedom by taking itself for an end escape all *situation?* Or on the contrary, will it remain situated? Or will it situate itself so much the more precisely and the more individually as it projects itself further in anguish as a conditioned freedom and accepts more fully its responsibility as an existent by whom the world comes into being? All these questions, which refer us to a pure and not an accessory reflection, can find their reply only on the ethical plane. We shall devote to them a future work.

From *Existentialism and Human Emotions*

Existentialism

What is meant by the term *existentialism?* . . .

Actually, it is the least scandalous, the most austere of doctrines. It is intended strictly for specialists and philosophers. Yet it can be defined easily. What complicates matters is that there are two kinds of existentialist; first, those who are Christian, among whom I would include Jaspers and Gabriel Marcel, both Catholic; and on the other hand the atheistic existentialists, among whom I class Heidegger, and then the French existentialists and myself. What they have in common is that they think that existence precedes essence, or, if you prefer, that subjectivity must be the starting point.

Just what does that mean? Let us consider some object that is manufactured, for example, a book or a paper-cutter: here is an object which has been made by an artisan whose inspiration came from a concept. He referred to the concept of what a paper-cutter is and likewise to a known method of production, which is part of the concept, something which is, by and large, a routine. Thus, the paper-cutter is at once an object produced in a certain way and, on the other hand, one having a specific use; and one can not postulate a man who produces a paper-cutter but does not know what it is used for. Therefore, let us say that, for the paper-cutter, essence—that is, the ensemble of both the production routines and the properties which enable it to be both produced and defined—precedes existence. Thus, the presence of the paper-cutter or book in front of me is determined. Therefore, we have here a technical view of the world whereby it can be said that production precedes existence.

When we conceive God as the Creator, He is generally thought of as a superior sort of artisan. Whatever doctrine we may be considering, whether one like that of Descartes or that of Leibnitz, we always grant that will more or less follows understanding or, at the very least, accompanies it, and that when God creates He knows exactly what He is creating. Thus, the concept of man in the mind of God is comparable to the concept of paper-cutter in the mind of the manufacturer, and, following certain techniques and a conception, God produces man, just as the artisan, following a definition and a technique, makes a paper-cutter. Thus, the individual man is the realization of a certain concept in the divine intelligence.

Atheistic existentialism, which I represent, . . . states that if God does not exist, there is at least one being in whom existence precedes essence, a being who exists before he can be defined by any concept, and that this being is man, or, as Heidegger says, human reality. What is meant here by saying that existence precedes essence? It means that, first of all, man exists, turns up, appears on the scene, and, only afterwards, defines himself. If man, as the existentialist conceives him, is indefinable, it is because at first he is nothing. Only afterward will he be something, and he himself will have made what he will be. Thus, there is no human nature, since there is no God to conceive it. Not only is man what he conceives himself to be, but he is also only what he wills himself to be after this thrust toward existence.

Man is nothing else but what he makes of himself. Such is the first principle of existentialism. It is also what is called subjectivity, the name we are labeled with when charges are brought against us. But what do we mean by this, if not that man has a greater dignity than a stone or table? For we mean that man first exists, that is, that man first of all is the being who hurls himself toward a future and who is conscious of imagining himself as being in the future. Man is at the start a plan which is aware of itself, rather than a patch of moss, a piece of garbage, or a cauliflower; nothing exists prior to this plan; there is nothing in heaven; man will be what he will have planned to be. Not what he will want to be. Because by the word "will" we generally mean a conscious decision, which is subsequent to what we have already made of ourselves. I may want to belong to a political party, write a book, get married; but all that is only a manifestation of an earlier, more spontaneous choice that is called "will." But if existence really does precede essence, man is responsible for what he is. Thus, existentialism's first move is to make every man aware of what he is and to make the full responsibility of his existence rest on him. And when we say that a man is responsible for himself, we do not only mean that he is responsible for his own individuality, but that he is responsible for all men.

The word subjectivism has two meanings, and our opponents play on the two. Subjectivism means, on the one hand, that an individual chooses and makes himself; and, on the other, that it is impossible for man to transcend human subjectivity. The second of these is the essential meaning of existentialism. When we say that man chooses his own self, we mean that every one of us does likewise; but we also mean by that that in making this choice he also chooses all men. In fact, in creating the man that we want to be, there is not a single one of our acts which does not at the same time create an image of man as we think he ought to be. To choose to be this or that is to affirm at the same time the value of what we choose, because we can never choose evil. We always choose the good, and nothing can be good for us without being good for all.

If, on the other hand, existence precedes essence, and if we grant that we exist and fashion our image at one and the same time, the image is valid for everybody and for our whole age. Thus, our responsibility is much greater than we might have supposed, because it involves all mankind. If I am a workingman and choose to join a Christian trade-union rather than be a communist, and if by being a member I want to show that the best thing for man is resignation, that the kingdom of man is not of this world, I am not only involving my own case—I want to be resigned for everyone. As a result, my action has involved all humanity. To take a more individual matter, if I want to marry, to have children; even if this marriage depends solely on my own circumstances or passion or wish, I am involving all humanity in monogamy and not merely myself. Therefore, I am responsible for myself and for everyone else. I am creating a certain image of man of my own choosing. In choosing myself, I choose man.

This helps us understand what the actual content is of such rather grandiloquent words as anguish, forlornness, despair. As you will see, it's all quite simple.

First, what is meant by anguish? The existentialists say at once that man is anguish. What that means is this: the man who involves himself and who realizes that he is not only the person he chooses to be, but also a lawmaker who is, at the same time, choosing all mankind as well as himself, can not help escape the feeling of his total and deep responsibility. Of course, there are many people who are not anxious; but we claim that they are hiding their anxiety, that they are fleeing from it. Certainly, many people believe that when they do something, they themselves are the only ones involved, and when someone says to them, "What if everyone acted that way?" they shrug their shoulders and answer, "Everyone doesn't act that way." But really, one should always ask himself, "What would happen if everybody looked at things that way?" There is no escaping this disturbing thought except by a kind of double-dealing. A man who lies and makes excuses for himself by saying "not everybody does that," is someone with an uneasy conscience, because the act of lying implies that a universal value is conferred upon the lie.

Anguish is evident even when it conceals itself. This is the anguish that Kierkegaard called the anguish of Abraham. You know the story: an angel has ordered Abraham to sacrifice his son; if it really were an angel who has come and said, "You are Abraham, you shall sacrifice your son," everything would be all right. But everyone might first wonder, "Is it really an angel, and am I really Abraham? What proof do I have?" . . .

There is no question here of the kind of anguish which would lead to quietism, to inaction. It is a matter of a simple sort of anguish that anybody who has had responsibilities is familiar with. For example, when a military officer takes the responsibility for an attack and sends a certain number of men to death, he chooses to do so, and in the main he alone makes the choice. Doubtless, orders come from above, but they are too broad; he interprets them, and on this interpretation depend the lives of ten or fourteen or twenty men. In making a decision he can not help having a certain anguish. All leaders know this anguish. That doesn't keep them from acting; on the contrary, it is the very condition of their action. For it implies that they envisage a number of possibilities, and when they choose one, they realize that it has value only because it is chosen. We shall see that this kind of anguish, which is the kind that existentialism describes, is explained, in addition, by a direct responsibility to the other men whom it involves. It is not a curtain separating us from action, but is part of action itself.

When we speak of forlornness, a term Heidegger was fond of, we mean only that God does not exist and that we have to face all the consequences of this. The existentialist is strongly opposed to a certain kind of secular ethics which would like to abolish God with the least possible expense. About 1880, some French teachers tried to set up a secular ethics which went something like this: God is a useless and costly hypothesis; we are discarding it; but, meanwhile, in order for there to be an ethics, a society, a civilization, it is essential that certain values be taken seriously and that they be considered as having an *a priori* existence. It must be obligatory, *a priori,* to be honest, not to lie, not to beat your wife, to have children, etc., etc. So we're going to try a little device which will make it possible to show that values exist all the same, inscribed in a heaven of ideas, though otherwise God does not exist. In other words— and this, I believe, is the tendency of everything called reformism in France—nothing will be changed if God does not exist. We shall find ourselves with the same norms of honesty, progress, and humanism, and we shall have made of God an outdated hypothesis which will peacefully die off by itself.

The existentialist, on the contrary, thinks it very distressing that God does not exist, because all possibility of finding values in a heaven of ideas disappears along with Him; there can no longer be an *a priori* Good, since there is no infinite and perfect consciousness to think it. Nowhere is it written that the Good exists, that we must be honest, that we must not lie; because the fact is we are on a plane where there are only men. Dostoievsky said, "If God didn't exist, everything would be possible." That is the very starting point of existentialism. Indeed, everything is permissible if God does not exist, and as a result man is forlorn, because neither within him nor without does he find anything to cling to. He can't start making excuses for himself.

If existence really does precede essence, there is no explaining things away by reference to a fixed and given human nature. In other words, there is no determinism, man is free, man is freedom. On the other hand, if God does not exist, we find no values or commands to turn to which legitimize our conduct. So, in the bright realm of values, we have no excuse behind us, nor justification before us. We are alone, with no excuses.

That is the idea I shall try to convey when I say that man is condemned to be free. Condemned, because he did not create himself, yet, in other respects is free; because, once thrown into the world, he is responsible for everything he does. The existentialist does not believe in the power of passion. He will never agree that a sweeping passion is a ravaging torrent which fatally leads a man to certain acts and is therefore an excuse. He thinks that man is responsible for his passion.

To give you an example which will enable you to understand forlornness better, I shall cite the case of one of my students who came to see me under the following circumstances: his father was on bad terms with his mother, and, moreover, was inclined to be a collaborationist; his older brother had been killed in the German offensive of 1940, and the young man, with somewhat immature but generous feelings, wanted to avenge him. His mother lived alone with him, very much upset by the half-treason of her husband and the death of her older son; the boy was her only consolation.

The boy was faced with the choice of leaving for England and joining the Free French Forces—that is, leaving his mother behind—or remaining with his mother and helping her to carry on. He was fully aware that the woman lived only for him and that his going-off—and perhaps his death—would plunge her into despair. He was also aware that every act that he did for his mother's sake was a sure thing, in the sense that it was helping her to carry on, whereas every effort he made toward going off and fighting was an uncertain move which might run aground and prove completely useless; for example, on his way to England he might, while passing through Spain, be detained indefinitely in a Spanish camp; he might reach England or Algiers and be stuck in an office at a desk job. As a result, he was faced with two very different kinds of action: one, concrete, immediate, but concerning only one individual; the other concerned an incomparably vaster group, a national collectivity, but for that very reason was dubious, and might be interrupted en route. And, at the same time, he was wavering between two kinds of ethics. On the one hand, an ethics of sympathy, of personal devotion; on the other, a broader ethics, but one whose efficacy was more dubious. He had to choose between the two.

Who could help him choose? Christian doctrine? No. Christian doctrine says, "Be charitable, love your neighbor, take the more rugged path, etc., etc." But which is the more rugged path? Whom should he love as a brother? The fighting man or his mother? Which does the greater good, the vague act of fighting in a group, or the concrete one of helping a particular human being to go on living? Who can decide *a priori?* Nobody. No book of ethics can tell him. The Kantian ethics says, "Never treat any person as a means, but as an end." Very well, if I stay with my mother, I'll treat her as an end and not as a means; but by virtue of this very fact, I'm running the risk of treating the people around me who are fighting, as means; and, conversely, if I go to join those who are fighting, I'll be treating them as an end, and, by doing that, I run the risk of treating my mother as a means.

If values are vague, and if they are always too broad for the concrete and specific case that we are considering, the only thing left for us is to trust our instincts. That's what this young man tried to do; and when I saw him, he said, "In the end, feeling is what counts. I ought to choose whichever pushes me in one direction. If I feel that I love my mother enough to sacrifice everything else for her—my desire for vengeance, for action, for adventure—then I'll stay with her. If, on the contrary, I feel that my love for my mother isn't enough, I'll leave."

But how is the value of a feeling determined? What gives his feeling for his mother value? Precisely the fact that he remained with her. I may say that I like so-and-so well enough to sacrifice a certain amount of money for him, but I may say so only if I've done it. I may say "I love my mother well enough to remain with her" if I have remained with her. The only way to determine the value of this affection is, precisely, to perform an act which confirms and defines it. But, since I require this affection to justify my act, I find myself caught in a vicious circle. . . .

From these few reflections it is evident that nothing is more unjust than the objections that have been raised against us. Existentialism is nothing else than an attempt to draw all the consequences of a coherent atheistic position. It isn't trying to plunge man into despair at all. But if one calls every attitude of unbelief despair, like the Christians, then the word is not being used in its original sense. Existentialism isn't so atheistic that it wears itself out showing that God doesn't exist. Rather, it declares that even if God did exist, that would change nothing. There you've got our point of view. Not that we believe that God exists, but we think that the problem of His existence is not the issue. In this sense existentialism is optimistic, a doctrine of action, and it is plain dishonesty for Christians to make no distinction between their own despair and ours and then to call us despairing.

From *The War Diaries, November 1939– March 1940*

Value, Freedom, and Responsibility

The characteristic of human reality, from the point of view which concerns us, is that it motivates itself without being its own foundation. What we call its freedom is that it is never anything without motivating itself to be it. Nothing can ever happen to it *from outside*. This comes from the fact that human reality is first of all consciousness: in other words, it's nothing that it isn't consciousness of being. It motivates its own reaction to the event from outside, and the event within it is that reaction. It only *discovers* the world, moreover, on the occasion of its own reactions. It is thus free in the sense that its reactions, and the way the world appears to it, are integrally attributable to it. But total freedom can exist only for a being which is its own foundation, in other words responsible for its facticity. Facticity is nothing other than the fact that there's a human reality in the world at every moment. It's a *fact*. It's not deduced from anything, as such, and isn't reducible to anything. And the world of values, necessity and freedom—all of it hangs on this primitive, absurd fact. If one examines any consciousness whatsoever, one will find nothing that's not attributable to it.

But the fact that *there* is a consciousness that motivates its own structure is irreducible and absurd. Each consciousness includes in itself the consciousness both of being responsible for itself and of not being the cause of its own being. This facticity is not an 'outside', but it's not an 'inside' either. It's not the passivity of a created and supported being, but neither is it the total independence of the *ens causa sui*. But if one considers things better, one sees clearly that this facticity doesn't mean that consciousness has its foundation in something other than itself—in God, for example—since any transcendent foundation of consciousness would kill consciousness with its own hands, while giving birth to it. It's merely the fact that consciousness exists *without* any foundation. It's a kind of nothingness proper to consciousness, which we shall call gratuitousness.

This impalpable gratuitousness is there, stretched out across the whole of consciousness, nowhere and everywhere. This gratuitousness could be compared to a fall into the world, and the motivations of consciousness to a kind of acceleration the falling stone would be free to impart to itself. Put otherwise, the speed of fall depends on consciousness, but not the fall itself. It's at the level of gratuitousness that the possibility of death intervenes for consciousness. And for that reason, it isn't one of *its* possibilities, or its innermost possibility, as Heidegger claims. But neither is it a possible external to it. The mortality of consciousness and its facticity are as one. Thus consciousness, which cannot *conceive* its death, since it still conceives like consciousness, encloses it existentially within itself at the very level of the nothingness that permeates it through and through. There's no being-about-to-die in the Heideggerian sense, but every consciousness is numbed by Nothingness and by death, without even being able to turn on this Nothingness and look it in the face.

The specific structure of consciousness is to throw itself forward into the world to escape this gratuitousness. But it throws itself there for its own purpose, in order to be its own foundation in the future. To say that human reality exists for its own purpose comes to the same thing as saying that consciousness throws itself towards the future in order to be its own foundation there. In other words, it projects a certain future of itself beyond the world, on the horizon, in the illusion that when it becomes that future, it will be so in the guise of its own foundation. This illusion is transcendental, and derives from the fact that consciousness, free foundation of its possibles, is the foundation of its being to come, without being able to be the foundation of its present being. For this being-*to-come,* as we've seen, though in relation to consciousness it doesn't have the transcendence of a real possible in relation to a thing, is nevertheless charged with a noematic transcendence, Being-to-come of consciousness, it's for that very reason no longer *itself* consciousness. And, consequently, it's in fact totally relative to the latter. That's what is called will. And here my description links up with the one I was giving on Thursday 23 and Friday 24. What escapes from consciousness here is the fact that when this future becomes present, be it exactly as it *had to* be, it will be consciousness—and will consequently draw its motivation from itself, despite being numbed by gratuitousness and nothingness.

Thus the first value and first object of will is: to be its own foundation. This mustn't be understood as an empty psychological desire, but as the transcendental structure of human reality. There is original fall and striving for redemption—and that fall with that striving constitutes human reality. Human reality is moral because it wishes to be its own foundation. And man is a 'being of distances' because it's only as a possible that he can be his foundation. Man is a being who flees from himself into the future. Throughout all his undertakings he seeks, not to preserve himself, as people have often said, nor to increase himself, but to found himself. And at the end of each undertaking he finds himself anew just as he was: gratuitous to the marrow. Whence those notorious disappointments after effort, after triumph, after love. Whence the creator's effort. Whence, as the lowest manifestation of this desire, the sense of ownership. (In these last two cases, there is a transfer to objects: the *created* object symbolically represents human reality founded upon itself; the *possessed* object symbolically represents human reality in possession of itself. Love is the effort of human reality to be a foundation of itself in the Other.) Whence the deep origins of the sense of having *rights:* the right consists in covering over the facticity of human reality by choosing ourselves as existent-that-exists-because-it-has-the-right-to-exist. But this grasping of oneself as existing by right can take place only on the occasion of particular objects over which we claim to have rights.

Thus the source of all value, and the supreme value, is the substantiality or nature of the being which is its own foundation. The substantiality forms part of human nature, but only in the capacity of a project, a constituent value. And human reality differs from pure consciousness inasmuch as it projects a value before itself: it is consciousness self-motivating itself [*se motivant elle-même*] towards this end.

Life is the transcendent, psychic object constructed by human reality in search of its own foundation.

However, this search for the absolute is also a flight before oneself. To found substantiality for the future is to flee the gratuitousness given at present. Human reality loses its way trying to found itself. The *life* it secretes is a totality only in appearance, it is gnawed backwards by death, *right* is an infamous lie, love is denied by *jealousy* or gripped by the impossibility of being for the Other the foundation of human reality. Human reality remains the prisoner of its unjustifiable facticity, with itself on the horizon of its search, everywhere.

It then comes to know weariness, and to deliver itself from the torment of freedom by pleading its facticity; in other words, it tries to conceal from itself the fact that it is condemned for ever to be its own motivation, by the fact that it is not its own foundation. It abandons itself; it makes itself a thing; it renounces its possibles, they're no longer its *own* possibles, it grasps them as external possibles analogous to those of things. For example, last year war was able to appear to everybody as an external possible, a mechanical eruption that escaped any particular human reality, just as the rolling marble is escaped by the fold in the carpet that will stop it. We shall designate this state buffeted human reality, for it realizes itself as buffeted amid the possibles, like a plank amid the waves.

But this state itself is inauthentic. For human reality, out of weariness, here conceals from itself the fact that it is condemned to self-motivate itself. And it self-motivates itself to conceal that fact. It resigns functions, it makes itself a thing, but it carries out this resignation by its own act. And this resignation itself is only one episode in its search for substantiality. It resigns to escape the constraint of values, to realize substantiality by some other means, etc. etc. It will, for example, refuse to assume an event on the pretext that it has refused the principle of it. From this point of view, the classic example of buffeted consciousness is Paul saying to me the other day: 'Me, a soldier? I consider myself a civilian in military disguise.' That would be all very fine if he weren't making himself a soldier—whatever he may say to the contrary—through his volitions, his perceptions, his emotions. A soldier: that's to say, adopting his superiors' orders as his own in order to execute them himself; hence complicit down to his arms that carry the rifle and his legs that march; a soldier in his perceptions, his emotions and his volitions. He thus stubbornly continues to *flee* what he's *making of himself*—which plunges him into a state of wretched, diffuse anguish.

This state of misery *can* be a reason for consciousness to return to an accurate view of itself and stop fleeing itself. It's not a question of its seeking any value other than substantiality if it did, it would cease to be *human* consciousness. The value that will assign it its new attitude remains the supreme value: being its own foundation. It will no more stop asserting—and willing—this value than cognitive consciousness, after Husserl's ἐποχή trans. "suspension",* ceases to posit the world. It is from the first impetus towards substantiality that human reality must draw the value-reason that allows it to recover itself. For buffeted consciousness can quite freely will, by its plenary authenticity, to accomplish its effort to found itself. And this not at all because authenticity is original value, superior to inauthenticity, but rather as one corrects a clumsy, ineffective effort by purifying it of all useless, parasitic actions. Thus authenticity is a value but not primary; it gives itself as a means to arrive at substantiality. It suppresses that which, in the search, is *flight*. But, of course, this value of authenticity is merely *proposed*. Consciousness alone can self-motivate itself to effect the conversion.

Which is this conversion? The search for a foundation requires that one *assume* that which one founds. If the act of founding is anterior to the existent one founds, as in the case of creation, assumption is contained a priori in the act of founding. But if, as in the case that concerns us, it's a question of an effort to found that which already exists in fact, assumption must precede foundation, as an intuition which reveals *what* one is founding. To assume does not at all mean to accept, though in certain cases the two go together. When I assume, I assume *in order* to make a given use of what I am assuming. Here, I am assuming *in order to* found. Moreover, to assume means to adopt as one's own, to claim responsibility. Thus the assumptive conversion that presents itself as a

---

* In Husserl, a 'placing in parenthesis' or suspension.

value for consciousness is, therefore, nothing other than an intuition of the will, which consists in adopting human reality as one's own. And, by that adoption, human reality is revealed to itself in an act of non-thematic comprehension. It is revealed, not as it would be known through concepts, but as it is *willed*.

But if assumption presents itself as a value of authenticity, it is because it already exists in advance. Value really only bids human freedom to do what it is doing. Consciousness self-motivates itself: it is free, except to acquire the freedom to be free no longer. We have seen that it renounces its possibles only by acquiring others. It can *freely make itself* akin to things, but it cannot *be* a thing. All that it is, it makes itself be. All that happens to it must happen to it by its own doing: that is the law of its freedom. Thus the first assumption that human reality can and must make, when looking back on itself, is the assumption of its freedom. Which can be expressed by the following formula: *one never has any excuse*. For it will be recalled that buffeted consciousness was a consciousness that pleaded the excuse of its facticity. But we should be clear that facticity has no relevance here. Granted, it is thanks to facticity that I'm thrown into war. But what war will be for me, what face it will reveal to me, what I shall myself be in war and for war—all this I shall be freely and am responsible for.

There is something intolerable here, but which one cannot complain of since it is also elusive: this obligation to *shoulder* what happens to me. This, no doubt, is what gave birth to the religious notion of *trial* sent me by Heaven. But, by refusing excuses and assuming my freedom, I appropriate it. Of course, it's a question not just of *recognizing* that one has no excuse, but also of *willing* it. For all my cowardices, all my stupidities, all my lies, I bear the responsibility. The point is not to say, with the saint: 'It's too much, O Lord, it's too much.' Nothing is ever too much. For—at the very moment when I lose my grip, when my body 'overcomes me', when under physical torment I confess what I wanted to keep secret—it is of my own accord, through the free consciousness of my torment, that I decide to confess. Jules Romains says that, in earlier wars, it was the defeated party who himself decided he'd been defeated (for those were not totalitarian wars, and he still had resources in men, weapons and wealth at his disposal). Well, similarly, it is always upon me that the terrible responsibility falls of acknowledging I am defeated; and, at whatever point I stop, it is I who have decided I couldn't go on any longer—hence, I could have gone on a bit longer still. But if I admit— and wish—never to have any excuse, my freedom becomes *mine,* I assume for ever that terrible responsibility.

The assumption of my freedom must, of course, be accompanied by that of my facticity. Which means, I must will it. And, no doubt, will it *in order to found it*. But we shall see what the result will be. What does it mean to will one's facticity? First, it is to acknowledge that one no more has rights than one has excuses. I grant myself no right for anything to happen to me other than what does happen to me. And, there again, I am only willing what is. All that happens to me has a dual nature: on the one hand, it is *given* me by virtue of my facticity and gratuitousness—and whatever it may be is still too much, in relation to what is due me, since my existence itself is *given;* on the other hand, I am responsible for it, since I self-motivate myself to discover it, as I noted above. Consequently, I have no *right* for it not to happen to me. For example, in the case of war.

6

Existential Ethics: Simone de Beauvoir and Albert Camus

SIMONE DE BEAUVOIR AND THE ETHICS OF AMBIGUITY

Simone de Beauvoir (1908–1986) had a close personal and intellectual relationship with Sartre for almost forty years. It is not surprising, therefore, that they influenced each other's thinking on certain fundamental issues in philosophy. Although de Beauvoir took over many Sartrean ideas, she accomplished a feat that Sartre never did, namely, she wrote a book on ethics. *The Ethics of Ambiguity* is an attempt to develop methods or principles that can help guide us in the practical problem of deciding what we ought to do. Her work is of particular interest to us, since in her attempt to address the question of how an existentialist ethics is possible she incorporates many of the central ideas of the philosophers we have considered. A useful way to approach de Beauvoir's ethics is by considering the ethical problems surrounding the tragically ambiguous human condition.

In our discussion of Sartre we saw that the existing individual is a being whose being is not to be. That is, by virtue of the intentional nature of consciousness, we are always separated from the object of consciousness, which constitutes the essence of consciousness. Thus, all attempts to achieve our goals must fail. A goal is a transcendent object of knowledge, and therefore we can never realize the synthesis of our consciousness of our goal with our goal. We are always at a distance from ourselves. Since we can never be for-ourselves what we are for others, we can never realize the type of being that we strive to be. Of course we can set goals for ourselves, but we can never merge our being qua for-itself or consciousness with the goals we set. For example, if I want to be a philosophy teacher I can perform actions that will lead to that result, but I can never be a philosophy teacher as an object in the world, that is, as a chair or a piece of chalk is an object in the world. I can never have the essence of "being a philosophy teacher," since that would be to deny that at any moment I have the possibility of giving up my choice to be a philosophy teacher. Thus, for Sartre, the ambiguity of the human condition is reflected in the paradox of each particular human being. Each of us, by virtue of our transcendence, is a lack of being and thus a continual striving to achieve a completeness of being that can never be attained. Since any attempt to achieve our ultimate goals must end in failure, existentialism seems to offer only an ethics of despair.

The situation is even worse, since the goals we set can have no external justification. Existentialists reject the spirit of seriousness which treats values as objective qualities of objects. However, if values are not qualities that attach themselves onto objects or goals independent of human consciousness, then it would appear that "existentialism encloses man in a sterile anguish, in an empty subjectivity. It is incapable of furnishing him with any principle for making choices" (p. 388). How can we hope to have an ethics that provides principles of conduct when we believe that no extrinsic justification can be given for our actions?

These problems arise from the Sartrean notion of freedom. If we are not what we are, then we can never exist as pure facticity—as a being-in-itself—whose essence is the source of our free and spontaneous choices. Our freedom always separates us from our essence and thus prevents us from being our essence. Furthermore, although our freedom, which is nothing other than consciousness itself, can never merge with being, our freedom can "disclose being." Consciousness discloses being, in that it is in virtue of consciousness that we structure the world and have goals and projects. Moreover, the value of a goal is created by the freedom that chooses it. For that very reason it would appear that whether we choose to be a drunkard or a leader of nations makes no difference to the value of a goal. Each human existence has the freedom to choose those values that will determine its actions, and for that reason there would seem to be nothing to choose between "good" and "bad" actions or goals. How, then, can an existential philosophy avoid despair and distinguish between moral and immoral actions?

De Beauvoir tackles these difficulties head on. At the outset she says we should realize that those who condemn existentialism as being a useless philosophy, and a philosophy of despair and absurdity, are making this judgment from an "objective" point of view. That is, they are treating these judgments as attributing objective properties to the pronouncements of existentialist philosophy. But such objections beg the question of whether or not objective value judgments can be given. The notions of "useful" and "useless" have no meaning apart from subjectivity. Whether existentialism is absurd or despairing depends on the life of the existing individual. Admittedly, the particular life of an existing individual

> *has* no reason to will itself. But this does not mean that it can not justify itself, that it can not *give itself* reasons for being that it does not *have*. And indeed Sartre tells us that man makes himself this lack of being *in order that* there might be being. The term *in order that* clearly indicates an intentionality. It is not in vain that man nullifies being. Thanks to him, being is disclosed and he desires this disclosure. There is an original type of attachment to being which is not the relationship "wanting to be" but rather "wanting to disclose being." (p. 389)

This passage is important for several reasons. First, it reveals that although we want to achieve the being that we will never be, our original attachment to being is that of "wanting to disclose being." We want to "disclose being," and that means we want to be the creator of the world and its values. Thus, although it may not be possible to be what we want to be, it is possible to disclose being.

To disclose being is to be at the center of the world where responsibilities lie, for it is the place from which meanings, values, and interpretations are made. De Beauvoir says that

> To wish for the disclosure of the world and to assert oneself as freedom are one and the same movement. Freedom is the source from which all significations and all values spring. . . . *To will oneself moral and to will oneself free are one and the same decision.* (p. 391: italics added)

To disclose being is to will oneself free, and to will oneself free is to will oneself master of the situation one has created. Thus, for example, in my capacity as a free being I may will a certain future or a certain goal. To will oneself free is to adhere to a definite set of concrete activities that reflect one's project. One creates values not merely by thinking them, but by living in accordance with them. This leads to the second important point in de Beauvoir's ethics.

Although no justification for our actions or goals can be found outside of us, we can justify our goals from the inside, as it were, by having the strength to persevere in our will. We can give ourselves reasons for our projects. As de Beauvoir puts it,

> The value of the chosen end is confirmed and, reciprocally, the genuineness of the choice is manifested concretely through patience, courage, and fidelity. . . . This living confirmation can not be merely contemplative and verbal. It is carried out in an act. The goal toward which I surpass myself must appear to me as a point of departure toward a new act of surpassing. (pp. 391–392)

To will oneself free and to be moral are the same thing. This is all very reminiscent of Nietzsche. We do not have an ethical theory that will tell us what do to in any given situation, but we have a general method for making decisions. One creates values through a genuine choice, and the genuineness of the choice is evidenced by the degree to which one is willing to stick to the project one affirms.

Yet if we are "essentially" free, then what moral content can there be in the idea of willing ourselves free? For "It is contradictory to set freedom up as something conquered if at first it is something given."[1] De Beauvoir has an answer to this. Although it is true that we cannot escape our freedom, "one can choose not to will himself free. In laziness, heedlessness, capriciousness, cowardice, impatience, one contests the meaning of the project at the very moment that one defines it."[2] There are two points here. First, one can choose goals, but not persevere in an attempt to realize them. Second, one can, in bad faith, try to avoid the anguish of having to make a choice. We have seen the mechanisms that allow us to avoid the consciousness of our freedom. Although these mechanisms do not enable us to avoid having to make a choice, they do enable us to avoid making a choice "rightly." A "right" choice does not deny freedom, but develops it. Indeed, insofar as the existentialist prescribes values we could say, "the value that we should strive for in our actions is the liberation or freedom of men". (p. 73)

For de Beauvoir, the freedom to be sought for is not simply one's own individual freedom, but the liberation of others as well. "To will oneself free is to will others free."[3] Perhaps what de Beauvoir has in mind is that my ability to choose projects and give meaning to certain tasks depends on the world containing a certain structure independently of me. In other words, those projects that I find meaningful will depend to some extent on others having already given meaning to certain projects in the world. But for others to introduce meaning and values into the world they must possess the freedom to do so. Thus, to be moral, to will oneself free, one must oppose oppression. As de Beauvoir puts it,

> Thus, we can set up point number one: the good of an individual or a

> group of individuals requires that it be taken as an absolute end of our action, but we are not authorized to decide upon this end *a priori.* To put the point positively, the precept will be to treat the other . . . as a freedom so that his end may be freedom. . . . (p. 399)

In the abstract this certainly seems right, but when we consider concrete cases the situation becomes ambiguous.

For example, one person's freedom almost always concerns that of other individuals. So, how are we to decide when we are choosing among freedoms, that is, when one person's freedom conflicts with that of another or others? And what are we to do when someone chooses to flee from their freedom in an effort to become a thing, or in some other way chooses a course of action we judge to be against their best interest? Are we justified in opposing willful acts that one considers perverted?

There are no a priori answers to such ethically ambiguous questions. On the one hand, we must not be an accomplice in flight, and yet on the other hand we must allow the Other freedom to make mistakes, for it is through failure that an individual can assert oneself as a freedom. To be moral is to take freedom as an end, but one must constantly question whether one's goal is a genuine assertion of freedom and whether or not the means justifies and is compatible with the end. Thus, Existentialist ethics is individualistic in

> that it accords to the individual an absolute value and that it recognizes in him alone the power of laying the foundations of his own existence. This individualism does not lead to the anarchy of personal whim. . . . Man is free, but he finds his law in his very freedom. [The individual] justifies his existence by a movement which, like freedom, springs from his heart but which leads outside of him. (p. 401)

CAMUS AND THE ABSURD

As we near the end of this book it is fitting to have a selection from Albert Camus' (1913–1960) famous work, *The Myth of Sisyphus,* for it brings us back to the starting point of our explorations, namely, the concrete, living, particular, existing individual. Camus approaches the existing individual through a consideration of the meaning of life, and the question of whether life is or is not worth living, that is, the question of suicide. Camus is concerned with the existential relevance of the absurd and with the consequences that follow from the existence of absurdity. What, then, is the absurd?

For Camus, the absurdity of life is encountered both emotionally and intellectually. We feel that life is absurd in several ways. The habitual and daily routine of life inevitably leads to us to the question, "Why?" What is it all for? Every day off to work, then back home, then watch TV, then get up again, and so on. What is the point of such a routine existence? There is, furthermore, the feeling of solitude and isolation that Camus expresses in the following passage:

> . . . in a universe suddenly divested of illusions and lights, man feels an alien, a stranger. His exile is without remedy since he is deprived of the memory of a lost home or the hope of a promised land. This divorce between man and his life, the actor and his setting, is properly the feeling of absurdity. (pp. 405–406)

Like Nietzsche, Camus recognizes the death of God and with it the isolation one must feel when values can no longer be believed to come from without. We seek some link that will ground our life in something greater, something solid, something true, something outside of ourselves, but all is illusion.

There is also a feeling of absurdity when we contemplate the passage of time. On the one hand, we live for the future. We think of ourselves as essentially what we will be. We make plans for ourselves and look forward to the future when our plans will be realized. On the other hand, "a day comes when a man notices or says that he is thirty" (p. 407). The passage of time is also the passage of our lives and the end of our future. Thus, what we long for is at the same time what we ought to reject. Death is a fact of life, and as such it can make us feel that none of our strivings and efforts make any sense or have any extrinsic justification. As Camus puts it,

> No code of ethics and no effort are justifiable *a priori* in the face of the cruel mathematics that command our condition. (p. 407)

Before drawing the implications of the absurdities of our condition, Camus recounts certain intellectual experiences of the absurd.

Ultimately, Camus is attempting to show that we have a desire to understand the universe, ourselves, and our place in it, but that such an understanding can never be achieved. He says that

> So long as the mind keeps silent in the motionless world of its hopes, everything is reflected and arranged in the unity of its nostalgia. But with its first move this world cracks and tumbles: an infinite number of shimmering fragments is offered to the understanding. We must despair of ever reconstructing the familiar, calm surface which would give us peace of heart. (p. 409)

Camus proceeds to define the absurd as the individual's desire for clarity linked with an irrational universe:

> The world in itself is not reasonable, that is all that can be said. But what is absurd is the confrontation of this irrational and the wild longing for clarity whose call echoes in the human heart. (p. 410)

Thus, Camus is certain of both his wish to reduce the world to a rational and intelligible principle and an intellectual recognition that such unity and clarity is impossible. What consequences are we to draw from the existence of absurdity? What is the existential relevance of this absurd situation? Is there any reason to go on living if all hopes and plans lead to death?

In the section on "Absurd Freedom" Camus attends to these questions. At the outset we can say that his answer is optimistic. According to Camus, there is a happiness, a joy, and a repose in living with a consciousness of the absurd. At the moment when one gives up all illusions of finding meaning in life and the universe

> This hell of the present is his Kingdom at last. All problems recover their sharp edge. . . . Spiritual conflicts become embodied and return to the abject and magnificent shelter of man's heart. None of them is settled. But all are transfigured. (p. 412)

Thus, the first consequence Camus draws from the truth of the absurd is *revolt*. Revolt is

> a constant confrontation between man and his own obscurity. It challenges the world anew every second. . . . It is that constant presence of man in his own eyes. It is not aspiration, for it is devoid of hope. That revolt is the certainty of a crushing fate, without the resignation that ought to accompany it. (p. 413)

The position of revolt does not solve the problems that lead to life's meaninglessness, but it involves a lucid contemplation of the absurd that provides freedom and happiness.

The freedom Camus refers to is not the metaphysical freedom that can be bestowed upon an individual by God. It is not the faculty of free will or the eternal freedom that encompasses the belief that "someday" one's aims will be fulfilled. The "absurd man" achieves an inner freedom when he abandons the illusion upon which he has been living. Previously we were restricted by the future, by our belief in what we could be, in what we could hope for. As Camus sees it, we become a slave to our goals:

> To the extent to which he imagined a purpose to his life, he adapted himself

> to the demands of a purpose to be achieved and became the slave of his liberty. Thus, I could not act otherwise than as the father (or the engineer or the leader of a nation, or the post-office sub-clerk) that I am preparing to be. (p. 415)

We achieve an "absurd freedom" when we realize that we cannot find meaning in the universe or in our connection with the universe, and that any meaning which we construct perishes with our death. Thus,

> the absurd man feels released from everything outside that passionate attention crystallizing in him. He enjoys a freedom with regard to common rules. . . . The return to consciousness, the escape from everyday sleep represent the first steps of absurd freedom. (p. 415)

Camus seems to be making the same point as Nietzsche: Objective values have a kind of power over us; we become slaves to them. Thus, once we give up the illusion of freedom we are liberated. An absurd freedom is liberating, but it is also absurd because it leaves us alone. And yet it is "the only reasonable freedom: that which a human heart can experience and live" (p. 416).

We can now turn to the question of suicide. Camus rejects suicide as the inevitable or even the proper outcome of his reflections on the absurd. To choose to solve the problem of meaninglessness by rushing toward the future is really a pseudo solution. One cannot overcome meaninglessness, but one can gain a measure of happiness from it by keeping it alive, by contemplating it. Thus, Camus claims that life will be lived all the better if it has no meaning. For the existence of absurdity leads to lucidity, an absurd freedom and happiness.

The hero Sisyphus is at once tragic and absurd, and yet it is his fate that ensures his happiness:

> The lucidity that was to constitute his torture at the same time crowns his victory. . . . One does not discover the absurd without being tempted to write a manual of happiness. (p. 418)

Recall that Sisyphus is condemned to push a huge stone up a mountain and then watch it fall, only to repeat the process forever. Camus says, "If the descent is thus sometimes performed in sorrow, it can also take place in joy" (p. 418). Once we have recognized the meaninglessness of life, and have become conscious of the absurd, we achieve a measure of victory over it. "One must imagine Sisyphus happy" (p. 419).

DE BEAUVOIR SELECTIONS

From *The Ethics of Ambiguity*

Ambiguity and Freedom

"The continuous work of our life," says Montaigne, "is to build death." He quotes the Latin poets: *Prima, quae vitam dedit, hora corpsit.* And again: *Nascentes morimur.* Man knows and thinks this tragic ambivalence which the animal and the plant merely undergo. A new paradox is thereby introduced into his destiny. "Rational animal," "thinking reed," he escapes from his natural condition without, however, freeing himself from it. He is still a part of this world of which he is a consciousness. He asserts himself as a pure internality against which no external power can take hold, and he also experiences himself as a thing crushed by the dark weight of other things. At every moment he can grasp the non-temporal truth of his existence. But between the past which no longer is and the future which is not yet, this moment when he exists is nothing. This privilege, which he alone possesses, of being a sovereign and unique subject amidst a universe of objects, is what he shares with all his fellow-men. In turn an object for others, he is nothing more than an individual in the collectivity on which he depends. . . .

At the present time there still exist many doctrines which choose to leave in the shadow certain troubling aspects of a too complex situation. But their attempt to lie to us is in vain. Cowardice doesn't pay. Those reasonable metaphysics, those consoling ethics with which they would like to entice us only accentuate the disorder from which we suffer. Men of today seem to feel more acutely than ever the paradox of their condition. They know themselves to be the supreme end to which all action should be subordinated, but the exigencies of action force them to treat one another as instruments or obstacles, as means. The more widespread their mastery of the world, the more they find themselves crushed by uncontrollable forces. Though they are masters of the atomic bomb, yet it is created only to destroy them. Each one has the incomparable taste in his mouth of his own life, and yet each feels himself more insignificant than an insect within the immense collectivity whose limits are one with the earth's. Perhaps in no other age have they manifested their grandeur more brilliantly, and in no other age has this grandeur been so horribly flouted. In spite of so many stubborn lies, at every moment, at every opportunity, the truth comes to light, the truth of life and death, of my solitude and my bond with the world, of my freedom and my servitude, of the insignificance and the sovereign importance of each man and all men. There was Stalingrad and there was Buchenwald, and neither of the two wipes out the other. Since we do not succeed in fleeing it, let us therefore try to look the truth in the face. Let us try to assume our fundamental ambiguity. It is in the knowledge of the genuine conditions of our life that we must draw our strength to live and our reason for acting.

From the very beginning, existentialism defined itself as a philosophy of ambiguity. It was by affirming the irreducible character of ambiguity that Kierkegaard opposed himself to Hegel, and it is by ambiguity that, in our own generation, Sartre, in *Being and Nothingness,* fundamentally defined man, that being whose being is not to be, that subjectivity which realizes itself only as a presence in the world, that engaged freedom, that surging of the for-oneself which is immediately given for others. But it is also claimed that existentialism is a philosophy of the absurd and of despair. It encloses man in a sterile anguish, in an empty subjectivity. It is incapable of furnishing him with any principle for making choices. Let him do as he pleases. In any case, the game is lost. Does not Sartre declare, in effect, that man is a "useless passion," that he tries in vain to realize the synthesis of the for-oneself and the in-oneself, to make himself God? . . .

That is true. And it is also true that in *Being and Nothingness* Sartre has insisted above all on the abortive aspect of the human adventure. It is only in the last pages that he opens up the perspective for an ethics. However, if we reflect upon his descriptions of existence, we perceive that they are far from condemning man without recourse.

The failure described in *Being and Nothingness* is definitive, but it is also ambiguous. Man, Sartre tells us, is "a being who *makes himself* a lack of being *in order that there might be* being." That means, first of all, that his passion is not inflicted upon him from without. He chooses it. It is his very being and, as such, does not imply the idea of unhappiness. If this choice is considered as useless, it is because there exists no absolute value before the passion of man, outside of it, in relation to which one might distinguish the useless from the useful. The word "useful" has not yet received a meaning on the level of description where *Being and Nothingness* is situated. It can be defined only in the human world established by man's projects and the ends he sets up. In the original helplessness from which man surges up, nothing is useful, nothing is useless. It must therefore be understood that the passion to which man has acquiesced finds no external justification. No outside appeal, no objective necessity permits of its being called useful. It *has* no reason to will itself. But this does not mean that it can not justify itself, that it can not *give itself* reasons for being that it does not *have*. And indeed Sartre tells us that man makes himself this lack of being *in order that* there might be being. The term *in order that* clearly indicates an intentionality. It is not in vain that man nullifies being. Thanks to him, being is disclosed and he desires this disclosure. There is an original type of attachment to being which is not the relationship "wanting to be" but rather "wanting to disclose being." Now, here there is not failure, but rather success. This end, which man proposes to himself by making himself lack of being, is, in effect, realized by him. By uprooting himself from the world, man makes himself present to the world and makes the world present to him. I should like to be the landscape which I am contemplating, I should like this sky, this quiet water to think themselves within me, that it might be I whom they express in flesh and bone, and I remain at a distance. But it is also by this distance that the sky and the water exist before me. My contemplation is an excruciation only because it is also a joy. I can not appropriate the snow field where I slide. It remains foreign, forbidden, but I take delight in this very effort toward an impossible possession. I experience it as a triumph, not as a defeat. This means that man, in his vain attempt to *be* God, makes himself exist *as* man, and if he is satisfied with this existence, he coincides exactly with himself. It is not granted him to exist without tending toward this being which he will never be. But it is possible for him to want this tension even with the failure which it involves. His being is lack of being, but this lack has a way of being which is precisely existence.

The first implication of such an attitude is that the genuine man will not agree to recognize any foreign absolute. When a man projects into an ideal heaven that impossible synthesis of the for-itself and the in-itself that is called God, it is because he wishes the regard of this existing Being to change his existence into being; but if he agrees not to be in order to exist genuinely, he will abandon the dream of an inhuman objectivity. He will understand that it is not a matter of being right in the eyes of a God, but of being right in his own eyes. Renouncing the thought of seeking the guarantee for his existence outside of himself, he will also refuse to believe in unconditioned values which would set themselves up athwart his freedom like things. Value is this lacking-being of which freedom *makes itself* a lack; and it is because the latter makes itself a lack that value appears. It is desire which creates the desirable, and the project which sets up the end. It is human existence which makes values spring up in the world on the basis of which it will be able to judge the enterprise in which it will be engaged. But first it locates itself beyond any pessimism, as beyond any optimism, for the fact of its original springing forth is a pure contingency. Before existence there is no more reason to exist than not to exist. The lack of existence can not be evaluated since it is the fact on the basis of which all evaluation is defined. It can not be compared to anything for there is nothing outside of it to serve as a term of comparison. This rejection of any extrinsic justification also confirms the rejection of an original pessimism which we posited at the beginning. Since it is unjustifiable from without, to declare from without that it is unjustifiable is not to condemn it. And the truth is that outside of existence there is nobody. Man exists. For him it is not a question of wondering whether his presence in the world is useful, whether life is worth the trouble of being lived. These questions make no sense. It is a matter of knowing whether he wants to live and under what conditions.

But if man is free to define for himself the conditions of a life which is valid in his own eyes, can he not choose whatever he likes and act however he likes? Dostoievsky asserted, "If God does not exist, everything is permitted." Today's believers use this formula for their own advantage. To re-establish man at the heart of his destiny is, they claim, to repudiate all ethics. However, far from God's absence authorizing all license, the contrary is the case, because man is abandoned on the earth, because his acts are definitive, absolute engagements. He bears the responsibility for a world which is not the work of a strange power, but of himself, where his defeats are inscribed, and his victories as well. A God can pardon, efface, and compensate. But if God does not exist, man's faults are inexpiable. If it is claimed that, whatever the case may be, this earthly stake has no importance, this is precisely because one invokes that in-human objectivity which we declined at the start. One can not start by saying that our earthly destiny *has* or *has not* importance, for it depends upon us to give it importance. It is up to man to make it important to be a man, and he alone can feel his success or failure. . . .

As for us, whatever the case may be, we believe in freedom. Is it true that this belief must lead us to despair? Must we grant this curious paradox: that from the moment a man recognizes himself as free, he is prohibited from wishing for anything?

On the contrary, it appears to us that by turning toward this freedom we are going to discover a principle of action whose range will be universal. The characteristic feature of all ethics is to consider human life as a game that can be won or lost and to teach man the means of winning. Now, we have seen that the original scheme of man is ambiguous: he wants to be, and to the extent that he coincides with this wish, he fails. All the plans in which this will to be is actualized are condemned; and the ends circumscribed by these plans remain mirages. Human transcendence is vainly engulfed in those miscarried attempts. But man also wills himself to be a disclosure of being, and if he coincides with this wish, he wins, for the fact is that the world becomes present by his presence in it. But the disclosure implies a perpetual tension to keep being at a certain distance, to tear oneself from the world, and to assert oneself as a freedom. To wish for the disclosure of the world and to assert oneself as freedom are one and the same movement. Freedom is the source from which all significations and all values spring. It is the original condition of all justification of existence. The man who seeks to justify his life must want freedom itself absolutely and above everything else. At the same time that it requires the realization of concrete ends, of particular projects, it requires itself universally. It is not a ready-made value which offers itself from the outside to my abstract adherence, but it appears (not on the plane of facility, but on the moral plane) as a cause of itself. It is necessarily summoned up by the values which it sets up and through which it sets itself up. It can not establish a denial of itself, for in denying itself, it would deny the possibility of any foundation. To will oneself moral and to will oneself free are one and the same decision.

    . . . But we also ought to ask ourselves whether one can will oneself free in any matter, whatsoever it may be. It must first be observed that this will is developed in the course of time. It is in time that the goal is pursued and that freedom confirms itself. And this assumes that it is realized as a unity in the unfolding of time. One escapes the absurdity of the clinamen only by escaping the absurdity of the pure moment. An existence would be unable to found itself if moment by moment it crumbled into nothingness. That is why no moral question presents itself to the child as long as he is still incapable of recognizing himself in the past or seeing himself in the future. It is only when the moments of his life begin to be organized into behaviour that he can decide and choose. The value of the chosen end is confirmed and, reciprocally, the genuineness of the choice is manifested concretely through patience, courage, and fidelity. If I leave behind an act which I have accomplished, it becomes a thing by falling into the past. It is no longer anything but a stupid and opaque fact. In order to prevent this metamorphosis, I must ceaselessly return to it and justify it in the unity of the project in which I am engaged. Setting up the movement of my transcendence requires that I never let it uselessly fall back upon itself, that I prolong it indefinitely. Thus I can not genuinely desire an end today without desiring it through my whole existence, insofar as it is the future of this present moment and insofar as it is the surpassed past of days to come. To will is to engage myself to persevere in my will. This does not mean that I ought not aim at any limited end. I may desire absolutely and forever a revelation of a moment. This means that the value of this provisional end will be confirmed indefinitely. But this living confirmation can not be merely contemplative and verbal. It is carried out in an act. The goal toward which I surpass myself must appear to me as a point of departure toward a new act of surpassing. Thus, a creative freedom develops happily without ever congealing into unjustified facticity. The creator leans upon anterior creations in order to create the possibility of new creations. His present project embraces the past and places confidence in the freedom to come, a confidence which is never disappointed. It discloses being at the end of a further disclosure. At each moment freedom is confirmed through all creation. . . .

It can be seen that, on the one hand, freedom can always save itself, for it is realized as a disclosure of existence through its very failures, and it can again confirm itself by a death freely chosen. But, on the other hand, the situations which it discloses through its project toward itself do not appear as equivalents. It regards as privileged situations those which permit it to realize itself as indefinite movement; that is, it wishes to pass beyond everything which limits its power; and yet, this power is always limited. Thus, just as life is identified with the will-to-live, freedom always appears as a movement of liberation. It is only by prolonging itself through the freedom of others that it manages to surpass death itself and to realize itself as an indefinite unity. Later on we shall see what problems such a relationship raises. For the time being it is enough for us to have established the fact that the words "to will oneself free" have a positive and concrete meaning. If man wishes to save his existence, as only he himself can do, his original spontaneity must be raised to the height of moral freedom by taking itself as an end through the disclosure of a particular content. . . .

It must again be called to mind that the supreme end at which man must aim is his freedom, which alone is capable of establishing the value of every end; thus, comfort, happiness, all relative goods which human projects define, will be subordinated to this absolute condition of realization. The freedom of a single man must count more than a cotton or rubber harvest; although this principle is not respected in fact, it is usually recognized theoretically. But what makes the problem so difficult is that it is a matter of choosing between the negation of one freedom or another: every war supposes a discipline, every revolution a dictatorship, every political move a certain amount of lying; action implies all forms of enslaving, from murder to mystification. Is it therefore absurd in every case? Or, in spite of everything, are we able to find, within the very outrage that it implies, reasons for wanting one thing rather than another?

Ambiguity

The notion of ambiguity must not be confused with that of absurdity. To declare that existence is absurd is to deny that it can ever be given a meaning; to say that it is ambiguous is to assert that its meaning is never fixed, that it must be constantly won. Absurdity challenges every ethics; but also the finished rationalization of the real would leave no room for ethics; it is because man's condition is ambiguous that he seeks, through failure and outrageousness, to save his existence. Thus, to say that action has to be lived in its truth, that is, in the consciousness of the antinomies which it involves, does not mean that one has to renounce it. In *Plutarch Lied* Pierrefeu rightly says that in war there is no victory which can not be regarded as unsuccessful, for the objective which one aims at is the total annihilation of the enemy and this result is never attained; yet there are wars which are won and wars which are lost. So is it with any activity; failure and success are two aspects of reality which at the start are not perceptible. That is what makes criticism so easy and art so difficult: the critic is always in a good position to show the limits that every artist gives himself in choosing himself; painting is not given completely either in Giotto or Titian or Cezanne; it is sought through the centuries and is never finished; a painting in which all pictorial problems are resolved is really inconceivable; painting itself is this movement toward its own reality; it is not the vain displacement of a millstone turning in the void; it concretizes itself on each canvas as an absolute existence. Art and science do not establish themselves despite failure but through it; which does not prevent there being truths and errors, masterpieces and lemons, depending upon whether the discovery or the painting has or has not known how to win the adherence of human consciousnesses; this amounts to saying that failure, always ineluctable, is in certain cases spared and in others not.

It is interesting to pursue this comparison; not that we are likening action to a work of art or a scientific theory, but because in any case human transcendence must cope with the same problem: it has to found itself, though it is prohibited from ever fulfilling itself. Now, we know that neither science nor art ever leaves it up to the future to justify its present existence. In no age does art consider itself as something which is paving the way for Art: so-called archaic art prepares for classicism only in the eyes of archaeologists; the sculptor who fashioned the Korai of Athens rightfully thought that he was producing a finished work of art; in no age has science considered itself as partial and lacunary; without believing itself to be definitive, it has however, always wanted to be a total expression of the world, and it is in its totality that in each age it again raises the question of its own validity. There we have an example of how man must, in any event, assume his finiteness: not by treating his existence as transitory or relative but by reflecting the infinite within it, that is, by treating it as absolute. There is an art only because at every moment art has willed itself absolutely; likewise there is a liberation of man only if, in aiming at itself, freedom is achieved absolutely in the very fact of aiming at itself. This requires that each action be considered as a finished form whose different moments, instead of fleeing toward the future in order to find there their justification, reflect and confirm one another so well that there is no longer a sharp separation between present and future, between means and ends.

But if these moments constitute a unity, there must be no contradiction among them. Since the liberation aimed at is not a *thing* situated in an unfamiliar time, but a movement which realizes itself by tending to conquer, it can not attain itself if it denies itself at the start; action can not seek to fulfill itself by means which would destroy its very meaning. So much so that in certain situations there will be no other issue for man than rejection. In what is called political realism there is no room for rejection because the present is considered as transitory; there is rejection only if man lays claim in the present to his existence as an absolute value; then he must absolutely reject what would deny this value. Today, more or less consciously in the name of such an ethics, we condemn a magistrate who handed over a communist to save ten hostages and along with him all the Vichyites who were trying "to make the best of things:" It was not a matter of rationalizing the present such as it was imposed by the German occupation, but of rejecting it unconditionally. The resistance did not aspire to a positive effectiveness; it was a negation, a revolt, a martyrdom; and in this negative movement freedom was positively and absolutely confirmed.

In one sense the negative attitude is easy; the rejected object is given unequivocally and unequivocally defines the revolt that one opposes to it; thus, all French anti-fascists were united during the occupation by their common resistance to a single oppressor. The return to the positive encounters many more obstacles, as we have well seen in France where divisions and hatreds were revived at the same time as were the parties. In the moment of rejection, the antinomy of action is removed, and means and end meet; freedom immediately sets itself up as its own goal and fulfills itself by so doing. But the antinomy reappears as soon as freedom again gives itself ends which are far off in the future; then, through the resistances of the given, divergent means offer themselves and certain ones come to be seen as contrary to their ends. It has often been observed that revolt alone is pure. Every construction implies the outrage of dictatorship, of violence. This is the theme, among others, of Koestler's *Gladiators*. Those who, like this symbolic *Spartacus,* do not want to retreat from the outrage and resign themselves to impotence, usually seek refuge in the values of seriousness. That is why, among individuals as well as collectivities, the negative moment is often the most genuine. Goethe, Barres, and Aragon, disdainful or rebellious in their romantic youth, shattered old conformisms and thereby proposed a real, though incomplete, liberation. But what happened later on? Goethe became a servant of the state, Barres of nationalism, and Aragon of Stalinist conformism. We know how the seriousness of the Catholic Church was substituted for the Christian spirit, which was a rejection of dead Law, a subjective rapport of the individual with God through faith and charity; the Reformation was a revolt of subjectivity, but Protestantism in turn changed into an objective moralism in which the seriousness of works replaced the restlessness of faith. As for revolutionary humanism, it accepts only rarely the tension of permanent liberation; it has created a Church where salvation is bought by membership in a party as it is bought elsewhere by baptism and indulgences. We have seen that this recourse to the serious is a lie; it entails the sacrifice of man to the Thing, of freedom to the Cause. In order for the return to the positive to be genuine it must involve negativity, it must not conceal the antinomies between means and end, present and future; they must be lived in a permanent tension; one must retreat from neither the outrage of violence nor deny it, or, which amounts to the same thing, assume it lightly. Kierkegaard has said that what distinguishes the pharisee from the genuinely moral man is that the former considers his anguish as a sure sign of his virtue; from the fact that he asks himself, "Am I Abraham?" he concludes, "I am Abraham;" but morality resides in the painfulness of an indefinite questioning. The problem which we are posing is not the same as that of Kierkegaard; the important thing to us is to know whether, in given conditions, Isaac must be killed or not. But we also think that what distinguishes the tyrant from the man of good will is that the first rests in the certainty of his aims, whereas the second keeps asking himself, "Am I really working for the liberation of men? Isn't this end contested by the sacrifices through which I aim at it?" In setting up its ends, freedom must put them in parentheses, confront them at each moment with that absolute end which it itself constitutes, and contest, in its own name, the means it uses to win itself.

It will be said that these considerations remain quite abstract. What must be done, practically? Which action is good? Which is bad? To ask such a question is also to fall into a naive abstraction. We don't ask the physicist, "Which hypotheses are true?" Nor the artist, "By what procedures does one produce a work whose beauty is guaranteed?" Ethics does not furnish recipes any more than do science and art. One can merely propose methods. Thus, in science the fundamental problem is to make the idea adequate to its content and the law adequate to the facts; the logician finds that in the case where the pressure of the given fact bursts the concept which serves to comprehend it, one is obliged to invent another concept; but he can not define *a priori* the moment of invention, still less foresee it. Analogously, one may say that in the case where the content of the action falsifies its meaning, one must modify not the meaning, which is here willed absolutely, but the content itself; however, it is impossible to determine this relationship between meaning and content abstractly and universally: there must be a trial and decision in each case. But likewise just as the physicist finds it profitable to reflect on the conditions of scientific invention and the artist on those of artistic creation without expecting any ready-made solutions to come from these reflections, it is useful for the man of action to find out under what conditions his undertakings are valid. We are going to see that on this basis new perspectives are disclosed.

In the first place, it seems to us that the individual as such is one of the ends at which our action must aim. Here we are at one with the point of view of Christian charity, the Epicurean cult of friendship, and Kantian moralism which treats each man as an end. He interests us not merely as a member of a class, a nation, or a collectivity, but as an individual man. This distinguishes us from the systematic politician who cares only about collective destinies; and probably a tramp enjoying his bottle of wine, or a child playing with a balloon, or a Neapolitan lazzarone loafing in the sun in no way helps in the liberation of man; that is why the abstract will of the revolutionary scorns the concrete benevolence which occupies itself in satisfying desires which have no morrow. However, it must not be forgotten that there is a concrete bond between freedom and existence; to will man free is to will there to *be* being, it is to will the disclosure of being in the joy of existence; in order for the idea of liberation to have a concrete meaning, the joy of existence must be asserted in each one, at every instant; the movement toward freedom assumes its real, flesh and blood figure in the world by thickening into pleasure, into happiness. If the satisfaction of an old man drinking a glass of wine counts for nothing, then production and wealth are only hollow myths; they have meaning only if they are capable of being retrieved in individual and living joy. The saving of time and the conquest of leisure have no meaning if we are not moved by the laugh of a child at play. If we do not love life on our own account and through others, it is futile to seek to justify it in any way.

However, politics is right in rejecting benevolence to the extent that the latter thoughtlessly sacrifices the future to the present. The ambiguity of freedom, which very often is occupied only in fleeing from itself, introduces a difficult equivocation into relationships with each individual taken one by one. Just what is meant by the expression "to love others"? What is meant by taking them as ends? In any event, it is evident that we are not going to decide to fulfill the will of every man. There are cases where a man positively wants evil, that is, the enslavement of other men, and he must then be fought. It also happens that, without harming anyone, he flees from his own freedom, seeking passionately and alone to attain the being which constantly eludes him. If he asks for our help, are we to give it to him? We blame a man who helps a drug addict intoxicate himself or a desperate man commit suicide, for we think that rash behavior of this sort is an attempt of the individual against his own freedom; he must be made aware of his error and put in the presence of the real demands of his freedom. Well and good. But what if he persists? Must we then use violence? There again the serious man busies himself dodging the problem; the values of life, of health, and of moral conformism being set up, one does not hesitate to impose them on others. But we know that this pharisaism can cause the worst disasters: lacking drugs, the addict may kill himself. It is no more necessary to serve an abstract ethics obstinately than to yield without due consideration to impulses of pity or generosity; violence is justified only if it opens concrete possibilities to the freedom which I am trying to save; by practising it I am willy-nilly assuming an engagement in relation to others and to myself; a man whom I snatch from the death which he had chosen has the right to come and ask me for means and reasons for living; the tyranny practised against an invalid can be justified only by his getting better; whatever the purity of the intention which animates me, any dictatorship is a fault for which I have to get myself pardoned. Besides, I am in no position to make decisions of this sort indiscriminately; the example of the unknown person who throws himself in to the Seine and whom I hesitate whether or not to fish out is quite abstract; in the absence of a concrete bond with this desperate person my choice will never be anything but a contingent facticity. If I find myself in a position to do violence to a child, or to a melancholic, sick, or distraught person the reason is that I also find myself charged with his upbringing, his happiness, and his health: I am a parent, a teacher, a nurse, a doctor, or a friend . . . So, by a tacit agreement, by the very fact that I am solicited, the strictness of my decision is accepted or even desired; the more seriously I accept my responsibilities, the more justified it is. That is why love authorizes severities which are not granted to indifference. What makes the problem so complex is that, on the one hand, one must not make himself an accomplice of that flight from freedom that is found in heedlessness, caprice, mania, and passion, and that, on the other hand, it is the abortive movement of man toward being which is his very existence, it is through the failure which he has assumed that he asserts himself as a freedom. To want to prohibit a man from error is to forbid him to fulfill his own existence, it is to deprive him of life. At the beginning of Claudel's *The Satin Shoe,* the husband of Dona Prouheze, the Judge, the Just, as the author regards him, explains that every plant needs a gardener in order to grow and that he is the one whom heaven has destined for his young wife; beside the fact that we are shocked by the arrogance of such a thought (for how does he know that he is this enlightened gardener? Isn't he merely a jealous husband?) this likening of a soul to a plant is not acceptable; for, as Kant would say, the value of an act lies not in its *conformity* to an external model, but in its internal truth. We object to the inquisitors who want to create faith and virtue from without; we object to all forms of fascism which seek to fashion the happiness of man from without; and also the paternalism which thinks that it has done something for man by prohibiting him from certain possibilities of temptation, whereas what is necessary is to give him reasons for resisting it.

Thus, violence is not immediately justified when it opposes willful acts which one considers perverted; it becomes inadmissible if it uses the pretext of ignorance to deny a freedom which, as we have seen, can be practised within ignorance itself. Let the "enlightened elites" strive to change the situation of the child, the illiterate, the primitive crushed beneath his superstitions; that is one of their most urgent tasks; but in this very effort they must respect a freedom which, like theirs, is absolute. They are always opposed, for example, to the extension of universal suffrage by adducing the incompetence of the masses, of women, of the natives in the colonies; but this forgetting that man always has to decide by himself in the darkness, that he must want beyond what he knows. If infinite knowledge were necessary (even supposing that it were conceivable), then the colonial administrator himself would not have the right to freedom; he is much further from perfect knowledge than the most backward savage is from him. . . .

However, the "enlightened elite" objects, one does not let a child dispose of himself, one does not permit him to vote. This is another sophism. To the extent that woman or the happy or resigned slave lives in the infantile world of ready-made values, calling them "an eternal child" or "a grown-up child" has some meaning, but the analogy is only partial. Childhood is a particular sort of situation: it is a natural situation whose limits are not created by other men and which is thereby not comparable to a situation of oppression; it is a situation which is common to all men and which is temporary for all; therefore, it does not represent a limit which cuts off the individual from his possibilities, but, on the contrary, the moment of a development in which new possibilities are won. The child is ignorant because he has not yet had the time to acquire knowledge, not because this time has been refused him. To treat him as a child is not to bar him from the future but to open it to him; he needs to be taken in hand, he invites authority, it is the form which the resistance of facticity, through which all liberation is brought about, takes for him. And on the other hand, even in this situation the child has a right to his freedom and must be respected as a human person. What gives *Emile* its value is the brilliance with which Rousseau asserts this principle. There is a very annoying naturalistic optimism in *Emile;* in the rearing of the child, as in any relationship with others, the ambiguity of freedom implies the outrage of violence; in a sense, all education is a failure. But Rousseau is right in refusing to allow childhood to be oppressed. And in practice raising a child as one cultivates a plant which one does not consult about its needs is very different from considering it as a freedom to whom the future must be opened.

Thus, we can set up point number one: the good of an individual or a group of individuals requires that it be taken as an absolute end of our action; but we are not authorized to decide upon this end *a priori*. The fact is that no behavior is ever authorized to begin with, and one of the concrete consequences of existentialist ethics is the rejection of all the previous justifications which might be drawn from the civilization, the age, and the culture; it is the rejection of every principle of authority. To put it positively, the precept will be to treat the other (to the extent that he is the only one concerned, which is the moment that we are considering at present) as a freedom so that his end may be freedom; in using this conducting-wire one will have to incur the risk, in each case, of inventing an original solution. Out of disappointment in love a young girl takes an overdose of pheno-barbital; in the morning friends find her dying, they call a doctor, she is saved; later on she becomes a happy mother of a family; her friends were right in considering her suicide as a hasty and heedless act and in putting her into a position to reject it or return to it freely. But in asylums one sees melancholic patients who have tried to commit suicide twenty times, who devote their freedom to seeking the means of escaping their jailers and of putting an end to their intolerable anguish; the doctor who gives them a friendly pat on the shoulder is their tyrant and their torturer. A friend who is intoxicated by alcohol or drugs asks me for money so that he can go and buy the poison that is necessary to him; I urge him to get cured, I take him to a doctor, I try to help him live; insofar as there is a chance of my being successful, I am acting correctly in refusing him the sum he asks for. But if circumstances prohibit me from doing anything to change the situation in which he is struggling, all I can do is give in; a deprivation of a few hours will do nothing but exasperate his torments uselessly; and he may have recourse to extreme means to get what I do not give him. . . .

We challenge every condemnation as well as every *a priori* justification of the violence practised with a view to a valid end. They must be legitimized concretely. A calm, mathematical calculation is here impossible. One must attempt to judge the chances of success that are involved in a certain sacrifice; but at the beginning this judgment will always be doubtful; besides, in the face of the immediate reality of the sacrifice, the notion of chance is difficult to think about. On the one hand, one can multiply a probability infinitely without ever reaching certainty; but yet, practically, it ends by merging with this asymptote: in our private life as in our collective life there is no other truth than a statistical one. On the other hand, the interests at stake do not allow themselves to be put into an equation; the suffering of one man, that of a million men, are incommensurable with the conquests realized by millions of others, present death is incommensurable with the life to come. It would be utopian to want to set up on the one hand the chances of success multiplied by the stake one is after, and on the other hand the weight of the immediate sacrifice. One finds himself back at the anguish of free decision. And that is why political choice is an ethical choice: it is a wager as well as a decision; one bets on the chances and risks of the measure under consideration; but whether chances and risks must be assumed or not in the given circumstances must be decided without help, and in so doing one sets up values. If in 1793 the Girondists rejected the violences of the Terror whereas a Saint-Just and a Robespierre assumed them, the reason is that they did not have the same conception of freedom. Nor was the same republic being aimed at between 1830 and 1840 by the republicans who limited themselves to a purely political opposition and those who adopted the technique of insurrection. In each case it is a matter of defining an end and realizing it, knowing that the choice of the means employed affects both the definition and the fulfillment.

Ordinarily, situations are so complex that a long analysis is necessary before being able to pose the ethical moment of the choice. We shall confine ourselves here to the consideration of a few simple examples which will enable us to make our attitude somewhat more precise. In an underground revolutionary movement when one discovers the presence of a stool-pigeon, one does not hesitate to beat him up; he is a present and future danger who has to be gotten rid of; but if a man is merely suspected of treason, the case is more ambiguous. We blame those northern peasants who in the war of 1914–18 massacred an innocent family which was suspected of signaling to the enemy; the reason is that not only were the presumptions vague, but the danger was uncertain; at any rate, it was enough to put the suspects into prison; while waiting for a serious inquiry it was easy to keep them from doing any harm. However, if a questionable individual holds the fate of other men in his hands, if, in order to avoid the risk of killing one innocent man, one runs the risk of letting ten innocent men die, it is reasonable to sacrifice him. We can merely ask that such decisions be not taken hastily and lightly, and that, all things considered, the evil that one inflicts be lesser than that which is being forestalled. . . .

It is apparent that the method we are proposing, analogous in this respect to scientific or aesthetic methods, consists, in each case, of confronting the values realized with the values aimed at, and the meaning of the act with its content. The fact is that the politician, contrary to the scientist and the artist, and although the element of failure which he assumes is much more outrageous, is rarely concerned with making use of it. May it be that there is an irresistible dialectic of power wherein morality has no place? Is the ethical concern, even in its realistic and concrete form, detrimental to the interests of action? The objection will surely be made that hesitation and misgivings only impede victory. Since, in any case, there is an element of failure in all success, since the ambiguity, at any rate, must be surmounted, why not refuse to take notice of it? In the first number of the *Cahiers d'Action* a reader declared that once and for all we should regard the militant communist as "the permanent hero of our time" and should reject the exhausting tension demanded by existentialism; installed in the permanence of heroism, one will blindly direct himself toward an uncontested goal; but one then resembles Colonel de la Roque who unwaveringly went right straight ahead of him without knowing where he was going. Malaparte relates that the young Nazis, in order to become insensitive to the suffering of others, practised by plucking out the eyes of live cats; there is no more radical way of avoiding the pitfalls of ambiguity. But an action which wants to serve man ought to be careful not to forget him on the way; if it chooses to fulfill itself blindly, it will lose its meaning or will take on an unforeseen meaning; for the goal is not fixed once and for all; it is defined all along the road which leads to it. Vigilance alone can keep alive the validity of the goals and the genuine assertion of freedom.

Conclusion

Is this kind of ethics individualistic or not? Yes, if one means by that that it accords to the individual an absolute value and that it recognizes in him alone the power of laying the foundations of his own existence. It is individualism in the sense in which the wisdom of the ancients, the Christian ethics of salvation, and the Kantian ideal of virtue also merit this name; it is opposed to the totalitarian doctrines which raise up beyond man the mirage of Mankind. But it is not solipsistic, since the individual is defined only by his relationship to the world and to other individuals; he exists only by transcending himself, and his freedom can be achieved only through the freedom of others. He justifies his existence by a movement which, like freedom, springs from his heart but which leads outside of him.

This individualism does not lead to the anarchy of personal whim. Man is free; but he finds his law in his very freedom. First, he must assume his freedom and not flee it; he assumes it by a constructive movement: one does not exist without doing something; and also by a negative movement which rejects oppression for oneself and others. In construction, as in rejection, it is a matter of reconquering freedom on the contingent facticity of existence, that is, of taking the given, which, at the start, *is there* without any reason, as something willed by man. A conquest of this kind is never finished; the contingency remains, and, so that he may assert his will, man is even obliged to stir up in the world the outrage he does not want. But this element of failure is a very condition of his life; one can never dream of eliminating it without immediately dreaming of death. This does not mean that one should consent to failure, but rather one must consent to struggle against it without respite.

Yet, isn't this battle without victory pure gullibility? It will be argued that this is only a ruse of transcendance projecting before itself a goal which constantly recedes, running after itself on an endless treadmill; to exist for Mankind is to remain where one is, and it fools itself by calling this turbulent stagnation progress; our whole ethics does nothing but encourage it in this lying enterprise since we are asking each one to confirm existence as a value for all others; isn't it simply a matter of organizing among men a complicity which allows them to substitute a game of illusions for the given world?

We have already attempted to answer this objection. One can formulate it only by placing himself on the grounds of an inhuman and consequently false objectivity; within Mankind men may be fooled; the word "lie" has a meaning by opposition to the truth established by men themselves, but Mankind can not fool itself completely since it is precisely Mankind which creates the criteria of true and false. In Plato, art is mystification because there is the heaven of Ideas; but in the earthly domain all glorification of the earth is true as soon as it is realized. Let men attach value to words, forms, colors, mathematical theorems, physical laws, and athletic prowess; let them accord value to one another in love and friendship, and the objects, the events, and the men immediately *have* this value; they have it absolutely. It is possible that a man may refuse to love anything on earth; he will prove this refusal and he will carry it out by suicide. If he lives, the reason is that, whatever he may say, there still remains in him some attachment to existence; his life will be commensurate with this attachment; it will justify itself to the extent that it genuinely justifies the world.

This justification, though open upon the entire universe through time and space, will always be finite. Whatever one may do, one never realizes anything but a limited work, like existence itself which tries to establish itself through that work and which death also limits. It is the assertion of our finiteness which doubtless gives the doctrine which we have just evoked its austerity and, in some eyes, its sadness. As soon as one considers a system abstractly and theoretically, one puts himself, in effect, on the plane of the universal, thus, of the infinite. That is why reading the Hegelian system is so comforting. I remember having experienced a great feeling of calm on reading Hegel in the impersonal framework of the Bibliothèque Nationale in August 1940. But once I got into the street again, into my life, out of the system, beneath a real sky, the system was no longer of any use to me: what it had offered me, under a show of the infinite, was the consolations of death; and I again wanted to live in the midst of living men. I think that, inversely, existentialism does not offer to the reader the consolations of an abstract evasion: existentialism proposes no evasion. On the contrary, its ethics is experienced in the truth of life, and it then appears as the only proposition of salvation which one can address to men. Taking on its own account Descartes' revolt against the evil genius, the pride of the thinking reed in the face of the universe which crushes him, it asserts that, despite his limits, through them, it is up to each one to fulfill his existence as an absolute. Regardless of the staggering dimensions of the world about us, the density of our ignorance, the risks of catastrophes to come, and our individual weakness within the immense collectivity, the fact remains that we are absolutely free today if we choose to will our existence in its finiteness, a finiteness which is open on the infinite. And in fact, any man who has known real loves, real revolts, real desires, and real will knows quite well that he has no need of any outside guarantee to be sure of his goals; their certitude comes from his own drive. There is a very old saying which goes: "Do what you must, come what may." That amounts to saying in a different way that the result is not external to the good will which fulfills itself in aiming at it. If it came to be that each man did what he must, existence would be saved in each one without there being any need of dreaming of a paradise where all would be reconciled in death.

CAMUS SELECTIONS

From *The Myth of Sisyphus*

An Absurd Reasoning

Absurdity and Suicide

There is but one truly serious philosophical problem, and that is suicide. Judging whether life is or is not worth living amounts to answering the fundamental question of philosophy. All the rest—whether or not the world has three dimensions, whether the mind has nine or twelve categories—comes afterwards. These are games; one must first answer. And if it is true, as Nietzsche claims, that a philosopher, to deserve our respect, must preach by example, you can appreciate the importance of that reply, for it will precede the definitive act. These are facts the heart can feel; yet they call for careful study before they become clear to the intellect.

If I ask myself how to judge that this question is more urgent than that, I reply that one judges by the actions it entails. I have never seen anyone die for the ontological argument. Galileo, who held a scientific truth of great importance, abjured it with the greatest ease as soon as it endangered his life. In a certain sense, he did right. That truth was not worth the stake. Whether the earth or the sun revolves around the other is a matter of profound indifference. To tell the truth, it is a futile question. On the other hand, I see many people die because they judge that life is not worth living. I see others paradoxically getting killed for the ideas or illusions that give them a reason for living (what is called a reason for living is also an excellent reason for dying). I therefore conclude that the meaning of life is the most urgent of questions. How to answer it? On all essential problems (I mean thereby those that run the risk of leading to death or those that intensify the passion of living) there are probably but two methods of thought: the method of La Palisse and the method of Don Quixote. Solely the balance between evidence and lyricism can allow us to achieve simultaneously emotion and lucidity. In a subject at once so humble and so heavy with emotion, the learned and classical dialectic must yield, one can see, to a more modest attitude of mind deriving at one and the same time from common sense and understanding.

Suicide has never been dealt with except as a social phenomenon. On the contrary, we are concerned here, at the outset, with the relationship between individual thought and suicide. An act like this is prepared within the silence of the heart, as is a great work of art. The man himself is ignorant of it. One evening he pulls the trigger or jumps. Of an apartment-building manager who had killed himself I was told that he had lost his daughter five years before, that he had changed greatly since, and that that experience had "undermined" him. A more exact word cannot be imagined. Beginning to think is beginning to be undermined. Society has but little connection with such beginnings. The worm is in man's heart. That is where it must be sought. One must follow and understand this fatal game that leads from lucidity in the face of existence to flight from light.

There are many causes for a suicide, and generally the most obvious ones were not the most powerful. Rarely is suicide committed (yet the hypothesis is not excluded) through reflection. What sets off the crisis is almost always unverifiable. Newspapers often speak of "personal sorrows" or of "incurable illness." These explanations are plausible. But one would have to know whether a friend of the desperate man had not that very day addressed him indifferently. He is the guilty one. For that is enough to precipitate all the rancors and all the boredom still in suspension.

But if it is hard to fix the precise instant, the subtle step when the mind opted for death, it is easier to deduce from the act itself the consequences it implies. In a sense, and as in melodrama, killing yourself amounts to confessing. It is confessing that life is too much for you or that you do not understand it. Let's not go too far in such analogies, however, but rather return to everyday words. It is merely confessing that that "is not worth the trouble." Living, naturally, is never easy. You continue making the gestures commanded by existence for many reasons, the first of which is habit. Dying voluntarily implies that you have recognized, even instinctively, the ridiculous character of that habit, the absence of any profound reason for living, the insane character of that daily agitation, and the uselessness of suffering.

What, then, is that incalculable feeling that deprives the mind of the sleep necessary to life? A world that can be explained even with bad reasons is a familiar world. But, on the other hand, in a universe suddenly divested of illusions and lights, man feels an alien, a stranger. His exile is without remedy since he is deprived of the memory of a lost home or the hope of a promised land. This divorce between man and his life, the actor and his setting, is properly the feeling of absurdity. . . .

All great deeds and all great thoughts have a ridiculous beginning. Great works are often born on a street-corner or in a restaurant's revolving door. So it is with absurdity. The absurd world more than others derives its nobility from that abject birth. In certain situations, replying "nothing" when asked what one is thinking about may be pretense in a man. Those who are loved are well aware of this. But if that reply is sincere, if it symbolizes that odd state of soul in which the void becomes eloquent, in which the chain of daily gestures is broken, in which the heart vainly seeks the link that will connect it again, then it is as it were the first sign of absurdity.

It happens that the stage sets collapse. Rising, streetcar, four hours in the office or the factory, meal, streetcar, four hours of work, meal, sleep, and Monday Tuesday Wednesday Thursday Friday and Saturday according to the same rhythm—this path is easily followed most of the time. But one day the "why" arises and everything begins in that weariness tinged with amazement. "Begins"—this is important. Weariness comes at the end of the acts of a mechanical life, but at the same time it inaugurates the impulse of consciousness. It awakens consciousness and provokes what follows. What follows is the gradual return into the chain or it is the definitive awakening. At the end of the awakening comes, in time, the consequence: suicide or recovery. In itself weariness has something sickening about it. Here, I must conclude that it is good. For everything begins with consciousness and nothing is worth anything except through it. There is nothing original about these remarks. But they are obvious; that is enough for a while, during a sketchy reconnaissance in the origins of the absurd. Mere "anxiety," as Heidegger says, is at the source of everything.

Likewise and during every day of an unillustrious life, time carries us. But a moment always comes when we have to carry it. We live on the future: "tomorrow," "later on," "when you have made your way," "you will understand when you are old enough." Such irrelevancies are wonderful, for, after all, it's a matter of dying. Yet a day comes when a man notices or says that he is thirty. Thus he asserts his youth. But simultaneously he situates himself in relation to time. He takes his place in it. He admits that he stands at a certain point on a curve that he acknowledges having to travel to its end. He belongs to time, and by the horror that seizes him, he recognizes his worst enemy. Tomorrow, he was longing for tomorrow, whereas everything in him ought to reject it. That revolt of the flesh is the absurd.

A step lower and strangeness creeps in: perceiving that the world is "dense," sensing to what a degree a stone is foreign and irreducible to us, with what intensity nature or a landscape can negate us. At the heart of all beauty lies something inhuman, and these hills, the softness of the sky, the outline of these trees at this very minute lose the illusory meaning with which we had clothed them, henceforth more remote than a lost paradise. The primitive hostility of the world rises up to face us across millennia. For a second we cease to understand it because for centuries we have understood in it solely the images and designs that we had attributed to it beforehand, because henceforth we lack the power to make use of that artifice. The world evades us because it becomes itself again. That stage scenery masked by habit becomes again what it is. It withdraws at a distance from us. Just as there are days when under the familiar face of a woman, we see as a stranger her we had loved months or years ago, perhaps we shall come even to desire what suddenly leaves us so alone. But the time has not yet come. Just one thing: that denseness and that strangeness of the world is the absurd.

Men, too, secrete the inhuman. At certain moments of lucidity, the mechanical aspect of their gestures, their meaningless pantomime makes silly everything that surrounds them. A man is talking on the telephone behind a glass partition; you cannot hear him, but you see his incomprehensible dumb show: you wonder why he is alive. This discomfort in the face of man's own inhumanity, this incalculable tumble before the image of what we are, this "nausea," as a writer of today calls it, is also the absurd. Likewise the stranger who at certain seconds comes to meet us in a mirror, the familiar and yet alarming brother we encounter in our own photographs is also the absurd.

I come at last to death and to the attitude we have toward it. On this point everything has been said and it is only proper to avoid pathos. Yet one will never be sufficiently surprised that everyone lives as if no one "knew." This is because in reality there is no experience of death. Properly speaking, nothing has been experienced but what has been lived and made conscious. Here, it is barely possible to speak of the experience of others' deaths. It is a substitute, an illusion, and it never quite convinces us. That melancholy convention cannot be persuasive. The horror comes in reality from the mathematical aspect of the event. If time frightens us, this is because it works out the problem and the solution comes afterward. All the pretty speeches about the soul will have their contrary convincingly proved, at least for a time. From this inert body on which a slap makes no mark the soul has disappeared. This elementary and definitive aspect of the adventure constitutes the absurd feeling. Under the fatal lighting of that destiny, its uselessness becomes evident. No code of ethics and no effort are justifiable *a priori* in the face of the cruel mathematics that command our condition.

Let me repeat: all this has been said over and over. I am limiting myself here to making a rapid classification and to pointing out these obvious themes. They run through all literatures and all philosophies.

Everyday conversation feeds on them. There is no question of reinventing them. But it is essential to be sure of these facts in order to be able to question oneself subsequently on the primordial question. I am interested—let me repeat again—not so much in absurd discoveries as in their consequences. If one is assured of these facts, what is one to conclude, how far is one to go to elude nothing? Is one to die voluntarily or to hope in spite of everything? Beforehand, it is necessary to take the same rapid inventory on the plane of the intelligence.

*   *   *

The mind's first step is to distinguish what is true from what is false. However, as soon as thought reflects on itself, what it first discovers is a contradiction. Useless to strive to be convincing in this case. Over the centuries no one has furnished a clearer and more elegant demonstration of the business than Aristotle: "The often ridiculed consequence of these opinions is that they destroy themselves. For by asserting that all is true we assert the truth of the contrary assertion and consequently the falsity of our own thesis (for the contrary assertion does not admit that it can be true). And if one says that all is false, that assertion is itself false. If we declare that solely the assertion opposed to ours is false or else that solely ours is not false, we are nevertheless forced to admit an infinite number of true or false judgments. For the one who expresses a true assertion proclaims simultaneously that it is true, and so on *ad infinitum*."

This vicious circle is but the first of a series in which the mind that studies itself gets lost in a giddy whirling. The very simplicity of these paradoxes makes them irreducible. Whatever may be the plays on words and the acrobatics of logic, to understand is, above all, to unify. The mind's deepest desire, even in its most elaborate operations, parallels man's unconscious feeling in the face of his universe: it is an insistence upon familiarity, an appetite for clarity. Understanding the world for a man is reducing it to the human, stamping it with his seal. The cat's universe is not the universe of the anthill. The truism "All thought is anthropomorphic" has no other meaning. Likewise, the mind that aims to understand reality can consider itself satisfied only by reducing it to terms of thought. If man realized that the universe like him can love and suffer, he would be reconciled. If thought discovered in the shimmering mirrors of phenomena eternal relations capable of summing them up and summing themselves up in a single principle, then would be seen an intellectual joy of which the myth of the blessed would be but a ridiculous imitation. That nostalgia for unity, that appetite for the absolute illustrates the essential impulse of the human drama. But the fact of that nostalgia's existence does not imply that it is to be immediately satisfied. For if, bridging the gulf that separates desire from conquest, we assert with

Parmenides the reality of the One (whatever it may be), we fall into the ridiculous contradiction of a mind that asserts total unity and proves by its very assertion its own difference and the diversity it claimed to resolve. This other vicious circle is enough to stifle our hopes.

These are again truisms. I shall again repeat that they are not interesting in themselves but in the consequences that can be deduced from them. I know another truism: it tells me that man is mortal. One can nevertheless count the minds that have deduced the extreme conclusions from it. It is essential to consider as a constant point of reference in this essay the regular hiatus between what we fancy we know and what we really know, practical assent and simulated ignorance which allows us to live with ideas which, if we truly put them to the test, ought to upset our whole life. Faced with this inextricable contradiction of the mind, we shall fully grasp the divorce separating us from our own creations. So long as the mind keeps silent in the motionless world of its hopes, everything is reflected and arranged in the unity of its nostalgia. But with its first move this world cracks and tumbles: an infinite number of shimmering fragments is offered to the understanding. We must despair of ever reconstructing the familiar, calm surface which would give us peace of heart. After so many centuries of inquiries, so many abdications among thinkers, we are well aware that this is true for all our knowledge. With the exception of professional rationalists, today people despair of true knowledge. If the only significant history of human thought were to be written, it would have to be the history of its successive regrets and its impotences.

Of whom and of what indeed can I say: "I know that!" This heart within me I can feel, and I judge that it exists. This world I can touch, and I likewise judge that it exists. There ends all my knowledge, and the rest is construction. For if I try to seize this self of which I feel sure, if I try to define and to summarize it, it is nothing but water slipping through my fingers. I can sketch one by one all the aspects it is able to assume, all those likewise that have been attributed to it, this upbringing, this origin, this ardor or these silences, this nobility or this vileness. But aspects cannot be added up. This very heart which is mine will forever remain indefinable to me. Between the certainty I have of my existence and the content I try to give to that assurance, the gap will never be filled. Forever I shall be a stranger to myself. In psychology as in logic, there are truths but no truth. Socrates' "Know thyself" has as much value as the "Be virtuous" of our confessionals. They reveal a nostalgia at the same time as an ignorance. They are sterile exercises on great subjects. They are legitimate only in precisely so far as they are approximate.

And here are trees and I know their gnarled surface, water and I feel its taste. These scents of grass and stars at night, certain evenings when the heart relaxes—how shall I negate this world whose power and strength I feel? Yet all the knowledge on earth will give me nothing to assure me that this world is mine. You describe it to me and you teach me to classify it. You enumerate its laws and in my thirst for knowledge I admit that they are true. You take apart its mechanism and my hope increases. At the final stage you teach me that this wondrous and multicolored universe can be reduced to the atom and that the atom itself can be reduced to the electron. All this is good and I wait for you to continue. But you tell me of an invisible planetary system in which electrons gravitate around a nucleus. You explain this world to me with an image. I realize then that you have been reduced to poetry: I shall never know. Have I the time to become indignant? You have already changed theories. So that science that was to teach me everything ends up in a hypothesis, that lucidity founders in metaphor, that uncertainty is resolved in a work of art. What need had I of so many efforts? The soft lines of these hills and the hand of evening on this troubled heart teach me much more. I have returned to my beginning. I realize that if through science I can seize phenomena and enumerate them, I cannot, for all that, apprehend the world. Were I to trace its entire relief with my finger, I should not know any more. And you give me the choice between a description that is sure but that teaches me nothing and hypotheses that claim to teach me but that are not sure. A stranger to myself and to the world, armed solely with a thought that negates itself as soon as it asserts, what is this condition in which I can have peace only by refusing to know and to live, in which the appetite for conquest bumps into walls that defy its assaults? To will is to stir up paradoxes. Everything is ordered in such a way as to bring into being that poisoned peace produced by thoughtlessness, lack of heart, or fatal renunciations.

Hence the intelligence, too, tells me in its way that this world is absurd. Its contrary, blind reason, may well claim that all is clear; I was waiting for proof and longing for it to be right. But despite so many pretentious centuries and over the heads of so many eloquent and persuasive men, I know that is false. On this plane, at least, there is no happiness if I cannot know. That universal reason, practical or ethical, that determinism, those categories that explain everything are enough to make a decent man laugh. They have nothing to do with the mind. They negate its profound truth, which is to be enchained. In this unintelligible and limited universe, man's fate henceforth assumes its meaning. A horde of irrationals has sprung up and surrounds him until his ultimate end. In his recovered and now studied lucidity, the feeling of the absurd becomes clear and definite. I said that the world is absurd, but I was too hasty. This world in itself is not reasonable, that is all that can be said. But what is absurd is the confrontation of this irrational and the wild longing for clarity whose call echoes in the human heart. The absurd depends as much on man as on the world. For the moment it is all that links them together. It binds them one to the other as only hatred can weld two creatures together. This is all I can discern clearly in this measureless universe where my adventure takes place. Let us pause here. If I hold to be true that absurdity that determines my relationship with life, if I become thoroughly imbued with that sentiment that seizes me in face of the world's scenes, with that lucidity imposed on me by the pursuit of a science, I must sacrifice everything to these certainties and I must see them squarely to be able to maintain them. Above all, I must adapt my behavior to them and pursue them in all their consequences. I am speaking here of decency. But I want to know beforehand if thought can live in those deserts. . . .

Absurd Freedom

Now the main thing is done, I hold certain facts from which I cannot separate. What I know, what is certain, what I cannot deny, what I cannot reject—this is what counts. I can negate everything of that part of me that lives on vague nostalgias, except this desire for unity, this longing to solve, this need for clarity and cohesion. I can refute everything in this world surrounding me that offends or enraptures me, except this chaos, this sovereign chance and this divine equivalence which springs from anarchy. I don't know whether this world has a meaning that transcends it. But I know that I do not know that meaning and that it is impossible for me just now to know it. What can a meaning outside my condition mean to me? I can understand only in human terms. What I touch, what resists me—that is what I understand. And these two certainties—my appetite for the absolute and for unity and the impossibility of reducing this world to a rational and reasonable principle—I also know that I cannot reconcile them. What other truth can I admit without lying, without bringing in a hope I lack and which means nothing within the limits of my condition?

If I were a tree among trees, a cat among animals, this life would have a meaning, or rather this problem would not arise, for I should belong to this world. I should *be* this world to which I am now opposed by my whole consciousness and my whole insistence upon familiarity. This ridiculous reason is what sets me in opposition to all creation. I cannot cross it out with a stroke of the pen. What I believe to be true I must therefore preserve. What seems to me so obvious, even against me, I must support. And what constitutes the basis of that conflict, of that break between the world and my mind, but the awareness of it? If therefore I want to preserve it, I can through a constant awareness, ever revived, ever alert. This is what, for the moment, I must remember. At this moment the absurd, so obvious and yet so hard to win, returns to a man's life and finds its home there. At this moment, too, the mind can leave the arid, dried-up path of lucid effort. That path now emerges in daily life. It encounters the world of the anonymous impersonal pronoun "one," but henceforth man enters in with his revolt and his lucidity. He has forgotten how to hope. This hell of the present is his Kingdom at last. All problems recover their sharp edge. Abstract evidence retreats before the poetry of forms and colors. Spiritual conflicts become embodied and return to the abject and magnificent shelter of man's heart. None of them is settled. But all are transfigured. Is one going to die, escape by the leap, rebuild a mansion of ideas and forms to one's own scale? Is one, on the contrary, going to take up the heart-rending and marvelous wager of the absurd? Let's make a final effort in this regard and draw all our conclusions. The body, affection, creation, action, human nobility will then resume their places in this mad world. At last man will again find there the wine of the absurd and the bread of indifference on which he feeds his greatness.

Let us insist again on the method: it is a matter of persisting. At a certain point on his path the absurd man is tempted. History is not lacking in either religions or prophets, even without gods. He is asked to leap. All he can reply is that he doesn't fully understand, that it is not obvious. Indeed, he does not want to do anything but what he fully understands. He is assured that this is the sin of pride, but he does not understand the notion of sin; that perhaps hell is in store, but he has not enough imagination to visualize that strange future; that he is losing immortal life, but that seems to him an idle consideration. An attempt is made to get him to admit his guilt. He feels innocent. To tell the truth, that is all he feels—his irreparable innocence. This is what allows him everything. Hence, what he demands of himself is to live *solely* with what he knows, to accommodate himself to what is, and to bring in nothing that is not certain. He is told that nothing is. But this at least is a certainty. And it is with this that he is concerned: he wants to find out if it is possible to live *without appeal.*

* * *

Now I can broach the notion of suicide. It has already been felt what solution might be given. At this point the problem is reversed. It was previously a question of finding out whether or not life had to have a meaning to be lived. It now becomes clear, on the contrary, that it will be lived all the better if it has no meaning. Living an experience, a particular fate, is accepting it fully. Now, no one will live this fate, knowing it to be absurd, unless he does everything to keep before him that absurd brought to light by consciousness. Negating one of the terms of the opposition on which he lives amounts to escaping it. To abolish conscious revolt is to elude the problem. The theme of permanent revolution is thus carried into individual experience. Living is keeping the absurd alive. Keeping it alive is, above all, contemplating it. Unlike Eurydice, the absurd dies only when we turn away from it. One of the only coherent philosophical positions is thus revolt. It is a constant confrontation between man and his own obscurity. It is an insistence upon an impossible transparency. It challenges the world anew every second. Just as danger provided man the unique opportunity of seizing awareness, so metaphysical revolt extends awareness to the whole of experience. It is that constant presence of man in his own eyes. It is not aspiration, for it is devoid of hope. That revolt is the certainty of a crushing fate, without the resignation that ought to accompany it.

This is where it is seen to what a degree absurd experience is remote from suicide. It may be thought that suicide follows revolt—but wrongly. For it does not represent the logical outcome of revolt. It is just the contrary by the consent it presupposes. Suicide, like the leap, is acceptance at its extreme. Everything is over and man returns to his essential history. His future, his unique and dreadful future—he sees and rushes toward it. In its way, suicide settles the absurd. It engulfs the absurd in the same death. But I know that in order to keep alive, the absurd cannot be settled. It escapes suicide to the extent that it is simultaneously awareness and rejection of death. It is, at the extreme limit of the condemned man's last thought, that shoelace that despite everything he sees a few yards away, on the very brink of his dizzying fall. The contrary of suicide, in fact, is the man condemned to death.

That revolt gives life its value. Spread out over the whole length of a life, it restores its majesty to that life. To a man devoid of blinders, there is no finer sight than that of the intelligence at grips with a reality that transcends it. The sight of human pride is unequaled. No disparagement is of any use. That discipline that the mind imposes on itself, that will conjured up out of nothing, that face-to-face struggle have something exceptional about them. To impoverish that reality whose inhumanity constitutes man's majesty is tantamount to impoverishing him himself. I understand then why the doctrines that explain everything to me also debilitate me at the same time. They relieve me of the weight of my own life, and yet I must carry it alone. At this juncture, I cannot conceive that a skeptical metaphysics can be joined to an ethics of renunciation.

Consciousness and revolt, these rejections are the contrary of renunciation. Everything that is indomitable and passionate in a human heart quickens them, on the contrary, with its own life. It is essential to die unreconciled and not of one's own free will. Suicide is a repudiation. The absurd man can only drain everything to the bitter end, and deplete himself. The absurd is his extreme tension, which he maintains constantly by solitary effort, for he knows that in that consciousness and in that day-to-day revolt he gives proof of his only truth, which is defiance. This is a first consequence.

* * *

If I remain in that prearranged position which consists in drawing all the conclusions (and nothing else) involved in a newly discovered notion, I am faced with a second paradox. In order to remain faithful to that method, I have nothing to do with the problem of metaphysical liberty. Knowing whether or not man is free doesn't interest me. I can experience only my own freedom. As to it, I can have no general notions, but merely a few clear insights. The problem of "freedom as such" has no meaning. For it is linked in quite a different way with the problem of God. Knowing whether or not man is free involves knowing whether he can have a master. The absurdity peculiar to this problem comes from the fact that the very notion that makes the problem of freedom possible also takes away all its meaning. For in the presence of God there is less a problem of freedom than a problem of evil. You know the alternative: either we are not free and God the all-powerful is responsible for evil. Or we are free and responsible but God is not all-powerful. All the scholastic subtleties have neither added anything to nor subtracted anything from the acuteness of this paradox.

This is why I cannot get lost in the glorification or the mere definition of a notion which eludes me and loses its meaning as soon as it goes beyond the frame of reference of my individual experience. I cannot understand what kind of freedom would be given me by a higher being. I have lost the sense of hierarchy. The only conception of freedom I can have is that of the prisoner or the individual in the midst of the State. The only one I know is freedom of thought and action. Now if the absurd cancels all my chances of eternal freedom, it restores and magnifies, on the other hand, my freedom of action. That privation of hope and future means an increase in man's availability.

Before encountering the absurd, the everyday man lives with aims, a concern for the future or for justification (with regard to whom or what is not the question). He weighs his chances, he counts on "someday," his retirement or the labor of his sons. He still thinks that something in his life can be directed. In truth, he acts as if he were free, even if all the facts make a point of contradicting that liberty. But after the absurd, everything is upset. That idea that "I am," my way of acting as if everything has a meaning (even if, on occasion, I said that nothing has)—all that is given the lie in vertiginous fashion by the absurdity of a possible death. Thinking of the future, establishing aims for oneself, having preferences— all this presupposes a belief in freedom, even if one occasionally ascertains that one doesn't feel it. But at that moment I am well aware that that higher liberty, that freedom *to be,* which alone can serve as basis for a truth, does not exist. Death is there as the only reality. After death the chips are down. I am not even free, either, to perpetuate myself, but a slave, and, above all, a slave without hope of an eternal revolution, without recourse to contempt. And who without revolution and without contempt can remain a slave? What freedom can exist in the fullest sense without assurance of eternity?

But at the same time the absurd man realizes that hitherto he was bound to that postulate of freedom on the illusion of which he was living. In a certain sense, that hampered him. To the extent to which he imagined a purpose to his life, he adapted himself to the demands of a purpose to be achieved and became the slave of his liberty. Thus I could not act otherwise than as the father (or the engineer or the leader of a nation, or the post-office sub-clerk) that I am preparing to be. I think I can choose to be that rather than something else. I think so unconsciously, to be sure. But at the same time I strengthen my postulate with the beliefs of those around me, with the presumptions of my human environment (others are so sure of being free, and that cheerful mood is so contagious!). However far one may remain from any presumption, moral or social, one is partly influenced by them and even, for the best among them (there are good and bad presumptions), one adapts one's life to them. Thus the absurd man realizes that he was not really free. To speak clearly, to the extent to which I hope, to which I worry about a truth that might be individual to me, about a way of being or creating, to the extent to which I arrange my life and prove thereby that I accept its having a meaning, I create for myself barriers between which I confine my life. I do like so many bureaucrats of the mind and heart who only fill me with disgust and whose only vice, I now see clearly, is to take man's freedom seriously.

The absurd enlightens me on this point: there is no future. Henceforth this is the reason for my inner freedom. I shall use two comparisons here. Mystics, to begin with, find freedom in giving themselves. By losing themselves in their god, by accepting his rules, they become secretly free. In spontaneously accepted slavery they recover a deeper independence. But what does that freedom mean? It may be said, above all, that they *feel* free with regard to themselves, and not so much free as liberated. Likewise, completely turned toward death (taken here as the most obvious absurdity), the absurd man feels released from everything outside that passionate attention crystallizing in him. He enjoys a freedom with regard to common rules. It can be seen at this point that the initial themes of existential philosophy keep their entire value. The return to consciousness, the escape from everyday sleep represent the first steps of absurd freedom. But it is existential *preaching* that is alluded to, and with it that spiritual leap which basically escapes consciousness. In the same way (this is my second comparison) the slaves of antiquity did not belong to themselves.

But they knew that freedom which consists in not feeling responsible. Death, too, has patrician hands which, while crushing, also liberate.

Losing oneself in that bottomless certainty, feeling henceforth sufficiently remote from one's own life to increase it and take a broad view of it—this involves the principle of a liberation. Such new independence has a definite time limit, like any freedom of action. It does not write a check on eternity. But it takes the place of the illusions of *freedom,* which all stopped with death. The divine availability of the condemned man before whom the prison doors open in a certain early dawn, that unbelievable disinterestedness with regard to everything except for the pure flame of life—it is clear that death and the absurd are here the principles of the only reasonable freedom: that which a human heart can experience and live. This is a second consequence. The absurd man thus catches sight of a burning and frigid, transparent and limited universe in which nothing is possible but everything is given, and beyond which all is collapse and nothingness. He can then decide to accept such a universe and draw from it his strength, his refusal to hope, and the unyielding evidence of a life without consolation.

The Myth of Sisyphus

The gods had condemned Sisyphus to ceaselessly rolling a rock to the top of a mountain, whence the stone would fall back of its own weight. They had thought with some reason that there is no more dreadful punishment than futile and hopeless labor.

If one believes Homer, Sisyphus was the wisest and most prudent of mortals. According to another tradition, however, he was disposed to practice the profession of highwayman. I see no contradiction in this. Opinions differ as to the reasons why he became the futile laborer of the underworld. To begin with, he is accused of a certain levity in regard to the gods. He stole their secrets. Ægina, the daughter of Æsopus, was carried off by Jupiter. The father was shocked by that disappearance and complained to Sisyphus. He, who knew of the abduction, offered to tell about it on condition that Æsopus would give water to the citadel of Corinth. To the celestial thunderbolts he preferred the benediction of water. He was punished for this in the underworld. Homer tells us also that Sisyphus had put Death in chains. Pluto could not endure the sight of his deserted, silent empire. He dispatched the god of war, who liberated Death from the hands of her conqueror.

It is said also that Sisyphus, being near to death, rashly wanted to test his wife's love. He ordered her to cast his unburied body into the middle of the public square. Sisyphus woke up in the underworld. And there, annoyed by an obedience so contrary to human love, he obtained from Pluto permission to return to earth in order to chastise his wife. But when he had seen again the face of this world, enjoyed water and sun, warm stones and the sea, he no longer wanted to go back to the infernal darkness. Recalls, signs of anger, warnings were of no avail. Many years more he lived facing the curve of the gulf, the sparkling sea, and the smiles of earth. A decree of the gods was necessary. Mercury came and seized the impudent man by the collar and, snatching him from his joys, led him forcibly back to the underworld, where his rock was ready for him.

You have already grasped that Sisyphus is the absurd hero. He *is,* as much through his passions as through his torture. His scorn of the gods, his hatred of death, and his passion for life won him that unspeakable penalty in which the whole being is exerted toward accomplishing nothing. This is the price that must be paid for the passions of this earth. Nothing is told us about Sisyphus in the underworld. Myths are made for the imagination to breathe life into them. As for this myth, one sees merely the whole effort of a body straining to raise the huge stone, to roll it and push it up a slope a hundred times over; one sees the face screwed up, the cheek tight against the stone, the shoulder bracing the clay-covered mass, the foot wedging it, the fresh start with arms outstretched, the wholly human security of two earth-clotted hands. At the very end of his long effort measured by skyless space and time without depth, the purpose is achieved. Then Sisyphus watches the stone rush down in a few moments toward that lower world whence he will have to push it up again toward the summit. He goes back down to the plain.

It is during that return, that pause, that Sisyphus interests me. A face that toils so close to stones is already stone itself! I see that man going back down with a heavy yet measured step toward the torment of which he will never know the end. That hour like a breathing-space which returns as surely as his suffering, that is the hour of consciousness. At each of those moments when he leaves the heights and gradually sinks toward the lairs of the gods, he is superior to his fate. He is stronger than his rock.

If this myth is tragic, that is because its hero is conscious. Where would his torture be, indeed, if at every step the hope of succeeding upheld him? The workman of today works every day in his life at the same tasks, and this fate is no less absurd. But it is tragic only at the rare moments when it becomes conscious. Sisyphus, proletarian of the gods, powerless and rebellious, knows the whole extent of his wretched condition: it is what he thinks of during his descent. The lucidity that was to constitute his torture at the same time crowns his victory. There is no fate that cannot be surmounted by scorn.

If the descent is thus sometimes performed in sorrow, it can also take place in joy. This word is not too much. Again I fancy Sisyphus returning toward his rock, and the sorrow was in the beginning. When the images of earth cling too tightly to memory, when the call of happiness becomes too insistent, it happens that melancholy rises in man's heart: this is the rock's victory, this is the rock itself. The boundless grief is too heavy to bear. These are our nights of Gethsemane. But crushing truths perish from being acknowledged. Thus, Œdipus at the outset obeys fate without knowing it. But from the moment he knows, his tragedy begins. Yet at the same moment, blind and desperate, he realizes that the only bond linking him to the world is the cool hand of a girl. Then a tremendous remark rings out: "Despite so many ordeals, my advanced age and the nobility of my soul make me conclude that all is well." Sophocles' Œdipus, like Dostoevsky's Kirilov, thus gives the recipe for the absurd victory. Ancient wisdom confirms modern heroism.

One does not discover the absurd without being tempted to write a manual of happiness. "What! by such narrow ways—?" There is but one world, however. Happiness and the absurd are two sons of the same earth. They are inseparable. It would be a mistake to say that happiness necessarily springs from the absurd discovery. It happens as well that the feeling of the absurd springs from happiness. "I conclude that all is well," says Œdipus, and that remark is sacred. It echoes in the wild and limited universe of man. It teaches that all is not, has not been, exhausted. It drives out of this world a god who had come into it with dissatisfaction and a preference for futile sufferings. It makes of fate a human matter, which must be settled among men.

All Sisyphus' silent joy is contained therein. His fate belongs to him. His rock is his thing. Likewise, the absurd man, when he contemplates his torment, silences all the idols. In the universe suddenly restored to its silence, the myriad wondering little voices of the earth rise up. Unconscious, secret calls, invitations from all the faces, they are the necessary reverse and price of victory. There is no sun without shadow, and it is essential to know the night. The absurd man says yes and his effort will henceforth be unceasing. If there is a personal fate, there is no higher destiny, or at least there is but one which he concludes is inevitable and despicable. For the rest, he knows himself to be the master of his days. At that subtle moment when man glances backward over his life, Sisyphus returning toward his rock, in that slight pivoting he contemplates that series of unrelated actions which becomes his fate, created by him, combined under his memory's eye and soon sealed by his death. Thus, convinced of the wholly human origin of all that is human, a blind man eager to see who knows that the night has no end, he is still on the go. The rock is still rolling.

I leave Sisyphus at the foot of the mountain! One always finds one's burden again. But Sisyphus teaches the higher fidelity that negates the gods and raises rocks. He too concludes that all is well. This universe henceforth without a master seems to him neither sterile nor futile. Each atom of that stone, each mineral flake of that night-filled mountain, in itself forms a world. The struggle itself toward the heights is enough to fill a man's heart. One must imagine Sisyphus happy.

Postscript

As we conclude this book it is useful to draw together several central themes that we have developed throughout the course of our discussion and to highlight some of the contributions of existentialism. Certainly one central theme, occurring in one form or another in all the philosophies we have discussed, is that of *authenticity*. Although Heidegger does not consider his analysis to be a moral imperative to do anything, it is clear that he and other existentialists do have (at least by implication) something to say about how we should approach the difficult task of living. As Sartre says, "existentialism is optimistic, a doctrine of action" (p. 372). What, then, constitutes authentic action, and what have we learned about human life from the existentialists?

Human beings are special creatures in several ways. We are conscious beings; consequently, we can reflect on ourselves and make choices about the way we should be. We have values, and we each give meaning to an intrinsically meaningless or absurd universe in our own particular way. Indeed, humans seem to be the only creatures that have values and make decisions. Furthermore, and most centrally, we are free. For Sartre, that means we must first exist and be conscious of our place in the world and then create what we will be. Our existence precedes our essence, in that at least part of human behavior, specifically human choices, are uncaused or spontaneous.

The emphasis on freedom and choice is relevant to several main themes in existentialism. One such theme concerns the nature of the self and personal identity. Existentialists reject the notion of the self as being a substance whose properties are limited by its essence or nature, and whose freedom is a static property of a substance. To think of the self in that way is to limit what we can be or become and thus to take away our freedom. A natured substance does not determine our identity, who we are and what we can become. Rather each person chooses his or her own individual essence. Thus, the question of what kind of self is an authentic self turns on an understanding of authentic choice, and that connects with the notion of freedom.

One chooses authentically and one leads an authentic life if one chooses freely. In Kierkegaard and Nietzsche, reason and objective values rob us of our freedom to choose, since a genuinely free choice must be one for which we accept full responsibility, and full responsibility is possible only if we view ourselves as the ultimate foundation for our choices. Thus, the existentialist emphasis is on *how* one chooses rather than *what* one chooses. And this is central, since if there are no objective values, then there is no obvious way in which the existentialist can say *what* the right way to choose will be.

For Kierkegaard, the *how* of authentic choice involves decisiveness, passionate interest, fear, and trembling. Since we are "constantly in process of becoming," our decisions, if they are to be made authentically, must be constantly renewed, and that in the light of their objective insecurity. In this context, a passage by Sartre is illuminating:

> . . . authenticity is achieved *en bloc,* one either is or is not authentic. But that doesn't at all mean that one acquires authenticity once and for good. I've already pointed out that the present has no purchase on the future, nor the past on the present. . . . The authenticity of your previous momentum doesn't protect you in any way against falling the next instant into the inauthentic. . . . The instant that arrives is novel: a new authenticity has to be invented. (p. 328)

The idea that authenticity is something which has to be recreated is present in Nietzsche's conception of freedom as an ongoing process of "growth." Freedom involves removing the chains of previously conditioned ways of thinking about values and setting our own goals and then overcoming them in an ongoing process of self-development and creation. This task, faced squarely and honestly, is bound to produce suffering and loneliness, but the powerful individual reaffirms life, this life, by overcoming the forces that restrain the instinct to freedom.

In Sartre and Heidegger the notion of the self, personal identity, and authentic choice take on new perspectives. Heidegger and Sartre, like Niezsche, reject the notion of personal identity as involving a separately existing entity or immaterial substance that remains the same through time and change. For Heidegger, the self is a "Being-in-the-world" and cannot be separated from either its dealings with the objects in the world or from its relations with other people. Still, we are unique, and our uniqueness is most clearly evident by the fact of our death, which separates us from others and individualizes us. Death is the end of our possibilities, the end of our future, and the way in which we view death can be taken to represent the difference between authentic and inauthentic Dasein. To view death as something that happens to everybody is one way of becoming lost in the crowd. More generally, to think of oneself solely in terms of the roles that one finds oneself, and to think of one's future as fixed by one's past essence, and thereby to lose sight of oneself as an existing individual, are all forms of inauthenticity. For existentialists, there is far more within the realm of choice than is usually admitted, and they claim that part of what makes a life authentic is that it be lived in full awareness of the choices available. Thus, in arguing that one should lead an authentic life, existentialists argue that one should not accept as inevitable things which as a matter of fact are within the realm of choice.

For Sartre, we are "condemned to be free" (p. 371). We are condemned because there are no excuses for our actions and choices. That is, "neither within him nor without does he find anything to cling to" (p. 371). The point is that if God does not exist then there are no objective values in front of us to provide a basis for choice and a clear-cut path to follow. And since we have no pre-determined essence within us, we cannot justify our actions by means of a human nature that determines our present and future decisions. We are alone, without recourse or excuse. According to Sartre, we are even responsible for our passions and emotions, and we cannot appeal to them to justify or excuse behavior. What, then, constitutes an authentic choice?

At the level of specific choices, there is no standard that one can appeal to that will justify the assertion that the action was the right action. And yet Sartre claims that one can still pass judgment, for "one can judge (and this is perhaps not a judgment of value, but a logical judgment) that certain choices are based on error and others on truth."[1] What Sartre is getting at is that one can pass judgment on a choice based on *how* the choice is made, although not on the basis of what is chosen.

Freedom is our real condition. That is a truth about us which, alas, we can deny. We can deny it or seek to hide it from ourselves by adopting a spirit of seriousness which treats values as coming to us from without (as being qualities that attach onto objects and actions), thus maintaining that our actions have an extrinsic justification. Or, we can hide in "deterministic excuses," thinking that our behavior is completely determined by our past, our environment, or our heredity. Such ways of choosing are in error, and the choices based on them are, in a certain sense, immoral. To choose authentically, on the other hand, is to take freedom as an ultimate value, to recognize freedom as the highest good.

Nevertheless, there are many devices we use to stand in the way of thinking about our freedom, our range of choices, and ourselves. For Kierkegaard, we avoid such thoughts by taking an objective attitude toward our own lives, that is, by thinking of ourselves in terms of, say, the contribution we make to the development of knowledge, or the betterment of the world. For Heidegger, it is the device of thinking of ourselves as a one like many. For Sartre, it involves thinking of ourselves as others see us, as having a fixed essence that determines our choices. And for Nietzsche, we avoid facing or realizing our freedom by thinking that values are objective and that we do not have to accept responsibility for values. Perhaps we can overcome these methods of escape by *living* certain existentialist ideas, as opposed to merely contemplating them. Indeed, to existentially understand existentialist attitudes toward freedom, authenticity, choice, and value, you must live with them and view them in relation to your own life. By applying to your own life the ideas of the existentialist philosophers we have considered, you will come in contact with the subject matter of existentialism: individual human existence. In our estimation, the discovery and elucidation of that subject matter is among the main contributions of existentialist philosophy.

Selected Bibliography

Survey Books on Existentialism

BARRETT, WILLIAM. *Irrational Man: A Study in Existential Philosophy.* New York: Doubleday Anchor Books, 1962. A classic.

GROSSMANN, REINHARDT. *Phenomenology and Existentialism: An Introduction.* Boston: Routledge & Kegan Paul, 1984. Concentrates on Husserl, Heidegger, and Sartre in relation to traditional philosophical problems.

SOLOMON, ROBERT C. *From Rationalism to Existentialism: The Existentialists and Their Nineteenth-Century Backgrounds.* Lanham, MD: University Press of America, 1985. Contains excellent discussions of Kierkegaard, Nietzsche, Heidegger, and Sartre.

Kierkegaard

ALASTAIR, HANNAY. *Kierkegaard.* Boston: Routledge & Kegan Paul, 1982. An advanced and comprehensive treatment of Kierkegaard's views.

ALLISON, HENRY E. "Christianity and Nonsense," in *Kierkegaard: A Collection of Critical Essays,* ed. Josiah Thompson. Garden City, NY: Anchor Books, pp. 289–323.

GARDINER, PATRICK L. *Kierkegaard.* Oxford: Oxford University Press, 1988. Intended for the reader with little background in philosophy.

PERKINS, ROBERT L. *Kierkegaard's "Fear and Trembling."* University of Alabama Press, 1981. Contains twelve articles on the philosophical issues raised in *Fear and Trembling.*

POJMAN, LOUIS P. *The Logic of Subjectivity: Kierkegaard's Philosophy of Religion.* University: University of Alabama Press, 1984. A clearly written advanced book that is well worth the effort to read.

Nietzsche

DANTO, ARTHUR C. *Nietzsche as Philosopher.* New York: Columbia University Press, 1980.

KAUFMANN, WALTER. *Nietzsche: Philosopher, Psychologist, Antichrist.* Princeton, NJ: Princeton University Press, 1974.

MAGNUS, BERND. "Perfectibility and Attitude in Nietzsche's Übermensch," *Review of Metaphysics,* 36 (March 1983), 633–660. Excellent discussion of Ubermensch and eternal recurrence.

NEHAMAS, ALEXANDER. *Nietzsche: Life as Literature.* Cambridge, MA: Harvard University Press, 1985.

PARUSH, ADI. "Nietzsche on the Skeptic's Life," *Review of Metaphysics,* 29 (March 1976), 532–542. An excellent discussion of Nietzsche's skepticism.

SCHACHT, RICHARD. *Nietzsche.* London: Routledge & Kegan Paul, 1983. A comprehensive interpretation and elaboration of Nietzsche's thought.

SOLOMON, ROBERT C., and HIGGINS, KATHLEEN M. (eds.). *Reading Nietzsche.* New York: Oxford University Press, 1968.

Heidegger

EDWARDS, PAUL. *Heidegger and Death: A Critical Evaluation.* La Salle, IL: Hegeler Institute, 1979.

ELLISTON, FREDERICK (ed.). *Heidegger's Existential Analytic.* New York: Mouton, 1978.

GELVEN, MICHAEL. *A Commentary on Heidegger's Being and Time.* New York: Harper & Row, 1970. A section-by-section explication of *Being and Time.*

OLAFSON, FREDERICK A. *Heidegger and the Philosophy of Mind.* New Haven, CT: Yale University Press, 1987.

SHAHAN, ROBERT W., and MOHANTY, J. N. (eds.). *Thinking About Being: Aspects of Heidegger's Thought.* Norman: University of Oklahoma Press, 1984.

Sartre

CAWS, PETER. *Sartre.* London: Routledge & Kegan Paul, 1979. A reading of the whole corpus of Sartre's philosophical writings.

FLYNN, THOMAS R. *Sartre and Marxist Existentialism: The Test Case of Collective Responsibility.* Chicago: University of Chicago Press, 1984. Attempts to show how Sartre combines existentialism and Marxism into a new social theory.

MORRIS, PHYLLIS SUTTON. "Sartre on the Transcendence of the Ego," *Philosophy and Phenomenonological Research,* XLVI, 2 (December 1985), 179–198.

SANTONI, RONALD E. "Bad Faith and 'Lying to Oneself,' " *Philosophy and Phenomenological Research,* 38 (March 1978), 384–398.

SCHILPP, PAUL A. (ed.). *The Philosophy of Jean-Paul Sartre.* La Salle, IL: Open Court, 1981. Contains an interview with Sartre and twenty-eight articles on all aspects of his philosophy.

SHROEDER, WILLIAM R. *Sartre and His Predecessors: The Self and the Other.* Boston: Routledge & Kegan Paul, 1984.

SILVERMAN, HUGH J., and ELLISTON, FREDERICK A. (eds.). *Jean-Paul Sartre: Contemporary Approaches to His Philosophy.* Pittsburgh: Duquesne University Press, 1980. Contains useful articles on bad faith, freedom, the self, and other topics.

Existentialist Ethics: de Beauvoir and Camus

KEEFE, TERRY. *French Existentialist Fiction: Changing Moral Perspectives.* London: Croom Helm, 1986. Discusses the ethics of Camus, Sartre, and de Beauvoir.

KEEFE, TERRY. *Simone de Beauvoir: A Study of Her Writings.* Totawa, NJ: Barnes & Noble, 1983.

LEE, SANDER H. "The Central Role of Universalization in Sartrean Ethics," *Philosophy and Phenomenological Research,* 46 (September 1985), 59–72.

Notes

CHAPTER 1

Introduction

1. Aristotle, *De Interpretatione, The Basic Works of Aristotle,* ed. Richard McKeon (New York: Random House, 1941). See also Steven M. Cahn, *Fate, Logic and Time* (New Haven: Yale University Press, 1967), and Richard Taylor, *Metaphysics,* 3rd ed. (Englewood Cliffs, NJ: Prentice-Hall, 1983), pp. 51–62.

2. *Ibid.,* p. 46. Note, however, that Aristotle himself does not endorse fatalism and offers a solution that seeks to avoid it. See, p. 48.

3. Soren Kierkegaard, *Concluding Unscientific Postscript,* trans. David F. Swenson and Walter Lowrie (Princeton, NJ: Princeton University Press, 1974), p. 68.

4. *Ibid.,* p. 72.

5. *Ibid.,* p. 71.

CHAPTER 2

Soren Kierkegaard

1. Kierkegaard, *Postscript,* Swenson and Lowrie, p. 173.

2. *Soren Kierkegaard's Journals and Papers,* ed. and trans. Howard V. Hong and Edna H. Hong (Bloomington: Indiana University Press,

1967). Reprinted in *Existentialism,* ed. Robert Solomon (New York: The Modern Library, 1974), p. 8.

3. René Descartes, *Meditations on First Philosophy, With Selections from the Objections and Replies,* trans. John Cottingham (New York: Cambridge University Press, 1986), p. 15; emphasis added.

4. Kierkegaard, *Postscript,* Swenson and Lowrie, p. 155.

5. *Ibid.,* p. 155.

6. *Ibid.,* p. 281.

7. Note, however, that there is another sense in which Kierkegaard's entire enterprise is to *indirectly* communicate the subjective encounter with existence by means of a new kind of philosophical writing. Kierkegaard's indirect form of communication takes the form of journal writing, or pseudo diary, carrying on a debate under pseudonyms, religious polemic, and commentary.

8. See John Locke, *Esssay Concerning Human Understanding,* ed. A. S. Pringle-Pattison (Oxford: University Press, 1964).

9. Kierkegaard, *Postscript,* Swenson and Lowrie, p. 135.

10. *Ibid.,* p. 209.

11. *Ibid.,* p. 198.

12. *Ibid.,* p. 218; emphasis added.

13. *Ibid.,* p. 185.

14. *Ibid.,* pp. 280, 281, 289, and 284; emphasis added.

CHAPTER 3

Friedrich Nietzsche

1. Friedrich Nietzsche, *Daybreak,* trans. R. J. Hollingdale (New York: Cambridge University Press, 1986), section 104.

2. Friedrich Nietzsche, *The Antichrist* in *The Portable Nietzsche,* ed. and trans. by Walter Kaufman (New York: The Viking Press, Inc., 1963), section 54.

3. Friedrich Nietzsche, *The Will to Power,* trans. by Walter Kaufman and R. J. Hollingsdale (New York: Random House, Inc., 1967), section 963.

4. Friedrich Nietzsche, *The Gay Science,* trans. by Walter Kaufman (New York: Random House, Inc., 1974), section 349.

5. Friedrich Nietzsche, *Beyond Good and Evil,* in *The Basic Writings of Nietzsche,* ed. and trans. by Walter Kaufman (New York: Random House, Inc., 1967), section 230.

6. *Ibid.,* section 44.

7. Nietzsche's view of the overman and the will to power has been

abused and distorted since those doctrines were first propounded. The most obvious case is that of the Nazis who took Nietzsche's writings and used them for their own purposes to justify their goals. They construed the overman as a racial notion whose values coincide with that of fascist ideology. We should note, however, that Nietzsche was opposed to anti-Semitism and German nationalism. Furthermore, his notion of a master race is simply a name for the collection of higher types; nothing racial, biological, or evolutionary is involved. In fact, Nietzsche seems to hold that race mixing (which was opposed by the Nazis) might even produce more overmen.

Nietzsche's overman has been interpreted by some as a power monger who legislates values that embody a new "higher" morality. But this is a mistaken interpretation of his views. For Nietzsche, there are no objective values, so that he cannot be interpreted as suggesting a higher morality, a morality represented by Nazism. Moreover, we have seen that Nietzsche rejects a morality which would involve suffering and injury to others. Thus, typical of overmen is that they restrain themselves from doing harm. The overman is a kind of ideal for which to strive, but this ideal was grossly misunderstood by the Nazis. In this connection see Walter Kaufmann, Nietzsche: Philosophy, Psychologist, Antichrist (Princeton, NJ: Princeton University Press, 1974): and Ronald Hayman, Nietzsche: A Critical Life (New York: Oxford University Press, 1980).

8. *Beyond Good and Evil,* section 209.

9. *The Will to Power,* section 488.

10. *Ibid.,* sections 488 and 490.

11. Friedrich Nietzsche, *Twilight of the Idols* in *The Portable Nietzsche,* "Skirmishes of an Untimely Man," section 38.

12. *The Will to Power,* section 558.

13. Excellent discussions of Nietzsche's doctrine of eternal recurrence from which I have benefited are Alexander Nehamas, *Nietzsche: Life as Literature* (Cambridge, MA: Harvard University Press, 1985), and Bernd Magnus, "Perfectibility and Attitude in Nietzsche's *Ubermensch,*" *Review of Metaphysics,* 36 (March 1983), pp. 633–659.

14. *Will to Power,* section 1066.

CHAPTER 4

Martin Heidegger

1. We should mention, however, that in Heidegger's "Letter on Humanism," in *Martin Heidegger Basic Writings,* ed. David Farrell Krell (New York: Harper & Row, 1977) written after *Being and Time,* Heidegger explicitly breaks with Sartre and gives essence priority over existence.

2. Martin Heidegger, *Being and Time,* trans. John Macquarrie and Edward Robinson (New York: Harper & Row, Pub., 1962), p. 92.

3. Of course, Heidegger is not maintaining that our being human (our being Dasein) is an accidental kind to which we belong. Rather, he is referring to those classifications about which we do have a choice, and the point is that we have a much greater choice than we realize. Whether I be a philosopher or a drunkard (or both) is not a necessary and inevitable consequence of the kind to which I belong, that is, the human kind.

CHAPTER 5

Jean-Paul Sartre

1. Jean-Paul Sartre, *The Transcendence of the Ego,* trans. Forrest Williams and Robert Kirkpatrick (New York: Farrar, Straus and Giroux, 1957). Jean-Paul Sartre, *Being and Nothingness,* trans. Hazel Barnes (New York: Washington Square Press, 1956).

2. Sartre, *Transcendence of the Ego,* pp. 53–54.

3. *Ibid.,* p. 89.

4. Sartre eventually came to have serious doubts about his theory of radical freedom expressed in *Being and Nothingness* and *The Transcendence of the Ego.* In *Search for a Method* he says,

> As soon as there exists *for everyone* a margin of *real* freedom beyond the production of life, Marxism will have lived out its span [and] a philosophy of freedom will take its place. But we now have no means, no intellectual instrument, no concrete experience that allows us to conceive of this freedom or this philosophy. (trans. Hazel Barnes, Knopf, 1963, p. 34)

In other words, one's freedom is ordinarily so limited that perhaps it does not deserve the name "freedom." Consider a factory worker. Is he free to work or not to work? In effect the choice is between starving and not starving. He still has a choice, but to speak of freedom here seems inappropriate. Existentialism may be the true philosophy for a true communist society, but that is in the future. In limiting this text to Sartre's concern with the individual, I have chosen not to include Sartre's writing on society and the "We" of the group as contained in *Critique of Dialectical Reason.* For a good discussion of Sartre's social philosophy, which contains an attempt to reconcile Sartre's existentialism and Marxism, see Thomas Flynn, *Sartre and Marxist Existentialism: The Test Case of Collective Responsibility* (Chicago: University of Chicago Press, 1984).

5. See, for example, Thomas Nagel, "Sexual Perversion," *The Journal of Philosophy,* 66, 1 (1969), pp. 5–17; Maurice Natanson, *A Critique of*

Jean-Paul Sartre's Ontology (Lincoln: University of Nebraska Press, 1951), pp. 42–46; *To Be and Not to Be: An Analysis of Jean-Paul Sartre's Ontology* (Detroit: Wayne State University Press, 1962), pp. 93–95; and Robert Solomon, "Sexual Paradigms," *The Journal of Philosophy,* 71, 11 (1974), pp. 336–345.

6. R. Solomon, "Sexual Paradigms," p. 342.

7. Furthermore, according to Sartre, sexual desire does not aim at, or have as its goal, engaging in sexual activity. See p. 346. Rather, its goal is to produce sexual desire in another person toward me. Indeed, for Sartre, to "have sex" is, in its most fundamental sense, not to engage in physical activity involving our sexual organs but to be in a state of double reciprocal incarnation, or mutual awareness. Thus, Sartre maintains our sexuality does not derive its origin from sex as a physiological and contingent determination of persons. Rather, sexuality is an ontological or necessary structure of our concrete relations with others.

8. T. Nagel, "Sexual Perversions," p. 10.

9. Solomon, "Sexual Paradigms," p. 342.

CHAPTER 6

Existential Ethics

1. Simone de Beauvoir, *The ethics of Ambiguity,* trans. Bernard Frechtman (Secaucus, NJ: Citadel Press, 1982), p. 24.

2. *Ibid.,* p. 25.

3. *Ibid.,* p. 73.

POSTSCRIPT

1. Jean-Paul Sartre, *Existentialism and Human Emotions,* trans. Bernard Frechtman (New York: Philosophical Library, 1985, p. 44).

Index